II. Consonants

i) Simple

Korean Letter	Romanization	English sound
ㄱ	k(g)	as *k*ing or *g*uy
ㄴ	n	as *n*ame
ㄷ	t(d)	as *t*oy or *d*ay
ㄹ	r(l)	as *r*ain or *l*ily
ㅁ	m	as *m*other
ㅂ	p(b)	as *p*in or *b*ook
ㅅ	s	as *s*peech
ㅇ	ng	as ki*ng*
ㅈ	ch(j)	as *J*ohn
ㅊ	ch'	as *ch*urch
ㅋ	k'	as *k*ite
ㅌ	t'	as *t*ank
ㅍ	p'	as *p*ump
ㅎ	h	as *h*igh

ii) Double

Korean Letter	Romanization	English sound
ㄲ	kk	as *sk*y or Ja*ck*
ㄸ	tt	as *st*ay
ㅃ	pp	as *sp*y
ㅆ	ss	as e*ss*ential
ㅉ	tch	as *tz*ar

BASIC KOREAN DICTIONARY

Korean-English/English-Korean

외국인을 위한 기초 한국어 사전

Compiled by
Sang-Oak LEE

Seoul National University

서울대학교 이 상억 편

with
Robert Fouser and David Baxter

HOLLYM
Elizabeth, NJ · SEOUL

Basic Korean Dictionary
KOREAN-ENGLISH/ENGLISH-KOREAN

외국인을 위한 기초 한국어 사전

Copyright © 1995
All rights reserved

First published in 1995
by the Ministry of Culture and Tourism
82-1 Sejongno, Chongno-gu, Seoul, Korea

First revised edition, 1996
Third printing, 2000
Published by Hollym International Corp.
18 Donald Place, Elizabeth, NJ 07208, U.S.A.
Phone: (908)353-1655   Fax: (908)353-0255
http://www.hollym.com

Published simultaneously in Korea
by Hollym Corporation; Publishers
13-13 Kwanchol-dong, Chongno-gu
Seoul 110-111, Korea
Phone: (02)735-7551~4   Fax:(02)730-5149, 8192
http://www.hollym.co.kr

ISBN: 1-56591-076-1

Printed in Korea

Table of Contents

Preface

Preface

Increasing interest in learning Korean as a foreign language has stimulated the publication of many Korean textbooks in recent years. Despite this positive development, learners of Korean lack a "learner's dictionary" that addresses their needs from the perspective of the non-native speaker of Korean. Learners of Korean often have difficulty in using standard Korean-English dictionaries in reading because these dictionaries were designed for native speakers of Korean for use in learning English. In writing, learners of Korean have difficulty in choosing the appropriate word from standard English-Korean dictionaries.

These compact English-Korean/Korean-English dictionaries for English speakers represent an attempt to overcome these problems through a combination of usable definitions and practical expressions. In the English-Korean part, Korean annotations are frequently translated in parentheses with English equivalents or synonyms for each Korean word to give easier choice of the appropriate word. By including idiomatic expressions, proverbs and set phrases, these dictionaries also address learners' practical need for natural vocabulary and expressions in speaking and listening. A list of suffixes as well as grammar and usage notes on topics that are particularly difficult for non-native speakers are included in an appendix.

Innovative Features

Based on several surveys of the frequency of vocabulary use, the most commonly used 5,000 words in each language are defined in the dictionaries. Of these words, the most common words are noted with "#", the next most common words with "*" and less commonly used words "+". This classification is an indication of the relative difficulty of words, and it helps learners acquire vocabulary in clearly defined stages.

Most standard dictionaries contain definitions that are not useful to non-native speakers and lack sufficient examples to illustrate meaning and usage. Every effort has been made to make the definitions simple and clear, and, in certain cases, additional explanations have been added for clarity. In certain cases, loose translations are placed next to literal translations to give learners a better idea of the nuances of the language.

Words related specifically to Korean culture and history-clothes, food, housing, ceremonies, folk culture-are explained as concisely as possible. "Difficulties with Korean Grammar" and "Usage Notes" in appendic explain important grammatical and cultural features of Korean, such as the system of honorifics and the various levels of language in Korean.

Difficult inflected forms, particularly irregular ones, are listed in their various forms in an appendix. Because Korean is an agglutinative language, forms such as "a-si-ŏt-ges-sŭm-ni-da," which are composed of a series of grammatical morphemes, are difficult for learners to analyze using standard dictionaries because only the basic form of the verb, "alda," is given. Derivations of various compound nouns are also listed as separate entries.

Idiomatic expressions and proverbs have been inserted or cross-referenced by the symbol ⓘ and [p.] in relevant entries and also in an appendix at the end of the dictionary because such terms require full listing. These dictionaries also include basic cultural and geographical information that learners ordinarily encounter in learning Korean.

Synonyms, parts of speech, and the morphological composition of each entry is noted for convenient reference, if necessary. This additional information is noted in a consistent coding system that serves as an index to various semantic references (→) and phonological changes (⟨) of Korean.

Because most learners are not familiar with the International Phonetic Alphabet (IPA), pronunciation is described in the *han'gŭl* letters with a transcription in the McCune-Reischauer system, which is basically identical to the official system of romanization in Korea. 's' before 'i' is not written as 'shi' since this causes people to pronounce the following vowel 'i' too far back and no great harm is done if the non-Korean fails to palatalize the 's'. Hyphens are used to show the boundary between nominals and particles.

It gives learners the most frequent words from *Koren Though English* (in particular, Book I & II) that have been published originally by the Ministry of Culture and Sports and later by Hollym Publishing Co.

With the above innovations, it is hoped that these dictionaries will be versatile enough to fit the diverse needs of learners of Korean in formal and informal settings. It is also hoped that more people will learn Korean by making it more accessible and interesting to learn.

Abbreviations

adj.	adjective	Amer.	American English
	(=descriptive verb)	Brit./Eng.	British English
adv.	adverb	C.	Chinese etymology
art.	article	ⓘ	cf. Idioms(Appendix)
cf.	confer	[p.7]	cf. Proverbs(Appen) no.7
conj.	conjunction	→ x	refer to the meaning of x
interj.	interjection	#	very frequent
lit.	literal meaning	*	quite frequent
n.	noun	+	frequent
pre-n.	pre-noun	x/y	x or y
prep.	preposition	~	(the entry item)
pron.	pronoun	x⟩y	sound changes
v.	verb		from x to y

References

Professor Samuel Martin's *New Korean-English Dictionary* (Yale University Press, 1968); B. J. Jones' *Standard English-Korean & Korean-English Dictionary for Foreigners* (Hollym Co. Publishers, 1991) and Professor Chong-wha Chung's *Dictionary of Korean-English Proverbs* (T'amgudang, 1991) were, along with several other dictionaries, the main references in compiling these dictionaries.

Acknowledgements

I would like to thank Professor Robert Ramsey for his help in setting up some of the guidelines for these dictionaries at the initial stage. Thereafter, Robert Fouser and David Baxter were extremely helpful in reading and commenting on the intial drafts of these dictionaries from the viewpoint of learners of Korean and in providing the useful appendix on difficulties in Korean grammar. I would also like to express my gratitude to the Ministry of Culture and Sports for supporting this project, which has developed from my experience teaching Korean to foreigners over a quarter of a century.

October 1995, Sydney   Sang-Oak Lee

Basic

KOREAN–ENGLISH DICTIONARY

≤ A ≥

\# **a** 아 interj. Ah!; O(h)!; O dear!

\# **-a** -아 other shapes: -ŏ -어, -yŏ -여. non-final tenseless (infinitive) ending of v. or adj. immediately following stems and used in combination with other endings. -a is the shape after a syllable containing o or a.

\# **abŏji** 아버지 n. father; papa; daddy; dad.

\# **ach'im** 아침 n. morning. *ach'im-e* 아침에 in the morning.

adong 아동 n.C. child; juvenile. *adong-ŭi* 아동의 children's; juvenile.

\# **adŭl** 아들 n. son; boy. *adŭlttal* 아들딸 son(s) and daughter.

aech'o-e 애초에 adv.C. (n.+particle) at first; at the start.

aeguk 애국 n.C. love of one's country; patriotism. *aegukka* 애국가 national anthem. *aegukchŏk* 애국 적 patriotic. *aeguktcha* 애국자 patriot.

aegyo 애교 n.C. charm. *aegyo innŭn* 애교 있는 attractive; charming.

aein 애인 n.C. (her) lover, girlfriend; (his) lover, boyfriend; sweetheart.

+ **aejŏng** 애정 n.C. love; affection. *aejŏng-i innŭn* 애정 이 있는 affectionate.

* **-aek** -액 n.C. (suffixal) amount; sum. *saengsan [sobi]aek* 생산[소비]액 amount of production [consumption].

* **aekch'e** 액체 n.C. liquid; fluid. *aekch'e yŏllyo* 액체 연료 liquid fuel.

aekssu 액수 n.C. sum; amount.

aemaehan 애매한 adj.C. vague; ambiguous.

aesŏkhada 애석하다 adj.C. sad; sorrowful; mournful; regrettable.

aessŭda 애쓰다 v. exert [strain] oneself; make an effort.

aet'ada 애타다 v. be anxious (about) ; be nervous [much worried] (about)

aewŏn 애원 n.C. supplication; entreaty. *aewŏnhada* 애원하다 entreat; implore; supplicate, beg.

+ **agassi** 아가씨 n. ① young lady; girl; maid(en) ② Miss; young lady!

* **agi** 아기 n. ① baby; infant ② (daughter; daughter -in-law) dear; darling.

+ **ahop** 아홉 n. nine. *ahoptchae* 아홉째 the ninth.

ahŭn 아흔 n. ninety *ahŭntchae* 아흔째 the nintieth.

\# **ai** 아이 child; kid; boy; girl. [p(ropverb).90,102]

\# **ajik** 아직 adv. yet; as yet; still.

ajikkaji 아직까지 adv. +particle. so [thus] far; up to now; till now; up to the present.

\# **aju** 아주 adv. very; quite; utterly; exceedingly.

+ **ajumŏni** n. 아주머니 aunt; auntie.

akkaptta adj. 아깝다 ① (be) pitiful; regrettable ② (be) dear; precious. *akkapkke-do* 아깝게도 regrettably; lamentably.

* **akki** 악기 n.C. musical instrument.

* **akkida** 아끼다 v. ① save; spare; be stingy ② value; prize; hold (a thing) dear.

akkimŏpshi 아낌없이 adv. unsparingly; generously; without stint.

akssu 악수 n.C. handshake. *akssuhada* 악수하다 shake hand (with).

\# **al** 알 n. egg; spawn; roe. [p.17] *ar-ŭl nat'a* 알을 낳다 lay an egg; spawn.

\# **alda** 알다 v. know. [p.87,88]

* **allida** 알리다 v. let (a person) know; inform; notify.

allyŏjida 알려지다 v. be [become] known (to); come to light. *chal allyŏjin* 잘 알려진 well-known; famous.

\# **almatta** 알맞다 adj. (be) fitting; becoming.

alt'a 앓다 v. suffer from (illness).

alttŭlhada 알뜰하다 adj. (be) thrifty; frugal; economical. *alttŭlhi* 알뜰히 frugally; thriftily.

* **ama** 아마 adv. probably; perhaps; maybe; possibly; presumably.

amnal 앞날 n. future; days ahead [to come].

* **amnyŏk** n.C. 압력 pressure; stress. *amnyŏg-ŭl kahada* 압력을 가하다 give[apply] pressure (to). *amnyŏksot* 압력솥 pressure cooker.

amsi 암시 n.C. hint; suggestion. *amsihada* 암시하다 hint (at); suggest.

\+ **amt'ak** 암탉 n. hen.

amugae 아무개 n. Mr. [Mrs., Miss] So and so; a certain person. *Kim amugae* 김 아무개 a certain Mr. Kim; one Kim.

amuraedo 아무래도 adv. anyhow; anyway; for anything; come what may.

\# **amuri** 아무리 adv. however much; no matter how.

amutchorok 아무쪼록 adv. by all means; as much as one can; in any case; at any cost.

\# **an** 안 n. ① inside; interior ② in; within; less than. [p.135] *an-e* 안에 within; inside; in. *an-ŭrobut'ŏ* 안으로부터 from the inside; from within.

\# **an** 안 adv. not. (*abbreviated from* 아니) [p.89,91] *an /ani ttaen kulttug-e yŏn'gi nalkka?* [=proverb. 89] 안/아니 땐 굴뚝에 연기 날까? Does smoke rise from a chimney where a fire has not been lit? = Where there is smoke, there is fire.

\# **anae** 아내 n. wife; better-half; spouse.

\+ **an'gae** 안개 n. fog; mist.

an'gida 안기다 v. (be) embraced; be in (a person's) arms [bosom].

an'gyŏng 안경 n.C. spectacles; glasses.

\# **ani(da)** 아니(다) adj. (be) not, no.

\+ **anjŏn** 안전 n.C. safety; security. *anjŏnhan* 안전한 safe; secure. *anjŏnhi* 안전히 safely; securely.

anjŏng 안정 n.C. stability; steadiness. *anjŏngdoeda* 안정되다 be stabilized.

anju 안주 n.C. side dish (with alcoholic beverages).

annae 안내 n.C. guidance; leading. *annaehada* 안내하다 guide; conduct. *annaeja* 안내자 (a) guide.

annyŏng 안녕 n.C. public peace. *Annyŏnghasimnikka* 안녕하십니까? ① How are you? ② Good morning[afternoon, evening]. *Annyŏnghi ka[kye]sipsio.* 안녕히 가[계]십시오. Good-bye.

ansaek 안색 n.C. complexion; countenance.

ansim 안심 n.C. relief; peace[ease] of mind. *ansimhada* 안심하다 feel at rest; feel easy (about).

+ **anssonnim** 안손님 n. lady visitor; woman caller.

ant'akkapta 안타깝다 adj. ① (be) impatient; irritated; frustrated ② (be) pitiful; pitiable; (feel) sad about.

antta 안다 v. ① hold[carry] in one's arm(s); embrace; hug. ② answer for; take charge of.

antta 앉다 v. sit down; take a seat; be seated.

ap n. 앞 front; fore. *ap'-ŭi* 앞의 front; preceding. *ap'-e* 앞에 in front of; ahead.

apch'uk 압축 n.C. compression; condensation. *apch'uk'ada* 압축하다 compress; condense.

appa 아빠 n. papa; daddy; dad; pop (Am.).

+ **appak** 압박 n.C. pressure; oppression. *appak'ada* 압박하다 oppress; suppress.

apssŏ 앞서 adv. before; previously; already.

apttanggida v. 앞당기다 move[carry] up; advance; make earlier.

apttohada 압도하다 v.C. overwhelm; overcome; overpower. *apttojŏk[ŭro]* 압도적[으로] overwhelming[ly]; sweeping[ly].

* **ap'ŭda** 아프다 adj. (be) sick, ill, painful; sore; have [feel] pain. ①

arae 아래 n. low part; foot; bottom; base. *arae-ŭi* 아래의 lower; under. *arae-e* 아래에 down; under; beneath; below.

arajuda 알아주다 v. acknowledge; recognize; appreciate.

aranaeda 알아내다 v. find out; make out; detect.

\# **arŭmdaptta** 아름답다 adj. (be) beautiful; pretty; lovely; fair. *arŭmdapkke* 아름답게 beautifully; prettily.

\# **-asŏ** -아서 infinitive ending with particle **-sŏ**. other shapes: **-ŏsŏ** -어서, **-yŏsŏ** -여서 ① reason marker. indicates that the state of affairs expressed by the following v. or adj. ② temporal precedence and continuing state marker. indicates that the action expressed by the preceding v. is prior to the action expressed by the following v., but the state resulting from the action of the preceding v. continues throughout the action of the following v.

\# **-ass-** -았- past tense marker. was. did. occus followed by **-ŏss-**, **-kess-**, **-sŭp-**, **-ta**, **-ŭmyŏ**, **-ŭni**, **-ŭn**. etc. The shape is -ass- if the last vowel of the stem is -o. It is -ss- after -a. cf. **-ŏss-**.

aswiptta 아쉽다 miss; feel the lack of; (be) inconvenient; (feel) regret.

\+ **au** 아우 man's younger brother; woman's younger sister.

-aya -아야 infinitive ending with particle **-ya**. other shapes: **-ŏya** -어야, **-yŏya** -여야. indicates that the proposition expressed by the preceding v. or adj. is a necessary condition for the following v. or adj. ① only to the extent that ... can one ..., you have to ... in order to ... ② to whatever extent.

$$\lesssim C [CH] \gtrsim$$

* **cha** 자 interj. (exclamation) well, come on.

* **cha** 자 n. ruler; measure.

  chabi 자비 n.C. mercy; charity; benevolence. *chabiroun* 자비로운 merciful; compassionate; tenderhearted. *mujabi* 무자비 without mercy.

* **chabon** 자본 n.C. capital; funds. *chabon-ga* 자본가 capitalist. *chabonjuŭi* 자본주의 capitalism.

* **chach'i** 자치 n.C. self-government; autonomy. *chach'ihada* 자치하다 govern oneself.

  chach'wihada 자취하다 v.C. do one's own cooking; cook; cook for oneself.

+ **chach'wi** 자취 n. traces; vestiges; marks.

chada 자다 v. sleep; go to bed; go to sleep; be in bed.

  chadongjŏgin 자동적인 adj.C. automatic. *chadong-jŏg-ŭro* 자동적으로 automatically. *chadongmun* 자동문 automatic door. *chadong p'anmaegi* 자동판매기 vending machine.

chadongch'a 자동차 n.C. motorcar;automobile (*Am.*)

+ **chae** 재 n. ashes. ① *tambaetchae* 담뱃재 cigarette ash.

+ **chaebae** 재배 n.C. cultivation;culture. * *chaebae-hada* 재배하다 cultivate, grow.

  chaebŏl 재벌 n.C. financial conglomerate [combine]; plutocracy.

* **chaeda** 재다 v. measure; weigh; gauge.

  chaegŏn 재건 n.C. reconstruction. *chaegŏnhada* 재건 하다 rebuild; reconstruct.

  chaeil-ŭi 재일의 adj.C. in Japan. *chaeil kyop'o* 재일 교포 Korean residents in Japan.

  chaejangnyŏn 재작년 n.C. the year before last.

chaejŏng 재정 n.C. finance; financial affairs.

* **chaeju** 재주 n.C. ability; talent; gifts. [p.117] *chaeju innŭn* 재주 있는 talented; able; gifted.

* **chaemi** 재미 n. interest; amusement; enjoyment; fun. + *chaemiitta* 재미있다 be interesting.

  chaemi 재미 n.C. *chaemi kyop'o* 재미 교포 Korean

residents in America. *chaemi yuhakssaeng* 재미
유학생 Korean students studying in America.

* **chaemok** 재목 n.C. wood; lumber (*Am.*); timber
  (*Eng.*) → **moktchae** 목재.

  chaeoe 재외. n.C. *chaeoe-ŭi* 재외의 abroad; overseas.
  chaeoe konggwan 재외 공관 embassies and
  legations abroad; diplomatic missions abroad.

* **chaep'an** 재판 n.C. trial; judgement. *chaep'anhada*
  재판하다 try; judge; decide on; pass judgement
  on. *chaep'anil* 재판일 day in court.

  chaeraesik 재래식 n.C. conventional type, old-
  fashioned.

chaeryo 재료 n.C. material; row material; stuff;
  data. *chaeryobi* 재료비 material costs.

* **chaesan** 재산 n.C. property; fortune; assets;
  wealth.

  chaesu 재수 n.C. luck; fortune.

chagi 자기 n.C. oneself; self; ego; my darling
  (between a young couple). *chagi-ŭi* 자기의 one's
  own (self); personal.

  chagŏp 작업 n.C. work; operations. *chagŏp'ada* 작업
  하다 work; conduct operations.

+ **chaguk** 자극 n.C. stimulus; impulse. *chaguk'ada* 자
  극하다 stimulate; irritate; incite; give an
  impetus.

* **chagŭm** 자금 n.C. funds; capital; fund.

+ **chagyŏk** 자격 n.C. qualification; eligibility. *cha-
  gyŏg-i itta* 자격이 있다 be qualified; be eligible
  (for).

chagyong 작용 n.C. action; operation. +*chagyong-
  hada* 작용하다 act; operate on.

  chaje 자제 n.C. self-control[-restraint]. *chajehada*
  자제하다 control [restrain] oneself.

  chajŏng 자정 n.C. midnight.

  chajŏn'gŏ 자전거 n.C. bicycle.

  chajonsim 자존심 n.C. pride.

* **chaju** 자주 adv. often; frequently.

+ **chakka** 작가 n.C. writer; author; artist. *inkki chakka* 인기 작가 popular [favorite] writer.

   chakkok 작곡 n.C. (musical) composition. *chakkok'ada* 작곡하다 compose. *chakkokka* 작곡가 composer.

* **chakku** 자꾸 adv. ① constantly; incessantly; always ② eagerly; strongly.

* **chakp'um** 작품 n.C. work, creation. *munhak chakp'um* 문학 작품 literary work.

+ **chaktchŏn** 작전 n.C. (military) operations; strategy. *chaktchŏnsang* 작전상 strategically; tactically.

chaktta 작다 adj. (be) small; little; tiny; young.

chal 잘 adv. well; nicely; skilfully.

   challhada 잘하다 v. ① do well [nicely, skillfully] ② do often; do a lot.

   challada 잘나다 adj. ① (be) handsome; good-looking ② (be) distinguished; great.

* **chalmot** 잘못 n. fault; mistake; error; blunder. *chalmot'ada* 잘못하다 do wrong; make a mistake.

cham 잠 n. sleep; nap; doze. ① *chamjada* 잠자다 sleep; go to sleep.

   chamae 자매 n.C. sisters. *chamae hakkyo* 자매 학교 sister school.

   chaman 자만 n.C. self-conceit; vanity; boast. *chamanhada* 자만하다 be conceited; be vain.

   chamdŭlda 잠들다 v. ① fall[drop] asleep; drop off to sleep ② lie (in the churchyard).

* **chamjak'o** 잠자코 adv. without a word; silently; without objection.

   chamjari 잠자리 n. dragonfly. *koch ujamjari* 고추 잠자리 red dragonfly. (Cf. **chamtchari** 잠자리〈잠＋자리 place for sleeping, bed.)

chamkkan 잠깐 n.C. (for) a while; (for) a moment; (for) some time; for a (short) time.

* **chamsi** 잠시 n.C. short time[while]; (little) while. *chamsi hu-e* 잠시 후에 after a while.

chamun 자문 n.C. consultation. *chamunhada* 자문하다 inquire; consult.

\# **chan** 잔 n.C. (wine) cup; glass. *ch´atchan* 찻잔 teacup.

* **chanaek** 잔액 n.C. balance; remainder.

chandi 잔디 n. lawn; sod. *chandibat* 잔디밭 lawn; grassplot.

\# **chane** 자네 pron. you.

chang 장 n.C. soy (sauce). *toenjang* 된장 bean paste.

chang 장 n.C. chest of drawers; cabinet; bureau (*Am.*). *otchang* 옷장 wardrobe.

\+ **changbu** 장부 n.C. (account) book; ledger.

* **changch´i** 장치 n.C. apparatus; equipment; installation. *changch´ihada* 장치하다 equip; install; fit.

\+ **changga** 장가 n. marriage. *changga kada [tŭlda]* 장가가다[들다] marry; get married; take a wife.

changgap 장갑 n.C. (a pair of) gloves [mittens].

changgi 장기 n.C. long time [period, term]. *changgi-ŭi* 장기의 long(-dated)

changgŏri 장거리 n.C. long distance [range]. *changgŏri chŏnhwa* 장거리 전화 long-distance call [telephone].

\# **changgun** 장군 n.C. general, admiral.

* **changgwan** 장관 n.C. grand sight; magnificent view [spectacle].

changgwan 장관 n.C. minister (of state); Cabinet member; secretary.

changhak 장학 n.C. *changhakkŭm* 장학금 scholarship. *changhakssaeng* 장학생 scholarship student [holder].

changma 장마 n. long rainy season (in July). *changmach´ŏl* 장마철 the rainy [wet] season.

changmi 장미 n.C. rose. *tŭltchangmi* 들장미 wild rose.

changmun 작문 n.C. composition.

* **changnae** 장래 n.C. furure. *changnae-ŭi* 장래의 future; prospective. *changnae-e* 장래의 in the future.
+ **changnan** 장난 n. game; play; joke. *changnanhada* 장난하다 do mischief; play a trick.
  changnankkam 장난감 n. toy; plaything.
  changnim 장님 n. blind person; the blind. [p.31,116]
+ **changnyŏ** 장려 n.C. encouragement. *changnyŏhada* 장려하다 encourage; promote.
* **changnyŏn** 작년 n.C. last year; the past year.
+ **changsa** 장사 n. trade; business; commerce. *changsahada* 장사하다 do [engage in] business.
  changsik 장식 n.C. decoration; adornment; ornament. *changsik'ada* 장식하다 ornament; decorate; adorn.
  changso 장소 n.C. place; spot; location; site.
  changtchŏm 장점 n.C. merit; strong [good] point; one's forte. *changdantchŏm* strong and weak points.
  changt'ŏ 장터 n. market place[site].
  chan'gŭm 잔금 n.C. balance; remainder.
+ **chanyŏ** 자녀 n.C. children; sons and daughters.
* **chap'ida** 잡히다 v. be caught; get captured.
+ **chaptchi** 잡지 n.C. magazine; journal; periodical.
  charang 자랑 n. pride. *charangsŭrŏptta* 자랑스럽다 worthy of pride, proud.
  chari 자리 n. seat, place. ①, [p.29].
  chase 자세 n.C. attitude.
-chi -지 ① sentence final ending used with casual statements, questions, suggestions, or commands. followed by *-yo* in polite speech. (I) suppose, I bet, don't-you-know ② used with *-man(ŭn)*: *kŭrŏch'iman* 그렇지만 but, however ③ used with *ant'a* 않다/*mot'hada* 못하다/*malda* 말다. attached to verb stem, makes the verb negative. *ant'a/mot'ada* are used for statements and

questions *malda* for commands and propositions.

chibang 지방 n.C. district, region; locality. *chibangjŏk* 지방적 local; provincial. *chibang sat'uri* 지방 사투리 local accent.

chibu 지부 n.C. branch (office); chapter.

* **chibul** 지불 n.C. payment; discharge. + *chibulhada* 지불하다 pay; discharge.

+ **chibung** 지붕 n. roof; roofing; housetop. *kiwa chibung* 기와 지붕 tiled roof.

chich'ida 지치다 v. be[get] tired; be exhausted; be worn out; be done up.

chich'ul 지출 n.C. expense; outgo. *chich'ulhada* 지출하다 expend; pay.

+ **chida** 지다 v. be [get] defeated; lose; yield (to). *kyŏnggi-e chida* 경기에 지다 lose in a contest.

+ **chida** 지다 v. ① bear; carry on the back ② owe; be indebted.

* **chida** 지다 v. ① fall; fade and fall: *nagyŏb-i chinda* 낙엽이 진다 Leaves are falling. ② set; sink; go down: *hae-ga chida* 해가 지다 The sun sets.

chidae 지대 n.C. zone; region; belt. *pimujang chidae* 비무장 지대 demilitarized zone [DMZ].

* **chido** 지도 n.C. map. *chidoch'aek* 지도책 atlas.

+ **chido** 지도 n.C. guidance; directions. *chidohada* 지도하다 guide; lead; coach.

chigak 지각 n.C. *chigak'ada* 지각하다 be[become] late; be behind time; be tardy.

chigap 지갑 n.C. purse; pocketbook.

* **chigŏp** 직업 n.C. occupation; calling; profession; vocation; business.

chigu 지구 n.C. the earth; the globe: *chigubon* 지구본 terrestrial globe.

+ **chigu** 지구 n.C. district; zone; region; area; section. *sangŏp[chut'aek] chigu* 상업[주택] 지구 business[residence] zone[area].

chigŭm 지금 n.C. now; the present; this moment. *chigŭm-kkaji* 지금까지 till now; up to the present.

chigŭm-but'ŏ 지금부터 from now on; after this.

chigwŏn 직원 n.C. personnel; staff-member; employee.

+ **chiha-ŭi(-e, -esŏ)** 지하의〔에, 에서〕 adj. underground. *chihach'ŏl* 지하철 subway.

chihwi 지휘 n.C. command; orders; direction. *chihwihada* 지휘하다 command; order; lead. *chihwija* 지휘자 conductor.

chihye 지혜 n.C. wisdom; intelligence. *chihye innŭn* 지혜 있는 wise; intelligent.

chijang 지장 n.C. obstacle; difficulty. *chijang-i ŏpsŭmyŏn* 지장이 없으면 if it is convenient to you.

chijŏbunhada 지저분하다 adj. (be) messy; disordered; untidy; dirty(-looking).

chijŏm 지점 n.C. branch shop 〔office, house〕. *chijŏmjang* 지점장 branch manager.

chijŏng 지정 n.C. appointment; designation. *chijŏnghada* 지정하다 appoint; fix; designate.

chik'ida 지키다 v. ① protect; defend ② watch; guard ③ keep; observe.

+ **chikkak** 직각 n.C. right angle.

* **chikkŏrida** 지껄이다 v. chatter; chat; engage in small talk.

chikssŏn 직선 n.C. straight line; beeline. *chikssŏn k'osŭ* 직선 코스 straight course.

chiktchang 직장 n.C. one's place of work.

chiktchŏp 직접 n.C. directly; firsthand; personally. *chiktchŏptchŏk* 직접적 direct; personal; firsthand.

chikt'ong 직통 n.C. direct communication, through traffic. *chikt'ong chŏnhwa* 직통 전화 direct telephone line 〔service〕.

chil 질 n.C. quality. *chiltchŏgin* 질적인 qualitative. *chiltchŏg-ŭro* 질적으로 qualitatively. *yang-kwa chil* 양과 질 quantity and quality.

chilgida 질기다 adj. (be) tough; durable; tenacious.

+ **chilli** 진리 n.C. truth. *kwahag-ŭi chilli* 과학의 진리 the truth of science.

+ **chilmun** 질문 n.C. question; inquiry. *chilmunhada* 질문하다 ask a question.
+ **chilssŏ** 질서 n.C. order; system. *chilssŏ innŭn* 질서 있는 orderly; systematic; methodical.
  chilt'u 질투 n.C. jealousy. *chilt'uhada* 질투하다 be jealous (of); envy; be envious of.
* **chim** 짐 n. load; cargo; luggage; baggage (*Am.*).
* **chimjak'ada** 짐작하다 v. guess; conjecture.
* **chimsŭng** 짐승 n. beast; brute; animal.
  chimyŏng 지명 n.C. nomination. *chimyŏnghada* 지명하다 nominate; name.
* **chinach'ida** 지나치다 v. ① go too far; exceed; do too much ② passthrough. *chinach'in* 지나친 excessive. *chinach'ige* 지나치게 excessively.
# **chinada** 지나다 v. ① pass by; go past; pass through ② expire; terminate; be out.
# **chinaeda** 지내다 v. ① spend [pass] one's time; get along ② hold; observe.
  chinanbŏn 지난번 n. last; last time; the other day. *chinanbŏn-ŭi* 지난번의 last; previous; recent.
  chinbo 진보 n.C. progress; advance. *chinbohada* 진보하다 make progress; improve.
  chinch'al 진찰 n.C. medical examination. *chinch'alhada* 진찰하다 examine. *chinch'alkkwŏn* 진찰권 consultation ticket.
  chindallae 진달래 n. azalea.
+ **chindong** 진동 n.C. vibration; shock. *chindonghada* 진동하다 shake; quake; vibrate.
  chinggŭrŏptta 징그럽다 adj. (be) creepy; disgusting; crawly; uncanny.
  chingmul 직물 n.C. cloth; textile fabrics. *chingmul kongjang* 직물 공장 textile factory [mill].
  chin'gong 진공 n.C. vacuum. *chin'gong-ŭi* 진공의 vacuous. *chin'gong ch'ŏngsogi* 진공청소기 vacuum cleaner *chin'gonggwan* 진공관 vacuum tube [bulb].
  chinhwa 진화 n.C. evolution. *chinhwahada* 진화하다

evolve. *chinhwaron* 진화론 evolutionism.

+ **chinjŏng** 진정 n.C. petition; appeal. *chinjŏnghada* 진정하다 make a petition; appeal. *chinjŏngsŏ* 진정서 written petition.

chinju 진주 n.C. pearl. [p.43] *chinju mokkŏri* 진주 목걸이 pearl necklace *chinju chogae* 진주 조개 pearl oyster.

chinsil 진실 n.C. fact; truth; reality. *chinsilhan* 진실한 true; real. + *chinsil- lo* 진실로 in fact; really.

chinsim 진심 n.C. true heart; sincerity. *chinsim-ŭro* 진심으로 heartily; sincerely.

chintcha 진짜 n. genuine article; real thing; real stuff.

chinŭng 지능 n.C intelligence; mental faculties; intellect *chinŭng chissu* 지능 지수 intelligence quotient [I.Q.].

chinyŏl 진열 n.C. exhibition; show; display. *chinyŏlhada* 진열하다 exhibit; display.

chip 집 n. house; home. *kiwa[ch'oga]jip* 기와[초가]집 tile [thatch] roofed house. *yangoktchip* 양옥집 Western style building.

* **chip** 짚 n. straw. *miltchip* 밀짚 wheat straw. *miltchip moja* 밀짚 모자 straw hat. *chipssin* 짚신 straw sandals.

chip'angi 지팡이 n. (walking) stick; cane.

chipp'il 집필 n.C. writing. *chipp'ilhada* 집필하다 write. *chipp'iltcha* 집필자 writer.

chiptta 집다 v. pick up; take up. *chipke-ro chiptta* 집게로 집다 pick up with tongs.

chiri 지리 n.C. geography.

* **chirŭda** 지르다 v. (sori-rŭl) *chirŭda* (소리를) 지르다 yell; cry aloud; scream; shout.

chisa 지사 n.C. branch (office).

+ **chisang** 지상 n.C. ground. *chisang-ŭi* 지상의 earthly; terrestrial. *chisangkkwŏn* 지상권 surface rights.

chisi 지시 n.C. directions; indication. *chisihada* 지시하다 direct; indicate; point out.

\# **chisik** 지식 n.C. knowledge; information; learning. *chisik kyegŭp* 지식 계급 the educated classes; the intelligentsia.

chisŏng 지성 n.C. intellect; intelligence. *chisŏngin* 지성인 intellectual.

chitta 짙다 adj. (be) dark; deep; thick; dense.

\# **chitta** 짓다 v. ①boil; cook(rice) ② compose(composition) ③ raise; grow (barley) ④ commit(crime) ⑤ wear(smile) ⑥ build; construct(house).

\# **chiuda** 지우다 v. erase; rub[wipe] out; cross out. *chiugae* 지우개 eraser.

* **chiwi** 지위 n.C. position; status; rank; post; situation.

chiwŏn 지원 n.C. application; volunteering. *chiwŏnhada* 지원하다 apply for; volunteer for. *chiwŏnja* 지원자 applicant; candidate.

\# **chiyŏk** 지역 n.C. area; region; zone. *chiyŏktchŏk* 지역적 local; regional.

\# **chŏ** 저 pron. ① (humble) I, me ② that. *chŏ saram* 저 사람 that man. + *chŏgŏt* 저것 that thing[one].

* **choahada** 좋아하다 v. ①like; love; prefer ② be pleased[delighted, glad].

* **chobu** 조부 n.C. grandfather. → harabŏji 할아버지.

chŏch'uk 저축 n.C. saving; savings. *chŏch'uk'ada* 저축하다 save; lay by[aside, up]; store up.

\# **choe** 죄 n.C. crime; sin; offense; guilt. *choe-rŭl pŏmhada/chitta* 죄를 범하다/짓다 commit a crime[sin].

choein 죄인 n.C. criminal; convict; offender; sinner.

\# **chogak** 조각 n.C. piece; bit; fragment; splinter.

* **chŏgi** 저기 pron. that place; there. *chŏgi-e* 저기에 there; over [up, down] there.

\+ **chŏgori** 저고리 n. coat; Korean jacket.

* **choguk** 조국 n.C. fatherland; one's native land.

chŏgŭm 저금 n.C. saving; savings; deposit. *chŏgŭmhada* 저금하다 save; deposit.

\+ **chogŭm** 조금 adv. ① small quantity; a little ②

small number; a few ③ somewhat; a bit.

chogyo 조교 n.C. assistant (teacher, instructor).

chŏhang 저항 n.C. resistance; opposition. *chŏhanghada* 저항하다 resist; oppose; fight against.

* **chohap** 조합 n.C. association; partnership; union; guild; league. *hyŏpttong chohap* 협동 조합 co-operative association[union]; co-op.

chohwa 조화 n.C. harmony. *chohwahada* 조화하다 harmonize (with); be in harmony.

chŏja 저자 n.C. writer; author.

chojak 조작 n.C. invention; fabrication. *chojak´ada* 조작하다 fabricate; invent.

chŏjang 저장 n.C. storage; storing. *chŏjanghada* 저장하다 store; preserve.

chojik 조직 n.C. organization; system. + *chojik´ada* 조직하다 organize; form; start up; compose.

+ **chojŏl** 조절 n.C. accommodation; adjustment. *chojŏlhada* 조절하다 adjust.

+ **chŏjŏllo** 저절로 adv. of itself; naturally; of its own accord; spontaneously; automatically.

chojong 조종 n.C. management; operation. *chojonghada* 조종하다 manage; operate. *chojongsa* 조종사 pilot.

chŏk 적 n.C. enemy; foe; opponent; rival. *chayu-ŭi chŏk* 자유의 적 enemy of freedom.

chŏktchŏlhan 적절한 adj.C. fitting; proper; adequate. *chŏktchŏlhi* 적절히 properly; aptly.

+ **chŏkkŭktchŏgin** 적극적인 adj.C. positive; active; constructive. *chŏkkŭktchŏg-ŭro* 적극적으로 positively; actively.

chokkŏn 조건 n.C. condition; term; stipulation. *nodong chokkŏn* 노동 조건 labor condition. *muchokkŏn* 무조건 unconditional.

chŏkssŏng 적성 n.C. aptitude. *chŏkssŏng kŏmsa* 적성 검사 aptitude test.

* **chŏktta** 적다 adj. write [put] down; record; describe.

chŏktta 적다 adj. (be) few; little; rare; scanty. *chŏktchianŭn* 적지않은 not a few [little].

chŏkttanghada 적당하다 adj.C. *chŏkttanghan* 적당한 suitable; fit(for); proper; competent; appropriate. * *chŏkttang[hi, hage]* 적당[히, 하게] suitably; properly; adequately.

* chŏl 절 n. Buddhist temple.

* chŏlch'a n.C. 절차 process; procedure; formalities. *segwan [yŏkkwŏn] chŏlch'a* 세관[여권] 절차 customs [passport] formalities.

chŏltchŏng 절정 n.C. summit; peak; zenith; climax. *inkki-ŭi chŏlchŏng* 인기의 절정 zenith of one's popularity.

cholda 졸다 v. doze; take a nap.

chŏllam 전람 n.C. exhibition; show. *chŏllamhoe* 전람회 exhibition; exposition.

chŏllyak 전략 n.C. strategy; tactics. *chŏllyaktchŏk* 전략적 strategic *chŏllyakssang* 전략상 strategically.

chŏllyŏk 전력 n.C. electric power; electricity.

+ chŏlttae-ŭi 절대의 adj.C. absolute; unconditional. *chŏlttae-ro* 절대로 absolutely; positively.

chŏm 점 n.C. ① spot; point ② mark; score.

chŏmch'a 점차 adv.C. gradually; by steps[degrees].

chŏmjant'a 점잖다 adj. (be) dignified; genteel; descent. *chŏmjanŭn saram* 점잖은 사람 descent person.

chŏmjŏm 점점 adv.C. by degrees; gradually; more and more; less and less.

+ chŏmnyŏng 점령 n.C. occupation. *chŏmnyŏnghada* 점령하다 occupy; take possession of; capture.

* chŏmsim 점심 n.C. lunch[eon]. *chŏmsim-ŭl mŏktta* 점심을 먹다 have [take] lunch.

chŏmtta 젊다 adj. (be) young; youthful. *chŏlmŭni* 젊은이 young man; youth.

chŏmwŏn 점원 n.C. shop-assistant; (shop) clerk. *yŏjŏmwŏn* 여점원 shopgirl.

chŏn 전 pre-n.C. all; whole; entire; total.

chŏn'gungmin 전국민 whole nation. *chŏnjaesan* 전 재산 entire fortune.

\# **chŏn** 전. pre-n.C. *chŏn-ŭi* 전의 previous; former; last. *chŏn-e* 전에 before; previously.

\+ **chŏnbo** 전보 n.C. telegram; wire. *chŏnbo ch'ida* 전보 치다 telegraph; send a telegram.

\# **chŏnbu** 전부 n.C. all; whole. *chŏnbu-ŭi* 전부의 all; whole; total. *chŏnbu hapch'yŏ* 전부 합쳐 in all; altogether; in full.

* **chŏnch'a** 전차 n.C. streetcar, tramcar *(Eng.)*; electric train.

\# **chŏnch'e** 전체 n.C. the whole; all. *chŏnch'e-ŭi* 전체 의 whole; entire; general. *chŏnch'ejŏg-ŭro* 전체적으 로 generally; as a whole.

chŏnch'ŏl 전철 n.C. subway, electric railway.

chŏnch'uk 전축 n.C. record player; electric phonograph.

* **chŏndŭng** 전등 n.C. electric light [lamp]. *hoejung chŏndŭng* 회중 전등 flashlight.

chong 종 n.C. bell. *chong-ŭl ullida* 종을 울리다 ring [strike, toll] a bell.

chŏngbo 정보 n.C. information; report; news. *chungang chŏngbobu* 중앙 정보부 Central Intelligence Agency (C.I.A). *chŏngbo sahoe* 정보 사회information society.

chŏngbu 정부 n.C. government; administration. *chŏngbu-ŭi* 정부의 governmental; ministerial. *Han-guk chŏngbu* 한국 정부 Korean government.

\# **chŏngch'aek** 정책 n.C. policy.

chŏngch'al 정찰 n.C. price tag [fixed price] system

\# **chŏngch'i** 정치 n.C. politics; government. *chŏngch'i-jŏgin* 정치적인 political.

\+ **chŏngdanghada** 정당하다 adj.C. *chŏngdanghan* 정당 한 just; fair; proper; right. *chŏngdanghage* 정당하 게 justly; rightly; lawfully.

\# **chŏngdo** 정도 n.C. grade; degree; standard; extent.

\+ **chŏnggi-ŭi** 정기의 n.C. regular; periodical. *chŏng-*

gijŏg-ŭro 정기적으로 regularly; periodically; at a fixed period. *chŏnggi kanhaengmul* 정기 간행물 periodical publications.

chŏnggu 정구 n.C. tennis. *chŏngguch'ida* 정구치다 play tennis. *chŏnggujang* 정구장 tennis court.

chŏngguk 정국 n.C. political sitution. *chŏnggug-ŭi puranjŏng[wigi]* 정국의 불안정[위기] unstable political situaion.

chonggyo 종교 n.C. religion. *chonggyosang-ŭi* 종교상의 religious. *chŏnggyo chaep'an* 종교 재판 the Inquisition.

chŏnghada 정하다 v.C. decide; fix; determine; settle; arrange; appoint.

chonghap 종합 n.C. synthesis. *chonghaptchŏk* 종합적 general; synthetic; composite. *chonghap pyŏngwŏn* 종합병원 general hospital.

* **chŏnghwakhada** 정확하다 n.C. correct; accurate; precise. *chŏnghwak'an[k'i]* 정확한[히] correct[ly]; exact[ly]; accurate[ly].

chongi 종이 n. paper. *chongi han chang* 종이 한 장 a sheet of paper. *saekchongi* 색종이 colored paper.

chŏn'gi 전기 n.C. electricity. *chŏn'gi-ŭi* 전기의 electric; electrical. *chŏn'gi-rŭl k'yŏda [kkŭda]* 전기를 켜다 [끄다] turn [switch] on [off] the electrical light.

+ **chongil** 종일 n.C. all day(long); whole day; from morning till night; throughout the day.

chŏngji 정지 n.C. stop; suspension. *chŏngjihada* 정지하다 stop; suspend.

+ **chŏngjŏn** 정전 n.C. ceasefire; truce; *chŏngjŏnhada* 정전하다 have a truce; suspend hostilities. *chŏngjŏn hoedam* 정전 회담 ceasefire conference [order].

chŏngmal 정말 n. the truth. *chŏngmal-lo* 정말로 really; quite; indeed; actually; truly.

chŏngmun 정문 n.C. front gate; main entrance.

chŏngni 정리 n.C. arrangement. *chŏngnihada* 정리하

다 put in order; adjust; arrange.

+ **chŏngnyŏl** 정열 n.C. passion; ardor. *chŏngnyŏltchŏgin* 정열적인 passionate; ardent.

chongnyu 종류 n.C. kind; sort. *on'gat chongnyu-ŭi* 온갖 종류의 all kinds[sorts] of.

+ **chongsahada** 종사하다 v.C. engage in; pursue; follow; devote; be employed.

chŏngsang 정상 n.C. normalcy; normality. *chŏngsangjŏk* 정상적 normal. *chŏngsanghwa* 정상화 normalization.

+ **chŏngse** 정세 n.C. situation; conditions. *kungnae [kukche] chŏngse* 국내[국제] 정세 domestic[international] situation.

+ **chŏngsik** 정식 n.C. formality. *chŏngsig-ŭi* 정식의 formal. *chŏngsik susok* 정식 수속 formal process [procedure].

chŏngsin 정신 n.C. mind; spirit; soul. *chŏngsinjŏgin* 정신적인 spiritual; mental.

chongtchŏm 종점 n.C. terminal(station); last stop (bus).

+ **chŏngŭi** 정의 n.C. justice; righteousness. *chŏngŭigam* 정의감 sense of justice.

* **chŏn'guk** 전국 n.C. whole country[nation]. *chŏn'gug-ŭi* 전국의 nationwide; national.

chŏngwŏl 정월 n.C. January. *chŏngwŏl ch'oharu* 정월 초하루 New Year's Day.

chŏnhada 전하다 v.C. ① convey[deliver] a message. ② hand down; transmit.

+ **chŏnhu** 전후 n.C. front and rear; before and behind.

chŏnhwa 전화 n.C. telephone; phone. *chŏnhwagi* 전화기 telephone (instrument). *chŏnhwahada* 전화하다 (tele)phone; call; call[ring] up.

+ **chŏnhyŏ** 전혀 adv. entirely; completely; utterly, quite.

chŏnja 전자 n.C. electron. *chŏnja kyesan'gi* 전자 계산기 calculator.

chŏnji 전지 n.C. electric cell; battery. *kŏnjŏnji* 건전

지 dry battery.

chŏnjin 전진 n.C. advance; progress. *chŏnjinhada* 전진하다 advance; march forward.

chŏnjung 존중 n.C. respect; esteem. +*chŏnjung-hada* 존중하다 respect; value.

+ **chŏnmun** 전문 n.C. speciality; major. *chŏnmun-ŭro* 전문으로 specially; professionally. *chŏnmun-ga* 전문가 specialist; professional; expert.

chŏnp'yo 전표 n.C. chit; ticket; slip. *maech'ul chŏnp'yo* 매출 전표 sales check.

chŏnse 전세 n.C. a contract to rent a house with a great amount of deposit. *chŏnsetchip* 전세집 house for rent *(Am.).*; house to let *(Eng.)*. *chŏnse pŏsŭ* 전세 버스 chartered bus.

chŏnsi 전시 n.C. exhibition; display. *chŏnsihada* 전시하다 exhibit. *chŏnsidoeda* 전시되다 be displayed.

+ **chŏnsi** 전시 n.C. wartime. *chŏnsi naegak* 전시 내각 war cabinet.

+ **chŏnsin** 전신 n.C. whole body. *chŏnsin-e* 전신에 all over the body.

* **chŏnsŏn** 전선 n.C. electric wire[cord]; cable.

+ **chŏnt'ong** 전통 n.C. tradition. *chŏnt'ongjŏgin[ŭro]* 전통적인[으로] traditional [ly].

chŏnyŏk 저녁 n. evening. *chŏnyŏkttae-e* 저녁때에 in the evening.

* **chŏnyŏn** 전연 adv.C.→ **chŏnhyŏ** 전혀.

chŏpch'ok 접촉 n.C. contact; touch. *chŏpch'ok'ada* 접촉하다 touch; come into contact[touch] (with).

chŏpkkŭn 접근 n.C. approach; access. *chŏpkkŭn-hada* 접근하다 approach; draw[get] near.

chŏpssi 접시 n. plate; dish; saucer; platter.

* **choptta** 좁다 adj. (be) narrow; small; limited.

+ **chŏpttae** 접대 n.C. reception. *chŏpttaehada* 접대하다 receive; entertain.

chorida 졸이다 v. ① boil down ② feel nervous [anxious]

chorŏp 졸업 n.C. graduation. *chorŏp'ada* 졸업하다

finish; graduate from. *chorŏpsaeng* 졸업생 graduate.

+ **chorŭda** 조르다 v. ① tighten; strangle ② importune; press.

chŏryak 절약 n.C. saving; economy; thrift. *chŏryak'ada* 절약하다 economize; save; spare.

* **chosa** 조사 n.C. investigation; inquiry.# *chosahada* 조사하다 inquire; investigate.

+ **chosang** 조상 n.C. ancestor; forefather.

chosim 조심 n.C. caution; heed; care. +*chosimhada* 조심하다 take care; be careful[cautious].

* **chŏt** 젖 n. milk. *chŏtkkoktchi* 젖꼭지 teat; nipple. *chŏsso* 젖소 milk cow.

chot'a 좋다 adj. (be) good; fine; nice. *kajang choŭn* 가장 좋은 best.

chŏtta 젖다 v. get wet; be damp; be soaked [drenched]. *chŏjŭn* 젖은 wet; damp.

choyak 조약 n.C. treaty; pact. *p'yŏnghwa choyak* 평화 조약 peace treaty.

+ **choyonghada** 조용하다 adj. (be) quiet; silent; still; tranquil; placid.

+ **choyonghi** 조용히 adv. quiet.

+ **chubu** 주부 n.C. housewife, mistress of a house.

chuch'a 주차 n.C. parking. *chuch'ahada* 주차하다 park.

chuda 주다 v. give; bestow; award. *kihoe-rŭl chuda* 기회를 주다 give [afford] a chance.

chugida 죽이다 v. kill; murder; slay.

+ **chugŭm** 죽음 n. death. *chugŭm-ŭl murŭpssŭgo* 죽음을 무릅쓰고 at the risk of one's death.

* **chuil** 주일 n.C week(day). *ibŏn [chinan, taŭm] chuil* 이번 [지난, 다음] 주일 this [last, next] week.

chuin 주인 n.C. master; employer; host.

* **chujang** 주장 n.C. assertion; claim. *chujanghada* 주장하다 assert; claim.

chuje 주제 n.C. main subject; theme; motif.

* **chuji** 주지 n.C. chief[head] priest.

chujŏnja 주전자 n.C. (copper, brass) kettle; tea-kettle.

+ **chuk** 죽 n.C. (rice) porridge; gruel. ①

chŭk 즉 adv. namely; that is; so to speak.

chuktta 죽다 v. die; pass away; be killed; lose one's life. [p.122,123] *chugŭn* 죽은 dead; deceased; the late.

chul 줄 n. rope; cord; string; line.

+ **chuldarigi** 줄다리기 n. tug of war. *chuldarigihada* 줄다리기하다 play at a tug of war.

* **chŭlgida** 즐기다 v. enjoy oneself; take pleasure in; amuse oneself.

* **chŭlgŏptta** 즐겁다 adj.(be) pleasant; delightful; glad. *chŭlgŏi/chŭlgŏpkke* 즐거이/즐겁게 happily; pleasantly; cheerfully.

chumal 주말 n.C. weekend. *chumar-e* 주말에 on weekends.

* **chumin** 주민 n.C. inhabitants; notice. *chumok'ada* 주목하다 pay attention to.

+ **chumun** 주문 n.C. order; request. *chumunhada* 주문하다 order; give an order.

chunbi 준비 n.C. preparation; arrangements; provision. * *chunbihada* 준비하다 prepare; arrange; provide for; get ready for.

* **chung** 중 n. Buddhist priest; monk.

chungang 중앙 n.C. center; middle; heart. *chungang-ŭi* 중앙의 central; middle.

chungbok 중복 n.C. duplication. *chungbok'ada* 중복하다 overlap; duplicate.

* **chungdaehada** 중대하다 v.C. importance. *chungdaehan* 중대한 important; serious; grave.

chungdan 중단 n.C. discontinuance. *chungdanhada* 중단하다 discontinue; suspend; break off.

+ **chŭngga** 증가 n.C. increase; addition. *chŭnggahada* 증가하다 increase; rise; grow.

* **chunggan** 중간 n.C. middle; interim; intermediate.

chŭnggŏ 증거 n.C. evidence; proof; testimony.

chungguk 중국 n.C. China.

chunghakkyo 중학교 n.C. middle school; junior high school *(Am.)*.

chungmae 중매 n.C. matchmaking. *chungmaehada/sŏda* 중매하다/서다 make a match.

+ **chŭngmyŏng** 증명 n.C. proof; evidence. * *chŭngmyŏnghada* 증명하다 prove; show; verify.

chŭngŏn 증언 n.C. testimony; witness; (verbal) evidence. *chŭngŏnsŏ* 증언서 written testimony.

chungsim 중심 n.C. center; focus; core. *kongŏb-ŭi chungsim* 공업의 중심 industrial center.

+ **chŭngsŏ** 증서 n.C. deed; bond; certificate; voucher.

+ **chungsun** 중순 n.C. second[middle] ten days of a month.

chungyohada 중요하다 adj.C. chungyohan 중요한 important; essentual; momentous. *chungyosihada* 중요시하다 make[think] much of. →chungsi 중시.

chuptta 줍다 v. pick up; gather (up); find.

+ **churida** 줄이다 v. reduce; decrease; diminish.

churo 주로 adj. mainly; chiefly; principally.

churŭm 주름 n. wrinkles; crumples. ① *churŭmjin ŏlgul* 주름진 얼굴 wrinkled [furrowed] face.

chusa 주사 n.C. injection; shot *(Am.)*. *chusahada* 주사하다 inject. *yebang chusa* 예방 주사 vaccination, preventive injection.

+ **chusik** 주식 n.C. shares *(Eng.)*; stock *(Am.)*.

chuso 주소 n.C. one's residence[abode]; address.

+ **chut'aek** 주택 n.C. house; residence. *hohwa chut'aek* 호화 주택 luxurious house [mansion].

chuŭi 주의 n.C. attention; care. *chuŭihada* 주의하다 be careful of; take care of.

* **chuwi** 주위 n.C. surroundings, circumference. *chuwiŭi* 주위의 neighboring.

chwach'uk 좌측 n.C. left(side). *chwach'uk t'onghaeng* 좌측 통행 "Keep to the left."

chwasŏk 좌석 n.C. seat. *chwasŏkssu* 좌석수 seating capacity.

* **chwau** 좌우 n.C. right and left. *chwau-e* 좌우에 on right and left. *chwauhada* 좌우하다 influence, determine.

chwi 쥐 n. rat; mouse. [p.27,124] *chwiyak* 쥐약 rat poison.

* **chwida** 쥐다 v. hold; take hold of; grasp; seize.

* **ch'a** 차 n.C. (motor)car; auto(mobile). *ch'a-rŭl t'ada* 차를 타다 take a car. *ch'asago* 차사고 car accident.

ch'abyŏl 차별 n.C. distinction; discrimination. *ch'abyŏlhada* 차별하다 discriminate.

+ **ch'ada** 차다 v. ① kick; give a kick. ② click(tongue).

ch'ada 차다 v. carry; wear; put on.

* **ch'ada** 차다 v. (be) full (of); be filled (with); be jammed [overcrowded].

ch'ada 차다 adj. (be) cold; chilly; icy. *ch'anbaram* 찬 바람 chilly [cold] wind.

ch'ado 차도 n.C. road; track.

* **ch'aegim** 책임 n.C. responsibility;liability. *ch'aegim chida* 책임지다 bear responsibility. *ch'aegim-i innŭn* 책임이 있는 responsible.

ch'aek 책 n.C. book; volume. *yŏngŏch'aek* 영어책 English book.

ch'aekppang 책방 n.C. bookstore; bookshop. → **sŏjŏm** 서점

* **ch'aekssang** 책상 n.C. desk; (writing) table [bureau].

ch'aektchang 책장 n.C. bookcase; bookshelf.

ch'aeso 채소 n.C. vegetables; greens. → **yach'ae** 야채.

ch'aeyong 채용 n.C. adoption. *ch'aeyonghada* 채용하다 adopt; decide to use.

ch'ago 차고 n.C. car shed; garage; carport.

* **ch'ai** 차이 n.C. difference; disparity. *ŭigyŏn-ŭi ch'ai* 의견의 차이 difference of opinion.

ch'ajanaeda 찾아내다 v. find out; discover; detect.

ch'ajihada 차지하다 v. occupy; hold; take; possess.

+ **ch'ak'ada** 착하다 v. (be) good; nice; kind-hearted.

ch'aksilhada 착실하다 v.C. (be) steady; trustworthy; faithful; sound. *ch'aksilhi* 착실히 steadily; faithfully.

+ **ch'amga** 참가 n.C. participation. *ch'amgahada* 참가하다 participate[take part] (in); join.

+ **ch'amgo** 참고 n.C. reference. *ch'amgohada* 참고하다 refer; consult. *ch'amgosŏ* 참고서 reference book.

+ **ch'ammal** 참말 n. true remark[story]; truth. *ch'ammallo* 참말로 truly; really; indeed.

+ **ch'amsŏk** 참석 n.C. cattendance. *ch'amsŏk'ada* 참석하다 attend; be present; take part in.

ch'amtta 참다 v. bear; endure; tolerate; stand.

* **ch'amŭro** 참으로 adv. really; truly; indeed.

* **ch'ang** 창 n.C. window. *yurich'ang* 유리창 glass window. *ch'angŭl yŏlda[tatta]* 창을 열다[닫다] open[close] a window.

+ **ch'anggo** 창고 n.C. warehouse; storehouse.

* **ch'angja** 창자 n. intestines; bowels; entrails.

ch'angjak 창작 n.C. original work; artistic creation. *ch'angjak'ada* 창작하다 create; write (a novel).

ch'angjo 창조 n.C. creation. *ch'angjohada* 창조하다 create. *ch'angjojŏk* 창조적 creative.

ch'angmun 창문 n.C. → ch'ang 창.

ch'ansŏng 찬성 n.C. approval; agreement. *ch'ansŏnghada* 찬성하다 approve of; agree.

ch'ap'yo 차표 n.C. ticket (Am.); return ticket (Eng.).

ch'arye 차례 n.C. order; turn. *ch'arye-ro* 차례로 in order; by[in] turns.

ch'atta 찾다 v. search[hunt, look] (for); seek (for, after); look out.

ch'ejung 체중 n.C. (body) weight. *ch'ejung-ŭl talda* 체중을 달다 weigh[measure] oneself. → mommuge 몸무게 weight.

ch'ejo 체조 n.C. gymnastics; gym; physical exercise. *kigye ch'ejo* 기계 체조 heavy gymnastics.

ch'eon 체온 n.C. (body)temperature. *ch'eon-gye* 체
온계 clinical thermometer.

ch'eyuk 체육 n.C. physical education. *ch'eyuk'oe* 체
육회 athletic association.

+ **ch'ida** 치다 v. strike; hit; beat. 〔p.62〕

+ **ch'ida** 치다 v. ① attack; assault ② cut; trim ③
denounce; charge.

+ **ch'ida** 치다 v. send (a telegram).

+ **ch'ida** 치다 v. put up; hang; draw. *k'ŏt'ŭn-ŭl ch'ida*
커튼을 치다 draw a curtain.

ch'ikkwa 치과 n.C. dentistry. *ch'ikkwa pyŏngwŏn* 치
과 · 병원 dental clinic. *ch'ikkwa ŭisa* 치과 의사
dentist; dental surgeon.

ch'ilgi 칠기 n.C. lacquer(ed) ware.

ch'ilp'an 칠판 n.C. blackboard.

ch'ilsip 칠십(70) n.C. seventy. *che ch'ilsib-ŭi* 제 칠십
의 the seventieth.

+ **ch'im** 침 n. saliva; spit. *ch'im-ŭl paetta* 침을 뱉다
spit.

ch'im 침 n.C. acupuncture. *ch'im-ŭl not'a* 침을 놓다
acupuncture; apply acupuncture.

* **ch'ima** 치마 n. skirt. 〔p.5〕

ch'imch'imhada 침침하다 v.C. (be) dark; gloomy;
dim. *ch'imch'imhan pang* 침침한 방 dimly-lit
room.

* **ch'imip** 침입 n.C. invasion. *ch'imip'ada* 침입하다
invade.

* **ch'imnyak** 침략 n.C. aggression; invasion.
ch'imnyak'ada 침략하다 invade.

ch'imsil 침실 n.C. bedroom.

ch'inch'ŏk 친척 n.C. relation; relative; kinsman.

ch'ingch'an 칭찬 n.C. praise; compliment.
ch'ingch'anhada 칭찬하다 praise; admire; speak
highly of.

ch'in-gu 친구 n.C. friend; companion; pal. *yŏja
ch'in-gu* 여자 친구 girl friend.

+ **ch'inhada** 친하다 v.C. (be) intimate; friendly.

ch'inhan pŏt 친한 벗 intimate friend.

ch'injŏl 친절 n.C. kindness. *ch'injŏlhan* 친절한 kind. *ch'injŏlhi* 친절히 kindly.

ch'insŏn 친선 n.C. goodwill; friendship; amity. *ch'insŏn kyŏnggi* 친선 경기 friendly match.

+ **ch'iril** 칠일 n.C. seventh (of the month); seven days.

* **ch'irwŏl** 칠월 n.C. July.

ch'iryo 치료 n.C. medical treatment. *ch'iryohada* 치료하다 treat; cure.

* **ch'iuda** 치우다 v. put in order; tidy up; clear away.

ch'issol 칫솔 n. toothbrush.

ch'o 초 n. candle. *ch'otppul* 촛불 candlelight.

ch'o 초 n.C. vinegar. *cho-rŭl ch'ida* 초를 치다 add vinegar.

ch'ŏ 처 n.C. wife. → anae 아내.

ch'obo 초보 n.C. first steps; rudiment. *ch'obo-ŭi* 초보의 elementary; rudimentary.

ch'odae 초대 n.C. invitation. *ch'odaehada* 초대하다 invite. *ch'odaekkwŏn* 초대권 complimentary ticket. *ch'odaetchang* 초대장 invitation card.

+ **ch'oech'o** 최초 n.C. first; beginning. *ch'oech'o-ŭi* 최초의 first. *ch'oech'o-e* 최초에 in the first place.

* **ch'oego** 최고 n.C. the highest, the best. *ch'oego-ŭi* 최고의 highest; maximum.

* **ch'oegŭn** 최근 n.C. (being) the nearest, the latest. *ch'oegŭn-ŭi* 최근의 recent; late; up-to-date. *ch'oegŭn-e* 최근에 recently; lately.

* **ch'oehu** 최후 n.C. the last; the end. *ch'oehu-ŭi* 최후의 the last; final. **ch'oesin** 최신 n.C. (being) the newest. *ch'oesin-ŭi* 최신의 newest; latest; up-to-date. *ch'oesinsik* 최신식 latest fashion; newest style.

* **ch'ogi** 초기 n.C. early days; first[early] stage.

ch'ogŭp 초급 n.C. beginner's class; junior course. *ch'ogŭp taehak* 초급 대학 junior college.

* **ch'ŏji** 처지 n.C. situation; circumstances; condition.

* **ch'ŏl** 철 n.C. iron; steel. *ch'ŏr-ŭi changmak* 철의 장막 the Iron Curtain. *ch'ŏlmun* 철문 iron gate.

  ch'ŏlhak 철학 n.C. philosophy. *ch'ŏlhak paksa* 철학 박사 doctor of philosophy.

  ch'ŏltchŏ 철저 n.C. thoroughness. *ch'ŏltchŏhan* 철저 한 thorough(going). *ch'ŏltchŏhi* 철저히 thoroughly.

ch'ŏltto 철도 n.C. railway; railroad (Am.). *ch'ŏltto sago* 철도 사고 railroad accident.

ch'ŏn 천(1,000) n.C. a thousand. *such'ŏn-ŭi* 수천의 thousands of. ch'ŏllian 천리안 clairvoyance.

+ **ch'ŏnch'ŏnhi** 천천히 adv. slowly; leisurely; without hurry.

+ **ch'ong** 총 n.C. gun; rifle. *ch'ong-ŭl ssoda* 총을 쏘다 shoot[fire] a gun.

  ch'ongaek 총액 n.C. all; whole; total; general. *ch'ongin'gu* 총인구 total population.

+ **ch'ŏngch'un** 청춘 n.C. youth; springtime of life. *ch'ŏngch'un'gi* 청춘기 adolescence.

  ch'ŏnggu 청구 n.C. demand; claim. *ch'ŏngguhada* 청 구하다 request; demand. *ch'ŏnggusŏ* 청구서 request; demand bill[draft, note. loan].

+ **ch'onggye** 총계 n.C. total amount; (sum) total. *ch'onggyehada* 총계하다 totalize; sum up.

  ch'ŏnggyŏl 청결 n.C. cleanliness; purity. *ch'ŏnggyŏlhada* 청결하다 (be) clean; pure; neat. *ch'ŏnggyŏlhi* 청결히 cleanly.

  ch'onghoe 총회 n.C. general meeting; plenary session.

+ **ch'ongni** 총리 n.C. premier; prime minster.

ch'ŏngnyŏn 청년 n.C. young man; youth.

  ch'ŏngso 청소 n.C. cleaning. *ch'ŏngsohada* 청소하다 clean; sweep. *ch'ŏngsobu* 청소부 janitor; scavenger. *ch'ŏngsoch'a* 청소차 refuse cart; sewage truck. *ch'ŏngsogi* 청소기 cleaning machine.

  chŏngsonyŏn 청소년 n.C. youth; younger generation; teenagers.

  ch'ŏn'guk 천국 n.C. Heaven; Paradise.

ch'ŏnjae 천재 n.C. genius. *ch'ŏnjaejŏk* 천재적 gifted; talented.

+ **ch'ŏnjang** 천장 n.C. ceiling.

+ **ch'ŏnji** 천지 n.C. ① heaven and earth; universe ② world ③ top and bottom.

ch'ŏnnal 첫날 n. first day; opening day.

* **ch'ŏnyŏ** 처녀 n.C. unmarried woman; maiden. *ch'ŏnyŏŭi* 처녀의 unmarried woman's; virgin; maiden. *ch'ŏnyŏji* 처녀지 virgin soil.

ch'ŏnyŏn-ŭi 천연의 adj. natural. *ch'ŏnyŏn kasŭ* 천연 가스 natural gas. *ch'ŏnyŏnsaek* 천연색 natural color.

+ **ch'ŏp** 첩 n.C. concubine; (secret, kept) mistress.

-**ch'ŏrŏm** 처럼 particle *following nouns*. like, (the same) as, as if.

ch'ŏt'ae 첫해 n. first year.

ch'ŏtchae 첫째 n. first (place); No.1; top. *ch'ŏtchae -ŭi* 첫째의 first; primary. *ch'ŏtchae-ro* 첫째로 first of all; to begin with.

+ **ch'ŏtppul** 촛불 n. candlelight.

ch'ŏŭm 처음 n. beginning; start[outset]; origin. *ch'ŏŭm-ŭi* 처음의 first; initial; early. *ch'ŏŭm-e* 처음에 at the beginning; first. *ch'ŏŭm-ŭn* 처음은 at first. *ch'ŏŭm-but'ŏ* 처음부터 from the first [beginning].

ch'uch'ŏn 추천 n.C. recommendation. *ch'uch'ŏnha-da* 추천하다 recommend.

ch'uch'ŭk 추측 n.C. guess; conjecture. *ch'uch'ŭk'-ada* 추측하다 guess; suppose.

ch'uk'a 축하 n.C. congratulation; celebration. *ch'uk'ahada* 축하하다 congratulate; celebrate.

ch'ukku 축구 n.C. football; soccer. *ch'ukku sŏnsu* 축구 선수 football player.

ch'ulbal 출발 n.C. departure; start. *ch'ulbalhada* 출발하다 start; set out; leave.

ch'ulgu 출구 n.C. exit; way out; outlet. pisang ch'ulgu 비상 출구 fire escape, emergency exit.

ch'ulgŭn 출근 n.C. attendance. *ch'ulgŭnhada* 출근하다 attend one's office.

ch'ulhyŏn 출현 n.C. appearance. *ch'ulhyŏnhada* 출현하다 appear; turn[show] up.

+ **ch'ulp'an** 출판 n.C. publication. *ch'ulp'anhada* 출판하다 publish; issue.

ch'ulssin 출신 n.C. ① native ② graduate ③ birth. *ch'ulssinida* 출신이다 come from; be a graduate of. *ch'ulssin-gyo* 출신교 one's Alma Mater.

ch'ulssŏk 출석 n.C. attendance; presence. *ch'ulssŏk'ada* 출석하다 attend; be present at.

ch'ultchang 출장 n.C. official [business] trip; working out of the office. *ch'ultchanggada* 출장가다 go on a business [an official] trip.

* **ch'um** 춤 n. dancing; dance. *ch'umch'uda* 춤추다 dance.

ch'ŭng 층 n.C. story; floor; stairs. *ilch'ŭng* 1층 first floor (Am.); ground floor (Eng.).

ch'ŭngbunhan 충분한 adj.C. sufficient; enough; full. *ch'ŭngbunhi* 충분히 enough; sufficiently; fully.

+ **ch'ŭngdol** 충돌 n.C. collision; conflict. *ch'ŭngdolhada* 충돌하다 collide with.

ch'ŭnggo 충고 n.C. advice; counsel. *ch'ŭnggohada* 충고하다 advice; counsel.

ch'ŭngnyang 측량 n.C. surveying; measuring. *ch'ŭngnyanghada* 측량하다 survey; measure.

ch'ŭngsil 충실 n.C. faithfulness. *ch'ŭngsilhan[hi]* 충실한[히] faithful[ly].

ch'uŏk 추억 n.C. memory; recollection.

ch'uptta 춥다 adj. (be) cold; chilly; feel cold.

ch'usŏk 추석 n.C. Harvest Moon Day [Festival] (15th of August by the lunar calendar).

+ **ch'uwi** 추위 n. cold; coldness. *simhan ch'uwi* 심한 추위 intense [bitter] cold.

ch'waryŏng 촬영 n.C. photographing. *ch'waryŏnghada* 촬영하다 take a photo(graph).

* **ch'wihada** 취하다 v.C. get drunk; become into-

   xicated [tipsy]; feel high.
ch'wihada 취하다 v.C. take, choose.
  ch'wijik 취직 n.C. employment. *ch'wijik´ada* 취직하
   다 find [get] employment; get a job [position].
+ **ch'wimi** 취미 n.C. taste; hobby. *ch'wimi saenghwal*
   취미 생활 leisure activities.
+ **ch'wiso** 취소 n.C. cancelation; withdrawl. *ch'wi-
   sohada* 취소하다 cancel; withdraw.
ch'yŏdaboda 쳐다보다 v. look up; stare [gaze] (at).

$\leqq E \geqq$

-e -에 particle for time, places and inanimate
   objects. at, in, on; to. ① marks the time of an
   action or state. at, in, on. *han si-e* 한 시에 at 1
   o'clock ② marks a place of static location. at, in,
   on. *chip-e itta* 집에 있다 stay at home ③ marks
   the destination of a movement. to. *hakkyo-e
   kada* 학교에 가다 go to school ④ marks an
   impersonal indirect object. to. *ŭnhaeng-e ponaeda* 은행에 보내다 send (someone) to a bank ⑤
   shows reference. per, for, to. *haru-e han pŏn* 하루
   에 한 번 once a day.
-ege -에게 follows animate nouns. for honorific
   people **-kke** -께. to; for; with; from.
  en'ganhada 엔간하다 adj. (be) proper; suitable; be
   considerable; passable.
  enuri 에누리 n . ① overcharge; two prices discount;
   reduction.
-esŏ -에서 particlemarks the location of an action.
   at, in. *hoesa-esŏ ilhada* 회사에서 일하다 work at a
   company ② from (a place, a position, a status, a
   group, a number); out of. *na-nŭn migug-esŏ*

watta 나는 미국에서 왔다 I came from the United States. ③ marks impersonal subject. *chŏngbu-esŏ kyŏltchŏnghan irida* 정부에서 결정한 일이다 It was decided by the government.

$$\leq H \geq$$

\# **hada** 하다 v. ① (transitive v.) do; act; try; play; practice ② (intransitive v.) say; tell. *kaji mallago haetta* 가지 말라고 했다 told (someone) not to go ③ (postnominal v.) do. *kongbu+hada* 공부하다. (do) study ④ (postnominal adj.) be. *haengbok +hada* 행복하다 be happy ⑤ (auxiliary transitive v.) occurs after the infinitive of an adj. expressing human feeling, when the subj. is 2nd or 3rd person. be. *musŏwŏhada* 무서워 하다 be afraid.

\# **hae** 해 n. sun. *hae-ga ttŭda [chida]* 해가 뜨다 [지다] sun rises [sets].

\# **hae** 해 n. year. *chinanhae* 지난해 last year. *haemada* 해마다 every year.

\# **hae** 해 n.C. injury; harm; damage. *hae-rŭl chuda* 해를 주다 do harm (to). *hae-rŭl iptta* 해를 입다 suffer damage.

\# **haean** 해안 n.C. seashore; coast; seaside.

\# **haebang** 해방 n.C. liberation; release. *haebanghada* 해방하다 liberate; release.

haebyŏn 해변 n.C. beach; seashore; coast.

\+ **haegyŏl** 해결 n.C. solution. *haegyŏlhada* 해결하다 solve.

\+ **haegun** 해군 n.C. navy. *haegun-ŭi* 해군의 naval; navy.

haek 핵 n.C. nucleus. *haekkajok* 핵가족 nuclear family. *haengmugi* 핵무기 nuclear weapons. *haek* *silhŏm* 핵실험 nuclear test. *haektchŏnjaeng* 핵전쟁 nuclear war.

\# **haengbok** 행복 n.C. happiness; welfare. *haengbok'-an* 행복한 happy; blessed; fortunate. *haengbok'-age* 행복하게 happily.

* **haengdong** 행동 n.C. action; conduct; deed. *haengdonghada* 행동하다 act.

* **haenghada** 행하다 v.C. act; do; carry out; practice.

* **haengjŏng** 행정 n.C. administration. *haengjŏng kwanch'ŏng* 행정 관청 governmemt office.

  haengun 행운 n.C. good fortune; good luck. *haengun-ŭi* 행운의 fortunate; lucky.

\+ **haengwi** 행위 n.C. act; action; deed. *pulppŏp haengwi* 불법 행위 illegal [unlawful] act.

\+ **haeoe** 해외 n.C. foreign countries. *haeoe-ŭi* 해외의 oversea(s); foreign. *haeoe-e* 해외에 abroad; overseas.

\+ **haeroptta** 해롭다 (be) injurious; harmful; bad.

* **haetppit** 햇빛 sunshine; sunlight.

\+ **haetppyŏt** 햇볕 n. sunbeams; heat of the sunlight.

  hakki 학기 n.C. (school) term; semester (Am.).

  hakkwa 학과 n.C. subject of study. *hakkwa sihŏm* 학과 시험 achievement test.

  hakkyo 학교 n.C. school; college; *hakkyo-e tanida* 학교에 다니다 attend [go to] school.

  hakppŏl 학벌 n.C. academic background.

  hakppumo(hyŏng) 학부모[형] n.C. parents of students.

  hakssaeng 학생 n.C. student. *hakssaeng sijŏl* 학생 시절 school days.

\# **haktcha** 학자 n.C. scholar; learned person.

  haktchang 학장 n.C. dean; rector; president.

  halmŏni 할머니 n. ① grandmother; grandma; granny ② old lady [woman].

\+ **hamburo** 함부로 adv. at random; indiscriminately; without reason.

\# **hamkke** 함께 adv. together (with, along); in

company with.
han 한 pre-n. ① one; a. *han saram* 한 사람 one man.
han madi 한 마디 one word * ② about; nearly;
some.
hana 하나 n. one. hana-ŭi 하나의 one; a.
hanbŏn 한번 n. once; one time. *tan hanbŏn* 단 한번
only once. *hanbŏn-e* 한번에 at a time. *hanbŏn tŏ* 한
번 더 once more.
handu 한두 pre-n. one or two; couple. *handu saram*
한두 사람 one or two persons. *handu pŏn* 한두 번
once or twice.
+ **hanggong** 항공 n.C. aviation; flight. * *hanggong
up´yŏn* 항공 우편 airmail.
hanggu 항구 n.C. port; harbor.
* **hangmun** 학문 n.C. learning; study. *hangmun-i
innŭn* 학문이 있는 educated.
+ **hangno** 항로 n.C. sea route; course; line.
* **hangnyŏn** 학년 n.C. school year; grade (Am.); form
(Eng.).
hangsang 항상 adv.C. always; at all times; usually.
han´guk 한국 n.C. Korea; Republic of Korea
(R.O.K).
han´gŭl 한글 n. the Korean alphabet.
+ **hankkŏbŏn-e** 한꺼번에 adv. at a time; at once; at a
clip.
* **hansum** 한숨 n. (heavy) sigh. *hansum swida* 한숨 쉬
다 (heavy) [draw] a sigh.
hantcha 한자 n.C. Chinese character.
hant´ŏk 한턱 n. treat; entertainment. *hant´ŏk
naeda* 한턱 내다 treat (someone).
hanŭl 하늘 n. sky; heaven. [p.48,138,139]
+ **hanŭnim** 하느님 n. (Lord of) Heaven; God.
+ **hao** 하오 n.C. afternoon. → **ohu** 오후.
+ **hapch´ida** 합치다 v.C. ① put together; joint
together; unite; combine ② sum up.
* **hapkkye** 합계 n.C. total; sum total. *hapkkyehada*
합계하다 sum [add] up.

hapkkyŏk 합격 n.C. passing an examination. *hapkkyŏk'ada* 합격하다 pass; be successful; be accepted.

* **harabŏji** 할아버지 n. ①grandfather; grandpa ② old man.

harin 할인 n.C. discount; deduction. *harinhada* 할인하다 discount; reduce.

haru 하루 n. a [one] day. *haru chongil* 하루 종일 all day long.

hasuk 하숙 n.C. lodging; boarding. *hasuk'ada* 하숙하다 lodge; board; room (Am.). *hasuktchip* 하숙집 lodging [boarding, rooming (Am.)] house.

* **hayat'a** 하얗다 adj. (be) pure white; snow white.

+ **hemaeda** 헤매다 v. wander[roam] about; rove.

him 힘 n. ① strength; force; might ② power; energy.

himdŭlda 힘들다 v. (be) tough; laborious; toilsome.

* **himssŭda** 힘쓰다 v. ① exert oneself; make efforts ② be industrious; be diligent (in).

+ **hobak** 호박 n. ① zucchini, pumpkin ① ② amber. *hobaksaeg-ŭi* 호박색의 ambercolored.

+ **hoebok** 회복 n.C. recovery; restoration. *hoebok'ada* 회복하다 restore; recover; get better.

* **hoedam** 회담 n.C. talk; conversation. *hoedamhada* 회담하다 have a talk; interview.

hoedap 회답 n.C. reply; answer. *hoedap'ada* 회답하다 reply; answer.

hoegap 회갑 n.C. one's 60th birthday anniversary.

hoego 회고 n.C. reflection; recollection. *hoegohada* 회고하다 look back; recollect.

+ **hoegye** 회계 n.C. account(ing); finance. *hoegyehada* 회계하다 account; count.

hoehwa 회화 n.C. conversation; talk; dialogue. *hoehwahada* 회화하다 converse [talk] (with). *Yŏngŏ hoehwa* 영어 회화 English conversation.

hoehwa 회화 n.C. → **kŭrim** 그림.

hoejang 회장 n.C. president, chairman.

\# **hoesa** 회사 n.C. company; corporation; firm. *hoesawŏn* 회사원 company employee; office worker.

\# **hoeŭi** 회의 n.C. meeting; conference. *hoeŭihada* 회의하다 confer (with); hold a conference.

hoewŏn 회원 n.C. member (of a society). *hoewŏn-i toeda* 회원이 되다 become a member.

hogisim 호기심 n.C. curiosity. *hogisim-i kanghan* 호기심이 강한 curious; inquisitive.

\+ **hohwasŭrŏun** 호화스러운 adj.C. splendid; luxurious. *hohwap'an* 호화판 de luxe edition.

hojumŏni 호주머니 n. pocket.

hollan 혼란 n.C. confusion; disorder. *hollanhada* 혼란하다 be confused.

homi 호미 n. weeding hoe.

hŏn 헌 adj. old; shabby; worn-out; secondhand. *hŏnot* 헌 옷 old clothes. *hŏn ch'aek* 헌 책 secondhand book.

honhap 혼합 n.C. mixture. *honhap'ada* 혼합하다 mix; compound.

hondong 혼동 n.C. confusion. *hondonghada* 혼동하다 confuse; mix up.

\+ **honja** 혼자 adv. alone; by oneself; for oneself. *honja salda* 혼자 살다 live alone.

honnada 혼나다 v.C. ① get frightened; become startled ② have bitter experiences.

* **hŏnpŏp** 헌법 n.C. constitution.

\+ **hŏrak** 허락 n.C. consent; assent; permission. *hŏrak'ada* 허락하다 consent to; permit.

horangi 호랑이 n. tiger. [p.71,142,143]

* **hŏri** 허리 n. lower back; waist; loins. *hŏritti* 허리띠 belt; sash; band.

horihorihada 호리호리하다 adj. (be) (tall and) slender; slim.

\# **hu** 후 n.C. after; afterward(s); later. *kŭ hu* 그 후 after that; since then.

hubae 후배 n.C. one's junior (in an organization).

hakkyo hubae 학교 후배 one's junior in school.

huban 후반 n.C. latter [second] half. *hubanjŏn* 후반 전 second half of game.

hubo 후보 n.C. candidate. *hubo sŏnsu* 후보 선수 substitute.

huhoe 후회 n.C. repentance; regret. *huhoehada* 후회 하다 repent of; regret.

\# **hŭida** 희다 adj. (be) white; fair.

* **hŭimang** 희망 n.C. hope; wish; desire. *hŭimanghada* 희망하다 hope (for); wish; desire.

\+ **hŭisaeng** 희생 n.C. sacrifice; victim. *hŭisaenghada* 희생하다 sacrifice. *hŭisaengjŏgin* 희생적인 sacrificial. *hŭisaengyang* 희생양 scapegoat, sacrificial lamb..

hujin 후진 n.C. *hujin-ŭi* 후진의 backward; underdeveloped. *hujin'guk* 후진국 underdeveloped nation.

\# **hŭk** 흙 n. earth; soil; ground.

hŭkp'an 흑판 n.C. blackboard.

\+ **hŭllida** 흘리다 v. ① spill; drop; shed ② lose ③ take no notice (of).

\# **hullyunghada** 훌륭하다 adj. (be) find; splendid. *hullyunghi* 훌륭히 nicely; splendidly.

humch'ida 훔치다 v. ① steal ② wipe (off).

\# **hŭndŭlda** 흔들다 v. shake; wave; swing; rock.

hŭngbun 흥분 n. excitement. *hŭngbunhada* 흥분하다 be [get] excited; be worked up.

\+ **hŭngmi** 흥미 n. interest; zest; intellectual stimulation. *hŭngmi innŭn* 흥미 있는 (be) interesting; stimulating.

\+ **hŭrida** 흐리다 adj. ① (be) cloudy; overcast ② (be) vague; dim; faint. v. ① get cloudy ② make muddy.

\# **hŭrŭda** 흐르다 v. flow; stream; run (down).

\# **hut'ŏjida** 흩어지다 v. be scattered; be dispersed.

hwa 화 n.C. disaster; calamity. *hwa-rŭl iptta* 화를 입 다 meet with a calamity.

hwabun 화분 n.C. flowerpot.

hwach'o 화초 n.C. flower; flowering plant. *hwach'o chaebae* 화초 재배 floriculture.

hwagin 확인 n.C. confirmation; affirmation. *hwaginhada* 확인하다 confirm; affirm.

\# **hwahak** 화학 n.C. chemistry. *hwahag-ŭi* 화학의 chemical. *hwahak yakp'um* 화학 약품 chemicals.

hwajang 화장 n.C. make up. *hwajanghada* 화장하다 make up one's face; make one's toilet.

hwaje 화제 n.C. subject [topic, theme] of conversation.

hwakttae 확대 n.C. magnify; expand; spread.

hwakssilhan 확실한 adj. sure; certain. *hwakssilhi* 확실히 certainly; surely.

\+ **hwakssin** 확신 n.C. conviction; firm belief. *hwakssinhada* 확신하다 be conviction of; be sure of.

hwalbalhada 활발하다 adj. active; vigorous; lively.

hwaltcha 활자 n.C. type; printing type.

\# **hwalttong** 활동 n.C. activity; action. *hwalttong-jŏgin* 활동적인 active; dynamic. *hwalttongga* 활동가 person of action.

\+ **hwan** 환 n.C. (note of) exchange; check; money order.

* **hwangje** 황제 n.C. emperor.

* **hwan'gyŏng** 환경 n.C. the environment; circumstances; surroundings. *hwan'gyŏng oyŏm* 환경 오염 environmental pollution.

\+ **hwanhada** 환하다 adj. (be) bright; light. *hwanhan pang* 환한 방 well-lighted room.

hwanja 환자 n.C. patient; case. *k'ollera hwanja* 콜레라 환자 cholera patient [case].

hwanyŏng 환영 n.C. welcome. *hwanyŏnghada* 환영하다 welcome; receive warmly. *hwanyŏnghoe* 환영회 reception.

* **hwanyul** 환율 n.C. exchange rate. *hwanyul insang* 환율 인상 raise in exchange rates.

* **hwap'ye** 화폐 n.C. money; currency; coinage.

\+ **hwasan** 화산 n.C. volcano.

hwayoil 화요일 n.C. Tuesday (Tues).

hwiballyu 휘발유 n.C. gasoline(Am.), petrol(Eng.); volatile oil.

* **hwŏlssin** 훨씬 adv. by far; very much; greatly.

* **hyanggi** 향기 n.C. fragrance; perfume; scent. *hyanggiroptta* 향기롭다 (be) fragrant; sweet-smelling.

+ **hyangsang** 향상 n.C. elevation; improvement. *hyangsanghada* 향상하다 rise; be elevated; improve.

hyet'aek 혜택 n.C. favo(u)r; benefit; benevolence. *munmyŏng-ŭi hyet'aek* 문명의 혜택 benefit of civilization.

* **hyŏ** 혀 n. tongue. *hyŏ-rŭl naemilda* 혀를 내밀다 stick out one's tongue.

* **hyokkwa** 효과 n.C. effect; efficacy. *hyokkwa innŭn* 효과 있는 effective.

+ **hyŏmnyŏk** 협력 n.C. cooperation. *hyŏmnyŏk'ada* 협력하다 cooperate with; work together.

* **hyŏndae** 현대 n.C. present age [day]; modern times; today. *hyŏndae-ŭi* 현대의 current; modern. *hyŏndaehwa* 현대화 modernization.

* **hyŏngje** 형제 n.C. brothers; sisters. *hyŏngje chamae* 형제 자매 brothers and sisters.

* **hyŏngp'yŏn** 형편 n.C. situation; condition; circumstance.

* **hyŏngsik** 형식 n.C. form; formality; mode. *hyŏngsiktchŏgin* 형식적인 formal; perfunctory.

* **hyŏngt'ae** 형태 n.C. form; shape.

hyŏn'gŭm 현금 n.C. cash; realy money. *hyŏngŭm-ŭro* 현금으로 in cash. *hyŏn'gum chibul* 현금 지불 cash payment.

hyŏnjae 현재 n.C. now; at present; currently. *hyŏnjae-kkaji* 현재까지 up to now. *hyŏnjae-ŭi* 현재의 present.

hyŏnjang 현장 n.C. scene (of action), the place of (of action). *hyŏnjang-esŏ* 현장에서 at the scene, on the spot.

hyŏnsang 현상 n.C. the present state [situation].

* **hyŏnsil** 현실 n.C. actuality. *hyŏnsir-ŭi* 현실의 actual;
real. *hyŏnsiltchŏg-ŭro* 현실적으로 actually; really.
hyŏsiljuŭi 현실주의 realism.

hyuga 휴가 n.C. holidays; vacation. *yŏrŭm hyuga* 여
름 휴가 summer vacation.

hyuji 휴지 n.C. toilet paper; tissue paper. *hyujit'ong* 휴지통 waste(paper) basket.

* **hyujŏn** 휴전 n.C. truce; armistice. *hyujŏnsŏn* 휴전선
truce line. *hyujŏn hoedam* 휴전 회담 truce
[armistice] talks.

hyuŏp 휴업 n.C. closing; going out of business
[trading]. *hyuŏp'ada* 휴업하다 close (office,
factory), go out of business.

hyusik 휴식 n.C. rest; time to relax; recess.
hyusik'ada 휴식하다 (take a) rest; relax.

$$\leq I \geq$$

\# **-i** -이 n. person. *kŭi* 그이 that person; he [him]; she
[her]. *chiŭni* 지은이 the author, the writer.

\# **i** 이 pre-n. this; present; current. *idal* 이 달 this
month. *i ch'aek* 이 책 this book.

\# **i** 이 n.C. 2, two.

* **i** 이 n. tooth.① *i-ŭi* 이의 dental. *i-ga ap'ŭda* 이가 아프
다 have a toothache.

\# **-i/ka** -이/가 particle. *-i* occurs after consonants,
-ga(⟨ka⟩) after vowels. ① marks the subject of a
v. or adj. expression. *hanŭl-i p'ŭrŭda* 하늘이 프르다
The sky is blue. ② marks the subject of a
phrase, possibly including another more
immediate subject of the v. of adj. *nae-ga ton-i
ŏptta* 내가 돈이 없다 I have no money. ③ marks the
complement of a negative copular expression.

igŏs-ŭn sagwa-ga anida 이것은 사과가 아니다 This is not an apple. ④ marks the complement (word) of a change of state (+*toeda* 되다) *mur-i ŏrŭm-i toenda* 물이 얼음이 된다 Ice becomes water.

ibal 이발 n.C. haircut(ting); hairdressing. *ibarhada* 이발하다 have one's hair cut. *ibalsso* 이발소 barbershop.

* **ibŏn** 이번 n. this time; now. *ibŏn-ŭi* 이번의 new; present. *ibŏn iryoil* 이번 일요일 this coming Sunday.

+ **ibul** 이불 n. Korean quilt; duvet(Eng.), comforter(Am.); coverlet.

ibwŏn 입원 n.C. hospitalization. *ibwŏnhada* 입원하다 enter [be sent to] hospital.

ibyŏl 이별 n.C. parting; separatirhada 이별하다 part; scparate.

* **ich'i** 이치 n.C. reason; principle. *ich'i-e matta* 이치에 맞다 be reasonable.

ich'ŭng 이층 n.C. second floor [story] *(Am.)*; first floor [storey] *(Eng.)*.

+ **idong** 이동 n.C. transfer; movement. *idonghada* 이동하다 move; transfer.

idŭn(ji) -이든(지) particle *(after n.)* whether ...or; either...or.

* **igida** 이기다 v. win; gain a victory; defeat.

igŏt 이곳 pron. this place; here. *igos-e* 이곳에 here; in this place.

igŏt 이것 pron. this; this one. *igŏs-ŭro* 이것으로 with this; now. *igŏt chom poseyo* 이것 좀 보세요 Please, look here.

* **iha** 이하 n.C. less than. *iha-ŭi* 이하의 less than; under; below.

* **ihae** 이해 n.C. understanding; comprehension. *ihaehada* 이해하다 understand; comprehend.

ihu 이후 n.C. after this; from now on; hereafter. *kŭ ihu* 그 이후 since then; thereafter.

* **iik** 이익 n.C. profit; gain; *iig-i innŭn* 이익이 있는 profitable; paying.

ija 이자 n.C. interest. *ija-ga putta* 이자가 붙다 yield interest.

ijŏbŏrida 잊어버리다 forget.

ijŏn 이전 n.C. being previous to. *ijŏn-ŭi* 이전의 previous; former. *ijŏn-e* 이전에 before; formerly; once.

+ **ijŏn** 이전 n.C. removal; moving (Am.); transfer. *ijŏnhada* 이전하다 remove; transfer.

ijung 이중 n.C. double. *ijung-ŭi* 이중의 double; twofold; dual. *ijung kuktchŏk* 이중 국적 dual nationality. *ijungju[ch'ang]* 이중주[창] duet.

ikkŭlda 이끌다 v. guide; conduct; lead; show [usher] in.

ikssuk'ada 익숙하다 adj.C. (be) familiar; be skilled in; be at home in.

iktta 읽다 v. read; persue. *chalmot iktta* 잘못 읽다 misread. *ta iktta* 다 읽다 read through.

* **iktta** 익다 v. ripen; mature; become [get] ripe; fermented; be cooked. *igŭn* 익은 ripe; mellow; cooked. *igŭn kimch'i* 익은 김치 fermented kimch'i.

il 일 n.C. 1 one. *cheil* 제일 the first.

il 일 n. work; task; labo(u)r.

ilban 일반 n.C. general. *ilban-ŭi* 일반의 general; universal. *ilbanjŏg-ŭro* 일반적으로 generally; in general.

Ilbon 일본 n.C. Japan. *Ilbon-ŭi* 일본의 Japanese. *ilbonmal* 일본말 Japanese (language). *Ilbonin* 일본인 Japanese (persons).

ilbŏn 일번 n.C. first; No.1. *ilbŏn-ŭi* 1번의 first; top.

* **ilbu** 일부 n.C. part; portion. *ilbu-ŭi* 일부의 partial; a part of; some.

+ **ilburŏ** 일부러 adv. on purpose; intentionally; purposely.

+ **ilch'e** 일체 n.C. ① all; everything. *ilch'e-ŭi* 일체의 all; every; whole. ② entirely; wholly; altogether. *ilch'e chungsaeng* 일체 중생 (Buddhistic term) all living beings.

+ **ilch'i** 일치 n.C. coincidence; agreement; consent. cooperation. *ilch'ihada* 일치하다 agree (with); accord (with); coincide (with); consent to; cooperate (with).

ilch'ŭng 일층 n.C. ① first floor *(Am.)*; gound floor *(Eng.)* ② more; still more.

ilgi 일기 n.C. weather. *ilgi yebo* 일기 예보 weather forecast [report].

ilgi 일기 n.C. diary; journal. *ilgitchang* 일기장 diary.

* **ilgop** 일곱 n. seven. *ilgoptchae* 일곱째 the seventh.

ilgŭp 일급 n.C. first class. *ilgŭb-ŭi* 일급의 first-class.

ilgwa 일과 n.C. daily lesson [work]; (daily) routine.

* **ilhada** 일하다 v. work; labor.

+ **ilhaeng** 일행 n.C. party; company; group.

ilhŭn 일흔 n. seventy; three score and ten.

‖ **-ilkka** -일까 particle *(after n.)* ① will it be? ② do you suppose ...? cf. *-ŭlkka*.

ilkkŏri 일거리 n. piece of work; task; things to do.

illiri 일일이 adv.C. one by one; in detail; everything.

‖ **illyu** 인류 n.C. human species; human beings. *illyu-ŭi* 인류의 human.

ilp'um 일품 n.C. a superior article. *ilp'um yori* 일품 요리 single-dish course, one-course dinner. *ch'ŏnha ilp'um* 천하 일품 article of unequaled quality.

* **ilssaeng** 일생 n.C. lifetime; one's (whole) life. *ilssaeng-ŭi* 일생의 lifelong.

+ **ilssang** 일상 n.C. every day; daily; usually. *ilssang-ŭi* 일상의 daily; everyday.

+ **ilssi** 일시 n.C. at one time; for a time [while]. *ilssijŏk* 일시적 momentary; temporary.

‖ **ilt'a** 잃다 v. lose; miss; be deprived [bereft] of.

iltchari 일자리 n. job; position. *iltchari-rŭl ŏtta* 일자리을 얻다 take [get] a job.

iltchehi 일제히 adv.C. altogether; in a chorus.

‖ **-iltchirado** 일지라도 particle *(after n.)* even though,

even if, regardless of. cf. *-ŭltchirado*.

+ **iltchong** 일종 n.C. kind; sort; *iltchong-ŭi* 일종의 a kind [sort] of.

iltchŏng 일정 n.C. (day's) schedule; itinerary.

iltchŏnghan 일정한 adj.C. fixed; definite; regular; settled.

iltchu 일주 n.C. round; tour. *iltchuhada* 일주하다 go [travel] round.

* **ilttae** 일대 n.C. whole area [distrct]; neighborhood (of).

ilttan 일단 adv.C. once (at least); for the moment; first.

ilttŭng 일등 n.C. first class; first rank [grade]. *ilttŭngsang* 일등상 first prize.

* **ima** 이마 n. forehead; brow.

imank'ŭm 이만큼 adv. this [so] much[many, big, long].

imdae 임대 n.C. lease. *imdaehada* 임대하다 lease [rent] out; let; hire out. *imdaeryo* 임대료 rent.

imgi 임기 n.C. term of service[office].

imgŭm 임금 n. king; sovereign.

imi 이미 adv. already; now; yet.

imin 이민 n.C. emigrate (to); immigration. *iminhada* 이민하다 emigrate (to); immigrate (from).

immatch'uda 입맞추다 v. kiss; give (a person) a kiss.

immyŏng 임명 n.C. appointment; nomination. *immyŏnghada* 임명하다 appoint to; nominate.

* **imsi** 임시 n.C. being temporary. *imsi-ŭi* 임시의 temporary; provisional. *imsi-ro* 임시로 specially; temporarily.

-(i)myŏn -(이)면 conditinal particle (*after n.*) if (when) it is, as for. other shapes: -(ŭ)myŏn, -(i)myŏn.

-in'ga -인가 particle (*after n.*) is it/he, etc.? (plain style question marker). cf. *-ŭn'ga*.

in'gan 인간 n.C. human being; person. *in'gan-ŭi* 인

간의 human.

in'gong 인공 n.C. human skill. *in'gong-ŭi(jŏk)* 인공의 〔적〕 artificial; unnatural. *in'gong wisŏng* 인공 위성 artificial satellite.

in'gu 인구 n.C. population. *in'gu chosa* 인구 조사 census.

* **inhada** 인하다 v. be due (to); be caused (by); be attributable (to). *inhayŏ* 인하여 because of.

inhyŏng 인형 n.C. doll. *inhyŏng kat'ŭn* 인형 같은 doll-like.

-ini -이니 particle (sentence final question marker used after n. when speaking to small children or close friends) is it/he, etc.? cf. *-ŭni*.

-ini(kka) -이니까 sequential particle (*after n.*) because/since it is. cf. *-ŭnikka*.

-(i)nji -(이)ㄴ지 particle ① copula -i- with -nji followed by verbs of knowing, telling, asking, if/whether it is ② (with *-ra* -라) since it is, as it is. other shape: -nji, -(nŭ)nji.

injong 인종 n.C. (human) race. *injong ch'abyŏl* 인종 차별 racial discrimination.

+ **injŏng** 인정 n.C. recognition; acknowledgement. *injŏnghada* 인정하다 recog- nize; acknowledge; approve.

inkki 인기 n.C. popularity. *inkki innŭn* 인기 있는 popular; favorite.

inkkwŏn 인권 n.C. human rights.

inkkyŏk 인격 n.C. personality; character. *inkkyŏk-tcha* 인격자 person of character.

* **inmul** 인물 n.C. person. *k'ŭn inmul* 큰 인물 great person 〔figure〕.

innae 인내 n.C. patience; endurance. *innaehada* 인내하다 endure; be patient with.

inp'um 인품 n.C. personality; character.

* **insa** 인사 n.C. greeting; salutation; bow. *insahada* 인사하다 greet; salute; (make a) bow.

insaeng 인생 n.C. life; human 〔person's〕 life.

insaenggwan 인생관 view of life.

insam 인삼 n.C. ginseng. *insamch'a* 인삼차 ginsaeng tea.

insim 인심 n.C. heart; feelings; emotions. *insim-i chot'a* 인심이 좋다 be good-hearted.

+ **inswae** 인쇄 n.C. printing; print. *inswaehada* 인쇄하다 print. *inswaemul* 인쇄물 printed matter.

inwŏn 인원 n.C. number of persons; staff; personnel.

inyŏm 이념 n.C. idea; ideology.

+ **inyŏn** 인연 n.C. affinity; connection; (Buddhistic term) karmic relation. *inyŏn-ŭl maetta* 인연을 맺다 form relations.

inyong 인용 n.C. quotation; citation. *inyonghada* 인용하다 quote; cite.

ip 입 n. mouth. ①, [p.74,112] *ib-ŭl pŏllida[tamulda]* 입을 벌리다 [다물다] open [shut] one's mouth.

* **ip'ak** 입학 n.C. (school) entrance. *ip'ak'ada* 입학하다 enter a school. *ip'ak sihŏm* 입학 시험 entrance examination.

ip'ida 입히다 v. ① dress; clothe; put on ② plate; coat; gild.

ipkku 입구 n.C. entrance; way in. *ipkku-esŏ* 입구에서 at the entrance[door].

ipkkuk 입국 n.C. entrance into a country. *ipkkuk'ada* 입국하다 enter a coutry. *ipkkuk satchŭng* 입국 사증 entry visa. *ipkkuk chŏlch'a* 입국 절차 formalities for entry.

* **ipkkŭm** 입금 n.C. deposit/receipt of money. payment on account. *ipkkŭm- hada* 입금하다 deposit/receive (some money).

ipssagwi 잎사귀 n. leaf; leaflet.

ipssi 입시 n.C. entrance examination. ←*ip'ak sihŏm* 입학 시험.

* **ipssul** 입술 n. lips. *win[araen] ipssul* 윗[아랫] 입술 upper [lower] lip.

iptchang 입장 n.C. entrance; admission. *iptchang-*

hada 입장하다 enter; be admitted. *iptchangkkwŏn* 입장권 admission ticket.

iptchŭng 입증 n.C. giving proof. *iptchŭnghada* 입증하다 prove; give proof; testify.

iptta 입다 v. ① put on; wear; be dressed in ② owe; be indebted to.

-ira -이라 particle (sentence final marker in assertive statements used after n.) it is. cf. *-ŭra.*

-iranŭn -이라는 particle (quotative modifier after n.) that is (called), someone/something (called). cf. *-ŭranŭn.*

irijŏri 이리저리 adv. this way and that; here and there; up and down.

irŏk'e 이렇게 adj. (adverbial form) thus; like; this; in this way; so.

irŏn 이런 adj. (modifying form) such; like this; of this kind.

+ **iron** 이론 n.C. theory. *ironsang(jŏgŭro)* 이론상[적으로] theoretically; in theory.

irŏnada 일어나다 v. ① rise; get up; stand up; arise ② happen; occur; break out.

irŏsŏda 일어서다 v. stand up; rise (to one's feet); get up.

iruda 이루다 v. accompilsh; achieve; attain.

* **irŭda** 이르다 adj. ① (be) early; premature. *irŭn ach'im* 이른 아침 early morning v. ② arrive ③ tell.

irŭm 이름 n. name; full name. [p.71]

+ **irŭnba** 이른바 pre-n. so-called; what is called.

irwŏl 일월 n.C. January.

iryoil 일요일 n.C. Sunday.

iryŏk 이력 n.C. one's personal history; one's career [record]. *iryŏkssŏ* 이력서 curriculum vitae, resume.

iryong 일용 n.C. everyday [daily] use. *iryongp'um* 일용품 daily necessities.

isa 이사 n.C. removal; moving. *isahada* 이사하다 move.

isa 이사 n.C. director; trustee. *isahoe* 이사회 board of directors.

isanhada 이산하다 v. be scattered; be dispersed. *isan kajok* 이산 가족 dispersed [separated] families. *isan kajok ch´atkki undong* 이산 가족 찾기 운동 Campaign for Reunion of Dispersed Family Members.

isang 이상 n.C. strangeness; abnormality. *isanghan/sŭrŏun* 이상한/스러운 odd; strange; queer.

+ **isang** 이상 n.C. ideal. *isangjŏg(ŭro)* 이상적(으로) ideal(ly). *isangjuŭi* 이상주의 idealism.

* **isang** 이상 n.C. more than; over; above; beyond. *simnyŏn isang* 십년 이상 more than 10 years.

isŏng 이성 n.C. reason. *isŏngjŏgin* 이성적인 rational.

issusigae 이쑤시개 n.C. toothpick.

isŭl 이슬 n. dew; dewdrops.

isŭlbi 이슬비 n. drizzle; mizzle; misty rain.

itchok 이쪽 n. this side[way]; our side.

itchŏm 이점 n.C. advantage; vantage point.

itta 있다 v. ① be; there is[are]; exist ② stay; remain ③ stand; be situated; be located ④ consist (in); lie (in) ⑤ have, possess.

itta 잇다 v. join; put together; connect; link.

itta 잊다 v. ① forget; slip one's mind ② leave behind. *ijŭl ssu ŏmnŭn* 잊을 수 없는 unforgettable.

ittagŭm 이따금 adv. from time to time; now and then; at times.

+ **it´ŭl** 이틀 n. ① two days ② second day (of month).

* **it´ŭnnal** 이튿날 n. next [following] day

* **iut** 이웃 n. neighbo(u)rhood. [p.1] *iutchip* 이웃집 neighbo(u)ring house; next door.

iwŏl 이월 n.C. February.

iyagi 이야기 n. talk; conversation; chat; discussion. *iyagihada* 이야기하다 speak; talk; have a conversation.

* **iyong** 이용 n.C. use; utilization. # *iyonghada* 이용하다 make use of; utilize. + *iyongdoeda* 이용되다 be

utilized.

iyu 이유 n.C. reason; cause; motive; grounds; pretext; why. *iyu ŏpssi* 이유없이 without (good) reason. *···ŭi iyu-ro* ···의 이유로 by reason of ···. *iyu-rŭl mutta* 이유를 묻다 inquire into the reason of.

iyul 이율 n.C. interest rate.

iyun 이윤 n.C. profit; gain. → **iik** 이익.

$$\leq K \geq$$

* **ka, kajangjari** 가, 가장자리 n. edge, verge, brink, margin.

-ka/i -가/이 particle. *-i* occurs after consonants, *-ga(⟨ka)* after vowels. ① marks the subject of a v. or adj. expression. *hanŭl-i p'ŭrŭda* 하늘이 프르다 The sky is blue. ② marks the subject of a phrase, possibly including another more immediate subject of the v. of adj. *nae-ga ton-i ŏptta* 내가 돈이 없다 I have no money. ③ marks the complement of a negative copular expression. *igŏs-ŭn sagwa-ga anida* 이것은 사과가 아니다 This is not an apple. ④ marks the complement (word) of a change of state (+*toeda* 되다) *mur-i ŏrŭm-i toenda* 물이 얼음이 된다 Ice becomes water.

* **-ka()ga** -가 suffix. street, block; district. *oga* 5가 the fifth street.

  kabang 가방 n. bag, briefcase, satchel, trunk, suitcase. *sonkkabang* 손가방 valise, handbag.

* **kabyŏptta** 가볍다 adj. (be) light, not serious.

* **kach'i** 가치 n.C. value, worth, merit. *kach'i innŭn* 가치 있는 valuable, worthy. *kach'i ŏmnŭn* 가치 없는 worthless, of no value.

kach'i ~ kaehyŏk 같이 adv. ① like, as, likewise, similary, in the same way, equally ② (along, together) with, in company with.

kach'uk 가축 n.C. domestic cattle, livestock. *kach'uk pyŏng'wŏn* 가축 병원 veterinary hospital, pet's hospital.

kada 가다 v. go, proceed. *aux.v.* do.

kaduda 가두다 v. shut in (up), lock in (up), confine, imprison.

kadŭk 가득 adv. full. *kadŭk ch'ada* 가득 차다 be full (to the brim).

* kae 개·n. dog, hound, puppy. [p.6] *suk'ae* 수캐 male dog *amk'ae* 암캐 bitch. *kaejosim* 개조심 Beware of the dog.

kae 개 n.C. piece, unit. *pinu tasŏt kae* 비누 다섯 개 five pieces[cakes] of soap.

+ kaebal 개발 n.C. development, exploitation, reclamation. *kaebalhada* 개발하다 develop, exploit, improve.

kaebang 개방 n.C. opening. *kaebanghada* 개방하다 (leave) open, free, throw open (a place) to the public.

kaech'ŏnjŏl 개천절 n.C. the National Foundation Day (of Korea): Oct. 3, the Foundation Day of Korea.

kaeda 개다 n. fold (up), wrap up. *ibujari-rŭl kaeda* 이부자리를 개다 fold up [turn down] the beddings [bedclothes].

kaeda 개다 n. clear up, become clear. *Piga kaetta* 비가 갰다 The rain is over.

kaegang 개강 n.C. opening a course. *kaeganghada* 개강하다 begin a class, begin (the first day of) the semester [series of one's lecture].

* kaeguri 개구리 n. frog. [p.7] *sigyong kaeguri* 식용 개구리 edible frog.

kaehak 개학 n.C. beginning of school. *kaehak'ada* 개학하다 begin school, school begins.

+ kaehyŏk 개혁 n.C. reform, innovation. *kaehyŏk'ada*

개혁하다 reform, innovate.

* **kaein** 개인 n.C. individual, private person. *kaeinjŏk* 개인적 individual, private, personal.

kaejŏng 개정 n.C. revision. *kaejŏnghada* 개정하다 revise. *kae'jŏngp'an* 개정판 revised edition, revision.

kaemi 개미 n. ant. *kaemitte* 개미떼 swarm of ants.

kaenyŏm 개념 n.C. concept, general idea, notion.

kaeron 개론 n.C. outline, introduction, survey. *yŏngmunhak kaeron* 영문학 개론 an introduction to English literature.

+ **kaeryang** 개량 n.C. improvement, renovation. *kaeryanghada* 개량하다 improve, reform, (make) better.

kaesŏn 개선 n.C. improvement, betterment. *kaesŏnhada* 개선하다 improve, amend, reform.

kage 가게 n. shop, store (*Am.*). *kumŏng kage* 구멍 가게 neighborhood [penny candy] store.

kagong 가공 n.C. processing. *kagonghada* 가공하다 process, work upon. *kagong sikp'um* 가공 식품 processed food(stuffs).

kagu 가구 n.C. furniture. *kagujŏm[sang]* 가구점[상] furniture store.

* **kagyŏk** 가격 n.C. price, cost. *tomae[somae] kagyŏk* 도매[소매] 가격 wholesale[retail] price.

+ **kahada** 가하다 n.C. add (up), sum up. *amnyŏg-ŭl kahada* 압력을 가하다 give [apply] pressure (to).

kaip 가입 n.C. joining, affiliation, subscription. *kaip'ada* 가입하다 join, become a member of, affiliate oneself with, subscribe for.

* **kajang** 가장 n.C. disguise, masquerade. *kajanghada* 가장하다 disguise oneself. *kajang haengnyŏl* 가장 행렬 fancy procession.

kajang 가장 adv. most, extremely, exceedingly. *kajang arŭmdaun* 가장 아름다운 the most beautiful.

kajang 가정 n.C. the head of a family.

+ **kaji** 가지 n. eggplant, egg apple.

\# **kaji** 가지 n. kind, sort, class. *se kaji* 세 가지 three kinds. *kajigaji-ŭi* 가지 가지의 various, diverse, sundry.

kaji 가지 n. branch, bough, limb.

\# **kajida** 가지다 v. have, hold, carry, process. *aux.v.*

\# **kojok** 가족 n.C. family, members of a family. *kajok kyehoek* 가족 계획 family planning.

\# **kajŏng** 가정 n.C. home, family. *kajŏng kyosa* 가정 교사 private teacher. *kajŏng kyoyuk* 가정 교육 home education, discipline.

kajŏng 가정 n.C. housekeeping, household management. *kajŏngkkwa* 가정과 department of domestic science. *kajŏngbu* 가정부 housekeeper.

\+ **kajuk** 가죽 n. skin, hide, leather. [p.72]

* **kajŭn** 갖은 pre-n. all, all sorts of, every. *kajŭn kosaeng* 갖은 고생 all sorts of hardship.

\# **kak-** 각- prefix/pre-n. each, every. *kakkuk* 각국 every country, each nation.

kakch'ŏ 각처 n.C. every[each] place, various places. *kakch'ŏ-e* 사처에 everywhere, in all[various] places.

\# **kakkai** 가까이 adv. near, close by[to], nearly, almost. *kakkai oda* 가까이 오다 come up close. *paengmyŏng kakkai* 백명 가까이 nearly one hundred persons.

\# **kakkak** 각각 adv. separately, respectively, apart. *kakkag-ŭi* 각각의 respective.

\# **kakkapta** 가깝다 adj. (be) near, be close by. [p.63]

kakki 각기 n.C. beriberi. *kakkai-e kŏllida* 각기에 걸리 다 have an attack of beriberi.

* **kakkŭm** 가끔 adv. occasionally, from time to time, now and then, sometimes.

kaktcha 각자 n.C. each, each [every] one, individually, respectively.

\+ **kaktchi** 각지 n.C. every [each] place, various places [quarters]

kaktchong 각종 n.C. every kind, various kinds, all

kinds [sorts]. *kaktchong-ŭi* 각종의 all sorts of, various.

+ **kaktto** 각도 n.C. angle, degrees of an angle.

  kalbi 갈비 n. ribs. *kalbit´ang* 갈비탕 beef-rib soup.

  kalda 갈다 v. ① sharpen, grind ② polish, burnish ③ rub, chafe. *k´ar-ŭl kalda* 칼을 갈다 sharpen a knife.

+ **kalda** 갈다 v. change, replace, substitute, alter. *irŭm-ŭl kalda* 이름을 갈다 change one's name.

* **kalda** 갈다 v. till, cultivate, plow. *pat´-ŭl kalda* 밭을 갈다 plow a field.

  kallae 갈래 n. fork, branch, division. *se kallae kil* 세 갈래 길 three forked [trifurcated] road, junction.

  kallida 갈리다 v. (bc) divided into, break into, fork. *kallimkkil* 갈림길 branch road, forked road.

  kalssaek 갈색 n.C. brown.

+ **kam** 감 n. persimmon.

+ **kam** 감 n.C. feeling, sense (of things).

* **kam** 감 n. material, stuff. *otkkam* 옷감 (dress) material, cloth.

  kama(sot) 가마(솥) n. iron pot, kettle, oven, kiln.

kamanhi 가만히 adv. still, quietly, silently. *kamanhi itta* 가만히 있다 keep still, be[remain] motionless[quiet].

* **kamch´uda** 감추다 v. ① hide, conceal, put out of sight, keep secret ② cover, veil, cloak, disguise.

  kamdong 감동 n.C. deep emotion, impression. *kamdonghada* 감동하다 (be) impressed (with, by), (be) moved[touched, affected] (by).

+ **kamgak** 감각 n.C. sense, sensation, feeling, sensibility. *kamgag-i yemin[tun]hada* 감각이 예민 [둔]하다 have keen[dull] senses.

  kamgi 감기 n.C. cold, influenza, flu. *kamgi-e kŏllida* 감기에 걸리다 catch[take] (a) cold. *kamgiyak* 감기약 medicine for a cold.

  kamgyŏk 감격 n.C. deep emotion, strong feeling. *kamgyŏk´ada* 감격하다 be deeply moved[touched].

* **kamja** 감자 n. potato, white potato.

kamjŏng 감정 n.C. judgement, appraisal. *kamjŏnghada* 감정하다 judge, appraise.

* **kamjŏng** 감정 n.C. feeling, emotion, passion, sentiment. *kamjŏngjŏk* 감정적 emotional, sentimental.

kamsa 감사 n.C. thanks, gratitude, appreciation. *kamsahada* 감사하다 thank, feel grateful[thankful].

kamsang 감상 n.C. appreciation. *kamsanghada* 감상하다 appreciate, enjoy.

kamso 감소 n.C. diminution, decrease, decline, drop. *kamsohada* 감소하다 diminish, decrease, lessen.

+ **kamt'an** 감탄 n.C. admiration, wonder. *kamt'anhada* 감탄하다 admire, marvel (at), wonder (at). *kamt'anhal manhan* 감탄할 만한 admirable, wonderful.

kamtta 감다 v. wind, roll (up), coil, twine.

* **kamtta** 감다 v. shut[close] (one's eyes).

kamtta 감다 v. wash, bathe, have a bath. *mŏri-rŭl kamtta* 머리를 감다 wash one's hair.

kamulda 가물다 v. (be) droughty, dry, have a spell of dry weather.

kan 간 n.C. ① a room (unit) ② a (building) space (180x180cm) ③ (as suffix, post-n.) relationship: *pujagan* 부자간 the relationship of father and son; (distance) between two points: *sŏul pusangan* 서울 부산간 between Seoul and Pusan

kan 간 ① liver. [p.47] *kanam* 간암 cancer of the liver, liver cancer. *kanyŏm* 간염 inflammation of the liver, hepatitis. ② courage, pluck.

kan 간 seasoning, salty taste, saltiness. *kan-ŭl ch'ida* 간을 치다 apply salt (to), season. *kan-ŭl poda* 간을 보다 check the seasoning.

kanan 가난 n. poverty, want. [p.2,4]

+ **kananhada** 가난하다 adj. (be) poor, needy.

kanch'ŏng 간청 n.C. entreaty, earnest request. *kanch'ŏnghada* 간청하다 entreat, implore, solicit.

* **kandan** 간단 n.C. brevity, simplicity. *kandanhan* 간단한 brief, simple, light. *kandanhan sikssa* 간단한 식사 light meal, quick meal, snack (lunch).
* **kandanhi** 간단히 adv.C. simply, briefly.
# **kang** 강 n.C. river. *kang kŏnnŏ* 강 건너 across the river. *kang-ŭl ttara* 강을 따라 along a river.
+ **kangaji** 강아지 n. pup, puppy.
# **kanghada** 강하다 adj.C. (be) strong, powerful, mighty. *kanghage* 강하게 hard, severely, strongly.
+ **kangje** 강제 n.C. compulsion, coercion, constraint. *kangjehada* 강제하다 force, compel, coerce. *kangjejŏgin* 강제적인 compulsory, forced.
  kangsŭp 강습 n.C. short training course. *kangsŭb-ŭl patta* 강습을 받다 take a course (in). *kangsŭpsso* 강습소 institute, training school.
  kangŭi 강의 n.C. lecture, discourse. *kangŭihada* 강의 하다 lecture (on), give a lecture.
  kangyŏn 강연 n.C. lecture, address. *kangyŏnhada* 강연하다 (give a) lecture, address (an audience). *kangyŏnhoe* 강연회 lecture meeting.
  kanho 간호 n.C. nursing, care (of the sick). *kanhohada* 간호하다 nurse, tend. *kanhosa /wŏn* 간호사/원 a nurse.
  kanjang 간장 n.C. liver. *kanjangppyŏng* 간장병 liver troubles [complaint].
+ **kanjang** 간장 n.C. soy(bean) sauce. *kanjangppyŏng* 간장병 a bottle for soy sauce.
+ **kanjik'ada** 간직하다 v. ① keep, store, save, treasure (up) ② hold in mind, cherish, entertain.
  kanjŏp 간접 n.C. indirectness. *kanjŏptchŏgin* 간접적인 indirect, round-about. *kanjŏptchŏg-ŭro* 간접적으로 indirctly.
  kanp'an 간판 n.C. signboard, billboard.
  kanpyŏn 간편 n.C. convenience, handiness. *kanp'yŏnhada* 간편하다 (be) convenient, simple, easy.
  kansŏp 간섭 n.C. interference, intervention. *kan-*

sŏp'ada 간섭하다 interfere, intervene. *muryŏk kansŏp* 무력 간섭 armed[military] intervention.

* **kanŭlda** 가늘다 adj. (be) thin, fine, slender. *kanŭn mokssori* 가는 목소리 thin voice. *kanŭn sil* 가는 실 fine thread. *kanŭn hŏri* 가는 허리 slender waist.

+ **kanŭnghan** 가능한 adj. possible. *kanŭnghadamyŏn* 가능하다면 if (it were) possible.

kaok 가옥 n.C. house, residence. *kaoksse* 가옥세 house tax.

kap 값 n. price, cost, charge. *kaps-i ssada[pissada]* 값이 싸다[비싸다] be cheap[expensive].

+ **kap** 갑 n.C. casket, box, pack. *tambaetkkap* 담뱃갑 cigarette case, tobacco box.

+ **kaptchŏl** 갑절 n. → **pae** 배.

kaptchagi 갑자기 adv. suddendly, all of a sudden, all at once, abruptly.

* **kaptta** 갚다 v. ① pay back, repay ② return, give (something) in return, reward ③ retaliate, revenge.

karaipta 갈아입다 v. change (one's) clothes.

karat'ada 갈아타다 v. change cars[trains], transfer (to another train).

'* **karida** 가리다 v. ① hide, conceal, screen, cover. ② hate, distinguish.

* **karik'ida** 가리키다 v. point to, indicate, point out, show.

karo 가로 n.C. street, road. *karodŭng* 가로등 street lamp. *karosu* 가로수 street[roadside] trees.

* **karo** 가로 n. width, breadth. *karo ip'it'ŭ* 가로 2피트 two feet in width.

* **karu** 가루 n. flour, meal, powder, dust. *karubinu* 가루비누 powder soap.

karŭch'ida 가르치다 v. teach, instruct, educate.

* **karŭda** 가르다 v. divide, part, sever, split, distribute.

karyŏptta 가렵다 adj. (be) itchy, itching, feel itchy.

kasa 가사 n.C. words [text] of a song.

kassŭ 가스 n. gas, natural gas, coal gas. *kassŭ chungdok* 가스 중독 gas-poisoning. *kassŭt'ong* 가스 통 gas cannister.

kasu 가수 n.C. singer, vocalist. *yuhaeng kasu* 유행 가수 popular singer.

\# **kasŭm** 가슴 n. breast, chest. [p.113] *kasŭm-i ap'ŭda* 가슴이 아프다 have a pain in the chest.

* **katch'uda** 갖추다 v. ① get ready, prepare, furnish, equip, provide ② possess, have, be endowed (with). *chunbi-rŭl katch'uda* 준비를 갖추다 prepare for, make full preparation.

\# **katta** 같다 adj. ① be the same, (be) identical ② (be) equal (to), uniform, equivalent ③ similar, like, alike. *ttokkatta* 똑같다 be the very same, be just the same. →**kach'i** 같이.

\# **kaŭl** 가을 n. autumn, fall (*Am.*). *kaŭl param* 가을 바 람 autumn wind.

\# **kaunde** 가운데 n. ① middle, midway, center ② interior, inside ③ between, among.

kawi 가위 n. scissors, shears, clippers.

* **kayŏpta** 가엾다 adj. (be) poor, pitiable, pitiful, sad, miserable.

* **ke** 게 n. crab. *kettaktchi* 게딱지 crust of crab.

\# **-ke** -게 adverbial ending following a verb stem, makes that v. and adv. meaning: -ly, so as to, so that, in such a manner.

kedaga 게다가 adv. besides, moreover, what is more, in addition (to that).

kesi 게시 n. notice, bulletin. *kesihada* 게시하다 post [put up] a notice. *kesip'an* 게시판 bulletin board.

\# **-kess-** -겠- prefinal ending ① (definite future marker, used with 1st person subject in statements and 2nd person subject in questions) will ② (conjecture marker, probable non-future, most often used with 3rd person subject) probably (is/does), must (be). cf. *-ŭl kŏsida* -을 것이다.

keŭrŭda 게으르다 adj. (be) idle, lazy, indolent.

ki 기 n.C. flag, banner, colo(u)rs. *ki-rŭl talda*[*nae-rida*] 기를 달다[내리다] hoist[lower] a flag.

kibon 기본 n.C. founation, basis. *kibonjŏgin* 기본적인 fundamental, basic, standard.

* **kich´a** 기차 n.C. train, railway carriage, railroad train. *kich´a-ro* 기차로 by train.

kich´im 기침 n. cough, coughing. *kich´imhada* 기침하다 have a cough.

* **kich´o** 기초 n.C. foundation, basis, base.

+ **kida** 기다 v. crawl, creep, go on all fours.

kidae 기대 n.C. expectation, anticipation. *kidaehada* 기대하다 expect, look forward to.

+ **kidaeda** 기대다 v. lean (against), rest against, recline on, lean over.

\# **kidarida** 기다리다 v. wait for, await, expect, look forward to.

kido 기도 n.C. prayer. *kidohada* 기도하다 pray, offer [give] prayers, say grace.

+ **kidung** 기둥 n. pillar, pole, post.

+ **kigu** 기구 n.C. utensil, implement, apparatus. *chŏngi kigu* 전기 기구 electrical appliance.

+ **kigu** 기구 n.C. strucure, organization, machinery. *kuktche kigu* 국제기구 international organization.

+ **kigwan** 기관 n.C. organ. *kamgak kigwan* 감각 기관 sense organs.

\# **kigwan** 기관 n.C. ① engine, machine ② organ, means, facilities. *kyoyuk kigwan* 교육 기관 educational faciliies.

kigye 기계 n.C. machine, machinery. *kigyejŏgin* 기계적인 mechanical. *kigyejŏg-ŭro* 기계적으로 mechanically, automatically.

\# **kigye** 기계 n.C. instrument, appliance, apparatus.

* **kihoe** 기회 n.C. opportunity, chance. *kihoe-rŭl chaptta* 기회를 잡다 seize a chance. *kihoejuŭija* 기회주의자 opportunist.

kihoek 기획 n.C. planning, plan. *kihoek´ada* 기획하다 (make a) plan, work out a program.

\# **kihu** 기후 n.C. weather, climate.

\+ **kiil** 기일 n.C. fixed date, time limit, appointed day.

* **kiiphada** 기입하다 v.C. enter, fill in (a blank), fill out (a form)..

* **kija** 기자 n.C. journalist, pressman (*Eng.*), newspaperman (*Am.*).

kijun 기준 n.C. standard, basis. *kijun-ŭi* 기준의 standard, basic, base.

\# **kil** 길 n. road, way, street. *kanŭn kir-e* 가는 길에 on the way. *kir-ŭl mutta* 길을 묻다 ask the way.

\# **kilda** 길다 adj. (be) long, lengthy. *kin tari* 긴 다리 long legs; long bridge.

kim 김 n. steam, vapor. ① *kim-i nada* 김이 나다 steam. *kimppajida* 김빠지다 lose its flavo(u)r.

kim 김 n. laver, dried seaweed.

kimch'i 김치 n. pickles, pickled and fermented vegetables (cabbage, radish, or cucumber spiced with red pepper, garlic, ginger, anchovy sauce, etc). [p.36]

kin'gŭp 긴급 n.C. emergency, urgency. *kin'gŭp'an* 긴급한 urgent, pressing, emergent.

kinjang 긴장 n.C. tension, strain. *kinjanghada* 긴장하다 become tense, be strained. *kinjangdoen* 긴장된 strained, tense.

* **kinŭng** 기능 n.C. ability, capacity, skill. *kinŭnggong* 기능공 skilled worker.

kinyŏm 기념 n.C. commemoration, memory. *kinyŏmhada* 기념하다 commem- orate, honor the memory of. *kinyŏm-ŭro* 기념으로 in memory [commemoration] of.

* **kiŏk** 기억 n.C. memory, rememberance. *kiŏk'ada* 기억하다 remember, bear in mind.

* **kion** 기온 n.C. (air) temperature. *kion pyŏnhwa* 기온 변화 change of temperature.

\+ **kiŏp** 기업 n.C. enterprise, undertaking. *kiŏpkka* 기업 가 entrepreneur, enter- priser.

* **kippŭda** 기쁘다 adj. (be) glad, delightful, happy,

pleased.

kiptta 깊다 adj. (be) deep, profound, close.

* **kip'i** 깊이 n. depth; adv. deep(ly).

kiri 길이 n. length, extent; adv. for ever.

* **kirok** 기록 n.C. record, document, archives. *kirok'ada* 기록하다 record, write down, register.

kirŭda 기르다 v. ① bring up, rear, breed, raise ② keep, grow, cultivate.

kirŭm 기름 n. ① oil ② fat, lard ③ grease, pomade.①

kisukssa 기숙사 n.C. dormitory.

kisul 기술 n.C. art, technique, skill. *kisultcha* 기술자 technician, engineer.

+ **kiulda** 기울다 v. incline (to), lean (to), slant, tilt. [p.33]

* **kiun** 기운 n.C. ① (physical) strength, energy, force ② vigor, spirit. *kiunch'an* 기운찬 vigorous, energetic.

kkach'i 까치 n. magpie.

+ **kkada** 까다 v. peel, husk, pare. *kyur-ŭl kkada* 귤을 까다 peel an orange.

kkadak 까닭 n. reason, cause. *musün kkadalg-ŭro* 무슨 까닭으로 why, for what reason.

kkadaroptta 까다롭다 adj. (be) particular, fastidious, picky.

kkae 깨 n. sesame (seed). *ch'amkkae* 참깨 sesame. *tŭlkkae* 들깨 wild sesame.

kkaeda 깨다 v. break, crush, smash. *kŭrŭs-ŭl kkaeda* 그릇을 깨다 break a dish.

kkaeda 깨다 v. ① wake up, awake ② become sober, sober (up) ③ have one's eyes opened.

* **kkaeda** 깨다 v. (be) hatched, hatch.

kkaedatta 깨닫다 v. see, perceive, realize, understand, sense, be aware of.

* **kkaekkŭsi** 깨끗이 adv. clean(ly), neatly, tidily. *kkaekkŭsi taktta* 깨끗이 닦다 wipe (a thing) clean.

* **kkaekkŭt'ada** 깨끗하다 adj. ① (be) clean, cleanly, tidy, neat ② (be) pure, clean, innocent, chaste ③

(be) fair, clean.

+ **kkaettŭrida** 깨뜨리다 adv. ① break, crush, destory, crash, smash ② baffle, frustrate, disturb, spoil.

kkaeuda 깨우다 adv. ① wake up, awaken, arouse ② bring (a person) to his sense, get[make] sober.

\# **-kkaji** -까지 particle ① (indicates that the preceding n. is the temporal or spatial ending point for an action) till, until, up to, by (*time*), as far as (*place*) ② (indicates that the following proposition extends to even the precedingn., often used as *-kkajido*) even, so far as (*extent*).

* **kkaktta** 깎다 v. shave, sharpen, cut down.

kkaktugi 깍두기 n. white-radish pickles.

* **kkalda** 깔다 v. ① spread, stretch ② pave, cover ③ sit on (a cushion).

kkamagwi 까마귀 n. crow, raven.

kkamkkamhada 깜깜하다 adj. ① (be) pitch-dark ② (be) ignorant.

* **kkamtchak(kamtchak)** 깜짝(깜짝) adv. with repeated starts. *kkamtchak*
kkamtchak nollada 깜짝깜짝 놀라다 be startled again and again.

kkangt'ong 깡통 n. can (*Am.*), tin (can) (*Eng.*). ① *kkangt'ong ttagae* 깡통 따개 can[tin] opener. *pin kkangt'ong* 빈 깡통 empty can[tin].

\# **kkida** 끼다 v. ① hold (a thing) (under one's arm); put on, pull on, wear (a ring, gloves); wedge in ② jam into ③ cloud up.

kkoda 꼬다 v. ① twist, twine ② writhe, wriggle. *saekki-rŭl kkoda* 새끼를 꼬다 make[twist] a rope.

kkoe 꾀 n. ① wit, resources ② trick, trap, artifice.

+ **kkŏjida** 꺼지다 v. ① go[die] out, be put out, be extinguished ② cave[fall] in, sink, subside.

\# **kkok** 꼭 adv. ① tightly, firmly, fast ② exactly, just ③ surely, without fail.

* **kkŏktta** 꺾다 v. ① break (off), snap ② make a turn, turn.

orŭnp'yŏn-ŭro kkŏkta 오른편으로 꺾다 turn to the right, turn right.

kkokttaegi 꼭대기 n. top, summit, peak, crown.

\# **kkol** 꼴 n. ① shape, form, appearance ② state, condition, situation ③ sight, spectacle. *chamdamhan kkol* 참담한 꼴 horrible sight[spectacle]. *kkolsanaun* 꼴사나운 un-sightly, shabby.

kkoma 꼬마 n. (little) kid, baby miniature. *kkoma chadongch'a* 꼬마 자동차 baby car. *kkoma chŏngu* 꼬마 전구 miniature bulb.

\# **kkŏnaeda** 꺼내다 v. pull[draw] out, take[bring] out, produce, whip out, pick out.

kkŏngch'ung 껑충 adv. with a jump[leap].

* **kkŏptchil** 껍질 n. ① bark ② rind, peel ③ husk, shell. *sagwa kkŏpchil* 사과 껍질 apple peel.

kkŏpttegi 껍데기 n. husk, hull, shell. →**kkŏptchil** 껍질.

* **kkori** 꼬리 n. tail, tag, brush (of fox), scut (of rabbit). *kkori-rŭl chaptta* 꼬리를 잡다 find (a person's) weak point, catch (a person) tripping.

kkŏrida 꺼리다 v. ① dislike, abhor ② avoid, shun ③ hesitate.

` * **kkot** 꽃 n. flower, blossom, bloom. *kkoch'-ŭi* 꽃의 floral. *kkottaun* 꽃다운 flowery, flowerlike. *kkotkage* 꽃가게 flowershop. *kkottabal* 꽃다발 bouquet, bunch of flowers.

kkŏt -껏 suffix. as far as possible, to the best (of), to the utmost (of). *sŏngŭikkŏt* 성의껏 heartily, from one's heart. *himkkŏt* 힘껏 as far as possible, to the best of one's ability. *maŭmkkŏt ulda* 마음껏 울다 cry one's heart out.

kkuda 꾸다 v. borrow, have[get] the loan (of).

kkuda 꾸다 v. dream.

\+ **kkŭda** 끄다 v. put out, extinguish.

kkujunhada 꾸준하다 adj. (be) steady, untiring, constant. *kkujunhi* 꾸준히 untiringly, steadily.

* **kkul** 꿀 n. honey, nectar. *kkulbŏl* 꿀벌 honeybee.

kkulmul 꿀물 honeyed water.

\# **kkŭlda** 끌다 v. ① draw, pull, tug, drag ② attract, catch ③ delay, protract.

\# **kkŭlt'a** 끓다 v. boil, simmer, seethe.

\# **kkum** 꿈 n. ① dream ② vision, illusion. *kkum kat'ŭn* 꿈 같은 dreamlike. *kkum-ŭl kkuda* 꿈을 꾸다 dream, have a dream.

* **kkumida** 꾸미다 v. ① decorate, ornament, adorn ② feign, pretend ③ invent, fabricate.

kkŭnimŏptta 끊임없다 adj. (be) continuous, ceaseless, incessant. *kkŭnimŏpsi* 끊임없이 adv. constantly, continually.

\# **kkŭnnada** 끝나다 v. (come to an) end, close, be over (up), be finished, expire.

kkŭnnaeda 끝내다 v. end, go[get] through (with), finish, complete.

\# **kkŭnt'a** 끊다 v. ① cut, cut off, sever ② give up (smoking), leave off.

\# **kkŭrida** 끓이다 v. ① boil (water), heat ② cook.

kkŭt 끝 n. ① end, close, final, last ② point, tip ③ result, consequence.

kkwae 꽤 adv. fairly, pretty, considerably.

kkwak 꽉 adv. ① tightly, fast, closely ② to the full. *mun-ŭl kkwak chamgŭda* 문을 꽉 잠그다 shut a door fast, lock a door tight.

kkwemaeda 꿰매다 v. sew, stitch, darn, patch up.

kkyŏantta 껴안다 v. embrace, hug, hold (a person) in one's arms.

\# **-ko** -고 ending① gerund. used to connect two v. or adj., with equal weight given to both. if there is a temporal relation between the two clauses, the prior one precedes *-ko* and the later one follows. (is or does) and/but also. Note: to connect two nouns use *-wa/kwa (colloq.) -hago, -(i)rang* ② *-ko itta* -고 있다 progressive v. ending. indicates that the action of the preceding v. is or was continuing. (he) is doing ③ *-ko siptta* -고 싶다 desire v. and adj. ending. indicates a desire to do the action or to be the state of the preceding stem. want to do or be.

koa 고아 n.C. orphan. *koawŏn* 고아원 orphanage.

kŏbu 거부 n.C. refusal, denial, rejection. *kŏbuhada* 거부하다 deny, refuse, reject, veto (a bill). *kŏbukkwŏn* 거부권 veto, veto power.

\# **koch'ida** 고치다 v. ① cure, heal, remedy ② mend, repair, fix (up) ③ correct, reform, rectify.

* **kŏch'ida** 거치다 v. pass by[through], go by way of.

\+ **kŏch'ilda** 거칠다 adj. (be) coarse, rough, harsh, violent.

koch'u 고추 n. red pepper, cayenne pepper. *koch'ukkaru* 고추 가루 red pepper powder. *koch'ujang* 고추장 hot pepper paste.

koch'ŭng 고층 n.C. higher stories, upper floors. *koch'ŭng kŏnmul* 고층 건물 high[lofty] building.

* **kodae** 고대 n.C. ancient[old] times, antiquity. *kodae-ŭi* 고대의 ancient, antique.

\+ **kodo** 고도 n.C. ① altitude, height ② high power[degree]. *kodo-ŭi* 고도의 high, high power.

kodok 고독 n.C. solitude, loneliness. *kodok'ada* 고독하다 (be) solitary, lonely, lone, isolated.

* **kŏduda** 거두다 v. ① gather, collect, harvest. *segŭm-ŭl kŏduda* 세금을 거두다 collect taxes ② gain, obtain ③ die, expire. *sum-ŭl kŏduda* 숨을 거두다 give up one's breath.

\+ **kodŭng** 고등 n.C. high grade, high class. *kodŭng-ŭi* 고등의 high, higher, advanced. *kodŭnghakkyo* 고등학교 high school.

kŏdŭp 거듭 adv. (over) again, repeatedly. *kŏdŭp'ada* 거듭하다 repeat, do again.

koemul 괴물 n.C. monster, goblin.

\+ **koengjanghada** 굉장하다 adj. grand, magnificent, splendid. *koengjanghi* 굉장히 extremely, awfully, terribly.

* **koeroptta** 괴롭다 adj. ① (be) troublesome, hard ② (be) onerous, distressing ③ (be) awkward, embarrassing.

kogae 고개 n. nape, scruff. ①, [p.11].

* **kogae** 고개 n. ① (mountain) pass ② crest, summit, peak, climax.

kogaek 고객 n.C. customer, client, patron. *oraen kogaek* 오랜 고객 old[regular] customer.

kogi 고기 n. ① # meat *takkoki* 닭고기 chicken. *twaejigogi* 돼지고기 pork. *soegogi* 쇠고기 beef. ② + fish *kogichaptta* 고기잡다 (*v.*) fish *mulkkogi* 물고기 (*n.*) fish.

kŏgi 거기 pron. that place, there. *kŏgi-e[esŏ]* 거기에 [에서] in that place, there. *kŏgiro* 거기로 to that place, there. *kŏgi-sŏbut'ŏ[robutŏ]* 거기서부터[로부터] from there.

koguk 고국 n.C. one's native land [country], one's home land.

* **koguma** 고구마 n. sweet potato *kun koguma* 군 고구마 roast [baked] sweet potato.

kogŭp 고급 n.C. high-class[-grade], higher, senior. *kogŭp kwalli* 고급 관리 higher [high-raking] officals. *kogŭp ch'a* 고급 차 deluxe car.

* **kohyang** 고향 n.C. one's home, one's native place, one's birth place.

kojang 고장 n. ① locality, district ② place of production ③ native place.

kojangnada 고장나다 v.C. get out of order, break down, go wrong.

kŏji 거지 beggar, mendicant.

* **kŏjinmal** 거짓말 n. lie, falsehood, fabrication, fake. *kŏjinmalhada* 거짓말하다 tell a lie, lie.

kojip 고집 n.C. stubbornness, abstinacy. *kojip'ada* 고집하다 hold fast (to), bywayadhere. *kojip sen* 고집 셴 stubborn, abstinate.

kŏjŏl 거절 n.C. refusal, rejection. *kŏjŏlhada* 거절하다 refuse, reject.

kŏkkuro 거꾸로 adv. reversely, (in) the wrong way, inside out, upside down.

* **kokssŏn** 곡선 n.C. curve, curved line. *koksŏnmi* 곡선 미 beauty of a curved line.
* **kŏktchŏng** 걱정 n. ① anxiety, apprehension ② uneasiness, fear ③ care, worry, trouble.
  kŏktchŏnghada 걱정하다 v. be anxious (about), (be) worried (by), trouble oneself about.
* **kŏlch'ida** 걸치다 v. extend (over), spread (over), range, cover.
# **kŏlda** 걸다 v. ① hang, suspend ② speak to. *saram-ege mar-ŭl kŏlda* 사람에게 말을 걸다 ③ pick, provoke. *saram-hant'e ssaum-ŭl kŏlda* 사람한테 싸움을 걸다 pick a quarrel with a person ④ call to, ring up, telephone.
+ **kŏlda** 걸다 adj. ① (be) rich, fertile ② abundant, plentiful.
+ **kollan** 곤란 n.C. difficulty, trouble, embarrassment.
* **kollanhan** 곤란한 adj.C. difficult, hard, troublesome.
  kŏlle 걸레 n. floor cloth, dustcloth, rag, mop. *kŏllejilhada* 걸레질하다 wipe with a damp cloth, mop (the floor).
kŏllida 걸리다 v. ① hang ② fall ill ③ (illness) be caught ④ * (time) take ⑤ make (a person) walk.
+ **kolmok** 골목 n. side street, alley. *twikkolmok* 뒷골목 back streets.
  kŏlsang 걸상 n. bench, stool, couch.
+ **koltchagi** 골짜기 n. valley, vale, ravine.
  kom 곰 n. bear. [p.117]
  kŏman 거만 n.C. arrogance, haughtiness, self-importance *kŏmanhada* 거만하다 be arrogant, haughty.
komaptta 고맙다 adj. ① (be) thankful, grateful ② (be) kind, nice, appreciated.
  kŏmbuktta 검붉다 adj. (be) dark red, blackish red.
  kŏmi 거미 n. spider. *kŏmijul* 거미줄 cobweb. [p.74]
+ **komin** 고민 n.C. agony, anguish. *kominhada* 고민하 다 (be) in agony, agonize.
  komo 고모 n.C. paternal aunt, one's father's sister.

komp'angi 곰팡이 n. mold, mildew, must.

kŏmp'urŭda 검푸르다 adj. (be) dark blue, blue-black.

kŏmsa 검사 n.C. public prosecutor, the prosecution, district attorney (*Am.*). *pujang kŏmsa* 부장 검사 chief public prosecutor.

+ **kŏmsa** 검사 n.C. inspection, examination, test. *kŏmsahada* 검사하다 inspect, examine, audit, condition (merchandise).

kŏmt'o 검토 n.C. examination, scrutiny. *kŏmt'ohada* 검토하다 examine, scrutinize.

* **kŏmtta** 검다 adj. (be) black, dark, sooty.

* **komu** 고무 n. rubber. *komugong* 고무공 rubber ball. *komusin* 고무신 rubber shoes.

komun 고문 n.C. adviser, counsel(l)or, consultant. *kisul komun* 기술 고문 technical adviser.

kŏmyŏl 검열 n.C. censorship, inspection, review. *kŏmyŏlhada* 검열하다 censor, inspect, examine.

-kŏna -거나 ending. whether ...or, whatever, however, whenever. *nŏya choahagŏna malgŏna* 너야 좋 아하거나 말거나 whether you like it or not.

kŏnban 건반 n.C. keyboard. *kŏnban akki* 건반 악기 keyboard instruments.

kŏnbangjida 건방지다 adj. (be) impertinent, insolent, haughty. *kŏnbangjin t'aedo* 건방진 태도 haughty bearing.

+ **kŏnch'uk** 건축 n.C. building, construction. *kŏnch'ukhada* 건축하다 build, construct, erect. *kŏnch'ukka* 건축가 architect. *kŏnch'uk hoesa* 건축 회사 building company. *kŏnch'ukppŏp* 건축법 building regulation.

konch'ung 곤충 n.C. insect, bug. *konch'ung ch'aejip* 곤충 채집 insect collecting.

* **kong** 공 n. ball, handball. *kong-ŭl ch'ada* 공을 차다 kick a ball.

* **kŏn'gang** 건강 n.C. health. *kŏn'gang sikp'um* 건강 식 품 health food.

* **kŏn'ganghada** 건강하다 adj. (be) well, healthy,

sound. *kŏn'gang chindan* 건강 진단 medical examination.

kongbak 공박 n.C. refutation, (wordy) attack, charge. *kongbak'ada* 공박하다 refute, confute, argue against.

\# **kongbu** 공부 n.C. study, learning. *kongbuhada* 공부하다 study, work at[on]. *sihŏm kongbu* 시험 공부 study for an examination.

+ **kongch'ae** 공채 n.C. public loan[debt]. *kongch'ae sijang* 공채 시장 bond market.

* **kongdong** 공동 n.C. association, cooperation, union. *kongdong-ŭi* 공동의 common, joint, public. *kongdong pyŏnso* 공동 변소 public lavatory. *kongdong myoji* 공동 묘지 public cemetery.

+ **konggan** 공간 n.C. space, room. *sigan-gwa konggan* 시간과 공간 time and space.

\# **konggi** 공기 n.C. air, atmosphere. *konggi oyŏm* 공기 오염 air pollution.

* **konggun** 공군 n.C. air force. *konggun kiji* 공군 기지 air base.

konghang 공항 n.C. airport. *kuktche konghang* 국제 공항 international airport. *Kimp'o konghang* 김포 공항 Kimpo Airport.

konghyuil 공휴일 n.C. legal holiday, red-letter day.

\# **kongjang** 공장 n.C. factory, plant, mill, workshop. *kunsu kongjang* 군수 공장 munitions factory. *kongjang p'yesu* 공장 폐수 industrial waste (water).

\# **kongju(nim)** 공주 n.C. (royal) princess.

kongjung 공중 n.C. public. [p.13] *kongjung-ŭi* 공중의 public, common. *kongjung chŏnhwa* 공중전화 public telephone.

+ **kongmuwŏn** 공무원 n.C. public official[servant].

kongnip 공립 n.C. public. *kongnip kakkyo* 공립 학교 public school.

kongno 공로 n.C. meritorious service, merits. *kongnoja* 공로자 person of merit. *kongnosang* 공로

상 distinguished service medal.

kongŏp 공업 n.C. industry. *kongŏp-ŭi* 공업의 industrial, technical. *kongŏp tanji* 공업 단지 industrial complex. *kongŏp hakkyo* 공업 학교 technical school. *chung[kyŏng]gongŏp* 중[경]공업 heavy [light] industry.

kongp'o 공포 n.C. fear, terror, dread, horror. *kongp'o-e chillin* 공포에 질린 terror-[horror-, panic-] stricken. *kongp'otchŭng* 공포증 phobia, morbid fear.

kongp'yŏng 공평 n.C. fairness. *kongp'yŏnghada* 공평하다 (be) fair, impartial, even-handed. *kongp'yŏnghage* 공평하게 fairly, impartially, justly.

+ kongsa 공사 n.C. construction work. *kongsabi* 공사비 cost of construction. *kongsajang* 공사장 site of construction.

* kongsandang 공산당 n.C. Communist Party. *kongsandangwŏn* 공산당원 a member of Communist Party.

+ kongsan'gun 공산군 n.C. communist army.

* kongsanjuŭi 공산주의 n.C. communism. *kongsanjuŭija* 공산주의자 communist.

kongsik 공식 n.C. formula. *kongsik-ŭi* 공식의 formal, official.

kongson 공손 n.C. politeness. *kongsonhan* 공손한 polite, courteous, civil. *kongsonhi* 공손히 politely, humbly, courteously.

kongtcha 공짜 n. thing got for nothing, free charge, gratuitousness.

kongt'ong 공통 n.C. commonness. *kongt'onghada* 공통하다 be common (to). *kongt'ong-ŭi* 공통의 common, mutual, general.

kongwŏn 공원 n.C. park, public garden. *kungnip kongwŏn* 국립 공원 national park.

kongye 공예 n.C. industrial arts, technology. *kongyega* 공예가 technologist. *kongyep'um* 공예품

industrial art products.

+ **kŏnjida** 건지다 v. ① take[bring] out of water, pick up ② save [rescue] a person from.

+ **kŏnjo** 건조 n.C. dryness. *kŏnjohan* 건조한 dry, dried, arid. *kŏnjogi* 건조기 drier, desiccator.

+ **kŏnjŏnhada** 건전하다 adj.C. (be) healthy, sound, wholesome. *kŏnjŏnhan sasang* 건전한 사상 wholesome ideas.

* **kŏnmul** 건물 n.C. building, structure. *sŏkcho [mokcho] kŏnmul* 석조[목조] 건물 stone[wooden] building.

kŏnnŏgada 건너가다 v. go[pass] over, go across, cross (over).

+ **kŏnsŏl** 건설 n.C. construction, building.

+ **kŏnsŏlhada** 건설하다 v. construct, build, establish. *kŏnsŏltchŏgin* 건설적인 constructive.

+ **kŏnŭrida** 거느리다 v. have (with one), lead, head, command.

* **kop** 곱 n. double, times. *kop'ada* 곱하다 multiply, double. *tu kop* 두 곱 double, twice, twofold.

* **kŏp** 겁 n.C. ① cowardice, timidity ② fear, awe, fright. *kŏb-i nada* 겁이 나다 be seized with fear.

* **kopta** 곱다 adj. ① (be) beautiful, lovely, fair, fine, nice ② (be) tender, kindly. *koun maŭmssi* 고운 마음씨 tender heart.

kop'ŭda 고프다 adj. (be) hungry. *pae-ga kop'ŭda* 배가 고프다 feel hungry.

kŏp'um 거품 n. bubble, foam, forth. *mulgŏp'um* 물거품 water bubble.

korae 고래 n. whale. *koraejabi* 고래잡이 whaling.

kŏrae 거래 n.C. transactions, dealings, business, trade. *kŏraehada* 거래하다 do[transact] business (with), have an account with.

kori 고리 n.C. high interest; usury. *koridaegŭm-ŏptcha* 고리 대금업자 usurer; loanshark (Am.)

kŏri 거리 n. street; road; quarter. *changkkŏri* 장거리 market street.

\# **kŏri** 거리 n. distance; range; interval.

korip 고립 n.C. isolation, *korip'ada* 고립하다 stand along; be isolated; be friendless. *koriptoen* 고립된 isolated; solitary; helpless.

koru 고루 adv. equally; evenly. *koru nanuda* 고루 나누다

\+ **kŏruk'ada** 거룩하다 adj. (be) divine; sacred; holy.

\# **kŏrŭm** 거름 n. manure; muck; fertilizer.

\# **kŏrŭm** 걸음 n. walking; stepping; step; pace. [p.126] *pparŭn kŏrŭmŭro* 빠른걸음으로 at a rapid pace.

\+ **koryŏhada** 고려하다 v.C. consider; deliberate; bear in mind.

\+ **kosaeng** 고생 n.C. ① hard[tough] life; hardships; sufferings ② toil; labor; pain. [p.9] *kosaenghada* 고생하다 go through hardship.

kosang 고상 n.C. *hosanghan* 고상한 noble; lofty; high; elegant; refined.

kŏseda 거세다 adj. (be) rough; wild; violent. *kŏsen mal* 거센 말 wild horse.

kosok 고속 n.C. high-speed; rapid trasit. *kosokttoro* 고속도로 espress highway; superhighway. *kosokppŏsŭ* 고속 버스 express bus.

kŏsŭrŭda 거스르다 v. ① oppose; go against; run counter to ② give (back) the change.

kŏsŭrŭmtton 거스름돈 n. change.

\# **kot** 곧 adv. ① at once; immediately; instantly ② easily; readily.

\# **kot** 곳 n. place; scene; locality. *kos-e ttara* 곳에 따라 in some places. *kotkos-e* 곳곳에 here and there.

\# **kŏt** 것 n. dependent noun. occurs after modifier. ① thing. *mŏgŭl kkŏt* 먹을 것 ② matter, fact. *sigan-i kanŭn kŏt* 시간이 가는 것 the fact that time passes ③ future (likely) fact. *ch'aeg-ŭl sal kkŏsida* 책을 살 것이다 (I) will buy a book ④ impersonal command. *sinipsaeng-ŭn samusil-lo ol kkŏt* 신입생은 사무실로 올 것 New students report to the office [expression written on a sign].

* **köt** 겉 face; surface; right side; exterior; outward appearance. *köt-ŭro* 겉으로 on the surface.

kot'ong 고통 n.C. pain; suffering; agony; anguish. *kot'ongsŭrŏun* 고통스러운 painful; afflicting.

+ **kotta** 곧다 adj. ① (be) straight; upright; erect ② (be) honest; upright.

kŏtta 걷다 v. walk; go on foot; stroll. [p.8] *kŏri-rŭl kŏtta* 거리를 걷다 walk the street.

* **kŏtta** 걷다 v. ① tuck[roll] up (one's sleeves); gather up (curtains); fold up ② take away; remove. *ppallae-rŭl kŏtta* 빨래를 걷다 gather up the laundry.

kŏŭi 거의 adv. ① almost; nearly; practically ② hardly; scarcely; little. *kŏŭi chŏnbu* 거의 전부 almost all.

+ **kŏul** 거울 n. mirror; (looking) glass. *sonkŏul* 손거울 hand mirror. *kŏur-ŭl poda* 거울을 보다 look in the mirror.

koyangi 고양이 n. cat; puss(y). *koyangi saekki* 고양이 새끼 kitten; kitty.

* **koyohada** 고요하다 adj. (be) quiet; still; tranquil; calm.

koyong 고용 n. employment. *koyonghada* 고용하다 hire; employ; engage. *koyongin* 고용인 employee. *koyongju* 고용주 employer.

ku 구 n. 9 nine. *chegu* 제구 the ninth. -> ahop 아홉

kŭ 그 pre-n. ① that; it. *kŭ saram* 그 사람 that person; he. *kŭ-ŭi* 그의 his. *kŭnyŏ* 그녀 she, her (literary only, not used in conversation). ② that; those; the; its. *kŭnal* 그날 that[the] day. *kŭttae* 그때 that time; then. *kŭgach'i* 그같이 thus; so; like that.

kubun 구분 n.C. division; demarcation; classification. *kubunhada* 구분하다 divide; classify; partition.

* **kubyŏl** 구별 n.C. distinction; difference; discrimination; division.

+ **kubyŏlhada** 구별하다 v.C. distinguish; discriminate.
* **kŭch'ida** 그치다 v. stop; cease; halt; be over; end.
# **kŭdaero** 그대로 adv. as it is[stands]; intact; just like that.
* **kudu** 구두 n. (dress) shoes. *kudu-rŭl sintta[pŏtta]* 구두를 신다[벗다] put on [take off, remove] shoes. *kududakki* 구두닦기 a shoeshine (boy).
  kugak 국악 n.C. Korean classical music.
* **kugŏ** 국어 n.C. (the national) language; one's mother tongue; Korean languge.
* **kugyŏnghada** 구경하다 v.C. see (a play); watch (a game); see the sight (of). *sinae-rŭl kugyŏnghada* 시내를 구경하다 do the sights of a city.
# **kuhada** 구하다 v.C. ① pursue; ask for ② buy; get ③ save; rescue.
  kuip 구입 n.C. purchase; buying. *kuip'ada* 구입하다 purchase; buy. *kuiptcha* 구입자 purchaser.
+ **kujo** 구조 n.C. rescue; aid; relief; succor. *kujohada* 구조하다 save; rescue; relieve.
  kŭjŏkke 그저께 n. the day before yesterday.
  kuk 국 n. soup; broth. *kug-ŭl masida* 국을 마시다 sip soup.
* **kŭk** 극 n.C. drama; play. *kŭktchŏgin* 극적인 dramatical. *kŭktchŏg-ŭro* 극적으로 dramatically.
* **kŭk** 극 n.C. ① pole(s) ② height; extreme; climax. *...ŭi kŭg-e talhada* ...의 극에 달하다 reach the climax.
+ **kukch'ae** 국채 n.C. national debt; national loan; government bond.
* **kŭk'i** 극히 adv.C. extremely; highly; most; quite.
# **kukka** 국가 n.C. state; nation; country. *kukkajŏk* 국가적 national; state.
* **kukkun** 국군 n.C. national army. *kukkun-ŭi nal* 국군의 날 (ROK) Armed Forces Day, Oct. 1.
* **kukkyŏng** 국경 n.C. border; national boundery.
# **kuk'oe** 국회 n.C. the National Assembly *kuk'veüiwŏn* 국회의원 a member of the National Assembly

[Congressman].

+ **kukppang** 국방 n.C. national defense. *kukppangbu* 국방부 Ministry of National Defence.

kukssa 국사 n.C. national history; history of Korea.

kukssu 국수 n. noodle. ①

+ **kŭktchang** 극장 n.C. theater; playhouse.

kuktche 국제 n.C. international (relationship). *kuktchejok* 국제적 internationally; universally.

* **kukt'o** 국토 n.C. country; territory; domain. *kukt'o pangwi* 국토 방위 national defense.

* **kuktta** 굵다 adj. (be) big; thick. *kulgŭn p'al* 굵은 팔 big arm.

+ **kŭktto** 극도 n.C. extreme. *kŭtto-ŭi* 극도의 extreme; utmost. *kŭktto-ro* 극도로 extremely; to the utmost.

+ **kul** 굴 n. ① cave; cavern ② den; lair ③ tunnel.

kŭl 글 n. writing; composition; prose; sentence.

kŭlp'i 글피 n. two days after tomorrow. cf. *more* 모레 the day after tomorrow.

* **kŭltcha** 글자 n. letter; character.

kulttuk 굴뚝 n. chimney.

kŭm 금 n.C. gold. *kŭm-ŭi* 금의 gold; golden; auric.

kŭm 금 n. ① line ① ② crack ①.

kŭmaek 금액 n.C. amount of money; sum (of money).

kŭmanduda 그만두다 v. quit; discontinue; cease.

kŭmbang 금방 adv.C. soon, in no time. → **panggŭm** 방금.

+ **kŭmhada** 금하다 v.C. ① → **kŭmjihada** 금지하다 ② suppress; restrain; check.

kŭmji 금지 n.C. prohibition; ban; embargo. *kŭmjihada* 금지하다 prohibit; forbid; ban.

kŭmjŏn 금전 n.C. money; cash; gold coin. *kŭmjŏnsang-ŭi* 금전상의 monetary; financial; pecuniary.

+ **kŭmnyŏn** 금년 n.C. this year; the current year. → **olhae** 올해.

\# **kumŏng** 구멍 n. hole; opening; chink. ① [p.139] *panŭl kumŏng* 바늘 구멍 eye of a needle. *kumŏng-ŭl ttult´a* 구멍을 뚫다 make[bore, drill] a hole.

\+ **kŭmsok** 금속 n.C. metal. *kyŭnggŭmsok* 경금속 light metals. *kwigŭmsok* 귀금속 precious metals.

* **kumtta** 굶다 v. starve; go hungry. *kulmŏ chuktta* 굶어 죽다 starve to death; die of hunger.

\+ **kŭmul** 그물 n. net; netting.

kŭmyoil 금요일 n.C. Friday.

\# **kun** 군 ① n. army; force; troops ② suffix. team. *che p´algun* 제 8군 the U. S. Eighth Army (stationed in South Korea). *paekkun* 백군 white team.

\+ **kŭnbon** 근본 n.C. foundation; basis; origin. *kŭnbonjŏk(ŭro)* 근본적(으로) foundational(ly); basical (ly).

* **kŭnch´ŏ** 근처 n.C. neighborgood; vicinity. *kŭnch´ŏ-ŭi* 근처의 neighboring; nearby; close by. *kŭnch´ŏ-e* 근처에 in the neighborhood[vicinity].

\+ **kŭndae** 근대 n.C. the modern ages; recent times. *kŭndaejŏgin* 근대적인 modernistic. *kŭndaehwahada* 근대화하다 moderize.

kŭne 그네 n. swing; trapeze. *kune-rŭl t´ada* 그네를 타다 get on a swing.

kungdungi 궁둥이 n. buttocks; hips; rump.

kungjŏn 궁전 n.C. (royal) palace.

\# **kungmin** 국민 n.C. nation; people. *kungmin-ŭi* 국민의 national. *kungmin sodŭk* 국민 소득 national income.

kungmun 국문 n.C. national [Korean] language. *kungmunppŏp* 국문법 Korean grammar.

kungnip 국립 n.C. *kungnib-ŭi* 국립의 national; state. *kungni kŭktchang [kongwŏn]* 국립극장[공원] national theater[park]

\+ **kŭn´gŏ** 근거 n.C. basis; base; foundation; ground. *kŭngŏ-ga ŏmnŭn* 근거가 없는 groundless; baseless.

* **kunin** 군인 n.C. soldier, serviceman. *chigŏp kunin*

　　직업 군인 professional soldier.
kunjung 군중 n.C. crowd; masses; multitude. *kunjung taehoe* 군중 대회 (mass) rally.
kŭnmu 근무 n.C. service; duty; work. *kŭnmuhada* 근무하다 work; serve.
\# **kunsa** 군사 n.C. soldier.
* **kunsa** 군사 n.C. military affairs. *kunsa komundan* 군사 고문단 the Military Advisory Group.
* **kŭnŭl** 그늘 n. shade. *namu kŭnŭl* 나무 그늘 shade of a tree.
\# **kŭnyang** 그냥 adv. as it is; just, as you find it; for no reason, in that condition.
kŭnyŏ 그녀 pron. she. *kŭnyŏ-ŭi(rŭl, ege)* 그녀의(를, 에게) her.
kŭnyuk 근육 n.C. muscle.
\+ **kŭp'ada** 급하다 adj.C. (be) urgent; pressing; hasty.
\+ **kŭp'i** 급히 adv.C. quickly; rapidly; hastly.
\+ **kuptta** 굽다 v. roast; broil; bake. *chal kuwŏjin* 잘 구워진 well-done; well baked. *tŏl kuwŏjin* 덜 구워진 medium. *sol kuwŏjin* 설 구워진 rare.
* **kuri** 구리 n. copper. *kuritppit* 구릿빛 copper-colored. *kuri ch'ŏlsa* 구리 철사 copper wire.
\+ **kŭrida** 그리다 v. picture; draw; paint; sketch.
\# **kŭrida** 그리다 v. yearn after(for); long(pine) for(after); thirst for(after)
\# **kŭrim** 그림 n. picture; painting; drawing. [p.19] *kŭrimnyŏpsŏ* 그림 엽서 picture(post) card. *kŭrim kat'ŭn* 그림 같은 picturesque.
kŭrimja 그림자 n. shadow; silhouette.
\# **kŭrŏhada** 그러하다 adj. (be)so; such; right.
kŭrŏl-ttŭt'ada 그럴듯하다 adj. (be) plausible, seems likely/reasonable.
\# **kŭrŏmŭro** 그러므로 adv. so; hence; therefore.
\# **kŭrŏmyŏn** 그러면 adv. if so; in that case; then.
\# **kŭrŏna** 그러나 adv. but; still; however; and yet.
* **kurŭm** 구름 n. cloud. *kurŭm kkin* 구름 낀 cloudy. *kurŭm ŏmnŭm* 구름 없는 cloudless.

kŭrŭt 그릇 n. vessel; container. *notkkŭrŭt* 놋그릇 brazen vessel.

kusil 구실 n. excuse; pretext; pretense. *...ŭl kusillo sama* ...을 구실로 삼아 on the pretext of.

kusok 구속 n.C. ① restriction; restraint ② detention; binding. *kusok'ada* 구속하다 detain (a person) in custody; restrict; restrain.

* kusŏk 구석 n. corner. *kusŏg-e* 구석에 in a corner.

kusŏng 구성 n.C. constitution; composition; organization. *kusŏnghada* 구성하다 constitute; organize.

kŭyamallo 그야말로 adv. indeed; really; quite.

-kwa -과 particle. *-kwa* occurs after consonants. and. cf. -wa

* -kwa -과 suffix.C. course; department; faculty. *Yŏngŏkkwa* 영어과 English course [department].

* (-)kwa (-)과 n./suffix.C. ① lesson; subject. *cheigwa [X cheikkwa]* 제 2과 Lesson two. ② section; department; division. *ch'ongmukkwa(jang)* 총무과 (장) (chief [head] of a) general affairs section.

kwabu 과부 n. widow.

+ kwaench'ant'a 괜찮다 adj. ① (be) passable; not so bad; will do ② do not care; be all right; be no problem.

* kwagŏ 과거 n.C. the past (days); bygone days. *kwagŏ-ŭi* 과거의 past; bygone.

kwahak 과학 n.C. science. *kwahaktchŏk(ŭro)* 과학적 (으로) scientific (-ally). *kwahak kisul* 과학 기술 science and technology. *kwahaktcha* 과학자 scientist.

kwail 과일 n. (edible) fruit. *kwail kage* 과일 가게 fruit shop[stand] → kwasil 과실.

kwaja 과자 n.C. confectionery; cake; sweets; candy; cookie; biscuit. *kwajajŏm* 과자점 sweetshop; candy store (Am.).

+ kwalli 관리 n.C. government official; public servant.

+ kwalli 관리 n.C. management; administration. *kwallihada* 관리하다 administer; manage. *kwalli-*

in[ja] 관리인[자] manager; superintendent.

* **kwamok** 과목 n.C. (school) subject; lesson; course.
  p'ilsu [sŏnt'aek'] kwamok 필수[선택]과목 required [optional, elective] subject.

  kwan'gaek 관객 n.C. spectator; audience.

  kwanggo 광고 n.C. advertisement, (TV) commercial.
  kwanggohada 광고하다 advertise; announce.

+ **kwanggyŏng** 광경 n.C. spectacle; sight; scene; view.

+ **kwangsan** 광산 n.C. mine. *kwangsan kisa* 광산 기사 mining engineer. *kwangsan nodongja* 광산 노동자 mine worker; miner.

* **kwangsŏn** 광선 n.C. light; ray; beam. *t'aeyang kwangsŏn* 태양 광선 sunlight. *eksŭ kwangsŏn* 엑스 광선 X rays.

  kwan'gwang 관광 n.C. sightseeing, tourism. *kwangwanghada* 관광하다 go sightseeing; do the sights (of). *kwan'gwanggaek* 관광객 sightseer; tourist. *kwan'gwangppŏsŭ* 관광버스 sightseeing bus. *kwangwang yŏhaeng* 관광여행 sightseeing tour. *kwangwangji[hot'el]* 관광지[호텔] tourist resort [hotel].

kwan'gye 관계 n.C. relation; concern(ment); connection. *kwan'gyehada* 관계하다 relate to; concern; participate in; be concerned in.

+ **kwanse** 관세 n.C. customs; customs duties. *suip [such'ul] kwanse* 수입[수출] 관세 import[export] duties. *kwansech'ŏng* 관세청 the Office of Customs Administration.

+ **kwansim** 관심 n.C. concern; interest; ...*e kwansim-ŭl kajida* ...에 관심을 가지다 be concerned (about), be interested in.

  kwanyong 관용 n.C. *kwanyong-ŭi* 관용의 common; customary. *kwan- yongŏ* 관용어 idiom.

  kwalho 괄호 n.C. parenthesis; bracket; brace.

kwasil 과실 n.C. fruit; *kwasilju* 과실주 fruit wine.

  kwasuwŏn 과수원 n.C. orchard; fruit garden.

kwi 귀 n. ear. *kwi-ga mŏktta* 귀가 먹다 be deaf. *kwi-ga mŏlda* 귀가 멀다 be hard of hearing.

kwich´ant´a 귀찮다 adj. (be) annoying; bothersome. *kwich´ank´e* 귀찮게 annoyingly.

kwiguk 귀국 n.C. *kwiguk´ada* 귀국하다 return to one's country; go home.

* **kwihada** 귀하다 adj.C. ① (be) noble; honorable ② (be) deer; lovable ③ (be) rare; uncommon. [p.18]

+ **kwijok** 귀족 n.C. noble(man); peer. *kwijok sahoe* 귀족 사회 aristocracy; nobility.

+ **kwijunghada** 귀중하다 adj. (be) precious; valuable. *kwijungp´um* 귀중품 valuables.

+ **kwiyŏpta** 귀엽다 adj. (be) lovely; charming; attractive; cute.

* **kwŏlli** 권리 n.C. right; claim; title; privilege.

kwŏllyŏk 권력 n.C. (political) power; authority. *kwŏllyŏk innŭn* 권력있는 influential; powerful. *kwŏllyŏkka* 권력가 man of power.

kwŏnch´ong 권총 n.C. pistol; revolver; gun (Am.). *kwŏnch´ong kangdo* 권총 강도 armed robber; gunman.

* **kwŏnhada** 권하다 v.C. ① recommend ② advise; ask ③ invite; urge.

kwŏnt´u 권투 n.C. boxing. *kwŏnt´u sihap* 권투 시합 boxing match[bout]; prize-fight.

kwŏnwi 권위 n.C. authority; power; dignity. *kwŏnwi innŭn* 권위 있는 authoritative.

kwŏnyu 권유 n.C. inducement; solicitation; canvassing.

* **kye** 계 ① n.C. section (in an office); (a person in) charge, duty. ② suffix. *-kye; ch´ullapkye* 출납계 cashier's section.

kyedan 계단 n.C. stairs; staircase; doorstep.

* **kyegŭp** 계급 n.C. class. *sangnyu[chungnyu, haryu] kyegŭp* 상류[중류, 하류] 계급 upper [middle, lower] class(es).

kyehoek 계획 n.C. plan; project; scheme; program(me). *kyehoek´ada* 계획하다 plan; project; scheme; intent. *kyehoektchŏgin* 계획적인 inten-

tional; planned. *kyehoektchŏg-ŭro* 계획적으로 intentionally; deliberately.

\# **kyejip** 계집 n. (*slang*) *woman;* female; one's wife.

* **kyejibai** 계집아이 n. girl. = *kyejibae* 계집애.

\+ **kyejŏl** 계절 n.C. season. *kyejŏr-ŭi* 계절의 seasonal.

\+ **kyesan** 계산 n.C. calculation; reckoning; counting; computation. *kyesanhada* 계산하다 count; sum up; calculate; reckon. *kyesan'gi* 계산기 adding machine; calculator. *kyesansŏ* 계산서 bill; account.

\# **kyesida** 계시다 (*honorific form of* -있다) be; stay.

* **kyesok** 계속 n.C. continuance; continuation.

\# **kyesok'ada** 계속하다 n.V. continue; last; go on with. *kyesoktchŏgin* 계속적인 continous; continual.

* **kyet'ong** 계통 n.C. ① system ② lineage ③ party. *kyet'ongjŏk* 계통적 systematic. *kyet'ongjŏg-ŭro* 계통적으로 systematically.

kyeyak 계약 n.C. contract; compact; covenant. *kyeyak'ada* 계약하다 contract; make a contract; *kyeyakkŭm* 계약금 contract deposit. *kyeyakssŏ* 계약서 (written) contract.

kyoch'a 교차 n.C. intersection; crossing. *kyoch'ahada* 교차하다 cross [intersect] (each other). *kyoch'aro* 교차로 crossroads; intersection.

kyodae 교대 n.C. alternation; change. *kyodaehada* 교대하다 take turns; alternate. *kyodaero* 교대로 by turns; alterantely.

kyŏgŏn 격언 n.C. maxim; proverb; saying.

\+ **kyogwasŏ** 교과서 n.C. textbook. *kŏmjŏng kyogwasŏ* 검정 교과서 authorized textbook.

\+ **kyohoe** 교회 n.C. church; chapel; cathedral. *kyohoedang* 교회당 church; chapel.

* **kyohwan** 교환 n.C. exchange; interchange; barter. *kyohwanhada* 교환하다 exchange; interchange; barter.

kyŏja 겨자 n. mustard.

\+ **kyojang** 교장 n.C. headmaster (Eng.); principal (Am.); director (of high school)

kyojŏng 교정 n.C. proofreading. *kyojŏnghada* 교정하다 read proofs; correct (the press).

+ **kyŏktta** 겪다 v. ① undergo; suffer; experience ② receive; entertain.

kyŏlbaek 결백 n.C. purity; innocence; integrity. *kyŏlbaek´ada* 결백하다 (be) pure; upright; innocent.

kyŏlguk 결국 n.C. after all; in the end; finally; in the long run; eventually.

kyŏlgwa 결과 n.C. result; consequence; effect; fruit. *...ŭi kyŏlgwa* ...의 결과 as a [the] result of.

* **kyŏllon** 결론 n.C. conclusion. *kyŏllon-ŭl naerida* 결론을 내리다 draw [form] a conclusion.

+ **kyŏlssan** 결산 n.C. settlement of accounts. *kyŏlssanhada* 결산하디 settle [balace] an account.

+ **kyŏlssim** 결심 n.C. determination; resolution.

+ **kyŏlssimhada** 결심하다 v.C. determine; be resolved; make up one´s mind.

kyŏlssŏk 결석 n.C. absence. *kyŏlssŏkk´ada* 결석하다 be absent [absent oneself] (from).

kyŏltan 결단 n.C. decision; determination; resolution.

+ **kyŏltchŏm** 결점 n.C. fault; defect; flaw.

* **kyŏltchŏng** 결정 n.C. decision; determination; conclusion; settlement.

* **kyŏltchŏnghada** 결정하다 v.C. decide (upon); conclude; settle.

+ **kyŏltchongtoeda** 결정되다 v.C. be decided.

+ **kyŏm** 겸 n.(between nouns). and; in addition; concurrently. *ach´im kyŏm chŏmsim* 아침 겸 점심 brunch. *ch´imsil kyŏm kŏsil* 침실 겸 거실 bed-sitting room, studio apartment. *susang kyŏm oesang* 수상 겸 외상 Prime Minister and (concurrently) Foreign Minister.

kyoman 교만 n.C. pride; elation; haughtiness. *kyomanhada* 교만하다 (be) proud; haughty; arrogant.

kyŏmim 겸임 n.C. an additional job appointment.

kyŏmimhada 겸임하다 hold an additional post
[office].

kyŏmson 겸손 n.C. modesty; humility. *kyŏmsonhada*
겸손하다 (be) modest; humble.

kyomyohan 교묘한 adj. clever; skil(l)ful; deft.

kyonae 교내 n.C. campus. *kyonae-ŭi* 교내의 interclass.
kyonae-esŏ 교내에서 on [within] the campus.

kyŏnbon 견본 n.C. sample; specimen.

* **kyŏndida** 견디다 v. ① bear; endure; stand ② wear;
last; be good for; be equal to.

* **-kyŏng** -경 post-n. suffix. about; toward(s);
around. *sesigyŏng* 세시경 about three o'clock.

kyŏng 경 n.C. ① Chinese classics of Confucianism
② sutra; *pulkyŏng* 불경 Buddhist scripture. [p.79]

* **kyŏngbi** 경비 n.C. expense; cost; expenditure. *kyŏngbi chŏryak [chŏlgam]* 경비 절약 [절감] curtail-
ment of expenditure.

kyŏngbi 경비 n.C. defense; guard. *kyŏngbihada* 경비
하다 defend; keep watch.

* **kyŏngch'al** 경찰 n.C. the police. *kyŏngch'alssŏ* 경찰서
police station. *kyŏngch'algwan* 경찰관 policeman;
police officer. *kyŏngch'algwan p'ach'ulsso* 경찰관
파출소 police box [station branch].

+ **kyŏngch'i** 경치 n.C. scenery; landscape; view.

+ **kyŏnggi** 경기 n.C. game; match; contest; event.
kyŏnggihada 경기하다 have [play] a game.
kyŏnggijang 경기장 ground; field; stadium.

kyŏnggi 경기 n.C. ① business(condition); market ②
the times; things. *pulgyŏnggi* 불경기 depression;
recession. *hogyŏnggi* 호경기 boom; prosperity.

kyŏnggo 경고 n.C. warning; caution. *kyŏnggohada* 경
고하다 warn(a person) against (of); give warning
(to).

kyŏnggwa 경과 n.C. ① progress (of a case);
development (of an event) ② lapse (of time).
kyŏnggwahada 경과하다 elapse; pass; go by; expire.

kyŏnggye 경계 n.C. guard; lookout; watch;

precaution. *kyŏnggyehada* 경계하다 guard against;
look out[watch] (for).

kyŏnggye 경계 n.C. boundary; border; frontier.
kyŏnggyesŏn 경계선 boundary line; borderline.

+ **kyŏnghŏm** 경험 n.C. experience. *kyŏnghŏmhada* 경험
하다 experience; go through; undergo. *kyŏng-
hŏm-i itta* 경험이 있다. have experience (in).

+ **kyŏnghyang** 경향 n.C. tendency; trend. ...*ŭi
kyŏnghyang-i itta* ...의 경향이 있다 tend towards;
tend to (do); have a tendency to.

kyŏngi 경이 n.C. wonder; miracle. *kyŏngijŏk(in)* 경이
적(인) wonderful; marvelous; sensational.

+ **kyŏngjaeng** 경쟁 n.C. competition; rivalry; contest. *kyŏngjaenghada* 경쟁하다 compete with;
contest; vie.

kyŏngjak 경작 n.C. cultivation; tillage; farming.
kyŏngjaktchi 경작지 land under cultivation.
kyŏngjakhada 경작하다 cultivate; till; plow; farm.

kyŏngje 경제 n.C. economy. *kyŏngje-ŭi* 경제의 econ-
omic. *kyŏngjejŏk (ŭro)* 경제적(으로) economical(ly).
kyŏngjehak 경제학 economics; political economy.

kyŏngju 경주 n.C. race; run. *kyŏngjuhada* 경주하다
have [run] a race (with).

kyŏngni 경리 n.C. accounting; management.

kyŏngnyŏ 격려 n.C. encouragement; urging. *kyŏng-
nyŏhada* 격려하다 encourage; spur (a person) on;
cheer up.

kyŏngnyŏk 경력 n.C. career; record; personal
history.

kyŏngsol 경솔 n.C. *kyŏngsolhada* 경솔하다 (be) rash;
hasty; careless. *kyŏngsolhage[hi]* 경솔하게[히]
rashly; hastily; thoughtlessly.

kyŏngu 경우 n.C. occasion; time; circumstances;
case. *kŭrŏn kyŏngu* 그런 경우 in such a case. *ŏttŏn
kyŏngu-edo* 어떤 경우에도 under any circumstances. *kyŏngu-e ttarasŏnŭn* 경우에 따라서는 according to [under some] circumstances.

+ **kyŏngyŏng** 경영 n.C. management; administration.
+ **kyŏngyŏnghada** 경영하다 v.C. manage; run; keep.
  kyŏngyu 경유 n. passing through, via. *kyŏngyuhada* 경유하다 go by way of; pass [go] through. ...*ŭl kyŏngyuhayŏ* 경유하여 via; by way of; through.
  kyŏnhae 견해 n.C. opinion; one's view.
  kyŏnjuda 견주다 v. compare (A) with (B); measure (one thing) against (another).
  kyŏnuda 겨누다 v. ① (take) aim at; level (a gun) at ② compare (A with B); measure.
  kyooe 교외 n.C. suburbs; outskirts. *kyooe saenghwal* 교외 생활 suburban life. *kyooesŏn* 교외선 suburban railway.
  kyŏp 겹 n. fold *tu kyŏp* 두 겹 two fold. *yŏrŏ kyŏp* 여러 겹 many folds.
* **kyŏre** 겨레 n. brethren; one's countrymen; compatriots; race, ethnic group.
* **kyŏlhon** 결혼 n.C. marriage; matrimony; wedding.
+ **kyŏlhonhada** 결혼하다 v.C. marry; be[get] married (to). *kyŏrhonsik* 결혼식 wedding [marriage] ceremony. *kyŏrhon p'iroyŏn* 결혼 피로연 wedding reception.
  kyŏruda 겨루다 v. compete with; contend; pit (one's skill against).
+ **kyŏrŭi** 결의 n.C. resolution; decision; vote.
  kyoryu 교류 n.C. interchange. *kyoryuhada* 교류하다 interchange. *Hanmi munhwa kyoryu* 한미 문화 교류 cultural exchange between Korea and America.
+ **kyosa** 교사 n.C. teacher; instructor.
+ **kyosil** 교실 n.C. classroom. *hwahak kyosil* 화학 교실 chemistry classroom.
+ **kyosŏp** 교섭 n.C. negotiation(s). *kyosŏp'ada* 교섭하다 negotiate; approach (a person on a matter).
* **kyosu(nim)** 교수 n.C. ① teaching; instruction; tuition ② professor. *pugyosu* 부교수 associate professor.
* **kyŏt** 곁 n. side. *kyŏt'-e* 곁에 by (the side of). *paro*

kyŏt'-e 바로 곁에 near [close] by.

kyot'ong 교통 n.C. traffic; communication.

kyŏu 겨우 adv. barely; narrowly; with difficulty; only.

kyŏul 겨울 n. winter. *kyŏur-ŭi[kat'ŭn]* 겨울의[같은] wintry. *kyŏul panghak* 겨울 방학 winter vacation.

kyowon 교원 n.C. teacher; schoolteacher; schoolmaster; instructor.

kyoyang 교양 n.C. culture; education; refinement. *kyoyang-i innŭn* 교양이 있는 educated; cultured; refined. *kyoyang-i ŏmnŭn* 교양이 없는 uneducated; uncultured.

kyoyuk 교육 n.C. education; schooling; instruction; training. *kyoyuk'ada* 교육하다 educate; instruct; train. *kajŏng kyoyuk* 가정 교육 home training.

kyuch'ik 규칙 n.C. rule; regulations. *kyuch'iktchŏk [ŭro]* 규칙적[으로] regular[ly]; systematical[ly].

kyul 귤 n.C. orange. kyulkkŏptchil 귤껍질 orange peel.

kyumo 규모 n.C. scale; scope; structure. *taegyumo-ro* 대규모로 on a large scale.

$$\leq K' \geq$$

k'aeda 캐다 v. dig up [out] ; unearth.

k'al 칼 n. knife; sword; saber. [p.35]

k'algukssu 칼국수 n. knife-cut noodles.

k'allal 칼날 n. blade of a knife [sword] .

+ **k'amk'amhada** 캄캄하다 adj. (be) dark; pitch-black.

* **k'i** 키 n. stature; height. *k'i-ga k'ŭda [chakta]* 키가 크다 [작다] be tall [short] .

* **k'iuda** 키우다 v. bring up; rear; raise; breed.

* **k'o** 코 n. nose. [p.91] *tŭlch'angk'o* 들창고 turned-up

nose. *maeburik'o* 매부리코 Roman [aquiline] nose.

* **k'ŏjida** 커지다 v. get big [large] ; grow up; expand.
* **k'ong** 콩 n. beans; peas; soybean. [p.130]
  k'ongkkaenmuk 콩깻묵 bean cake.
k'ŭda 크다 adj. (be) big; large; great. ① *nŏmu k'ŭda* 너무 크다 be too large.
+ **k'ŭgi** 크기 n. size; dimension. *kat'ŭn k'ŭgi-ŭi* 같은 크기의 of the same size.
  kuk'oe 국회 n.C. National Assembly.
  kŭnil-nada 큰일나다 v. serious thing happens; be in trouble.
* **k'yŏda** 켜다 v. light; kindle; turn [switch] on.
  k'yŏlle 켤레 n. pair. *kudu han k'yŏlle* 구두 한 켤레 a pair of shoes.

$\leqslant$ M $\geqslant$

mach'i 마치 adv. as if [though] ; just like.
* **mach'ida** 마치다 v. finish; complete. *hagŏb-ŭl mach'ida* 학업을 마치다 finish a school course.
* **mach'im** 마침 adv. luckily; fortunately; just in time.
* **mach'imnae** 마침내 adv. finally; at last; eventually.
# **-mada** -마다 *particle*. each, every, all (inclusive).
* **madang** 마당 n. garden; yard; court. *ammadang* 앞마당 front yard. *anmadang* 안마당 courtyard.
# **madi** 마디 n. joint; knot; knob. phrase; clause.
  maebu 매부 n.C. husband of one's sister; one's brother-in-law.
* **maeda** 매다 v. tie (up); bind; fasten.
* **maeil** 매일 n.C. (adverbial use) every day; each day; daily. *maeir-ŭi* 매일의 (adjectival) everyday; daily. *maeil maeil* 매일 매일 day after day; day by

day.

maejŏm 매점 n.C. stand; stall; booth; small shop.

maek 맥 n.C. pulse; pulsation. *maeg-i ttwida* 맥이 뛰다 pulsate; pulse beats.

maektchu 맥주 n.C. beer; ale. *pyŏngmaektchu* 병맥주 bottled beer. *saengmaektchu* 생맥주 draft beer.

+ **maemae** 매매 n.C. trade; dealing; bargain. *maemaehada* 매매하다 deal [trade] (in).

+ **maenyŏn** 매년 n.C. every [each] year; annually; yearly.

maeptta 맵다 adj. be hot (spicy).

maep'yoso 매표소 n.C. ① ticket [booking] office ② box office.

maeryŏk 매력 n.C. charm; fascination. *maeryŏk innŭn* 매력 있는 charming; attractive.

maetta 맺다 v. ① tie (up); (make a) knot ② bear fruit ③ contract; enter relations (with).

maeu 매우 adv. very (much); greatly; awfully.

maewŏl 매월 n.C. every month; each month; monthly.

* **magu** 마구 adv. recklessly; at random〉 **mak** 막 (abbr.)

magyŏnhada 막연하다 adj.C. (be) vague; obscure; ambiguous.

mahŭn 마흔 n.C. forty. →**saship** 사십.

* **majimak** 마지막 n. the last; the end.

* **maju** 마주 adv. face to face. *maju poda* 마주 보다 look at each other.

majuch'ida 마주치다 v. collide with; clash with; run into.

* **mak** 막 adv. 〈 **magu** 마구.

+ **mak** 막 adv. just; just now; (be) about to.

+ **mak'ida** 막히다 v. be stopped by; be clogged [chocked].

makkŏlli 막걸리 n. unrefined [raw] rice liquor [wine].

maktta 막다 v. ① stop (up); plug ② intercept; block ③ defend; keep off [away].

maktta 맑다 adj. (be) clear; clean; pure (*water*); (be) resonant (*sound*); (be) fine; clear(*weather*).

+ **makttae(gi)** 막대(기) n. stick; rod; bar; club.

mal 말(short vowel) n. horse. *mar-ŭl t'ada* 말을 타다 ride [get on] a horse. cf. *chongma* 종마 stallion.

mal 말(long vowel) n. word; speech; language; term. [p.59,97,143] *malhada* 말하다 to speak.

+ **mal** -말(short vowel) n. the end. *samwŏlmal* 삼월말 the end of March.

+ **mal** 말(short vowel) n. a unit of measure [=about 18 litres]. [p.42] *ssal se mal* 쌀 세 말 three **mal** of rice.

mallida 말리다 v. dissuade (a person from doing); stop. *ssaum-ŭl mallida* 싸움을 말리다 stop a quarrel.

* **mallida** 말리다 v. make dry; dry. *pur-e mallida* 불에 말리다 dry (a thing) over the fire.

malssŏng 말썽 n. trouble; dispute; complaint. *malssŏngŭl purida* 말썽을 부리다 complain; cause trouble.

mamuri 마무리 n. finish; finishing (touches). *mamurihada* 마무리하다. finish (up); complete.

man 만 n.C. ten thousand; myriad. *suman* 수만 tens of thousands. *susimman* 수십만 hundreds of thousands.

-man -만 particle after n. and adjectival n. only, just, this much.

manch'an 만찬 n.C. supper; dinner. *manch'anhoe* 만찬회 dinner party.

mandŭlda 만들다 v. make; manufacture; create; form.

mang 망 n.C. ① net; casting a net ② network. *t'ongsin [pangsong] mang* 통신 [방송] 망 communication [radio] network.

mangch'i 망치 n. hammer.

mangch'ida 망치다 v. spoil; ruin; destroy; make a mess (of).

* **manghada** 망하다 v. go to ruin; be ruined; perish.

  mangsŏrida 망설이다 v. hesitate; scruple; be at a loss.

  mangwŏn'gyŏng 망원경 n.C. telescope.

  manhwa 만화 n.C. caricature; cartoon.

mani 많이 adv. much; lots; plenty; in abundance.

manil 만일 n.C. (adverbial use) if; in case; supposing (that).

+ **manjok** 만족 n.C. satisfaction; contentment. *manjok'ada* 만족하다 be satisfied with.

mannada 만나다 v. see; meet; interview.

  mannyŏnp'il 만년필 n.C. fountain pen.

  manse 만세 n.C. ① cheers; hurrah ② long live.

mant'a 많다 adj. (be) many; much; lots of; plenty of.

  mantchŏm 만점 n.C. a perfect score.

manŭl 마늘 n. garlic.

  manwŏn 만원 n.C. full [packed] house; capacity audience. *manwŏn pŏssŭ* 만원 버스 jam-packed bus.

mari 마리 n. number of animals; head. *kae han mari* 개 한 마리 a dog.

marŭda 마르다 v. (be) dry (up); get dry; run dry.

  maryŏnhada 마련하다 v. prepare; arrange; raise; make shift.

* **massŏda** 맞서다 v. ① stand opposite each other ② stand against.

mat 맛 n. taste; flavor; savor. *matchoŭn* 맛좋은 tasty; savory; delicious.

  match'uda 맞추다 v. fix [fit] into; assemble; put together.

+ **matkkida** 맡기다 v. place in custody; deposit with; put in charge of; entrust.

matta 맞다 v. be hit.

* **matta** 맞다 adj. ① be right [correct] ② match ③ fit; suit ④ agree (with).

matta 맡다 v. ① be entrusted with ② take [be in]

charge of.

+ **mattanghada** 마땅하다 adj. be proper.

* **maŭl** 마을 n. village; hamlet. *maŭl saram* 마을 사람 villagers.

maŭm 마음 n. mind; spirit; heart; will. *maŭmsog-ŭro* 마음속으로 inwardly; in one's heart.

mayak 마약 n.C. narcotic; (illegal) drug. *mayak chungdoktcha* 마약 중독자 drug addict.

meari 메아리 n. echo. *mearich'ida* 메아리치다 echo; be echoed; resound.

meda 메다 v. shoulder; carry on one's shoulder [back].

meuda 메우다 v. fill up [in] ; stop (up); reclaim.

* **mi** 미 n.C. beauty; grace. *yukch'emi* 육체미 physical beauty. *chayŏnmi* 자연미 natural beauty.

* **mianhada** 미안하다 v.C. (be) sorry; regrettable; repentant.

* **mich'ida** 미치다 v. go mad [crazy] ; become insane; lose one's senses.

midŏpta 미덥다 adj. (be) trustworthy; reliable; dependable; promising; hopeful.

Miguk 미국 n.C. (the United States of) America; U.S.A. *Migug-ŭi* 미국의 American; U.S.

mihon 미혼 n.C. single. *mihon-ŭi* 미혼의 unmarried; single. *mihonmo* 미혼모 unwed [unmarried] mother.

* **miin** 미인 n.C. beautiful woman [girl] ; beauty.

mijangwŏn 미장원 n.C. beauty salon [parlor, shop] .

mijigŭnhada 미지근하다 adj. (be) tepid; lukewarm.

mikkŭrŏpta 미끄럽다 adj. (be) smooth; slippery.

* **mil** 밀 n. wheat.

* **milda** 밀다 v. push; shove; thrust; jostle.

+ **milkkaru** 밀가루 n. wheat flour.

mimyohada 미묘하다 adj. (be) delicate; subtle.

+ **min'gan** 민간 n.C. civilian, private. *min'gan-ŭi* 민간의 civil; civilian; non-government.

minjok 민족 n.C. race; nation; people; ethnic group.

minjok undong 민족 운동 national movement.
* **minju** 민주 n.C. democracy. *minjujŏgin* 민주적인 democratic.
+ **minjujuŭi** 민주주의 n.C. democracy.
* **minjung** 민중 n.C. the (common) people; masses.
  minsok 민속 n.C. folklore; folkways. *minsok pangmulgwan* 민속 박물관 folklore museum.
  minyo 민요 n.C. folk song; ballad.
  minyŏ 미녀 n.C. beautiful woman; beauty; belle.
+ **miptta** 밉다 adj. (be) hateful; abominable; detestable.
* **miri** 미리 adv. beforehand; in advance; previously; in anticipation; prior to; earlier than.
  miruda 미루다 v. ① put off; postpone; delay; defer ② shift; shuffle off.
  misin 미신 n.C. superstition; superstitious belief.
  miso 미소 n.C. smile. *miso(-rŭl) chitta* 미소(를) 짓다 smile; beam.
+ **misul** 미술 n.C. art; fine arts. *misur-ŭi* 미술의 artistic. *misulga* 미술가 artist.
# **mit** 밑 n. lower part; bottom; base; foot. [p.46] *mit'ŭi* 밑의 lower; subordinate; inferior. *mit'-ŭro* 밑으로 down(ward). *mit'-ŭrobut'ŏ* 밑으로부터 from under [below] .
# **mit** 및 adv. and; also; as well as; in addition.
# **mitta** 믿다 v. believe; be convinced; trust; credit. [p.56] *midŭl ssu innŭn* 믿을 수 있는 believable.
  miwŏhada 미워하다 v. hate; detest; loathe.
  moch'in 모친 n.C. mother (in honorific term). → **ŏmŏni** 어머니.
  mŏdŏpta 멋없다 adj. (be) not smart [stylish] ; insipid.
  modu 모두 adv. ① all; everything; everybody; everyone ② in all; all told ③ altogether.
modŭn 모든 pre-n. all; every; each and every.
  mogi 모기 n. mosquito. *mogijang* 모기장 mosquito net. *mogihyang* 모기향 mosquito repellent [coil] .

mŏgi 먹이 n. feed; food (for animals).

* mŏgida 먹이다 v. let someone eat; feed (cattle on grass).

moguk 모국 n.C. one's mother country; one's native country. *mogugŏ* 모국어 one's mother tongue.

mogyok 목욕 n.C. bathing; bath. *mogyok'ada* 목욕하다 bathe (oneself) in; take [have] a bath.

mohŏm 모험 n.C. adventure; risk. *mohŏmhada* 모험하다 adventure; take a risk [chance]. *mohŏmjŏgin* 모험적인 adventurous; risky.

moida 모이다 v. gather; come [get] together; flock; crowd.

* moja 모자 n. hat, cap. *moja-rŭl ssŭda [pŏtta]* 모자를 쓰다 [벗다] put on [take off] a [one's] hat.

+ mojarada 모자라다 v. be not enough; be insufficient; be short of.

+ mojori 모조리 adv. all; wholly; entirely; altogether; without (an) exception.

mok 목 n. neck. ①, [p.43].

+ mok 몫 n. share; portion; lot; allotment. *nae mok* 내 몫 my share.

mŏk 먹 n. inkstick; Chinese ink; Indian ink.

mokkŏri 목걸이 n. necklace. *chinju mokkŏri* 진주 목걸이 pearl necklace.

mokkong 목공 n.C. carpenter.

mokkumŏng 목구멍 n. throat. [p.52] cf. *siktto* 식도 gullet; *kido* 기도 windpipe.

* mokkyŏk 목격 n.C. observation; witnessing. *mokkyŏk'ada* 목격하다 witness; observe.

mokp'yo 목표 n.C. mark; target; object; aim. *mokp'yohada* 목표하다 aim at; set the goal at.

mokssa(nim) 목사 n.C. pastor; minister; clergyman; rector; chaplain.

mokssori 목소리 n. voice; tone (of voice).

mokssu 목수 n.C. carpenter. → mokkong 목공.

mokssum 목숨 n. life. *mokssum-ŭl kŏlgo* 목숨을 걸고 at the risk of one's life.

moktchae 목재 n.C. timber, lumber, wood.

moktchang 목장 n.C. pasture; stockfarm; meadow; ranch(*Am.*).

\# **moktchŏk** 목적 n.C. purpose; aim; object; end. *mokchŏg-ŭl talssŏnghada* 목적을 달성하다 attain one's object; fulfil one's purpose.

\# **mŏktta** 먹다 v. eat; take; have. *pab-ŭl mŏktta* 밥을 먹다 eat rice; take a meal.

mokttori 목도리 n. muffler; neckerchief; scarf.

* **molda** 몰다 v. drive; urge; chase; run after. *ch'a-rŭl molda* 차를 몰다 drive a car.

mŏlda 멀다 adj. (be) far. [p.63]

\+ **mollae** 몰래 adv. secretly; in secret; on the sly.

\# **mom** 몸 n. body ①; physique; build; frame. *mom-i k'ŭn* 몸이 큰 big-bodied.

\+ **mŏmch'uda** 멈추다 v. stop; cease; put a stop; halt.

\+ **mŏmurŭda** 머무르다 v. stay; stop; put up (at an inn). *hot'er-e mŏmurŭda* 호텔에 머무르다 stop [put up] at a hotel. 〉 **mŏmulda** 머물다 (abbr).

mongnok 목록 n.C. catalog(ue); list.

\# **mŏnjŏ** 먼저 adv. first; first of all; above all.

* **mopssi** 몹시 adv. very (much); hard; greatly; awfully; extremely.

* **morae** 모래 n. sand; grit. *moraettang* 모래땅 sandy soil. *moraet'op* 모래톱 sand-bank.

more 모레 n. the day after tomorrow.

\# **mŏri** 머리 n. ① head ② brain ③ hair. ①

mŏrik'arak 머리카락 n. hair. *hŭin mŏrik'arak* 흰 머리카락 white hair.

\# **morŭda** 모르다 v. not know; be ignorant.

mosun 모순 n.C. contradiction; conflict; inconsistency. *mosunttoeda* 모순되다 be inconsistent (with).

* **mosŭp** 모습 n. appearance; one's features; one's image; face; look. *yenmosŭp* 옛모습 one's former self.

\+ **mot** 못 n. nail; peg. *mos-ŭl paktta/ch'ida [ppaeda]*

못을 박다/치다 [빼다] drive in [pull out] a nail.

mŏt 멋 n. (good) taste, (elegant) style, class; dandyism. *mŏdinnŭn* 멋있는 smart-looking; stylish; chic; fashionable.

mot'ada 못하다 ① v. cannot, be unable ② adj. (be) inferior; be worse than; fall behind.

mŏtchangi 멋장이 n. stylish person; chic thing; dandy, fop, dude.

moŭda 모으다 v. ① gather; get (things, people) together; collect ② concentrate; focus.

moyang 모양 n.C. shape; form; appearance; look; figure. *k'omoyang* 코모양 shape of one's nose.

moyok 모욕 n.C. insult; contempt. *moyok'ada* 모욕하다 insult.

+ **mudae** 무대 n.C. stage; field. *mudae changch'i* 무대 장치 stage setting; set(s).

+ **mudang** 무당 n.C. 'shaman'; witch; sorceress; exorcist.

mudŏm 무덤 n. grave; tomb.

mudŏptta 무덥다 adj. (be) ot and humid, sultry; sweltering; muggy.

muge 무게 n. weight; heaviness; burden. *muge-rŭl talda* 무게를 달다 weigh (a thing).

+ **mugi** 무기 n.C. arms; weapon; ordnance.

* **mugŏptta** 무겁다 adj. (be) heavy; weighty. *mugŏun chim* 무거운 짐 heavy [weighty] burden.

mugunghwa 무궁화 n.C. rose of Sharon (*national flower of Korea*).

mujilssŏ 무질서 n.C. disorder. *mujilssŏhada* 무질서하다 (be) disordered; chaotic; lawless.

muktta 묶다 v. bind; tie; fasten (together).

mul 물 n. water. ①, [p.54,55,105,140] *ch'anmul* 찬물 cold water. *tŏunmul* 더운물 hot water.

mulch'e 물체 n.C. body; object.

* **mulda** 물다 v. ① bite; snap; sting ② hold [put] in the mouth.

+ **mulkka** 물가 n.C. prices (of commodities). *mulkkago*

물가고 high prices of commodities.

* **mulkki** 물기 n. moisture. *mulkki-ga itta* 물기가 있다 be moist; damp; wet.

* **mulkkogi** 물고기 n. fish. →**saengsŏn** 생선.

* **mulkkyŏl** 물결 n. wave; billow; surf; ripple.

* **mullich′ida** 물리치다 v. ① decline; refuse; reject ② drive back [away] ; beat off [back] ③ keep away.

  mullida 물리다 v. get bitten. *mogi-e mullida* 모기에 물리다 be bitten by a mosquito.

  mullihak 물리학 n.C. physics; physical science.

+ **mullŏgada** 물러가다 v. move backward; step back; retreat; withdraw.

mullon 물론 n.C. (adverbial use) of course; to say nothing of; not to speak of; no doubt; needless to say; naturally.

  mulp′um 물품 n.C. articles; things; goods; commodities.

* **multcha** 물자 n.C. material, goods; things; (raw) materials.

multchil 물질 n.C. matter; substance. *multchiljŏgin* 물질적인 material; physical.

  mult′ong 물통 n. water pail [bucket] .

* **mumyŏng** 무명 n. cotton. *mumyŏngsil* 무명실 cotton thread. *mumyŏngot* 무명옷 cotton clothes.

mun 문 n.C. gate; door; gateway. ① *chadongmun* 자동문 automatic door. *am [twin] mun* 앞 [뒷] 문 front [back] door.

  munbanggu 문방구 n.C. stationery; writing materials. *munbanggujŏm* 문방구점 stationery shop; stationer′s.

  mungch′i 뭉치 n. bundle; roll; lump.

* **munhak** 문학 n.C. literature; letters. *munhag-ŭi* 문학의 literary. *munhaktcha* 문학자 literary person.

munhwa 문화 n.C. culture; civilization. *munhwa saenghwal* 문화 생활 cultural life. *munhwachae* 문화재 cultural assets.

munjang 문장 n.C. sentence; composition; writing.

\# **munje** 문제 n.C. question; problem; issue. *sahoe munje* 사회 문제 social problem.

* **munmyŏng** 명명 n.C. civilization; culture. *munmyŏnghan* 명명한 civilized; enlightened.

\+ **munŏjida** 무너지다 v. crumble; collapse; go [fall] to pieces; give way.

munppŏp 문법 n.C. grammar.

munsŏ 문서 n.C. document; paper. *munsŏro* 문서로 in writing.

* **muntcha** 문자 n.C. letters; character; alphabet. [p.12]

\+ **munŭi** 무늬 n. pattern; design; figure.

munye 문예 n.C. leterary arts; art and literature. *munyeran* 문예란 literary column. *munyepyŏngnon* 문예평론 literary criticism.

\# **muŏt** 무엇 pron. what; something; anything. *muŏsidŭn* 무엇이든 anything; whatever. *muŏtppodado* 무엇보다도 above all (things); first of all.

* **muri** 무리 n.C. irrational(ity). *murihan* 무리한 unreasonable; unjust; immoderate.

muryo 무료 n.C. free of charge. *muryo-ŭi* 무료의 free (of charge); gratuitous; cost-free.

\+ **muryŏp** 무렵 n. time; about; around; towards. *haejil muryŏb-e* 해질 무렵에 toward evening.

musimusihada 무시무시하다 adj. (be) dreadful; awful; frightful; horrible.

\# **musŏptta** 무섭다 adj. (be) fearful; terrible; dreadful; horrible.

musŏwŏhada 무서워하다 v. (be) afraid (of); fear; be fearful (of); be frightened (at).

\# **musŭn** 무슨 pre-n. what; what sort [kind] of. *musŭn illo* 무슨 일로 on what business; why.

\# **mutta** 묻다(long vowel) v. ask; question; inquire.

* **mutta** 묻다(short vowel) v. bury.

* **mutta** 묻다(short vowel) v. stick; be stained (with).

\# **muyŏk** 무역 n.C. trade; commerce. *muyŏk'ada* 무역

하다 trade (with); engage in foreign trade.

muyong 무용 n.C. dancing; dance. *muyonghada* 무용 하다 dance; perform a dance.

* **myŏch'il** 며칠 n. what day of the month; how many days; how long; a few days. *myŏch'il chŏn* 며칠 전 a few days ago.

myoji 묘지 graveyard; cemetery. *kongdong myoji* 공 동 묘지 public cemetery.

\# **-myŏn** -면 conditional ending for v. or adj. **-myŏn** occurs after stems that end on vowel or *l* consonant. if, when, whenever. other shapes: -(ŭ)myŏn, -(i)myŏn.

myŏndo 면도 n.C. shaving. *myŏndohada* 면도하다 shave (oneself); get a shave. *myŏndonal* 면도날 razor blade. *chŏngi myŏndogi* 전기면도기 electric shaver.

myŏngham 명함 n.C. (name) card; business card; calling card (*Am.*).

\+ **myŏngnanghan** 명랑한 adj. cheerful; merry; bright; happy; light- hearted.

* **myŏngnyŏng** 명령 n.C. order; command. *myŏng-nyŏnghada* 명령하다 order; command.

\+ **myŏnhada** 면하다 v.C. escape; avoid; get rid of.

myŏnhoe 면회 n.C. interview. *myŏnhoehada* 면회하다 meet; see; have an interview.

\# **myŏnjŏk** 면적 n.C. area. *kyŏngjak myŏnjŏk* 경작 면적 area under cultivation.

myŏnmyŏt 몇몇 pre-n. some; several.

myŏnse 면세 n.C. tax exemption. *myŏnsehada* 면세하 다 exempt (a person) from taxes. *myŏnsep'um* 면 세품 tax-exempt [duty-free] articles.

\+ **myŏnŭri** 며느리 n. daughter-in-law; one's son's wife.

\# **myŏtnk** 몇 pre-n. ① some; a few; several ② how many; how much.

⪤ N ⪥

na 나 pron. I; myself. *naǔi* 나의 my. *na-ege/rǔl* 나에게/를 me.
* **naagada** 나아가다 v. advance; proceed; march; go forward; move on.

  naajida 나아지다 v. become [get] better; improve; make a good progress.
* **nabi** 나비 n. butterfly.
# **nada** 나다 v. ① be born ② be out; come into (*bud, leaf*) ③ produce; yield ④ smell; taste.

  nae 내(long vowel) n. stream; brook; creek(*Am.*).
nae 내(short vowel) pron. ① I. *nae-ga ganda* 내가 간다 I go. ② (abbreviated form of *na-ǔi* 나의) my. [p.28]
naebin 내빈 n.C. guest. *naebinsǒk* 내빈석 guests' seat. *naebinsil* 내빈실 reception room.
+ **naebonaeda** 내보내다 v. ① let out; let go out ② dismiss; fire(*Am.*).
+ **naebu** 내부 n.C. inside; interior. *naebu-ǔi* 내부의 inside; internal; inner. *naebu-e* 내부에 inside; within.

  naehunyǒn 내후년 n.C. the year after next.
naeil 내일 tomorrow. *naeil chǒnyǒk* 내일 저녁 tomorrow evening.

  naejuda 내주다 v. ① take [bring] (a thing) out and give it; give away ② resign [surrender] (one's seat to a person).
* **naemsae** 냄새 n. smell; odo(u)r; scent; stink; reek. *naemsaenada* 냄새나다 smell (of tobacco). *choǔn [nappǔn] naemsae* 좋은 [나쁜] 냄새 sweet [bad] smell. → **hyanggi** 향기 fragrance; perfume.
+ **naemu** 내무 n.C. home [domestic] affairs. *naemubu* 내무부 Ministry of Home Affairs; Home Office

(*Eng.*); Department of the Interior (*Am.*)

naengbang 냉방 n.C. air conditioning; air-conditioned room. *naengbang changch'i* 냉방 장치 air conditioning; air conditioner; air cooler. *naengbang chung* 냉방 중 air-conditioned.

naengdong 냉동 n.C. freezing. *naengdongsil* 냉동실 deep-freezer. *naengdong- hada* 냉동하다 freeze. *naengdong sikp'um* 냉동 식품 frozen food(stuffs).

naengjang 냉장 n.C. cold storage; refrigeration. *naengjanggo* 냉장고 refrigerator; icebox.

\# **naerida** 내리다 v. ① descend; come down; drop; fall. ② get off; dismount.

* **naeyong** 내용 n.C. contents; substance.

\# **nagada** 나가다 v. go [come, get] out; be present; leave.

\+ **nagyŏp** 낙엽 n.C. fallen [dead] leaves.

nahŭl 나흘 n. four days; the fourth day of the month.

\# **nai** 나이 age.

\# **najung-e** 나중에 adj. later (on); afterwards; after some time. *najung kkŏt* 나중 것 the latter.

nakkwan 낙관 n.C. optimism. *nakkwanjŏk* 낙관적 (be) optimistic.

nakssijil 낚시질 n. fishing. *nakssijilhada* 낚시질하다 (*v.*) fish.

nakssŏ 낙서 n.C. graffitti; scribbles; scrawl.

naktta 낡다 adj. ① (be) old; used; worn ② (be) old-fashioned; be out of date.

naktche 낙제 n.C. failure in an examination. *naktchehada* 낙제하다 fail in an exam.

\# **nal** 날 n. ① day; date; time ① ② time when; in time of. *nallo* 날로 day by day.

nal 날 n. edge; blade. *k'allal* 칼날 blade of a knife.

\# **nalda** 날다 v. fly; soar; flutter [flit] about.

\# **nalgae** 날개 n. wing. *nalgae tallin* 날개 달린 winged. [p.100]

nalk'aropta 날카롭다 adj. (be) sharp; keen; acute;

pointed. *nalk'aropke* 날카롭게 sharply; stingingly.

nallo 난로 n.C. stove; fireplace; heater.

+ **nalssi** 날씨 n. the weather.

+ **naltcha** 날짜 n. date. *kyeyak naltcha* 계약 날짜 date of a contract.

\# **nam** 남 n. another person; others; unrelated person(s); stranger(s); outsider(s). [p.22, 23, 24, 25]

nam 남 n.C. south. *nam-ŭro* 남으로 to the south. *namtchog-e* 남쪽에 in the south.

nambuk 남북 n.C. north and south. *nambuk taehwa* 남북 대화 the South-North dialogue. *nambuk t'ongil* 남북 통일 reunification of Korea.

Namdaemun 남대문 n.C. the South Gate (of Seoul). *Namdaemun sijang* 남대문 시장 Namdaemun market.

\# **namgida** 남기다 v. ① leave (behind); bequeath ② make [get, obtain, realize] a profit (of).

Namhan 남한 n.C. South Korea. cf. *Pukhan* 북한 North Korea.

\# **namja** 남자 n.C. man; male. *namja-ŭi* 남자의 male; masculine. *namja-daun* 남자다운 manly.

* **namnyŏ** 남녀 n.C. man and woman; male and female.

* **namŏji** 나머지 n. ① the rest; the remainder; the balance ② excess.

\# **namp'yŏn** 남편 n.C. husband.

+ **namsŏng** 남성 n.C. male (sex); the masculine gender. *namsŏngjŏk(in)* 남성적(인) manly; masculine.

\# **namtta** 남다 v. be left over; remain.

* **namu** 나무 n. ① tree; plant ② wood; timber; lumber. [p.96,106,115] *namunnip* 나뭇잎 leaf; foliage.

namurada 나무라다 v. scold; reproach; reprimand.

nanbang 난방 n.C. heating. *nanbang changch'i* 난방 장치 heating apparatus.

nangbi 낭비 n.C. waste; extravagance. *nangbihada*

낭비하다 waste; squander.
nanuda 나누다 v. ① divide ② share ③ classify.
aoda 나오다 v. go [come, get] out; be present; leave.
nap´al 나팔 n. trumpet, bugle.①
nappajida 나빠지다 v. grow worse; go bad.
nappu 납부 n.C. delivery; payment. *nappuhada*
납부하다 pay; deliver; supply (goods). *nappu-jŭngmyŏngsŏ* 납부 증명서 certificate of payment.
nappŭda 나쁘다 adj. bad; evil; wrong; wicked;
inferior (*quality*); unwell (*health*); poor, weak
(*memory*); nasty, foul (*weather*).
naptchak´ada 납작하다 adj. (be) flat.
nara 나라 n. ① country; state; land; nation ②
world; realm. *uri nara* 우리 나라 our country.
tallara 달나라 lunar world.
* **naranhi** 나란히 adv. in a row [line] ; side by side.
narŭda 나르다 v. carry; convey; transport.
nassŏlda 낯설다 adj. (be) strange; unfamiliar.
* **nat** 낯 n. face; features; looks. [p.104] → **ŏlgul** 얼굴.
* **nat** 낮 n. daytime. [p.27] *naj-e* 낮에 in the daytime.
nat 낫 n. sickle; scythe. [p.26]
nat´a 낳다 v. ① bear; give birth to; be delivered of
(a child) ② produce.
nat´anada 나타나다 v. come out; turn up; appear.
natcham 낮잠 n. nap; siesta. *natcham chada* 낮잠 자
다 take a nap[siesta].
* **natta** 낫다 v. (be) better (than); preferable. [p.61]
+ **natta** 낫다 v. recover; get well; be cured (of); heal.
natta 낮다 adj. ① (be) low ② humble.
ne 네(long vowel) n. four. *ne saram* 네 사람 four
people. *ne si* 네 시 four o'clock.
ne 네(short vowel) pron. ① you. *ne-ga ganda* 네가 간
다 You go. ② (abbreviated form of *nŏ-ŭi* 너의)
your. [p.28] *ne adŭl* 네 아들 your son.
ne 네(short vowel) interj. (positive answer using
around Seoul area) yes; certainly. → **ye** 예.
negŏri 네거리 n. crossroads; street crossing.

nemo 네모 n. square. *nemonan* 네모난 four-cornered; square.

netchae 네째 n. the fourth; No.4; the fourth place.

\# **-nji** -ㄴ지 ending ① present adj. or past v. with **-nji** followed by verbs of knowing, telling, asking. if/whether it is (adj.) or did (v.) ② (with *-ra* -라) since it is or did, as it is or did. other shape: -(i)nji, -(ŭ)nji.

\# **nŏ** 너 pron. you (informal, intimate style).

nŏbi 너비 n. width; breadth.

+ **nodong** 노동 n.C. manual labor; work. *nodonghada* 노동하다 manual labor; work; toil.

+ **nodongja** 노동자 n.C. laborer; worker; working people; labor.

nŏgŭrŏpta 너그럽다 adj. (be) lenient; generous. *noŏgŭrŏi* 너그러이 generously; leniently.

* **nŏhŭi** 너희 pron. (pl.) you all; you people [folk] .

* **noin** 노인 n.C. old [aged] man. *noinppyŏng* 노인병 disease of old age.

nokssaek 녹색 n.C. green; green color.

\# **noktta** 녹다 v. melt; dissolve; thaw.

nol 놀 n. glow (in the sky). *chŏnyŏngnol* 저녁놀 evening glow.

\# **nolda** 놀다 v. play; amuse oneself.

nŏlda 널다 v. spread out; stretch.

nollada 놀라다 v. be surprised [astonished] ; be startled; be stunned. *nollal manhan* 놀랄 만한 surprising; amazing.

nolli 논리 n.C. logic. *nollijŏk(ŭro)* 논리적(으로) log-ical(ly). *nollihak* 논리학 logic.

* **nŏlli** 널리 adv. widely; far and wide; generally.

\# **nollida** 놀리다 v. tease; kid; laugh at; make fun of; banter; chaff; rally; ridicule.

nŏlp'ida 넓히다 v. widen; enlarge; broaden; extend.

\# **nŏltta** 넓다 adj. (be) broad; wide; roomy; extensive.

nŏmch'ida 넘치다 v. ① overflow; flow [run] over; be full of ② exceed; be above [beyond] .

nŏmgida 넘기다 v. ① hand (over); turn over; transfer; pass ② throw down; overthrow ③ pass; exceed ④ turn a page.

nŏmŏ 너머 n. opposite [other] side; across; beyond.

+ **nŏmŏgada** 너머가다 v. ① cross; go across [over] ② sink; set; go down ③ be transferred ④ fall; be thrown down ⑤ be swallowed.

nŏmŏjida 너머지다 v. fall (down); come down; tumble down.

\# **nŏmtta** 넘다 v. ① cross; go over; go [get] beyond ② exceed; pass.

\# **nŏmu** 너무 adv. too (much); over; excessively.

+ **nongbu** 농부 n. farmer; peasant.

* **nongch'on** 농촌 n.C. farm village; rural community.

nongdam 농남 n.C. joke; fun; prank. *nongdamhada* 농담하다 jest; crack a joke; poke fun at.

* **nongga** 농가 n.C. farmhouse; farm household.

nonggu 농구 n.C. basketball. *nonggu sŏnsu* 농구 선수 basketball player.

nongjang 농장 n.C. farm.

\# **nongjangmul** 농작물 n.C. crops; harvest; farm produce.

* **nongmin** 농민 n.C. farmer; peasant.

nŏngnŏk'ada 넉넉하다 adj. (be) enough; sufficient. *nŏngnŏk'i* 넉넉히 enough; sufficiently; fully.

\# **nongŏp** 농업 n.C. agriculture; farming. *nongŏb-ŭi* 농업의 agricultural.

* **nongsanmul** 농산물 n.C. agricultural products; farm produce.

nonmun 논문 n.C. research report; dissertation; thesis.

nonsŏl 논설 n.C. discussion; opinion article; editorial(in case of newspaper). *nonsŏl wiwŏn* 논설 위원 editorial writer.

* **nop'i** 높이 n. ① (*noun*) height; altitude ② (*adverb*) high; highly.

\# **noptta** 높다 adj. (be) high; tall; lofty; elevated.

norae 노래 n. song; ballad; singing. *noraehada* 노래
하다 sing (a song).

norat'a 노랗다 adj. (be) yellow. *noran saek* 노란색
yellow (color).

nori 놀이 n. play; game; sport. *minsongnori* 민속놀이
folk games; traditional games. *norit'ŏ* 놀이터
playground; pleasure resort.

norida 노리다 v. stare at; watch (for); fix the eye
on; aim at.

norŭm 노름 n. gambling; gaming; betting. *norŭmha-
da* 노름하다 gamble; play for money. *norŭmkkun*
노름꾼 gambler; gamester.

* **noryŏk** 노력 n.C. endeavo(u)r; effort.

* **noryŏk'ada** 노력하다 v.C. endeavor; strive; make
efforts.

noryŏnhan 노련한 adj. experienced; veteran; expert;
skilled.

not'a 놓다 v. ① put; place; lay; set ② let go; set
free; release.

nŏt'a 넣다 v. ① put in [into] ; set [let] in; stuff ②
send [put] (to); admit ③ include.

+ **noye** 노예 n.C. slave; slavery. *noye kŭnsŏng* 노예 근
성 servile spirit.

noyŏum 노여움 n. anger; offence; displeasure. *no-
yŏum-ŭl sada* 노여움을 사다 incur (a person's)
displeasure.

nuda 누다 v. ① urinate ② defecate.

nŭdadŏpsi 느닷없이 adv. abruptly; all of a sudden;
unexpectedly.

nugu 누구 pron. who. *nugu-ŭi* 누구의 whose. *nugu-rŭl*
누구를 whom.

nuguŏjida 누그러지다 v. get milder; calm down;
abate; subside.

nui 누이 n. sister; elder sister; younger sister.

nŭkkida 느끼다 v. ① feel; be aware [conscious] (of)
② be impressed (by, with).

nŭktta 늙다 v. grow old; age; advance in age.

\# **nŭl** 늘 adv. → **ŏnjena** 언제나.

    nŭllida 늘리다 v. ① increase; add to; multiply ② extend; enlarge.

    nŭlssinhada 늘씬하다 adj. (be) slender; slim; slender and elegant.

\# **nun** 눈(long vowel) n. snow; snowfall. *nun-ŭi* 눈의 snowy.

\# **nun** 눈(short vowel) n. eye. ①. [p.31,119] *nun-ŭl ttŭda [kamta]* 눈을 뜨다 [감다] open [close] one's eyes.

\# **-nŭn/ŭn** -는/은 topic particle. **-nŭn** -는 occurs after vowels, **-ŭn** -은 after consonants. ① marks the topic, reducing the emphasis on the preceding word(s) in order to highlight the rest of the sentence because the sentence is long (or the item has already been mentioned, etc.) *tar-ŭn han hae-e yŏlttu pŏn tonda* 달은 한 해에 열두 번 돈다 The moom rotates twelve times a year. ② marks two contrasting items *na-nŭn hakssaengijiman, kŭ pŭn-ŭn kyosunimisida* 나는 학생이지만 그분은 교수님이시다 I am a student but he is a professor. ③ marks exclusion *kŭ saram(man)ŭn an minnŭnda* 그 사람(만)은 안 믿는다 (Only) he does not believe it. *or* I do not believe him (but others).
    cf. **-i/ga.**

\# **-nŭn** *processive modifier* -는 occurs after verb stems and *it-/ŏm((p)-* 있-/없-. marks the end(ing) of a present tense verbal in a modifying clause. corresponds to relative pron. (that, who, which, etc.) in English. *nae-ga t'anŭn ch'a* 내가 타는 차 the car (that) I ride, *or* the tea (that) I prepare.

    nŭnghi 능히 adv.C. well; easily; ably.

    nungnuk'ada 눅눅하다 adj. (be) damp; humid.

* **nŭngnyŏk** 능력 n.C. ability; capacity; faculty. *nŭngnyŏg-e ttara* 능력에 따라 according to ability. *nŭngnyŏg-i itta* 능력이 있다 be able to do.

\# **-nŭnji** ending ① present v. with **-nŭnji** followed by verbs of knowing, telling, asking. if/whether it does

② (with -ra -라) since it does, as it does. other shape: -(i)nji, -(ŭ)nji.

nŭrinnŭrit 느릿느릿 adv. slowly; sluggishly; idly.

nŭrŏnot'a 늘어놓다 v. ① scatter about; leave (things) lying about ② arrange; place (things) in a row.

nŭrŏsŏda 늘어서다 v. stand in a row; form in a line; stand abreast.

\# **nurŭda** 누르다 v. ① press (down); weigh on; hold (a person) down ② stamp; seal.

nŭtcham 늦잠 n. late rising; morning sleep. *nŭtchamjada* 늦잠자다 rise [get up] late.

nŭtch'uda 늦추다 v. ① loosen; unfasten; slacken ② put off; postpone; delay; defer.

* **nŭtta** 늦다 adj. (be) late; behind time; be slow. *nŭtkke* 늦게 late. *nŭjŏdo* 늦어도 at (the) latest.

\+ **nyŏsŏk** 녀석 n. fellow; guy; chap. *I pabo nyŏsŏk* 이 바보 녀석 You fool!

⪯ O ⪰

\# **o** 오 n. 5 five; *cheo* 제 5 the fifth.

\# **-ŏ** -어 other shapes: -a -아, -yŏ -여. non-final tenseless (infinitive) ending of v. or adj. immediately following stems and used in combination with other endings.

ŏbŏi 어버이 n. parents; father and mother. *ŏbŏinal* 어버이날 Parents' Day, May 8.

och'an 오찬 n.C. luncheon; (heavy) lunch. *och'anhoe* 오찬회 luncheon party. → **chŏmsim** 점심 (informal) lunch.

\# **oda** 오다 v. come; come up [down]; come over [along].

\# **ŏdi** 어디 pron. where; what place. *ŏdi-ena* 어디에나 anywhere; everywhere.

ŏduptta 어둡다 adj. (be) dark; dim; gloomy. [p.46]

oebu 외부 n.C. outside; exterior. *oebu-ŭi* 외부의 outside; outward; external.

+ **oech´ida** 외치다 v. shout out; cry (out); exclaim.

oech´ul 외출 n.C. going out. *oech´ulhada* 외출하다 go out. *oech´uljung* 외출중 while (one is) out.

\# **oeguk** 외국 n.C. foreign country [land]. *oegug-ŭi* 외국의 foreign; alien. *oegugin* 외국인 n.C. foreigner. *oegugŏ* 외국어 foreign language.

+ **oegyo** 외교 n.C. diplomacy. *oegyo munje* 외교 문제 diplomatic problem. *oegyo chŏngch´aek* 외교 정책 diplomatic policy. *oegyogwan* 외교관 diplomat.

oehwa 외화 n.C. foreign currency [money].

oekkwa 외과 n.C. surgery; surgical department. *oekkwa ŭisa* 외과 의사 surgeon.

oemu 외무 n.C. foreign affairs. *oemubu* 외무부 Ministry of Foreign Affairs.

* **oentchok** 왼쪽 n. left (side). *oentchog-ŭi* 왼쪽의 left (-hand). *oentchog-e* 왼쪽에 on the left side.

+ **oeroptta** 외롭다 adj. (be) lonely; lonesome; solitary.

oesang 외상 n.C. credit; trust. *oesang kŏrae* 외상 거래 credit transaction.

* **oet´u** 외투 n.C. overcoat; topcoat.

ŏgida 어기다 v. go against; disobey; break.

ŏgŭnnada 어긋나다 v. ① cross each other ② pass each other ③ go amiss; go wrong with.

ŏgwi 어귀 n. entrance; entry(Am.) *maŭl ŏgwi* 마을 어귀 entrance to a village.

ohae 오해 n.C. misunderstanding; misconception. *ohaehada* 오해하다 misunderstand.

ŏhak 어학 n.C. language study; philology; linguistics.

\# **ohiryŏ** 오히려 adv. rather; preferably; on the contrary; instead.

* **ohu** 오후 n.C. afternoon; p.m.; P.M.

ŏhwi 어휘 n.C. vocabulary; glossary; lexicon.

+ **oi** 오이 n. cucumber. *oiji* 오이지 cucumbers pickled in

salt.

+ **oil** 오일 n.C. five days; the fifth day (of the month).

ŏje 어제 n. yesterday. *ŏje ach'im* 어제 아침 yesterday morning.

ŏjiröptta 어지럽다 adj. (be) dizzy; feel light-headed; feel giddy.

+ **ojŏn** 오전 n.C. forenoon; morning; a.m.; A.M.

+ **ojum** 오줌 n. urine. *ojum nuda* 오줌 누다 urinate.

* **ŏk** 억 n.C. one hundred million. *sibŏk* 십억 billion.

* **ŏkkae** 어깨 n. shoulder. *ŏkkae-rŭl ŭssŭk'ada* 어깨를 으쓱하다 perk up [raise] one's shoulders.

ŏkku 어구 n. phrase; words and phrases.

+ **ŏktchiro** 억지로 adv. by force; forcibly.

+ **ol** 올 n. ply; texture; strand.

olch'aengi 올챙이 n. tadpole. [p.7]

* **ŏlda** 얼다 v. freeze; be frozen (over); be benumbed with cold.

ŏlgul 얼굴 n. face; features; looks. *ŏlgur-ŭl tollida* 얼굴을 돌리다 look away; look aside. *ŏlgur-ŭl pulk'ida* 얼굴을 붉히다 blush.

olhae 올해 n. this year; the current year.

ollagada 올라가다 v. go up; mount; climb; rise; ascend.

ollida 올리다 v. raise; lift up; put [hold] up; elevate; hoist.

ŏllon 언론 n.C. speech; the press. *ŏllon-ŭi chayu* 언론의 자유 freedom of speech [press].

ŏllŭn 얼른 adv. fast; quickly; rapidly; promptly; at once.

ŏlma 얼마 n. ① how much; what price ② how many; what number [amount].

ŏlmana 얼마나 adv. ① how much; what; how many ② how (far, large, old, etc.).

olt'a 옳다 adj. ① (be) right; rightful ② (be) righteous; just ③ (be) correct; accurate ④ (be) proper.

omgida 옮기다 v. remove; move; transfer.

ŏmji 엄지 n. *ŏmjisonkkarak* 엄지손가락 thumb.

ŏmkkyŏk 엄격 n.C. *ŏmkyŏk´ada* 엄격하다 (be) strict; stern.

* **ŏmma** 엄마 n. ma; mama; mommy; mummy.

ŏmmu 업무 n.C. business. *ŏmmuyong* 업무용 for buisiness use.

\# **ŏmŏni** 어머니 n. mother. *ŏmŏni-ŭi* 어머니의 mother's; motherly; maternal.

ŏmsuk 엄숙 n.C. solemnity; gravity; sternly. *ŏmsuk´ada* 엄숙하다 (be) grave; solemn; stern. *ŏmsuk´age* 엄숙하게 solemnly.

\# **on** 온 pre-n. all; whole. *on sesang* 온 세상 all the world. *on chiban* 온 집안 whole family. *on kajok* 온 가족 whole family.

ondae 온대 n.C. Temperate Zone; warm latitudes.

\# **ondo** 온도 n.C. temperature. *ondogye* 온도계 thermometer; mercury.

ondol 온돌 n.C. Korean hypocaust; under-floor heating system. *ondolppang* 온돌방 room with a heated floor; *ondol* room.

\+ **on´gat** 온갖 pre-n. all; every; all sorts of; various.

ŏngk´ŭmhada 엉큼하다 adj. (be) wily [insidious]; crafty.

ŏngt´ŏri 엉터리 n. ① fake; sham ② ground; foundation. *ŏngt´ŏri ŭisa* 엉터리 의사 quack (doctor). *ŏngt´ŏriŏmnŭn* 엉터리없는 gruondless; absurd.

* **ŏnje** 언제 pron. when. *ŏnje-rado* 언제라도 at any time. *ŏnjetchŭm* 언제쯤 about when.

* **ŏnjena** 언제나 adv. always; all the time; usually.

onjongil 온종일 n. all day (long); the whole day.

* **ŏnni** 언니 n. elder sister.

\+ **ŏnŏ** 언어 n. language; speech; words. *ŏnŏ changae* 언어 장애 speech impediment.

\+ **ŏntta** 얹다 v. put on; place [lay, set] on; load.

\# **ŏnŭ** 어느 pre-n. ① a; one; certain; some ② which; what. *ŏnŭ nal* 어느 날 one day. *ŏnŭ ch´aek* 어느 책 which book. → **ŏnŭsae** 어느새 already.

onŭl 오늘 n. today; this day. *onŭllal* 오늘날 these days.

ŏnŭsae 어느새 adv. ① already; now; by this time ② so soon; before one knows; unnoticed.

ŏpssi 없이 adv. without. *hyuil-do ŏpssi* 휴일도 없이 without holidays.

+ **ŏptcha** 업자 n.C. business people; traders.

ŏptta 없다 adj. ① there is no ···; cannot be found ② have no ... ; lack.

+ **ŏptta** 업다 v. carry on one's back.

ŏptta 엎다 v. overturn; turn over; turn upside down.

* **ŏpttŭrida** 엎드리다 v. postrate oneself; lie flat.

* **orae** 오래 adv. long; for a long while [time].

+ **orak** 오락 n.C. amusement(s); recreation; pastime; *orakssil* 오락실 amusement hall, video arcade (Am.).

ŏrida 어리다 adj. (be) young; juvenile; infant; childish.

* **ŏrini** 어린이 n. child; little one; youngster; infant.

+ **ŏrisŏktta** 어리석다 adj. (be) foolish; childish; silly; stupid.

+ **oroji** 오로지 adv. alone; only; solely; exclusively.

orŭda 오르다 v. go up; climb; ascend; rise; mount.

ŏrŭm 얼음 n. ice. *sarŏrŭm* 살얼음 thin ice. *ŏrŭm chumŏni* 얼음 주머니 ice pack [bag].

orŭn 오른 pre-n. right. *orŭntchok* 오른쪽 right side. *orŭntchog-e* 오른쪽에 on the right (side of). *orŭntchog-ŭro* 오른쪽으로 to the right (of). *orŭnson* 오른손 right hand. *orŭnp'yŏn* 오른편 right side.

* **ŏrŭn** 어른 n. adult; grown-up (person). [p.90] *ŏrŭn-ŭi* 어른의 adult; grown-up.

ŏryŏptta 어렵다 adj. (be) hard; difficult.

ŏsaekhada 어색하다 adj. feel awkward [embarrassed]; clumsy.

osip 오십 n. 50 fifty. *osimnyŏn* 50년 fifty years.

ŏsŏ 어서 adv. ① quickly; without delay ② (if you) please; right. *ŏsŏ tŭrŏosipssio* 어서 들어오십시오

Come right in, please.

-**ŏsŏ** -어서 infinitive ending with particle -**sŏ**. other shapes: -**asŏ** -아서, -**yŏsŏ** -여서. ① reason marker. indicates that the state of affairs expressed by the following v. or adj. ② temporal precedence and continuing state marker. indicates that the action expressed by the preceding v. is prior to the action expressed by the following v., but the state resulting from the action of the preceding v. continues throughout the action of the following v.

-**ŏss**- -었- past tense marker. was, did. occurs followed by -**ŏss**-, -**kess**-, -**sŭp**-, -**ta**, -**ŭmyŏ**, -**ŭni**. cf. -**ass**-, -**ss**-.

ot 옷 n. clothes; dress; garment. *okkam* 옷감 cloth. [p.100]

* **ŏtchaesŏ** 어째서 adv. why; for what reason; how.

* **ŏtchaettŭn** 어쨌든 adv. anyhow; anyway; at any rate.

otchang 옷장 n. wardrobe; clothes chest.

ŏtchi 어찌 adv. how; in what way; by what means.

otkkam 옷감 n. cloth; stuff; dry goods.

otkkŏri 옷걸이 n. coat hanger; clothes rack.

ŏtkkŭje 엊그제 n. the day before yesterday; a few days ago.

ŏtta 얻다 v. get; gain; obtain; earn; achieve; win.

ŏttŏk'e 어떻게 adv. how; in what manner [way]. *ŏttŏk'e haesŏrado* 어떻게 해서라도 at any cost; by any means.

ŏttŏn 어떤 pre-n.what; what like; what sort [kind] of; any. *ŏttŏn iyu-ro* 어떤 이유로 why; for what reason.

ŏullida 어울리다 v. become; match; be becoming [suitable, fitting].

ŏŭm 어음 n. draft; bill; note. *yakssok ŏŭm* 약속 어음 promissory note. *pudo ŏŭm* 부도 어음 dishonored bill.

-**ŏya** -어야 infinitive ending with particle -**ya**. other

shapes: **-aya** -아야, **-yŏya** -여야. indicates that the proposition expressed by the preceding v. or adj. is a necessary condition for the following v. or adj. ① only to the extent that ... can one ..., you have to ... in order to ... ② to whatever extent.

oyŏm 오염 n.C. pollution. *oyŏmhada* 오염하다 pollute. *oyŏmdoeda* 오염되다 be polluted.

pabo 바보 n. fool; idiot; dunce. *pabo kat´ŭn* 바보 같은 silly; foolish.

\# **pach´ida** 바치다 v. give; offer; present; dedicate.

\# **pada** 바다 n. sea; ocean. *pada kŏnnŏ* 바다 건너 beyond [across] the sea.

* **padak** 바닥 n. flat surface; bottom; bed.

padakka 바닷가 n. seashore, the beach.

\# **pae** 배(short vowel) n. vessel; ship; boat; steamer. [p.70] *pae-ro* 배로 by ship.

\# **pae** 배(short vowel) n. belly; stomach. ① *pae-ga ap´ŭda* 배가 아프다 have a stomachache; be green with envy.

* **pae** 배(short vowel) n. pear. *paenamu* 배나무 pear tree.

pae 배(long vowel) n.C. double, (multiple) times, fold. *sam pae* 삼 배 three times.

* **paech´u** 배추 n. Chinese cabbage. *paech´u kimch´i* 배추 김치 pickled cabbage.

paedal 배달 n.C. delivery. *paedalhada* 배달하다 deliver; distribute. *paedalbu* 배달부 delivery person; carrier; mail carrier.

\# **paegŭp** 배급 n.C. distribution. *paegŭp´ada* 배급하다 distribute.

paegyŏng 배경 n.C. ① background; setting ② backing; pull.

paekkop 배꼽 n. navel; belly button.

paek'wajŏm 백화점 n.C. department store.

paem 뱀 n. snake; serpent.

paengman 백만 n.C. million.

\# **paeuda** 배우다 v. learn; take lessons (in, on); study.

paeuja 배우자 n.C. spouse.

paji 바지 n. trousers; pants.

pak 박 n. gourd; calabash.

\# **pak** 밖 n. ① → **pakkat** 바깥 ② outside of; except; but.

* **pakkat** 바깥 n. outside; exterior; out-of-doors. *pakkat'-ŭi* 바깥의 outside; outdoors; outer; external. *pakkat'-esŏ* 바깥에서 in the open (air).

* **pakkuda** 바꾸다 v. ① change; exchange; barter ② replace; alter; shift.

* **pakssa** 박사 n. doctor [Dr.]; doctorate. *pakssa hagwi* 박사 학위 doctor's degree.

paktcha 박자 n. time; rhythm; beat.

* **paktta** 박다 v. drive in; hammer (in); set; inlay.

\# **paktta** 밝다 adj. (be) light; bright.

* **pak'wi** 바퀴 n. wheel; round [turn]. *ap[twit]pak'wi* 앞[뒤]바퀴 front [back] wheel.

\# **pal** 발(short vowel) n. foot; paw; leg ①, [p.56,59,121].

pal 발(long vowel) n. blind.

\+ **palgyŏn** 발견 n.C. discovery. \# *palgyŏnhada* 발견하다 find(out); discover.

palmyŏng 발명 n.C. invention. *palmyŏnghada* 발명하다 invent; devise.

\+ **palp'yo** 발표 n.C. announcement; publication. * *palp'yohada* 발표하다 announce; make public.

\+ **palssang** 발생 n.C. occurrence; outbreak; origination; generation.

* **palssaenghada** 발생하다 occur; break out; originate.

paltchŏn 발전 n.C. development; growth. #*paltchŏnhada* 발전하다 develop; grow.

palt'op 발톱 n. toenail; claw.

palttal 발달 n.C. development; growth; progress; advance. # *palttalhada* 발달하다 develop; grow; advance; make progress.

pam 밤(short vowel) n. night; evening. *pam-e* 밤에 at night.

pam 밤(long vowel) n. chestnut.

pamsaeuda 밤새우다 v. sit [stay] up all night.

* **pan** 반 n.C. half; halfway. [p.83] *pan sigan* 반 시간 half an hour; half hour.

panbal 반발 n.C. repulsion; resistance. *panbalhada* 반발하다 repel; repulse; resist.

panbok 반복 n.C. repetition; reiteration. *panbok'ada* 반복하다 repeat; reiterate.

panch'an 반찬 n.C. sidedish (with rice). [p.84] *kogi panch'an* 고기 반찬 meat dish. *panch'an kkage* 반찬 가게 grocery store.

pandae 반대 n.C. contrary; opposition; reverse; objection. +*pandaehada* 반대히디 v. oppose; object to. *pandae-ŭi* 반대의 opposite; contrary. *pandae-ro* 반대로 on the contrary.

pando 반도 n.C. peninsula. *Hanbando* 한반도 Korean Peninsula.

pandŭsi 반드시 adv. certainly; surely; without fail; necessarily; by all means. *pandŭsi ···hajinŭn ant'a* 반드시 하지는 않다 not always; not necessarily.

pang 방 n.C. room; chamber; apartment *setppang* 셋방 room to let.

* **pan'gapta** 반갑다 adj. (be) happy; glad; be pleased [delighted].

pangbŏp 방법 n.C. way; method; means.

+ **pangch'im** 방침 n.C. course; line; policy; principle. *yŏngŏp pangch'im* 영업 방침 business policy.

pangch'ŏng 방청 n.C. hearing; attendance. *pang-

ch'ŏnghada 방청하다 hear; attend; listen to.

panggong 방공 n.C. air defense. *panggongho* 방공호 dugout; air-raid shelter. *panggong yŏnsŭp* 방공 연습 anti-air raid (air defence) drill.

* **panggŭm** 방금 adv. just now; a moment ago.

panghae 방해 n.C. obstruction; disturbance. *panghaehada* 방해하다 obstruct; disturb; interrupt.

\# **panghyang** 방향 n.C. direction; course.

\+ **pangji** 방지 n.C. prevention; check. *pangjihada* 방지하다 prevent; check; stop.

pangmulgwan 박물관 n.C. museum. *kungnip pangmulgwan* 국립박물관 National Museum.

\+ **pangmun** 방문 n.C. call; visit. *pangmunhada* 방문하다 (pay a) visit; make a call on; call at.

pangmyŏn 방면 n.C. direction; quarter; district. *Cheju pangmyŏn* 제주 방면 the Cheju districts.

pangnamhoe 박람회 n.C. exhibition; exposition (EXPO); fair (*Am.*) *pangnamhoejang* 박람회장 n.C. fair ground; exhibition site.

\+ **pangsong** 방송 n.C. broadcasting; broadcast. *pangsonghada* 방송하다 broadcast; go on the air.

pangwi 방위 n.C. defense; protection. *pangwihada* 방위하다 defend; protect.

panhang 반항 n.C. resistance; opposition; defiance. *panhanghada* 반항하다 resist; oppose; rebel (against).

panji 반지 n.C. ring. *panji-rŭl kkida* 반지를 끼다 put a ring on one's finger. *kyŏlhon(yak'on) panji* 결혼 (약혼) 반지 wedding (engagement) ring.

\+ **panmyŏn** 반면 n.C. the other side; the reverse. *panmyŏn-e* 반면에 on the other hand; on the contrary.

pansa 반사 n.C. reflection. *pansahada* 반사하다 reflect; reverberate.

pansŏng 반성 n.C. reflection; self-examination. *pansŏnghada* 반성하다 reflect on (oneself);

reconsider.

* **panŭl** 바늘 n.C. needle; pin; hook. [p.57,58] *ttŭgae panŭl* 뜨개 바늘 knitting needle. *naksi panŭl* 낚시 바늘 fishhook. *panŭl pangsŏk* 바늘 방석 uncomfortable situation (*lit.* a bed of nails).

  panyŏk 반역 n.C. treason; rebelion. *panyŏk'ada* 반역 하다 rebel (against); rise in rovolt. *panyŏktcha* 반 역자 traitor.

pap 밥 n. boiled [cooked] rice. *pab-ŭl chitta* 밥을 짓 다 cook [boil] rice.

* **pappŭda** 바쁘다 adj. (be) busy; (be) pressing; urgent. *pappŭge* 바쁘게 busily; hurriedly.

* **paptta** 밟다 v. ① step [tread] on ② set foot on.

paraboda 바라보다 v. see; look (at); look out over; watch; gaze (at)

parada 바라다 v. ① expect; hope for; look forward to ② want; wish; desire.

param 바람 n. wind; breeze; gale; storm. ①, [p.57] *param-i pulda* 바람이 불다 wind blows.

  parhaeng 발행 n.C. publication; issue. *palhaenghada* 발행하다 publish; issue; bring out.

paro 바로 adv. ① rightly; correctly; straight ② just; exactly ③ at once; immediately; right away.

  parŏn 발언 n.C. utterance; speaking. *parŏnhada* 발 언하다 utter; speak.

* **parŭda** 바르다 v. ① (be) straight; upright ② (be) right; righteous; just; correct.

  parŭm 발음 n.C. pronunciation; articulation. *parŭmhada* 발음하다 pronounce; articulate.

* **pat'ang** 바탕 n. ① nature; character; natural disposition ② texture; ground, background.

pat 밭 n. field. *okssusubat* 옥수수밭 corn field. cf. **non** 논 paddy(field).

patta 받다 v. receive; accept; be given [granted].

* **pawi** 바위 n. rock; crag, boulder.

* **peda** 베다 v. cut; chop; saw; carve.

  pegae 베개 n. pillow.

\# **pi** 비 n. rain *piga oda[mŏtta/kŭch'ida]* 비가 오다[멎다/
그치다] (It) rains [stops raining].

pi 비 n. broom. *pitcharu* 빗자루 broom stick.

pich'amhan 비참한 adj.C. miserable; wretched;
tragic; distressful.

* **pich'ida** 비치다 v. ① shine ② be reflected [mirrored]
(in) ③ show through.

\+ **pich'uda** 비추다 v. ① shed [throw] light (on); light
(up); illuminate ② reflect; mirror ③ hint;
suggest.

* **pidan** 비단 n.C. silk fabrics; silk.

pidulgi 비둘기 n. dove; pigeon. *pidulgip'a* 비둘기파
(politics) dove; soft-liner.

\+ **pigŭk** 비극 n.C. tragedy. *pigŭktchŏk* 비극적 tragic.

* **pigyo** 비교 n.C. comparison. *pigyohada* 비교하다
compare (A with B). * *pigyojŏk(ŭro)* 비교적(으로)
comparative(ly)

\+ **pihaeng** 비행 n.C. flying; flight; aviation. *pihaeng-
hada* 비행하다 fly; make a flight; take the air.

\# **pihaenggi** 비행기 n.C. aeroplane(*Eng.*); airplane
(*Am.*); aircraft. ①

pihaengjang 비행장 n.C. airfield; airport.

pijopta 비좁다 adj. (be) narrow and close
[confined]; cramped.

* **pilda** 빌다 v. ① pray; wish ② beg; solicit ③ ask;
request; entreat.

* **pilda, pillida** 빌다, 빌리다 v. borrow; have [get] the
loan (of); hire; rent; lease; charter.

* **pimil** 비밀 n.C. secrecy; secret. *pimir-ŭi* 비밀의
secret; confidential.

pimyŏng 비명 n.C. scream; shriek. *pimyŏng-ŭl
chirŭda* 비명을 지르다 scream; shriek.

pinan 비난 n.C. blame; censure. *pinanhada* 비난하다
blame; censure; accuse.

pinbŏnhan 빈번한 adj. frequent; incessant. *pinbŏnhi*
빈번히 frequently.

pindaettŏk 빈대떡 n. mung bean [green-bean]

    pancake.

pin′gon 빈곤 n.C. poverty; want. *pin′gonhan* 빈곤한 poor; needy; destitute.

pinnada 빛나다 v. ① shine; be bright; gleam ② be brilliant.

pinnaeda 빛내다 v. light up; make (a thing) shine; brighten.

* **pinu** 비누 n. soap. *karu pinu* 가루 비누 soap powder.

+ **pip′an** 비판 n.C. critcism. *pip′anhada* 비판하다 criticize; comment (on); pass[give] judgment (on).

pip′yŏng 비평 n.C. review; critique; comment. *pip′yŏnghada* 비평하다 criticize; review.

* **pirok** 비록 adv. through; if; even if.

piroso 비로소 adv. for the first time; not … until [till].

pirye 비례 n.C. proportion; ratio. *piryehada* 비례하다 be in proportion.

+ **piryo** 비료 n.C. fertilizer; manure.

pisŏ 비서 n.C. (private) secretary. *pisŏsil* 비서실 secretary′s office.

pissada 비싸다 adj. (be) expensive; costly.

* **pisŭt′ada** 비슷하다 adj. (be) like; similar; look like.

pit 빛 n. ① light; rays; beam ② color; hue. [p.69]

+ **pit** 빚 n. debt; loan. *pij-ŭl chida* 빚을 지다 run [get] into debt; borrow money.

pit 빗 n. comb. hairbrush.

+ **pit′al** 비탈 n. slope; incline. *pit′alkkil* 비탈길 slope.

* **pitkkal** 빛깔 n. color; shade; hue; tint.

pit′ŭlda 비틀다 v. twist; wrench; screw.

piutta 비웃다 v. laugh at; deride; jeer (at).

* **piyong** 비용 n.C. cost; expense(s).

piyul 비율 n.C. ratio; percentage; rate. *…ŭi piyul-lo* …의 비율로 at the rate [ratio] of.

+ **poch′ung** 보충 n.C. supplement; replacement. *poch′unghada* 보충하다 supplement; fill up.

poda 보다 v. see; look at; witness; stare [gaze] at;

watch; read; look over; view. [p.64]

-**poda** -보다 particle. marks the standard against which somthing else is being compared. than (used after the second member of a comparison, usually accompanied by *tŏ* 더 more), rather than.

+ **podo** 보도 v.C. report; news.

pogi 보기 v. example.

+ **pogo** 보고 n.C. report. *pogohada* 보고하다 report; inform; brief. *pogosŏ* 보고서 report.

+ **pogŏn** 보건 n.C. (preservation of) health; sanitation; hygiene. *segye pogŏn kigu* 세계 보건 기구 World Health Organization (WHO).

pogŭp 보급 n.C. diffusion; distribution; popularization. *pogŭphada* 보급하다 diffuse; distribute; pervade; popularize.

pogwan 보관 n.C. (safe) keeping; custody. *pogwanhada* 보관하다 keep (a thing); look after (a thing).

* **poho** 보호 n.C. protection; safeguard. * *pohohada* 보호하다 protect; shelter; safeguard.

* **pohŏm** 보험 n.C. insurance. pohŏmnyo 보험료 premium. *pohŏm hoesa* 보험 회사 insurance company.

poida 보이다 v. ① be seen [visible]; appear; seem ② show; let (a person) see.

+ **pojang** 보장 n.C. guarantee; security. *pojanghada* 보장하다 guarantee; secure. *sahoe pojang* 사회 보장 social security.

pojon 보존 n.C. preservation; conservation. *pojonhada* preserve conserve.

pojŭng 보증 n.C. guarantee; assurance; security. *pojŭnghada* 보증하다 guarantee; assure; warrant. *pojŭng sup'yo* 보증 수표 certified check. *pojŭngin* 보증인 guarantor.

+ **pok** 복 n.C. good fortune; blessing; good luck. *pokttoen* 복된 lucky; happy; blessed.

pokssa 복사 n.C. copy. *pokssssahada* 등사하다 copy; make a copy.

pokssu 복수 n.C. revenge; avenge; vengeance. *pok-*

ssuhada 복수하다 get revenge (on); avenge.

+ **pokssunga** 복숭아 n. peach. *pokssungakkot* 복숭아꽃 peach blossoms.

* **poktchap** 복잡 n.C. complexity; complication. *poktchap'an* 복잡한 (be) complicated; complex; tangled.

poktchong 복종 n.C. obedience; submisson. *poktchonghada* 복종하다 obey; submit.

+ **poktto** 복도 n.C. corridor; passage; lobby; hallway(*Am*.).

pokttŏkppang 복덕방 n.C. real estate agency.

+ **pŏl** 벌(long vowel) n. bee. *pŏltte* 벌떼 swarm of bees. *pŏltchip* 벌집 honeycomb. *pŏl(tchip)t'ong* 벌(집)통 beehive. *pŏlkkul* 벌꿀 honey.

pŏl 벌(short vowel) n.C. punishment; penalty. *pŏlhada* [*chuda*] 벌하다[주다] punish; penalize.

+ **pŏlda** 벌다 v. earn; make (money); gain.

+ **pollae** 본래 n.C. (adverbial use) originally; primarily; naturally; by nature. *pollae-ŭi* 본래의 original; natural.

pŏlle 벌레 n. insect; bug; worm; moth. *pŏlle mŏgŭn* 벌레 먹은 worm [moth]-eaten.

+ **pŏllida** 벌리다 v. open; widen; leave a space.

pom 봄 n. spring(time). *pom-ŭi* 봄의 spring; vernal

+ **pŏmjoe** 범죄 n.C. crime; criminal act. *pŏmjoe-ŭi* 범죄의 criminal.

* **pŏmnyul** 법률 n.C. law; statute. *pŏmnyul-ŭi* 법률의 legal. *pŏmnyulga* 법률가 lawyer. *pŏmnyulhaktcha* 법률학자 jurist.

* **pŏmwi** 범위 n.C. extent; scope; sphere; range; limit; bounds. *pŏmwi nae*[*oe*]*e* 범위 내[외]에 within [beyond] the limit [scope].

ponaeda 보내다 v. send; forward; transmit.

+ **ponbu** 본부 n.C. headquarters; main [head] office.

ponggŭp 봉급 n.C. salary; pay; wages.

+ **pongji** 봉지 n.C. paper bag.

pongsa 봉사 n.C. service; attendance. *pongsahada*

봉사하다 serve; render service; attend on.

pongt'u 봉투 n.C. envelope.

+ **pŏnho** 번호 n.C. number; make; *pŏnhopyo* 번호표 number ticket [plate].

+ **ponin** 본인 n.C. the person in question; the person himself [herself]; principal.

ponmun 본문 n.C. body (of a letter); text (of a treaty).

ponsim 본심 n.C. one's real intention; one's heart; one's inner mind.

pont'o 본토 n.C. mainland; the country proper.

pŏnyŏk 번역 n.C. translation; *pŏnyŏkhada* 번역하다 translate [render] into; put (into).

pŏp 법 n.C. law; rule; custom; practice. [p.63]

* **pori** 보리 n. barley. *porich'a* 보리차 barley tea.

pŏrida 버리다 v. ① throw [cast, fling] away ② abandon; forsake; give up.

* **pŏrŏjida** 벌어지다 v. ① split; crack ② open; smile ③ occur; come about ④ become wide.

* **pŏrŭt** 버릇 n. habit; acquired tendency; propensity. [p.77,120] ···*hanŭn pŏrŭs-i itta* ···하는 버릇이 있다 have a habit of doing.

posang 보상 n.C. compensation; indemnity. *posanghada* 보상하다 compensate for; make up for.

posŏk 보석 n.C. jewel; gem; precious stone. *posŏkssang* 보석상 jeweler's (shop).

+ **pŏt** 벗 n. friend; companion; mate; company.

+ **pŏt'ida** 버티다 v. endure; stand; bear.

* **pŏtkkita** 벗기다 v. ① peel; rind; pare ② take [strip] off; strip of; help off.

pot'ong 보통 n.C. ordinarily; commonly; normally. *pot'ong-ŭi* 보통의 usual; ordinary; common.

pŏtta 벗다 v. take [put] off; slip [fling] off.

poyŏjuda 보여 주다 v. show; let (a person) see; display.

ppaeatta 빼앗다 v. take away from; snatch from; plunder; deprive of.

ppaeda 빼다 v. ① pull [take] out; draw; extract ② subtract [deduct] (from) ③ remove; wash off ④ omit; exclude.

ppajida 빠지다 v. fall [get] into; sink; go down.

* ppalda 빨다 v. ① sip; suck; luck ② wash.

* ppallae 빨래 n. wash; washing; laundary. *ppallaehada* 빨래하다 wash. *ppallaetchul* 빨랫줄 clothesline.

ppalli 빨리 adv. quickly; fast; rapidly; in haste; soon; immediately.

+ ppang 빵 n. bread; *ppang-kuptta* 빵을 굽다 bake [toast] bread.

* pparŭda 빠르다 adj. ① (be) quick; fast; swift; speedy ② (be) early; premature.

ppoptta 뽑다 v. ① pull [take] out; draw; extract ② select; pick [single] out; elect ③ enlist; enroll.

* ppŏtta 뻗다 v. ① lengthen; stretch; extend ② collapse; knock out ③ develop.

ppun 뿐 particle (preceded by n. or *kŭ* 그, usually followed by *-ida* -이다) only, nothing but; alone; merely. *ppun(man) anira* 뿐(만) 아니라 (indicates that the preceding n. is all there is, and implies that is insufficient.) besides; moreover; in addition.

ppuri 뿌리 n. root. *ppuri kip'ŭn* 뿌리 깊은 deep-rooted. *ppur-rŭl paktta/naerida* 뿌리를 박다/내리다 put down roots.

ppurida 뿌리다 v. sprinkle; strew; scatter; diffuse.

ppyŏ 뼈 n. bone. *ppyŏdae* 뼈대 frame.

pubu 부부 n.C. man [husband] and wife; married couple.

pubun 부분 n.C. part; portion; section. *pubunjŏg-ŭro* 부분적으로 partially.

puch'ida 부치다 v. send; mail; remit; forward. *ton-ŭl puch'ida* 돈을 부치다 remit money.

+ Puch'ŏ(nim) 부처(님) n. Buddha.

* pudae 부대 n.C. unit; corps; detachment. *pudae-*

jang 부대장 commander.

+ **pudam** 부담 n.C. burden; charge; responsibility. *pudamhada* 부담하다 bear; shoulder; stand; share. *pudamsŭrŏptta* 부담스럽다 be burdensome.

* **pudich'ida** 부딪히다 v. collide with; bump against [into]

  pudongsan 부동산 n.C. immovable property; real estate; realty. *pudongsanŏptcha* 부동산업자 realtor (*Am.*.)

  pudŭrŏptta 부드럽다 adj. (be) soft; tender; mild; gentle. *pudŭrŏpkke* 부드럽게 softly; mildly; tenderly.

+ **pugi** 부기 n.C. book-keeping.

  pugŭn 부근 n.C. neighborhood; vicinity. *pugŭn-ŭi* 부근의 nighboring; nearby; adjacent.

  puho 부호 n.C. sign; make; cipher; symbol.

  puin 부인 n.C. woman; lady. *puinppyŏng* 부인병 woman's disease [ailments].

puin 부인 n.C. denial; disapproval. *puinhada* 부인하다 deny; disapprove; say no.

+ **puja** 부자 n.C. rich person; wealthy person.

  pujirŏnhada 부지런하다 adj. (be) industrious; diligent. *pujirŏnhi* 부지런히 diligently; industriously; hard.

+ **pujok** 부족 n.C. shortage; deficiency; deficit; lack. * *pujokhada* 부족하다 be short (of); lack.

+ **pukkŭk** 북극 n.C. the North Pole. *pukkŭk-ŭi* 북극의 arctic; polar. *pukkŭkssŏng* 북극성 n.C. North Star.

* **pukkŭrŏpta** 부끄럽다 adj. (be) shameful; disgraceful.

puktta 붉다 adj. (be) red; crimson scarlet.

pul 불 n. fire; flame; blaze. ①. [p.121] *pur-ŭl puthida* 불을 붙이다 light a fire.

  pulch'injŏl 불친절 n.C. unkindness; unfriendliness. *pulch'injŏlhan* 불친절한 unkind; unfriendly.

pulda 불다 v. blow; breathe. *nap'ar-ŭl pulda* 나팔을 불다 blow a trumpet.

pulganŭng 불가능 n.C. impossibility. *pulganŭnghada* 불가능하다 (be) impossible [unattainable]

pulgu 불구 n.C. deformity. *pulgu-ŭi* 불구의 deformed; crippled; disabled. *pulguja* 불구자 n.C. disabled [deformed] person; handicapped person.

* **pulgyo** 불교 n.C. Buddhism. *pulgyodo* 불교도 Buddhist.

+ **pulhaeng** 불행 n.C. unhappiness; misfortune; bad-luck. *pulhaeng* 불행한 unhappy; unfortunate. *pulhaenghi(do)* 불행히(도) unfortunately.

pulhwa 불화 n.C. trouble; discord. *pulhwahada* 불화하다 be on bad terms (with); be in discord (with); be at strife [odds] (with).

pulk'wae 불쾌 n.C. unpleasantness; displeasure. *pulk'waehada* 불쾌하다 feel unpleasant [displeased].

pullyang 분량 n.C. quantity; measure; dose.

pulp'iryo 불필요 n.C. *pulp'iryohan* 불필요한 unnecessary; needless. *pulp'iryohage* 불필요하게 n.C. unnecessarily; needlessly.

pulp'yŏn 불편 n.C. inconvenience. + *pulp'yŏnhada* 불편하다 (be) inconvenient.

pulp'yŏng 불평 n.C. discontent; complaint; grievance. *pulp'yŏnghada* 불평하다 grumble; complain.

+ **pulssanghada** 불쌍하다 adj. (be) poor; pitiful; miserable.

pumo 부모 n.C. father and mother; parents. [p.141] *pumo-ŭi* 부모의 parental.

pumun 부문 n.C. section; department; class; group; category.

pun 분 n. minute (of an hour). *sibobun* 15분 quarter; fifteen minutes.

punbae 분배 n.C. distribution; sharing. *punbaehada* 분배하다 distribute; divide; allot.

+ **pun'gae** 분개 n.C. indignation; resentment. *pungaehada* 분개하다 (be) indignant; resent.

punhae 분해 n.C. analysis. *punhaehada* 분해하다 analyze; dissolve.

+ **punji** 분지 n.C. basin; hollow; valley.

punjŏm 분점 n.C. branch shop; branch office.

+ **punmyŏnghada** 분명하다 adj.C. (be) clear; distinct; obvious. * *punmyŏnghi* 분명히 clearly; apparently.

punno 분노 n.C. fury; rage; indignation. *punnohada* 분노하다 get [be] angry; be enraged.

punsik 분식 n.C. powdered food; flour.

punsŏk 분석 n.C. analysis. *punsŏk'ada* 분석하다 analyze; make an analysis (of).

punya 분야 n.C. sphere; field; province. *yŏn'gu punya* 연구 분야 field [area] of study.

* **puŏk** 부엌 n. kitchen.

* **pup'i** 부피 n. bulk; volume; size.

purak 부락 n.C. village; village community. *purangmin* 부락민 people of a village.

+ **puran** 불안 n.C. uneasiness; anxiety; unrest. *puranhada* 불안한 uneasy; anxious.

+ **purida** 부리다 v. ① keep (person, horse. etc.) at work; set [put] to work; hire; employ ② manage; handle; run ③ exercise; yield.

purŏptta 부럽다 adj. (be) enviable. *purŏun dŭsi* 부러운 듯이 enviously; with envy.

purŭda 부르다 v. ① call; hail ② name; designate ③ bid (a price); offer ④ sing. *norae-rŭl purŭda* 노래를 부르다 ⑤ shout ⑥ send for; invite.

purŭda 부르다 v. be full; be inflated. *pae-ga purŭda* 배가 부르다 have eaten one's fill; be pregnant.

* **purŭjitta** 부르짖다 v. shout; cry; exclaim.

pusang 부상 n.C. wound; injury; cut; bruise. *pusanghada* 부상하다 be wounded; get hurt.

pusok 부속 n.C. attachment. *pusok'ada* 부속하다 belong (to); be attached to. *pusog-ŭi* 부속의 attached; belonging to; dependent.

+ **put** 붓 n. writing brush; brush; pen.

put'ak 부탁 n.C. request; favor; solicitation.
+*put'ak'ada* 부탁하다 ask; request; beg.

−**put'ŏ** −부터 particle. indicates that the preceding
n. is the temporal or spatial starting point for an
action. from, since, starting from.

+ **putchaptta** 붙잡다 v. seize; grasp; catch; take hold
of.

putta 붙다 v. stick (to); adhere [cling] (to); attach
oneself to; glue; paste.

* **putta** 붓다 v. pour (into, out); fill with; put (water
in a bowl); feed (a lamp with oil).

* **puttŭlda** 붙들다 ① catch; seize; take hold of; grasp
[grab] ② arrest; capture.

* **pyŏ** 벼 n. rice plant; paddy.

* **pyŏk** 벽 n.C. wall; partition. *pyŏkppo* 벽보 bill;
poster.

pyŏl 별 n. star. *pyŏlppit* 별빛 starlight.

* **pyŏllo** 별로 adv. (with negetive) especially; particularly; in particular.

pyŏndong 변동 n.C. change; fluctuation.
pyŏndonghada 변동하다 charge; alter.

pyŏng 병 n.C. bottle; jar.
pyŏng 병 n.C. disease, sickness. [p.51,112]

* **pyŏngwŏn** 병원 n.C. ospital; nursing home.
pyŏngwŏn-e ibwŏnhada 병원에 입원하다 go into
hospital.

pyŏn'gyŏng 변경 n.C. charge; alteration.
pyŏn'gyŏnghada 변경하다 charge; alter.

pyŏnhada 변하다 v. charge; undergo a change; vary.
pyŏnho 변호 n.C. defense; justification. *pyŏnhohada*
변호하다 plead; defend; speak for.

pyŏnhosa 변호사 n.C. lawyer; attorney(Am.);
barrister(Eng.). the bar;

pyŏnhwa 변화 n.C. charge; variation; alteration.
pyŏnhwahada 변화하다 change; turn.

+ **pyŏnso** 변소 n.C. lavatory; water closet (WC);
toilet; wash room; rest room.

+ **pyŏsŭl** 벼슬 n. government post [service] (in the traditional Korean society).
+ **pyŏt** 볕 n. sunshine; sunlight. [p.124]

≤ P' ≥

* **p'a** 파 n. ① branch of a family [clan] ② party; faction; sect. *churyup'a* 주류파 main stream faction.
* **p'a** 파 n. scallion; (Welsh) green onion.
* **p'ada** 파다 v. dig; excavate; drill.
  p'ado 파도 n.C. waves; billows; surge.
+ **p'ae** 패 n.C. ① tag; tablet ② group; gang; company.
  p'agoe 파괴 n.C. destruction. *p'agoehada* 파괴하다 destory; break. *p'agoejŏgin* 파괴적인 destructive. *p'agoeja* 파괴자 destroyer.
p'al 팔 n. arm. [p.135] *p'ar-ŭl kkigo* 팔을 끼고 with folded arms; (walk) arm in arm (with).
p'alda 팔다 v. sell; deal in.
* **p'alssip** 팔십 n.C. 80 eighty. *chep'alssip* 제80 the eightieth.
  p'andan 판단 n.C. judgment; decision. *p'andanhada* 판단하다 judge.
+ **p'anmae** 판매 n.C. sale; selling. *p'anmaehada* 판매하다 sell; deal in.
  p'ansa 판사 n.C. judge; justice.
  p'anssori 판소리 n. Korean (classical) solo opera drama.
  p'arang 파랑 n. blue (color); green. *p'arangsae* 파랑새 bluebird.
* **p'arat'a** 파랗다 adj. ① (be) blue; green ② (be) pale; pallid.
  p'ari 파리 n. fly. ① *p'ariyak* 파리약 fly posion. *p'ari-*

ch'ae 파리채 fly swatter.

p'arwŏl 팔월 n.C. August.

p'ayŏl 파열 n.C. explosion; bursting. *p'ayŏlhada* 파열하다 explode; burst (up); rupture.

p'i 피 n. blood. ① [p.136] *p'i-ga nada* 피가 나다 bleed; blood runs [flows] out.

p'ibu 피부 n.C. skin. *p'ibusaek* 피부색 skin color.

p'igon 피곤 n.C. fatigue; tiredness. *p'igonhada* 피곤하다 (be) tired; fatigued.

* **p'ihada** 피하다 v. avoid; dodge; evade; keep away from; shirk; shun.

+ **p'ihae** 피해 n.C. damage; injury; harm. *p'ihae-rŭl iptta* 피해를 입다 be damaged [injured] (by).

p'inan 피난 n.C. refuge. *p'inanhada* 피난하다 take refuge. *p'inanmin* 피난민 refugee.

p'inggye 핑계 n. excuse; pretext; *p'inggye-rŭl taeta* 핑계를 대다 make [find] an excuse.

p'iro 피로 n.C. fatigue; weariness; exhaustion. *p'irohan* 피로한 (be) tired; weary.

p'iryo 필요 n.C. necessity; need. *p'iryohan* 필요한 necessary; essential.

p'isŏ 피서 n.C. get away from the summer heat; summering. *p'isŏ kada* 피서 가다 go to a summer resort.

p'iuda 피우다 v. ① make [build] a fire ② smoke; burn (incense) ③ bloom.

+ **p'odo** 포도 n.C. grape. *p'odobat* 포도밭 vineyard. *p'odoju* 포도주 (grape) wine.

+ **p'ogi** 포기 n.C. abandonment. *p'ogihada* 포기하다 give up; abandon.

+ **p'oham** 포함 n.C. inclusion. *p'ohamhada* 포함하다 contain; include. ···*ŭl p'ohamhayŏ* ···를 포함하여 including.

p'ojang 포장 n.C. packing. *p'ojanghada* 포장하다 pack; wrap (up). *p'ojangji* 포장지 n.C. packing [wrapping] paper.

p'ojang 포장 n.C. pavement; paving. *p'ojanghada* 포

장하다

* **p'ŏjida** 퍼지다 v. spread out; get broader; be propagated; get abroad.

p'ok 폭 n.C. width; breadth. *p'og-i nŏlbŭn* 폭이 넓은 wide; broad. *p'og-i chobŭn* 폭이 좁은 narrow.

* **p'ŏk** 퍽 adv. very (much); quite; awfully; highly.

p'ok'aeng 폭행 n.C. (act of) violence. *p'ok'aenghada* 폭행하다 do violence; commit an outrage.

p'okp'ung 폭풍 n.C. storm; typhoon; hurricane. *p'okp'ung chuŭibo* 폭풍 주의보 storm alert.

* **p'okt'an** 폭탄 n.C. bomb. *wŏnja(suso)p'okt'an* 원자〔수소〕폭탄 atomic 〔hydrogan〕 bomb.

* **p'oro** 포로 n.C. prisoner of war (POW). *p'oro suyongso* 포로 수용소 prisoner's 〔concentration〕 camp.

p'ul 풀 n. paste; starch. *p'ul-lo puch'ida* 풀로 붙이다 stick with paste; paste (up).

p'ulda 풀다 v. ① untie; unpack; undo ② solve.

* **p'umjil** 품질 n.C. quality. *p'umjil kwalli* 품질 관리 quality control.

* **p'umtta** 품다 v. hold in one's bosom; embrace; hug.

+ **p'ungbu** 풍부 n.C. abundance; plenty. *p'ungbuhan* 풍부한 abundant; rich; wealthy.

p'unggyŏng 풍경 n.C. landscape; scenery; view.

* **p'ungsŏk** 풍속 n.C. manners; customs; climate.

p'urŭda 푸르다 adj. (be) blue; azure; pale.

p'ye 폐 n.C. lungs. *p'yeam* 폐암 cancer of lung. *p'yeppyŏng(kyŏlhaek)* 폐병〔결핵〕 tuberculosis.

p'yehoe 폐회 n.C. closing of meeting. *p'yehoesa* 폐회사 closing address. *p'yehoesik* 폐회식 closing ceremony.

p'yo 표 n.C. table; list. *siganp'yo* 시간표 time table. *chŏngkkap'yo* 정가표 price list.

* **p'yŏda** 펴다 v. spread (out); open; unfold.

p'yohyŏn 표현 n.C. expression. *p'yohyŏnhada* 표현하다 express; be representative 〔expressive〕 of.

+ **p'yojŏng** 표정 n.C. expression; look. *sŭlp'ŭn p'yojŏng* 슬픈 표정 sad expression.

* **p'yojun** 표준 n.C. standard; level. *p'yojunŏ* 표준어
  standard language.

\# **p'yŏlli** 편리 n.C. convenience; facilities. *p'yŏllihan*
  편리한 convenient; expedient.

  p'yŏnan 편안 n.C. being well. *p'yŏnanhi* 편안히
  peacefully; quietly.

  p'yŏnch'ant'a 편찮다 adj. (be) ill; unwell.

  p'yŏngbŏmhan 평범한 adj.C. common; ordinary;
  mediocre; flat; featureless.

  p'yŏngdŭng 평등 n.C. equality; parity. *p'yŏng-
  dŭnghan[hage]* 평등한[하게] equal[ly]; even[ly].

\# **p'yŏnghwa** 평화 n.C. peace. *p'yŏnghwasŭrŏn* 평화스런
  peaceful; tranquil. *p'yŏnghwajŏg-ŭro* 평화적으로
  peacefully; at [in] peace.

  p'yŏngil 평일 n.C. weekday. *p'yŏngir-e(nŭn)* 평일에
  (는) on weekdays; on business [ordinary] days.

* **p'yŏnggyun** 평균 n.C. average. *p'yŏnggyunhayŏ* 평균
  하여 on average.

* **p'yŏngmyŏn** 평면 n.C. plain; level. *p'yŏngmyŏndo*
  평면도 plane figure.

  p'yŏngnon 평론 n.C. review; criticism. *p'yŏngnon-
  hada* 평론하다 review; criticize; comment (on).

\# **p'yŏngya** 평야 n.C. plain; open field.

\# **p'yŏnji** 편지 n.C. litter. *p'yŏnji-rŭl puch'iada* 편지를
  부치다 mail [post] a letter.

  p'yŏnjip 편집 n.C. editing. compilation. *p'yŏnjip'ada*
  편집하다 edit; compile.

  p'yŏnŭi 편의 n.C. convenience; facilities. *p'yŏnŭisang*
  편의상 for convenience' sake.

≤ R ≥

\+ **radio** 라디오 n. radio.

raemp'u 램프 n. lamp. *sŏgyu raemp'u* 석유 램프 oil lamp.

rait'ŏ 라이터 n. (cigarette) lighter.

rek'odŭ 레코드 n. record.

renjŭ 렌즈 n. (contact) lens; lenses.

ridŭm 리듬 n. rhythm.

\# **-ro** -로 particle. to; with; by.

\# **-rŭl/ŭl**-를/을 particle. -**ŭl** occurs after consonants; -**rŭl** or abbreviated form -l after vowels. ① marks the direct object of a transitive v. *pab-ŭl mŏktta* 밥을 먹다 eat rice/a meal ② marks the direct object of a passive-transitive v., indicating 'suffer- ing' or 'undergoing' an action. *ttang-ŭl ppaekkida* 땅을 뺏기다 have one's land taken away ③ marks certain direct objects ending in -*m* ㅁ that are cognate with the (usually intransitive) v. used in the expression. *kkum-ŭl kkuda* 꿈을 꾸다 dream (a dream) ④ marks the location of a verb of movement, with or without particle -*e* -에 preceding. *hakkyo-(e)rŭl kada* 학교(에)를 가다 go to school ⑤ emphasizes a negative expression when inserted between -*chi* -지 and the negative auxiliary. *oji-rŭl ant'a* 오지를 않다 just won't come.

⪦ S ⪧

* **sa** 사 n.C. 4 four. *chesa* 제 4 the fourth.

* **sabang** 사방 n.C. four sides; all directions [quarters].

\+ **sabyŏn** 사변 n.C. accident; incident. *yugio sabyŏn* 6 ·25 사변 the Korean War.

sach'i 사치 n.C. luxury; extravagance. *sach'isŭrŏptta* 사치스럽다 (be) luxurious; extravagant.

sach'on 사촌 n.C. cousin. *oesach'on* 외사촌 cousin on one's mother's side. [p.72]

sada 사다 v. buy; purchase. [p.72]

sadon 사돈 n.C. relatives by marriage.

sae 새(long vowel) n. bird; fowl; poultry.

sae 새(short vowel) pre-n. new; fresh; novel; recent.

* **saebyŏk** 새벽 n. dawn; daybreak. *saebyŏg-e* 새벽에 at dawn [daybreak].

saeda 새다 v. ① dawn; break ② leak (out); run.

saegin 색인 n.C. index.

saek, saekch'ae 색, 색채 n.C. colo(u)r; hue; tinge.

saekki 새끼 n. ① young; litter; cub ② guy; fellow. [p.10,142] *kaesaekki* 개새끼 You beast!

+ **saekssi** 색시 n. ① bride ② wife ③ maiden; girl ④ barmaid; hostess.

saenggak 생각 n. ① thinking; thought; ideas ② opinion ③ mind; intention.

saenggangnada 생각나다 v. come to mind; occur to one; be reminded of.

saenghwal 생활 n.C. life; living; livelihood. *saenghwarhada* 생활하다 live; make a living.

saengil 생일 n.C. birthday. *saengil chanch'i* 생일 잔치 birthday party.

saengjon 생존 n.C. existence; survival. *saengjonhada* 생존하다 exist; live; survive.

* **saengmul** 생물 n.C. living thing; creature; life. *saengmulhak* 생물학 biology.

saengmyŏng 생명 n.C. life; soul; vitality.

saengnyak 생략 n.C. omission; abbreviation. *saengnyak'ada* 생략하다 omit; abbreviate.

saengsan 생산 n.C. production; manufacture.

* **saengsŏn** 생선 n.C. fish; fresh [raw] fish. *saengsŏnhoe* 생선회 sliced raw fish.

* **saero** 새로 adv. newly; new; anew.

saeroptta 새롭다 adj. (be) new; fresh; vivid. *saeropkke* 새롭게 newly.

saeu 새우 n. prawn; shrimp. *saeujŏt* 새우젓 pickled shrimp.

* **saeuda** 새우다 v. sit [stay] up all night; keep vigil.

sago 사고 n.C. incident; accident; trouble.

* **sagwa** 사과 n.C. apple. *sagwaju* 사과주 hard cider.

sagwa 사과 n.C. apology. *sagwahada* 사과하다 apologize; beg (a person) pardon.

sagyo 사교 n.C. social intercourse [life]. *sagyojŏgin* 사교적인 social.

\# **sahoe** 사회 n.C. society; world; public. *sahoejŏk* 사회적 social.

+ **sahŭl** 사흘 n. ① three days ② the third day. *sahŭnnal* 사흗날 the third day of the month.

\# **sai** 사이 n. ① interval; distance; space ② time; during ③ between; among.

sajang 사장 n.C. president (of company). *pusajang* 부사장 vice- president (of company).

* **sajin** 사진 n.C. photograph; picture; photo; snapshot. *sajin-ŭl tchiktta* 사진을 찍다 take a photograph of. *sajin'ga* 사진가 photographer.

sajŏn 사전 n.C. dictionary; lexicon. *sajŏn-ŭl ch'atta* 사전을 찾다 consult [refer to] a dictionary.

\# **sajŏng** 사정 n.C. circumstances; conditions; reasons.

* **sakkŏn** 사건 n.C. event; matter; occurrence; affair; case. *sarin sakkŏn* 살인사건 murder case.

\# **salda** 살다 v. ① live; be alive ② make a living; get along ③ dwell; inhabit; reside.

* **sallida** 살리다 v. save, spare (a person's life).

* **sallim** 살림 n. living; housekeeping. *sallimhada* 살림하다 run the house; manage a household.

sallim 산림 n.C. forest. *sallim poho* 산림 보호 forest conservation.

\# **salp'ida** 살피다 v. take a good look at; look about; inspect closely.

+ **sam** 삼 n. hemp.

* **samak** 사막 n.C. desert.

samang 사망 n.C. death. *samanghada* 사망하다 die; decease; pass away.

samch'on 삼촌 n.C. uncle (on the father's side). *oesamch'on* 외삼촌 uncle (on the mother's side). → *sukppu* 숙부.

\# **samgak** 삼각 n.C. triangle. *samgag-ŭi* 삼각의 triangular *samgak'yŏng* 삼각형 triangle.

\# **samsip** 삼십 n.C. 30 thirty. *chesamsip(ŭi)* 제30(의) the thirtieth.

* **samtta** 삶다 v. boil; cook. *talgyar-ŭl samtta* 달걀을 삶다 boil an egg. **samu** 사무 n.C. business; affairs; office work. *samusil* 사무실 office (room). *samuwŏn* 사무원 clerk; deskworker.

\+ **samwŏl** 삼월 n.C. March.

\+ **samyŏng** 사명 n.C. mission; commission; errand. *samyŏnggam* 사명감 sense of purpose.

\# **san** 산(short vowel) n.C. mountain.

\+ **san** 산(long vowel) n.C. acid.

\+ **sanai** 사나이 n. man; male. *sanaidaun* 사나이다운 manly; manlike.

sanbuinkkwa 산부인과 n.C. obsterics and gynecology. *sanbuinkkwa ŭisa* 산부인과 의사 ladies' doctor.

sang 상 n.C. prize; reward. *sang-ŭl t'ada* 상을 타다 win [get] a prize.

* **sang** 상 n.C. (dining, eating) table; small table.

\+ **sangch'ŏ** 상처 n.C. wound; injury; cut; scar.

\+ **sangdae** 상대 n.C. ① companion; mate ② the other party; opponent.

sangdam 상담 n.C. consultation; counsel; conference. *sangdamhada* 상담하다 consult (with); confer.

* **sangdanghan** 상당한 adj.C. respectable; decent. *sangdanghi* 상당히 pretty; fairly; considerably.

\+ **sanggwan** 상관 n.C. senior [superior] officer; higher officer [official].

* **sangin** 상인 n.C. merchant; trader; dealer; tradesman; shopkeeper.

+ **sangja** 상자 n.C. box; case.

+ **sangjŏm** 상점 n.C. shop; store (*Am.*). *sangjŏm chuin* 상점 주인 shopkeeper (*Eng.*); storekeeper (*Am.*).

sangk'waehan 상쾌한 adj.C. refreshing; exhilarating; invigorating; bracing.

+ **sangnyu** 상류 n.C. ① upper stream (of a river) ② upper [higher] classes. *sangnyu sahoe* 상류사회 high society.

sangŏp 상업 n.C. commerce; trade; business. *sangŏb-ŭi* 상업의 commercial; business.

sangp'um 상품 n.C. goods; merchandise; commodity.

sangsang 상상 n.C. imagination; fancy. *sangsanghada* 상상하다 imagine.

sangsik 상식 n.C. common sense; good sense.

sangsok 상속 n.C. succession; inheritance. *sangsok'ada* 상속하다 succeed (to); inherit.

sangt'ae 상태 n.C. condition; state; situation. *kŏngang sangt'ae* 건강 상태 state of health.

* **sanji** 산지 n.C. place of production. *ssar-ŭi sanji* 쌀의 산지 rice-producing district.

sanmaek 산맥 n.C. mountain range.

+ **sanmul** 산물 n.C. product; production; produce.

sanŏp 산업 n.C. industry. *sanŏb-ŭi* 산업의 industrial.

sanso 산소 n.C. oxygen.

sanyang 사냥 n. hunting; shooting. *sanyanghada* 사냥하다 hunt; shoot.

saŏp 사업 n.C. enterprise; undertaking; business. *saŏpkka* 사업가 entrepre- neur.

* **sarajida** 사라지다 v. disappear; vanish; be gone.

saram 사람 n. man; person; human being.

sarang 사랑 n. love; affection. *saranghada* 사랑하다 love; be fond of; be attached to.

sarip 사립 n.C. private establishment. *sarib-ŭi* 사립의 private. *sarip hakkyo* 사립 학교 private school.

sasaek 사색 n.C. contemplation; meditation.

sasaek'ada 사색하다 contemplate; speculate.

sasang 사상 n.C. thought; idea. *sasangga* 사상가 thinker. *sasangbŏm* 사상범 political offense [offender].

sasil 사실 n.C. fact; actual fact; truth. *sasilssang* 사실상 in fact; actually.

sasip 사십 n.C. 40 forty. *chesasip* 제40 the fortieth. **sasŏl** 사설 n.C. editorial.

sat'ang 사탕 n.C. candy. → **sŏlt'ang** 설탕 sugar.

+ **sawŏl** 사월 n.C. April.

+ **sayong** 사용 n.C. use; employment. *sayonghada* 사용하다 use; employ; apply.

se 세 n.C. tax; duty (on goods). *sodŭksse* 소득세 individual income tax.

se 세 pre-n. three. *se saram* 세 사람 three people.

* **seda** 세다 v. count; calculate; enumerate.

* **seda** 세다 adj. (be) strong; powerful; mighty. *sege* 세게 hard; strongly; powerfully.

* **segŭm** 세금 n.C. tax. → **se** 세.

segwan 세관 n.C. customhouse; customs. *segwan chŏlch'a* 세관 절차 customs formalities.

segye 세계 n.C. world. *segyejŏk* 세계적 world-wide; international; universal.

* **sep'o** 세포 n.C. cell. *sep'o-ŭi* 세포의 cellular.

seppang 셋방 n.C. room to let; room for rent.

seryŏk 세력 n.C. power; influence. *seryŏk innŭn* 세력 있는 powerful; influential.

sesang 세상 n.C. world; society. *sesang-e* 세상에 in the world; on earth.

sesu 세수 n.C. *sesuhada* 세수하다 wash one's face; have a wash.

* **set** 셋 n. three. *setchae(ro)* 세째(로) third(ly).

set'ak 세탁 n.C. wash(ing); laundry. *set'ak'ada* 세탁하다 wash; do the washing. *set'akki* 세탁기 washing machine.

seuda 세우다 v. ① raise; set [put] up; erect ② stop; hold up ③ build; construct.

* **sewŏl** 세월 n.C. time; time and tide; years. [p.3,78]
  -seyo/siŏyo/syŏyo -세요/시어요/셔요 polite informal imperative v. ending. the *-seyo* form is favored in Seoul.
  si 시(short vowel) n.C. poetry; poem; verse.
si 시(short vowel) n.C. o'clock; hour; time. *tusi* 두시 two o'clock.
si 시(long vowel) n.C. city; town. *si-ŭi* 시의 municipal; city. *sich'ŏng* 시청 city hall.
  sich'al 시찰 n.C. inspection. *sich'arhada* 시찰하다 inspect; observe.
  sida 시다 adj. (be) sour; acid; tart.
sidae 시대 n.C. age; era; period; times; days. *uju sidae* 우주 시대 space age. *silla sidae* 신라 시대 *Silla* period, period of the *Silla* kingdom.
  sido 시도 n.C. attempt. *sidohada* 시도하다 attempt; try out.
+ **siga** 시가 n.C. streets of a city; city; town. *sigaji* 시가지 urban district.
# **sigan** 시간 n.C. time; hour. *yŏngŏp sigan* 영업 시간 business hours. *siganp'yo* 시간표 time table.
* **sigi** 시기 n.C. season; time; period; occasion.
# **sigol** 시골 n. country (side) ; rural district. *sigol saram* 시골 사람 country-dweller; rustic.
* **sigye** 시계 n.C. clock; watch. *sonmok sigye* 손목 시계 wristwatch. *t'akssang sigye* 탁상 시계 table clock.
  sihap 시합 n.C. match; game. → **kyŏnggi** 경기.
* **sihŏm** 시험 n.C. examination; exam; test. *sihŏmhada* 시험하다 examine; test. *sihŏm(-ŭl) poda* 시험 (을) 보다 take a test.
  siil 시일 n.C. ① time; days; hours ② data; the time. *siil-gwa changso* 시일과 장소 time and place.
+ **siin** 시인 n.C. poet. *yŏryu siin* 여류 시인 poetess.
+ **sijak** 시작 n.C. beginning; commencement. [p.83] *sijak'ada* 시작하다 begin; com- mence; start.
* **sijang** 시장 n.C. market (place); fair.
  sijang 시장 n.C. mayor. *Sŏul sijang* 서울 시장 Mayor

of Seoul.

+ **sijip** 시집 n. collection of poems; anthology.

sijip 시집 n. one's husband's home or family. ⓘ

sijung 시중 n. attendance; service. *sijungdŭlda* 시중
들다 attend; wait on; serve.

sik'ida 시키다 v. make [let] a person do; have [get]
a person do.

+ **sik'ida** 식히다 v. cool; let (a thing) cool.

sikkŭrŏpta 시끄럽다 adj. (be) noisy; boisterous.
sikkŭrŏpkke 시끄럽게 noisily; clamorously.

sikssa 식사 n.C. meal; diet. *sikssahada* 식사하다
have [take] a meal; eat.

sikt'ak 식탁 n.C. (dinner) table. *sikt'akppo* 식탁보
table cloth.

+ **siktta** 식다 v. (become) cool; get cold; cool off.

sikttang 식당 n.C. dining room [hall]; mess hall;
restaurant; eating house; lunch counter.

* **sil** 실 n. thread; yarn; string.

silch'ŏn 실천 n.C. practice. *silch'ŏnhada* 실천하다
practice; put into practice.

silhaeng 실행 n.C. practice; execution; fulfil(l)
ment. *silhaenghada* 실행하다 practice; put into
practice; carry out, execute.

silhŏm 실험 n.C. experiment; laboratory work.
silhŏmhada 실험하다 experiment (on)

silhyŏn 실현 n.C. realization. *silhyŏnhada* 실현하다
realize; materialize; come true.

silloe 신뢰 n.C. confidence; trust; reliance. *si-
lloehada* 신뢰하다 trust; believe in.

sillye 실례 n.C. rudeness; discourtesy

sillyŏk 실력 n.C. real ability. *sillyŏg-i innŭn* 실력이
있는 able; capable; talented.

silmang 실망 n.C. disappointment. *silmanghada* 실
망하다 be disappointed in [at].

+ **silp'ae** 실패 n.C. failure; mistake; error; blunder.
silp'aehada 실패하다 fail; go wrong.

* **silssi** 실시 n.C. execution; enforcement. *silssihada*

실시하다 enforce; put in operation [force].

silssu 실수 n.C. mistake; blunder; fault. *silssuhada* 실수하다 make a mistake; commit a blunder.

* **silssŭp** 실습 n.C. practice; exercise; drill. *silssŭphada* 실습하다 practice; have (practical) training.

\# **silt'a** 싫다 adj. (be) disagreeable; disgusting; reluctant.

* **siltche** 실제 n.C. truth; fact; reality. *siltche-ŭi* 실제의 real; true; actual; practical. *siltche-ro* 실제로 really; actually.

simburŭm 심부름 n. errand; message. *simburŭmhada* 심부름하다 do errands.

\# **simhada** 심하다 adj.C. (be) violent; intense; excessive; severe.

\+ **simin** 시민 n.C. citizen; townfolks.

simjang 심장 n.C. heart. *simjang mabi* 심장마비 heart attack.

simni 심리 n.C. mental state; psychology. *simnijŏk(ŭro)* 심리적(으로) mental(ly); psychological(ly).

* **simsa** 심사 n.C. inspection; examination. *simsahada* 심사하다 examine; judge; investigate.

simsimhada 심심하다 adj. be bored; be at loose ends.

* **sin** 신 n.C. god. *yŏsin* 여신 goddess. *sin-ŭi* 신의 divine; godly.

\+ **sin(bal)** 신(발) n. shoes; boots. → **kudu** 구두

\+ **sinae** 시내 n.C. (in, within) the city. *sinae ppŏsŭ* 시내 버스 urban bus. *sinae chŏnhwa* 시내 전화 local phones.

sinang 신앙 n.C. faith; belief. *sinang saenghwal* 신앙 생활 life of faith; religious life.

sinbu 신부 n.C. bride; newly-wed wife.

sinbu(nim) 신부(님) n.C. priest.

sinch'e 신체 n.C. body. *sinch'e-ŭi* 신체의 bodily; physical. *sinch'e kŏmsa* 신체 검사 physical check-up (Am.).

sinch'ŏng 신청 n.C. application. *sinch'ŏnghada* 신청

하다 apply (for). *sinch'ŏngsŏ* 신청서 (written) application. *sinch'ŏngin* 신청인 applicant.

singgŏptta 싱겁다 adj. (be) insipid; taste flat.

singmin 식민 n.C. colonization; settlement. *singminji* 식민지 colony.

singmul 식물 n.C. plant; vegetation. *singmulssŏng* 식물성 vegetability; vegetable property.

sin'go 신고 n.C. report; statement. *sin'gohada* 신고 하다 state; report; make [file] a return.

singsinghada 싱싱하다 adj. (be) fresh; lively; full of life.

* **sin'gyŏng** 신경 n.C. nerves. *sin'gyŏngssŏng(ŭi)* 신경 성(의) nervous. *sin'gyŏngjil* 신경질 nervous temperament.

sinho 신호 n.C. signal; signal(l)ing. *sinhohada* 신호 하다 (make a) signal.

sinhon 신혼 n.C. new marriage. *sinhon-ŭi* 신혼의 newly married [wedded]. *sinhon yŏhaeng* 신혼 여 행 honeymoon.

sinmun 신문 n.C. newspaper; paper; press.

sinnada 신나다 v. get in high spirits; get elated.

sinsok 신속 n.C. quickness. *sinsok'an* 신속한 rapid; swift. *sinsok'i* 신속히 rapidly; promptly; quickly.

+ **sintta** 신다 v. wear (on one's feet); put [have] on. *kudu-rŭl [yangmar- ŭl] sintta* 구두를 [양말을] 신다 put on one's shoes [socks].

+ **sinyong** 신용 n.C. confidence; trust. *sinyonghada* 신 용하다 trust (in); give credit to; rely on.

sip 십 n.C. 10 ten. *chesip* 제10 the tenth.

sipkku 십구 n.C. 19 nineteen. *sipkkusegi* 19세기 the nineteenth century.

sipssa 십사 n.C. 14 fourteen. *chesipssa* 제14 the fourteenth.

sipssam 십삼 n.C. 13 thirteen. *chesipssam* 제13 the thirteenth.

siptta 싶다 adj. want, wish; hope; desire; would [should] like to (do).

siryŏk 시력 n.C. (eye) sight; vision. *siryŏk kŏmsa* 시력 검사 eyesight test.

siryong 실용 n.C. practical use. *siryongjŏgin* 실용적인 practical; useful.

* **sisŏl** 시설 n.C. establishment; facilities; equipment. *sisŏlhada* 시설하다 establish; equip.

* **sitta** 싣다 v. load; take on; take on board; ship.

* **siwŏnhada** 시원하다 adj. (be) feel cool [refreshing].

so 소 n. cow; bull; ox; cattle. [p.57,58,79,80,81]

soakkwa 소아과 n.C. pediatrics. *soakkwa ŭisa* 소아과 의사 child specialist; pediatrician.

* **sobi** 소비 n.C. consumption. *sobihada* 소비하다 consume; spend; expend.

sŏda 서다 v. ① stand (up); rise (to one's feet) ② stop; halt; run down ③ be built [erected].

sodŭk 소득 n.C. income; earnings. *kungmin sodŭk* 국민 소득 national income.

sŏdurŭda 서두르다 v. hurry (up); hasten; make haste. *sŏdullŏ* 서둘러 hurriedly; in haste.

soegogi 쇠고기 n. beef. *soegogisŭp'ŭ* 쇠고기스프 beef soup.

sogae 소개 n.C. introduction. *sogaehada* 소개하다 introduce. *sogaetchang* 소개장 letter of introduction.

* **sŏgi** 서기 n.C. Anno Domini (A.D.); western calendar.

* **sogida** 속이다 v. deceive; cheat; swindle.

sogot 속옷 n. underwear; underclothes; undergarment; undershirt (*Am.*).

sogŭm 소금 n. salt. [p.65] *sogŭm-e chŏrin* 소금에 절인 salted; pickled with salt.

sŏgyu 석유 n.C. oil; petroleum; kerosene. *sŏgyu nallo* 석유 난로 kerosene stove; oil stove.

+ **sohwa** 소화 n.C. digestion. *sohwahada* 소화하다 digest.

sohyŏng 소형 n.C. small size. *sohyŏng-ŭi* 소형의 small(-sized); tiny; pocket(-size).

sojihada 소지하다 v.C. have; possess. *sojip'um* 소지품 one's belongings.

sŏjŏk 서적 n.C. books. *sŏjŏkssang* 서적상 bookseller's; bookshop; bookstore.

sŏjŏm 서점 n.C. bookshop; bookstore.

sok 속 n. interior; inner part; inside. *sog-e* 속에 in; within; amid(st).

* **sok'ada** 속하다 v.C. belong (to); be part of.

* **sŏk'oe** 석회 n.C. lime. *sŏk'oesŏk* 석회석 limestone.

* **sŏkt'an** 석탄 n.C. coal. *sŏkt'anjae* 석탄재 coal cinders.

soktta 속다 v. be cheated [deceived, fooled].

soktta 솎다 v. thin (out); weed out.

sŏktta 섞다 v. mix; blend.

sokttal 속달 n.C. express [special] delivery (mail).

sokttam 속담 n.C. proverb; (common) saying; maxim.

* **soktto** 속도 n.C. speed; velocity; tempo.

sol 솔 n. brush. *soljil* 솔질 brushing. *sol-lo t'ŏlda* 솔로 털다 brush off.

+ **sŏlbi** 설비 n.C. equipment(s); arrangements; facilities. *sŏlbihada* 설비하다 equip; provide; install.

+ **sŏlch'i** 설치 n.C. establishment; installation. *sŏlch'ihada* 설치하다 establish; set up; found; install.

+ **sŏlmyŏng** 설명 n.C. explanation. *sŏlmyŏnghada* 설명하다 explain; account for.

sŏlssa 설사 n.C. diarrhea; loose bowels. *sŏlssahada* 설사하다 have loose bowels.

* **sŏlt'ang** 설탕 n.C. sugar. *kaksŏlt'ang* 각설탕 sugar cube. *hŭksŏlt'ang* 흑설탕 brown sugar.

soltchik'an 솔직한 adj. plain; frank; candid; straight and honest.

+ **som** 솜 n. cotton; cotton wool.

sŏm 섬 n. island; isle.

+ **somae** 소매 n. sleeve. *somae-ga kin [tchalbŭn]* 소매

가 긴 [짧은] long [short]-sleeved.

somssi 솜씨 n. skill; make; workmanship. *somssi-innŭn* 솜씨 있는 skillful; dexterous.

+ **somun** 소문 n.C. rumo(u)r; hearsay. [p.21] *somunnan* 소문난 (very) famous.

sŏmyŏng 서명 n.C. signature; autograph. *sŏmyŏng-hada* 서명하다 sign one's name.

son 손 n. hand. ① [p.44] *orŭn [oen] son* 오른[왼]손 right [left] hand. *son-e nŏt'a* 손에 넣다 get; obtain.

sŏn 선 n.C. line; route. *p'yŏnghaengsŏn* 평행선 parallel line. *kyŏngbusŏn* 경부선 *kyŏngbu* (Seoul-Pusan) line.

sonagi 소나기 n. shower. *sonagi-rŭl mannada* 소나기 를 만나다 be caught in a shower.

+ **sonamu** 소나무 n. pine(tree). → **sol** 솔 (abbr.).

sŏnbae 선배 n.C. senior; elder.

sŏnbak 선박 n.C. vessel; ship; shipping; marine. *sŏnbakhoesa* 선박 회사 shipping company.

sŏnbal 선발 n.C. selection; choice. *sŏnbalhada* 선발 하다 select; choose.

* **sŏng** 성(short vowel) n.C. castle; fortress; citadel.

+ **sŏng** 성(long vowel) n.C. family name; surname.

* **sŏngbun** 성분 n.C. ingredient; component; con-stituent.

sŏngdang 성당 n.C. cathedral; catholic church.

sŏnggong 성공 n.C. success. *sŏnggonghada* 성공하다 succeed; be successful.

+ **songgŭm** 송금 n.C. remittance. *songgŭmhada* 송금하 다 send money; remit money.

sŏnggyŏng 성경 n.C. (Holy) Bible; Scriptures.

+ **songi** 송이 n. cluster; bunch; flake (of snow).

sŏngjang 성장 n.C. growth. *sŏngjanghada* 성장하다 grow (up). *sŏngjanghan* 성장한 grown-up.

sŏngjil 성질 n.C. nature; character.

+ **sŏngjŏk** 성적 n.C. result; record; merit; grades. *sŏngjŏkp'yo* 성적표 list of students' record; grade sheet, report card.

* **sŏngkyŏk** 성격 n.C. character; personality.
* **sŏngmyŏng** 성명 n.C. declaration; statement. *sŏngmyŏnghada* 성명하다 declare; announce.

sŏngmyŏng 성명 n.C. (full) name.

+ **sŏngnip** 성립 n.C. formation. *sŏngnip´ada* 성립하다 be formed [organized]; be effected.

* **sŏngnyang** 성냥 n. matches. *sŏngnyangkkap* 성냥갑 match box. *sŏngnyang kkaebi* 성냥 개비 match stick.

* **songnyŏk** 속력 n.C. → **soktto** 속도. *chŏnsongnyŏg- ŭro* 전속력으로 (at) full speed.

sŏn´gŏ 선거 n.C. election. *sŏn´gŏhada* 선거하다 elect; vote for.

sŏngsil 성실 n.C. sincerity; honesty. *sŏngsilhan* 성실 한 sincere; faithful.

sŏngsukhada 성숙하다 v.C. ripen; get ripe. *sŏng- suk´an* 성숙한 ripe; mature.

sŏngt´anjŏl 성탄절 n.C. Christmas (day).

* **sonhae** 손해 n.C. damage; injury; loss. *sonhae paesang* 손해 배상 compensation for damages.

+ **sŏnjŏn** 선전 n.C. propaganda; publicity; advertise- ment. *sŏnjŏnhada* 선전하다 propagandize; ad- vertise.

* **sonkkarak** 손가락 n. finger. *ŏmjisonkkarak* 엄지손가 락 thumb. *chipke[kaundet, yak. saekki]sonkarak* 집게[가운뎃, 약, 새끼]손가락 index [middle, ring, little] finger.

sŏnmul 선물 n.C. present; gift. *sŏnmurhada* 선물하다 give [send] a present.

sonnim 손님 n. ① guest; caller; visitor ② customer; client; audience ③ passenger.

sonnyŏ 손녀 n.C. granddaughter.

sŏnp´unggi 선풍기 n.C. fan; electric fan

sŏnsaeng(nim) 선생(님) n.C. teacher; instructor.

+ **sonsil** 손실 n.C. loss; disadvantage; damage. *k´ŭn sonsil* 큰 손실 great [heavy, serious] loss.

* **sŏnsu** 선수 n.C. player; athlete; champion.

+ **sonssugŏn** 손수건 n.C. handkerchief.

+ **sŏnt'aek** 선택 n.C. selection; choice; option. *sŏnt'aek'ada* 선택하다 select; choose.

sont'op 손톱 n. finger nail. *sont'op kkakki* 손톱 깎이 nail clipper.

+ **sŏnŭlhada** 서늘하다 adj. (be) cool; refreshing; chilly.

sŏnŏn 선언 n.C. declaration; proclamation. *sŏnŏnhada* 선언하다 declare; proclaim.

* **sonyŏ** 소녀 n.C. (young) girl.

* **sonyŏn** 소년 n.C. boy. *sonyŏn-ŭi* 소년의 juvenile.

sŏpsŏp'ada 섭섭하다 adj. (be) sorry; sad; disappointed.

sop'ung 소풍 n.C. outing; excursion; picnic. *sop'ung kada* 소풍 가다 go on an excursion [a picnic].

sori 소리 n. ① sound; noise ② voice; cry. ①, [p.44] *k'ŭn [chagŭn] soriro* 큰 [작은] 소리로 in a loud [low] voice.

+ **sŏri** 서리 n. frost; white frost.

sorijirŭda 소리지르다 v. shout; cry [call] (out); scream; roar; yell.

sŏro 서로 adv. mutually; each other; one another.

sŏrŭn 서른 n. thirty. *sŏrŭn sal* 서른 살 thirty years of age.

soryang 소량 n.C. small quantity [amount]. *soryang-ŭi* 소량의 litter; small quality [amount] of.

+ **sŏryu** 서류 n.C. documents; papers. *sŏryu kabang* 서류 가방 briefcase.

* **sosik** 소식 n.C. news. [p.53]

sŏsŏhi 서서히 adv. slowly. → *ch'ŏnch'ŏnhi* 천천히.

sosok 소속 n.C. belongings. *sosok'ada* 소속하다 belong to; be attached to. *sosog-ŭi* 소속의 attached [belonging] to.

sosŏl 소설 n.C. novel; story; fiction. *sosŏlga* 소설가 novelist.

sosong 소송 n.C. lawsuit; legal action. *sosonghada* 소송하다 sue; bring a lawsuit.

sot 솥 n. iron pot; kettle. *sottukkŏng* 솥뚜껑 lid of a kettle.

* **sotta** 솟다 v. ① rise [soar, tower] high ② gush [spring] out; well out.

sŏt'urŭda 서투르다 adj. (be) unfamiliar; (be) awkward; clumsy; unskil(l)ful; stiff; poor.

Sŏul 서울 n. Seoul (capital of Korea). [p.50]

sowi 소위 pre-n. so-called.

sŏyang 서양 n.C. the West; the Occident. *sŏyang-ŭi* 서양의 Western; Occidental. *sŏyang saram* 서양 사람 Westerner; European. cf. **tongyang** 동양.

+ **soyu** 소유 n.C. possession. *soyuhada* 소유하다 have; possess; own; hold.

-ss- -ㅆ- past tense marker. was, did. The shape is -ss- after -a, and -ass- after -o, followed by -ŏss-, -kess-, -sŭp-, -ta, -ŭmyŏ, -ŭni, etc.

ssada 싸다 v. rap up [in]; do up; bundle; pack up.

+ **ssada** 싸다 adj. (be) inexpensive; cheap; low-priced. *ssage* 싸게 cheaply; at a low cost.

ssak 싹 n. bud; sprout; shoot. ① *ssag-i t'ŭda* 싹이 트다 bud; shoot; sprout.

ssal 쌀 n. (raw, uncooked) rice. *ssalkkage* 쌀가게 rice store. *ssalt'ong* 쌀통 rice chest.

ssalssalhada 쌀쌀하다 adj. ① (be) chilly; (rather) cold ② distant; coldhearted; indifferent.

* **ssat'a** 쌓다 v. ① pile [heap] (up); stack; lay ② accumulate; store up.

ssauda 싸우다 v. fight; make war; struggle; quarrel.

ssaum 싸움 n. fight (*n.*).

ssi 씨 n. seed; stone; kernel; pit; pip. *ssi ŏmnŭn* 씨 없는 seedless.

+ **ssikssik'ada** 씩씩하다 adj. (be) manly; brave.

+ **ssiptta** 씹다 v. chew; masticate.

ssirŭm 씨름 n. wrestling; wrestling match. *ssirŭm-hada* 씨름하다 wrestle.

* **ssitta** 씻다 v. wash, wash away; cleanse.

   ssoda 쏘다 v. shoot; fire; discharge.

* **ssŏktta** 썩다 v. go bad; rot; decay; corrupt. *ssŏgŭn* 썩은 bad; rotten; stale.

+ **ssotta** 쏟다 v. ① pour out; spill; shed; drop ② concentrate; devote; effort.

ssŭda 쓰다 v. use; make use of; spend (money) on.

ssŭda 쓰다 v. write; compose.

* **ssŭda** 쓰다 v. put/wear on one's head; cover.

+ **ssŭlda** 쓸다 v. sweep (up, away, off). *pang-ŭl ssŭlda* 방을 쓸다 sweep a room.

+ **ssŭlssŭlhada** 쓸쓸하다 adj. (be) lonely; lonesome.

   ssŭregi 쓰레기 n. garbage; rubbish (*Eng.*); trash (*Am.*). *ssŭregit'ong* 쓰레기통 garbage can (*Am.*); dustbin (*Eng.*).

* **ssŭrŏjida** 쓰러지다 v. ① collapse; fall down ② sink [break] down ③ fall dead ④ go bankrupt.

su 수 n. (possibility) *hal (s)su itta* be able to.

   subak 수박 n. watermelon.

+ **subun** 수분 n.C. moisture; juice; water. *subun-i manŭn* 수분이 많은 watery; juicy.

   such'i 수치 n.C. shame; disgrace. *such'isŭrŏn* 수치스런 shameful; disgraceful.

* **such'ul** 수출 n.C. export; exportation. *such'ulhada* 수출하다 export; ship abroad.

   sudan 수단 n.C. means; way; measure; step.

* **sudo** 수도 n.C. capital. *sudokkwŏn* 수도권 metropolitan area around the capital.

   sudong 수동 n.C. passivity. *sudongjŏg(ŭro)* 수동적(으로) passive(ly).

   sugo 수고 n.C. trouble; pains; efforts. *sugohada* 수고하다 take pains [trouble].

+ **sugŏn** 수건 n.C. towel. *sesu sugŏn* 세수 수건 face towel. *sugŏn kŏri* 수건 걸이 towel rack.

+ **suhak** 수학 n.C. mathematics.

* **suip** 수입 n.C. importation; import. *suiphada* 수입하다 import. *suipp'um* 수입품 imported articles [goods].

sujŏng 수정 n.C. amendment; modification. *sujŏnghada* 수정하다 amend; modify.

sukppak 숙박 n.C. lodging. *sukppakhada* 숙박하다 lodge; stay. *sukppangnyo* 숙박료 room charge; hotel charge.

suktche 숙제 n.C. homework; home task. *panghak suktche* 방학 숙제 holiday tesk.

sul 술 n. liquor; wine; rice wine. *sur-ŭl masida* 술을 마시다 have a drink. *sur-e ch'wihada* 술에 취하다 get drunk.

* **sŭlp'ŭda** 슬프다 adj. (be) sad; sorrowful; pathetic.

\+ **sŭlp'ŭm** 슬픔 n. sorrow; sadness; grief.

* **sultchip** 술집 n. bar (room); saloon(*Am.*); pub(lic house)(*Eng.*).

sum 숨 n. breath; breathing; *sum-ŭl swida* 숨을 쉬다 breathe.

* **sumtta** 숨다 v. hide [conceal] oneself; take cover. *sumŭn* 숨은 hidden; unknown.

sumgida 숨기다 v. hide; conceal; shelter.

-(su)mni(da) -(스)ㅂ 니(다) ending (polite formal style marker, followed by -da [statements], -kka [questions]) is, does.

* **sun'gan** 순간 n.C. moment; instant; second. *sun'ganjŏk* 순간적 momentary; admire; adore.

sŭnggaek 승객 n.C. passenger.

sungmyŏng 숙명 n.C. fate; destiny; fatality.

* **sŭngni** 승리 n.C. victory; triumph. *sŭngnihada* 승리 하다 win; win [gain] a victory.

sungnyŏ 숙녀 n.C. lady. *sungnyŏdaun* 숙녀다운 ladylike.

sun'gyŏl 순결 n.C. purity; chastity; virginity. *sun'gyŏlhan* 순결한 pure; clean; chaste.

\+ **sŭnim** 스님 n. Buddhist priest [monk].

\+ **sunsŏ** 순서 n.C. order; sequence. *sunsŏ-rŭl ttara* 순 서를 따라 in proper sequence.

sunyŏ(nim) 수녀(님) n.C. nun; sister. *sunyŏwŏn* 수녀원 nunnery; convent. *sunyŏwŏnjang* 수녀원장 abbess.

suŏp 수업 n.C. class; lesson; lecture. *suŏp'ada* 수업
하다 teach; lecture.

* **sup** 숲 n. wood; forest; grove.

supi'l 수필 n.C. essay. *sup'ilga* 수필가 essayist.

* **sŭpkki** 습기 n.C. humidity; moisture; dampness.

\+ **sŭpkkwan** 습관 n.C. habit; custom. *sŭpkkwanjŏgin*
습관적인 habitual; customary. *sŭpkkwanjŏg-ŭro* 습
관적으로 habitually; from habit.

* **sup'yo** 수표 n.C. check (*Am.*); cheque (*Eng.*).
pojŭng sup'yo 보증 수표 certifide check. *pudo
sup'yo* 부도 수표 bad [dishonored] check.

suri 수리 n.C. repair; mending. *surihada* 수리하다
repair; mend; have (a thing) mended. *surigong*
수리공 repairman.

* **suryang** 수량 n.C. quantity; volume.

\+ **susan(mul)** 수산(물) n.C. marine products. *susan
sijang* 수산 시장 fish market. *susanŏp* 수산업
fisheries.

\+ **susang** 수상 n.C. prime minister; premier.

susanghada 수상하다 adj.C. be suspicious.

susŏn 수선 n.C. repair; mending. *susŏnhada* 수선하
다 repair; mend; have (a shoe)

susul 수술 n.C. (surgical) operation. *susulhada* 수술
하다 operate on; perform a surgical operation.
susulsil 수술실 operating room

sŭsŭng 스승 n. teacher; master; mentor.

* **sŭsŭro** 스스로 adv. (for) oneself; in person. *sŭsŭro-ŭi*
스스로의 one's own; personal.

susuryo 수수료 n.C. commission; fee; service
charge.

\+ **sut** 숯 n. charcoal. [p.82] *sutppul* 숯불 charcoal fire.

* **sutcha** 숫자 n.C. figure; numeral.

suwi 수위 n.C. guard; doorkeeper; gatekeeper.

suyo 수요 n.C. demand. *suyo konggŭp* 수요 공급
demand and supply. *suyoja* 수요자 user.

suyoil 수요일 n.C. Wednesday.

suyŏng 수영 n.C. swimming; swim. *suyŏnghada* 수영

하다 swim; have a swim. *suyŏngbok* 수영복 swimming suit.

swida 쉬다 v. rest; take a rest.

swiptta 쉽다 v. ① (be) easy; simple; without difficulty [effort] ② be apt to; be liable to.

\# **-syŏyo/seyo/siŏyo** -셔요/세요/시어요 polite informal imperative v. ending. the *-seyo* form is favored in Seoul.

$$\leq T \geq$$

\# **ta** 다 adv. ① all; everything; everybody ② utterly; completely. *tahaesŏ* 다해서 in all; all told. *tagach'i* 다같이 together.

\# **-ta** -다 ending ① citation (dictionary) form. indicative ending in plain style. follows v., adj. and copula stem. is, does (only in the literary language attached directly to v. stem; colloq. *-nŭnda* -는다) ② interruption v. ending. indicates that the action of the preceding v. was interrupted. frequently followed by particle *-ka* -가: *-taga* -다가.

tabang 다방 n.C. tearoom; teahouse; coffee house; coffee shop (of hotel)

tach'ida 다치다 v. be [get, become] wounded [hurt, injured, damaged]; bruised.

\+ **tae(namu)** 대(나무) n. bamboo. *taebaguni* 대바구니 bamboo basket.

\# **taebubun** 대부분 n.C. most; major part (of); mostly; largely; for the most part.

taebyŏn 대변 n.C. excrement; feces. *taebyŏn-ŭl poda* 대변을 보다 have a bowel movement; defecate.

\+ **taech'aek** 대책 n.C. countermeasure. *taech'aeg-ŭl*

seuda 대책을 세우다 work out a countermeasure, plan to solve a problem.

\# **taech'ejŏgin** 대체적인 adj.C. general; main; rough. *taech'e-ro* 대체로 generally; as a whole.

taech'ung 대충 adv.C. nearly; about; roughly.

* **taedanhada** 대단하다 adj.C. (be) enormous; severe; intense; grave.

\# **taedanhi** 대단히 adv.C. very; seriously; exceedingly; awfully.

\# **taedap** 대답 n.C. answer; reply. *taedap'ada* 대답하다 answer; reply; respond (to); give an answer.

taedasu 대다수 n.C. large majority; greater part.

\# **taegae** 대개 adv.C. mostly; for the most part; in general.

\+ **taegang** 대강 n.C. ① general principles; outline; general features; the gist. ② generally; roughly.

* **taehak** 대학 n.C. university; college. *taehakssaeng* 대학생 university student. *taehagwŏn* 대학원 graduate school; (post) graduate course; *taehakppyŏngwŏn* 대학병원 university hospital.

Taehan 대한 n.C. (great) Korea. *Taehanmin'guk* 대한민국 Republic of Korea.

taehang 대항 n.C. opposition; rivalry. *taehanghada* 대항하다 oppose; cope with.

* **taehoe** 대회 n.C. great [grand] meeting; mass meeting; rally; convention; athletic meeting; competetion. *taehoe-rŭl yŏlda* 대회를 열다 hold a mass meeting.

taehwa 대화 n.C. conversation; dialogue. *taehwahada* 대화하다 talk [converse] with.

* **taejang** 대장 n.C. general (*army, air*); admiral (*navy*).

taeji 대지 n.C. site; lot; plot. *kŏnch'uk taeji* 건축 대지 building [housing] site [lot, land].

taejo 대조 n.C. contrast; collation. *taejohada* 대조하다 contrast; check; collate.

\# **taejŏn** 대전 n.C. great war; the World War. *cheich'a*

segye taejŏn 제 2차 세계 대전 World War II

taejŏp 대접 n.C. treatment; entertainment; reception. *taejŏp'ada* 대접하다 treat; entertain; receive.

+ **taejung** 대중 n.C. the common people, masses; populace; multitude. *kŭllotaejung* 근로 대중 working people.

taek 댁 n.C. ① (your, his, her) house; residence ② you ③ the wife of (a person); Mrs ...

taemŏri 대머리 n.C. bald head; bald-headed person.

taemuntcha 대문자 n.C. capital letter.

taep'o 대포 n.C. gun; cannon; artillery. *taep'o-rŭl ssoda* 대포를 쏘다 fire a gun.

* **taep'yo** 대표 n.C. representation; representative. *taep'yohada* 대표하다 represent; stand [act] for.

taerip 대립 n.C. opposition; rivalry; confrontation; antagonism. *taerip'ada* 대립하다 be opposed to.

taeryang 대량 n.C. large quantity; *taeyang saengsan* 대량 생산 mass production.

taeryuk 대륙 n.C. continent. *taeryukkan t'andot'an* 대륙간 탄도탄 intercontinental ballistic missile.

taesa 대사 n.C. ambassador. *chumi [chuil, chuyŏng] taesa* 주미[주일, 주영] 대사 ambassador to the United States [Japan, Great Britain]

taesagwan 대사관 n.C. embassy. *Miguk taesagwan* 미국 대사관 American Embassy.

+ **taesang** 대상 n.C. object; subject; target.

taet'ongnyŏng 대통령 n.C. president. *taet'ongnyŏng-ŭi* 대통령의 presidential. *taet'ongnyŏng sŏn'gŏ* 대통령 선거 presidential election. *taet'ongnyŏng yŏngbuin* 대통령 영부인 first lady.

taeu 대우 n.C. treatment; reception; pay; service. *taeuhada* 대우하다 treat; receive; pay. *nomuja taeu kaesŏn* 노무자 대우 개선 improvement of labor conditions.

taeyong 대용 n.C. substitution. *taeyongp'um* 대용품 substitute article.

-taga -다가 interruption v. ending, indicates that

the action of the preceding v. was interrupted.

tagwa 다과 n.C. tea and cake; light refreshments.

tahaeng 다행 n.C. good fortune [luck]. *tahaenghada* 다행하다 (be) happy; lucky; fortunate. *tahaenghi* 다행히 happily; fortunately; luckily.

tajida 다지다 v. ① ram; harden (the ground) ② mince; chop (up) ③ make sure of; press (a person) for a definite answer.

tak 닭 n. hen; cock [rooster]. [p.34] *takkogi* 닭고기 chicken. *taktchang* 닭장 coop; henhouse.

taktta 닦다 v. ① polish; shine; burnish; brush; wipe; scrub ② improve; cultivate; train.

tal 달 n. ① moon. *porŭmttal* 보름달 full moon ② month. [p.33] *k'ŭn[chagŭn] dal* 큰[작은] 달 odd [even] month. *chinandal* 지난달 last month.

* **talda** 달다 v. weigh. *chŏul-lo talda* 저울로 달다 weigh (a thing) on a scale.

+ **talda** 달다 adj. (be) sweet; sugary.

talda 달다 v. ① attach; affix; fasten. ② fix; set up ③ put on; wear ④register ⑤ burn.

tallaeda 달래다 v. appease; soothe; coax; beguile; calm; amuse; pacify; dandle.

tallida 달리다 v. run; dash; gallop.

+ **tallyŏdŭlda** 달려들다 v. pounce on; fly at; jump [leap, spring] at [on].

tallyŏk 달력 n.C. calendar.

talssŏng 달성 n.C. achievement. *talssŏnghada* 달성하다 accomplish; achieve; attain.

talt'a 닳다 v. ① be worn out [down]; be rubbed off [down]; wear threadbare ② be boiled down ③ lose (one's) modesty.

+ **tam** 담 n. wall; fence. ① *toldam* 돌담 stone [brick] wall. *hŭkttam* 흙담 mud [earthen] wall.

taman 다만 adv. ① only; merely; simply ② but; however; and yet; still.

tambae 담배 n. tobacco; cigaret(te). *tambae-rŭl p'iuda* 담배를 피우다 smoke (tobacco). *tambae kage*

담배 가게 cigar store.

tambo 담보 n.C. security; mortgage; guarantee; warrant. *tambo-rŭl chaptta* 담보를 잡다 take security.

+ **tamdang** 담당 n.C. charge. *tamdanghada* 담당하다 take charge (of); be in charge of.

* **tamgŭda** 담그다 v. ① soak [steep, dip, immerse] (in water) ② pickle; brew.

tamhwa 담화 n.C. talk; conversation; statement. *tamhwamun* 담화문 official statement.

\# **tamtta** 담다 v. put in; fill. *kwangjuri-e tamtta* 광주리에 담다 put into a basket.

tamulda 다물다 v. shut; close (one's lips). *ib-ŭl tamulda* 입을 다물다 hold one's tongue.

+ **tan** 단 n. bundle; bunch; sheaf.

* **tanch'e** 단체 n.C. group; organization. *tanch'e haengdong* 단체 행동 united action. *tanch'e yŏhaeng* 단체 여행 group trip.

tantchŏm 단점 n.C. weak point; shortcoming; defect; fault.

tanch'u 단추 n. button; stud. *tanch'u-rŭl ch'aeuda* 단추를 채우다 button up; fasten a button. *tanch'u-rŭl kkŭrŭda* 단추를 끄르다 unbutton (a coat)

tanch'uk 단축 n.C. reduction; shortening. *tanch'uk'ada* 단축하다 reduct; shorten; curtail.

+ **tandanhada** 단단하다 adj. (be) hard; solid; strong; firm. *tandanhi* 단단히 hard; solidly; firmly.

tandok 단독 n.C. singleness. *tandog-ŭro* 단독으로 independently; seperately; individually; alone; singly.

+ **tanggida** 당기다 v. pull; draw; tug; haul.

tanggu 당구 n.C. billiards. *tanggu-rŭl ch'ida* 당구를 치다 play billiards.

tangguk 당국 n.C. authorities (concerned). *hakkyo tangguk* 학교 당국 school authorities.

tan'gi 단기 n.C. short term [time]. *tan'gi-ŭi* 단기의

short(-term); short-dated.

tan'gol 단골 n. custom; connection; patronage. *tan'gol sonnim* 단골 손님 regular customer [client].

\# **tangsi** 당시 n.C. then; that time; those days *tangsi-ŭi* 당시의 of those days; then.

tangsŏn 당선 n.C. winning an election. *tangsŏnhada* 당선하다 be elected; win the election.

tan'gyŏl 단결 n.C. union; combination; cooperation; *tan'gyŏlhada* 단결하다 unite [hold, get] (together); combine [cooperate] (with a person).

tangyŏnhan 당연한 adj. reasonable; proper; natural. *tangyŏnhi* 당연히 justly; naturally; deservedly.

\# **tanida** 다니다 v. ① go to and from (a place); go [walk] about [around]; commute ② work at [in], attend regularly ③ drop in; stop at .

tanji 단지 n.C. housing development [estate (*Eng.*)]; collective [public] housing area. *kongŏp tanji* 공업 단지 industrial complex.

tanjo 단조 n.C. monotony; dullness. *tanjoropta* 단조롭다 monotonous; flat; dull.

tanŏ 단어 n.C. word; vocabulary. *kibon tanŏjip* 기본 단어집 collection of basic words; basic wordbook.

tanp'ung 단풍 n.C. autumn colors/leaves; maple (tree). *tanp'ung tŏlda* 단풍 들다 (leaves) turn red [cirmson, yellow]. *tanp'ungnip* 단풍잎 maple leaves.

tanp'yŏn 단편 n.C. short piece; sketch. *tanp'yŏn sosŏl* 단편 소설 short story.

tansik 단식 n.C. fast; fasting. *tansik'ada* 단식하다 fast; abstain from food. *tansiknongsŏng* 단식농성 hunger strike.

+ **tansun** 단순 n.C. simplicity. *tansunhada* 단순하다 (be) simple; simple-minded. *tansunhi* 단순히 simply; merely.

* **tanwi** 단위 n.C. unit; denomination.

+ **tap** 답 n.C. answer; reply; solution

taphada 답하다 adj.C. answer; reply; give an answer; respond.

taptchang 답장 n.C. witten reply; letter in reply.

tapttap´ada 답답하다 adj.C. ① be stifling; suffocating; stuffy. ② feel frustrated [aggravated, upset] *kasŭm-i taptap´ada* 가슴이 답답하다 feel heavy in the chest.

* **taranada** 달아나다 v. run away; flee; escape; take to flight; break [get] loose; fly away.

+ **tari** 다리 n. bridge. ① *tari-rŭl kŏnnŏda* 다리를 건너다 cross a bridge.

tari 다리 n. leg. ①

tarida 달이다 v. boil down; decoct; infuse. *yag-ŭl tarida* 약을 달이다 make a medical decoction.

tarimi 다리미 n. iron; flatiron. *chŏn´gi tarimi* 전기 다리미 electriciron.

taruda 다루다 v. handle; manage; deal with; treat.

tarŭda 다르다 v. differ (from, with); be different (from, with); vary; unlike.

tasi 다시 adv. again; overagain; once more [again]; again and again.

tasŏt 다섯 n. five. *tasŏtchae* 다섯째 the fifth *tasŏt pae(ŭi)* 다섯 배(의) fivefold.

+ **tasu** 다수 n.C. large [great] number; many; majority. *tasu-ŭi* 다수의 many; large number of; numerous.

tat´uda 다투다 v. ① brawl; quarrel; have words (with) ② contend; compete; struggle.

taŭm 다음 n. (adverbial use) next; following; second. *taŭmnal* 다음날 next [following] day.

tchada 짜다 v. wring; squeeze. *sugŏn-ŭl tchada* 수건을 짜다 wring a towel.

* **tchada** 짜다 adj. (be) salty; briny. [p65]

+ **tchak** 짝 n. pair; couple; partner.

tchakssarang 짝사랑 n. one-sided love; unrequited love. *tchak- ssaranghada* 짝사랑하다 love in vain [without return]; be in a state of unrequited love.

* **tchaltta** 짧다 adj. (be) short; brief. *tchalkke* 짧게 short; briefly.

   tchaptchalhada 짭짤하다 adj. ① (be) nice and salty; saltish ② suitable.

   tchinggŭrida 찡그리다 v. frown; scowl; (make a) grimace [wry face]

   tchiktta 찍다 v. ① stamp; seal; impress ② stab; stick ③ (take a) photograph. *sajin(-ŭl) tchiktta* 사진을 찍다 take a photograph.

+ **tchip´urida** 찌프리다 v. ① grimace; frown [scowl] ② cloud over; get cloudy.

+ **tchirŭda** 찌르다 v. pierce; stab; thrust; prick.

+ **tchitta** 찢다 v. tear; split; cleave; rip.

   tchoeda 쬐다 v. ① shine on [over] ② bask in the sun.

tchok 쪽 n. direction; side; way. *orŭn[oen]tchok* 오른[왼]쪽 right [left] side.

tchotta 쫓다 v. ① drive away ② chase; pursue.

   teuda 데우다 v. warm; heat (up).

-to 도 particle ① also, too, neither. *na-do kagetta* 나도 가겠다 I will go too. ② both ... and ... (positive); (n)either ... (n)or ... (negative) *Kkwŏng-do mŏkko al-do mŏkko* 꿩도 먹고 알도 먹고 eat both the pheasant and the egg (=to have one's cake and eat it too) ③ even, yet, still *hana-do ŏptta* 하나도 없다 There is not even one.

tŏ 더 adv. more (quantity); longer (time); farther (distance). *tŏ manhi* 더 많이 much more *tŏ hanch´ŭng* 더 한층 more and more; still more.

   toan 도안 n.C. design; sketch. *toan´ga* 도안가 designer.

   tobo 도보 n.C. walking. *tobo-ro* 도보로 on foot. *tobo-yŏhaeng* 도보 여행 walking tour.

* **tŏburŏ** 더불어 adv. together; with; together with.

+ **toch´ak** 도착 n. arrival. *toch´ak´ada* 도착하다 arrive (in, at, on); reach; get to.

todaech'e 도대체 adv. on earth; in the world.

* **todŏk** 도덕 n.C. morality; virtue; morals. *todŏktchŏk* 도덕적 moral; ethical. *todŏkssang* 도덕상 morally.

toduk 도둑 n. thief; burglar; robber; sneak. [p.37, 58] *toduk matta* 도둑 맞다 be stolen; be robbed (of).

tŏdŭmtta 더듬다 v. feel [grope] for; grope about [around] for; fumble for.

toeda 되다 v. ① become; get; grow ② turn [change] into; develop ③ be realized; be accomplished ④ turn out; result; prove ⑤ come to; reach.

toeda 되다 adj. (be) thick; tough; hard. *toen chuk* 된죽 thick gruel.

toenjang 된장 n. soybean paste.

toep'uri 되풀이 n. repetition; reiteration. *toep'urihada* 되풀이하다 repeat.

togu 도구 n.C. tool; implement; utensil; instrument.

+ **tŏhada** 더하다 n. ① add (up); sum up ② get worse; grow harder.

tojang 도장 n.C. seal; stamp. *tojang-ŭl tchiktta* 도장을 찍다 seal; put one's seal to.

tojung 도중 n.C. on the way; on one's way.

tok 독 n.C. poison; venom. *tog-i innŭn* 독이 있는 poisonous; venomous; harmful.

toktcha 독자 n.C. reader; subscriber.

tokch'ok 독촉 n.C. demand. *tokch'ok'ada* 독촉하다 press [urge] (a person to do).

toktchŏm 독점 n.C. monopoly; exclusive possession.

tokkam 독감 n.C. influenza; bad cold; flu.

tokppack 독백 n.C. monolog(ue); soliloquy. *tokppaek'ada* 독백하다 talk [speak] to oneself.

tokssŏ 독서 n.C. reading *tokssŏhada* 독서하다 read (books). *toksŏ chugan* 독서 주간 book week.

tŏkt'aek 덕택 n.C. *tŏkt'aeg-ŭro* 덕택으로 due to; thanks to; by (a person's) favor [help, aid].

\# **tol** 돌 n. stone; pebble. [p.14,41] *toldam* 돌담 stone wall. *tolsot* 돌솥 stone bowl (for rice).

\+ **tolboda** 돌보다 v. take care of; care for; look after; attend to; back up; assist; protect.

tolda 돌다 v. turn round; rotate; revolve.

tŏlda 덜다 v. ① diminish; reduce; mitigate; lighten ② subtract; deduct; take off.

\# **tollida** 돌리다 v. ① turn; revolve; roll; spin ② pass (round); hand round. *sultchan-ŭl tollida* 술잔을 돌리다 pass a glass round.

tomae 도매 n.C. wholeasale. *tomaehada* 도매하다 sell wholeasale. *tomaesang.* 도매상 wholeasale dealer.

\+ **tomang** 도망 n.C. escape; flight; desertion. *tomang-ch'ida[hada]* 도망치다[하다] ɪun away; flee; fly; desert. *tomangja* 도망자 fugitive.

\# **ton** 돈 n. money; cash; coin. [p.38,39,40,117] *ton-ŭl pŏlda* 돈을 벌다 make [earn] money; make a fortune.

tonan 도난 n.C. *tonandanghada* 도난당하다 be robbed; have (one's money) stolen; be stolen.

\# **tongan** 동안 n. ① period; span; interval ② time; space ③ for; during; while.

tongch'ang 동창 n.C. classmate; school fellow; fellow student. *tongch'anghoe* 동창회 alumni [almunae] association.

tongch'imi 동치미 n. sliced turnips with garlic and scallion pickled in salt water.

tongdŭng 동등 n.C. equality; parity. *tongdŭnghada* 동등하다 (be) equal.

tonggam 동감 n.C. same opinion; sympathy. *tong-gamida* 동감이다 agree; be of the same opinion.

tonggi 동기 n.C. motive; incentive; motivation.

tonggi 동기 n.C. same class, same year in school. *tonggisaeng* 동기생 classmate; graduates of the same year.

tonggul 동굴 n.C. cavern; cave; grotto.

tonghwa 동화 n.C. fairy tale; nursery story [tale].

tongjak 동작 n.C. action; movement(s); manners.

tongji 동지 n.C. the winter solstice.

-tŏni -더니 recollection sequential v. ending. used when recalling past events. indicates that the action of the preceding v. was followed by the action of the following v.; likewise indicates the state with adj. ... and /but now (or then).

tŏnjida 던지다 v. throw; hurl; fling; cast.

tongjŏn 동전 n. (copper) coin.

tongjŏng 동정 n.C. sympathy; compassion. *tongjŏnghada* 동정하다 sympathize; have compassion (on).

+ **tongmaeng** 동맹 n.C. alliance; union; league. *tongmaenghada* 동맹하다 ally with; be allied [leagued] with; combine. *tongmaengguk* 동맹국 allied power. *tongmaeng p'aŏp* 동맹 파업 allied strike.

tongmu 동무 n. friend; companion; (in North Korea) comrade. *ŏkkaedongmu* 어깨동무 childhood friend, bossom buddy; putting arms around each other's shoulder.

tongmul 동물 n.C. animal; beast.

tongmurwŏn 동물원 n.C. zoological garden; zoo.

tongnan 동란 n.C. disturbance; upheaval; riot; war.

tongnip 독립 n.C. independence; self-reliance; self-support.

tongnip'ada 독립하다 v. become independent (of); stand alone. *tongnib-ŭi* 독립의 independent.

tongnyo 동료 n.C. associate; colleague; fellow; co-worker; companion. worker.

tongnyŏk 동력 n.C. (motive) power. *tongnyŏkssŏn* 동력선 power vessel. *tongnyŏk chawŏnbu*. 동력 자원 부 Ministry of Energy and Resource.

* **tŏngŏri** 덩어리 n. lump; mass; clod.

* **tongp'o** 동포 n.C. member of the same race/nation; one's fellow countryman.

tongsi 동시 n.C. the same time. *tongsi-ŭi* 동시의 simultaneous; concurrent. *tongsi-e* 동시에 at the

same time; simultaneously with.

* **tongtchok** 동쪽 n. east. *tongtchog-ŭi* 동쪽의 east; eastern; easterly. *tongtchog-ŭro* 동쪽으로 to [in, on] the east.

tongwŏn 동원 n.C. mobilization. *tongwŏnhada* 동원하다 mobilize. *tongwŏn haeje* 동원 해제 demobilization

* **tongyang** 동양 n.C. the Orient; the East, Asia. *tongyangin* 동양인 Asian, Oriental; Asians. cf. **sŏyang** 서양.

tongyo 동요 n.C. shake; quake; tremble. *tongyohada* 동요하다 shake; quake; stir; tremble.

tongyo 동요 n.C. children's song; nursery rhyme.

\# **toptta** 돕다 v. ① help; aid; assist ② relieve; give relief to ③ promote.

* **toraboda** 돌아보다 v. look back; turn one's head; turn round.

toradanida 돌아다니다 v. wander [roam] about; walk [go] around; make one's rounds.

\# **toragada** 돌아가다 v. go back; return; turn back.

\# **toriŏ** 도리어 adv. on the contrary; instead; rather; all the more.

* **toro** 도로 n.C. road; street; highway.

* **tŏrŏpta** 더럽다 adj. (be) unclean; dirty; filthy; foul; soiled.

toryŏn 돌연 adv. suddenly; on [all of] a sudden; all at once. *toryŏnhan* 돌연한 sudden; abrupt; unexpected; unlooked-for.

\# **tosi** 도시 n.C. cities; towns.

tosŏ 도서 n.C. books. *tosŏgwan* 도서관 library.

totpogi 돋보기 n. long-distance glasses; magnifying glass.

\# **tŏuk** 더욱 adv. more; more and more; still more.

towajuda 도와주다 v. help; assist [aid]; relieve; give relief to; support.

tŏwi 더위 n. heat; hot weather.

* **ttada** 따다 v. ① pick (flower, fruit); pluck; nip ②

open (can, bottle); cut out ③ get (prize, title);
take; obtain.

\# **ttae** 때 n. ① time; hour; moment ② case; occasion
③ chance; opportunity.

* **ttae** 때 n. dirt; filth; grime.

\# **ttaemun** 때문 n. because (of) *-ki ttaemune* -기 때문
에 on account of; because of; owing to.

* **ttaerida** 때리다 v. strike; bit; hit; slap.

ttaettaero 때때로 adv. occasionally; now and then;
at times; from time to time.

\+ **ttajida** 따지다 v. ① distinguish (between right and
wrong); demand an explanation for ② calculate.

\+ **ttak** 딱 adv. ① accurately; exactly; just ② firmly;
stiffly ③ flatly; positively.

\+ **ttak'ada** 딱하다 adj. ① (be) annoying; embarrassing
② (be) pitiable; pitiful; sorry; regrettable.

ttaktchi 딱지 n. ① stamp; sticker; label; tag ② picture card. *up'yottaktchi* 우표딱지 postage stamp.

ttakttak'ada 딱딱하다 adj. ① (be) hard; solid; stiff;
tough ② rigid, (be) stiff; formal (person) ③
bookish; formal (writing).

ttalgi 딸기 n. strawberry.

* **ttam** 땀 n. sweat; perspiration. *ttam-ŭl hŭllida* 땀을
흘리다 sweat; perspire.

* **ttan** 딴 pre-n. another; other; different. *ttande
[got]* 딴데〔곳〕 another place. *ttansaram* 딴사람
another person; someone else.

\# **ttang** 땅 n. ① earth; ground ② land; territory; soil.
〔p.72〕

ttanim 따님 n. (*honorific*) your [his] (esteemed)
daughter.

\# **ttarasŏ** 따라서 adv. ① accordingly; therefore ② in
accordance with; according to.

* **ttaro** 따로 adv. apart; separately; besides; in
addition; additionally.

* **ttarŭda** 따르다 v. ① accompany; follow; go along
with ② model (after) ③ obey; yield to.

ttattŭt´ada 따뜻하다 adj. ① (be) mild; warm; genial ② (be) kindly; cordial; warm (person).

ttawi 따위 n. ① and such like; such (a thing) like [as]··· ② and so on [forth]; and [or] the like.

* tte 떼 n. group; crowd; throng; herd; flock. *tte-rŭl chiŏsŏ* 떼를 지어서 in crowds [flocks].

tteda 떼다 v. ① take off[away]; remove [p.144] ② part; pull apart; pluck[tear] off ③ break[open] the seal; cut (a letter) open.

tti 띠 n. belt; sash; girdle; band.

tto 또 adv. ① again; once more; repeatedly ② too; also; as well ③ and; moreover.

* ttŏdŭlda 떠들다 v. make a noise; clamo(u)r; make a fuss [disturbance].

* ttŏk 떡 n. rice cake. [p.22,30,36,64] *ttŏkkuk* 떡국 rice-cake soup.

ttokttok´ada 똑똑하다 adj. ① (be) clever; sharp; bright ② (be) distinctive; vivid; plain.

* ttŏlda 떨다 v. shake; tremble; shiver; quake; shudder.

ttŏnada 떠나다 v. ① leave; start from; set out; depart ② quit; resign (from); part from [with].

+ ttong 똥 n. feces; stool; excrement; dung.

ttŏrŏjida 떨어지다 v. ① fall; drop; come down ② come [fall] off ③ go down; decline.

+ ttŏrŏttŭrida 떨어뜨리다 v. ① drop; throw down; let fall ② lose; miss.

ttŭda 뜨다 v. ① float (on the water, in the air) ② rise; come up.

* ttŭda 뜨다 v. open (one's eyes); wake up; awake. [p.31]

* ttŭgŏptta 뜨겁다 adj. (be) hot; heated; burning.

+ ttŭiuda 띄우다 v. fly; let fly; make fly. *yŏn-ŭl ttŭiuda* 연을 띄우다 fly a kite.

+ ttukkŏng 뚜껑 n. lid; cover; cap; shield; case. *ttukkŏng-ŭl yŏlda* 뚜껑을 열다 lift [take off] a lid; uncover. *ttukkŏng-ŭl tatta* 뚜껑을 닫다 put on the lid.

* **ttult´a** 뚫다 v. bore; punch; make [drill] a hole.

ttungttunghada 뚱뚱하다 adj. (be) fat [plump, overweight]. *ttungttungbo* 뚱뚱보 fatty [plump] person.

tturyŏt´ada 뚜렷하다 adj. (be) clear; vivid; evident; obvious.

ttŭt 뜻 n. ① intention ② meaning; sense. [p.45]

* **ttŭtta** 뜯다 v. ① take down; tear apart ② pluck; pick ③ play (zither, etc.); perform on ④ bite [gnaw] off ⑤ clamor for; importune.

ttwida 뛰다 v. ① run; dash ② jump; leap; skip. [p.8]

ttwiŏgada 뛰어가다 v. run; rush; dash; dart.

tuda 두다 v. put; place; lay; set.

* **tŭdiŏ** 드디어 adv. finally; at last; eventually; at length.

tudŭrida, ttudŭrida 두드리다, 뚜드리다 v. strike; beat; hit; knock.

* **tukkŏptta** 두껍다 adj. (be) thick; thick and heavy. *tukkŏpkke* 두껍게 thickly; heavily. *tukkŏun ch´aek* 두꺼운 책 thick book.

tul 둘 n. two. *tulssik* 둘씩 by [in] two´s.

* **tŭl** 들 n. field; plain; green.

-tŭl -들 suffix. ① plural marker. -s ② and others. etc.

tŭlda 들다 v. take [have, carry] in one´s hand; hold.

* **tulle** 둘레 n. circumference; girth. *tulle-e* 둘레에 round; around; about.

tŭllŭda 들르다 v. drop [look] in at; stop by [in] (*Am.*); visit; stop over.

tultchae 둘째 n. the second; number two (No. 2). *tultchae-ro* 둘째로 second(ly); in the second place.

+ **tŭmulda** 드물다 v. (be) rare; scarce; unusual; uncommon. *tŭmulge* 드물게 rarely; seldom.

* **tŭng** 등 n. ① back ①, [p.47] ② ridge.

tŭngdae 등대 n.C. lighthouse; beacon.

* **tunggŭlda** 둥글다 adj. (be) round; circular; globular.

tŭnggi 등기 n.C. registration; registry. *tŭnggi up'yŏn* 등기 우편 registered mail.

+ **tŭngnok** 등록 n.C. registration; entry. *tŭngnok'ada* 등록하다 register; enroll.

tŭngsan 등산 n.C. mountain climbing; mountaineering. *tŭngsanhada* 등산하다 climb a mountain.

-**tŭnji** -든지 ending. indicates that the following proposition is true, regardless of any possible state of affairs expressed by the preceding phrase. wh--(so)ever, no matter wh--, (regardless) whether ... or ....

tunoe 두뇌 n.C. head; brains. *chŏnja tunoe* 전자 두뇌 electronic brain.

* **tŭrida** 드리다 v. (*honorific*) give; offer up; present; dedicate.

tŭrŏgada 들어가다 v. ① enter; go (get, walk, step) in (into) ② join; enter.

* **turŭda** 두르다 v. enclose; encircle; surround.

* **tŭryŏdaboda** 들여다보다 v. ① peep (look, peek) into; see through (into) ② gaze (stare) (at); observe; watch.

tut'ong 두통 n.C. headache. *tut'ong-i nada* 두통이 나다 have a (bad, slight) headache.

tŭtta 듣다 v. ① hear; listen (to); lend an ear to ② obey; accede to ③ be good (effective) (for).

twaeji 돼지 n. pig; swine; hog. [p.43] *twaejigogi* 돼지고기 pork. *twaejigirŭm* 돼지기름 lard.

twi 뒤 n. back; rear; next; after; future; tail; reverse. *twi-e* 뒤에 ① behind; in back of ② afterwards; later.

twich'uk 뒤축 n. heel. *twich'ug-i nop'ŭn (najŭn)* 뒤축이 높은 (낮은) high(low)-heeled.

twidŏptta 뒤덮다 v. cover; overspread; veil; hang over; wrap; muffle.

twisŏktta 뒤섞다 v. mix up; mingle together.

twitchotta 뒤쫓다 v. follow; go after; pursue; chase.
twittŏrŏjida 뒤떨어지다 v. ① fall [drop] behind; be backward ② stay behind.

⪕ T′ ⪖

* **t'ada** 타다 v. burn; blaze.
# **t'ada** 타다 v. ride; take; take [have] a ride in; get in [on]; go [get] abroad; embark in [on].
t'ada 타다 v. play on (organ, etc.); perform on.
t'aedo 태도 n.C. attitude; manner; behavior; bearing.
t'aegŭkki 태극기 n.C. flag of Republic of Korea.
+ **t'aeŏnada** 태어나다 v. be born; come into the world.
t'aesaeng 태생 n.C. ① viviparity ② birth; origin; lineage. *oeguk t'aesaeng-ŭi* 외국 태생의 foreign-born.
+ **t'aeuda** 태우다 v. ① carry; let ride; take on board ② burn (something). [p.67]
* **t'aeyang** 태양 n.C. sun. *t'aeyang-ŭi* 태양의 solar. *t'aeyangnyŏl* 태양열 solar heat. *t'aeyangnyŏl chut'aek* 태양열 주택 solar house.
t'ain 타인 n.C. another person; stranger.
t'ajagi 타자기 n.C. typewriter. *yŏngmun t'ajagi* 영문 타자기 English character typewriter.
t'aktcha 탁자 n.C. table; desk.
t'akku 탁구 n.C. ping-pong; table tennis.
+ **t'al** 탈 n. mask. *t'ar-ŭl ssŭda* 탈을 쓰다 wear a mask.
t'alssŏn 탈선 n.C. ① derailment ② digression. *t'alssŏnhada* 탈선하다 (be) derailed; make a digression.
t'amgu 탐구 n.C. search; investigation. *t'amguhada* 탐구하다 search for; seek for.

t'amhŏm 탐험 n.C. exploration; expedition. *t'amhŏmhada* 탐험하다 explore.

t'amnaeda 탐내다 v.C. want; wish; covet; be greedy [hanker] for (money).

t'anap 탄압 n.C. oppression; suppression. *t'anap'ada* 탄압하다 suppress; oppress; bring pressure upon.

t'ansaeng 탄생 n.C. birth; nativity. *t'ansaenghada* 탄생하다 be born; come into the world.

t'ansik 탄식 n.C. sigh; lamentation. *t'ansik'ada* 탄식하다 (heave [draw] a) sigh; lament; deplore.

+ **t'anso** 탄소 n.C. carbon. *t'anso-ŭi* 탄소의 carbonic.

t'anyak 탄약 n.C. (a round of) ammunition. *t'anyakko* 탄약고 (powder) magazine.

+ **t'ap** 탑 n.C. tower; pagoda; steeple.

t'arak 타락 n.C. degradation; corruption. *t'arak'ada* 타락하다 be corrupted; degenerate. *t'arak'an* 타락한 corrupt; depraved.

t'arŭi 탈의 n.C. *t'arŭisil* 탈의실 dressing [changing] room. *t'arŭijang* 탈의장 bathing booth.

t'ŏ 터 n. site; place; ground; lot. *chipt'ŏ* 집터 building lot [site, land].

t'odae 토대 n.C. foundation; base; groundwork.

t'oegŭn 퇴근 n.C. leaving one's office. *t'oegŭnhada* 퇴근하다 leave one's office; go home from work.

t'oehak 퇴학 n.C. leaving school. *t'oehak'ada* 퇴학하다 leave [give up, quit] school (halfway).

t'oewŏn 퇴원 n.C. leaving the hospital. *t'oewŏnhada* 퇴원하다 leave (the) hospital.

t'oji 토지 n.C. land; soil; earth.

* **t'ŏjida** 터지다 v. explode; burst; erupt; blow up; break out; rip; tear; collapse; disclosed; be struck; split.

+ **t'ŏk** 턱 n. jaw; chin. *t'ŏkppyŏ* 턱뼈 jawbone. *araet'ŏk* 아래턱 lower jaw.

* **t'okki** 토끼 n. rabbit; hare. [p.133]

t'ŏl 털 n. (body) hair, fur. *t'ŏr-i manŭn* 털이 많은

hairy; haired.

+ **t'ŏlda** 털다 v. shake off; throw off; dust; brush up.

t'omak 토막 n. piece; bit; block. *t'omangnaeda* 토막내다 sever; cut in pieces.

t'omok 토목 n.C. engineering works. *t'omok kongsa* 토목 공사 public (engineering) works.

* **t'ong** 통 n.C. tub; barrel; pail; bucket. *mult'ong* 물통 water bucket. *sult'ong* 술통 wine-barrel.

t'ongdak 통닭 n.C. (abbr. of *t'ongdakkui*). ⟨*t'ongdakkui* 통닭구이⟩ roast chicken; chicken roasted whole.

t'onggŭn 통근 n.C. commuting. *t'onggŭnhada* 통근하다 attend office; commute. *t'onggŭn ppŏsŭ [yŏlch'a]* 통근 버스[열차] commuters' bus [train].

+ **t'onggwa** 통과 n.C. passage; passing. *t'onggwahada* 통과하다 pass; pass by [through].

t'onggwan 통관 n.C. customs clearance. *t'onggwanhada* 통관하다 pass (through) customs. *t'onggwan chŏlch'a* 통관 절차 customs formalities; clearance.

+ **t'onggye** 통계 n.C. statistics. *t'onggye(sang)-ŭi* 통계 (상)의 statistic(al).

t'onghada 통하다 v.C. ① run [lead] to ② be understood ③ be familiar (with). [p.16]

t'onghaeng 통행 n.C. passing; traffic. *t'onghaenghada* 통행하다 pass (by); go along. *t'onghaenggŭmji* 통행금지 no through traffic.

t'onghak 통학 n.C. attending school. *t'onghak'ada* 통학하다 attend [go to] school.

t'onghwa 통화 n.C. (telephone) call. *t'onghwajung* 통화중 The line is busy.

* **t'ongil** 통일 n.C. unity; unification. *t'ongilhada* 통일하다 unify. *nambuk t'ongil* 남북 통일 unification of North and South (Korea).

t'ongjang 통장 n.C. passbook. *yegŭm t'ongjang* 예금 통장 bankbook; deposit passbook.

t'ongjorim 통조림 n. canned goods. *t'ongjorimhan* 통 조림한 canned; tinned. *soegogi t'ongjorim* 쇠고기 통

조림 canned [tinned] beef.

t′ongno 통로 n.C. passage; passageway; way; path; aisle.

+ **t′ongsang** 통상 n.C. commerce; trade; commercial relations. *t′ongsanghada* 통상하다 v.C. trade with. *t′ongsang choyak* 통상 조약 commercial treaty.

+ **t′ongsin** 통신 n.C. correspondence; communication. *t′ongsinhada* 통신하다 correspond (with).

t′ongtchae(ro) 통째(로) adv. whole; wholly; bodily. *t′ongtchaero mŏkta* 통째로 먹다 eat (something) whole.

t′ongt′onghada 통통하다 adj. (be) plump; chubby.

t′oron 토론 n.C. discussion; debate. *t′oronhada* 토론하다 debate (on); discuss (with). *t′oronhoe* 토론회 forum; debate.

t′oŭi 토의 n.C. discussion; debate. *t′oŭihada* 토의하다 discuss; debate [deliberate] upon.

t′oyoil 토요일 n.C. Saturday.

* **t′ŭda** 트다 n. ① sprout; bud out ② be chapped.

t′uja 투자 n.C. investment. *t′ujahada* 투자하다 invest; put [sink] in; lay out.

t′ujaeng 투쟁 n.C. fight; strife; struggle. *t′ujaenghada* 투쟁하다 fight; struggle.

* **t′ŭktching** 특징 n.C. characteristic; special feature; unique point. *tŭktching innŭn* 특징 있는 characteristic; peculiar.

t′ŭkkŭp 특급 n.C. limitted [special] express. *tŭkkŭp yŏlch′a* 특급 열차 special express(train). *tŭkkŭp hot′el* 특급 호텔 five-starred hotel.

* **t′ŭkppyŏlhan** 특별한 adj. special; particular.

* **t′ŭkppyŏlhi** 특별히 particularly; especially.

+ **t′ŭkssaek** 특색 n.C.→ **t′ŭktching** 특징.

+ **t′ŭkssuhan** 특수한 adj. special; particular; specific; peculiar.

t′ŭl 틀 n. ① frame; framework ② mold.

* **t′ŭllida** 틀리다 v. go wrong [amiss]; be mistaken [erroneous]. *t′ŭllin* 틀린 mistaken; wrong; false.

t'ŭm 틈 n. crevice; crack; gap; opening. ①

* **t'ŭnt'ŭnhada** 튼튼하다 adj. ① (be) robust; sturdy; stout ② solid; firm; strong.

+ **t'up'yo** 투표 n.C. vote. *t'up'yohada* 투표하다 vote; ballot (for); give [cast] a vote [ballot].

t'wida 뛰다 v. ① spring; bound; hop; bounce ② run away; flee; sneak away.

t'wigim 튀김 n. (batter) fried food; deep fried dish; frying.

≤ U ≥

–ŭ– –으– euphonic vowel in between stem-final consonants and some endings which start with consonants. cf. -(ŭ)lkka, -(ŭ)m, -(ŭ)ni, -(ŭ)nikka, etc.

ua 우아 n.C. elegance. *uahan* 우아한 elegant; graceful.

uch'eguk 우체국 post office; *uch'et'ong* 우체통 post; mailbox (*Am.*).

uch'ŭk 우측 n.C. right side. *uch'ŭk t'onghaeng* 우측 통행 keep to the right.

udŭng 우등 n.C. top [superior] grade; excellency. *udŭng-ŭi* 우등의 excellent; superior. *udŭngsang* 우 등상 honor prize.

ugida 우기다 v. demand one's own way; force; persist in; assert; stick to; be obstinate.

–ŭi particle. possessive or genitive marker for modification or subordination. indicates that the entity referred to by the following n. belongs to, was made or done by, etc. usually pronounced -*e* in Seoul. …'s, of.

* **ŭibok** 의복 n.C. clothes; garments; clothing.

ŭido 의도 n.C. intention; design; aim. *ŭidohada* 의도
하다 intend (to do); aim at.

* **ŭigyŏn** 의견 n.C. opinion; view; idea. *ŭigyŏn-ŭi
taerip [ch'ungdol]* 의견의 대립 [충돌] disagree
[opposition, conflict, split, clash] of opinion.

+ **ŭihoe** 의회 n.C. Parliament (*Eng.*); Congress (*Am.*);
Diet (*Jap. ·Swed.*). → **kuk'oe** 국회 National
Assembly (*Korea*).

+ **ŭija** 의자 n.C. chair. *kin ŭija* 긴의자 sofa; couch.

+ **ŭijang** 의장 n.C. chairman; speaker.

ŭiji 의지 n.C. will; volition.

ŭiji 의지 n.C. leaning; trust; reliance. *ŭijihada* 의지
하다 lean on; depend [rely] on [upon].

ŭikkwa 의과 n.C. medical department. *ŭikkwa-
daehak* 의과 대학 medical college.

ŭimi 의미 n.C. meaning; sense; significance.

* **ŭimihada** 의미하다 mean; imply; signify.

* **ŭimu** 의무 n.C. duty; obligation. *ŭimujŏk* 의무적 obli-
gatory; compulsory.

ŭimun 의문 n.C.question; doubt. *ŭimun-ŭi* 의문의
doubtful; questionable.

ŭinon 의논 n.C. consultation; conference. *ŭinonhada*
의논하다 consult (with); counsel (with).

+ **ŭioe** 의외 n.C. *ŭioe-ŭi* 의외의 unexpected; unforeseen.
ŭioe-ro 의외로 unexpectedly.

ŭiryo 의료 n.C. medical treatment. *ŭiryo pohŏm* 의료
보험 medical (care) insurance. *ŭiryobi* 의료비
medical expenses [fee].

* **ŭisa** 의사 n.C. doctor; physician; surgeon. *ŭisa
chindansŏ* 의사 진단서 medical certificate.

ŭisa 의사 n.C. intention; mind; purpose.

ŭisang 의상 n.C. clothes; dresses; garments; cos-
tume.

+ **ŭisik** 의식 n.C. consciousness; senses. *ŭisik'ada* 의식
하다 be conscious [aware] of.

+ **ŭisim** 의심 n.C. doubt; question. *ŭisimhada* 의심하다
doubt; suspect. *ŭisim- sŭrŏptta* 의심스럽다 be

doubtful of; be suspected of.

ŭiwŏn 의원 n.C. member of an assembly; assemblyman; Congressman; Senator (Am.); Member of Parliament (M.P.).

ŭiyok 의욕 n.C. volition; will; desire. *ŭiyoktchŏgin* 의욕적인 ambitious; aspiring.

ujŏng 우정 n.C. friendship; fellowship. *ujŏng-i innŭn* 우정이 있는 amicable; friendly.

uju 우주 n.C. universe; cosmos. *uju-ŭi* 우주의 universal; cosmic. *uju yŏhaeng* 우주 여행 (outer) space travel [flight].

-ŭl/rŭl -을/를 -ŭl particle. **-ŭl** occurs after consonants; **-rŭl** or abbreviated form **-l** after vowels. ① marks the direct object of a transitive v. *pab-ŭl mŏktta* 밥을 먹다 eat rice/a meal ② marks the direct object of a passive-transitive v., indicating 'suffer- ing' or 'undergoing' an action. *ttang-ŭl ppaekkida* 땅을 뺏기다 have one's land taken away ③ marks certain direct objects ending in -*m* -ㅁ that are cognate with the (usually intransitive) v. used in the expression. *kkum-ŭl kkuda* 꿈을 꾸다 dream (a dream) ④ marks the location of a verb of movement, with or without particle -*e* -에 preceding. *hakkyo-(e) rŭl kada* 학교(에)를 가다 go to school ⑤ emphasizes a negative expression when inserted between -*chi* -지 and the negative auxiliary. *oji-rŭl ant'a* 오지를 않다 just won't come.

ulda 울다 v. cry; weep. [p.92,102]

-(ŭ)lkka -(으)ㄹ까 ending (after v. and adj.) ① will it be? will it (do)? ② do you suppose ...? cf. *ilkka*.

-(ŭ)ltchirado -(으)ㄹ지라도 ending (after v. and adj.) even though; regardless of. cf. *-iltchirado*.

-(ŭ)m -(으)ㅁ nominalizing ending which changes a v./adj. into a n. *ch'uda → ch'um* 춤 dance. *chada → cham* 잠 sleep(ing); *noptta → nop'ŭm* 높음

highness.

\# **ŭmak** 음악 n.C. music. *ŭmaktchŏk* 음악적 musical, melodious. *ŭmakka* 음악가 musician.

ŭmhyang 음향 n.C. sound; noise. *ŭmhyang hyokkwa* 음향 효과 sound effect.

\# **umjigida** 움직이다 v. ① move; stir; shift ② work; operate; run ③ be moved [touched, affected].

ŭmjŏl 음절 n.C. syllable. *taŭmjŏrŏ* 다음절어 polysyllable.

ŭmnyo 음료 n.C. beverage; drink. *ŭmnyosu* 음료수 drinking water.

ŭmnyŏk 음력 n.C. lunar calendar.

\# **ŭmsik** 음식 n.C. food; foodstuff; diet. *ŭmsingmul* 음식물 food-stuff.

+ **ŭmsŏng** 음성 n.C. voice. *ŭmsŏnghak* 음성학 phonetics. → **mokssori** 목소리.

* **umul** 우물 n. well. [p.103] *umulmul* 우물물 well-water.

\# **-(ŭ)myŏn** -(으)면 conditional ending for v. or adj. **-ŭ-** occurs after stems that end on a non-*l* consonant. if, when, whenever. other shapes: **-(ŭ)myŏn**, **-(i)myŏn**.

un 운 n.C. fortune; luck. *un-i chok´e* 운이 좋게 fortunately; luckily; by good luck. *un-i nappŭge* 운이 나쁘게 unluckily; unfortunately; by ill luck.

* **ŭn** 은 n.C. silver. *ŭn-gŭrŭt* 은그릇 silverware.

\# **-ŭn/nŭn** -은/는 topic particle. **-ŭn** -은 occurs after consonants, **-nŭn** -는 after vowels. ① marks the topic, reducing the emphasis on the preceding word(s) in order to highlight the rest of the sentence because the sentence is long (or the item has already been mentioned, etc.) *tar-ŭn han hae-e yŏlttu pŏn tonda* 달은 한 해에 열두 번 돈다 The moom rotates twelve times a year. ② marks two contrasting items *na-nŭn hakssaengijiman, kŭ pŭn-ŭn kyosunimisida* 나는 학생이지만 그분은 교수님이시다 I am a student but he is a professor. ③ marks exclusion *kŭ saram* *(man)ŭn an minnŭnda* 그 사람(만)은 안 믿는다 (Only) he does not believe it. *or* I do not believe him (but others).

    cf. -i/ga.

-(ŭ)n -(으)ㄴ modifier ending. indicates that the following noun (phrase) is characterized by the preceding v. or adj. ① (present tense with adj., copular) ...that (which) is, ...who is ② (past tense with v.) ...that (who) has done, ...that (one) did.

unban 운반 n.C. conveyance; transportation. *unbanhada* 운반하다 carry; convey; transport.

-(ŭ)nji -은지 ending ① adj. stem with -(ŭ)nji followed by verbs of knowing, telling, asking. if/whether it is ② (period of time) since, from the time when (*with verb + time word + ida or toeda*). other shape: -(i)nji, -(nŭ)nji.

undong 운동 n.C. ① motion; (political or physical) movement ② sports; exercise. *undonghada* 운동하다 take exercise; move. *undonghoe* 운동회 athletic meet. *undong kyŏnggi* 운동 경기 athletic event.

+ **undongjang** 운동장 n.C. playground.

undonghwa 운동화 n.C. sports shoes; sneakers (*Am.*).

-(ŭ)n´ga -(으)ㄴ가 ending (after v. and adj.) does or is it/he, etc.? (plain style question marker). cf. -in´ga.

ŭnggŭp 응급 n.C. emergency. *ŭnggŭp ch´iryŏ* 응급 치료 first aid; first-aid treatment. *ŭnggŭpssil* 응급실 emergency room.

ŭngyong 응용 n.C. (practical) application. *ŭngyonghada* 응용하다 apply. *ŭngyong munje* 응용 문제 applied question.

+ **unha** 운하 n.C. canal.

ŭnhaeng 은행 n.C. bank. *ŭnhaengkkwŏn* 은행권 bank bill [note]. *ŭnhaengju* 은행주 bank stock.

+ **ŭnhye** 은혜 n.C. favor; benefit; grace.

-(ŭ)ni -(으)니 ending(sentence final question marker used after v. and adj. when speaking to small children or close friends) does or is it/he, etc.? *ap'ŭni?* 아프니 are you sick? cf. *-ini.*

-(ŭ)ni(kka) -(으)니(까) ending (sequential ending after v. and adj.) because/since it does or is. cf. *-inikka.*

unjŏn 운전 n.C. driving. *unjŏn myŏnhŏtchŭng* 운전면 허증 drivers license. *unjŏnhada* 운전하다 drive; operate.

unjŏn(ki)sa 운전(기)사 n.C. driver; chauffeur.

* **unmyŏng** 운명 n.C. fate; destiny; fortune; one's lot.

unyŏng 운영 n.C. operation; management. *unyŏng-hada* 운영하다 manage; run; operate.

up'yo 우표 n.C. postage-stamp; stamp.

up'yŏn 우편 n.C. post (*Eng.*); mail (*Am.*). *up'yŏn paedalbu* 우편 배달부 mail carrier. *up'yŏn yogŭm* 우편요금 postage. *up'yŏn ham* 우편함 a letter box.

-(ŭ)ra -(으)라 ending (sentence final ending in attentive command used after v.) Do!. cf. *-ira.*

-(ŭ)ranŭn -(으)라는 ending (quotative modifier after v.) to do. *kisa-rŭl ssŭranŭn put'ag-ŭl padatta* 기사를 쓰라는 부탁을 받았다 I received a request to write an article. cf. *-iranŭn.*

uri 우리 pron. we. *uri-ŭi* 우리의 our. *uri-ege* 우리에게 us. *uri-rŭl* 우리를 us. *uri nara* 우리나라 our country.

-(ŭ)ro -(으)로 particle. to; with; by.

urŭm 울음 n. crying; weeping. *urŭm-ŭl t'ŏttŭrida* 울음을 터뜨리다 burst out crying.

uryŏ 우려 n.C. worry; anxiety; fear. *uryŏhada* 우려하다 worry over; be anxious about.

usan 우산 n.C. umbrella. *usan-ŭl ssŭda* 우산을 쓰다 put up [raise] an umbrella.

use 우세 n.C. superiority; predominance. *usehada* 우세하다 (be) superior [in a strong position].

usŏn 우선 adv.C. first (of all); in the first place.

+ **usuhan** 우수한 adj.C. good; excellent; superior.

usŭm 웃음 n. laugh; laughter; smile; ridicule.
usŭng 우승 n.C. victory; championship. *usŭnghada* 우승하다 win the championship.
usŭptta 우습다 v. (be) funny; amusing; laughable.
utta 웃다 v. ① laugh; smile; chuckle; grim ② laugh [sneer] at; ridicule; jeer at. [p.104]
uurhan 우울한 adj.C. melancholy; gloomy.
uyŏn 우연 n.C. chance; accident. *uyŏnhan* 우연한 casual; accidental; unexpected. *uyŏnhi* 우연히 accidentally; by chance [accident]; incidental.
* **uyu** 우유 n.C. (cow's) milk. *punmal uyu* 분말 우유 milk powder.

$$\leqslant W \geqslant$$

-wa -와 -wa occurs after vowels. and. cf. -kwa
wae 왜 adv. why; how; for what reason.
wang 왕 n.C. king; monarch. *wang-ŭi* 왕의 royal.
wangbi 왕비 n.C. wife of male monarch. cf. yŏwang 여왕 queen.
wangbok 왕복 n.C. going and returning; round trip. *wangbok'ada* 왕복하다 go and return. *wangbok ch'ap'yo* 왕복 차표 return ticket, round-trip ticket.
wangbi 왕비 n.C. queen; empress.
wanggung 왕궁 n.C. king's [royal] palace.
wangja 왕자 n.C. (Royal, Imperial) prince.
* **wanjŏn** 완전 n.C. perfection; completeness, *wanjŏnhada* 완전하다 *wanjŏnhan* [hi] 완전한(히) perfect[ly]; complete[ly].
+ **wansŏng** 완성 n.C. completion; perfection; accomplishment. *wansŏng- hada* 완성하다 complete; accomplish; finish. *wansŏngdweda* 완성되다 be completed.

wennil 웬일 n. what matter; what business. wennirinya 웬일이냐? what is up [the matter]?

we 위 n. upside; upper part. wi-ŭi 위의 upper; upward. wi-e 위에 above; over; on; upon; up.

wiban 위반 n.C. violation. wibanhada 위반하다 violate; disobey; break; be against.

wich'i 위치 n.C. situation; location; position; place; site. wich'ihada 위치하다 be situated [located].

* widae 위대 n.C. greatness; mightiness. widaehan 위대한 great; mighty; grand.

+ wigi 위기 n.C. crisis; critical moment.

wihada 위하다 v. do for the sake of; respect; value. wihayŏ 위하여 for; for the sake of.

+ wihŏm 위험 n.C. danger; peril; risk. wihŏmhan 위험한 dangerous; perilous.

wihyŏp 위협 n.C. menace; threat; intimidation wihyŏp'ada 위협하다 menace; threaten; frighten.

wiim 위임 n.C. trust; commission; charge. wiimhada 위임하다 entrust; delegate to.

wimun 위문 n.C. consolation; consolatory visit. wimunhada 위문하다 console.

wiro 위로 n.C. consolation; solace; comfort. wirohada 위로하다 console; comfort.

wisaeng 위생 n.C. hygiene; sanitation. wisaengjŏk 위생적 sanitary; hygienic.

wisŏng 위성 n.C. satellite. wisŏngdosi 위성도시 satellite city. wisŏng chungge 위성 중계 satellite telecast.

* wiwŏn 위원 n.C. member for a committee. wiwŏnhoe 위원회 committee; commission.

wŏlgan 월간 n.C. monthly publication. wŏlgan-ŭi 월간의 monthly. wŏlgan chaptchi 월간 잡지 monthly magazine.

wŏlgŭp 월급 n.C. monthly salary [pay].

* wŏlli 원리 n.C. principle; fundamental principles (of life).

* wŏllyŏ 원료 n.C. raw material; materials.

wŏlmal 월말 n.C. end of the month.

wŏlse 월세 n.C. mŏnthly rent.

+ **wŏn** 원 n.C. desire; wish. *wŏnhada* 원하다 desire; wish.

* **wŏnch´ik** 원칙 n.C. principle; general rule.

wŏn´go 원고 n.C. manuscript (MS.); copy; draft. *wŏn´goryo* 원고료 renumeration for writing.

wŏnin 원인 n.C. cause; origin. *wŏnin-gwa kyŏlgwa* 원인과 결과 cause and effect.

* **wŏnja** 원자 n.C. atom. *wonjaryŏk* 원자력 atomic energy. *wŏnja p´okt´an* 원지폭탄 atom(ic) bomb; A-bomb.

wŏnjo 원조 n.C. help; support; assistance; aid. *wŏnjohada* 원조하다 assist; help; support.

wŏnmang 원망 n.C. grudge; resentment. *wŏnmang-hada* 원망하다 reproach; bear a grudge against.

wŏnsi 원시 n.C. genesis. *wŏnsiin* 원시인 primitive human. *wŏnsijŏgin* 원시적인 primitive. *wŏnsi sidae* 원시 시대 primitive times.

* **wŏnsu** 원수 n.C. general of the army; fleet admiral (*Am.*); (field) marshal; admiral of fleet (*Eng.*)

* **wŏnsu** 원수 n.C. enemy.

wŏnsungi 원숭이 n.C. monkey; ape.

wŏryoil 월요일 n.C. Monday.

$$\leq Y \geq$$

ya interj. 야 Oh, dear!; O my!; Hey (you)!; Hi; Hello.

yach´ae 야채 n.C. vegetables; greens. *yach´ae kage* 야채 가게 green grocery.

yagan 야간 n.C. night; night time. *yagan-ŭi* 야간의 night; nocturnal. *yagan-e* 야간에 at night.

\# **yak** 약 n.C. medicine; drug; remedy. [p.51, 73, 78, 112] *yakppang* 약방 drugstore (*Am.*); chemist (*Eng.*); pharmacy.

yak 약 pre-n.C. about; some; nearly; around (*Am.*).

yak´ada 약하다 adj.C. (be) weak; frail; delicate; faint. *yak´age* 약하게 weakly; feebly; faintly.

* **yakkan** 약간 n.C. some; little; bit; few; somewhat.

yakkuk 약국 n.C. pharmacy; drugstore (*Am.*); chemist(*Eng.*).

yakppang 약방 n.C. yakkuk 약국.

\+ **yakssok** 약속 n.C. promise; engagement. *yakssok´ada* 약속하다 promise. *yakssog-ŭl chik´ida* 약속을 지키다 keep one's promise.

yaktto 약도 n.C. rough sketch; sketch map.

yamjŏnhada 얌전하나 adj. (be) gentle; wellbehaved; modest. *yamjŏnhi* 얌전히 gently; modestly.

* **yang** 양 n.C. sheep; lamb.

\# **yang** 양 n.C. a pair; both; two.

\# **yang** 양 n.C. quantity; capacity.

* **-yang** -양 suffix.C. Miss. *Kim yang* 김양 Miss Kim.

* **yangban** 양반 n.C. nobility; nobleman. *chuin yangban* 주인 양반 master (of a the house).

yangbo 양보 n.C. concession; compromise. *yangbohada* 양보하다 concede (to); make a concession.

\+ **yangbok** 양복 n.C. Western [European] clothes, (two-piece) suit. *yangbok-tchŏm* 양복점 tailor; tailor's (shop).

\# **yangbun** 양분 n.C. nourishment; nutriment.

yanghae 양해 n.C. understanding; comprehension. *yanghaehada* 양해하다 understand; comprehend.

yangmal 양말 n.C. socks; stockings.

yangnyŏm 양념 n. spices; flavo(u)r; seasoning; condiment.

yangnyŏk 양력 Western (solar) calendar.

yangp'um 양품 foreign articles [goods]. *yangp'um-jŏm* 양품점 fancy(-goods) store.

yangsik 양식 Western food; foreign dishes; foreign

cookery. *yangsiktchip* 양식집 foreign-style [Western] restaurant.

yangsik 양식 provisions; food. *yangsig-ŭl taeda* 양식을 대다 provide (a person) with food.

+ **yangsim** 양심 n.C. conscience. *yangsim-ŭi kach'aek* 양심의 가책 pangs [pricks] of conscience.

yangsŏ 양서 n.C. foreign [Western] book.

yangtchok 양쪽 n.C. both sides; either side. *yangtchog-ŭi* 양쪽의 both; either.

yaoe 야외 n.C. field; open air. *yaoe-ŭi* 야외의 outdoor; open air. *yaoe-esŏ* 야외에서 in the open air.

yasim 야심 n.C. ambition; designs; treason; treachery. *yasimjtchŏk* 야심적 ambitious.

+ **yatta** 얕다 adj. (be) shallow. *yat'ŭn kaeul [kŭrŭt, mot]* 얕은 개울 [그릇, 못] shallow stream [dish, pond].

yayŏng 야영 n.C. camp; camping. *yayŏnghada* 야영하다 camp (out); encamp.

ye 예 n.C. instance; example; practice; custom; precedent.

ye 예 interj. yes; certainly.

+ **yebang** 예방 n.C. prevention; protection. *yebanghada* 예방하다 prevent. *yebang chusa* 예방주사 vaccine, (lit.) preventive injection.

yegam 예감 n.C. premonition; presentiment. *yegami tŭlda* 예감이 들다 have a presentiment (of).

yegŭm 예금 n.C. deposit; bank account. *yegŭmhada* 예금하다 deposit money.

+ **yejŏng** 예정 n.C. plan; program; schedule. *yejŏngdaero* 예정대로 according to program.

yemae 예매 n.C. advance sale. *yemaehada* 예매하다 buy/sell (ticket) in advance.

yennal 옛날 n. ancient/previous times; old days. *yennare* 옛날에 once upon a time.

+ **yeppŭda** 예쁘다 adj. (be) pretty; lovely; shapely; nice.

yesan 예산 n.C. estimate; budget.

yesang 예상 n.C. expectation; forecast; anticipation. *yesanghada* 예상하다 expect; foresee. *yesang oero* 예상 외로 beyond all expectations.

* **yesul** 예술 n.C. art; fine arts. *yesulga* 예술가 artist.

yesŭp 예습 n.C. preparation for lessons. *yesŭphada* 예습하다 prepare for lessons.

yey 옛 pre-n. old.

yeyak 예약 n.C. booking; reservation. *yeyak´ada* 예약하다 reserve; subscribe.

yo 요 n. mattress; baddings.

-yŏ -여 infinitive ending of v. or adj. immediately following stems and used in combination with other endings. the irregular conjugational ending of **hada** 하다, which has **hayŏ** 하여 (abbr. 해) as its infinitive. other shapes: **-a** -아, **-ŏ** -어. non-final tenseless.

yŏbo 여보 interj. my darling (between an old couple). *yŏboseyo* 여보세요 hello; (telephone); hey (there).

yotchŏm 요점 n.C. point; essential [main] point.

yoch´ŏng 요청 n.C. demand; request. *yoch´ŏnghada* 요청하다 request; claim; demand.

yŏdang 여당 n.C. government [ruling] party.

yŏdongsaeng 여동생 n.C. younger sister.

yŏga 여가 n.C. leisure; spare time; off hours. *yŏga-e* 여가에 at one's leisure.

* **yŏgan** 여간 n.C. (adverbial use, with negative) *yŏgan anida* 여간 아니다 (be) uncommon; unusual; remarkable.

yŏgi 여기 pron. this place; here; *yŏgi-e[esŏ]* 여기에 [에서] here; at [in] this place. *yŏgi-sŏbut´ŏ* 여기서부터 from here. *yŏgi-ro* 여기로 to this place.

yŏgijŏgi 여기저기 pron. here and there; from place to place; up and down; back and forth.

* **yogu** 요구 n.C. demand; claim; request. *yoguhada* 요구하다 demand; request.

yogŭm 요금 n.C. charge; fee; fare; *chŏn´gi[sudo] yogŭm* 전기[수도] 요금 power [water] rates.

* **yŏgwan** 여관 n.C. inn. *yŏgwan-e muktta* 여관에 묵다 stay [put up] at an inn. *yŏgwan chuin* 여관 주인 hotel keeper; landlady.

+ **yŏhaeng** 여행 n.C. travel; travelling; journey; tour. *yŏhaenggada* 여행가다 travel; make a trip to.

yŏhakkyo 여학교 n.C. girls school.

yŏhakssaeng 여학생 n.C. girl student; schoolgirl.

yŏil 요일 n.C. day of the week; weekday.

* **yŏin** 여인 n.C. woman. *pamkkŏri-ŭi yŏin* 밤거리의 여인 streetwalker; woman of the street.

yŏja 여자 n.C. woman; girl; female. *yŏja-ŭi* 여자의 female; feminine.

yŏjŏmwŏn 여점원 n.C. saleswoman; shop girl.

yŏjuin-gong 여주인공 n.C. heroine.

yok 욕 n.C. abuse; slander. *yog-ŭl hada* 욕을 하다 call names; speak ill of.

* **yŏk** 역 n.C. (railroad; railway) station.

+ **yŏk'al** 역할 n.C. part; role.

yokkŏn 요건 n.C. necessary [indispensable] condition; essential factor; important matter.

yŏkssa 역사 n.C. history. *yŏkssasang-ŭi* 역사상의 historical. *yŏkssajŏgin* 역사적인 historical.

yŏkssi 역시 adv. ① too; also; not either ② still; all[just] the same ③ after all.

yokssil 욕실 n.C. bathroom.

+ **yokssim** 욕심 n.C. greed; avarice. *yokssim(-i) manŭn* 욕심(이) 많은 greedy; avaricious.

yŏkkwŏn 여권 n.C. passport; *yŏkkwŏn-ŭl sinch'ŏng [palbu]hada* 여권을 신청[발부]하다 apply for [issue, take out] a passport.

yŏl 열 n. ten. *yŏlppŏntchae* 열번째 the tenth.

yŏl 열 n.C. heat; temperature; fever.

yŏl 열 n.C. line; row; rank; column; queue. *yŏr-ŭl chitta* 열을 짓다 form a line [queue]; line up.

yŏlch'a 열차 n.C. train. *yŏlch'a sago* 열차 사고 train [railroad] accident. kich'a 기차.

yŏlda 열다 v. ① open; uncover; unlock ② hold (a

party, etc.); give.
yŏlda 열다 v. bear (fruit); grow.
  yŏlgi 열기 n.C. heat; hot air.
  yŏlgwang 열광 n.C. (wild) excitement; frenzy; craze. *yŏlgwanghada* 열광하다 be [grow] wildly excited.
+ **yŏllak** 연락 n.C. connection; liaison; communication; correspondence. *yŏllak'ada* 연락하다 connect; contact, liaise. *yŏllakssŏn* 연락선 ferryboat.
* **yŏllida** 열리다 v. ① open; be opend; be unlocked ② be held; take place.
+ **yŏllyo** 연료 n.C. fuel. *yŏllyobi* 연료비 cost of fuel.
+ **yŏllyŏlhan[hi]** 열렬한[히] adj.[adv.] ardent[ly]; fervent[ly].
  yŏllyŏng 연령 n.C. age; years. *p'yŏnggyun yŏllyŏng* 평균 연령 average age.
* **yŏlmae** 열매 n. fruit; nut; seed.
  yŏlssim 열심 n.C. eagerness; enthusiasm. *yŏlssimin* 열심인 eager; earnest; enthusiastic. *yŏlssimhi* 열심히 eagerly, enthusiastically.
  yŏlssoe 열쇠 n. key. *yŏlssoe-rŭl ch'aeuda* 열쇠를 채우다 lock; turn a key on.
  yŏlssŏng 열성 n.C. ardo(u)r; zeal; devotion. *yŏlssŏngjŏgin* 열성적인 warm; earnest.
  yŏltta 엷다 adj. (be) thin. *yŏlkke* 엷게 thinly.
+ **yŏlttae** 열대 n.C. the tropics, Torrid Zone. *yŏlttae-ŭi* 열대의 tropical. *yŏlttae singmul* 열대식물 tropical plants [flora].
* **yŏmnyŏ** 염려 n.C. anxiety; worry; care. *yŏmnyŏhada* 염려하다 be [feel] anxious about; worry.
  yŏmsaek 염색 n.C. dyeing. *yŏmsaek'ada* 염색하다 dye.
  yŏmso 염소 n. goat.
+ **yŏnae** 연애 n.C.love. *yŏnaehada* 연애하다 be [fall] in love with; lose one's heart to.
* **yŏnan** 연안 n.C. coast; shore. *yŏnan-e* 연안에 on [along] the coast. *yŏnan-ŭi* 연안의 coastal.

yŏnbong 연봉 n.C. annual [yearly] salary.

yŏnch'ul 연출 n.C. (dramatic) production. *yŏnch'urhada* 연출하다 produce; perform; represent.

yŏndae 연대 n.C. age; epoch; era. *yŏndaep'yo* 연대표 chronological table.

yŏng 영 n.C. zero; nill. *ilttae yŏng-ŭro* 1대 0으로 by score of one to zero.

yongdo 용도 n.C. use; service. *yongdoga mant'a* 용도가 많다 have various [many] uses.

\# **yŏnggam** 영감 n.C. inspiration; brain wave.

* **yonggi** 용기 n.C. courage; bravery. *yonggi innŭn* 용기 있는 courageous; brave.

yŏngguk 영국 n.C. England; (Great) Britain; United Kingdom. *yŏnggug-ŭi* 영국의 English; British. *yŏnggugin* 영국인 Englishman; the English.

yŏnggwang 영광 n.C. hono(u)r; glory. *yŏnggwangsŭrŏun* 영광스러운 glorious; honorable.

yŏngha 영하 n.C. below zero; sub-zero. cf. *yŏngsang* 영상.

\+ **yŏnghon** 영혼 n.C. soul; spirit.

* **yŏnghwa** 영화 n.C. movie; (motion) picture; film. *yŏnghwa paeu* 영화 배우 movie actor[actress]. yŏnghwagwan 영화관 movie theatre; cinema.

\# **yŏnghyang** 영향 n.C. influence; effect. *yŏnghyang-ŭl mich'ida* 영향을 미치다 influence; affect.

* **yŏn'gi** 연기 n.C. smoke. *yŏn'gi-ga nanŭn* 연기가 나는 smoky; smoking.

yŏn'gi 연기 n.C. postponement; deferment. *yŏn'gihada* 연기하다 postpone; put off; adjourn; suspend.

yongji 용지 n.C. paper (to use); (bland) form; printed form.

yŏngju 영주 n.C. permanent residence. *yŏngjuhada* 영주하다 reside permanently; settle down.

yongmo 용모 n.C. face; looks; features.

yongmu 용무 n.C. business; matter of business.

yŏngnihan 영리한 adj.C. wise; clever; smart; bright.

yongnyang 용량 n.C. capacity; volume.

yongŏ 용어 n.C. term; terminology. *chŏnmun yongŏ* 전문 용어 technical terms.

yŏngŏ 영어 n.C. English; English language. *yŏngŏ-ŭi* 영어의 English. *yŏngŏ-ro* 영어로 in English.

+ **yŏngŏp** 영업 n.C. business; trade. *yŏngŏp'ada* 영업하다 do [carry on] business.

yongpŏp 용법 n.C. way to use; usage; direction for use.

yongsa 용사 n.C. brave man; warrior; hero.

+ **yongsŏ** 용서 n.C. pardon; forgiveness. *yongsŏhada* 용서하다 pardon; forgive; excuse.

yŏngsujŭng 영수증 n.C. receipt.

yŏngtchang 영장 n.C. warrant; writ. *kusok yŏngchang* 구속 영장 warrant of arrest.

* **yŏngt'o** 영토 n.C. territory; domain.

yŏn'gu 연구 n.C. research; study. *yŏn'guhada* 연구하다 conduct research, make a study of.

yŏn'gŭk 연극 n.C. play; drama. *yŏn'gŭg-ŭl hada* 연극을 하다 play; act (a play).

yŏn'gŭm 연금 n.C. annuity; pension.

yŏngung 영웅 n.C. hero. *yŏngungjŏgin* 영웅적인 heroic.

+ **yŏngwŏn** 영원 n.C. eternity; permanence. *yŏngwŏnhan[hi]* 영원한[히] eternal[ly].

* **yŏngyang** 영양 n.C. nourishment; nutrition.

yŏn'gyŏl 연결 n.C. connection. *yŏn'gyŏlhada* 연결하다 connect; attach; join.

+ **yŏnhada** 연하다 v.C. ① (be) tender (*meat*); soft ② (be) light (*color*). *yŏnhan pitkkal* 연한 빛깔 light color.

+ **yŏnhap** 연합 n.C. combination; incorporation; alliance. *yŏnhap'hada* 연합하다 combine; join; union.

yŏnjang 연장 n. tool; inplement; utensil.

yŏnjang 연장 n.C. extension. *yŏnjanghada* 연장하다 extend; lengthen; prolong; continue.

yŏnju 연주 n.C. musical performance. *yŏnjuhada* 연주하다 perform; play. *yŏnjuhoe* 연주회 concert.

yŏnmaeng 연맹 n.C. league; federation; union.

yŏnmal 연말 n.C. end of the year; year-end. cf. *chumal* 주말 weekend, *wŏlmal* 월말 end of the month.

yŏnp'il 연필 n.C. (lead) pencil. *yŏnp'ilkkakki* 연필깎이 pencil sharpener.

yŏnsok 연속 n.C. continuity; continuation. *yŏnsok'ada* 연속하다 continue; last.

yŏnsŏl 연설 n.C. (public) speech; address. *yŏnsŏlhada* 연설하다 make a speech.

+ **yŏnsŭp** 연습 n.C. practice; exercise; training. *yŏnsŭp'ada* 연습하다 practice; exercise.

yŏnt'an 연탄 n.C. (coal) briquet. *yŏnt'an kkasŭ chungdok* 연탄 가스 중독 briquet gas poisoning.

yŏp 옆 n. side; flank. *yŏp'-ŭi* 옆의 side; next; adjoining. *yŏp'-esŏ* 옆에서 by the side (of); by. *yŏp'-ŭro* 옆으로 on [to] one side; aside, sideways.

yŏptchip 옆집 n. next door [house]; neighbo(u)ring house. *yŏptchip saram* 옆집 사람 neighbo(u)r.

yŏpssŏ 엽서 n.C. postcard; postal card.

+ **yori** 요리 n.C. ① cooking; cookery ② dish; food; fare. *yorisa* 요리사 cook. *yoritchip* 요리집 restaurant.

yŏrŏ 여러 pre-n. many; several; various.

yŏrŏgaji 여러 가지 n. various; all kinds of; several.

* **yŏron** 여론 n.C. public [general] opinion. *yŏron chosa* 여론 조사 public opinion poll [survey].

yŏrŭm 여름 n. summer; summertime.

yŏsa 여사 n.C. Lady; Madame; Mrs; Miss. *Kim yŏsa* 김여사 Mrs. [Miss] Kim; Madame Kim.

* **yosae** 요새 n. recently; lately; these days.

* **yoso** 요소 n.C. element; factor; essential part.

yŏsŏng 여성 n.C. womanhood; women. *yŏsŏng-ŭi* 여성의 female. *yŏsŏngyong-ŭi* 여성용의 for ladies' use.

-yŏsŏ -여서 infinitive ending with particle -**sŏ**. the irregular conjugational ending of **hada** 하다, which

has **hayŏ** 하여 (abbr. 해) as its infinitive. other shapes: **-asŏ** -아서, **-ŏsŏ** -어서. ① reason marker. indicates that the state of affairs expressed by the following v. or adj. ② temporal precedence and continuing state marker. indicates that the action expressed by the preceding v. is prior to the action expressed by the following v., but the state resulting from the action of the preceding v. continues throughout the action of the following v.

* **yŏsŏt** 여섯 n. six. *yŏsŏtchae* 여섯째 the sixth.

+ **yŏt'ae(kkaji)** 여태(까지) adv. till [until] now; up to the present; by this time; hitherto.

+ **yŏtppoda** 엿보다 v. watch [look] for; spy on; steal a glance at.

yŏwang 여왕 n.C. queen, female monarch. *mi-ŭi yŏwang* 미의 여왕 queen of beauty.

yŏu 여우 n.C. fox. *yŏu kat'ŭn* 여우 같은 foxy; sly.

-yŏya -여야 infinitive ending with particle -ya. the irregular conjugational ending of **hada** 하다: **hayŏya** 하여야 (abbr. 해야). other shapes: **-aya** -아야, **-ŏya** -어야. indicates that the proposition expressed by the preceding v. or adj. is a necessary condition for the following v. or adj. ① only to the extent that ... can one ..., you have to ... in order to ... ② to whatever extent.

yoyak 요약 n.C. summary; digest. *yoyak'ada* 요약하다 summarize; epitomize; abridge.

+ **yŏyu** 여유 n.C. (emotional) space, room; surplus, composure; relaxed feeling. *yŏyu-ga itta* 여유가 있다 have in reserve; have time [money] to spare.

yubang 유방 n.C. (woman's) breast(s).

yudo 유도 n.C. judo.

yugam 유감 n.C. regret; pity. *yugamsŭrŏun* 유감스러운 regrettable; deplorable; pitiful.

yugoe 유괴 n.C. kidnap(p)ing; abduction. *yugoehada* 유괴하다 abduct; kidnap; carry off.

yugyo 유교 n.C. Confucianism.

yuhaeng 유행 n.C. fashion; vogue; trend. *yuhaeng-hada* 유행하다 be in fashion [vogue]; prevail; be prevalent.

yuhak 유학 n.C. studying abroad. *yuhak'ada* 유학하다 study abroad; go abroad to study.

yuhok 유혹 n.C. temptation; lure. *yuhok'ada* 유혹하다 tempt; allure; entice; seduce.

yuhwa 유화 n.C. oil painting [color].

yuhyo 유효 n.C. validity; efficiency. *yuhyohada* 유효하다 be effective; hold good; remain valid. *yuhyohage* 유효하게 effectively; efficiently.

yuik 유익 n.C. *yuik'an* 유익한 profitable; beneficial. *yuik'age* 유익하게 usefully; profitably.

yujŏk 유적 n.C. remains; relics; ruins; historic spots.

\# **yuk** 육 n.C. six; *che yuk* 제6 the sixth.

yukch'e 육체 n.C. flesh; body. *yukch'e-ŭi[jŏk]* 육체의[적] bodily; physical.

\+ **yuktchi** 육지 n.C. land; shore.

\+ **yukkun** 육군 n.C. army; military service. *yukkun-ŭi* 육군의 military.

yukssang 육상 n.C. land; ground. *yukssang kyŏnggi* 육상 경기 track and field, athletic sports.

* **yukssip** 육십 n.C. 60, sixty. *che yukssip* 제 60 the sixtieth.

\+ **yuk'waehan** 유쾌한 adj.C.pleasant; cheerful; joyful; jolly.

yukwŏnja 유권자 n.C. voter.

yumul 유물 n.C. relic; historical remains.

\# **yumyŏnghan** 유명한 adj.C. famous; noted; renowned.

yurae 유래 n.C. origin; history; source. *yuraehada* 유래하다 originate (in).

* **yurihan** 유리한 adj.C. profitable; advantageous. *yurihage* 유리하게 profitably.

yuryŏng 유령 n.C. ghost.

yusa 유사 n.C. similarity; resemblance; likeness;

analogy. *yusahada* 유사하다 be similar (to).

yusan 유산 n.C. inheritance; legacy; bequest.

yut 윷 n. Four-Stick Game; *Yut*.

yuŭihada 유의하다 v.C. bear [keep] in mind; care about; be mindful of; take care [notice].

* **yuwŏl** 유월 n.C. June.

yuyonghan 유용한 adj.C. useful; valuable; serviceable.

Basic

ENGLISH –KOREAN DICTIONARY

≲ A ≳

a *art.* no exact equivalent in Korean: *a person* saram 사람, *a week* chuil 주일. [When *a* positively means *one*, it may be translated by *han* 한 or *il* 일: ~ *person* han saram 한 사람, ~ *week* il chuil 일 주일; but when *a* means a generic member of a group, it is usually omitted in Korean translation: ~ *dog is a faithful animal.* kae-nŭn ch'ungsilhan tongmurida. 개는 충실한 동물이다]; (*a certain*) ŏttŏn 어떤, han 한: ~ (*certain*) *person* ŏttŏn saram 어떤 사람; (*per*) -e -에, -mada -마다: *three meals* ~ *day* haru-e se pŏn sikssa 하루에 세번 식사.

abacus *n.* chup'an 주판.

abalone *n.* chŏnbok 전복.

abandon *v.* p'ogihada 포기하다, pŏrida 버리다.

abbreviate *v.* churida 줄이다, ch'ugyakhada 축약하다.

* **abbreviation** *n.* saengnyak⟨ryak 생략, (*word*) yakch'ing 약칭, yagŏ 약어.

* **ability** *n.* nŭngnyŏk⟨ryŏk 능력.

* **able** *adj.* yunŭnghan 유능한, nŭngnyŏk/sillyŏk innŭn ⟨itnŭn 능력/실력 있는. *be* ~ *to* ...ŭl hal ssu itta … 을 할 수 있다. → **can.**

aboard *adv. & prep.* (*on board*) ...ŭl t'ago (itta) 타고 (있다): *get* ~ t'ada 타다.→ **to board.**

abolish *v.* ŏpssaeda 없애다, p'yejihada 폐지하다.

abortion *n.* nakt'ae 낙태. → **miscarriage** *n.* yusan 유산(流産).

about *prep.* (*concerning*) ...e taehaesŏ …에 대해서, ...e tae/kwanhayŏ …에 대/관하여. —*adv.* (*approximately*) yak 약. *a book* ~ *Korea* han'gug-e kwanhan ch'aek 한국에 관한 책. *The train was* ~ *to*

start. kich'a-ga mak ttŏnaryŏnŭn ch'amiŏtta. 기차
가 막 떠나려는 참이었다.

+ **above** *prep.* ...wi-e …위에. —*adv.* wi-ro 위로. —*adj.*
  (*above-mentioned*) wi-ŭi 위의, wi-esŏ malhan 위에
  서 말한. ~ *all* muŏtppodado 무엇보다도.

  abroad *adv.* (*overseas*) haeoe-e 해외에; (*widely*) nŏlli 널리.

  abruptly *adv.* kaptchagi 갑자기.

  absence *n.* pujae 부재, kyŏlssŏk 결석; (*lack*) ŏpssŭm
  없음.

  absent *adj.* kyŏlssŏkhan 결석한; ŏmnŭn〈ŏpnŭn 없는.
  --*v.* kyŏlssŏkhada 결석하다, ŏptta 없다. *He is ~
  from home* chib-e ŏptta 그는 집에 없다.

  absent-minded *adj.* mŏnghani innŭn〈itnŭn 멍하니
  있는.

  absolute *adj.* chŏlttaejŏgin 절대적인.

+ **absolutely** *adv.* chŏlttae-ro 절대로.

  absorb *v.* hŭpssuhada 흡수하다.

  absorbed *adj.* (*fascinated*) ...e yŏltchunghan …에 열
  중한.

  abstain *v.* chŏltchehada 절제하다, samgada 삼가다.

+ **abstract** *adv.* ch'usangjŏgin 추상적인. —*n.* ch'usang
  추상; (*summary*) kaeyo 개요, yoyak 요약.

  absurd *adj.* (*unreasonable*) pulhamnihan〈pulhapri-
  han 불합리한; (*foolish*) ŏiŏmnŭn〈ŏiŏpnŭn 어이없는.

  abundant *adj.* manŭn〈manhŭn 많은, p'ungbuhan 풍
  부한.

  abuse *n.* (*of authority*) namyong 남용; (*verbal*)
  yokssŏl 욕설. —*v.* (*revile*) moyokhada 모욕하다;
  (*misuse*) namyonghada 남용하다.

  academy *n.* hagwŏn 학원, hakkyo 학교. *the Military
  ~* yukkunsagwanhakkyo 육군사관학교.

+ **academic** *adj.* hangmunjŏgin〈hagmunjŏgin 학문적인,
  hakkujŏgin 학구적인..

  accede *v.* tongŭihada 동의하다.

  accent *n.* aekssent'ŭ 액센트, malssi 말씨.

* **accept** *v.* (*a gift*) patta 받다, (*a position*) padadŭr-

ida 받아들이다: ~ *Catholicism (come to believe in)*
k'at'ollikkyo-rŭl padadŭrida/mitta 카톨릭교를 받아
들이다/믿다.

+ **acceptable** *adj.* padadŭril ssu innŭn〈itnŭn 받아들일
수 있는, maŭm-e tŭnŭn 마음에 드는, manjokhan 만족
한, surakhal manhan 수락할 만한.

accessible *adj.* swipkke ssŭl ssu innŭn〈itnŭn 쉽게 쓸
수 있는, chŏpkkŭnhagi swiun 접근하기 쉬운.

accessory *n.* pusokp'um 부속품, aekssesŏri 액세서리.
—*adj.* pojojŏgin 보조적인.

ı **accident** *n.* *(unexpected event)* sago 사고, *(chance)*
uyŏn 우연 : *by ~* uyŏnhi 우연히.

+ **accidentally** *adv.* uyŏnhi 우연히.

accommodation *n.(adjustment)* chŏgŭng 적응;
(lodgings) suksso 숙소.

accompany *v.* …wa hamkke/kach'i kada …와 함께/같
이 가다.

accomplice *n.* kongbŏmja 공범자.

accomplish *v.* iruda 이루다, wansŏnghada 완성하다.

accord *n.* ilch'i 일치.—*v.* ilch'ihada 일치하다.

+ **according** *adv.* ~ *to* …e ttara …에 따라(서), …e
ŭihamyŏn …에 의하면.

+ **account** *n.* kyesan 계산, *(bank)* kyejwa 계좌, *(report)*
pogo 보고, *(explanation)* sŏlmyŏng 설명. —*v.* …(i)
rago saenggakhada …(이)라고 생각하다.

accumulate *v.* ch'uktchŏkhada 축적하다, moŭda 모으다.

+ **accurate** *adj.*chŏnghwakhan 정확한, chŏngmilhan 정
밀한.

+ **accused** *n.* p'igo(in) 피고(인).

accustom *v.* ikssukhaejige hada 익숙해지게 하다, ik-
hida 익히다, *(habituate)* sŭpkkwandŭrida 습관들이
다.

accustomed *n.* ikssukhan 익숙한.

ache *v.* ap'ŭda 아프다.—*n.* ap'ŭm 아픔.

* **achieve** *v.* iruda 이루다, talssŏnghada 달성하다, sŏng-
sasik'ida 성사시키다, wansŏngsik'ida 완성시키다.

+ **achievement** *n.* *(aim)* sŏngch'wi 성취, sŏngkkwa 성

과, talssŏng 달성; (*merit*) kongjŏk 공적, (*work,
publication*) ŏptchŏk 업적.

acid *n*. san 산(酸). → **sour** *adj*. sin 신.

acknowledge *v*. (*recognize, admit*) injŏnghada 인정
하다; (*a gift*) kamsahada 감사하다.

acne *n*. yŏdurŭm 여드름.

acorn *n*. tot´ori 도토리. ~ *jelly* (*starch paste*)
tot´orimuk 도토리묵.

acquaintance *n*. anŭn saram 아는 사람, ch´inji 친지. *I
am happy to make your* ~. sŏnsaengnim-ŭl
poepkke toeŏ kippŭmnida. 선생님을 뵙게 되어 기쁩니다.

acquaint *v*. (*make familiar*) ...ŭl alge hada …을 알게
하다, (*inform*) allida 알리다.

acquire *v*. ŏtta 얻다, sŭpttŭkhada 습득하다.

+ **across** *adv*. kŏnnŏsŏ 건너서. —*prep*. kŏnnŏpyŏn-ŭro
건너편으로, majŭn pyŏn-ŭro 맞은 편으로.

* **act** *v*. haengdonghada 행동하다. —*n*.(*deed, behavior*)
haengdong 행동; (*law*) pŏmnyŏng⟨pŏpryŏng 법령;
(*drama*) mak 막.

+ **acting** *adj*. (*substitute*) taeri-ŭi 대리의. ~ *manager*
chibaein taeri 지배인 대리. --*n*. (*play, movie, etc.*)
yŏngi 연기 (演技).

* **action** *n*. haengdong 행동, haengwi 행위; (*play*) yŏngi 연기. *Actions speak louder than words*. Haeng-
dong-ŭn mal-poda kanghada. 행동은 말보다 강하다.

+ **active** *adj*. hwalttongjŏgin 활동적인, hwalbalhan 활발
한; chŏkkŭktchŏgin 적극적인.

* **activity** *n*. hwalttong 활동, hwaryak 활약.

+ **actor** *n*. paeu 배우.

+ **actual** *adj*. siltche-ŭi 실제의; (*present*) hyŏnhaeng-ŭi
현행의.

actually *adv*. siltchero 실제로.

acupuncture *n*. ch´imsul 침술.

acute *adj*. (*sharpness*) nalk´aroun 날카로운: ~ *angle*
yegak 예각, (*keen*) mojin 모진, (*medical*)
kŭpssŏngin 급성인.

adapt *v*. chŏgŭngsik´ida 적응시키다. *He will easily* ~

himself to any circumstances. kŭ-nŭn ŏttŏn
hwan´gyŏng-edo swipkkye chŏgŭnghal kŏsida. 그
는 어떤 환경에도 쉽게 적응할 것이다.

adaptability *n.* yungt´ongsŏng 융통성.

adaptable *adj.* yungt´ongsŏng-i innŭn⟨itnŭn 융통성이
있는.

* **add** *v.* tŏhada 더하다, ch´ugahada 추가하다, tŏt-
ppuch´ida⟨tŏsput´ida 덧붙이다: *"I think so, too," he
added.* "chŏ-to kŭrŏk´e saenggakhamnida"rago
kŭ-nŭn (mar-ŭl) tŏtppuch´ŏtta. "저도 그렇게 생각 합
니다"라고 그는 (말을) 덧붙였다.

addict *v.* ppajige hada 빠지게 하다.—*n.* chungdoktcha 중독자: *an opium/drug* ~ ap´yŏn chungdoktcha 아편/약물 중독자.

+ **addition** *n.* puga 부가: tŏssem⟨tŏtsem 덧셈. *in* ~
kedaga 게다가.

+ **additional** *adj.* ch´uga-ŭi 추가의: ~ *tax* pugasse 부가세.

+ **address** *v.* (*speak to*) ...ege mar-ŭl kŏlda …에게 말을
걸다, (*public speaking*) ...ege yŏnsŏlhada …에게 연
설하다; (*a letter*) chuso sŏngmyŏngŭl ssŭda 주소 성
명을 쓰다.—*n.* (*a letter*) chuso 주소, (*speech*) yŏnsŏl
연설.

adequate *adj.* pujok´aji anhŭn 부족하지 않은, ch´ung-
bunhan 충분한.

adjacent *adj.* pugŭn-ŭi 부근의, injŏphan 인접한.

* **adjective** *n.* hyŏngyongsa 형용사.

+ **adjust** *v.* chojŏnghada 조정하다, chŏngdonhada 정돈하
다; ...e sunŭnghada …에 순응하다.

+ **administrative** *adj.* haengjŏng-ŭi 행정의.

admirable *adj.* hullyunghan 훌륭한.

+ **admiration** *n.* kamt´an 감탄, sungbae 숭배; ch´ing-
ch´an 칭찬.

+ **admire** *v.* kamt´anhada 감탄하다, sungbaehada 숭배
하다; (*praise*) ch´ingch´anhada 칭찬하다. ~ *Korean
dance* han´gug-ŭi muyong-ŭl ch´anmihada 한국의
무용을 찬미하다.

admission *n.* (*school*) iphak 입학, (*theater, etc.*) iptchang 입장. ~ *fee* iptchangnyo 입장료, (*school entrance fee*) iphakkŭm 입학금

+ **admit** *v.* (*let in*) tŭrŏoge hada 들어오게 하다. *get/be admitted to college* taehag-e iphaktoeda 대학에 입학되다; (*recognize*) injŏnghada 인정하다; (*permit*) hŏyonghada 허용하다.

adolescence *n.* sach'un'gi 사춘기, ch'ŏngnyŏn'gi 청년기, ch'ŏngch'un'gi 청춘기.

adolescent *adj.* ch'ŏngnyŏn'gi-ŭi 청년기의, ch'ŏngch'un'gi-ŭi 청춘기의.

adopt *v.* yangja/yangnyŏ-ro samda 양자/양녀로 삼다. (*accept*) ch'aet'aekhada 채택하다.

adopted *adj.* yangja/nyŏ-ga toen 양자/녀가 된. *an ~ son* yangja 양자, *an ~ daughter* yangnyŏ 양녀.

adore *v.* sungbaehada 숭배하나, saranghada 사랑하다.

adult *n.* ŏrŭn 어른, sŏngin 성인: ~ *education* sŏngingyoyuk 성인교육.

adutery *n.* kant'ong 간통, kanŭm 간음.

+ **advance** *v.* (*move forward*) chŏnjinhada 전진하다; (*propose*) chujanghada 주장하다; (*promote*) sŭngjinsik'ida 승진시키다. *in ~* miri 미리.

+ **advanced** *adj.* chinbohan 진보한, kogŭp-ŭi 고급의. *an ~ country* sŏnjinguk 선진국.

+ **advantage** *n.*iik 이익, changtchŏm 장점. *the advantages of city life* tosisaenghwar-ŭi p'yŏnŭi 도시생활의 편의.

advantageous *adj.* yurihan 유리한.

adventure *n.* mohŏm 모험.

+ **adverb** *n.* pusa 부사.

advertise/tize *v.* kwanggohada 광고하다.

advertise/tizement *n.* kwanggo 광고, kongsi 공시.

+ **advice** *n.* ch'unggo 충고 ; (*information*) allim 알림.

advise *v.* ch'unggohada 충고하다.

adviser *n.* choŏnja 조언자, (*academic supervisor*) chidogyosu 지도교수, komun 고문(顧問) : *a legal ~* pŏmnyul〈pŏpryul komun 법률 고문.

advocate *v.* chuch'anghada 주창하다. —*n.* (*uphold-*

er) chuch'angja 주창자; (*lawyer*) pyŏnhosa 변호사.
+ **aeroplane** *n*. (British spelling) pihaenggi 비행기.
+ **affair** *n*. (*business*) il 일. *a private ~* sasaroun il 사사로운 일; (*event*) sakkŏn 사건. *a love ~* yŏnae-sakkŏn 연애사건. *have an ~ with (someone)* -wa param-ŭl p'iuda -와 바람을 피우다. *international affairs* kuktche sajŏng 국제 사정.
+ **affect** *v*. ① ...ege yŏnghyang-ŭl chuda/kkich'ida ...에게 영향을 주다/끼치다 ② (*pretend*) ...in ch'ehada ··· 인 체하다.
  affected *adj*. (*be ~*) ilburŏ kkumin 일부러 꾸민.
+ **affection** *n*. (*love*) aejŏng 애정, jŏng 정, (*feeling*) kamjŏng 감정. → **disease** *n*. chilbyŏng 질병.
  affinity *n*. inch'ŏk 인척.
  affliction *n*. (*suffering*) kot'ong 고통; (*calamity*) chaenan 재난.
+ **afford** *v*. ...hal ch'ungbunhan ton-i itta ···할 충분한 돈이 있다, ...ŭi yŏyu-ga itta ···의 여유가 있다. *I cannot afford a car*. na-nŭn ch'a-rŭl kajil yŏyu-ga ŏptta. 나는 차를 가질 여유가 없다.
  afloat *adj*. ttŏinnŭn⟨ttŏitnŭn 떠있는. --*adv*. ttŏsŏ 떠서.
+ **afraid** *adj*. (may be used as predicate/complement) musŏwŏhada/hayŏ 무서워하다/하여, uryŏhada/hayŏ 우려하다/하여; (*sorry*) mianhajiman 미안하지만, yugamsŭrŏpkke 유감스럽게. *I'm ~ I can't attend*. mianhajiman ch'amsŏkhal ssu ŏpssŭmnida. 미안하지만 참석할 수 없습니다. ch'amsŏkhal ssu ŏpssŏ mian hamnida. 참석할 수 없어 미안합니다.
  afresh *adv*. saeroi 새로이, saeropkke 새롭게.
* **after** *adv*. (*behind*) twi-e 뒤에; (*time*) hu-e 후에. — *prep*. ...ŭi twi-e ···의 뒤에. *~ a long time (of absence)* *adv*. oraeganman-e 오래간만에. *~ all* *adv*. kyŏlgug-ŭn 결국은. *~ (a) while* *adv*. chogŭm ittaga 조금 있다가.
+ **afternoon** *n*. ohu 오후.
  afterward(s) *adv*. najung-e 나중에, kŭhu-e 그후에. (in narration) *They lived happily ever ~*. kŭ twi-e

haengbokhage sarattamnita. 그 뒤에 행복하게 살았답니다.

* **again** adv. tasi 다시, tto 또.
* **against** prep. ‴e pan(dae)hayŏ ‴에 반(대)하여: be ~ me na-hant'e pandaehayŏ 나한테 반대하여.
+ **age** n. (year) nai 나이, yŏllŏng〈yŏnryŏng 연령, (to senior) yŏnse 연세: middle ~ chungnyŏn 중년; (period) yŏndae 연대: the Atomic A~ wŏnjaryŏksidae 원자력시대.

  agency n. taeri(jŏm) 대리(점): a general ~ ch'ongdaerijŏm 총대리점; (of government) kigwan 기관. travel ~ yŏhaengsa 여행사.

  agent n. taeriin 대리인: secret ~ kanch'ŏp 간첩.

  aggravating adj. akhwasik'inŭn 악화시키는.
+ **aggressive** adj. chŏkkŭktchŏk 직극적, ch'imnyaktchŏk〈ch'imryakchŏk 침략적.

  aggression n. konggyŏk 공격; ch'imnyak〈ch'imryak 침략.

  agitate v. tongyosik'ida 동요시키다.
+ **ago** adv. (chigŭm-but'ŏ) ‴chŏn-e (지금부터) ‴전에: ten years ~ simnyŏn chŏn〈sipnyŏn chŏn(-e) 10년 전(에).

  agony n. konoe 고뇌.
+ **agree** v. tongŭihada 동의하다. I quite ~ with him. (na-nŭn) kŭ-ege chŏntchŏg-ŭro tongŭihanda. (나는) 그에게 전적으로 동의한다.

  agreeable adj. kibunjoŭn 기분좋은, (pleasant) kwaejŏkhan 쾌적한.
+ **agreement** n. (treaty) hyŏbyak 협약; (assent) tongŭi 동의; (concord) ilch'i 일치.

  agriculture n. nongŏp 농업; (science) nonghak 농학.

  ahead adv. ap'-e 앞에: gets ~ chŏnjinhada 전진하다.

  aid n. toum 도움. --v. toptta 돕다.

  AIDS n. eijŭ 에이즈, huch'ŏnssŏng myŏnyŏkkyŏlp'iptchŭng 후천성 면역결핍증.
+ **aim** v. (at a person) ‴ŭl kyŏnuda ‴을 겨누다. —n. moktchŏk 목적.

* **air** *n.* (*atmosphere*) konggi 공기, (*open space*) kong-jung 공중; (*draft*) param 바람; (*manner*) t'aedo 태도.
  air base *n.* konggun kiji 공군기지.
  air conditioned *n.* naengbang changch'idoen 냉방 장치 된.
  air conditioner *n.* eŏk'ŏn 에어컨, naengbanggi 냉방기.
  air conditioning *n.* naengbang 냉방.
+ **aircraft/airplane** *n.* pihaenggi 비행기.
  air force *n.* konggun 공군.
  airmail *n.* hanggongup'ŏn 항공우편.
+ **airport** *n.* konghang 공항.
  airsickness *n.* pihaenggi mŏlmi 비행기 멀미.
  aisle *n.* (chwasŏk sai-ŭi) t'ongno⟨t'ongro (좌석 사이의) 통로.
  alarm *v.* (*frighten*) kkamtchak nollage hada 깜짝놀라게 하다; (*warn*) wigŭpham-ŭl allida 위급함을 알리다. —*n.* nollam 놀람, kyŏngbo 경보.
  album *n.* aelbŏm 앨범, (*photo*) sajinch'ŏp 사진첩, (*stamp*) up'yoch'ŏp 우표첩.
+ **alcohol** *n.* alk'ol 알콜, sul 술.
+ **alcoholic** *n.* alk'ol/sul chungdoktcha 알콜/술 중독자.
  alert *adj.* (*watchful*) pint'ŭm ŏmnŭn⟨ŏpnŭn 빈틈없는. —*n.* kyŏnggye 경계.
  alien *n.* (*foreigner*) oegugin 외국인, (*extraterrestrial*) oegyein 외계인. —*adj.* oegugin-ŭi 외국인의, oegyein-ŭi 외계인의.
  alike *adj.* (*like each other*) pisŭthan 비슷한: *be exactly* ~ kkok talmŭn/pisŭthan 꼭 닮은/비슷한. —*adv.* (*similarly*) pisŭthage 비슷하게.
  alimony *n.* ihon sudang 이혼 수당.
+ **alive** *adj.* (*living*) sarainnŭn⟨itnŭn 살아있는: *be* ~ sara itta 살아 있다. (*active*) hwalbaran⟨hwalbalhan 활발한.
* **all** *adj.* modŭn 모든. —*n.* chŏnbu 전부. —*adv.* (*completely* used with negatives) chŏnhyŏ 전혀, (*both*) yangtchok ta 양쪽 다, (*wholly*) t'ongt'ŭrŏ 통틀어. ~ *kinds of* modŭn chongnyu-ŭi⟨chongryuŭi 모든 종류

의. ~ *over* ta kkŭnna〈kkŭt′na 다 끝나; toch′ŏ-e 도 처에; aju 아주: *He is his father ~ over* kŭ-nŭn abŏji-rŭl aju talmatta 그는 아버지를 아주 닮았다. ~ *right* choa 좋아! musahi 무사히. ~ *the time* hangsang 항상. ~ *the way* tojung naenae 도중 내내. at ~ (used in question and conditional clause) chŏgŏdo 적어도. *not at* ~ chŏnhyŏ ... anta〈anhta. 전혀 ···않다.

allergy *n.* allergi 알레르기, kwamintchŭng 과민증.

alley *n.* (*aisle*) t′ongno〈t′ongro 통로, (*back street*) twitkkolmok 뒷골목.

alliance *n.* (*union*) yŏnhap 연합, (*treaty*) tong-maeng 동맹.

+ **allow** *v.* (*permit*) hŏrakhada 허락하다, (*grant*) chigŭp-hada 지급하다. *Smoking is not allowed here.* yŏgisŏ-nŭn kŭmyŏn(imnida). 여기서는 금연(입니다).

allowance *n.* sudang 수당.

+ **almost** *adv.* kŏŭi 거의, taech′ero 대체로.

+ **alone** *adj.* honjain 혼자인.—*adv.* honja 혼자.

* **along** *prep. & adv.* ...ŭl ttarasŏ ...을 따라서.

+ **aloud** *adv.* (*audibly*) tŭllil chŏngdo-ro 들릴 정도로, (*loudly*) k′ŭn sori-ro 큰 소리로, sorinop′i 소리 높이.

+ **alphabet** *n.* alp′abet 알파벳, muntcha ch′egye 문자 체계.

+ **already** *adv.* pŏlssŏ 벌써, imi 이미.

also *adv.* yŏkssi 역시, mach′angajiro 마찬가지로.

alter *v.* pyŏngyŏnghada 변경하다, (*clothes*) koch′ida 고치다.

alternate *v.* kyodae/kyoch′ehada 교대/교체하다.

+ **alternative** *adj.* yangja t′aegil-ŭi 양자 택일의. —*n.* yangjachung-ŭi sŏnt′aek 양자 중의 선택, tarŭn-pangdo 다른 방도.

* **although** *conj.* pirok ···iltchirado 비록 ···일지라도.

altitude *n.* kodo 고도, nop′i 높이.

altogether *adv.* (*wholly*) aju 아주, chŏnyŏn 전연, (*all included*) modu 모두.

+ **always** *adv.* hangsang 항상, nŭl 늘, ŏnjena 언제나.

a.m. (*before noon*) ojŏn 오전.

amateur *n.* amat´yuŏ 아마튜어.

amaze *v.* mopssi nollage hada 몹시 놀라게 하다.

ambassador *n.* taesa 대사(大使).

ambiance *n.* punwigi 분위기.

ambiguous *adj.* aemaehan 애매한.

ambition *n.* yasim 야심, yamang 야망.

amend *v.* sujŏnghada 수정하다.

America *n.* miguk 미국, amerik´a 아메리카.

* **American** *adj.* migug-ŭi 미국의.—*n.* (*person*) migugin 미국인. ~ *English* (migungnyŏngŏ⟨⟩migukyŏngŏ 미국 영어.

amid *prep.* kaunde 가운데.

+ **among(st)** *prep.* kaunde 가운데.

* **amount** *n.* (*altogether*) ch´onggye 총계; (*quantity*) aeksu 액수, yang 양(量).—*v.* irŭda 이르다, toeda 되다. *The hotel bill amounted to 150 dollars.* hoter-ŭi kyesan-ŭn hapkye paegosip dallayŏtta. 호텔의 계산은 합계 백오십 달러였다.

ample *adj.* ch´ungbunhan 충분한.

amuse *v.* chaeminage hada 재미나게 하다, chŭlgŏpkke hada 즐겁게 하다.

amusement *n.* 오락. ~ *park* yuwŏnji 유원지.

+ **amusing** *adj.* (*stimulating*) chaemiinnŭn⟨itnŭn 재미 있는, (*entertaining*) chŭlgŏpkkehanŭn 즐겁게 하는, (*funny*) ukkinŭn⟨utkinŭn 웃기는.

analysis *n.* punsŏk 분석, punhae 분해.

analyze/lyse *v.* punsŏkhada 분석하다.

+ **ancestor** *n.* chosang 조상.

ancestry *n.* chosang 조상; (*family descent*) kagye 가계(家系), munbŏl 문벌.

anchor *n.* tat 닻.

ancient *adj.* kodae-ŭi 고대의, yennar-ŭi⟨yetnal-ŭi 옛날의. → **old** *adj.* oraedoen 오래된.

and *conj.* (*between noun and n.*) ...wa/kwa ⋯와/과, (*everywhere else*) tto 또, kŭrigo 그리고, (*literary*) mit 및, (*colloq.*) hago 하고. ~ *so on* ...ttawi ⋯따위,

tŭngdŭng 등등. ~ *yet* kŭrŏndedo 그런데도.

anew *adv.* saero 새로, tasi han bŏn 다시 한번.

angel *n.* ch'ŏnsa 천사.

+ **anger** *n.* *hwa* 화, punno 분노, noyŏum 노여움. —*v.* nohage hada 노하게 하다.

+ **angle** *n.* ① kaktto 각도; (*corner*) mot'ungi 모퉁이 ② (*fishhook*) nakssi 낚시.—*v.* (*fish*) nakssijilhada 낚시질하다; kkoeŏnaeda 꾀어내다.

* **angry** *adj.* hwanan 화난, sŏngnan 성난, nohan 노한.

anguish *n.* simhan komin 심한 고민, koeroum 괴로움.

* **animal** *n.* tongmul 동물. → **beast** *n.* chimsŭng 짐승.

animate *v.* hwalgi-rŭl chuda 활기를 주다. --*adj.* hwalgich'an 활기찬.

ankle *n.* palmok 발목: ~ *bone* poksappyŏ 복사뼈.

announce *v* (*give notice of*) allida 일리나; (*publish, proclaim*) palp'yohada 발표하다. *This is an announcement.* annae malssŭm-ŭl turigessŭmnida. 안내 말씀을 드리겠습니다.

+ **annoy** *v.* koerophida 괴롭히다, sokt'aeuda 속태우다, kwich'annk'e kulda 귀찮게 굴다.

+ **annoyance** *n.* koerophim 괴롭힘, kwich'anŭnil/saram 귀찮은 일/사람.

annonymous *adj.* ingmyŏng-ŭi⟨ikmyŏng-ŭi 익명의.

annual *adj.* maenyŏn-ŭi 매년의.

* **another** *adj.* tto hana-ŭi 또 하나의, (*different*) tarŭn 다른. —*n.* (*one more thing or person*) tto hana 또 하나, tto han saram 또 한 사람.

+ **answer** *v.* taedaphada 대답하다: ~ *the phone/door* chŏnhwa-rŭl patta 전화를 받다/mun-e nagada 문에 나가다. —*n.* taedap 대답, (*test*) chŏngdap 정답.

ant *n.* kaemi 개미.

antartic *adj.* namgŭg-ŭi 남극의. --*n.* namgŭk 남극.

antecedent *adj.* sŏnhaeng-ŭi 선행의.

antenna *n.* ant'ena 안테나.

anthropology *n.* illyuhak⟨inryuhak 인류학.

anti-American *adj.* panmi-ŭi 반미의, panmijŏk 반미적.

antibiotic(s) *n.* hangsaengje 항생제.

anticipate *v.* kidaehada 기대하다, yesanghada 예상하다.

anticipation *n.* kidae 기대, (*forecast*) yesang 예상.

anti-Communist *adj.* pan'gong-ŭi 반공의: *an ~ policy* pan'gong chŏngch'aek 반공정책.

antidote *n.* haedoktche 해독제.

antique *adj.* kodae-ŭi 고대의; (*old-fashioned*) kusik -ŭi 구식의.—*n.* kolttongp'um 골동품.

antiwar *adj.* panjŏn-ŭi 반전의.

antonym *n.* panŭiŏ 반의어, pandaemal 반대말.

+ **anxiety** *n.* (*uneasiness*) kŏktchŏng 걱정, kŭnsim 근심; (*eager desire*) yŏlmang 열망.

+ **anxious** *adj.* (*uneasy*) kŏktchŏngdoenŭn 걱정되는; (*eager*) kalmanghanŭn 갈망하는. *All of us are anxious for peace.* uri-nŭn modu pyŏnghwa-rŭl kalmanghago itta. 우리는 모두 평화를 갈망하고 있다.

* **any** *adj.* (with negatives) ŏttŏn …to 어떤 …도, (in questions or conditions) musŭn 무슨.

anyhow *adv.* amut'ŭn 아무튼, chwaugan 좌우간.

+ **anyone** *pron.* (positive) nugudŭnji 누구든지, (negative) amudo 아무도, (question) nugun'ga 누군가.

* **anything** *pron.* (positive) muŏsidŭnji 무엇이든지, (negative) amugŏt-to 아무것도, (question) muŏnga 무언가.

anytime *adj.* ŏnjedŭnji 언제든지, ŏnjena 언제나, amuttaena 아무때나.

anyway *adv.* ŏtchaettŭn 어쨌든, hayŏt'ŭn 하여튼.

anywhere *adv.* (positive) ŏdidŭnji 어디든지, amudena 아무데나, (negative) amude-to 아무데도: *Don't go ~.* amude-to kajimara. 아무데도 가지마라, (question) ŏdin'ga 어딘가.

+ **apart** *adv.* ttŏrŏjyŏsŏ 떨어져서, ttarottaro 따로따로:*live ~* ttaro salda 따로 살다. *~ from* …ŭn pyŏlttoro hago … 은 별도로 하고.

apartment *n.* ap'at'ŭ 아파트. → **room** *n.* pang 방.

ape *n.* wŏnsungi 원숭이.

apiece *adv.* kakkak 각각, ttarottaro 따로따로.

apologize *v.* (*excuse*) sagwahada 사과하다, (*explain*)

pyŏnmyŏnghada 변명하다.

apparent *adj.* nun-e poinŭn 눈에 보이는, (*obvious*) myŏngbaekhan 명백한; (*seeming*) p'yomyŏnsang-ŭi 표면상의.

apparently *adv.* (*clearly*) myŏngbaekhi 명백히; (*seemingly*) oegyŏnsang 외견상.

appeal *v.* hosohada 호소하다.

+ **appear** *v.* nat'anada 나타나다, ···ro poida ···로 보이다.

+ **appearance** *n.* ch'ulhyŏn 출현; oemo 외모.

appetite *n.* sigyok 식욕: *have a good ~* pammas-i⟨ papmas-i itta 밥맛이 있다; (*craving*) kalmang 갈망.

appetizers *n.* (*to go with drinks*) (sul)anju (술)안주.

applaud *v.* pakssuch'ida 박수치다.

apple *n.* sagwa 사과. → nŭnggŭm 능금.

application *n.* chŏgyong 적용, chiwŏn 지원, sinch'ŏng (sŏ) 신청(서).

+ **apply** *v.* (*a theory to a case*) ŭngyonghada 응용하다, (*submit an application*) sinch'ŏnghada 신청하다.

appoint *v.* chijŏnghada 지정하다.

+ **appointed** *adj.* chijŏngdoen 지정된, yakssokhan 약속한: *at the ~ time* yakssok(han) sigan-e 약속(한) 시간에; (*equipped*) sŏlbidoen 설비된.

appointment *n.* (*nomination*) immyŏng 임명; (*designation*) chijŏng 지정; (*promise*) yakssok 약속.

appreciate *v.* kamsanghada 감상하다.

+ **appreciation** *n.* kamsang 감상; kamsa 감사.

apprehend *v.* (*fear*) uryŏhada 우려하다; (*seize*) ch'ep'ohada 체포하다; (*understand*) ihaehada 이해하다.

apprentice *n.* toje 도제(徒弟), kyŏnsŭpssaeng 견습생, (*novice*) ch'osimja 초심자.

approach *v.* kakkai kada 가까이 가다, chŏpkkŭnhada 접근하다. —*n.* chŏpkkŭn 접근. *a new ~ to the study of Korean* han'gugŏ hakssŭb-ŭl wihan saeroun pangbŏp 한국어 학습을 위한 새로운 방법.

+ **appropriate** *adj.* chŏkttanghan 적당한.—*v.* ch'ungdanghada 충당하다.

+ **approval** *n.* sŭngin 승인, (*sanction*) in'ga 인가.

+ **approve** v. sŭnginhada 승인하다, (*permit*) hŏgahada 허가하다.
+ **approximate** v. chŏpkkŭnhada 접근하다, ŏrimchaptta 어림잡다.
+ **approximately** adv. taegang 대강, taech'ung 대충. → **almost** adv. kŏŭi 거의.
  apricot n. salgu 살구.
  April n. sawŏl 사월.
  apt adj. ... hagi swiun ... 하기 쉬운. *He is apt to forget.* kŭ-nŭn itkki〈ichki-rŭl chal handa. 그는 잊기를 잘 한다. *He is apt at languages.* kŭ-nŭn ŏhag-e chaenŭng-i itta. 그는 어학에 재능이 있다.
  aptitude n. chŏkssŏng 적성.
  aquarium n. sujokkwan 수족관, yangŏjang 양어장.
  archery n. kungsul 궁술, kungdo 궁도.
  archipelago n. kundo 군도.
  architect n. kŏkŭnch'ukka 건축가.
  architecture n. kŏnch'uk 건축.
  arctic adj. pukkŭg-ŭi 북극의.-n. (*the A~*) pukkŭk 북극.
* **area** n. (*space*) myŏnjŏk 면적: *What is the area of Seoul?* sŏur-ŭi myŏnjŏg-ŭn ŏlmana toemnikka? 서울의 면적은 얼마나 됩니까?; (*district*) kuyŏk 구역, chigu 지구, (*nearby area*) kŭnch'ŏ 근처.
+ **argue** v. (*discuss*) nonhada 논하다, nonjaenghada 논쟁하다; (*contend*) chujanghada 주장하다.
+ **argument** n. nonjaeng 논쟁, malssaum 말싸움; (*reason*) nonjŭng 논증.
  arise v. irŏnada 일어나다, palsaenghada 발생하다.
+ **arm** n. ① (*body part*) p'al 팔. ② (pl. *weapons*) pyŏnggi 병기, mugi 무기. —v. mujanghada 무장하다.
  armament n. kunbi 군비.
+ **armed** adj. mujanghan 무장한.
  armo(u)r n. kabot 갑옷.
+ **army** n. yukkun 육군.
* **around** adv. & prep. tulle-e 둘레에; (*about*) yak 약, tchŭm 쯤, (only with time words) kyŏng 경.
  arouse v. (*awaken*) kkaeuda 깨우다; (*excite*)

chagŭkhada 자극하다.

+ **arrange** v. (*put in order*) chŏngnihada⟨chŏngrihada 정리하다, chŏngdonhada 정돈하다; (*make ready for*) chunbihada 준비하다. *arranged marriage* chungmae kyŏlhon 중매결혼.

+ **arrangement** n. chŏngdon 정돈; (*preparation*) chunbi 준비; (*agreement*) t'ahyŏp 타협. *flower* ~ kkokkoji 꽃꽂이.

  arrest v. ch'ep'ohada 체포하다.—n. ch'ep'o 체포.

  arrival n. toch'ak 도착.

+ **arrive** v. toch'akhada 도착하다, todalhada 도달하다.

  arrogant adj. kŏmanhan 거만한, k'ottae-ga sen 콧대가 센.

  arrow n. hwasal 화살.

+ **art** n. yesul 예술, misul 미술; (*craft*) kisul 기술; (*trick*) kigyo 기교.

+ **article** n. (*newspaper*) kisa 기사; (*things*) mulp'um 물품; (*provision*) chohang 조항; (*grammar*) kwansa 관사.

+ **artificial** adj. ingongjŏk 인공적, mojo-ŭi 모조의.

+ **artist** n. yesulga 예술가, misulga 미술가. → **painter** n. hwaga 화가.

+ **artistic** adj. yesultchŏgin 예술적인.

as adv. ···wa katkke ···와 같게, (*as much as*) ···kat'ŭlmank'ŭm ···같을 만큼.—conj. ...mank'ŭm ···만큼, ... chŏngdo ···정도. —prep. ...ch'ŏrŏm ···처럼, ...wa kach'i ···와 같이, ...rosŏ ···로서. —rel. pron. ...wa kat'ŭn ···와 같은, ...hanŭn pa-ŭi ···하는 바의, (*as soon as*) haja maja 하자 마자. ~ *a matter of fact* sasil-ŭn 사실은. ~ *a rule* taegae 대개. ~ ... ~ *possible/one can* toel su innŭn⟨itnŭn han 될 수 있는 한. *I use this dictionary as often as possible.* na-nŭn i sajŏn-ŭl kagŭptchŏk chaju sajonghanda. 나는 이 사전을 가급적 자주 사용 한다. ~ *far* ~ ...e kwanhan han ...에 관한 한. ~ *for/to* ...e kwanhaesŏ-nŭn ...에 관해서는. ~ *if/though* mach'i ...in kŏtch'ŏrŏm 마치 ...인 것처럼. ~ *much* ~ mank'ŭm 만큼. ~ *well* ...to tto ...도 또. ~

  well ~ ...kwa mach'angajiro ...과 마찬가지로.

ascend *v.* ollagada 올라가다.

ascertain *v.* hwaginhada 확인하다, (*find out*) aranaeda 알아내다.

ash *n.* chae 재; (*pl.*) (*remains*) yugol 유골.

+ ashamed *adj.* sujupŏhanŭn 수줍어 하는, pukkŭrŏun 부끄러운: *He ought to be ashamed of himself.* kŭ-nŭn chasin-ŭl pukkŭrŏpkke saenggakhaeya handa. 그는 자신을 부끄럽게 생각해야 한다.

ashtray *n.* chaettŏri 재떨이.

Asian *n.* asia saram 아시아사람. --*adj.* asia (saram) -ŭi 아시아(사람)의.

aside *adv.* yŏp'-e 옆에.

* ask *v.* (*inquire*) mutta 묻다, (*honorific form*) yŏtchuptta 여쭙다; (~ *a favor of a person*) ···ege put'ak/ch'ŏngt'akhada ···에게 부탁/청탁하다. ~ *for a person* amu-rŭl ch'ajaoda/ch'atta 아무를 찾아오다/찾다.

+ asleep *adv.* chamdŭrŏ 잠들어: *be* ~ chago itta 자고 있다.

+ aspect *n.* (*phase*) kungmyŏn⟨kukmyŏn 국면; (*look*) yongmo 용모, (*appearance*) moyang 모양.

aspiration *n.* yŏlmang 열망.

aspire *v.* yŏlmanghada 열망하다.

assemble *v.* moida 모이다, moŭda 모으다.

assembly *n.* ŭihoe 의회, (*convention*) taehoe 대회.

assent *n.* tongŭi 동의. --*v.* tongŭihada 동의하다.

assert *v.* (*maintain*) chujanghada 주장하다; tanŏnhada 단언하다.

assist *v.* toptta 돕다, wŏnjohada 원조하다.

assistance *n.* wŏnjo 원조, choryŏk 조력. → **help** *n.* toum 도움.

assistant *n.* (*in general*) chosu 조수, (*univesity*) chogyo 조교, pojoja 보조자.

associate *v.* (*keep company*) kyojehada 교제하다; (*combine*) yŏnhaphada 연합하다; yŏnsanghada 연상하다.

+ associated *adj.* yŏnhaphan 연합한.

association n. (*connection*) yŏnhap 연합; (*society*) hyŏphoe 협회, (*academic*) hakhoe 학회.

assume v. (*suppose*) kajŏnghada 가정하다, (*pretend*) kajanghada 가장하다.

assumption n. kajŏng 가정.

assure v. hwakssilhage hada 확실하게 하다.

astonish v. nollage hada 놀라게 하다.

astronomer n. ch'ŏnmunhaktcha 천문학자.

astronomy n. ch'ŏnmunhak 천문학.

\# **at** prep. ...e …에, ...esŏ …에서, ...uro …으로, ...chung-e …중에, ...ŭl …을. ~ *any rate* yŏhat'ŭn 여하튼. ~ *best* kikkŏtthaeya 기껏해야. ~ *ease* p'yŏnanhi 편안히. ~ *last* tŭdiŏ 드디어. ~ *least* chŏgŏdo 적어도; amut'ŭn 아무튼. ~ *once* (*soon*) kot 곧; (*at the same time*) tongsi-e 동시에.

athlete n. sŏnsu 선수: ~'*s foot* mujŏm 무좀.

athletics n. undong kyŏnggi 운동 경기.

Atlantic n. taesŏyang 대서양.

+ **atmosphere** n. (*air*) taegi 대기(大氣). → **environment** n. hwangyŏng 환경.

atom n. wŏnja 원자.

atomic adj. wŏnja-ŭi 원자의. ~ *energy* wŏnjaryŏk 원자력. ~ *bomb* wŏnjat'an 원자탄.

+ **attach** v. puch'ida 붙이다, ch'ŏmbuhada 첨부하다.

+ **attack** v. konggyŏkhada 공격하다.—n. konggyŏk 공격, sŭpkkyŏk 습격.

attain v. ...ŭl talssŏnghada ...을 달성하다.

+ **attempt** v. sidohada 시도하다.—n. kido 기도(企圖). *make an* ~ *to do* ... hae poda ... 해 보다.

attend v. ch'ulsŏkhada 출석하다, ch'amsŏkhada 참석하다.

attendance n. ch'ulssŏk 출석; (*service*) sijung 시중.

* **attention** n. chuŭi 주의, sinkyŏng-ŭl ssŭm 신경을 씀: *A* ~! Ch'aryŏ 차려! *pay* ~ *to* ...e chuŭihada/ sinkyŏng-ŭl ssŭda ...에 주의하다/신경을 쓰다.

+ **attitude** n. t'aedo 태도, chase 자세.

+ **attract** v. kkŭlda 끌다, yuinhada 유인하다; (*entice*)

maehokhada 매혹하다.

attraction *n*. maeryŏk 매력.

* **attractive** *adj*. maeryŏginnŭn⟨itnŭn 매력있는.

attribute *v*. ...ttaemunirago hada ...때문이라고 하다.
—*n*. sokssŏng 속성, t'ŭkssaek 특색.

+ **audience** *n*. ch'ŏngjung 청중, kwan'gaek 관객.

auditorium *n*. (*hall*) kangdang 강당; ch'ŏngjungsŏk
청중석.

August *n*. p'arwŏl 팔월.

aunt *n*. (*the wife of one's father's younger brother*)
sungmo⟨sukmo 숙모, (*one's mother's sister*) imo
이모, (*one's father's sister*) komo 고모, (*in
general*) ajumŏni 아주머니.

Australia *n*. hoju 호주, ostreillia 오스트레일리아.

authentic *adj*. (*trustworthy*) mitŭl manhan 믿을 만
한; (*genuine*) chintcha-ŭi 진짜의.

author *n*. chŏja 저자, chakka 작가.

* **authority** *n*. (*concept*) kwŏnwi 권위, kwŏnhan 권한;
(*person, organization*) tangguk 당국.

autobiography *n*. chasŏjŏn 자서전.

automatic *adj*. chadong-ŭi 자동의.

+ **automatically** *adv*. chadongjŏk-ŭro 자동적으로.

automobile *n*. chadongch'a 자동차.

+ **autumn** *n*. kaŭl 가을.

+ **auxiliary** *adj*. pojo-ŭi 보조의.

+ **available** *adj*. iyonghal ssu innŭn⟨itnŭn 이용할 수 있는.

avant-garde *n*. chŏnwi 전위.

+ **average** *n*. p'yŏnggyun 평균.—*adj*. p'yŏnggyun-ŭi 평
균의.

+ **avoid** *v*. p'ihada 피하다, hoep'ihada 회피하다.

awake *v*. cham-ŭl kkaeda 잠을 깨다. —*adj*. kkaeŏ in
nŭn⟨itnŭn 깨어 있는.

awaken *v*. cham-ŭl kkaeuda 잠을 깨우다.

award *n*. sangp'um 상품(賞品). *the highest* ~
ch'oego sang 최고상. —*v*. (*adjudge*) suyŏhada 수여
하다, sang-ŭl chuda 상을 주다. *be awarded* sang-ŭl
patta 상을 받다.

+ **aware** *adj.* algosŏ 알고서 ; kkaedatkko 깨닫고: *be ~ of* …ŭl algo itta …을 알고 있다.

* **away** *adv.* (*off*) ttŏrŏjyŏsŏ 떨어져서; (*far*) mŏlli 멀리.
  awe *n.* turyŏum 두려움, musŏum 무서움, (*reverential fear*) kyŏngoe 경외.
  awesome *adj.* musimusihan 무시무시한, (*size*) kŏdaehayŏ turyŏun 거대하여 두려운.
  awful *adj.* (*impressive*) wiŏmminnŭn〈wiŏmitnŭn 위엄있는, (*dreadful*) turyŏun 두려운, (*ugly*) ch'uakhan 추악한, (*very bad*) hyŏngp'yŏnŏmnŭn〈ŏpnŭn 형편없는.

+ **awkward** *adj.* (*embarrassing*) kŏbukhan 거북한; (*clumsy*) sŏt'urŭn 서투른, kkolsanaun 꼴사나운; (*human relations*) sŏmŏksŏmŏkhan 서먹서먹한.
  awl *n.* songgot 송곳.
  ax(e) *n.* tokki 도끼—*v.* tokki-ro charŭda 도끼로 자르다.
  axis *n.* kulttae 굴대, ch'uk 축(軸).
  azalea *n.* chindallae 진달래, ch'ŏltchuk 철쭉.

⪬ B ⪭

+ **baby** *n.* agi 아기, aegi 애기; yua 유아; (*girl friend*) aein 애인.
  bachelor *n.* ch'onggak 총각, tokssin(nam)ja 독신(남)자, (*university degree*) haksa 학사: *a ~ of arts* munhakssa 문학사.

* **back** *n.* (*of body*) tŭng 등, twi 뒤. —*adj. & adv.* twi-ŭi 뒤의, twi-ro 뒤로. —*v.* hut'oehada 후퇴하다. *I'll be back soon.* kot toraogessŏyo. 곧 돌아오겠어요.

+ **background** *n.* paegyŏng 배경, imyŏn 이면.

+ **backward(s)** *adv.* twi-ro 뒤로, kkŏkku-ro 거꾸로. —*adj.* twitchok-i 뒤쪽의, (*late*) twijin 뒤진: *a ~ country* 후진국.

+ **bacteria** *n.* segyun 세균, pakt'eria 박테리아.

* **bad** *adj.* nappŭn 나쁜, (*incorrect*) t'ŭllin 틀린, (*severe*) simhan 심한: *It is bad to steal.* humch'inŭn kŏs-ŭn nappŭda. 훔치는 것은 나쁘다.

\+ **badly** *adv.* (*wrongly*) nappŭge 나쁘게: *Things went badly.* ir-i chal an toeŏtta. 일이 잘 안 되었다; (*very much*) tae-danhi 대단히, maeu 매우.

\+ **bad-tempered** *adj.* simsulgujŭn 심술궂은.

\+ **bag** *n.* kabang 가방, paek 백, charu 자루.

  baggage *n.* chim 짐, suhamul 수하물.

\+ **baked** *adj.* kuŭn 구은.

  bakery *n.* ppangtchip 빵집, chegwajŏm 제과점.

\+ **balance** *n.* (*equality*) kyunhyŏng 균형: ~ *of trade* muyŏk suji kyunhyŏng 무역 수지 균형; (*scales*) chŏul 저울; (*bank*) chanaek 잔액. —*v.* kyunhyŏng/chungsim-ŭl chaptta 균형/중심을 잡다; (*weigh*) (muge-rŭl) talda (무게-를) 달다; (*settle*) kyŏlssanhada 결산하다.

  bald *adj.* taemŏri-ŭi 대머리의.

\+ **ball** *n.* ① (*sports equipment*) kong 공, pol 볼. ② (*social dancing*) mudohoe 무도회.

  bamboo *n.* tae 대(竹), taenamu 대나무: ~ *shoots* chuksun 죽순.

  banana *n.* panana 바나나.

\+ **band** *n.* ① (*sash*) tti 띠, kkun 끈. ② (*group*) tte 떼, muri 무리; (*music*) akttae 악대. —*v.* kkŭn-ŭro muktta 끈으로 묶다, (*unite*) tan'gyŏlhada 단결하다.

  bandage *n.* pungdae 붕대. --*v.* pungdae-ro kamtta 붕대로 감다.

\+ **bank** *n.* ① (*money*) ŭnhaeng 은행. ② (*of river*) tuk 둑, chebang 제방.

\+ **bar** *n.* (*stick*) makttaegi 막대기; (*for drinks*) sultchip 술집, pa 바; (*court*) pŏptchŏng 법정. —*v.* (karo) maktta (가로)막다.

  barbarian *n.* yamanin 야만인.

  barber *n.* ibalssa 이발사: ~'*s shop* ibalsso 이발소, ibalgwan 이발관.

  bare *adj.* (*naked*) pŏlgŏpŏsŭn 벌거벗은.

barely *adv.* kyŏu 겨우.

bargain *n.* hŭngjŏng 흥정. ssan mŭlgŏn 싼 물건.

barge *n.* kŏrutppae 거룻배, pajisŏn 바지선.

bark ① *v.* chitta 짖다. ② *n.* (namu)kkŏptchil (나무)껍질.

barometer *n.* kiapkkye 기압계.

barren *adj.* pulmo-ŭi 불모의.

+ **barrier** *n.* ult'ari 울타리, pangch'aek 방책; (*obstacle*) changae 장애: *a ~ of education* kyoyug-ŭi changae 교육의 장애.

+ **base** *n.* kich'o 기초, (*of operations*) kiji 기지(基地). — *adj.* (*mean*) ch'ŏnhan 천한. -*v.* kich'o-rŭl tuda 기초를 두다. *It is based on a serious study.* kugos-ŭn sinjunghan yon'gu-e kich'o-rŭl tugo itta. 그것은 신중한 연구에 기초를 두고 있다.

baseball *n.* yagu 야구, (*ball*) yagugong 야구공.

+ **basic** *adj.* kibonjŏk 기본적, kich'ojŏk 기초석. *a ~ salary* kibon'gŭp 기본급.

basin *n.* (*for washing*) taeya 대야.

+ **basis** *n.* kich'o 기초, kŭn'gŏ 근거: *What ~ do you have for this judgment?* musŭn kŭn'gŏ-esŏ irŏn p'andan-ŭl naeryŏnnŭn'ga? 무슨 근거에서 이런 판단을 내렸는가?

basket *n.* (*bamboo*) paguni 바구니, (*round wicker*) kwangjuri 광주리: *a ~ of fruit* kwail han paguni 과일 한 바구니.

bat *n.* ① (*baseball*) pangmangi 방망이, paet'ŭ 배트. ② (*animal*) paktchwi 박쥐.

+ **bath** *n.* mogyok 목욕. *a public ~* taechung (mogyok)t'ang 대중(목욕)탕.

bathe *v.* mogyokhada 목욕하다; (*swim*) suyŏnghada 수영하다.

bathing suit *n.* suyŏngbok 수영복.

bathroom *n.* mogyokssil 목욕실, (American) hwajangsil 화장실.

battery *n.* (*electric*) chŏnji 전지; (*artillery*) p'obyŏngjungdae 포병중대; (*law*) kut'a 구타.

+ **battle** *n.* (*fight*) ssaum 싸움, chŏnt'u 전투. — *v.*

ssauda 싸우다, punt'uhada 분투하다.

bay *n.* man 만.

be *v.* (*existence*) itta 있다; (*predicative*) ida 이다; (*honorfic*) kyesida 계시다.

beach *n.* haesuyoktchang 해수욕장. → **seashore** *n.* haebyŏn 해변, mulkka 물가, padatkka 바닷가.

+ **beak** *n.* (*bill*) chudungi 주둥이, puri 부리.

beam *n.* kwangsŏn 광선.

+ **bean** *n.* k'ong 콩.

+ **bear** *n.* kom 곰. --*v.* (*endure*) kyŏndida 견디다; (*yield*) maetta 맺다; (*a child*) nat'a 낳다; (*carry*) narŭda 나르다; (*relation*) kwangye(-ga) itta 관계 (가) 있다. *This information may ~ on the case.* i chŏngbo-nŭn kŭ sakkŏn-gwa kwan'gye-ga issŭl kŏsida. 이 정보는 그 사건과 관계가 있을 것이다.

beard *n.* (t'ŏk)suyŏm (턱)수염; (*awn, on a plant*) kkakkŭrŏgi 꺼끄러기.

bearing *n.*(*manner*) t'aedo 태도.

beast *n.* chimsŭng 짐승.

+ **beat** *v.* (*hit*) ttaerida 때리다, p'aeda 패다. (*defeat*) chiuda 지우다. —*n.* (*of music*) paktcha 박자.

+ **beautiful** *adj.* arŭmdaun 아름다운.

+ **beauty** *n.* arŭmdaum 아름다움, mi 미(美); miin 미인: ~ *contest* miin taehoe 미인 대회, ~ *parlor/ shop/salon* miyongwŏn 미용원, miyongsil 미용실.

because *conj.* ...igi ttaemun-e ···이기 때문에, waenya-hamyŏn 왜냐하면, *because of* ttaemun-e 때문에, ...(ŭ)nikka ···(으)니까: *He cannot work ~ of his age.* kŭ-nŭn nai-ga manhasŏ/nai ttaemun-e ir-ŭl mothanda. 그는 나이가 많아서/나이 때문에 일을 못한다.

* **become** *v.* ...i/ka toeda ...이/가 되다. *I wonder what has ~ of him.* kŭ-nŭn ŏttŏhke toenŭnji kunggŭmhada. 그는 어떻게 됐는지 궁금하다; (*suit*) ŏullida 어울리다.

+ **becoming** *adj.* (*suitable*) ŏullinŭn 어울리는.

+ **bed** *n.* ch'imdae 침대; (*flower*) hwadan 화단.

bedroom *n.* ch'imsil 침실.

bee *n.* pŏl 벌, (*honey bee*) kkulbŏl 꿀벌: *a queen ~* yŏwangbŏl 여왕벌. *~ hive* pŏlt'ong 벌통.

beef *n.* soegogi 쇠고기/sogogi 소고기, kogi 고기.

beefsteak *n.* pip'ŭsŭt'eik'ŭ 비프스테이크.

+ **beer** *n.* maektchu 맥주: *~ hall* piŏ hol 비어 홀, maektchutchip 맥주집. *draft ~* saengmaektchu 생맥주.

befall *v.* (-ŭi sinbyŏn-e) takch'ida (의 신변에) 닥치다.

* **before** *adv.* ap'-e 앞에, mŏnjŏ 먼저. —*prep.* (*time*) (i)chŏn-e (이)전에; (*place*) ap'-e 앞에. — *conj.* ...hagi chŏn-e …하기 전에.

beforehand *adv.* miri 미리. → **already** *adv.* pŏlssŏ 벌써.

beg *v.* ch'ŏnghada 청하다. *I ~ your pardon.* sillyechiman tasi malssŭm hae chuseyo. 실례지만 다시 말씀해 주세요.

beggar *n.* kŏji 거지, pirŏngbaengi 비렁뱅이.

+ **begin** *v.* sijakhada 시작하다, kaesihada 개시하다. *What shall we ~ with?* muŏt-but'ŏ sijak halkka? 무엇부터 시작할까? *to ~ with* usŏn 우선.

+ **beginning** *n.* sijak 시작, sich'o 시초, palttan 발단. *at the ~ of this term* i hakkich'o-e 이 학기 초에.

+ **behalf** *n.* (*interest*) iik 이익: *on ~ of* ...ŭl taesinhayŏ ...을 대신하여; *in/on ~ of* ...ŭl wihayŏ …을 위하여.

* **behave** *v.* haengdonghada 행동하다, ch'ŏsinhada 처신하다; (*work*) (kigye-ga) umjigida (기계가) 움직이다.

* **behaviour** *n.* haengdong 행동, ch'ŏsin 처신, p'umhaeng 품행; (*conduct*) haengwi 행위.

+ **behind** *adv.* twi-e 뒤에. —*prep.* ...ŭi twi-e ...의 뒤에. *I am behind him in Korean.* na-nŭn han'gugo-esŏ kŭege twittŏrŏjinda. 나는 한국어에서 그에게 뒤떨어진다.

+ **being** *n.* (*existence*) siltchae 실재, (*human life*) insaeng 인생, (*human being*) in'gan 인간, (*essence*) ponjil 본질.

* **belief** *n.* (*convinction*) hwaksin 확신, (*trust*) sinyong 신용, (*faith*) mitŭm 믿음, sinang 신앙.

* **believe** *v.* mitta 믿다; (*think*) saenggakhada 생각하다. *~ in a god* sin-ŭl mitta. 신을 믿다.

+ **bell** n. (*temple, gate*) chong 종, pel 벨.
+ **belong** v. ...e sokhada ...에 속하다, ...(ŭi) kŏsida ···
  (의) 것이다. *The book belongs to me.* kŭ ch'aeg-ŭn
  nae kŏsida. 그 책은 내 것이다.
+ **below** adv. & prep. arae-e 아래에, (*unworthy of*) ...
  hal kach'i-ga ŏmnŭn〈ŏpnŭn ...할 가치가 없는. →
  under adv. (paro) mit'-e (바로) 밑에.
  belt n. hŏritti 허리띠, hyŏkttae 혁대, pelt'ŭ 벨트,
  (*area*) chidae 지대: *green* ~ noktchidae 녹지대.
  bench n. pench'i 벤치.
+ **bend** v. kuburida 구부리다, (*twist*) hwida 휘다.
+ **benefit** n. (*profit*) iik 이익, (*favor*) hyet'aek 혜택. —v.
  ...ege iroptta ···에게 이롭다.
+ **beside** prep. ...yŏp'-e ···옆에, kyŏt'-e ···곁에.
  besides prep. (*otherwise*) kŭbakke 그밖에; (*moreover*) tŏugi 더욱이, kedaga 게다가.
  best adj. kajang/cheil choŭn 가장/제일 좋은.—adv.
  kajang chal 가장 잘. —n. ch'oesŏn 최선, ch'oesang
  최상.
  bestow v. (sŏnmul-lo) chuda (선물로) 주다.
+ **bet** n. naegi 내기.—v. (ton-ŭl) kŏlda (돈을) 걸다.
  better adj. tŏ(uk) choŭn 더(욱) 좋은.—adv. tŏ(uk)
  chok'e 더(욱) 좋게. —n. poda naŭn kŏt 보다 나은 것.
  --v. kaesŏnhada 개선하다. *You had better see a
  doctor.* ŭisa-rŭl ch'ajaga poaja toegetta 의사를 찾아
  가 보아야 되겠다.
* **between** prep. ...sai-e ...사이에. —adv. sai-e 사이에.
  beverage n. ŭmnyo〈ŭmryo〈su〉 음료〈수〉.
  beware v. chosimhada 조심하다. *Beware of fire.*
  puljosim hasio. 불조심 하시오.
+ **beyond** prep. ...ŭi chŏtchog-e ...의 저쪽에, (*past*)
  ...ŭl nŏmŏsŏ ...을 넘어서.—adv. chŏtchog-e 저쪽 에.
  ~ doubt ŭsimhal yŏjiŏpsi 의심할 여지없이.
+ **Bible** n. sŏnggyŏng 성경.
+ **bicycle** n. chajŏngŏ 자전거.
  bid v.(*command*) myŏngnyŏnghada〈myŏngryŏnghada
  명령하다. (*tell*) malhada 말하다. (*price*) kaps-ŭl

maegida 값을 매기다.

+ **big** adj. k'ŭn 큰, kŏdaran 커다란; chungyohan 중요한; kwajanghan 과장한.

+ **bill** n. kyesansŏ 계산서; (of bank) ŏŭm 어음, (paper money) chipye 지폐; (deed) chŭngsŏ 증서: ~ of lading sŏnha chŭngkkwŏn 선하증권; (animal's) puri 부리.

billiards n. tanggu 당구: ~ table tanggudae 당구대.

bind v. (tie) maeda 매다. (oblige) ŭimu-rŭl chiuda 의무를 지우다.

biography n. chŏn'gi 전기.

biological adj. saengmulhag-ŭi 생물학-의, saengmulhak- tchŏk 생물학적.

* **bird** n. sae 새, naltchimsŭng 날짐승.

+ **birth** n. ch'ulssan 출산, t'ansaeng 탄생; (descent) t'aesaeng 태생.

+ **bit** n. chogŭm 조금. → end n. kkŭt 끝.

+ **bite** v. (snap, sting) mulda 물다. —n. mulgi 물기. a ~ (of snack) hannip 한입

+ **bitter** adv. (taste) ssŭn 쓴; (extremely) simhage 심하게: bitter cold mopssi ch'uun 몹시 추운.

+ **black** adj. kŏmŭn 검은.—v. kkamak'e hada 까맣게 하다. —n. hŭkssaek 흑색, hŭgin 흑인.

+ **blade** n. (of knife) k'allal〈nal 칼날, (sword) k'al 칼; (of grass) p'ullip〈p'ulnip〈p'ulip 풀잎.

+ **blame** v. pinanhada 비난하다, t'athada 탓하다. —n. pinan 비난, t'at 탓.

+ **blanket** n. tamnyo 담요.

blemish n. hŭm 흠.

blind adj. nunmŏn 눈먼, changnim-ŭi 장님의.

blink v. nun-ŭl kkamppakkŏrida 눈을 깜박거리다.

blister n. muljip 물집. —v. muljip-i saenggida 물집이 생기다.

blizzard n. nunbora 눈보라.

+ **block** n. (of wood) namut'omak 나무토막; (lump) tŏngŏri 덩어리; (area) kuhoek 구획. —v. (obstruct) maktta 막다, (check) panghaehada 방해하다.

blond adj. kŭmbar-ŭi 금발의.

+ **blood** n. p'i 피; (lineage) hyŏlt'ong 혈통. ~ pressure hyŏrap 혈압.

bloom n. kkot 꽃. --v. kkoch'-i p'ida 꽃이 피다; (prosper) pŏnyŏnghada 번영하다.

blot n. ŏlluk 얼룩, otchŏm 오점, kyŏltchŏm 결점. --v. (stain) ŏlluktchige hada 얼룩지게 하다.

blouse n. pŭllausŭ 블라우스, yŏja syassŭ 여자 샤쓰.

+ **blow** v. pulda 불다; (explode) p'okppalhada 폭발하다. --n. (knock) t'agyŏk 타격.

+ **blue** adj. p'urŭn 푸른; (depressed) uulhan 우울한, ch'imulhan 침울한.

blueprint n. ch'ŏngsajin 청사진, (architecture) sŏlgyedo 설계도.

blunt adj. (dull) mudin 무딘; (outspoken) soltchikhan 솔직한. → stern n. muttukttukhan 무뚝뚝한.

blush v. (be shamed) nach'-ŭl pulk'ida 낯을 붉히다, ppalgaejida 빨개지다.--n. (rosy glow) hongjo 홍조, pulgŭreham 불그레함.

+ **board** n. (thin plank) p'anja 판자; (committee) wiwŏn-hoe 위원회: ~ of directors isahoe 이사회. --v. (embark on) ollat'ada 올라타다; (lodge) hasukhada 하숙하다.

boast v. charanghada 자랑하다, ttŏbŏrida 떠벌리다. --n. charang 자랑; hŏp'ung 허풍.

+ **boat** n. chakŭn pae/kisŏn 작은 배/기선, pout'ŭ 보우트.

boch beer n. hŭngmaektchu(hŭkmaektchu 흑맥주.

* **body** n. mom 몸, yukch'e 육체; (corpse) sich'e 시체; (group) tanch'e 단체; (letter, composition) ponmun 본문.

boil v. (liquid) kkŭlt'a 끓다; (solids) samda 삶다. --n. (tumor) chonggi 종기, pusŭrŏm 부스럼.

boiler n. poillŏ 보일러.

+ **boiling** adj. kkŭllŭn 끓는.

bold adj. taedamhan 대담한.

bolt n. (screw) poltŭ 볼트; (of a gate) pitchang 빗장; (lightning) pŏngaetppul 번갯불.

+ **bomb** n. p'okt'an 폭탄: hydrogen ~ suso p'okt'an 수소 폭탄/incendiary ~ soit'an 소이탄. —v. p'okgyŏk-hada 폭격하다.

bomber n. p'okkyŏkki 폭격기.

bond n. (tie) kyŏlssok 결속; (fetters) sokppak 속박; (finance) chŭnkkwŏn 증권.

+ **bone** n. ppyŏ 뼈, kolgyŏk 골격.

bonfire n. modakppul 모닥불, hwat'otppul 화톳불.

bonito n. kadaraengi 가다랭이.

bonus n. sangyŏgŭm 상여금, pounŏsŭ 보우너스; paedanggŭm 배당금.

* **book** n. ch'aek 책.—v. (record) kiiphada 기입하다; (reserve) yeyakhada 예약하다.

bookcase/shelf n. ch'aektchang 책장, ch'aekkoji 책꽂이, sŏga 서가.

bookkeeping n. pugi 부기(簿記).

bookshop n. sŏjŏm 서점.

boom n. (in market value) pyŏrak kyŏnggi 벼락 경기; kŭpssŏngjang 급성장, kŭpttŭng 급등.

booth n. (stand) nojŏm 노점, pusŭ 부스, telephone ~ kongjung chŏnhwa (paksŭ) 공중 전화 (박스).

boot n. changhwa 장화, panjanghwa 반(半)장화, puch'ŭ 부츠; (of an automobile) t'ŏrŏngk'ŭ 트렁크.

+ **border** n. (fringe) kajangjari 가장자리, t'eduri 테두리; (borderline) kyŏnggye 경계. —v. (adjoin) chŏp-hada 접하다.

+ **boring** adj. chiruhan 지루한, chaemiŏmnŭn 재미없는, simsimhan 심심한.

+ **born** adj. t'agonan 타고난, ch'ŏnsŏng-ŭi 천성의.

borrow v. pillida 빌리다, ch'ayonghada 차용하다.

bosom n. kasŭm 가슴. —adj. (cherished) kasŭm-e kanjikhan 가슴에 간직한.

boss n. chuin 주인, tumok 두목, posŭ 보스. —v. (control) t'ongsolhada 통솔하다.

* **both** adj. yangtchog-ŭi 양쪽의.—pron. tul ta 둘다. —adv. ...do ...do …도 …도.

bother v. (annoy) kwich'ank'e kulda/hada 귀찮게 굴

다/하다 : ~ about kŏktchŏnghada 걱정하다.
bothersome adj. kwich'anŭn 귀찮은, (colloquial)
kolch'i ap'ŭn 골치 아픈.
+ **bottle** n. pyŏng 병: a ~ opener pyŏngmagae ppobi 병
마개 뽑이.
+ **bottom** n. mitppadak 밑바닥; kich'o 기초; (pl. buttocks) kungdungi 궁둥이.
bounce v. t'wida 튀다, ttwiŏorŭda 뛰어오르다.
bound v. (leap) t'wida 튀다. n. (boundary) kyŏnggye
경계, (range) pŏmwi 범위. ③ adj. mukkin 묶인.
+ **boundary** n. kyŏnggye 경계. → range n. pŏmwi 범위.
bouquet n. kkottabal 꽃다발; (wine) hyanggi 향기.
+ **bown**. ① (archery) hwal 활. ② (of the head) chŏl 절.
—v. (for salutation) chŏlhada 절하다.
+ **bowl** n. (in general) sabal 사발, (rice) konggi 공기;
(stew) ttukppaegi 뚝배기.
+ **box** n. sangja 상자; (theater) t'ŭkppyŏlsŏk 특별석;
(witness box) chŭnginsŏk 증인석.
+ **boy** n. sonyŏn 소년, namja ai 남자 아이; (son) adŭl 아
들, (young man) chŏlmŭn namja 젊은 남자; (young
servant) kŭpsa 급사.
bracelet n. p'altchi 팔찌.
+ **brain** n. noe 뇌, tunoe 두뇌; chiryŏk 지력.
brake n. chedonggi 제동기, pŭreik'ŭ 브레이크.
+ **branch** n. (of tree) kaji 가지; (office) chijŏm 지점.
—v. kallajida 갈라지다.
+ **brass** n. notssoe 놋쇠.
+ **brave** adj. yonggamhan 용감한. —v. yonggamhage
mat- ssŏda 용감하게 맞서다.
brazier n. hwaro 화로.
+ **bread** n. ppang 빵, sikppang 식빵: ~ crumbs ppang-
kkaru 빵가루.
+ **break** v. (destroy) pusuda 부수다, (chop) tchogaeda
쪼개다; (violate) wibanhada 위반하다; (stop)
chungjihada 중지하다. —n. (rupture) p'agoe 파괴;
(gap) kallajin t'ŭm 갈라진 틈; (pause) chungdan
중단.

breakable adj. kkaejigi swiun 깨지기 쉬운.

+ **breakfast** n. ach'im(pap) 아침(밥), choban 조반.

bream n. ingŏ 잉어: sea ~ tomi 도미.

+ **breast** n. kasŭm 가슴.

+ **breath** n. sum 숨, hohŭp 호흡.

+ **breathe** v. sumswida 숨쉬다, hohŭphada 호흡하다.

breeze n. sandŭlbaram 산들바람, mip'ung 미풍.

brewery n. yangjojang 양조장.

bribe n. noemul 뇌물. —v. noemul-ŭl chuda 뇌물을 주다.

brick n. pyŏkttol 벽돌.

bride n. sinbu 신부(新婦), saesaekssi 새색시.

bridegroom n. sillang 신랑.

+ **bridge** n. tari 다리, kyoryang 교량.

+ **brief** adj. kandanhan 간단한, (concise) kan'gyŏlhan 간결한, (short) tchalbŭn 짧은.

briefly adv. kandanhi 간단히.

brigade n. tae 대(隊); yŏdan 여단.

+ **bright** adj. palgŭn 밝은; pinnanŭn⟨pitnanŭn 빛나는, malgŭn 맑은; k'waehwalhan 쾌활한; ch'ongmyŏng-han 총명한.

brightly adv. palkke 밝게, ch'ongmyŏnghage 총명하게.

+ **bring** v. (of things) kajyŏoda 가져오다, (of person) teryŏoda 데려오다 ; ch'oraehada 초래하다.

+ **British** adj. yŏnggug-ŭi 영국의.

broad adj.(wide) nŏlbŭn 넓은, (extensive) kwangdae-han 광대한; (obvious) myŏngbaekhan 명백한.

+ **broadcast** v. pangsonghada 방송하다; (spread) yup'o-hada 유포하다. —n. pangsong 방송: ~ing station pangsongguk 방송국.

+ **broken** adj. pusŏjin 부서진; (weakened) naksimhan 낙심한: ~ hearted siryŏn⟨silyŏnhan 실연한, kijugŭn 기죽은.

broker n. chunggaein 중개인, p'urouk'ŏ 브로우커.

bronze n. ch'ŏngdong 청동. —adj. ch'ŏngdong-ŭi 청동의.

brook n. sinae 시내, silgaech'ŏn 실개천.

broom n. pi 비. —v. (sweep) ssŭlda 쓸다, ch'ŏngsohada 청소하다.

+ **brother** n. hyŏngje 형제: elder ~ (for men) hyŏngnim 형님: (for women) oppa 오빠/younger ~ tongsaeng 동생, au 아우.

brow n. (forehead) ima 이마: (eye) nunssŏp 눈썹.

+ **brown** n. & adj. kalssaek(-ŭi) 갈색(의), kodongsaek(-ŭi) 고동색(의).

+ **brush** n. sol 솔, pŭrŏssi 브러시, (for painting, calligraphy) put 붓. —v. soljilhada 솔질하다.

brutal adj. yasujŏgin 야수적인: (cruel) chaninhan 잔인한, yabihan 야비한.

+ **bubble** n. kŏp'um 거품, konggibangul 공기방울.

bucket n. yangdongi 양동이, pŏk'it 버킷.

buckle n. mulrimsoe 물림쇠, hyŏkdaesoe 혁대쇠, pŏk'ŭl 버클.

buckwheat n. memil 메밀.

bud n. pongori 봉오리, ssak 싹.

Buddha n. puch'ŏ(nim) 부처(님).

Buddhism n. pulgyo 불교.

Buddhist n. pulgyodo 불교도, pulgyosinja 불교신자.

buddy n. (co-worker) tongnyo〈tongryo 동료, tchakp'ae 짝패, (friend) ch'in'gu 친구, tongmu 동무.

budget n. yeasn 예산, yesanan 예산안.

bug n. pŏlle 벌레: (bedbug) pindae 빈대.

bugle n. nap'al 나팔, kaktchŏk 각적.

+ **build** v. chitta 짓다, seuda 세우다, kŏnsŏlhada 건설하다.

* **building** n. kŏnmul 건물, pilding 빌딩.

bulb n. (plant) kugŭn 구근, (electric) chŏngu 전구.

bulk n. (volume) yongjŏk 용적, pup'i 부피: (size) k'ŭgi 크기: (cargo) paetchim 뱃짐.

bulldozer n. puldojŏ 불도저.

+ **bullet** n. ch'ongal 총알, t'anhwan 탄환.

bulletin n. kongbo 공보, hoebo 회보: a ~ board kesip'an 게시판.

bum n. (buttocks) ŏngdŏngi 엉덩이: (person) purangja 부랑자.

bump v. puditch'ida 부딪치다.—n. ch'ungdol 충돌. (swelling) hok 혹.

bunch n. songi 송이, tabal 다발: a ~ of flower kkottabal 꽃다발.

bundle n. tabal 다발, kkurŏmi 꾸러미.

bureau n. (dresser) otchang 옷장; (office) ...kuk ...국(局): the weather ~ kisangdae/guk 기상대/국, annaeso 안내소: an employment ~ chigŏpsogaeso 직업소개소.

burglar n. kangdo 강도, (pam)toduk (밤)도둑.

+ **burn** v. pult'ada 불타다, hwasang-ŭl iptta 화상을 입다, kŭŭlda 그을다.—n. hwasang 화상(火傷).

burp n. t'ŭrim 트림.—v. t'ŭrimhada 트림하다.

burst v. t'ŏjida 터지다; pyŏrangan nat'anada 별안간 나타나다.—n. p'okppal 폭발.

+ **bury** v. mutta 묻다.

+ **bus** n. pŏssŭ 버스.

+ **bush** n. sup'ul 수풀, tŏmbul 덤불. rose ~ changmi namu 장미나무.

* **business** n. chigŏp 직업; ŏmmu〈ŏpmu 업무; chang-sa 장사; saŏp 사업.

businessman n. saŏpkka 사업가.

bust n. pansinsang 반신상, hyungsang 흉상. ② (failure) silp'ae 실패.

+ **busy** adj. pappŭn 바쁜, pŏnch'anghan 번창한.

* **but** conj. kŭrŏna 그러나, hajiman 하지만. —prep. ...oe-e nŭn ···외에는. —adv. taman 다만, tanji 단지.

butcher n. paekchŏng 백정, p'ujuhan 푸주한. a ~ shop chŏngyuktchŏm 정육점.

butt n. ① (bottom part) mittung 밑둥, (stub of cigarette) kkongch'o 꽁초. ② (large cask) k'ŭn t'ong 큰통. ③ v. toltchinhada 돌진하다.

+ **butter** n. bŏt'ŏ 버터.

butterfly n. nabi 나비: ~ stroke chŏbyŏng 접영(蝶泳).

buttock n. (pl.) ŏngdŏngi 엉덩이.

+ **button** n. tanch'u 단추.

* **buy** v. sada 사다, kuiphada 구입하다. —n. maeip 매입.

by adv. kyŏt′-e 곁에. —prep. ...yŏp′-e …옆에; (by means of) ...e ŭihayŏ …에 의하여, ...ŭl kajigo …을 가지고; (before) ...kkaji-enŭn …까지에는.

≤ C ≥

cab n. t′aeksi 택시.
cabaret n. k′yabare 캬바레.
cabbage n. yangbaech′u 양배추, k′aebiji 캐비지.
cable n. (rope) kulgŭn patchul 굵은 밧줄, k′eibŭl 케이블; (underwater) haejŏ chŏnsŏn 해저 전선.
cafe n. (coffee shop, restaurant) k′yap′e 캬페.
cage n. (bird) saejang 새장; (slang) kamok 감옥.
+ cake n. k′eik′ŭ 케이크; (solid mass) tŏngŏri 덩어리.
    → pastry n. kwaja 과자.
calamity n. chaenan 재난, pulhaeng 불행.
+ calculate v. kyesanhada 계산하다, yesanghada 예상하다; → rely n. kidaehada 기대하다.
+ calculation n. kyesan 계산; (forecast) yesang 예상.
calculator n. kyesan′gi 계산기.
+ calendar n. tallyŏk 달력, k′aellindŏ 캘린더.
* call v. purŭda 부르다; (visit) pangmunhada 방문하다; (telephone) chŏnhwa-rŭl kŏlda 전화를 걸다. —n. (visit) pangmun 방문.
calligraphy n. sŏdo 서도.
calling n. sojip 소집; (occupation) chigŏp 직업.
+ calm adj. koyohan 고요한, onhwahan 온화한.
camel n. nakt′a 낙타.
+ camera n. k′amera 카메라, sajinkki 사진기.
camp n. yayŏng 야영. v. yayŏnghada 야영하다.
+ campaign n. (military) kunsahaengdong 군사행동, (political) chŏngch′i undong 정치 운동: an election ~ sŏngŏ undong 선거 운동, a ~ for charity

funds chasŏn mogŭm undong 자선 모금 운동.

camping *n.* yayŏng 야영, k′aemp′ŭ saenghwal 캠프 생
활, ch′ŏnmak saenghwal 천막 생활.

campus *n.* hakkyo kunae 학교 구내, k′aemp′ŏsŭ 캠퍼스.

\# **can** *n.* kkangt′ong 깡통.

can *aux. v.* ···hal ssu itta ···할 수 있다, (*may*) hayŏdo
chot′a 하여도/해도 좋다.

Canadian *n.* k′aenadasaram 캐나다사람. —*adj.* k′ae-
nadaŭi 캐나다의.

canary *n.* k′anaria 카나리아.

cancel *v.* ch′wisohada 취소하다, malssalhada 말살하다.

cancellation *n.* malssal 말살, p′yegi 폐기.

cancer *n.* am 암: ~ *of the lung* p′yeam 폐암/ ~ *of
the stomach* wiam 위암/ *uterine* ~ chagungam 자
궁암; (*C*~) haiisŏn 하지선(夏至線).

\+ **candidate** *n.* huboja 후보자 ; chiwŏnja 지원자.

candle *n.* yangch′o 양초; ch′okkwang 촉광.

candy *n.* sat′ang 사탕, k′aendi 캔디.

cane *n.* chip′angi 지팡이, tanjang 단장; (*stem*) chulgi
줄기: *sugar* ~ sat′angsusu 사탕수수.

canned goods *n.* t′ongjorim chep′um 통조림 제품.

cannon *n.* taep′o 대포, kigwanp′o 기관포.

\+ **cannot** *v.* ···hal ssu ŏptta ···할 수 없다.

canvas *n.* hwap′o 화포(畵布), k′aenbŏsŭ 캔버스.

cap *n.* (*baseball*) moja 모자; ttukkŏng 뚜껑.

\+ **capable** *adj.* ···hal ssu innŭn〈itnŭn ···할 수 있는.

cape *n.* ① ŏkkae mangt′o 어깨 망토, k′eip′ŭ 케이프. ②
(*headland*) kot 곶(岬).

\+ **capital** *adj.* (Brit. *chief*) chuyohan 주요한. —*n.*
(*city*) sudo 수도; (*money*) chabon 자본; (*letter*)
taemuntcha 대문자.

capitalism *n.* chabonjuŭi 자본주의.

capitalist *n.* chabon′ga 자본가; chabonjuŭija 자본주
의자.

capsule *n.* k′aepsyul 캡슐; kkot′uri 꼬투리.

captain *n.* (*army*) taewi 대위; (*navy*) taeryŏng 대령;
(*of warship*) hamjang 함장; (*of merchant ship*) sŏn-

jang 선장; (*of sport*) chujang 주장.

* **car** *n.* ch'a 차, chadongch'a 자동차.
  carbarn *n.* (Brit.) ch'ago 차고.
  carbolic acid *n.* sŏkt'ansan 석탄산.
+ **card** *n.* k'adŭ 카드, (*playing*) t'ŭrŏmp'ŭ 트럼프, (*business*) myŏngham 명함.
+ **cardboard** *n.* mabunji 마분지.
+ **care** *v.* kŏktchŏnghada 걱정하다. —*n.* (*anxiety*) kŏktchŏng 걱정, chosim 조심: *take* ~ chuŭihada 주의하다.
+ **career** *n.* (*background, experience*) kyŏngnyŏk⟨kyŏngryŏk 경력; (*occupation*) chigŏp 직업.
+ **careful** *adj.* chosimsŭrŏun 조심스러운, chuŭigip'ŭn 주의 깊은, sojunghi hanŭn 소중히 하는.
* **carefully** *adv.* chosimsŭrŏpkke 조심스럽게.
+ **careless** *adj.* chosimssŏng ŏmnŭn⟨chosimsŏng ŏpnŭn 조심성 없는, kyŏngsolhan 경솔한.
+ **carelessly** *adv.* soholhage 소홀하게, kyŏngsolhage 경솔하게.
  cargo *n.* hwamul 화물, paetchim 뱃짐.
  carp *n.* ingŏ 잉어: *the silver* ~ pungŏ 붕어. → **goldfish** *n.* kŭmpungŏ 금붕어.
‘ **carpenter** *n.* mokssu 목수, mokkong 목공.
+ **carpet** *n.* yangt'anja 양탄자, yungdan 융단.
  carrot *n.* tanggŭn 당근.
+ **carry** *v.* (*take*) narŭda 나르다, unbanhada 운반하다; (*on the head*) ida 이다; (*on the back*) chida 지다; (*in the arms*) antta 안다; (*on the shoulder*) meda 메다; (*in the hand*) tŭlda 들다; (*at the waist*) ch'ada 차다; hyudaehada 휴대하다.
  cart *n.* ch'a 차, chimch'a 짐차, (son)sure (손)수레.
  cartoon *n.* (p'ungja)manhwa (풍자)만화.
  carve *v.* chogak'ada 조각하다, saegida 새기다.
  carving *n.* chogak 조각, chogaksul 조각술.
* **case** *n.* (*box*) sangja 상자; (*condition*) kyŏngu 경우; (*affair, suit*) sakkŏn 사건. → **patient** *n.* hwanja 환자.
  cash *n.* hyŏn'gŭm 현금, hyŏnch'al 현찰. —*v.* (*ex-*

change) hyŏn′gŭm-ŭro pakkuda 현금으로 바꾸다.

cashier *n.* ch′ulnapkye 출납계, hoegyewŏn 회계원.

cask *n.* t′ong 통: *a wine* ~ sult′ong 술통.

cast *v.* (*throw*) tŏnjida 던지다; (*found, mold*) chujo-hada 주조하다. —*n.* (*mold*) chuhyŏng 주형(鑄型); (*of play*) paeyŏk 배역.

castle *n.* sŏng 성(城), sŏnggwak 성곽, (*mansion*) kungjŏn 궁전.

+ **casual** *adj.* (*accidental*) uyŏnhan 우연한, ttŭtppakk-ŭi 뜻밖의; (*inadvertant*) musimhan 무심한. ~ *wear* pyŏng-sangbok 평상복.

+ **cat** *n.* koyangi 고양이.

catalog(ue) *n.* mongnok〈mokrok 목록, k′at′allogŭ 카탈로그.

+ **catch** *v.* (*seize*) chaptta 잡다. (*grab*) patta 받다; (*overtake*) ch′uwŏlhada 추월하다; (*be infected by disease*) kamyŏmdoeda 감염되다; (*attract*) chuŭi-rŭl kkŭlda 주의를 끌다. → **understand** *v.* ihaehada 이해하다.

caterpillar *n.* p′ulsswaegi 풀쐐기, moch′ung 모충.

catfish *n.* megi 메기.

+ **Catholic** *adj.* (*Roman*) ch′ŏnjugyo-ŭi 천주교의, k′at′ollik-ŭi 카톨릭의. —*n.* ch′ŏnjugyodo 천주교도, kugyodo 구교도, k′at′ollik 카톨릭.

cattle *n.* so 소; (*livestock*) kach′uk 가축.

* **cause** *v.* irŭk′ida 일으키다. —*n.* (*reason*) wŏnin 원인; (*motive*) tonggi 동기; taeŭi 대의.

cautious *adj.* chosimssŏng innŭn〈itnŭn 조심성 있는.

cave *n.* kul 굴, tonggul 동굴, tonghyŏl 동혈.

cedar *n.* himallaya sammok 히말라야 삼목(杉木).

+ **ceiling** *n.* ch′ŏnjang 천장; (*top limit*) sanghan 상한.

celebrate *v.* ch′uk′ahada 축하하다.

celery *n.* sellŏri 셀러리.

+ **cell** *n.* sep′o 세포, (*jail*) tokppang 독방.

cellar *n.* chihasil 지하실; um 움.

cement *n.* siment′ŭ 시멘트, yanghoe 양회.

cemetery *n.* (kongdong)myoji (공동)묘지.

censor n. kŏmyŏl 검열.

cent n. sent'ŭ 센트.

+ **centimetre/centimeter** n. sent'imit'ŏ 센티미터.

centipede n. chine 지네.

+ **central** adj. chungang-ŭi 중앙의, chungsim-ŭi 중심의.

+ **centre/center** n. chungsim 중심, sent'ŏ 센터.

+ **century** n. segi 세기, paengnyŏn〈paeknyŏn 100년.

+ **ceremony** n. yesik 예식, ŭisik 의식(儀式): *a marriage* ~ kyŏlhonsik 결혼식.

* **certain** adj. (*sure*) hwaksilhan 확실한; (*one, some*) ŏttŏn 어떤; (*fixed*) iltchŏnghan 일정한.

certainly adv. hwaksilhi 확실히; (*exclamation*) kŭrŏk'omalgo 그렇고말고.

+ **chain** n. soesasŭl 쇠사슬; (*a long line*) yŏnsok 연속.

+ **chair** n. ŭija 의자, kŏlsang 걸상; (*chairperson*) ŭijang 의장.

+ **chalk** n. punp'il 분필.

+ **chance** n. (*opportunity*) ki-hoe 기회.

* **change** n. pyŏnhwa 변화, pyŏn'gyŏng 변경, (*small money*) chandon 잔돈, (*returned money*) kŏsŭrŭmtton 거스름돈. —v. pyŏnhada 변하다, pakkuda 바꾸다.

+ **character** n. sŏngkkyŏk 성격, inkkyŏk 인격; sŏngjil 성질; inmul 인물; myŏngsŏng 명성; (*letter*) kŭltcha 글자.

+ **characteristic** adj. t'ŭktchiljŏk 특질적. —n. t'ŭktching 특징.

charcoal n. sut 숯, mokt'an 목탄.

+ **charge** n. ch'aegim 책임, (*price demanded*) pudam 부담, yogŭm 요금; (*accusation*) pinan 비난, kobal 고발. —v. (*attack*) chingyŏkhada 진격하다.

+ **charity** n. chabisim 자비심, chaae 자애, (*love*) sarang 사랑; chasŏn 자선:*I work for a charity*. na-nŭn chasŏn hwalttong-ŭl handa. 나는 자선활동을 한다.

charm v. maehok'ada 매혹하다. —n. maeryŏk 매력.

charming adj. maeryŏktchŏgin 매력적인.

chase v. twi-rŭl tchotta 뒤를 쫓다. —n. ch'ugyŏk 추격.

chaste adj. sun'gyŏlhan 순결한; kosanghan 고상한.

chat *n.* & *v.* chapdam(hada) 잡담(하다).

chatter *v.* chaejaljaejal chikkŏrida 재잘재잘 지껄이다. *n.* chikkŏrinŭn sori 지껄이는 소리.

chauffeur *n.* unjŏn kisa 운전 기사, unjŏnsu 운전수.

+ **cheap** *adj.* (*price*) ssan 싼, kapssan 값싼; (*quality*) chir-i nappŭn 질이 나쁜.

cheat *v.* sogida 속이다; sogyŏ ppaeatta 속여 빼앗다; (*examination*) kŏnninghada 컨닝하다.

+ **check** *v.* (*prevent*) chŏjihada 저지하다, (*control*) ŏktchehada 억제하다; (*collate*) taejohada 대조하다, ch'ek'ŭhada 체크하다. —*n.* panghae 방해; chŏmgŏm 점검, ch'ek'ŭ 체크; (*bank*) sup'yo 수표.

checkers *n.* sŏyangjanggi 서양장기.

cheek *n.* ppyam 뺨, pol 볼.

+ **cheerful** *adj.* kibunjoŭn 기분좋은; yuk'waehan 유쾌한, k'waehwalhan 쾌활한.

+ **cheese** *n.* ch'ijŭ 치즈.

chef *n.* yorisa 요리사.

+ **chemical** *adj.* hwahak-ŭi 화학의. —*n.* hwahakjep'um 화학 제품, yakp'um 약품.

chemistry *n.* hwahak 화학.

+ **cheque** *n.* sup'yo 수표: *traveler's* ~ yŏhaengja sup'yo 여행자 수표.

cherry *n.* pŏtchi 버찌; (*blossom*) pŏtkkot 벚꽃; (*tree*) pŏnnamu⟨pŏtnamu 벚나무. —*adj.* chinbunhong-ŭi 진분홍의.

+ **chess** *n.* sŏyangjanggi 서양장기, ch'essŭ 체스.

+ **chest** *n.* (*breast*) kasŭm 가슴; (*box*) kwe 궤, sangja 상자. → **fund** *n.* chagŭm 자금.

chestnut *n.* pam 밤(栗), (*tree*) pamnamu 밤나무.

+ **chew** *v.* ssiptta 씹다.

chicken *n.* tak 닭, takkogi 닭고기.

chief *adj.* chuyohan 주요한, ŭttŭmganŭn 으뜸가는. —*n.* udumŏri 우두머리, -chang -장: *the* ~ *of a section* kwajang 과장.

* **child** *n.* ai 아이, ŏrini 어린이, adong 아동.

childhood *n.* ŏrin sijŏl 어린 시절, yunyŏn'gi 유년기.

chill *n*. naenggi 냉기.

chimney *n*. kulttuk 굴뚝, yŏnt'ong 연통.

+ **chin** *n*. t'ŏk턱, t'ŏkkŭt 턱끝.

China *n*. chungguk 중국.

Chinese *adj*. chungguk-ŭi 중국의, chungguksig-ŭi 중국식의. —*n*. (*people*) chungguksaram 중국사람, chunggugin 중국인: (*language*) chunggugŏ 중국어.

chip *n*. t'omak 토막, namutchogak 나뭇조각. —*v*. chalge ssŏlda 잘게 썰다, kkaktta 깎다.

chisel *n*. kkŭl 끌, chŏng 정.

chlorine *n*. yŏmso 염소(鹽素).

chocolate *n*. ch'ok'ollet 초콜렛.

+ **choice** *n*. sŏnt'aek 선택, korŭn kŏt 고른 것.

choir *n*. hapch'angdae 합창대, (*in church*) sŏnggadae 성가대.

choke *v*. summak'ige hada 숨막히게 하다; ŏngnurŭda⟨ŏknurŭda 억누르다. —*n*. chilssik 질식.

cholera *n*. hoyŏltcha 호열자, k'ollera 콜레라.

+ **choose** *v*. sŏnt'aekhada 선택하다; (*elect*) sŏnch'ulhada 선출하다. → **want** *v*. wŏnhada 원하다.

chop *v*. (*cut*) charŭda 자르다. —*n*. kogitchŏm 고깃점. *pork* ~ toejigalbisal 돼지갈비살.

chopping board *n*. toma 도마.

chopsticks *n*. chŏtkkarak 젓가락.

Christ *n*. yesu(nim) 예수(님), kŭrisŭdo 그리스도.

+ **Christian** *n*. kidokgyosinja 기독교신자, kidokkgyoin 기독교인.

+ **Christianity** *n*. kidokkyo 기독교.

+ **Christmas** *n*. k'ŭrisŭmasŭ 크리스마스, sŏngt'anjŏl 성탄절.

chrysanthemum *n*. kuk'wa 국화.

+ **church** *n*. kyohoe 교회, yebaedang 예배당.

cider *n*. (*apple juice*) sagwajussŭ 사과주스; (Korean, *a very fizzy soda pop*) saida 사이다.

cigar *n*. yŏsongyŏn 여송연, siga 시가.

+ **cigaret(te)** *n*. tambae 담배.

cinder *n*. sŏkt'an chae 석탄 재, ttŭn sut 뜬 숯.

+ **cinema** n. (*theater*) kŭktchang 극장, yŏnghwagwan 영화관; (*movies*) yŏnghwa 영화.

cinnamon n. kyep'i 계피.

+ **circle** n. (*round*) wŏnhyŏng 원형, tongŭrami 동그라미; (*group*) chipttan 집단; ···kye ···계(界); (*range*) pŏmwi 범위. —v. hoejŏnhada 회전하다.

+ **circular** adj. wŏnhyŏng-ŭi 원형의, tunggŭn 둥근; sunhwan- hanŭn 순환하는. —n. hoeramjang 회람장.

circulate v. sunhwanhada 순환하다, tollida 돌리다.

+ **circumstances** n. sanghwang 상황.

circus n. kongmadan⟨kokmadan 곡마단, sŏk'ŏsŭ 서커스.

+ **city** n. tosi 도시, (suffix) -si -시(市): *Cheju ~* 제주시.

civilian n. min'ganin 민간인, mun'gwan 문관.

civilization n. munmyŏng 문명, (*in imperialist contexts*) kaehwa 개화.

+ **claim** n. yogu 요구. —v. (*insist*) chujanghada 수장하다; (*demand*) yoguhada 요구하다.

clan n. ssijok 씨족; tangp'a 당파.

clap v. (*hands*) paksuhada 박수하다; kabyŏpkke ch'ida 가볍게 치다. —n. paksu 박수. *a ~ of thunder* ch'ŏndungsori 천둥소리.

+ **class** n. kyegŭp 계급: *upper ~* sangnyuch'ŭng⟨sangryuch'ŭng 상류층; (*school*) pan 반; (*dignity*) p'umwi 품위: *He has ~.* kŭ-nŭn p'umwi-ga itta. 그는 품위가 있다.

classic adj. kojŏn-ŭi 고전의. —n. kojŏn chakp'um 고전작품. → **first-rate** adj. illyu-ŭi 일류의.

+ **clause** n. (*provision*) cho-hang 조항; (*sentence*) chŏljŏl 철절; (*music*) akku 악구(樂句).

+ **claw** n. palt'op 발톱.

+ **clay** n. chinhŭk 진흙, ch'alhŭk 찰흙.

+ **clean** adj. kkaekkŭthan 깨끗한. —v. kkaekkŭsi hada 깨끗이 하다, ch'ŏngsohada 청소하다, taktta 닦다.

+ **cleaning** n. ch'ŏngso 청소; *dry ~* tŭrai k'ŭllining 드라이 클리닝.

+ **clear** adj. malgŭn 맑은. —v. malkke hada 맑게 하다.

+ **clearly** adv. malkke 맑게, punmyŏnghi 분명히.

+ **clergy** n. sŏngjiktcha 성직자. → **minister** n.(pro-
  testant church) mokssa 목사.
  clerk n. samuwŏn 사무원, chŏmwŏn 점원.
+ **clever** adj. (bright) yŏngnihan〈yŏngrihan 영리한,
  ttokttok'an 똑똑한. → **wise** adj. hyŏnmyŏnghan 현명한.
+ **cliff** n. nangttŏrŏji 낭떠러지, chŏlbyŏk 절벽.
  climate n. kihu 기후, p'ungt'o 풍토.
  climb v. kiŏorŭda 기어오르다. —n. tŭngban 등반.
+ **climbing** n. tŭngsan 등산. —adj. sangsŭnghanŭn 상승
  하는
  clip ① n. k'ŭllip 클립. —② v. (cut) kawi-ro charŭda
  가위로 사르다. → **grip** v. kkwak chwida 꽉 쥐다.
+ **clock** n. (kwaejong)sigye (괘종)시계.
+ **close** v. (shut) tatta 닫다; (finish) mach'ida 마치다.
  close adv. kakkai 가까이. —adj. (near) kakkaun 가까
  운; (intimate) ch'inhan 친한.
+ **closely** adv. (nearly) kakkapkke 가깝게; (strictly) ŏ
  mmilhi 엄밀히; (tightly) tandanhi 단단히: look ~
  kkomkkomhi poda 꼼꼼히 보다.
  closet n. pyŏktchang 벽장, (W.C.) pyŏnso 변소.
* **cloth** n. ch'ŏn 천, otkkam 옷감.
* **clothes** n. ot 옷: Korean ~ Hanbok 한복. →
  bedclothes n. ch'imgu 침구.
  clothesbrush n. otsol 옷솔.
* **clothing** n. (collective) ŭiryu 의류, ŭibok 의복.
+ **cloud** n. kurŭm 구름. → **sky** n. hanŭl 하늘.
  cloudy adj. kurŭmkkin 구름낀, hŭrin 흐린.
+ **club** n. (heavy stick) konbong 곤봉, (association)
  k'ŭllŏp 클럽, tonghohoe 동호회, (student club)
  tongari 동아리.
  clue n. silmari 실마리, tansŏ 단서.
+ **clumsy** adj. (unskillful) sŏt'urŭn 서투른, ŏsaekhan 어
  색한, (tactless) ŏlppajin 얼빠진.
  cluster n. songi 송이; (crowd) muri 무리, tte 떼. —v.
  (round) tte-rŭl jiŏ moida 떼를 지어 모이다.
  coach v. chidohada 지도하다, k'och'ihada 코치. —n.
  taehyŏngmach'a 대형마차, (railway) kaekch'a 객차.

(*motor* ~) bŏs 버스: (*atheletic*) k′och′i 코치.

+ **coal** *n.* sŏkt′an 석탄: ~ *field* t′anjŏn 탄전.
+ **coast** *n.* haean 해안, yŏnan 연안.
+ **coat** *n.* udot 웃옷, sangŭi 상의, oet′u 외투.
  cobweb *n.* kŏmijul 거미줄, kŏmijip 거미집.
  cock *n.* sut′ak 수탉: (*bird*) suk′ŏt 수컷: (*tap, faucet*) kkoktchi 꼭지.
  cockroach *n.* pak′wi(bŏlle) 바퀴(벌레).
  cocktail *n.* k′akt′eil 칵테일.
  coconut *n.* yaja yŏlmae 야자 열매, k′ok′onŏt 코코넛.
  cocoon *n.* (*silkworm*) koch′i 고치.
  cod *n.* (*codfish*) taegu 대구.
  co-educational *adj.* namnyŏ konghak-ŭi 남녀 공학의.
+ **coffee** *n.* kŏp′i 커피.
+ **coin** *n.* (*copper* ~) tongiŏn 동전: *small* ~ chandon 잔돈. (*metal money*) kyŏnghwa(p′ye) 경화(폐).
* **cold** *adj.* ch′an 찬, ch′uun 추운, ch′agaun 차가운: *be* ~ ch′uptta 춥다: (*of hands and feet*) sirida 시리다. —*n.* kamgi 감기: *catch* ~ kamgi tŭlda 감기 들다.
  collapse *v.* munŏjida 무너지다: soet′oehada 쇠퇴하다.
+ **collar** *n.* k′alla 칼라, kit 깃.
+ **collect** *v.* moŭda 모으다, sujiphada 수집하다.
+ **collection** *n.* sujip 수집, sujipp′um 수집품.
+ **college** *n.* tankkwadaehak 단과대학.
  collision *n.* ch′ungdol 충돌, sangch′ung 상충.
  colloquial *adj.* kuŏ(ch′e)-ŭi 구어(체)의.
  colonel *n.* yukkundaeryŏng 육군대령.
  colony *n.* singminji〈sikminji 식민지: (*group*) chipttan 집단.
* **colo(u)r** *n.* saekkal 색깔, pitkkal 빛깔, k′ŏllŏ 컬러, (*art*) saekch′ae 색채: (*pl.*) kun′gi 군기(軍旗). —*v.* saekch′ilhada 색칠하다.
+ **colourful** *adj.* tach′aeroun 다채로운.
+ **colourless** *adj.* t′oesaekhan 퇴색한: p′itkki-ga ŏmnŭn 〈ŏpnŭn 핏기가 없는.
+ **column** *n.* (*pillar*) kidung 기둥: (*of newspaper*) nan 난 (欄): (*mil.*) chongdae 종대.

comb n. pit 빗. —v. pitta 빗다.

+ **combination** n. kyŏlhap 결합, tchangmatch'ugi
  〈tchakmach'ugi 짝맞추기, (*clothes*) k'ombi(neisyŏn)
  콤비(네이션).

+ **combine** v. paehaphada 배합하다, tchangmach'uda
  〈tchakmatch'uda 짝맞추다.

* **come** v. oda 오다: (*be caused by*) yuraehada 유래하
  다: (*become*) ...i toeda ...이 되다: (*amount to*) ...e
  talhada ...에 달하다. → **happen** v. irŏnada 일어나다.
  comedian n. hŭigŭk paeu 희극 배우.
  comet n. hyesŏng 혜성, salbyŏl 살별.

+ **comfort** n. (*consolation*) wian 위안: (*ease*) allak
  〈anrak 안락.

+ **comfortable** adj. p'yŏnanhan 편안한, allak'an
  〈anrakhan 안락한.
  comic adj. hŭigŭg-ŭi 희극의.
  command n. myŏngnyŏng〈myŏngryŏng 명령. —v. myŏng-
  nyŏnghada〈myŏngryŏnghada 명령하다, chihwihada
  지휘하다.
  commander n. chihwigwan 지휘관, saryŏnggwan 사령
  관: (*navy*) chungnyŏng〈chungryŏng 중령: ~ *in*
  chief ch'ongsaryŏnggwan 총사령관.

+ **comment** v. nonp'yŏnghada 논평하다. —n. nonp'yŏng 논평.
  commerce n. sangŏp 상업, (*trade*) muyŏk 무역.

+ **commit** v. (*entrust*) wit'akhada 위탁하다: (*do*
  wrong) pŏmhada 범하다, chŏjirŭda 저지르다.

+ **committee** n. wiwŏnhoe 위원회.

+ **common** adj. kongt'ong-ŭi 공통의: (*average*) pot'ongŭi
  보통의.

+ **communicate** v. allida 알리다, chŏnhada 전하다:
  t'ongsinhada 통신하다.
  communism n. kongsanjuŭi 공산주의.

+ **community** n. sahoe 사회, kongdongsahoe 공동사회,
  chiyŏksahoe 지역사회.
  commute v. t'onggŭnhada 통근하다.
  companion n. tongnyo〈tongryo 동료, ch'in'gu 친구,
  tongbanja 동반자.

* **company** *n.* (*association*) kyoje 교제; (*companions*) tongnyo〈tongryo 동료; (*firm*) hoesa 회사; (*army*) chungdae 중대.

+ **comparative** *adj.* pigyo-ŭi 비교의.

+ **compare** *v.* pigyohada 비교하다, piyuhada 비유하다.

compass *n.* nach'imban 나침반; (*extent*) pŏmwi 범위.

+ **compete** *v.* kyŏngjaenghada 경쟁하다.

+ **competition** *n.* kyŏngjaeng 경쟁, sihap 시합.

+ **complain** *v.* pulp'yŏnghada 불평하다; hosohada 호소하다.

complaint *n.* pulp'yŏng 불평.

+ **complete** *v.* wansŏnghada 완성하다. —*adj.* wanjŏnhan 완전한, (*whole*) chŏnbu-ŭi 전부의.

+ **complex** *adj.* poktchaphan 복잡한; pokhap-ŭi 복합의.

+ **complicated** *adj.* poktchaphan 복잡한.

compliment *n.* (*praise*) ch'ingch'an 칭찬, ch'ansa 찬사; (*greetings*) insa(mal) 인사(말). —*v.* ch'ingch'anhada 칭찬하다.

compromise *n.* & *v.* t'ahyŏp(hada) 타협(하다).

+ **computer** *n.* k'ŏmp'ut'ŏ 컴퓨터: *an electronic ~* chŏnja kyesan'gi 전자 계산기. → **calculator** *n.* kyesan'gi 계산기.

comrade *n.* pŏt 벗, tongji 동지.

conceal *v.* kamch'uda 감추다, sumgida 숨기다.

+ **concentrate** *v.* chipjunghada 집중하다.

+ **concern** *n.* (*anxiety*) kŭnsim 근심. —*v.* (*relate to*) kwan'gyehada 관계하다, kwansim-ŭl katta 관심을 갖다. → **relation** *n.* kwangye 관계.

+ **concerning** *prep.* ...e kwanhayŏ ...에 관하여, ...ŭl tullŏ ssago ...을 둘러 싸고.

+ **concert** *n.* ŭmakhoe 음악회, k'onsŏt'ŭ 콘서트.

+ **conclusion** *n.* (*thesis*) kyŏllon 결론, (*speech*) chonggyŏl 종결; (*treaty*) ch'egyŏl 체결.

+ **concrete** *adj.* kuch'ejŏgin 구체적인. —*n.* k'onk'ŭrit'ŭ 콘크리트. → **solidify** *v.* kuch'ida 굳히다.

* **condition** *n.* (*state*) sangt'ae 상태; (*in contracts*) chokkŏn 조건; (*rank*) sinbun 신분.

conductor *n.* (*orchestra*) chihwija 지휘자; (*train*)

ch'ajang 차장.

conference *n.* hoeŭi 회의.

confess *v.* chabaek'ada 자백하다, kobaek'ada 고백하다; (*recognize*) chainhada 자인하다.

+ confidence *n.* (*trust*) sinyong 신용; (*self-assurance*) chasin 자신, hwakssin 확신.

+ confident *adj.* hwakssinhada/hayŏ 확신하다/하여, chasininnŭn〈itnŭn 자신있는.

Confucianism *n.* yugyo 유교.

Confucius *n.* kongja(nim) 공자(님).

+ confuse *v.* hondonghada 혼동하다: *be ~d with* (...ŭ ro) hondongdoeda (...으로) 혼동되다, *be ~d at* (...ŭ ro) tanghwanghada (...으로) 당황하다.

+ confusion *n.* (*disorder*) hollan〈honran 혼란, (*embarrassment*) tanghwang 당황.

congratulation *n.* ch'uk'a 축하; ch'ukssa 축사.

conjunction *n.* kyŏlhap 결합; (*grammar*) chŏpsokssa 접속사.

+ connect *v.* yŏn'gyŏlhada 연결하다, itta 잇다.

+ connection *n.* yŏn'gyŏl 연결; kwan'gye 관계; (*relative*) yŏntchul 연줄, yŏn'go 연고.

conscience *n.* yangsim 양심, toŭisim 도의심.

conscientious *adj.* yangsimjŏgin 양심적인.

+ consciousness *n.* ŭisik 의식, chagak 자각.

consent *v.* sŭngnak'ada〈sŭngrakhada 승락하다, tongŭihada 동의하다. —*n.* sŭngnak〈sŭngrak 승락; tongŭi 동의.

conserve *v.* pojonhada 보존하다.

+ consequence *n.* kyŏlgwa 결과; chungyossŏng 중요성.

considerable *adj.* sangdanghan 상당한.

* consider *v.* saenggakhae poda 생각해 보다, koryŏhada 고려하다, (*ponder*) sukkohada 수고하다, paery ŏhada 배려 하다.

+ consideration *n.* koryŏ 고려, koryŏ-ŭi taesang 고려의 대상.

+ consist *v.* ...jida ...으로 이루어지다; ... e itta ...에 있다; yangnip'ada〈yangriphada 양립하다.

console *v.* wirohada 위로하다.

consonant *n.* chaŭm 자음. —*adj.* ilch´ihanŭn 일치하는.

constant *adj.* (*same*) han´gyŏlgatŭn 한결같은: (*continuous*) kkŭnimŏmnŭn 끊임없는, pudanhan 부단한.

constipation *n.* pyŏnbi 변비.

construction *n.* kujo 구조: kŏnsŏl 건설.

consul *n.* yŏngsa 영사(領事).

consulate *n.* yŏngsagwan 영사관.

consume *v.* sobihada 소비하다.

+ **contact** *n.* chŏpch´ok 접촉, kyoje 교제. —*v.* yŏllakhada 연락하다.

+ **contain** *v.* p´ohamhada 포함하다, tamkko itta 담고 있다.

* **container** *n.* kŭrŭt 그릇, kŏnt´einŏ 컨테이너.

+ **content** ① *adj.* (*satisfied*) manjokhan 만족한. —*n.* manjok 만족. ② *n.* naeyong 내용.

+ **contest** *n.* nonjaeng 논쟁, tat´um 다툼. —*v.* tat´uda 다투다, kyŏruda 겨루다.

continent *n.* taeryuk 대륙: *the* ~ *of Asia* asia taeryuk 아시아 대륙.

+ **continually** *adv.* pinbŏnhi 빈번히.

* **continue** *v.* kyesok/yŏnsokhada 계속/연속하다.

+ **continuous** *adj.* kyesoktchŏgin 계속적인, kyesokttoenŭn 계속되는.

+ **contract** *n. & v.* kyeyak(hada) 계약(하다).

contradict *v.* panbak´ada 반박하다, mosundoeda 모순되다.

contradiction *n.* mosun 모순.

+ **contrast** *n.* taejo 대조, taebi 대비(對比).

* **control** *v.* chibaehada 지배하다; (*hold in check*) ŏktchehada 억제하다. —*n.* t´ongje 통제.

convenient *adj.* p´yŏllihan⟨p´yŏnrihan 편리한.

convent *n.* sunyŏwŏn 수녀원, sudowŏn 수도원.

+ **conversation** *n.* hoehwa 회화, iyagi 이야기, tamhwa 담화.

convert *v.* chŏnhwanhada 전환하다.(*religion*) kaejongsik´ida 개종시키다.

+ **cook** *v.* pabŭl hada 밥을 하다, (*fancy food*) yorihada 요리하다. —*n.* yorisa 요리사.

+ **cool** *adj.* (*weather*) sŏnŭlhan 서늘한; (*person*) naengjŏnghan 냉정한. *as* ~ *as a cucumber* naengjŏnghan

냉정한, —v. sikhida 식히다.

cooperate v. hyŏpttong/hyŏptchohada 협동/협조하다, hyŏmnyŏk´ada〈hyŏpryŏkhada 협력하다.

cooperation n. hyŏmnyŏk〈hyŏpryŏk 협력.

+ **cope** v. taehanghada 대항하다, matssŏda 맞서다; taech´ŏhada 대처하나.

copper n. kuri 구리, tong 동(銅): ~plate tongp´an 동판.

+ **copy** v. pokssahada 복사하다, pekkida 베끼다. —n. pokssa 복사, sabon 사본: a rough ~ ch´ogo 초고; (book) -kwŏn -권

coral n. sanho 산호.

cord n. (thick string) kulgŭn kkŭn 굵은 끈: (small rope) kanŭn patchul 가는 밧줄.

core n. sok 속, haekssim 핵심, koltcha 골자.

cork n. k´orŭk´ŭ 코르크.

+ **corn** n. okssusu 옥수수. → **grain** n. kokssik 곡식, kongmul〈kokmul 곡물.

corner n. mot´ungi 모퉁이, k´onŏ 코너: (angle) kusŏk 구석.

corporal n. hasa 하사(下士), sangbyŏng 상병.

corps n. kundan 군단, pyŏngdan 병단.

corpse n. sich´e 시체, songjang 송장.

* **correct** adj. parŭn 바른. —v. koch´ida 고치다.

+ **correctly** adv. chŏnghwakhi 정확히, parŭge 바르게.

correspondence n. (agreement) ilch´i 일치, sangŭng 상응; (communication) t´ongsin 통신.

corridor n. pokdo 복도, hoerang 회랑.

corrode v. pusikhada 부식하다.

cosmetic adj. (beautifying) miyong-ŭi 미용의, hwajang-yong-ŭi 화장용의. —n. hwajangp´um 화장품.

+ **cost** v. kamnagada〈kapnagada 값나가다; (require) tŭlda 들다, yohada 요하다; hŭisaengsik´ida 희생시키다. —n. (expense) piyong 비용, (price) kap 값.

+ **cotton** n. som 솜; (cloth) myŏn 면, mumyŏng 무명.

cough n. kich´im 기침. —v. kich´imhada 기침하다.

+ **could** aux. v. (past tense) ...hal ssu issŏtta ...할 수 있었다, (honorific form) ...hal ssu itta ...할 수 있다: Could you give me a ring tonight? onŭl pam-e chŏn-

hwahae chusilssu issŭmnikka? 오늘밤에 전화해 주 실
수 있습니까?

+ **council** *n.* p'yŏngŭihoe 평의회, hyŏpŭihoe 협의회.
+ **count** ① *v.* seda 세다, kyesanhada 계산하다: ~ *for much* chungyohada 중요하다. —*n.* kyesan 계산. ②
  n. (*title*) paektchak 백작.
* **country** *n.* (*rural district*) sigol 시골, (*region*)
  chibang 지방, (*district*) chiyŏk 지역: (*nation*) nara
  나라, kukka 국가.
+ **countryside** *n.* sigol 시골, chibang 지방.
  county *n.* kun 군(郡), (*British*) chu 주(州).
  couple *n.* han ssang 한 쌍, pubu 부부.
+ **courage** *n.* yonggi 용기, paetchang 배짱.
+ **course** *n.* (*route*) chillo〈chinro 진로, k'osŭ 코스: (*of study*) kangjwa 강좌, kwajŏng 과정.
+ **court** *n.* (*law*) chaep'anso 재판소: k'ot'ŭ 코트: *a tennis* ~ t'enisŭ k'ot'ŭ 테니스 코트.
+ **cover** *v.* tŏptta 덮다, (*hide*) kamch'uda 감추다:
  (*extend over*) chŏnmyŏn-e kŏlch'ida 전면에 걸치다:
  p'ohamhada 포함하다. —*n.* tŏpkkae 덮개.
+ **cow** *n.* amso 암소: ~ *boy* mokttong 목동.
  crab *n.* ke 게.
+ **crack** *n.* (*crevice*) t'ŭm 틈, kŭm 금, (*shot*) palssa 발사. —*v.* (*break*) tchogaeda 쪼개다, kkaejida 깨지다.
  cracker *n.* (*firecracker*) p'oktchuk 폭죽: p'aswaegi 파쇄기: (*biscuit*) k'ŭraek'ŏ 크래커.
  cradle *n.* yoram 요람(搖籃); palssangji 발상지.
  crater *n.* punhwagu 분화구.
  crazy *adj.* (*insane*) mich'in 미친: (*madly eager*) yŏl-gwanghanŭn 열광하는.
+ **cream** *n.* k'ŭrim 크림, yuji 유지.
+ **create** *v.* ch'angjohada 창조하다: sŏlliphada 설립하다.
+ **creature** *n.* (*anything in existence*) ch'angjomul 창조물: (*living being*) saengmul 생물: (*domestic animal*) kach'uk 가축: (*human being*) in'gan 인간.
+ **cricket** *n.* (*insect*) kwitturami 귀뚜라미: (*game*) k'ŭrik'et 크리켓.

* **crime** *n.* pŏmjoe 범죄, (*ethic*) choe 죄.
+ **criminal** *adj.* pŏmjoe-ŭi 범죄의, hyŏngsasang-ŭi 형사
  상의. —*n.* pŏmin 범인, choein 죄인.
  cripple *n.* chŏllŭmbari 절름발이, pulguja 불구자.
+ **criticism** *n.* pip'yŏng 비평, (*article*) p'yŏngnon〈ron
  평론.
+ **criticize** *v.* pipyŏnghada 비평하다, pipanhada 비판하
  다; pinanhada 비난하다.
+ **crop** *n.* suhwakmul 수확물. —*v.* suhwakhada 수확하
  다; (*clip, trim*) kkaktta 깎다.
+ **cross** *n.* siptchaga 십자가. —*v.* kŏnnŏda 건너다;
  (*intersect*) kyoch'ahada 교차하다.
+ **crowd** *n.* kunjung 군중; (*throng*) honjap 혼잡. —*v.*
  (*swarm*) pumbida 붐비다.
  crown *n.* wanggwan 왕관. —*v.* kwan-ŭl ssŭiuda 관을
  씌우다. → **top** *n.* kkokkttaegi 꼭대기
+ **cruel** *adj.* chaninhan 잔인한; mujŏnghan 무정한
+ **crush** *v.* nullŏ pusŭrŏttŭrida 눌러 부스러뜨리다, tchigŭ-
  rŏttŭrida 찌그러뜨리다.
  crust *n.* (*bread*) ppang kkŏptchil 빵 껍질; (*hardened
  surface*) kudŏjin p'yomyŏn 굳어진 표면.
  crutch *n.* mokppal 목발; (*prop*) pŏt'im 버팀.
+ **cry** *v.* ulda 울다; (*shout*) sori chirŭda 소리 지르다. —
  n. urŭmssori 울음소리; purŭjijŭm 부르짖음.
  cuckoo *n.* ppŏkkuksae 뻐꾹새, ppŏkkugi 뻐꾸기.
  cucumber *n.* oi 오이:
+ **culture** *n.* munhwa 문화; (*refinement*) kyoyang 교양.
+ **cup** *n.* chan 잔, k'ŏp 컵; sangbae 상배(賞杯).
+ **cupboard** *n.* ch'antchang 찬장.
  cure *n.* (*remedy*) ch'iryo 치료, ch'iyu 치유. —*v.*
  (*heal*) koch'ida 고치다, natta 낫다.
  curio *n.* kolttongp'um 골동품, misulp'um 미술품: ~
  dealer kolttongp'umsang 골동품상.
  curious *adj.* hogisim-e ch'an 호기심에 찬; (*eccentric*)
  koesanghan 괴상한, chin'gihan 진기한.
+ **currency** *n.* yut'ong 유통, t'onghwa 통화.
+ **current** *n.* hŭrŭm 흐름, p'ungjo 풍조; (*electricity*) chŏl-

lyu〈chŏnryu 전류. —adj. yut'ongdoenŭn 유통되는:
(present) hyŏnjae-ŭi 현재의.

curry n. k'are 카레.

curtain n. k'ŏtŭn 커튼, changmak 장막.

+ **curve** n. koksŏn 곡선. —v. (bend) kuburida 구부리다.

cushion n. pangsŏk 방석, k'ussyŏn 쿠션.

+ **custom** n. sŭpkkwan 습관, kwansŭp 관습, kwallye
〈kwanrye 관례: (import duties, pl.) kwansse 관세.

customer n. kogaek 고객, tan'golsonnim 단골손님.

* **cut** v. (oneself) peda 베다, (a string) kkŭnt'a 끊다,
(delete) sakkamhada 삭감하다: (carve) saegida 새
기다: (absent from) kyŏlssŏkhada 결석하다. —n.
(gash, wound) sangch'ŏ 상처.

cute adj. (pretty) kwiyŏun 귀여운: (sharp) pint'ŭmŏm-
nŭn 〈pint'ŭmŏpnŭn 빈틈없는, (shrewd) kiminhan 기민한.

cuttlefish n. ojingŏ 오징이.

D

dairy n. nangnongjang〈naknongjang 낙농장, nang-
nongŏp〈naknongŏp 낙농업.

dam n. taem 댐, tuk 둑. —v. (block up) maktta 막다.

+ **damage** n. sonhae 손해, sonhaebaesang 손해배상. —
v. sonhae-rŭl iphida 손해를 입히다.

+ **damp** adj. ch'ukch'ukhan 축축한, p'ul-i chugŭn 풀이
죽은. —n. sŭpkki 습기. → **fog** n. angae 안개.

+ **dance** n. ch'um 춤, muyong 무용, mudohoe 무도회.
— v. ch'um-ŭl ch'uda 춤을 추다.

dandruff n. pidŭm 비듬.

+ **danger** n. (risk) wihŏm 위험: (menace) wihyŏp 위협,
wihŏmmul 위험물.

* **dangerous** adj. wihŏmhan 위험한, wit'aeroun 위태로운.

+ **dark** adj. ŏduun 어두운, (dismal) ŭmch'imhan 음침한.
--n. ŏdum 어둠, amhŭk 암흑.

+ **darkness** *n.* ŏdum 어둠, amhŭk 암흑.
+ **date** *n.* naltcha 날짜; teit'ŭ 데이트; mannal yakssok 만날 약속. —*v.* ¨esŏ pirottoeda ¨에서 비롯되다.
+ **daughter** *n.* ttal 딸.
  dawn *n.* saebyŏk 새벽. —*v.* nal-i saeda 날이 새다.
* **day** *n.* nal 날, haru 하루; (*daytime*) nat 낮; (*epoch*) sidae 시대.
+ **dead** *adj.* chugŭn 죽은; hwalbalch'i mothan 활발치 못한; *a ~ season* hansanhan ch'ŏl 한산한 철.
  deaf *adj.* kwimŏgŭn 귀먹은, kwimŏgŏri-ŭi 귀머거리의.
* **deal** *v.* (*treat*) taruda 다루다; (*trade*) kŏraehada 거래하다; (*deliver*) chuda 주다. —*n.* (*treatment*) ch'wigŭp 취급; (*amount*) pullyang〈punryang 분량.
+ **death** *n.* chugŭm 죽음, samang 사망.
  debt *n.* pit 빚, puch'e 부채, (*obligation*) ŭnhye 은혜.
+ **deceive** *v.* sogida 속이다; hyŏnhoksik'ida 현혹시키다.
  December *n.* sibiwŏl 12월, sŏttal 섣달.
* **decide** *v.* kyŏltchŏnghada 결정하다.
+ **decision** *n.* kyŏltchŏng 결정, (*judgment*) p'angyŏl 판결.
  decline *v.* (*bend down*) kiur(i)da 기울(이)다, soet'oehada 쇠퇴하다; (*refuse*) kŏjŏlhada 거절하다. —*n.* kyŏngsa 경사, soet'oe 쇠퇴.
+ **decorate** *v.* kkumida 꾸미다.
+ **decoration** *n.* changsik 장식; (*medal*) hunjang 훈장.
+ **decorative** *adj.* changsig-ŭi 장식의.
+ **decrease** *n.* kamso 감소. --*v.* chulda 줄다.
+ **deep** *adj.* kip'ŭn 깊은, simwŏnhan 심원한.
+ **deer** *n.* sasŭm 사슴.
+ **defeat** *n.* p'aebae 패배. —*v.* ch'yŏbusuda 쳐부수다; chiuda 지우다.
+ **defend** *v.* pangŏhada 방어하다, (*in court*) pyŏnhohada 변호하다.
+ **definite** *adj.* myŏnghwakhan 명확한, iltchŏnghan 일정한; hanjŏngdoen 한정된.
+ **definitely** *adv.* myŏngbaekhi 명백히.
* **degree** *n.* (*extent*) to 도(度), chŏngdo 정도; (*school*) hagwi 학위; (*rank*) tŭnggŭp 등급.

+ **delay** v. yŏngisik´ida 연기시키다; kkumulgŏrida 꾸물거리다.—n. chich´e 지체, yŏn´gi 연기.

delegate n. taep´yo 대표. —v. taep´yo-ro naeseuda 대표로 내세우다. (commit) wiimhada 위임하다.

+ **deliberate** v. (consider) sinjunghi saenggakhada 신중히 생각하다; (debate) toŭihada 토의하다. —adj. sinjunghan 신중한.

* **deliberately** adv. sinjunghage 신중하게, koŭi-ro 고의로.

+ **delicate** adj. chŏnggyohan 정교한; (slender) kanyalp´ŭn 가냘픈; (sensitive) mingamhan 민감한.

delicious adj. masinnŭn〈masitnŭn 맛있는.

delightful adj. (maeu) chŭlgŏun (매우) 즐거운, kippŭn 기쁜.

deliver v. (distribute) paedalhada 배달하다; (utter) chinsulhada 진술하다; (throw) tŏnjida 던지다; (relieve) kuhaenaeda 구해내다.

+ **demand** n. & v. yogu(hada) 요구(하다).

democracy n. minjujuŭi 민주주의, minjujŏngch´e 민주정체.

dentist n. ch´ikkwaŭisa 치과의사.

deny v. puinhada 부인하다, (refuse)`kŏjŏlhada 거절하다.

+ **department** n. (part) pumun 부문; (suffixes of government structure, large) ...pu …부, (middle) ...kuk …국(局), (small) …kwa …과; (university) ...kakkwa …학과.

department store n. paek´wajŏm〉paekhwajŏm 백화점.

deposit n. (in a bank) yegŭm 예금; (sediment) anggŭm 앙금, tchikki 찌끼. —v. yegŭm/kongt´akhada 예금/공탁하다.

+ **depressed** adj. naerinullin 내리눌린, uulhan 우울한.

* **describe** v. sŏsulhada 서술하다, myosahada 묘사하다. (trace) kŭrida 그리다.

+ **description** n. sŏsul 서술, sŏlmyŏngsŏ 설명서.

desert ① n. samak 사막. —adj. pulmo-ŭi 불모의. ② v. (forsake) pŏrida 버리다; t´alch´ulhada 탈출하다.

+ **deserve** v. (after verbs) ...hal manhada ···할 만하다, ···hal kach'i-ga itta ···할 가치가 있다, (after nouns) ...ŭl padŭl manhada ···을 받을 만하다, ...ŭl padŭl kach'i-ga itta ···을 받을 가치가 있다.

+ **design** n. sŏlgye 설계, kusang 구상; ŭido 의도. —v. sŏlgyehada 설계하다, tijainhada 디자인하다.

+ **desirable** adj. paramjik'an 바람직한, somangsŭrŏn 소망스런.

+ **desire** n. yongmang⟨yokmang 욕망, somang 소망, yogu 요구. —v. parada 바라다, yomanghada 요망하다.

desk n. ch'aeksang 책상.

desperate adj. chŏlmangjŏgin 절망적인, p'ilsajŏgin 필사적인, chap'ojagi-ŭi 자포자기의.

dessert n. tijŏt'ŭ 디저트, husik 후식.

destiny n. unmyŏng 운명.

+ **destroy** v. p'agoehada 파괴하다, munŏttŭrida 무너뜨리다; (kill) chugida 죽이다.

+ **detail** v. sangsehi malhada 상세히 말하다; t'ŭkp'ahada 특파하다. —n. sebu 세부(細部).

detective n. t'amjŏng 탐정; hyŏngsa 형사.

+ **determination** n. kyŏlssim 결심.

+ **determined** adj. kyŏlssimhada/hayŏ 결심하다/하여.

detour n. uhoe 우회.

+ **develop** v. palttalhada 발달하다; (photo) hyŏnsanghada 현상하다.

+ **development** n. palttal 발달, kae-bal 개발, (photo) hyŏnsang 현상.

* **device** n. (scheme) koan 고안, (apparatus) changch'i 장치; kungni⟨kungri 궁리; ŭijang 의장(意匠), kyech'aek 계책.

devil n. angma⟨akma 악마, kwisin 귀신.

dew n. isŭl 이슬; pangul 방울: the ~ of tears nunmulppangul 눈물방울.

diabetes n. tangnyoppyŏng 당뇨병.

+ **diagram** n. (figure) top'yo 도표, tohyŏng 도형, tosik 도식; (drawing) chaktto 작도.

+ **dial** n. p'yosip'an 표시판, (sundial) haesigye 해시계.

(*telephone*) taiŏl 다이얼.

dialect *n.* sat'uri 사투리; kwanyongŏ 관용어.

+ **diamond** *n.* taiamondŭ 다이아몬드, kŭmgangsŏk 금강석.

diaper *n.* (*breech-cloth*) kijŏgwi 기저귀; marŭmmokkol munŭi 마름모꼴 무늬.

diarrhoea *n.* sŏlsa 설사: *have* ~ sŏlsahada 설사하다.

diary *n.* ilgi 일기, iltchi 일지.

dictation *n.* padassŭgi 받아쓰기; (*command*) myŏngnyŏng〈myŏngryŏng 명령.

dictator *n.* toktchaeja 독재자, chiryŏngja 지령자.

+ **dictionary** *n.* sajŏn 사전, chajŏn 자전.

+ **die** *v.* chuktta 죽다. —*n.* chusawi 주사위.

diet *n.* ① (*weight-loss program*) taiŏtŭ 다이어트; (food) ŭmsingmul〈ŭmsikmul 음식물. ② (*Swedish, Japanese, etc.*) kuk'oe 국회.

+ **difference** *n.* ch'ai 차이; (*discord*) pulhwa 불화.

* **different** *adj.* tarŭn 다른, sangihan 상이한.

* **difficult** *adj.* ŏryŏun 어려운, kkadaroun 까다로운.

+ **difficulty** *n.* ŏryŏum 어려움, kollan〈konran 곤란.

dig *v.* p'ada 파다, k'aeda 캐다; t'amguhada 탐구하다.

digest *v.* sohwahada 소화하다; (*summarize*) yoyak'ada 요약 하다. —*n.* kaeyo 개요.

dike/dyke *n.* torang 도랑, tuk 둑; chebang 제방.

dimple *n.* pojogae 보조개; (*the water surface*) chanmulkkyŏl 잔물결.

dining *n.* siksa 식사: ~ *car* sikttangch'a 식당차, ~ *room* sikttang 식당, ~*table* sikt'ak 식탁.

+ **dinner** *n.* chŏngch'an 정찬, manch'an 만찬: *a* ~ *party* manch'anhoe 만찬회, och'anhoe 오찬회.

diplomat *n.* oegyogwan 외교관, oegyoga 외교가.

+ **direct** *adv.* (*immediate*) chiktchŏptchŏgin 직접적인; (*frank*) soltchikhan 솔직한; (*straight*) ttokpparŭn 똑바른. —*v.* (*order*) chisihada 지시하다, myŏngnyŏng〈myŏngryŏnghada 명령하다; (*guide*) chidohada 지도하다; (*orchestra*) chihwihada 지휘하다.

* **direction** *n.* panghyang 방향; (*instruction*) chisisŏ 지시서; sayongppŏp 사용법.

+ **directly** *adv.* chiktchŏp 직접, chŭkssi 즉시.
  directory *n.* inmyŏngnok〈inmyŏngrok 인명록, (*telephone*) chŏnhwa pŏnhobu 전화 번호부.
+ **dirt** *n.* ssŭregi 쓰레기; chinhŭk 진흙; omul 오물.
+ **dirty** *adj.* (*unclean*) tŏrŏun 더러운, (*base*) ch'ŏnhan 천한, sangsŭrŏun 상스러운.
+ **disagree** *v.* (*differ*) ŭigyŏn-i tarŭda 의견이 다르다; (*unsuitable*) chŏkhaphaji ant'a 적합하지 않다.
+ **disagreement** *n.* purilch'i 불일치.
+ **disappear** *v.* sarajida 사라지다, somyŏlhada 소멸하다.
+ **disappoint** *v.* silmangk'e hada 실망케 하다, chŏbŏrida 저버리다, chwajŏlsik'ida 좌절시키다.
+ **disappointment** *n.* silmang 실망, nakssim 낙심.
* **disapproval** *n.* pulch'ansŏng 불찬성, pulman 불만.
+ **disapprove** *v.* ch'ansŏngha-ji ant'a 찬성하지 않다; (*condemn*) pinanhada 비난하다.
+ **disaster** *n.* chaenan 재난, pulhaeng 불행.
  discipline *n.* hullyŏn〈hunryŏn 훈련; (*public morals*) p'unggi 풍기. —*v.* (*train*) hullyŏnhada〈hunryŏnhada 훈련하다; (*reprimand*) chinggyehada 징계하다.
  discount *n.* & *v.* harin(hada) 할인(하다).
  discourtesy *n.* sillye 실례, (*rude act*) murye 무례.
+ **discover** *v.* palgyŏnhada 발견하다, kkaedatta 깨닫다.
+ **discuss** *v.* ŭinonhada 의논하다, t'oronhada 토론하다.
+ **discussion** *n.* ŭinon 의논, t'oŭi 토의.
+ **disease** *n.* pyŏng 병, chilhwan 질환.
  disgraceful *adj.* such'isŭrŏun 수치스러운.
+ **disgust** *n.* siltchŭng 싫증, hyŏmo 혐오.
+ **dish** *n.* chŏpssi 접시; yori 요리.
+ **dishonest** *adj.* chŏngjikhaji mothan 정직하지 못한.
+ **dislike** *n.* sirŭm 싫음, hyŏmo 혐오. —*v.* sirŏhada 싫어하다, (*people*) miwŏhada 미워하다.
+ **disorder** *n.* nanjap 난잡, mujilsŏ 무질서. —*v.* ŏjirŏphida 어지럽히다.
+ **disorganize** *v.* ⋯ŭi chojig-ŭl p'agoehada ⋯의 조직을 파괴하다, hollansik'ida〈honransikhida 혼란시키다.
  dispense *v.*(*distribute*) nanwŏjuda 나눠주다, (*do*

without) ŏpssi kyŏndida 없이 견디다, (*put up*) chojehada 조제하다.

+ **display** *n.* chinyŏl 진열. *v.* (*show*) chŏnsihada 전시하다, (*reveal*) nat'anaeda 나타내다.

  disposition *n.* (*temperament*) kijil 기질; (*management*) ch'ŏri 처리.

+ **dispute** *n.* maldat'um 말다툼, nonjaeng 논쟁. —*v.* maldat'umhada 말다툼하다.

  dissipated *adj.* pangt'anghan 방탕한.

  dissolve *v.* (*melt*) noktta 녹다; (*terminate*) haesanhada 해산하다.

+ **distance** *n.* kŏri 거리, kangyŏk 간격.

  distant *adj.* (*space*) mŏlli innŭn⟨itnŭn 멀리 있는; (*time*) oraen 오랜; (*relationship*) ch'onsu-ga mŏn 촌수가 먼; (*not familiar*) sŏrŭmhan 서름한.

+ **distinct** *adj.* (*clear*) myŏngbaekhan 명백한, sŏnmyŏnghan 선명한; (*seperate*) pyŏlgae-ŭi 별개의.

  distress *n.* kŭnsim 근심, kot'ong 고통; kon'gung 곤궁. *v.* koerop'ida 괴롭히다, sŭlp'ŭge hada 슬프게 하다.

  distribute *v.* nanuŏjuda 나누어주다.

  district *n.* kuyŏk 구역; (*region*) chibang 지방.

+ **disturb** *v.* ŏjirŏpkke hada 어지럽게 하다, kyoranhada 교란하다; panghaehada 방해하다.

  ditch *n.* torang 도랑, kaech'ŏn 개천.

+ **divide** *v.* nanuda 나누다, pullihada⟨punrihada 분리하다.

+ **division** *n.* punhal 분할; (*boundary*) kyŏnggye 경계; (*portion*) kuhoek 구획; (*military*) sadan 사단.

  divorce *n.* ihon 이혼. —*v.* ihonhada 이혼하다.

do *v.* (*act*) hada 하다; (*make*) mandŭlda 만들다; (*finish*) kkŭnnaeda⟩kkŭtnaeda 끝내다; (*enough*) ch'ungbunhada 충분하다: *This will ~ me very well.* igŏs-ŭro ch'ungbunhamnida 이것으로 충분합니다; (*confer, give*) haechuda 해주다: *Will you ~ me a favor?* put'ak hana tŭrŏ jusigessŭmnikka? 부탁 하나 들어 주시겠습니까?

  dock *n.* ① (*artificial basin*) tok'ŭ 도크, sŏngŏ 선거(船

渠), (*wharf*) pudu 부두. ② (*law*) p'igosŏk 피고석.

+ **doctor** *n*. (*medical*) ŭisa 의사, (*degree*) pakssa 박사. —*v*. ch'iryohada 치료하다.

+ **document** *n*. munsŏ 문서, chŭngsŏ 증서.

+ **dog** *n*. kae 개: *a dirty* ~ (slang) tŏrŏun nyŏsŏk 더러운 녀석.

    doll *n*. inhyŏng 인형. → **puppet** *n*. kkokttugakssi 꼭두각시.

    dollar *n*. tallŏ 달러, -pul -불(弗): *five* ~*s* obul 5불.

    done *v*. (imi) ⋯han (이미) ⋯한: *well*-~ ta kuun 다구운.

    donkey *n*. tangnagwi 당나귀.

    Don't! Haji maseyo! 하지 마세요!

    dormitory *n*. kisuksa 기숙사, hapsuksso 합숙소.

+ **door** *n*. mun 문, ch'uripkku 출입구: ~ *keeper* munjigi 문지기, suwi 수위. ~ *knob* sonjabi 손잡이. *out of* ~*s* yaoe-esŏ 야외에서, chip pakk-esŏ 집 밖에서.

    dot *n*. chŏm 점. —*v*. chŏm-ŭl tchiktta 점을 찍다.

    double *adj*. tu kob-ŭi 두 곱의, tu pae-ŭi 두 배의. —*v*. pae-ro hada 배로 하다. —*n*. kop 곱, pae 배(倍).

+ **doubt** *n*. ŭisim 의심, ŭihok 의혹. —*v*. ŭisimhada 의심하다.

    dough *n*. milkkaru panjuk 밀가루 반죽.

    dove *n*.(*pigeon*) pidulgi 비둘기. → **Holy Spirit** *n*. sŏngnyŏng〈sŏngryŏng 성령.

* **down** *adv*. & *adj*. arae-ro(-ŭi) 아래로(의).

+ **downward** *adv*. araetchog-ŭro 아래쪽으로.

    drag *v*. kkŭlda 끌다, kkŭrŏdanggida 끌어당기다.

    dragon *n*. yong 용.

    drain *n*. paesu 배수(排水). —*v*. mur-ŭl ppaeda 물을 빼다; tchuk tŭrik'ida 쭉 들이키다.

    drape *n*. p'ojang 포장, hwijang 휘장. —*v*. tŏptta 덮다.

+ **draw** *v*. (*pull*) kkŭlda 끌다; (*pictures*) kŭrida 그리다; (*inhale*) sum-ŭl swida 숨을 쉬다.

+ **drawer** *n*. (*chest*) sŏrap 서랍; (*pl. pants*) p'aench'ŭ 팬츠.

+ **drawing** *n*. chedo 제도(製圖), kŭrim 그림.

    dreadful *adj*. musŏun 무서운, (*terrible*) turyŏun 두려운; (*disagreeable*) mopssi silhŭn 몹시 싫은.

dream *n.* kkum 꿈; kongsang 공상. —*v.* kkum-ŭl kkuda 꿈을 꾸다, mongsanghada 몽상하다.

+ **dress** *n.* ot 옷, ŭibok 의복. —*v.* (*put on*) iptta 입다; (*adorn*) kkumida 꾸미다, sonjilhada 손질하다.

dressmaker *n.* yangjaesa 양재사.

* **drink** *v.* masida 마시다. —*n.* (*generic*) ŭmnyo〈ŭmryo 음료, (*alcoholic*) sul 술.

drinking *n.* sulmasigi 술마시기, ŭmju 음주.

+ **drive** *v.* molda 몰다, (*car, etc.*) unjŏnhada 운전하다. *n.* tŭraibŭ 드라이브; (*path*) ch'ado 차도; (*campaign*) undong 운동.

+ **driver** *n.* unjŏnsu 운전수.

driveway *n.* ch'ado 차도.

+ **drop** *n.* pangul 방울, mulppangul 물방울. —*v.* ⋯ŭl ttŏrŏttŭrida ⋯을 떨어뜨리다. (*fall*) ⋯i (ttokttok) ttŏrŏjida ⋯이 (똑똑) 떨어지다.

drown *v.* mur-e ppajida 물에 빠지다, ikssahada 익사하다.

+ **drug** *n.* yak 약, yakp'um 약품; (*narcotic*) mayak 마약. *v.* yak-ŭl mŏgida 약을 먹이다.

drugstore *n.* yakkuk 약국.

drum *n.* puk 북, tŭrŏm 드럼; (*eardrum*) komak 고막.

drunk *adj.* sulch'wihan 술취한.

+ **dry** *v.* mallida 말리다.—*adj.* marŭn 마른, kŏnjohan 건조한.

duck *n.* ori 오리: *a domestic* ~ chibori 집오리.

due *adj.* man'gi-ga toen 만기가 된; chidanghan 지당한; toch'ak yejŏngin 도착 예정인. —*adv.* chŏng- 정-: ~ *south* chŏngnam 정남.

+ **dull** *adj.* (*insensitive*) tunhan 둔한, (*blunt*) mudin 무딘; (*boring*) chaemi ŏmnŭn〈ŏpnŭn 재미없는.

dummy *n.* (*imitation*) mojop'um 모조품; (*stupid person*) pabo 바보; (*figurehead*) kkokttugakssi 꼭두각시.

dumpling *n.* mandu 만두.

dung *n.* ttong 똥; (*manure*) kŏrŭm 거름.

* **during** *prep.* ⋯hanŭn tongan ⋯하는 동안.

+ **dust** *n*. mŏnji 먼지.—*v*. mŏnji-rŭl ttŏlda 먼지를 떨다.
  dustbin *n*. ssŭregit'ong 쓰레기통.
+ **duty** *n*. ŭimu 의무; (*tax*) segŭm 세금.
  dwarf *n*. nanjangi 난장이. —*adj*. waesohan 왜소한,
  chagŭn 작은. —*v*. (*keep small*) chakke hada 작게
  하다.
  dwindle *v*. (chŏmjŏm) chagajida (점점) 작아지다,
  chulda 줄다; (*waste away*) yawida 야위다.
  dye *v*. muldŭrida 물들이다. —*n*. mulkkam 물감.

≤ E ≥

* **each** *adj*. kakkag-ŭi 각각의, kaktcha-ŭi 각자의. *pron*.
  kaktcha 각자, chegakki 제각기.
+ **eager** *adj*. yŏltchunghanŭn 열중하는, yŏlssimin 열심인.
+ **eagerly** *adv*. yŏlssimhi 열심히, kanjŏlhi 간절히.
  eagle *n*. toksuri 독수리; (*emblem*) toksurip'yo 독수리
  표.
  ear *n*. kwi 귀, (*corn, etc.*) isak 이삭.
+ **early** *adj*. irŭn 이른. —*adv*. iltchigi 일찍이.
+ **earn** *v*. (*by labor*) pŏlda 벌다, (*obtain*) ŏtta 얻다;
  (*deserve*) padŭl manhada 받을 만하다.
+ **earth** *n*. (*globe*) chigu 지구; (*ground*) taeji 대지;
  (*soil*) hŭk 흙; (*this world*) i sesang 이 세상.
  earthenware *n*. chilgŭrŭt 질그릇, t'ogi 토기(土器).
  earthquake *n*. chijin 지진.
+ **east** *n*. tongtchok 동쪽. —*adv*. tongtchog-ŭro 동쪽으로:
  E~ *Asia* tongasia 동아시아 /*Far E*~ kŭkttong 극동.
+ **easy** *adj*. swiun 쉬운 ; p'yŏnhan 편한 ; nŏgŭrŏun 너그
  러운. —*adv*. swipkke 쉽게. E~ *come, ~ go.*
  swipkke ŏdŭn kŏs-ŭn swipkke ilnŭnda 쉽게 얻은 것
  은 쉽게 잃는다.
* **eat** *v*. mŏktta 먹다, (*honorific, meal*) chapsusida 잡수

시다, (*honorific, meal & drink*) tŭsida 드시다;
(*gnaw*) pusikhada 부식하다.

echo *n.* meari 메아리, panhyang 반향. —*v.* mearich'ida 메아리치다.

+ **economic** *adj.* kyŏngje-ŭi 경제의, kyŏngjehag-ŭi 경제
학의.

economics *n.* kyŏngjehak 경제학.

economize *v.* kyŏngjejŏg-ŭro ssŭda 경제적으로 쓰다,
chŏryak'ada 절약하다.

+ **economy** *n.* kyŏngje 경제, (*frugality*) chŏryak 절약.

+ **edge** *n.* kajangjari 가장자리, (*blade*) nal 날. —*v.*
nar-ŭl seuda 날을 세우다, kalda 갈다.

+ **education** *n.* kyoyuk 교육, hunyuk 훈육.

eel *n.* paemjangŏ 뱀장어.

* **effect** *n.* (*result*) kyŏlgwa 결과; (*efficacy*) hyokkwa
효과; (*influence*) yŏnghyang 영향. —*v.* irŭk'ida 일으
키다, talsŏnghada 달성하다.

+ **effective** *adj.* yuhyohan 유효한, hyokkwajŏgin 효과적인.

efficiency *n.* hyoyul 효율, nŭngnyul〈nŭngryul 능률.

+ **efficient** *adj.* hyoyultchŏgin 효율적인, (*person*) yunŭnghan 유능한.

* **effort** *n.* noryŏk 노력, sugo 수고, nogo 노고.

+ **egg** *n.* al 알, (*of hen*) kyeran 계란, talgyal 달걀.

+ **eight** *n.* yŏdŏl 여덟, p'al 팔(8).

eighteen *n.* yŏlyŏdŏl 열여덟, sipp'al 십팔(18).

eighty *n.* yŏdŭn 여든, p'alsip 팔십(80).

+ **either** *pron. & adj.* ŏnŭ han tchok 어느 한 쪽. —*adv.
& conj.* ···kŏna ···kŏna ···거나 ···거나.

+ **elaborate** *adj.* (*work*) chŏngsŏngdŭrin 정성들인,
chŏnggyohan 정교한. —*v.* (*plan*) chŏnggyohage
mandŭlda 정교하게 만들다, tadŭmtta 다듬다, (*topic,
subject*) chasehi malhada 자세히 말하다.

elastic *n.* komukkŭn 고무끈. —*adj.* t'allyŏk'ssŏng in-
nŭn〈t'anryŏksŏng itnŭn 탄력성있는, sinch'ukssŏng
innŭn〈sinch'uksŏng itnŭn 신축성있는.

elbow *n.* p'alkkumch'i 팔꿈치. —*v.* p'alkkumch'i-ro
ttŏmilda 팔꿈치로 떠밀다.

+ **elect** v. (*choose*) ppoptta 뽑다, sŏn´gŏhada 선거하다.
  —*adj.* tangsŏndoen 당선된. *president* ~ taet´ong-
  nyŏng tangsŏnja 대통령 당선자, ch´agi taet´ong-
  nyŏng 차기 대통령.
+ **election** n. sŏn´gŏ 선거: *a general* ~ ch´ongsŏn´gŏ 총
  선거.
+ **electric** adj. chŏn´gi-ŭi 전기의: ~ *appliance* chŏn´gi-
  jep´um 전기제품. ~ *bulb* chŏn´gu 전구. ~ *current*
  chŏllyu〈chŏnryu 전류. ~ *engineering* chŏn´gigong-
  hak 전기공학. ~ *fan* sŏnp´unggi 선풍기. ~ *heater*
  chŏngi nallo〈nanro 전기난로. ~ *light* chŏn´gi(ppul)
  전기(불), chŏndŭng 전등. ~ *power house* paltchŏnso
  발전소. ~ *rice cooker* chŏn´gibapssot 전기밥솥.
+ **electricity** n. chŏn´gi 전기, chŏn´gihak 전기학.
+ **electronic** adj. chŏnja-ŭi 전자의: ~ *organ* chŏnja orŭgan 전자 오르간.
  elegant adj. uahan 우아한, kosanghan 고상한.
  element n. yoso 요소.**elephant** n. k´okkiri 코끼리.
  elevator n. sŭngganggi 승강기, ellibeit´ŏ 엘리베이터.
  eleven n. yŏlhana 열하나, sibil 십일(11).
* **else** adv. kŭbakke 그밖에: *or* ~ kŭrŏch´i anŭmyŏn 그
  렇지않으면.
+ **embarrass** v. (*perplex*) nanch´ŏhage hada 난처하게
  하다, ch´angp´ihage hada 창피하게 하다: (*complic-
  ate*) poktchaphagehada 복잡하게 하다: (*hinder*)
  panghaehada 방해하다.
+ **embarrassment** n. tanghwang 당황, kollan〈konran
  곤란.
  embassy n. taesagwan 대사관.
+ **emotion** n. kamjŏng 감정; chŏngsŏ 정서; kamdong 감동.
+ **emotional** adj. kamjŏngjŏgin 감정적인, chŏng-e yakhan 정에 약한 .
  emperor n. hwangje 황제, chewang 제왕.
+ **emphasis** n. kangjo 강조.
* **emphasize** v. kangjohada 강조하다, yŏksŏlhada 역설
  하다.
+ **emphatic** adj. kangjohan 강조한.

+ **employ** v. ch´aeyonghada 채용하다; (use) sayonghada 사용하다. —n. koyong 고용; kŭnmu 근무.
+ **employer** n. koyongju 고용주, chuin 주인.
empress n. hwanghu 황후, wangbi 왕비.
+ **empty** adj. (t´ong) pin (텅) 빈; hŏttoen 헛된. —v.
piuda 비우다.
+ **enable** v. ···hal ssu itkke hada ···할 수 있게 하다.
+ **enclose** v. ponghae nŏt´a 봉해 넣다, ewŏssada 에워싸다.
+ **encourage** v. yonggi-rŭl chuda 용기를 주다; changryŏ-
hada 장려하다; chojanghada 조장하다.
* **end** n. kkŭt 끝; (purpose) moktchŏk 목적; (close) kyŏlmal 결말. —v. kkŭnnada⟨kkŭtnada 끝나다; (stop)
kkŭnnaeda⟨kkŭtnaeda 끝내다.
+ **ending** n. (termination) kyŏlmal 결말, majimak 마지
막; (death) chugŭm 죽음.
+ **enemy** n. chŏk 적, (forces) chŏkkun 적군, (country)
chŏkkuk 적국.
+ **energetic** adj. hwalgich´an 활기찬, chŏngnyŏktchŏg-
in⟨chŏngryŏkchŏgin 정력적인.
* **energy** n. him 힘, enŏji 에너지.
engage v. chongsahada 종사하다, yaksok´ada 약속하
다, (betroth) yakhonhada 약혼하다.
` **engagement** n. yak´on 약혼, yaksok 약속.
+ **engine** n. enjin 엔진, kigwan 기관: a locomotive ~ 기
관차, palttonggi 발동기.
engineer n. kisa 기사, konghakja 공학자(工學者).
England n. yŏngkuk 영국, inggŭllaendŭ 잉글랜드.
* **English** n. & adj. (language) yŏngŏ(-ŭi) 영어(의).
Englishman n. yŏngguksaram 영국사람.
+ **enjoy** v. chŭlgida 즐기다: ~ a visit pangmunhayŏ
chŭlgŏwŏhada 방문하여 즐거워 하다, (possess) nuri-
da 누리다.
+ **enjoyable** adj. chŭlgŏun 즐거운, kwaejŏkhan 쾌적한.
ensign n. (badge) kijang 기장, (flag) ki 기.
* **enough** adj. ch´ungbunhan 충분한. —adv. nŏngnŏk-
hage⟨nŏknŏkhage 넉넉하게. —n. ch´ungbunham 충
분함.

+ **enter** v. (*go into*) tŭrŏgada 들어가다; (*start*) sijak-hada, 시작하다, (*join*) kaiphada 가입하다, (*record*) kiiphada 기입하다.

entertain v. (*amuse*) hŭnggyŏpkke hada 흥겹게 하다, (*hospitality*) hwandaehada 환내하나, (*harbor*) maŭm-e p'umtta 마음에 품다.

+ **entertainment** n. chŏpttae 접대, hwandae 환대; (*amusement*) yŏhŭng 여흥.

+ **enthusiasm** n. yŏlgwang 열광, yŏlssim 열심.

+ **enthusiastic** adj. yŏlgwangjŏgin 열광적인.

entire adj. (*total*) chŏnch'e-ŭi 전체의, (*complete*) wanjŏnhan 완전한: *He is an ~ believer in Christianity.* kŭ-nŭn wanjŏnhan kŭrisŭdogyoinida 그는 완전한 그리스도교인이다.

+ **entrance** n. iptchang 입장(入場), iphoe 입회, (*door*) ipkku 입구: ~ *fee* iptchangnyo⟨iptchangryo 입장료.

+ **entry** n. ch'amga 참가, (*organization*) kaip 가입; (*vestibule*) hyŏn'gwan 현관: *No ~.* tŭrŏgaji motham. 들어가지 못함. iptchanggŭmji. 입장금지; ~ *fee* iptchangnyo⟨ryo 입장료; kiip 기입.

+ **envelope** n. pong'u 봉투. → **wrapper** n. ssagae 싸개.

+ **environment** n. hwangyŏng 환경.

envy n. chilt'u 질투, sigi 시기, sŏnmang 선망. —v. purŏwŏhada 부러워하다.

+ **equal** adj. kat'ŭn 같은, tongdŭnghan 동등한; p'yongdŭnghan 평등한.

+ **equally** adv. ttokgach'i 똑같이, kyundŭnghage 균등하게.

* **equipment** n. sŏlbi 설비, changgu 장구(裝具).

erase v. chiuda 지우다, sakjehada 삭제하다.

eraser n. chiugae 지우개, komujiugae 고무지우개.

erect adj. kodŭn 곧은.—v. seuda 세우다.

errand n. simburŭm 심부름; (*mission*) samyŏng 사명; (*business*) pollil⟨polil 볼일, yongkkŏn 용건.

error n. chalmot 잘못, (*fault*) erŏ 에러.

+ **escape** n. & v. (*flee*) tomang(gada) 도망(가다), (*avoid*) momyŏn(hada) 모면하다.

* **especially** *adv.* t'ŭkhi 특히.

\+ **essential** *adj.* ponjiltchŏgin 본질적인; (*necessary*) kinyohan 긴요한. —*n.* (chu)yotchŏm (주)요점.

establish *v.* (*found*) sŏlliphada 설립하다; (*constitute*) chejŏnghada 제정하다; (*prove*) hwaktchŭnghada 확증하다.

etiquette *n.* yeŭi pŏmjŏl 예의 범절, et'ik'et 에티켓.

Europe *n.* yurŏp 유럽, kuju 구주.

evaporate *v.* chŭngbalhada 증발하다, sosanhada 소산 (消散)하다; t'alsuhada 탈수하다.

\+ **even** *adj.* (*level*) p'yŏngp'yŏnghan 평평한. —*adv.* (*just*) paro 바로; ⋯choch'ado ⋯조차도: *E~ a child could understand it.* ŏrin ai-joch'ado/rado kŭgŏs -ŭn alssu itta. 어린 아이조차도/라도 그것은 알 수 있다.

\+ **evening** *n.* chŏnyŏk 저녁, haejillyŏk⟨haejilnyŏk 해질녘.

* **event** *n.* sakkŏn 사건; (*outcome*) sŏngkkwa 성과; (*in sport*) kyŏnggi chongmok 경기 종목.

\+ **eventually** *adv.* kyŏlguk 결국. → **finally** *adv.* ma- ch'im nae 마침내.

\+ **ever** *adv.* yŏt'aekkŏt 여태껏, iltchigi 일찍이; (*always*) ŏnjena 언제나.

\+ **every** *adj.* modŭn 모든, (*all possible*) ongat 온갖; (*prefix*) mae⋯ 매⋯: ~ *day* maeil 매일, (*suffix*) ⋯mada ⋯마다 : ~ *other day* it'ŭltchae-mada 이틀 째 마다, kyŏgil-lo 격일로.

everybody *pron.* nuguna 누구나, chegakki 제각기.

\+ **everyone** *pron.* nuguna 누구나, modŭn saram 모든 사 람, (*honorific*) yŏrŏbun 여러분, kaktcha 각자.

\+ **everything** *pron.* modŭn kŏt 모든 것, muŏsidŭnji 무엇 이든지. —*n.* kajang chungyohan kŏt 가장 중요한 것: *Art was his* ~. yesur-ŭn kŭ-ege kajang chungyo- han kŏsiŏtta. 예술은 그에게 가장 중요한 것이었다.

everywhere *adv.* ŏdidŭnji 어디든지, toch'ŏ-e 도처에.

\+ **evidence** *n.* chŭnggŏ 증거, (*sign*) chinghu 징후.

\+ **evil** *adj.* (*wicked*) saakhan 사악한, (*unlucky*) pulgil- han 불길한. —*n.* ak 악, chaehae 재해. → **wrong** *adj.* nappŭn 나쁜.

- **exact** *adj.* (*accurate*) chŏnghwakhan 정확한, chŏng-milhan 정밀한: (*strict*) ŏmkkyŏkhan 엄격한.
+ **exactly** *adv.* chŏnghwakhage 정확하게, t'ŭllimŏpsi 틀림없이.
+ **exaggerate** *v.* kwajanghada 과장하다.
+ **examination** *n.*(*test*) sihŏm 시험; kŏmsa 검사, (*scrutiny*) kŏmt'o 검토: (*court*) simmun 심문.
+ **examine** *v.* sihŏmhada 시험하다, simsahada 심사하다; (*scrutinize*) kŏmt'ohada 검토하다, chosahada 조사하다.
* **example** *n.* ye 예, pogi 보기, (*instance*) sillye 실례; (*model*) mobŏm 모범. ~ *sentences* yemun 예문.
+ **excellent** *adj.* usuhan 우수한, hullyunghan 훌륭한.
+ **except** *prep.* ⋯ŭl cheoehago ⋯을 제외하고. —*v.* cheoehada 제외하다.
  exception *n.* yeoe 예외, cheoe 제외.
  excess *n.* ch'ogwa 초과, kwada 과다: yŏbun 여분.
+ **exchange** *n.* & *v.* kyohwan(hada) 교환(하다), pakkuda 바꾸다.
  excite *v.* chagŭk'ada 자극하다, irŭk'ida 일으키다.
+ **excitement** *n.* hŭngbun 흥분, chagŭk 자극.
+ **exciting** *adj.* chagŭktchŏgin 자극적인, (*stirring*) hŭng-bun sikhinŭn 흥분시키는, (*thrilling*) sinnanŭn 신나는.
  excursion *n.* sop'ung 소풍, yuram 유람.
+ **excuse** *n.* p'inggye 핑계, (*justification*) pyŏnmyŏng 변명, (*pretext*) kusil 구실. —*v.* (pardon) yongsŏhada 용서하다: (justify) pyŏnmyŏnghada 변명하다.
+ **exercise** *n.* (*physical*) undong 운동 ; (*practice*) yŏn-sŭp 연습, (*military*) hullyŏn 〈hunryŏn 훈련. —*v.* undonghada 운동하다; yŏnsŭphada 연습하다.
* **exist** *v.* chonjaehada 존재하다, (*live*) saraitta 살아있다.
+ **existence** *n.* chonjae 존재, siltchae 실재.
  exit *n.* (*way out*) ch'ulgu 출구: (*departure*) t'oejang 퇴장. —*v.* nagada 나가다, t'oejanghada 퇴장하다.
+ **expect** *v.* kidaehada 기대하다, yegihada 예기하다.
+ **expensive** *adj.* kappissan 값비싼.
* **experience** *n.* kyŏnghŏm 경험, (*physical*) ch'ehŏm 체

험. —v. kyŏnghŏm/ch'ehŏmhada 경험/체험하다.

expert *adj.* ikssuk'an 익숙한, noryŏnhan 노련한. —*n.* chŏnmun'ga 전문가, myŏngsu 명수.

+ **explain** *v.* sŏlmyŏnghada 설명하다, palk'ida 밝히다.

+ **explanation** *n.* sŏlmyŏng 설명, haesŏl 해설.

+ **explosion** *n.* p'okppal 폭발: *population* ~ in'gu p'okpal 인구폭발, p'ayŏl 파열.

+ **explosive** *adj.* p'okppalssŏng-ŭi 폭발성의. *n.* p'ogyak 폭약.

export *v.* such'ulhada 수출하다. —*n.* such'ulp'um 수출품.

* **express** *v.* p'yohyŏnhada 표현하다, nat'anaeda 나타내다. —*adj.* t'ŭkppyŏlhan 특별한. —*n.* (*bus*) kŭphaengppŏssŭ 급행버스, (*train*) kŭphaengyŏlch'a 급행열차; (*mail*) sokttal 속달.

* **expression** *n.* (*verbal, artistic*) p'yohyŏn 표현; (*facial*) p'yojŏng 표정.

+ **extend** *v.* nŭrida 늘이다, hwakjanghada 확장하다; (*reach*) ``e irŭda ``에 이르다.

+ **extent** *n.* nŏlbi 넓이, pŏmwi 범위; chŏngdo 정도.

+ **extra** *adj.* yŏbun-ŭi 여분의. —*n.* (*newspaper*) hooe 호외; (*actor*) eksŭt'ŭrŏ 엑스트러.

+ **extreme** *adj.* (*excessive*) kŭkttanjŏgin 극단적인; (*radical*) kwagyŏkhan 과격한; (*final*) ch'oejong-ŭi 최종의. —*n.* kŭkttan 극단.

* **eye** *n.* nun 눈: *artificial* ~ ŭian 의안(義眼).

eyebrow *n.* nunssŏp 눈썹: ~ *pencil* nunssŏp kŭrigae 눈썹그리개.

≦ F ≧

+ **fabric** *n.*(*cloth*) otkkam 옷감, ch'ŏn 천, (*textile*) chingmul⟨chikmul 직물; (*structure*) kujo 구조. →

building n. kŏnmul 건물.

* **face** n. ŏlgul 얼굴; (*surface*) p'yomyŏn 표면. —v. ...
kwa maju poda …과 마주보다; (*confront*) …e
chingmyŏnhada⟨chikmyŏnhada …에 직면하다.

* **fact** n. sasil 사실, silche 실제, chinsang 진상.

+ **factory** n. kongjang 공장, chejaksso 제작소.

fade v. sidŭlda 시들다, paraeda 바래다.

+ **fail** v. (*not succeed*) silp'aehada 실패하다; (*be insufficient*) pujokhada 부족하다; (*not pass*) naktchehada 낙제하다.

+ **failure** n. silp'ae 실패; naktche 낙제.

faint adj. (*vague, dim*) hŭimihan 희미한; (*weak,
feeble*) kanyalp'ŭn 가냘픈; (*fainting*) hyŏn'gitchŭng
nanŭn 현기증 나는. —v. hŭimihaejida 희미해지다;
kijŏlhada 기절하다.

+ **fair** ① adj. (*just*) kongp'yŏnghan 공평한, (*poetic,
beautiful*) arŭmdaun 아름다운. ② n. sijang 시장(市
場); (*exhibition*) kongjinhoe 공진회.

+ **fairly** adv. (*justly*) kongjŏnghage 공정하게; (*pass-
ably*) sangdanghi chok'e 상당히 좋게; (*pretty*)
kkwae 꽤.

fake n. katcha 가짜.

+ **fall** v. ttŏrŏjida 떨어지다. —n. ch'urak 추락;(*autumn*)
kaŭl 가을; (*pl. waterfall*) p'okp'o 폭포: *the ~s of
Niagara* naiaegara p'okp'o 나이애가라 폭포.

+ **false** adj. (*untrue*) kŏjis-ŭi 거짓의, (*wrong*)
kŭrŭttoen 그릇된, (*unfaithful*) pulssŏngsilhan 불성
실한.

+ **familiar** adj. (*intimate*) ch'in(mil)han 친(밀)한;
(*wellknown*) chal algo innŭn⟨itnŭn 잘 알고 있는,
nannigŭn⟨natigŭn 낯익은, (*common*) hŭnhan 흔한.

+ **family** n. kajok 가족, kajŏng 가정.

+ **famous** adj. yumyŏnghan 유명한.

fan ① n. (*admirer*) p'aen 팬. ② n. (*hand-held*)
puch'ae 부채; *an electric* ~ sŏnp'unggi 선풍기. —v.
puch'aejilhada 부채질하다; sŏndonghada 선동하다.

+ **far** adj. mŏn 먼; yowŏnhan 요원한.—adv. mŏlli 멀리:

~ *away* mŏlli-e 멀리에.

+ **farm** *n.* nongjang 농장; (*animal*) yangsiktchang 양식장. —*v.* (*cultivate*) (t´oji-rŭl) kyŏngjakhada (토지를) 경작하다; (intransitive) nongsa-rŭl chitta 농사를 짓다.

farmer *n.* nongbu 농부, (*group*) nongmin 농민.

+ **fashionable** *adj.* yuhaeng-e matnŭn 유행에 맞는.

+ **fast** ① *adj.* (*quick*) pparŭn 빠른, (*speedy*) sinsokhan 신속한; (*firm*) tandanhan 단단한; (*unfading*) pulbyŏn-ŭi 불변의. —*adv.* (*quickly*) ppalli 빨리, (*swiftly*) sinsokhi 신속히; (*tightly*) tandanhi 단단히. ② *n.* tansik 단식. —*v.* tansikhada 단식하다. → *break* ~ *n.* choban 조반.

+ **fasten** *v.* tongyŏmaeda 동여매다, chamgŭda 잠그다.

+ **fat** *adj.* saltchin 살찐, (*fleshy*) ttungttunghan 뚱뚱한; (*fertile*) piokhan 비옥한. —*n.* kutkkirŭm 굳기름, chibang 지방, (*meat*) pigye 비계.

fate *n.* (*destiny*) unmyŏng 운명; (*doom*) agun 악운. → **death** *n.* chugŭm 죽음.

+ **father** *n.* abŏji 아버지, (*honorific*) abŏnim 아버님, puch´in 부친; (*founder*) sijo 시조; (*priest*) sinbu (nim) 신부(님).

+ **fault** *n.* (*defect*) hŭm 흠, kyŏltchŏm 결점, (*mistake*) kwao 과오, silssu 실수, oryu 오류, (*sin*) choe 죄.

+ **favo(u)r** *n.* put´ak 부탁; hoŭi 호의, ch´ongae 총애. —*v.* ch´ansŏnghada 찬성하다; ch´injŏlhi taehada 친절히 대하다, toptta 돕다.

favo(u)rite *adj.* kajang maŭm-e tŭnŭn 가장 마음에 드는, aju choahanŭn 아주 좋아하는. —*n.* (*thing*) kajang maŭm-e tŭnŭn kŏt 가장 마음에 드는 것; (*person*) ch´onga 총아.

+ **fear** *n.* (*dread*) kongp´o 공포; (*anxiety*) kŏktchŏng 걱정. —*v.* turyŏwŏhada 두려워하다; kŏktchŏnghada 걱정하다.

+ **feather** *n.* (*plume*) kit 깃, kitt´ŏl 깃털.

+ **feature** *n.* (*characteristic*) t´ŭktching 특징; (*appearance*) yongmo 용모; (*scoop*) t´ŭktchonggisa 특종기

사; (*TV program*) inkki p'ŭro 인기 프로.

February *n.* iwŏl 2월.

feeble *adj.* yak'an 약한, kanyalp'ŭn 가냘픈.

feed *v.* mŏgida 먹이다; kirŭda 기르다; (*supply*) konggŭphada 공급하다. —*n.*(*for fowl*) moi 모이; (*for cattle, horses*) kkol 꼴, yŏmul 여물; (*for dogs, cats*) pap 밥.

* **feel** *v.* manjyŏ poda 만져 보다; (*with senses*) nŭkkida 느끼다. —*n.* nŭkkim 느낌.

* **feeling** *n.* nŭkkim 느낌, (*artistic sense*) kamgak 감각, (*pl. emotion*) kamjŏng 감정.

+ **feet** *n.* (*measure*) p'it'ŭ 피트. → foot.

fellow *n.* ch'in'gu 친구, tongnyo〈tongryo 동료; (*intimate*) nyŏsŏk 녀석; (*man*) namja 남자, sanai 사나이.

+ **female** *n.* yŏsŏng 여성, yŏja 여자. —*adj.* (*used as animals*) amk'ŏs-ŭi 암컷의; (*people*) yŏsŏng-ŭi 여성의: ~ *dress* puinbok 부인복.

+ **fence** *n.* (*hedge*) ult'ari 울타리, (*wall*) tam 담.

fencing *n.* kŏmsul 검술.

ferryboat *n.* narutppae 나룻배, yŏllaksŏn〈yŏnraksŏn 연락선.

festival *n.* ch'uktche(il) 축제(일), chanch'i 잔치.

feudal *adj.* yŏngji-ŭi 영지의, ponggŏnjŏgin 봉건적인: *the* ~ *system* ponggŏnjedo 봉건제도.

fever *n.* (*temperature*) koyŏl 고열, (*disease*) yŏlbyŏng 열병; (*craze*) yŏlgwang 열광.

+ **few** *adj.* sosu-ŭi 소수의, kŏŭi ŏmnŭn〈ŏpnŭn 거의 없는. —*n.* sosu 소수, tusŏnŏt 두서넛. *a* ~ chogŭm 조금, myŏtkkae(-ŭi) 몇개(의).

fickle *adj.* (*changeable*) pyŏndŏksŭrŏun 변덕스러운, pyŏnhagi swiun 변하기 쉬운.

+ **field** *n.* tŭl 들; (*scope, academic area*) punya 분야.

fierce *adj.* (*savage*) sanaun 사나운, (*violent*) maengnyŏlhan〈maengryŏlhan 맹렬한; (*very bad*) chidok'an 지독한, salbŏlhan 살벌한.

fifteen *n.* yŏldasŏt 열다섯, sibo 15.

fifty *n.* swin 쉰, osip 50. —*adj.* osip-ŭi 오십의.

+ **fight** *v.* ssauda 싸우다. —*n.* ssaum 싸움, kyŏkt'u 격투; (*contest*) sŭngbu 승부.

+ **figure** *n.* (*form*) hyŏngsang 형상, moyang 모양; (*appearance*) oemo 외모, oegwan 외관; (*design*) tohae 도해, kŭrim 그림; (*numeral*) sutcha 숫자. —*v.* (*think*) sanggakhada 생각하다; (*reckon*) hearida 헤아리다. (*imagine*) maŭm sog-e kŭrida 마음 속에 그리다.

file *v.* (*papers*) ch'ŏlhada 철하다; (*submit*) chech'ulhada 제출하다. —*n.* (*tool*) chul 줄; (*for papers*) sŏryuch'ŏl 서류철; (*mil.*) taeyŏl 대열.

+ **fill** *v.* (*kadŭk*) ch'aeuda (가득) 채우다, meuda 메우다. —*n.* ch'ungbun 충분; (*satiety*) p'osik 포식.

* **film** *n.* p'illŭm 필름; yŏlbŭn mak 엷은 막.

filthy *adj.* aju tŏrŏun 아주 더러운, pulgyŏlhan 불결한, (*vile*) ch'ujap'an 추잡한.

+ **final** *adj.* majimag-ŭi 마지막의, kyŏltchŏngjŏgin 결정적인.

+ **finally** *adv.* mach'imnae 마침내, (*lastly*) ch'oehu-ro 최후로, (*at last*) tŭdiŏ 드디어.

finance *n.* chaejŏng 재정, (*science*) chaejŏnghak 재정학, (*pl. funds*) chaewŏn 재원. —*v.* chaejŏng-ŭl chiwŏnhada 재정을 지원하다.

+ **financial** *adj.* chaejŏng(sang)-ŭi 재정(상)의.

* **find** *v.* ch'ajanaeda 찾아내다, (*discover*) palgyŏnhae naeda 발견해 내다, (*something lost*) ch'atta 찾다: *I found my lost ring.* irhŭn panji-rŭl ch'ajatta 잃은 반지를 찾았다; (*learn*) alda 알다.

+ **fine** ① *adj.* (*excellent*) hullyunghan 훌륭한, usuhan 우수한; (*satisfactory*) chohŭn 좋은; (*very thin*) kanŭdaran 가느다란; (*handsome*) arŭmdaun 아름다운. ② *n.* pŏlgŭm 벌금.

+ **finger** *n.* sonkkarak 손가락: *the first* ~ chipkke sonkkarak 집게손가락. *the middle* ~ kaundesonkkarak 가운데손가락. *the ring* ~ mumyŏngji 무명지, yaksonkkarak 약손가락. *the little* ~ saekkisonkkarak 새끼손가락.

+ **finish** *v.* (*end*) ...ŭl mach'ida ⋯을 마치다, ...ŭl kkŭnnaeda〈kkŭtnaeda ⋯을 끝내다, ...i kkŭnnada〈kkŭt-

nada …이 끝나다; (*consume*) ta mŏktta 다 먹다;
(*complete*) wansŏngsik´ida/hada 완성시키다/하다.
—*n.* (*end*) kkŭt 끝, chonggyŏl 종결; (*perfection*)
mamuri 마무리.

+ **fire** *n.* pul 불, (*conflagration*) hwajae 화재.—*v.* (*a
gun*) ssoda 쏘다; (*from job*) haegohada 해고하다;
(*set fire to*) pul not´a 불 놓다.

  fireman *n.* sobangsu 소방수; hwabu 화부.

  fireworks *n.* pulkkonnori〈pulkkotnori 불꽃놀이.

+ **firm** *n.* sangsa 상사, hoesa 회사.—*adj.* kyŏngohan 견
고한, anjŏngdoen 안정된.

* **first** *adj.* ch´ŏtchae-ŭi 첫째의, cheil-ŭi 제일의. —*adv.*
ch´ŏtchae-ro 첫째로.—*n.* ch´ŏtchae 첫째, cheil 제일.

+ **fish** *n.* (*live ~*) mulkkogi 물고기, (*~ to eat*) saengsŏn 생선. —*v.* naktta 낚다, nakssi-rŭl hada 낚시를
하다, kogi-rŭl chaptta 고기를 잡다.

  fisherman *n.* ŏbu 어부; (*angler*) naksikkun 낚시꾼.

  fishing *n.* kogijabi 고기잡이, ŏŏp 어업: *~ boat* ŏsŏn 어
선/*~ line* naksitchul 낚싯줄/*~ rod* naksittae 낚싯대
/*~ village* ŏch´on 어촌.

  fist *n.* chumŏk 주먹. → **punch** *v.* chumŏg-ŭro ch´ida
주먹으로 치다.

+ **fit** *adj.* (*suitable*) chŏkttanghan 적당한, (*suited*)
almajŭn 알맞은; (*going with match, fitting*) ŏullinŭn 어울리는. —*v.* (*suit*) almatta 알맞다, (*tailor*)
match´uda 맞추다. —*n.* (*convulsion*) paltchak 발작.

+ **five** *n.* tasŏt 다섯, o 오(5).

+ **fix** *v.* (*repair*) koch´ida 고치다, surihada 수리하다;
(*secure, establish*) kojŏngsik´ida 고정시키다.

  flag *n.* ki 기, kippal 깃발: *national ~* kukki 국기
(國旗).

+ **flame** *n.* pulkkot 불꽃; chŏngnyŏl〈chŏngyŏl 정열.

  flash *v.* pŏntchŏgida 번쩍이다, hoek chinagada 획 지나
가다. —*n.* sŏmgwang 섬광(閃光).

* **flat** ① *adj.* (*even*) p´yŏngp´yŏnghan 평평한; (*uniform*) kyunilhan 균일한. —*n.* p´yŏngmyŏn 평면. ②
(*apartment in England*) ap´at´ŭ 아파트.

+ **flavo(u)r** v. yangnyŏmhada 양념하다. —n. mat 맛,
p'ungmi 품미. → **fragrance** n. hyanggi 향기.

flea n. pyŏruk 벼룩. ~ *market* pyŏruksijang 벼룩시장.

+ **flesh** n. (*meat*) kogi 고기, sal 살; (*human body*)
yukch'e 육체.

+ **flexible** adj. (*bend*) hwigi swiun 휘기 쉬운, (*pliant*)
tarugi swiun 다루기 쉬운, yuyŏnhan 유연한;
(*personal relations*) mal chal tŭnnŭn〈tŭtnŭn 말 잘
듣는.

+ **float** n. (*buoy*) pup'yo 부표. —v. ttŭda 뜨다.

+ **floor** n. (*wooden*) maru 마루, (*heated floor*) ondol
온돌; (*story*) ch'ŭng 층; (*bottom*) (mit)ppadak
(밑)바닥.

florist n. kkotchangsu 꽃장수.

+ **flour** n. milkkaru 밀가루, karu 가루, punmal 분말.

+ **flow** v. hŭrŭda 흐르다, nŏmch'yŏhŭrŭda 넘쳐 흐르다.
—n. hŭrŭm 흐름, yuch'ul 유출, yut'ong 유통.

+ **flower** n. kkot 꽃: *artificial* ~ chohwa 조화/~
arrangement kkotkkoji 꽃꽂이.

flowerpot n. hwabun 화분.

+ **fly** ① n. (*insect*) p'ari 파리. ② v. (*bird*) nalda 날다;
(*kite*) nallida 날리다, (*operate a plane*)
chojonghada 조종하다; (*run away*) taranada 달아나
다. → **flight** n. pihaeng 비행.

foam n. kŏp'um 거품.—v. kŏp'um-i ilda 거품이 일다.

focus n. ch'otchŏm 초점, p'ouk'ŏsŭ 포우커스.

fog n. an'gae 안개, yŏnmu 연무(煙霧).

+ **fold** n. churŭm 주름. —v.(*paper*) chŏptta 접다,
(*laundry*) kaeda 개다.

folk n. (*people*) saramdŭl 사람들, (*pl.*) kajok 가족. ~
dance minsok muyong 민속무용.

+ **follow** v. ttaragada 따라가다, ttarŭda 따르다; (*pursue*) ch'uguhada 추구하다.

following adj. taŭm-ŭi 다음의.

+ **fond** adj. choahanŭn 좋아하는, chŏngdaun 정다운.

* **food** n. ŭmsik 음식: ~ *stuff* singnyang〈sikryang 식량,
singnyop'um〈sikryop'um 식료품.

fool n. pabo 바보, mŏngch'ŏngi 멍청이. —v. sogida 속이다.

+ **foolish** adj. (silly) ŏrisŏgŭn 어리석은, pabogat'ŭn 바보같은; (immature) yuch'han 유치한.

+ **foot** n. (of the body) pal 발; (bottom) mit 밑; (measure) p'it'ŭ 피트; (infantryman, ~ soldier) pobyŏng 보병.

+ **football** n. (soccer) ch'ukku 축구, (American ~) misik ch'ukku 미식축구, p'utppol 풋볼; ch'ukku-gong 축구공.

for prep. ···ŭl wihayŏ ···을 위하여; (on account of) ttaemun-e 때문에; (during) ···tongan ···동안.

forbid v. kŭmhada 금하다; panghaehada 방해하다.

* **force** n. him 힘; (pl.) (troops) kundae 군대. (effect) hyoryŏk 효력. —v. ŏktchi-ro ···hage hada 억지로 ···하게 하다, kangyohada 강요하다.

+ **forceful** adj. himsen 힘센, kangnyŏkhan⟨kangryŏkhan 강력한.

+ **foreign** adj. oeguk-ŭi 외국의, oerae-ŭi 외래의.

foreigner n. oegugin 외국인, oegukssaram 외국사람.

+ **forest** n. sup 숲, samnim⟨samrim 삼림.

+ **forget** v. ijŏbŏrida 잊어버리다, manggakhada 망각하다.

forgive v. yongsŏhada 용서하다; (remit) myŏnjehada 면제하다, t'anggamhada 탕감하다.

* **form** n. (shape) moyang 모양, hyŏngt'ae 형태, (figure) mosŭp 모습, (appearance) oegwan 외관; (blank) sŏsik 서식. —v. hyŏngt'ae-rŭl iruda 형태를 이루다.

* **formal** adj. chŏngsig-ŭi 정식의; (in form) hyŏngsiktchŏgin 형식적인.

+ **former** adj. (previous) ap'-ŭi 앞의; yennar-ŭi⟨yetnal-ŭi 옛날의, ijŏn-ŭi 이전의: ~ president chŏntaet'ongnyŏng⟨ryŏng 전대통령. —n. (the ~) chŏnja 전자.

fortune n. (chance) un 운, unsu 운수, (good luck) haengun 행운; (wealth) chaesan 재산, pu 부(富).

forty n. mahŭn 마흔, sasip 사십(40).

+ **forward** *adj.* ap′-ŭi 앞의. —*adv.* ap′-ŭro 앞으로. —*v.* ch′oktchinhada 촉진하다; chŏnsonghada 전송하다.

foul *adj.* tŏrŏun 더러운, pulgyŏlhan 불결한; ŭmt′anghan 음탕한. —*n.* kyuch′ik wiban 규칙 위반, panch′ik 반칙.

fountain pen *n.* mannyŏnp′il 만년필.

+ **four** *n.* net 넷, sa 4: *in ~s* sayollo〈sayŏl-ro 4열로.

fourteen *n.* yŏlnet 열넷, sipsa 십사(14).

fox *n.* yŏu 여우; (slang. *sly person*) kyohwalhan in′gan 교활한 인간: *a silber ~* ŭnyŏu 은여우.

fragile *adj.* pusŏjigi swiun 부서지기 쉬운.; hŏyak′an 허약한.

+ **frame** *n.* (*framework*) kujo 구조, (*building*) ppyŏdae 뼈대, (*skeleton*) kolgyŏk 골격; (*system*) ch′egye 체계, (*structure*) ch′eje 체제; (*window*) t′ŭl 틀, (*picture*) aektcha 액자.

France *n.* p′ŭrangsŭ 프랑스.

+ **free** *adj.* chayu-ŭi 자유의, chayuroun 자유로운; (*without payment*) muryo-ŭi 무료의, kongtcha-ŭi 공짜의. —*v.* haebanghada 해방하다, (*prisoners*) p′urŏjuda 풀어주다.

+ **freedom** *n.* chayu 자유.

freely *adv.* chayuropkke 자유롭게.

freeze *v.* ŏlda 얼다; ŏllida 얼리다, tonggyŏlsik′ida 동결시키다.

frequent *adj.* pinbŏnhan 빈번한, (*habitual*) sangsŭptchŏgin 상습적인. —*v.* chaju kada 자주 가다.

+ **fresh** *adj.* sinsŏnhan 신선한, singsinghan 싱싱한.

+ **friend** *n.* ch′ingu 친구, tongmu 동무, pŏt 벗.

+ **friendly** *adj.* ch′inhan 친한, (*amicable*) uhojŏgin 우호적인; (*kindly*) ch′injŏlhan 친절한.

+ **friendship** *n.* ujŏng 우정, uae 우애, ch′in′gyo 친교.

+ **frighten** *v.* kkamtchak nollage hada 깜짝 놀라게 하다, (*scare*) kŏb-ŭl chuda 겁을 주다.

frog *n.* kaeguri 개구리.

from *prep.* ¨¨ro-but′ŏ ¨¨로부터, ¨¨esŏ ¨¨에서, ¨¨egesŏ ¨¨에게서, (colloq) ¨¨hantesŏ ¨¨한테서 .

* **front** *n.* ap 앞, (*forward part*) chŏngmyŏn 정면, ammyŏn⟨apmyŏn 앞면; (*fighting*) chŏnsŏn 전선, ilssŏn 일선.

frost *n.* sŏri 서리. —*v.* sŏri-ga naerida 서리가 내리다. → **freeze** *v.* ŏlge hada 얼게 하다.

+ **fruit** *n.* kwail 과일, kwasil 과실; (*plant products*) sanmul 산물: ~ *shop* kwail kage 과일 가게.

+ **fry** *v.* kirŭm-e t'wigida 기름에 튀기다, p'ŭraihada 프라이하다. —*n.* t'wigimnyori⟨t'wigimyori 튀김요리: *french* ~ *ies* kamjatwigim 감자튀김.

+ **fuel** *n.* yŏllyo⟨yŏnryo 연료, (*firewood*) changjak 장작.

* **full** *adj.* kadŭkch'an 가득찬, (*complete*) ch'ungbunhan 충분한. --*adv.* kadŭkhi 가득히. —*n.* chŏnbu 전부.

+ **fun** *n.* changnan 장난, (*joking*) nongdam 농담, (*amusement*) chaemi 재미. --*adj.*(*amusing*) chaemiinnŭn⟨itnŭn 재미있는.

+ **function** *n.* kinŭng 기능, yŏkhal 역할, chingnŭng⟨chiknŭng 직능. —*v.* (*work*) chakyong/kinŭnghada 작용/기능 하다.

funeral *n.* changryesik 장례식. —*adj.* changrye-ŭi 장례의.

+ **funny** *adj.* usŭun 우스운, (*comical*) ikssalmajŭn 익살맞은, utkkinŭn 웃기는, (*amusing*) chaemiinnŭn⟨chaemiitnŭn 재미있는, (*strange*) isanghan 이상한, (*queer*) koesanghan 괴상한, (*odd*) kimyohan 기묘한.

+ **fur** *n.* mop'i 모피, t'ŏl 털.

furnace *n.* hwaro 화로; (*smelter*) yonggwangno⟨yonggwangro 용광로.

furnish *v.* (*supply*) konggŭp'ada 공급하다, taejuda 대주다, (*equip*) pich'ihada 비치하다.

+ **furniture** *n.* kagu 가구, segan 세간, pip'um 비품.

+ **further** *adj.* kŭ wi-ŭi 그 위의, kŭ isang-ŭi 그 이상의. —*adv.* kŭ wi-e 그 위에, kedaga 게다가.

* **future** *n.* changnae⟨changrae 장래, mirae 미래. —*adj.* mirae-ŭi 미래의; (*next life*) naese-ŭi 내세의.

≶ G ≷

+ **gain** v. (*get*) ŏtta 얻다, (*in weight*) saltchida 살찌다, (*win*) igida 이기다: ~ *a battle* ssaum-e igida 싸움 에 이기다. —*n.* idŭk 이득.

gamble *n. & v.* tobak(hada) 도박(하다).

* **game** *n.*(*sport*) yuhŭi 유희, (*play*) nori 놀이, (*amusement*) orak 오락; (*prey*) sanyangkkam 사냥감.

+ **gap** *n.* (*opening*) t'ŭm 틈, (*interval*) kan'gyŏk 간격.

garbage *n.* ssŭregi 쓰레기, tchikkŏgi 찌꺼기.

+ **garden** *n.* chŏngwŏn 정원, ttŭl 뜰, kkotppat 꽃밭, yach'aepat 야채밭. *pleasure* ~s yuwŏnji 유원지.

gardener *n.* chŏngwŏnsa 정원사.

garlic *n.* manŭl 마늘.

garter *n.* yangmal taenim 양말 대님.

+ **gas** *n.* gasŭ 가스: *natural* ~ ch'ŏnyŏn'gasŭ 천연가스.

gasoline *n.* hwibalyu 휘발유, kasollin 가솔린.

gasp *v.* hŏlttŏkkŏrida 헐떡거리다. → **desire** *v.* kalmanghada 갈망하다.

gate *n.* mun 문, taemun 대문, (*portal*) ch'urimmun⟨ch'uripmun 출입문.

+ **gather** *v.*(*assemble*) moŭda 모으다, moida 모이다; (*crease, pleat*) churŭm-ŭl chaptta 주름을 잡다.

gaudy *adj.* yahan 야한, hwaryŏhan 화려한.

gay *adj.* (*cheerful*) k'waehwalhan 쾌활한; (*showy*) yahan 야한; (*homosexual*) (namsŏng) tongsŏng yŏnaeja-ŭi (남성) 동성 연애자의.

* **general** ① *n.* changgun 장군. ② *adj.* ilbanjŏgin 일반적 인, chŏnbanjŏgin 전반적인.

+ **generous** *adj.* kwandaehan 관대한, (*magnanimous*) nŏgŭrŏun 너그러운; (*unsparing*) akkimŏmnŭn⟨akkimŏpnŭn 아낌없는.

+ **gentle** *adj.* chŏmjanŭn 점잖은, (*mild*) onhwahan 온화한,(*soft*) pudŭrŏun 부드러운.

gentleman *n.* sinsa 신사.

+ **gently** *adv.* chŏmjank'e 점잖게, (*kindly*) sangnyanghage 상냥하게, (*softly*) pudŭrŏpkke 부드럽게; (*quietly*) choyonghage 조용하게.

+ **genuine** *adj.* chinjŏnghan 진정한, chintcha-ŭi 진짜의.

geography *n.* chiri(hak) 지리(학), chiji 지지(地誌); chise 지세(地勢).

geology *n.* chijilhak 지질학.

+ **germ** *n.* (*microbe*) pyŏnggyun 병균, segyun 세균; (*origin*) kŭnwŏn 근원, kiwŏn 기원: *the ~ of intelligence* chisŏng-ŭi kiwŏn 지성의 기원.

German *adj.* togir-ŭi 독일의.—*n.* (*people*) togilsaram 독일 사람; (*language*) togirŏ 독일어.

Germany *n.* togil 독일.

+ **gesture** *n.* momtchit 몸짓, sonjit 손짓, chesŭch'ŏ 제스처.

* **get** *v.* (*acquire*) ŏtta 얻다; (*arrive*) irŭda 이르다; (*induce*) hage hada 하게 하다; (*become*) …i toeda …이 되다: ~ *up* irŏnada 일어나다.

ghost *n.* yuryŏng 유령, mangnyŏng〈mangryŏng 망령, kwisin 귀신.

gift *n.* sŏnmul 선물; (*natural ability*) ch'ŏnbu-ŭi chaenŭng 천부의 재능.

ginger *n.* saeang 새앙, saenggang 생강: ~ *group* (British) (*radicalists*) kŭpjinp'a 급진파.

girdle *n.* tti 띠, hŏritti 허리띠.—*v.* turŭda 두르다.

+ **girl** *n.* sonyŏ 소녀, (*derogatory*) kyejibai 계집아이. → **sweetheart** *n.* aein 애인.

gist *n.* yoji 요지.

* **give** *v.* chuda 주다, (from elders) chusida 주시다, (to elders) tŭrida 드리다, pep'ulda 베풀다; (*hold*) yŏlda 열다; (*entrust*) matkkida 맡기다: ~ *up* p'ogihada 포기 하다, tannyŏmhada 단념하다.

glad *adj.* kippŭn 기쁜, chŭlgŏun 즐거운.

+ **glass** *n.* yuri 유리; k'ŏp 컵; (*spectacles*) an'gyŏng 안경.

gloomy *adj.* ŏduun 어두운, ch'imulhan 침울한.

glove *n.* changgap 장갑, (*baseball*) kŭllŏbŭ 글러브.

glow *v.* pinnada 빛나다, ppalgak'e taraorŭda 빨갛게 달아 오르다.

+ **glue** *n.* p'ul 풀, agyo 아교, —*v.* p'ul/agyo-ro puch'ida 풀/아교로 붙이다.

* **go** *v.* (*proceed*) kada 가다; (*work, run*) umjigida 움직이다; (*elapse*) chinagada 지나가다.

+ **goal** *n.* kyŏlssŭngjŏm 결승점, mokp'yo 목표, (*destination*) moktchŏktchi 목적지.

goat *n.* yŏmso 염소.

+ **god** *n.* sin 신(神), (*G~*) hanŭnim 하느님. *My ~!* ŏmŏna, hananim! 어머나, 하나님!

+ **gold** *n.* kŭm 금, (*coin*) kŭmhwa 금화; (*color*) kŭmppit 금빛.

+ **golf** *n.* kolp'ŭ 골프.

* **good** *n.* ch'akham 착함. —*adj.* choŭn 좋은, (*kind*) ch'injŏlhan 친절한; (*skilled*) nŭngsukhan 능숙한.

+ **goodby(e)** *n.* chakppyŏl insa 작별 인사. —*int.* (*go in peace, to departing person*) annyŏnghi kasipssio 안녕히 가십시오, (*stay in peace, to person staying*) annyŏnghi kyesipsio 안녕히 계십시오.

* **goods** *n.* mulp'um 물품, (*merchandise*) sangp'um 상품, (*products*) chep'um 제품.

goose *n.* kŏwi 거위: *wild ~* kirŏgi 기러기.

gorgeous *adj.* ch'allanhan⟨ch'anranhan 찬란한, hwaryŏhan 화려한; hullyunghan 훌륭한.

gossip *n.* chapttam 잡담, twitkkongnon⟨twitkongron 뒷공론, kosip 고십: *the ~ column* kosipnan⟨kosipran 고십란(欄).

* **government** *n.* chŏngbu 정부, (*politics*) chŏngch'i 정치.

governor *n.* t'ongch'ija 통치자, chisa 지사.

+ **graceful** *adj.* uahan 우아한, chŏmjanŭn 점잖은.

+ **gradual** *adj.* chŏmch'ajŏgin 점차적인.

graduate *n.* chorŏpsaeng 졸업생. —*v.* chorŏphada 졸업하다, hagwi-rŭl suyŏhada 학위를 수여하다.

+ **grain** n. koksik 곡식, kongmul〈kokmul 곡물, (cereal seeds) nadal 낟알; (piece) algaengi 알갱이; (wood) namutkkyŏl 나뭇결; kŭkssoryang 극소량: have not a ~ of common sense sangsig-i chŏnhyŏ ŏptta 상식이 전혀 없다. → **temper** n. kijil 기질.

+ **grammar** n. munppŏp 문법, ŏppŏp 어법.

  grand adj. ungdaehan 웅대한, (majestic) tangdanghan 당당한; hohwaroun 호화로운.

  granddaughter n. sonnyŏ 손녀.

  grandfather n. harabŏji 할아버지, chobu 조부.

  grandmother n. halmŏni 할머니, chomo 조모.

  grandson n. sonja 손자.

  grape n. p'odo 포도: ~ sugar (dextrose) p'ododang 포도당.

+ **grass** n. p'ul 풀, mokch'o 목초; (meadow) moktchang 목장; (lawn) chandi 잔디. a blade of ~ p'ullip 풀잎.

+ **gratitude** n. kamsa 감사, saŭi 사의(謝意), komaum 고마움.

  grease v. kirŭm 기름, chibang 지방, (mechanics) kŭrisŭ 그리스. —v. kirŭm-ŭl ch'ida 기름을 치다.

* **great** adj. k'ŭn 큰, (remarkable) hullunghan 훌륭한, widaehan 위대한; (numerous) manhŭn 많은; (important) chungdaehan 중대한.

+ **greatly** adv. taedanhi 대단히, maeu 매우, k'ŭge 크게.

  greedy adj. yoksimmanŭn 욕심많은, kalmanghanŭn 갈망하는.

+ **green** adj. ch'orokssaeg-ŭi 초록색의, nokssaeg-ŭi 녹색의; (unripe) sŏrigŭn 설익은. —n. ch'orok(ssaek) 초록(색), nokssaek 녹색. ~ vegetables p'urŭnnip ch'aeso 푸른잎 채소.

+ **greeting** n. insa 인사, (pl.) insamal 인사말: New Year's ~s sinnyŏn insamal 신년 인사말.

+ **grey/gray** n. hoesaek 회색. —adj. hoesaeg-ŭi 회색의; (dull) ujungch'unghan 우중충한.

  grill n. (gridiron) sŏksoe 석쇠.

  grind v. kalda 갈다.

groan *n.* sinŭmsori 신음소리.—*v.* sinŭmhada 신음하다.

grocery *n.* (*pl.-ies*) singnyop'um〈sikryop'um 식료품〉. ~ *store* sikp'umjŏm 식품점.

* **ground** *n.* ttang 땅. *play~* undongjang 운동장.

* **group** *n.* muri 무리, chipttan 집단. (*aggregation*) tanch'e 단체. —*v.* tte-rŭl chitta 떼를 짓다; (*classify*) pullyuhada〈punryuhada 분류하다〉.

+ **grow** *v.* (*thrive*) charada 자라다; k'ŏjida 커지다, (*cultivate*) chaebaehada 재배하다; (*become*) ...ge toeda …게 되다.

gruel *n.* (mulgŭn) chuk (묽은) 죽.

guard *n.* (*sentry*) p'asukkun 파수꾼; (*protector*) suwi 수위; —*v.* p'asuboda 파수보다, chik'ida 지키다, (*defend*) pangwihada 방위하다. → **conductor** *n.* ch'ajang 차장.

+ **guess** *v.* (*surmise*) ch'uch'ŭkhada 추측하다, aramach'ida 알아맞히다: ~ *who* nugunga mach'ida 누군가 맞히다. —*n.* ch'uch'ŭk 추측. → **think** *v.* saenggakhada 생각하다.

+ **guest** *n.* sonnim 손님, naebin 내빈, kaek 객(客).

guide *n.* (*person*) annaeja 안내자, kaidŭ 가이드, (*book*) p'yŏllam〈p'yŏnram 편람〉. —*v.* annaehada 안내하다, indohada 인도하다.

+ **guilty** *adj.* yujoe-ŭi 유죄의, choeinnŭn〈choeitnŭn 죄있는〉.

+ **guitar** *n.* kit'a 기타.

gulf *n.* man 만(灣).

gull *n.* kalmaegi 갈매기. → **dupe** *n.* ŏlgani 얼간이.

gulp *v.* samk'ida 삼키다.

gum *n.* ① komu 고무: ~ *boots* komusin 고무신; (*of theeye*) nunkkop 눈곱; (*chewing ~*) kkŏm 껌. ② (pl. *of the mouth*) inmom〈itmom 잇몸〉.

+ **gun** *n.* ch'ong 총: *air ~* konggich'ong 공기총, *machine ~* kigwanch'ong 기관총, *squirt ~* mulch'ong 물총.

gutter *n.* (*groove*) homt'ong 홈통, (*ditch*) hasudo 하수도.

≲ H ≳

+ **habit** *n*. pŏrŭt 버릇, sŭpkkwan 습관, (*biological*) sŭp-ssŏng 습성.

  hail *n*. ssarangnun⟨ssaraknun 싸락눈, (*hailstone*) ubak 우박. —*v*. ssarangnun-i⟨ssaraknun-i naerida 싸락눈이 내리다; (*call*) purŭda 부르다.

* **hair** *n*. t′ŏl 털, mŏrit′ŏl 머리털, mŏri(k′arak) 머리(카락) tubal 두발.

  hairdresser *n*. ibalssa 이발사, miyongsa 미용사.

+ **half** *n*. & *adj*. pan 반, chŏlban(-ŭi) 절반(의).

  hall *n*. (*auditorium*) kangdang 강당; (*corridor*) poktto 복도, t′ongno⟨t′ongro 통로: *city* ~ sich′ŏng 시청 /*music* ~ ŭmaktang 음악당.

  halt *v*. (*army*) chudunhada 주둔하다; (*stop*) mŏmch′uda 멈추다. —*n*. chŏngji 정지: *Company,* ~! chungdae sŏ 중대 서!

  ham *n*. haem 햄.

  hammer *n*. mangch′i 망치, haemŏ 해머. —*v*. mangch′ijilhada 망치질하다.

+ **hand** *n*. (*of the body*) son 손; (*laborer*) ilsson 일손, (*skill*) somssi 솜씨; (*timepiece*) sigyebanŭl 시계바늘. —*v*. kŏnnejuda 건네주다.

  handkerchief *n*. sonsugŏn 손수건.

+ **handle** *n*. sonjapi 손잡이, (*car*) haendŭl 핸들. —*v*. (*deal with*) taruda 다루다; (*control*) chojonghada 조종 하다, (*manage*) ch′ŏrihada 처리하다; (*deal in*) maemaehada 매매하다.

  handy *adj*. p′yŏllihan⟨p′yŏnrihan 편리한, kanp′yŏn-han 간편한.

+ **hang** *v*. kŏlda 걸다, maedalda 매달다; (*remain in suspense*) mangsŏrida 망설이다.

* **happen** v. irŏnada 일어나다, saenggida 생기다. ~ touyŏnhi ⋯hada 우연히 ⋯하다.

+ **happiness** n. haengbok 행복. → **luck** n. haengun 행운.

+ **happy** adj. haengbokhan 행복한, (glad) kippŭn 기쁜, 한. kibun chohŭn 기분 좋은; (lucky) tahaenghan 다행

* **hard** adj. (solid) ttakttakhan 딱딱한 tandanhan 단단한; (difficult) ŏryŏun 어려운. —adv. (earnestly) yŏlssimhi 열심히.

+ **hardly** adv. kŏŭi ⋯anida 거의 ⋯아니다.

  hardware n. (ironmongery) ch'ŏlmul 철물, (computer)hadŭweŏ 하드웨어.

+ **harm** n. hae 해, sonhae 손해, sonsang 손상. —v. haech'ida 해치다, sonsanghada 손상하다.

+ **harmful** adj. haeroun 해로운.

  harp n. hap'ŭ 하프.

+ **harsh** adj. kŏch'in 거친; kahokhan 가혹한; (discordant) kwi-e kŏsŭllinŭn 귀에 거슬리는.

  hasten v. sŏdurŭda 서두르다, (speed up) moraseuda 몰아 세우다, chaech'ok'ada 재촉하다.

+ **hat** n. moja 모자.

  hatchet n. sondokki 손도끼.

  hate v. (detest) miwŏhada 미워하다, (dislike) sirŏhada 싫어하다. —n. chŭngo 증오.

+ **hatred** n. (strong dislike) hyŏmo 혐오, (hate) chŭngo 증오.

have v. (possess) kajida 가지다, itta 있다; I have a car. na-nŭn ch'a-ga itta 나는 차가 있다; (eat) mŏktta 먹다; (drink) masida 마시다; (obtain) ŏtta 얻다. ~ a jacket on (wear) chak'es-ŭl ipkko itta 자켓을 입고 있다.

  hawk n. mae 매(鷹).

  hay n. kŏnch'o 건초, kkol 꼴.

* **he** pron. kŭ-nŭn/-ga 그는/가, chŏsaram-ŭn/-i 저사람은/이.—n. namja 남자, suk'ŏt 수컷.

* **head** n. mŏri 머리, (intellect) tunoe 두뇌, chiryŏk 지력; (chief) suryŏng 수령, chang 장(長).

headquarters *n.* ponbu 본부, saryŏngbu 사령부: *general* ~ ch'ongsaryŏngbu 총사령부.

+ **health** *n.* kŏn'gang 건강; (*hygiene*) wisaeng 위생.

+ **healthy** *adj.* kŏn'ganghan 건강한, t'ŭnt'ŭnhan 튼튼한.

+ **hear** *v.* tŭtta 듣다; (*law*) simmunhada 심문하다.

+ **hearing** *n.* tŭtkki 듣기, ch'ŏngch'wi 청취.

+ **heart** *n.* simjang 심장, (*mind*) maŭm 마음.

+ **heat** *n.* yŏl 열(熱); (*temparature*) ondo 온도; (*hotness*) tŏwi 더위; (*anger*) punno 분노, kyŏngno⟨kyŏkno 격노; (*zeal*) yŏlssim 열심. —*v.* teuda 데우다, ttŭgŏpkke hada 뜨겁게 하다.

heater *n.* nanbangjangch'i 난방장치, (*portable*) hit'ŏ 히터.

heating *n.* nanbang 난방.

heaven *n.* hanŭl 하늘, ch'ŏn'guk 천국.

* **heavy** *adj.* mugŏun 무거운; (*violent*) maengnyŏlhan⟨maengryŏlhan 맹렬한: *a* ~ *rain* p'oku 폭우.

+ **heavily** *adv.* mugŏpkke 무겁게; simhage 심하게.

hedge *n.* sanult'ari 산울타리; (*barrier*) changbyŏk 장벽.

heel *n.* twikkumch'i 뒤꿈치, kup 굽, (*shoe*) twich'uk 뒤축.

+ **height** *n.* nop'i 높이; (*stature*) k'i 키; koji 고지.

+ **held** *v.* (past form of *hold*) chinin 지닌, kaech'oedoen 개최된.

hello *int.* (*telephone*) yŏboseyo 여보세요; (*greetings*)annyŏnghasimnikka⟨annyŏnghasipnikka 안녕하십니까?/annyŏnghaseyo 안녕하세요?

* **help** *n.* toum 도움, (*remedy*) kujech'aek 구제책. —*v.* toptta 돕다, towajuda 도와주다, (*honorific*) towadŭrida 도와드리다.

+ **helpful** *adj.* toum-i toenŭn 도움 이 되는, (*useful*) yuyonghan 유용한, p'yŏllihan 편리한.

* **her** *pron.* kŭ yŏja-ŭi/rŭl/ege 그 여자의/를/에게, kŭnyŏŭi/rŭl/ege 그녀의/를/에게.

here *adv.* yŏgi-e 여기에, igos-e 이곳에.

+ **herself** *pron.* kŭ yŏja chasin 그 여자 자신.

hesitate *v.* chujŏhada 주저하다, mangsŏrida 망설이다,
kyŏldan-ŭl mot naerida 결단을 못 내리다.

hey *int.* ibwa 이봐, ŏi 어이; ya 야.

hiccough hiccup *n.* ttalkkuktchil 딸꾹질.

+ **hidden** *adj.* sumgyŏjin 숨겨진, pimil-ŭi 비밀의.

+ **hide** *v.* kamch'uda 감추다, sumda 숨다. —*n.* (*animal*)
kajuk 가죽, p'ihyŏk 피혁.

* **high** *adj.* nop'ŭn 높은; (*superior*) kogŭp-ŭi 고급의;
(*intense*) kangnyŏlhan⟨kangryŏlhan 강렬한: *ex-*
change ~ *words* kwagyŏkhan mal-ŭl chugobatta
과격한 말을 주고 받다. —*adv.* nop'i 높이.

+ **high-pitched** *adj.* karag-i nop'ŭn 가락이 높은, kŭp-
kkyŏngsa-ŭi 급경사의.

+ **highly** *adv.* nop'i 높이, (*very*) maeu 매우: ~ *enter-*
taining maeu chaemiinnŭn⟨itnŭn 매우 재미있는 .

highway *n.* kosok/kansŏn toro 고속/간선 도로, (*public*
road) kongno⟨kongro 공로.

+ **hill** *n.* ŏndŏk 언덕, chakŭn san 작은 산.

+ **him** *pron.* kŭ-rŭl 그를, kŭ-ege 그에게.

+ **himself** *pron.* kŭ chasin 그 자신.

+ **hip** *n.* yŏbŏngdŏngi 옆엉덩이, hŏri 허리. → **buttocks**
n. kungdungi 궁둥이.

hire *n.* koyong 고용; imdae 임대(賃貸); sak 삯.—*v.*
(*engage*) koyonghada 고용하다.

+ **his** *pron.* kŭ-ŭi 그의.

historical *adj.* yŏksa-ŭi 역사의, yŏksajŏk 역사적,
sahag-ŭi 사학(史學)의.

+ **history** *n.* yŏksa 역사; kyŏngnyŏk⟨kyŏngryŏk 경력,
naeryŏk 내력.

* **hit** *v.* (*strike*) ch'ida 치다, myŏngjunghada 명중하다.

+ **hobby** *n.* ch'wimi 취미, torak 도락; (*hobbyhorse*)
mongma ⟨mokma 목마.

+ **hockey** *n.* (*field*) hak'i 하키: *ice* ~ aisŭ hak'i 아이스
하키.

* **hold** *v.* (*keep*) chinida 지니다, kajida 가지다; (*open*)
kaech'oehada 개최하다; (*grasp*) putchaptta 붙잡다;
(*support*) chit'aenghada 지탱하다. —*n.*(*grasp*)

p'och'ak 포착; (*ship*) sŏnch'ang 선창.

+ **hole** *n*. kumŏng 구멍.

+ **holiday** *n*. hyuil 휴일, (*public~*) konghyuil 공휴일,
(*festival*) ch'uktcheil 축제일, myŏngjŏl 명절.

+ **hollow** *n*. umukhan kot 우묵한 곳.—*adj*. (*empty*)
(sogi) pin (속이) 빈, (*sunken, concave*) omokhi tŭr-
ŏgan 오목히 들어간. —*v*. (*excavate*) toryŏnaeda 도려
내다.

+ **holy** *adj*. sinsŏnghan 신성한, kŏrukhan 거룩한.

+ **home** *n*. (chagi)jip (자기)집, kajŏng 가정: *the joys of*
~ kajŏngsanghwal-ŭi kippŭm 가정생활의 기쁨; (*na-
tive land*) pon'guk 본국 ~*town* kohyang 고향.

  homesick *adj*. hyangsuppyŏng-ŭi 향수병의, mang-
hyang-ŭi 망향의.

+ **honest** *adj*. chŏngjikhan 정직한, sŏngsilhan 성실한;
(*legitimate*) chŏngdanghan 정당한.

  honey *n*. (pŏl)kkul (벌)꿀; (*my darling*) yŏbo 여보! →
  lover *n*. aein 애인.

  hono(u)r *n*. myŏngye 명예, (*esteem*) kyŏngŭi 경의;
(*pl. medal*) hunjang 훈장; (*top grade*) udŭng 우등.
—*v*. (*repect*) chon'gyŏnghada 존경하다.

+ **hook** *n*. kalgori 갈고리, huk 훅, (*for fishing*) naksi-
banŭl 낚시바늘.—*v*. kuburŏjida 구부러지다, kalgori-
ro kŏlda 갈고리로 걸다.

+ **hope** *n*. hŭimang 희망, somang 소망, kidae 기대. —*v*.
parada 바라다, hŭimanghada 희망하다, kidaehada
기대하다..

  horizon *n*. (*land*) chip'yŏngsŏn 지평선, (*water*) su-
p'yŏngsŏn 수평선.

+ **horizontal** *adj*. sup'yŏng-ŭi 수평의, (*level*) p'yŏng-
p'yŏnghan 평평한: ~ *bar* ch'ŏlbong 철봉.

+ **horn** *n*. ppul 뿔; (*bugle*) nap'al 나팔, (*french ~*) ho-
rŭn 호른.

+ **horrible** *adj*. (*dreadful*) musŏun 무서운, musimusihan 무시 무시한; (*unpleasant*) chingŭrŏun 징그
러운, chinjŏrinanŭn 진저리나는.

+ **horse** *n*. mal 말: ~ *race* kyŏngma 경마.

+ **hospital** *n.* (chonghap) pyŏngwŏn (종합) 병원.

+ **hostile** *adj.* chŏgŭi-e ch'an 적의에 찬, (*opposed*) pandaehanŭn 반대하는, chŏg-ŭi 적의.

* **hot** *adj.* (*temperature*) tŏun 더운, ttŭgŏun 뜨거운; (*taste by red pepper*) maeun 매운, ŏlk'ŭnhan 얼큰한; (*fresh*) kannaon⟨katnaon 갓나온.

+ **hotel** *n.* hot'el 호텔, yŏgwan 여관.

+ **hour** *n.* sigan 시간; (*o'clock*) si 시(時).

* **house** *n.* chip 집, kaok 가옥; (*H~*) ŭihoe 의회.

  housewife *n.* chubu 주부.

* **how** *adv.* (*in what state*) ŏttŏk'e 어떻게; (*to what extent*) ŏnŭ chŏngdo 어느 정도; (*why*) wae 왜; (*interjection*) ya 야, ai ch'am 아이 참: *H~ fast he runs!* ya ppalli tallinda! 야 빨리 달린다. —*n.* (*means*) pangbŏp 방법, pangsik 방식.

  however *adv.* amuri ...haedo 아무리 …해도. —*conj.* (*though*) kŭrŏna 그러나, kŭrŏch'iman 그렇지만.

+ **human** *n.* in'gan 인간. —*adj.* in'gan-ŭi 인간의, in'ganjŏgin 인간적인, in'gandaun 인간다운.

  humble *adj.* (*lowly*) pich'ŏnhan 비천한; (*modest*) kyŏmsonhan 겸손한.

  humid *adj.* sŭpkki-ga manhŭn 습기가 많은, (*damp*) ch'ukch'uk'an 축축한, nungnuk'an⟨nuknukhan 눅눅한.

+ **humorous** *adj.* ikssalsŭrŏun 익살스러운, chaemi innŭn ⟨itnŭn 재미있는, (*funny*) ukkinŭn⟨utkinŭn 웃기는.

  hundred *n.* paek 백.

  hungry *adj.* paegop'ŭn 배고픈, kumjurin 굶주린: *go/be ~* paegop'ŭda 배고프다.

  hunt *n.* sanyang 사냥, (*search*) ch'ujŏk 추적. —*v.* sanyanghada 사냥하다: *~ for* ch'atta 찾다.

  hurrah/hurray *int.* manse 만세, hura 후라.

  hurricane *n.* p'okp'ung 폭풍, (*typhoon*) t'aep'ung 태풍.

+ **hurry** *v.* sŏdurŭda 서두르다.—*n.* (*haste*) sŏdurŭm 서두름, kŭpssok 급속: *in a ~* kŭphi 급히, pappi 바삐.

+ **hurt** *v.* tach'igehada 다치게 하다: *~ one's feelings* kamjŏng-ŭl tach'igehada 감정을 다치게 하다, (*inju-*

re) haech'ida 해치다, (*feel pain*) ap'ŭda 아프다. *get*
~ pusanghada 부상하다. —*n.* (*wound*) pusang 부상,
sangch'ŏ 상처; (*damage*) sonhae 손해; (*pain*)
kot'ong 고통, ap'ŭm 아픔.
+ **husband** *n.* namp'yŏn 남편.
  hygiene *n.* kŏn'gangppŏp 건강법; (*sanitary science*)
  wisaenghak 위생학, sŏpssaengppŏp 섭생법.

+ **I** *pron.* na-nŭn 나는, nae-ga 내가.
+ **ice** *n.* ŏrŭm 얼음, pingsu 빙수.**freeze** *n.* ŏllida 얼리다.
  ice cream *n.* aisŭk'ŭrim 아이스크림.
* **idea** *n.* (*conception*) kwannyŏm 관념, (*thought*)
  sasang 사상, (notion) saenggak 생각, (*opinion*) ŭigyŏn 의견, (*plan*) kyehoek 계획.
+ **identity** *n.* chuch'essŏng 주체성.
# **if** *conj.* (*in case that*) manil ...iramyŏn 만일 …이라면,
  (*even if*) ...iltchirado …일지라도; (*whether*) ...inji
  ŏttŏnji …인지 어떤지.
+ **ignore** *v.* musihada 무시하다, morŭn ch'ehada 모른 체
  하다.
* **ill** *adj.* (*sick*) ap'ŭn 아픈, pyŏngdŭn 병든; (*bad*)
  nappŭn 나쁜; ~ *nature* (*malevolent nature*)
  simsulgujŭm 심술 궂음. —*n.* (*evil*) ak 악, (pl.
  misfortune) pulhaeng 불행.
+ **illegal** *adj.* pulppŏp-ŭi 불법의, pihappŏptchŏgin 비합
  법적인: *an* ~ *act* pulppŏp haengwi 불법 행위.
* **illness** *n.* (*disease*) pyŏng 병, p'yŏnch'anŭm 편찮음.
  illustrate *v.* (*example*) ye-rŭl tŭrŏ sŏlmyŏnghada 예
  를 들어 설명하다, yejŭnghada 예증(例證)하다; (*pictu-
  re*) kŭrim-ŭl nŏt'a 그림을 넣다.
+ **image** *n.* yŏngsang 영상, (*statue*) chosang 조상(彫像),

(*symbol*) sangjing 상징; (*form*) moyang 모양.

+ **imaginary** *adj.* sangsangjŏgin 상상적인.

+ **imagination** *n.* sangsang 상상, sangsangnyŏk〈sangsangryŏk 상상력.

+ **imagine** *v.* sangsanghada 상상하다, (*think*) saenggakhada 생각하다.

   imitate *v.* hyungnaenaeda 흉내내다, mobanghada 모방하다.

+ **immediately** *adv.* kot 곧, paro 바로, chŭkssi 즉시.

+ **immoral** *adj.* pudodŏkhan 부도덕한.

+ **impatient** *adj.* ch'amŭlssŏngŏmnŭn〈ŏpnŭn 참을성없는, sŏnggŭphan 성급한, sŏngmarŭn 성마른.

   imperial *adj.* (*of an empire*) chegug-ŭi 제국의, hwangjeŭi 황제의; (*majestic*) tangdanghan 당당한.

   impolite *adj.* pŏrŭtŏmnŭn〈pŏrŭtŏpnŭn 버릇없는.

   import *v.* (*bring in*) suip'ada 수입하다. —*n.* suip 수입. (*meaning*) ŭimi 의미. (*importance*) chungyossŏng 중요성.

+ **importance** *n.* chungyo(sŏng) 중요(성).

* **important** *adj.* chungyohan 중요한, chungdaehan 중대한.

+ **impossible** *adj.* pulganŭnghan 불가능한.

+ **impress** *v.* insang-ŭl chuda 인상을 주다.

+ **impression** *n.* insang 인상, kammyŏng 감명.

+ **impressive** *adj.* insangjŏgin 인상적인.

+ **improve** *v.* kaesŏnhada 개선하다, choajida 좋아지다. (*use well*) iyonghada 이용하다: *I~ your time bystudying.* sikan-ŭl hwaryonghaesŏ kongbuhada 시간을 활용해서 공부하시오.

in *prep.* ...e(sŏ) …에(서); ...ŭi an-e …의 안에. —*adv.* an-e/ŭro 안에/으로.

   incense *n.* hyang 향: ~ *burner* hyangno〈hyangro 향로.

   inch *n.* inch'i 인치(=2.54cm).

+ **include** *v.* p'ohamhada 포함하다: *postage* ~ usongnyo〈usongryo p'ohamhayŏ 우송료 포함하여.

+ **income** *n.* suip 수입, sodŭk 소득.

   inconvenient *adj.* pulp'yŏnhan 불편한; (*causing*

trouble) p'ye-ga toenŭn 폐가 되는.

+ **incorrect** *adj.* pujŏnghwakhan 부정확한, t'ŭllin 틀린, olch'i anŭn 옳지 않은.

+ **increase** *v.* chŭnggahada 증가하다, orŭda 오르다. —*n.* chŭngga 증가.

 indecent *adj.* (*ill-bred*) pŏrŭdŏmnŭn〈pŏrŭtŏpnŭn 버릇 없는; (*immodest*) ch'ujaphan 추잡한.

+ **indeed** *adv.* ch'am-ŭro 참으로, kwayŏn 과연.

+ **indepedent** *adj.* tongnip'an〈tokriphan 독립한.

 India *n.* indo 인도: ~ *ink* mŏk 먹.

* **indicate** *v.* chijŏkhada 지적하다, karik'ida 가리키다; (*show*) p'yosihada 표시하다.

 indigestion *n.* sohwa pullyang 소화 불량.

+ **indirect** *adj.* kanjŏptchŏgin 간접적인; (*roundabout*) uhoejŏgin 우회적인.

+ **individual** *adj.* kaeintchŏgin 개인적인, tandoktchŏg-in 단독적인, (*characteristic*) toktchajŏgin 독자적인. —*n.* kaein 개인, kaech'e 개체.

 indoors *adv.* ongnae-esŏ〈oknae-esŏ 옥내에서, sillae-esŏ〈silnae-esŏ 실내에서.

+ **industrial** *adj.* sanŏp-ŭi 산업의, kongŏp-ŭi 공업의.

+ **industry** *n.* sanŏp 산업; (*diligence*) kŭnmyŏn 근면.

 industrious *adj.* kŭnmyŏnhan 근면한.

 infant *n.* (kannan)aegi (갓난)애기, yua 유아, soa 소아, adong 아동.

+ **infect** *v.* chŏnyŏmsik'ida 전염시키다.

+ **infectious** *adj.* chŏnyŏmssŏng-ŭi 전염성의.

+ **inferior** *adj.* (*lower*) hawi-ŭi 하위의; (*second rate*) iryuin 이류인, yŏlttŭnghan 열등한. —*n.* araet-ssaram 아랫사람, yŏlttŭnghan cha 열등한 자.

+ **influence** *n.* yŏnghyang 영향; yŏnghyangnyŏk〈ryŏk 영향력. —*v.* yŏnghyang-ŭl kkich'ida 영향을 끼치다.

 inform *v.* allida 알리다, t'ongjihada 통지하다.

+ **informal** *adj.* pigongsik-ŭi 비공식의, yaksik-ŭi 약식의.

* **information** *n.* (*personal news*) sosik 소식; (*intelligence*) chŏngbo 정보: ~ *bureau* chŏngboguk 정보국, annaeso 안내소; ~ *office* annaeso 안내소. (*knowl-*

　　　edge) chisik 지식. → **report** *n*. pogo 보고.

　injection *n*. chusa 주사, chuip 주입, kwanjang 관장
　　(灌腸).

+ **injure** *v*. haech'ida 해치다; (*hurt*) tach'ida 다치다.

+ **injury** *n*. (*harm*) sanghae 상해, (*wound*) pusang 부
　　상; (*damage*) sonhae 손해; kwŏllich'imhae〈kwŏnri-
　　ch'imhae 권리침해.

+ **ink** *n*. ingk'ŭ 잉크: *India* ~ mŏk 먹.

　inland *n*. & *adj*. naeryuk(-ŭi) 내륙(의); (*domestic*)
　　kungnae〈kuknae(-ŭi) 국내(의): *an* ~ *duty* naeguk-
　　sae 내국세.

　inn *n*. yŏinsuk 여인숙, yŏgwan 여관.

　inquire *v*. (*ask*) mutta 묻다; (*investigate*) chosa-
　　hada 조사하다.

　insane *adj*. (*crazy*) mich'in 미친.

+ **insect** *n*. pŏlle 벌레, konch'ung 곤충.

* **inside** *n*. antchok 안쪽, naebu 내부. —*adj*.& *prep*.
　　an-ŭi 안의. —*adv*. antchog-ŭro 안쪽으로, an-e 안에.

+ **instead** *adv*. taesin-e/ŭro 대신에/으로.

+ **institution** *n*. (*system*) chedo 제도; (*custom, prac-*
　　tice) sŭpkkwan 습관; (*association, society*) hakhoe
　　학회, hyŏphoe 협회. → **establishment** *n*. sŏllip 설립.

　instruct *v*. (*teach*) karŭch'ida 가르치다; (*direct*)
　　chisihada 지시하다; (*inform*) allida 알리다.

+ **instruction** *n*. (*teaching*) karŭch'im 가르침; (*knowl-*
　　edge) chisik 지식; (*directions*) sayongppŏp 사용법,
　　(*orders*) hullyŏng 훈령.

　instructor *n*. kyosa 교사, kangsa 강사.

+ **instrument** *n*. (*tool*) kigu 기구; (*musical*) akki 악
　　기;(*means*) sudan 수단.

+ **insult** *v*. moyokhada 모욕하다.—*n*. (*insolence*) moyok
　　모욕; (*impoliteness*) murye 무례.

+ **insurance** *n*. pohŏm 보험, (*fee*) pohŏmnyo〈pohŏmryo
　　보험료.

+ **intelligence** *n*. (*sagacity*) chihye 지혜; (*intellect*)
　　ihaeryŏk 이해력, (*psychological term*) chinŭng 지
　　능; (*information*) chŏngbo 정보.

+ **intelligent** *adj.* chitchŏgin 지적인, (*rational*) ijijŏgin 이지적인; (*acute*) ch'ongmyŏnghan 총명한, (*discerning*) ttokttokhan 똑똑한.

+ **intend** *v.* ...hal chaktchŏngida ···할 작정이다, ...haryŏhada ···하려 하다.

+ **intense** *adj.* (*violent*) kyŏngnyŏlhan〈kyŏkryŏlhan 격렬한, (*fervent*) yŏllyŏlhan 열렬한. → **tense** *adj.* kinjangdoen 긴장된.

  intensely *adv.* simhage 심하게.

+ **intensity** *n.* kangdo 강도(强度).

+ **intention** *n.* ŭido 의도, ŭiji 의지, ŭihyang 의향.

+ **interest** *n.* hŭngmi 흥미, (*concern*) kwansim 관심; (*money*) ija 이자.

* **interesting** *adj.* hŭngmi/chaemiinnŭn〈itnŭn 흥미/재미있는.

  interfere *v.* kansŏphada 간섭하다; chojŏnghada 조정하다.

+ **international** *adj.* kuktchejŏgin 국제적인.

  interpreter *n.* haesŏltcha 해설자; t'ongyŏktcha 통역자.

+ **interrupt** *v.* (*block, divide*) karomaktta 가로막다, (*hinder*) panghaehada 방해하다; (*stop*) chungdanhada 중단하다.

+ **interval** *n.* kan'gyŏk 간격; (*break*) hyusikkigan 휴식기간; (*between acts*) makkan 막간.

  intestines *n.* naejang 내장.

  intimate *adj.* ch'inmilhan 친밀한, kakkaun 가까운. —*n.* ch'inu 친우.—*v.* (*hint*) amsihada 암시하다.

* **into** *prep.* an-ŭro 안으로, (an)-e (안)에.

  intoxicate *v.* ch'wihage hada 취하게 하다; toch'wi/hŭngbunhada 도취/흥분하다.

* **introduce** *v.* sogaehada 소개하다; (*bring in*) toiphada 도입하다, ikkŭrŏ tŭrida 이끌어 들이다.

+ **introduction** *n.* sogae 소개; (*preface*) sŏmun 서문, mŏrimal 머리말; (*basic textbook*) immun〈ipmun 입문.

+ **invent** *v.* palmyŏnghada 발명하다 ; kkumyŏnaeda 꾸며내다; (*make up*) naltchohada 날조하다.

invention *n.* palmyŏng(p´um) 발명(품).

investigate *v.* chosahada 조사하다, yŏn´guhada 연구
하다.

+ **investigation** *n.* chosa 조사. → **research** *n.* yŏn´gu
연구.

invite *v.* ch´odaehada 초대하다; (*tempt*) kkoeda 꾀다.

+ **involve** *v.* (*include*) p´ohamsik´ida 포함시키다, (*im-plicate*) kkŭrŏnŏt´a 끌어넣다; (*imply*) ttŭthada 뜻하다.

+ **inward** *adj.* naebu-ŭi 내부의; (*mental*) simtchŏgin 심
적인.

iodine *n.* yodŭ 요드.

+ **iron** *n.* soe 쇠, ch´ŏl 철, (*clothes iron*) tarimi 다리미.
—*adj.* ch´or-ŭi 철의, kyŏn´gohan 견고한.

+ **irregular** *adj.* pulgyuch´iktchŏgin 불규칙적인, (*un-even*) korŭji anŭn 고르지 않은, pyŏnch´ig-ŭi 변칙의.

+ **irritate** *v.* (*provoke*) tchajŭngnagehada 짜증나게 하
다, chagŭkhada 자극하다, yagollida 약올리다, an-dallage〈andalnage hada 안달나게 하다.

it *pron.* (no exactly equivalent word in Korean.)
kŭgŏsŭn 그것은, kŭgŏs-i 그것이, kŭgŏs-ŭl 그것을.

Italy *n.* it´allia 이탈리아.

itch *n.* karyŏum 가려움; (*disease*) om 옴. —*v.* karyŏ-wŏhada 가려워하다.

+ **item** *n.* chohang 조항, hangmok 항목.

itinerary *n.* yŏjŏng 여정(旅程).

* **its** *pron.* kŭgŏs-ŭi 그것의.

+ **itself** *pron.* kŭ chasin 그 자신, kŭ chach´e 그 자체.

ivory *n.* sanga 상아; *artificial* ~ injo sanga 인조 상아,
~ *tower* sangat´ap 상아탑.

$$\leqslant J \geqslant$$

+ **jacket** *n.* chak´et 자켓, jamba 잠바.

jade *n.* pich'wi 비취, ok 옥.

jail *n.* kamok 감옥, (*prison*) kyodoso 교도소.

+ **jam** *n.* ① chaem 잼: *strawberry* ~ ttalgi chaem 딸기잼. ② (*crowdedness*) honjap 혼잡; (*machinery*) kojang 고장. —*v.* (*press, squeeze*) ssusyŏnŏt'a 쑤셔넣다; (*crowd*) kkwak ch'ada 꽉 차다; (*machinery*) kŏllida 걸리다.

janitor *n.* (*doorkeeper*) munjigi 문지기, (*guard*) suwi 수위, (*building, apartment*) kwalliin⟨kwanriin 관리인.

january *n.* chŏngwŏl 정월, irwŏl 일월.

Japan *n.* ilbon 일본(日本).

Japanese *n.* (*people*) ilbonsaram 일본사람. (*lang.*) ilbonmal 일본말. —*adj.* ilbon-ŭi 일본의.

jar *n.* tok 독, tanji 단지, hangari 항아리.

jaundice *n.* hwangdal 황달.

jaw *n.* t'ŏk 턱: *Hold your* ~! takch'yŏ 닥쳐!

jealous *adj.* chilt'usimmanŭn 질투심많은, sigihanŭn 시기하는, t'ugihanŭn 투기하는.

jelly *n.* hanch'ŏn 한천, umu 우무; chelli 젤리.

jellyfish *n.* haep'ari 해파리.

Jew *n.* yut'aein 유태인; yut'aegyo sinja 유태교 신자.

jewel *n.* posŏk 보석, pook 보옥.

+ **jewelry** *n.* posŏngnyu⟨posŏkryu 보석류.

* **job** *n.* (*work*) il 일; (*employment*) chigŏp 직업; (*post*) chiwi 지위.

+ **join** *v.* kaiphada 가입하다, (*unite*) kyŏlhaphada 결합하다, (*connect,*) yŏn'gyŏlhada 연결하다; (*participate*)ch'amgahada 참가하다.

+ **joke** *n.* nongdam 농담.—*v.* nongdamhada 농담하다.

+ **journey** *n.* yŏhaeng 여행. —*v.* yŏhaenghada 여행하다.
→ **itinerary** *n.* yŏjŏng 여정(旅程).

+ **judge** *n.* p'ansa 판사, chaep'an'gwan 재판관. —*v.* p'angyŏlhada 판결하다, p'andan-ŭl naerida 판단을 내리다.

+ **judg(e)ment** *n.* (*court case*) chaep'an 재판; (*discernment*) p'andan 판단; (*opinion*) ŭigyŏn 의견.

juice *n*. chŭp 즙, chyusŭ 쥬스: *fruit* ~ kwail chyusŭ 과일쥬스, kwajŭp 과즙.

juicy *adj*. subun-i manhŭn 수분이 많은.

July *n*. ch'irwŏl 7월.

+ jump *v*. (*up*) ttwiŏorŭda 뛰어오르다, (*over*) ttwiŏnŏmtta 뛰어넘다, (*down*) ttwiŏnaerida 뛰어내리다. —*n*. (*leap*) toyak 도약, chŏmp'ŭ 점프.

jumper *n*. jamba 잠바.

* just *adj*. (*right*) chŏngdanghan 정당한, kongjŏnghan 공정한.—*adv*. (*exactly*) paro 바로, ttak 딱; (*hardly*) kakkasŭro 가까스로.

$\leq K \geq$

* keep *v*. (*guard*) chik'ida 지키다; (*raise*) kirŭda 기르다; (*preserve*) pojonhada 보존하다; pokwanhada 보관하다.

+ keeping *n*. (*retaining*) yuji 유지; (*preservation*) pojon 보존; (*safe-keeping*) pokwan 보관, (*support*) puyang 부양.

ketchup *n*. k'ech'ŏp 케첩.

kettle *n*. chujŏnja 주전자, (*pot*) sot 솥.

+ key *n*. yŏlsoe 열쇠; (*piano*) kŏn 건; (*clue*) silmari 실마리; (*secret*) pigyŏl 비결.

kick *v*. ch'ada 차다.—*n*. pal-lo ch'agi 발로 차기.

kidney *n*. sinjang 신장(腎臟), k'ongp'at 콩팥.

+ kill *v*. (*slay*) chugida 죽이다; (*suppress*) ŏknurŭda 억누르다.

* kind *n*. (*sort*) chongnyu〈chongryu 종류, (*character*) sŏngjil 성질.—*adj*. ch'injŏlhan 친절한.

kindergarten *n*. yuch'iwŏn 유치원.

+ king *n*. wang 왕, kugwang 국왕, kunju 군주.

kiss *n*. immach'um〈ipmach'um 입맞춤, k'isŭ 키스,

ppoppo 뽀뽀. —v. immach′uda⟨ipmach′uda 입맞추다.

+ **kitchen** n. puŏk 부엌, chubang 주방.

kite n. (toy) yŏn 연(鳶); (bird) solgae 솔개; (impostor) sagikkun 사기꾼.

+ **knee** n. murŭp 무릎: on one′s ~s murŭp-ŭl kkulk′o 무릎을 꿇고

+ **knife** n. (chumŏni)k′al (주머니)칼, naip′ŭ 나이프. → **sword** n. k′al 칼.

knit v. (yarn) ttŭda 뜨다, (weaving) tchada 짜다, (joint) chŏp′ap′ada⟨chŏphaphada 접합하다.

knitting n. ttŭgaejil 뜨개질, p′yŏnmul 편물.

+ **knock** v. (strike) tudŭrida 두드리다.—n. (stroke) t′a-gyŏk 타격, (blow) kut′a 구타; (door) nok′ŭ 노크.

knot n. (tie) maedŭp 매듭; (nautical mile, speed) haeri 해리(海里), (speed) not′ŭ 노트.—v. maedŭp-chitta 매듭짓다, (entangle) ŏlk′ida 얽히다.

* **know** v. (understand) alda 알다; (recognize) injŏng-hada 인정하다; (be acquainted with) ...wa anŭn-saida …와 아는 사이다.

+ **knowledge** n. (information) chisik 지식, insik 인식; ihae 이해 ; (learning) hangmun⟨hakmun 학문.

+ **known** adj. allyŏjyŏ innŭn⟨itnŭn 알려져 있는: make ~ allida 알리다, palp′yohada 발표하다.

Korea n. han′guk 한국: taehanmin′guk 대한민국.

Korean n. & adj. (people) han′guksaram(-ŭi) 한국사람(의); (language) han′gukmal(-ŭi) 한국말(의).

≤ L ≥

labo(u)r n. nodong 노동, (toil) kodoen il 고된 일. —v. ilhada 일하다, nodonghada 노동하다.

lace n. (fabric) reisŭ 레이스, (shoe) kkŭn 끈.

+ **lack** n. (want) pujok 부족, (deficiency) kyŏlp′ip 결핍.

—*v.* pujokhada 부족하다, mojarada 모자라다.

lacquer *n.* raek'ŏ 래커, ch'il 칠(漆), ot 옻.

ladder *n.* sadakttari 사닥다리.

lady *n.* kwibuin 귀부인, sungnyŏ〈suknyŏ 숙녀: *a ~ clerk* yŏsamuwŏn 여사무원.

+ **lake** *n.* hosu 호수 ; (*pond*) mot 못, yŏnmot 연못.

lamb *n.* (*young sheep*) ŏrin yang 어린 양.

lame *adj.* chŏllŭmbari-ŭi 절름발이의; (*imperfect*) purwanjŏnhan 불완전한.

lamp *n.* tŭng 등, namp'o 남포: *a street ~* karodŭng 가로등, *a safety ~* anjŏndŭng 안전등.

* **land** *n.* ttang 땅, (*estates*) t'oji 토지; (*country*) nara 나라. —*v.* (*disembark*) sangryukhada 상륙하다, (*airplane*) ch'angnyukhada〈ch'akryukhad 착륙하다; (*alight*) hach'ahada 하차하다; (*arrive*) toch'akhada 도착하다.

landlord *n.* (*house*) chiptchuin 집주인; kajang 가장, (*property*) chiju 지주.

* **language** *n.* mal 말, ŏnŏ 언어: *national ~* kugŏ 국어.

lantern *n.* ch'orong 초롱, k'andella 칸델라.

lap ① *v.* (*lick*) haltta 핥다. ② *n.* murŭp 무릎.

* **large** *adj.* k'ŏdaran 커다란, (*spacious*) nŏlbŭn 넓은, (*copious*) manŭn 많은, (*liberal*) kwandaehan 관대한.

+ **last** *v.* (*continue*) kyesokhada 계속하다. *adj.* ch'oehu-ŭi 최후의; (*most recent*) ch'oegŭn-ŭi 최근의; (*past*)chinan 지난. —*adv.* ch'oehu-ro 최후로.

+ **late** *adj.* nŭjŭn 늦은, chigakhan 지각한, (*recent*) ch'oegŭn-ŭi 최근의, (*dead*) ko 고(故): *the ~ Mr.E* ko issi 고(故) E씨. —*adv.* nŭtkke 늦게.

latrine *n.* (*privy*) pyŏnso 변소.

+ **laugh** *v.* utta 웃다.—*n.* usŭm 웃음.

+ **laughter** *n.* usŭm 웃음, usŭmssori 웃음소리.

lavatory *n.* semyŏnso 세면소, hwajangsil 화장실.

* **law** *n.* pŏp 법, pŏmnyul〈pŏpryul 법률: *constitutional ~* hŏnppŏp 헌법, *martial ~* kunppŏp 군법.

lawn *n.* chandi 잔디, chandibat 잔디밭: *~ mower* chandi kkangnŭn〈kkaknŭn kigye 잔디 깎는 기계.

+ **lawyer** n. pŏmnyulga〈pŏpryulga 법률가; pyŏnhosa 변호사.

+ **lay** v. (*put down*) not'a 놓다, tuda 두다; (*produce eggs*) nat'a 낳다; (*prepare*) chunbihada 준비하다: ~ *a table for dinner* siksa chunbi-rŭl hada 식사 준비를 하다.

+ **layer** n. ch'ŭng 층; kyŏp 겹; nonnŭn〈notnŭn saram 놓는 사람: *a brick* ~ pyŏkttol ssannŭn〈ssatnŭn saram 벽돌 쌓는 사람.

+ **lazy** adj. keŭrŭn 게으른, kumttŭn 굼뜬, nŭrin 느린.

+ **lead** ① v. ikkŭlda 이끌다, indohada 인도하다, aptchang sŏ kada 앞장서 가다. —n. (*direction*) sŏndo 선도, (*command*) chihwi 지휘. ② (*metal*) nap 납.

+ **leader** n. sŏndoja 선도자, t'ongsoltcha 통솔자, chidoja 지도자.

+ **leaf** n. (*of tree*) namunnip〈namutip 나뭇잎, (*of book*) han chang 한 장, p'eiji 페이지.

  leak n. saenŭn kot 새는 곳. —v. saeda 새다.

+ **learn** v. paeuda 배우다; alda 알다 ; (*hear*) tŭtta 듣다.

+ **learned** adj. pakssikhan 박식한, yusikhan 유식한.

+ **learning** n. hangmun〈hakmun 학문; hakssŭp 학습.

+ **leather** n. kajuk 가죽, p'ihyŏk 피혁: ~ *belt* kajuk hyŏkttae 가죽혁대.

* **leave** ① v. (*go away*) ttŏnada 떠나다; (*cease*) kŭmanduda 그만두다; (*abandon*) naebŏryŏ tuda 내버려 두다. ② n. (*permission*) hŏga 허가; (~ *of absence*) hyuga 휴가.

  lecture n. kangŭi 강의, (*speech*) kangyŏn 강연; hun'gye 훈계.—v. kangŭihada 강의하다.

  left adv. oenp'yŏn-ŭro 왼편으로. —adj. oentchog-ŭi 왼쪽의. —n. oenp'yŏn 왼편.

+ **leg** n. tari 다리. (*prop*) pŏt'imttae 버팀대.

+ **legal** adj. pŏmnyulssang-ŭi〈pŏpryulsang-ŭi 법률상의, (*lawful*) happŏptchŏgin 합법적인, chŏngdanghan 정당한.

  legend n. chŏnsŏl 전설; (*map*) pŏmnye〈pŏmrye 범례 (凡例).

leisure *n.* yŏga 여가, t'ŭm 틈, (*ease*) anil 안일.

lemon *n.* lemon 레몬; (*pale yellow*) tamhwangsaek 담황색.

lend *v.* pillyŏjuda 빌려주다; (*add*) ch'ŏmgahada 첨가하다; (*furnish*) chegonghada 제공하다.

+ **length** *n.* kiri 길이; (*time*) tongan 동안; (*space*) kŏri 거리.

lens *n.* renjŭ 렌즈, sujŏngch'e 수정체.

* **less** *adj.* poda chŏgŭn 보다 적은. —*adv.* poda chŏkke 보다 적게.

+ **let** *v.* (*allow*) hŏrakhada 허락하다.—*v.* (*allow to*) ‥hage hada ‥하게 하다, (*lend*) pillyŏjuda 빌려주다: *house to* ~ setchip 셋집.

* **letter** *n.* (*written message*) p'yŏnji 편지, (*alphabet*)munja 문자; (*pl.*) (*literature*) munhak 문학. → **learning** *n.* hangmun⟨hakmun 학문.

* **level** *adj.* p'yŏngp'yŏnghan 평평한, korŭn 고른.—*n.* sup'yŏng 수평, (*standard*) sujun 수준.

lever *n.* chirettae 지렛대, (*mechanical*) rebŏ 레버.

lewd *adj.* ŭmtanghan 음탕한, ch'ujap'an 추잡한.

library *n.* tosŏgwan/sil 도서관, (*study*) sŏjae 서재, changsŏ 장서, ch'ongsŏ 총서.

lice *n.* i 이.

licence/license *n.* hŏga 허가, in'ga 인가; myŏnhŏtchang 면허장, hŏgatchŭng 허가증.

lick *v.* haltta 핥다. → **beat** *n.* ttaerida 때리다.

+ **lid** *n.* ttukkŏng 뚜껑; (*eyelid*) nunkkap'ul 눈까풀.

+ **lie** ① *n.* kŏjinmal⟨kŏjitmal 거짓말. —*v.* kŏjinmalhada⟨kŏjitmalhada 거짓말하다. ② (*recline*) nuptta 눕다; (*be situated*) wich'ihada 위치하다. → **exist** *v.*chonjaehada 존재하다.

* **life** *n.* saengmyŏng 생명; (*span of* ~) ilssaeng 일생; (*human* ~) insaeng 인생; (*biography*) chŏngi 전기 (傳記); (*state of living*) saenghwal 생활; (*energy*) hwalgi 활기.

+ **lift** *v.* tŭrŏollida 들어올리다; nop'ida 높이다; (*fog*)kŏthida 걷히다. —*n.* tŭroolligi 들어올리기; sŭngjin 승진;

(*elevator*) sŭngganggi 승강기.

* **light** ① *n.* pit 빛; (*lamp*) pul 불. —*v.* pul-ŭl k'yŏda 불을 켜다, (*fire*) pulp'iuda 불피우다. ② *adj.* kabyŏun 가벼운.

   lighter *n.* (*cigarette*) rait'ŏ 라이터.

+ **lightly** *adv.* kabyŏpkke 가볍게, (*easily*) swipkke 쉽게.

   lightning *n.* pŏn'gaetppul 번갯불. —*adj.* kŭpssok'an 급속한, chŏn'gwangsŏk'wa-ŭi 전광석화의.

   likable *adj.* (*congenial*) maŭm-e tŭnŭn 마음에 드는.

* **like** *v.* choahada 좋아하다. —*prep.* ...wa kach'i …와 같이, ch'ŏrŏm 처럼. —*adj.* talmŭn 닮은.

* **likely** *adj.* kŭrŏlttŭthan 그럴듯한, issŭmjikhan 있음직한. —*adv.* ama 아마, tabunhi 다분히.

   liking *n.* choaham 좋아함.

   lily *n.* nari 나리, paek'ap 백합: ~ *of the vally* ŭnbangulkkot 은방울꽃, *water* ~ suryŏn 수련.

+ **limit** *v.* chehanhada 제한하다. —*n.* chehan 제한; (*range*) pŏmwi 범위.

* **line** *n.* sŏn 선, (*row*) chul 줄, yŏl 열(列), haeng 행.

   linen *n.* amap'o 아마포, rinnerŭ 린네르.

   linguist *n.* ŏnŏhaktcha 언어학자, ŏhaktcha 어학자.

   linguistics *n.* ŏnŏhak 언어학.

   lining *n.* (*of dresses*) an 안, ankkam 안감; (*contents*) naeyong 내용, almaengi 알맹이.

+ **link** *v.* yŏn'gyŏlhada 연결하다, yŏn'gyŏlsik'ida 연결시키다. —*n.* (*loop*) kori 고리.

   lion *n.* saja 사자.

+ **lip** *n.* ipssul 입술: ~ *service* malppunin hoŭi 말뿐인 호의. → **mouth** *n.* ip 입.

* **liquid** *n.* aekch'e 액체.—*adj.* aekch'e-ŭi 액체의.

   liquor *n.* alk'ool ŭmnyo〈ŭmryo 알코올 음료, sul 술.

+ **list** *n.* (*table*) p'yo 표, (*roster*) myŏngdan 명단, (*roll*) myŏngbu 명부. —*v.* myŏngbu-e chŏktta/nayŏlhada 명부에 적다/나열하다, myŏngdan-e ollida 명단에 올리다.

+ **listen** *v.* tŭtta 듣다, kwi-rŭl kiurida 귀를 기울이다.

+ **literature** *n.* munhak 문학, munye 문예; (*works*) chŏsul 저술; (*documents*) munhŏn 문헌.

* **little** *adj.* (*size*) chagŭn 작은, (*amount*) chŏgŭn 적은;

(*young*) ŏrin 어린. —*adv. & n.* chogŭm-pakke … ant'a 조금밖에 … 않다.

* **live** *v.* salda 살다, saenghwalhada 생활하다. —*adj.* sarainnŭn〈saraitnŭn 살아있는, hwalgiinnŭn〈hwalgiitnŭn 활기있는.

+ **lively** *adj.* hwalbalhan 활발한, hwalgiinnŭn〈hwalgiitnŭn 활기있는.; (*vivid*) saengsaenghan 생생한.— *adv.* kiunch'age 기운차게.

   liver *n.* kanjang 간장, kan 간: ~ *oil* kanyu 간유.

   loan *n.* taebu 대부(貸付), kongch'ae 공채, ch'agwan 차관. —*v.* taebuhada 대부하다.

   lobster *n.* padagajae 바다가재, k'ŭn saeu 큰 새우.

+ **local** *adj.* chibang-ŭi 지방의: ~ *color* chibangsaek 지방색, a ~ *paper* chibangsinmun 지방신문.

+ **lock** *n.* chamulssoe 자물쇠, (*water*) sumun 수문. —*v.* chamulssoe-rŭl ch'aeuda 자물쇠를 채우다, chamgŭda 잠그다.

   locker *n.* rok'ŏ 로커, (*cabinet to be locked*) chang 장.

   log *n.* t'ongnamu 통나무: ~ *cabin* t'ongnamujip 통나무 집, (*diary*) hanghaeiltchi 항해일지.

* **long** *adj.* kin 긴, (*time*) oraen 오랜. —*adv.* kilge 길게, orae 오래. —*v.* (*yearn*) kŭriwŏhada 그리워하다, tonggyŏnghada 동경하다; yŏlmanghada 열망하다.

* **look** *v.* paraboda 바라보다, chŏdaboda 쳐다보다,(*stare*) yusimhi poda 유심히 보다; (*face*) hyanghada 향하다. —*n.* (*facial expression*) p'yochŏng 표정; (*glance*) ilgyŏn 일견; (*aspect*) yongmo 용모.

+ **loose** *adj.* (*slack*) hŏlgŏwŏjin 헐거워진, (*not tight*) tanjŏngch'i mothan 단정치 못한.

   loosen *v.* (*slacken*) nŭtch'uda 늦추다, p'urŏjuda 풀어 주다.

+ **lorry** *n.* hwamulchadongch'a 화물자동차, t'ŭrŏk 트럭.

+ **lose** *v.* ilt'a 잃다; (*be defeated*) chida 지다, p'aebae-hada 패배하다; (*late watch*) nŭrida 느리다; (*miss*) noch'ida 놓치다; (*waste*) hŏbihada 허비하다.

+ **loss** *n.* punsil 분실, (*deficit*) sonsil(aek) 손실(액).

+ **lost** *adj.* irŭn 잃은, haengbangbulmyŏng-ŭi 행방불명의.

* **lot** *n.* (*house*) puji 부지, (*plenty*) manŭm 많음.
  lottery *n.* ch'uch'ŏm 추첨, (*fortune*) un 운.
  lotus *n.* yŏn(kkot) 연(蓮)(꽃).
* **loud** *adj.* sori-ga k'ŭn 소리가 큰; (*noisy*) sikkŭrŏun 시끄러운, (*showy*) yahan 야한.
  loudspeaker *n.* hwaksŏnggi 확성기.
  louse *n.* i 이(蝨), kisaengch'ung 기생충.
+ **love** *n.* sarang 사랑, aejŏng 애정; (*person*) yŏnin 연인, aein 애인. —*v.* saranghada 사랑하다. → **liking** *n.* choaham 좋아함.
  lover *n.* aein 애인, yŏnin 연인; (*dovotee*) aehoga 애호가, ch'anmija 찬미자.
+ **low** *adj.* najŭn 낮은; (*mean, humble*) pich'ŏnhan 비천한. —*adv.* natkke 낮게, ssage 싸게.
+ **luck** *n.* un 운, haengun 행운, yohaeng 요행.
+ **lucky** *adj.* unjoŭn 운좋은, haengun-ŭi 행운의.
  luggage *n.* suhamul 수하물, yŏhaenghamul 여행하물.
  lumber ① *n.* chaemok 재목. ② *v.* (*rumble*) k'ung-k'ung kŏtta 쿵쿵 걷다.
+ **lump** *n.* tŏngŏri 덩어리, hok 혹.
  lunch *n.* chŏmsim 점심, (*box*) tosirak 도시락.
+ **lung** *n.* p'ye 폐(肺), hŏp'a 허파.
  luxurious *adj.* sach'isŭrŏn 사치스런.
  luxuriously *adv.* sach'isŭrŏpkke 사치스럽게.
  luxury *n.* sach'i 사치, hosa 호사.
+ **lying** *adj.* ① nuwŏinnŭn〈nuwŏitnŭn 누워있는 ② hŏwi-ŭi 허위의.

≤ M ≥

* **machine** *n.* kigye 기계, (*structure*) kigu 기구.
+ **machinery** *n.* kigye 기계, (*mechanism*) kigye changch'i 기계 장치.

+ **mad** *adj.* (*crazy*) mich'in 미친; (*furious*) maengnyŏl-han 〈maengryŏlhan 맹렬한; (*angry*) hwa-ga nan 화가 난.

made *adj.* (*artificially produced*) mandŭn 만든, ...che ···제(製): ~ *in Korea* han'guktche 한국제, ~ *in U.S.A.* miguktche 미국제.

+ **magazine** *n.* (*periodical*) chaptchi 잡지, chŏnggi kan-haengmul 정기 간행물, (*army*) t'anyakko 탄약고.

+ **magic** *n.* masul 마술, mappŏp 마법, yosul 요술; maryŏk 마력. —*adj.* mappŏp-ŭi 마법의, yosur-ŭi 요술의.

magician *n.* masulsa 마술사.

maid *n.* (*servant*) hanyŏ 하녀. → **girl** *n.* sonyŏ 소녀, agassi 아가씨.

mail *n.* up'yŏnmul 우편물. —*v.* usonghada 우송하다.

* **main** *adj.* chungyohan 중요한; (*leading*) yuryŏkhan 유력한. —*n.* (*main pipe*) pon'gwan 본관(本管).

+ **mainly** *adv.* churo 주로, taegae 대개, taech'ero 대체로.

major *n.* (*army*) yukkun soryŏng 육군 소령. —*adj.* k'ŭn p'yŏn-ŭi 큰편의, chuyohan 주요한. —*v.* (*specialize*) chŏn'gonghada 전공하다.

\# **make** *v.* mandŭlda 만들다; (*compel*) ...hage hada ···하게 하다; (*become*) ...i toeda ···이 되다; (*gain*) hoek-dŭkhada 획득하다. —*n.* chejo 제조.

+ **male** *n.* & *adj.* namsŏng(-ŭi) 남성(의); (*of animal*) suk'ŏt(-ŭi) 수컷(의): *a* ~ *dog* suk'ae 수캐.

* **man** *n.* (*male*) namja 남자. → **people** *n.* saram 사람.

+ **manage** *v.* kwallihada 관리하다; (*handle*) taruda 다루다; (*business*) kyŏngyŏnghada 경영하다.

Manchuria *n.* manju 만주.

+ **manner** *n.* pangbŏp 방법; yejŏl 예절; t'aedo 태도.

* **many** *adj.* manhŭn 많은, tasu-ŭi 다수의.

+ **map** *n.* chido 지도, yaktto 약도, ch'ŏnch'edo 천체도.

maple *n.* tanp'ung(namu) 단풍(나무).

March *n.* samwŏl 3월.

marine *adj.* pada-ŭi 바다의; (*of the navy*) haegun-ŭi 해군의: ~ *insurance* haesangbohŏm 해상보험, ~ *force* haebyŏngdae 해병대. —*n.* sŏnbak 선박.

+ **mark** n. (*trace*) p'yojŏk 표적, chaguk 자국; (*pl.*) kiho 기호; (*point*) chŏmsu 점수, (*grade*) sŏngjŏk 성적. —v. p'yohada 표하다, mak'ŭ-rŭl hada 마크를 하다.

market n. sijang 시장(市場), chang 장: *black* ~ amsijang 암시장, *fish* ~ ŏmulsijang 어물시장, *fruit* ~ ch'ŏnggwasijang 청과시장.

+ **marriage** n. kyŏlhon 결혼, (*wedding*) kyŏlhonsik 결혼식.

+ **marry** v. kyŏlhonhada 결혼하다, kyŏlhonsik'ida 결혼 시키다; (*for men*) changgadŭlda 장가들다; (*for women*) sijipkkada 시집가다.

marvel(l)ous adj. nollaun 놀라운, kiihan 기이한, mŏtchin 멋진.

mask n. t'al 탈, kamyŏn 가면, pongmyŏng〈pokmyŏn 복면. —v. kamyŏn-ŭl ssŭda 가면을 쓰다, (*disguise*) kajanghada 가장하다, (*hide*) kamch'uda 감추다.

+ **mass** ① n. tŏngŏri 덩어리; (*large number*) tasu 다수, (*great quality*) taryang 다량; (*crowd*) kunjung 군중, (*group*) chipttan 집단; (*bulk*) pup'i 부피. —v. moŭda 모으다. ② n. misa 미사.

mat n. (*straw*) totchari 돗자리; (*bamboo*) taejari 대자리, kŏjŏk 거적, kkalgae 깔개.

+ **match** n. ① sŏngnyang 성냥. ② (*athletic*) kyŏnggi 경기, (*game*) sihap 시합; (*rival*) chŏkssu 적수. —v. (*be equal to*) …e p'iltchŏkhada …에 필적하다; (*be arival to*) sangŏn-ŭdae-ga toeda 상대가 되다; (*fit*) chohwahada 조화하다, ŏullida 어울리다.

* **material** adj. multchir-ŭi 물질의; (*essential*) chung yohan 중요한. —n. chaeryo 재료.

+ **mathematics** n. suhak 수학.

+ **matter** n. (*substance*) multchil 물질; (*affair*) sakkŏn 사건; (*material*) chaeryo 재료; (*constituents*) yoso 요소. —v. sangkwan-i/kwan'gye-ga itta 상관이/관계가 있다.

May n. owŏl 5월.

* **may** aux. v. (*guess*) …iltchido morŭnda …일지도 모 른다; (*permit*) …haedo chot'a/toeda …해도 좋다/되 다; (*ability*) …hal ssu itta …할 수 있다; (*wish*) wŏnk′ondae ⋯hagi-rŭl 원컨대 ⋯하기를.

mayor *n*. sijang 시장(市長).

me *pron*. (dative, *to* ~) na-ege 나에게, (accusative) na-rŭl 나를, (*humble*) chŏ-ege 저에게, chŏ-rŭl 저를.

+ **meal** ① *n*. (*food*) sikssa 식사. ② (*corn*) kulgŭn karu 굵은 가루.

mean ① *v*. (*signify*) ŭimihada 의미하다; (*intend*) ye-jŏnghada 예정하다. ② *adj*. (*base*) ch′ŏnhan 천한; (*nasty*) chikkujŭn 짓궂은; (*stingy*) insaekhan 인색한. ③(*average*) p′yŏnggyun-ŭi 평균의. ––*n*. chung gan 중간; (*average*) p′yŏnggyun-ŭi 평균; (*pl*.) su-dan 수단, pangbŏp 방법.

+ **meaning** *n*. ttŭt 뜻, ŭimi 의미.

meaningful *adj*. (*significant*) ŭimisimjanghan 의미심장한.

+ **measure** *n*. ch′issu 치수, ch′ŭktchŏng 측정; (*pl*.) su-dan 수단. ––*v*. chaeda 재다, ch′ŭktchŏnghada 측정하다.

+ **measure** *n*. ch′issu 치수, ch′ŭktchŏng 측정; (*pl*.)
measurement *n*. ch′ŭngnyang⟨ch′ŭkryang 측량.

+ **measure** *n*. ch′issu 치수, ch′ŭktchŏng 측정; (*pl*.)
meat *n*. kogi 고기: *tender* ~ yŏnhan kogi 연한 고기.

+ **medical** *adj*. ŭihak-ŭi 의학의, ŭisul-ŭi 의술의: *a ~ college* ŭikkwa taehak 의과대학, *a ~ examination/ check-up* kŏngang chindan 건강 진단.

+ **medicine** *n*. yak 약; (*science*) ŭihak 의학.

medium *n*. chunggan 중간; maegae 매개, (*means*) sudan 수단. ––*adj*. chungch′i-ŭi 중치의.

+ **meet** *v*. mannada 만나다; majihada 맞이하다; (*join*) hapch′ida 합치다.

+ **meeting** *n*. (*assembly*) hoeŭi 회의, hoehap 회합, moim 모임, (*blind date*) 미팅.

melon *n*. mellon 멜론, ch′amoe 참외.

melt *v*. noktta 녹다, nogida 녹이다, yonghaehada 용해하다.

* **member** *n*. irwon 일원; (*of a company*) sawŏn 사원; (*of an association*) hoewŏn 회원.

+ **memory** *n*. kiŏk 기억, kiŏngnyŏk⟨kiŏkryŏk 기억력;

(*recollection*) ch'uŏk 추억.

mend v. koch'ida 고치다, susŏnhada 수선하다.

menstruation n. wŏlgyŏng 월경, mensŭ 멘스.

+ **mental** adj. chŏngsin-ŭi 정신의, tunoe-ŭi 두뇌의.

+ **mention** v. (*speak of*) ...ŭl malhada …을 말하다, ŏngŭphada 언급하다.

merchant n. sangin 상인.—adj. sangŏp-ŭi 상업의.

mess n. (*food*) ŭmsingmul〈ŭmsikmul 음식물; (*mixture*) honhap 혼합, (*medley*) twijukbaktchuk 뒤죽박죽: ~ hall sikttang 식당.

+ **message** n. t'ongsin 통신, chŏn'gal 전갈, mesiji 메시지, (*communication*) sosik 소식; (*mission*) samyŏng 사명.

messy adj. ŏjirŏun 어지러운, chijŏbunhan 지저분한.

* **metal** n. kŭmsok 금속, soebuch'i 쇠붙이.

method n. pangbŏp 방법; (*order*) sunsŏ 순서.

+ **metre/ter** n. (*measure*) mit'ŏ 미터; (*instrument*) kyeryanggi 계량기; (*rhyme*) unyul 운율, (*rhythm*) paktcha 박자.

midnight n. chajŏng 자정, hanbamtchung 한밤중, yaban 야반.

+ **middle** n. kaunde 가운데, chungang 중앙. —adj. chungang-ŭi 중앙의, hangaunde-ŭi 한가운데의.

* **might** n. (*power*) him 힘, nŭngnyŏk〈nŭngryŏk 능력: M~ is right. Him-ŭn chŏngŭida 힘은 정의다.

+ **mile** n. mail 마일 (1,609.3m).

+ **military** adj. kun(sa)-ŭi 군사의: ~ attache taesagwan sosok mugwan 대사관소속 무관, ~ academy yukkunsagwan hakkyo 육군사관학교, ~ strength kunsaryŏk 군사력.

+ **milk** n. (*cow's*) uyu 우유, (*mother's*) chŏt 젖, milk'ŭ 밀크.

million n. & adj. paekman(-ŭi) 백만(의).

* **mind** n. maŭm 마음, saenggak 생각; (*intent*) ŭihyang 의향. —v. (*heed, be careful*) chosimhada 조심하다.

mine pron. na-ŭi kŏt 나의 것. —n. kwangsan 광산; (*land*) chiroe 지뢰: a coal ~ t'an'gwang 탄광.

minister n. (*government*) changgwan 장관, (*church*)

mok'ssa(nim) 목사(님); (*envoy*) kongsa 공사(公使): *the Prime M~* kungmuch'ongni〈kukmuch'ongri 국무총리.

+ **minor** *adj.* (*lesser*) sosu-ŭi 소수의, (*inferior*) hach'anŭn 하찮은. —*n.* misŏngnyŏnja 미성년자.

+ **minute** ① *adj.* misehan 미세한, (*detailed*) sangsehan 상세한. ② *n.* pun 분(分), sun'gan 순간.

+ **mirror** *n.* kŏul 거울, (*pattern*) mobŏm 모범. —*v.* (*reflect*) panyŏnghada 반영하다.

  miss *v.* noch'ida 놓치다; kŭriwŏhada 그리워하다, …i ŏpssŏsŏ sŏunhada …이 없어서 서운하다. —*n.*(*failure*) silch'aek 실책; (*omission*) t'allak 탈락.

  Miss *n.* yang 양: ~ *Kim* kimyang 김양.

+ **missile** *n. & adj.* misail(-ŭi) 미사일(의), naraganŭn-mugi(-ŭi) 날아가는 무기(의).

  missionary *n.* sŏngyosa 선교사, sŏnjŏnja 선전자, sajŏl 사절.

+ **mistake** *n.* chalmot 잘못, silssu 실수. —*v.* t'ŭllida 틀리다, (*misunderstand*) chalmot saenggakhada 잘못 생각 하다.

+ **mix** *v.* sŏktta 섞다, honhaphada 혼합하다; (*mingle with*) sŏkkida 섞이다.

+ **mixture** *n.* honhap 혼합, honhapmul 혼합물.

+ **model** *n.* (*pattern*) mŏhyŏng 모형; (*for behavior*) mobŏm 모범; (*ideal specimen*) p'yobon 표본; (*fashion*) model 모델. —*v.* ponttŭda 본뜨다.

+ **modern** *adj.* hyŏndae-ŭi 현대의, (*up-to-date style*) sinsik-ŭi 신식의. —*n.* hyŏndaein 현대인.

  modest *adj.* (*humble*) kyŏmsonhan 겸손한, yamjŏnhan 얌전한; (*shy*) sujubŭn 수줍은.

  mold *n.* ① (*fungus*) komp'angi 곰팡이. ② (*model*) hyŏng 형.

+ **moment** *n.* sungan 순간; (*occasion*) kihoe 기회, kyŏngu 경우.

  Monday *n.* wŏryoil 월요일.

* **money** *n.* ton 돈, kŭmjŏn 금전. → **wealth** *n.* pu 부(富).

  monkey *n.* wŏnsungi 원숭이.

+ **month** *n*. tal 달, wŏl 월 : *this* ~ idal 이달, *last* ~
  chinandal 지난달, *next* ~ taŭmdal 다음달, naedal
  내 달; *at the beginning/end of the* ~ ch'osun-e 초/
  하순 에, *in the middle of the* ~chungsun-e 중순에.

+ **mood** *n*. kibun 기분, (*temper*) simjŏng 심정; (*social
  atmosphere*) p'ungjo 풍조.

+ **moon** *n*. tal 달: *a full* ~ porŭmttal 보름달, manwŏl 만
  월, *a new* ~ ch'osŭngttal 초승달, *an old* ~ kŭmŭm-
  ttal 그믐달, *a half* ~ pandal 반달.

  mop *n*. charu kŏlle 자루 걸레.

+ **moral** *adj*. (*ethical*) yullijŏgin 윤리적인, (*virtuous*)
  todŏktchŏgin 도덕적인. —*n*. kyohun 교훈, yulli〈
  yunri 윤리.

* **more** *adj*. tŏ manhŭn 더 많은. —*adv*. tŏ manhi 더 많
  이. —*n*. tŏ manhŭn kŏt 더 많은 것.

+ **morning** *n*. ach'im 아침, (*before noon*) ojŏn 오전.

  mosquito *n*. mogi 모기.

  mosquito net *n*. mogijang 모기장.

  moss *n*. ikki 이끼: *stones covered with* ~ ikki kkin
  tol 이끼 낀 돌.

* **most** *adj*. kajang manhŭn 가장 많은. —*n*. ch'oedae-
  ryang 최대량.

  moth *n*. nabang 나방; (*clothes moth*) chomppŏlle 좀벌레.

+ **mother** *n*. ŏmŏni 어머니, (*honorific*) moch'in 모친. —*v*.
  (*bring up*) poyukhada 보육하다.

+ **motor** *n*. palttonggi 발동기, mout'ŏ 모우터.

+ **motorcycle** *n*. ot'obai 오토바이.

+ **mountain** *n*. san 산: ~ *range* sanmaek 산맥.

  mouse *n*. saengjwi 생쥐: ~ *trap* chwidŏt 쥐덫.

+ **mouth** *n*. ip 입: *with one* ~ igudongsŏng-ŭro 이구동
  성으로.

* **move** *v*. umjigida 움직이다; (*touch emotionally*)
  kamdongsik'ida 감동시키다; (*propose*) cheŭihada
  제의하다; (*move*) isahada 이사하다.

* **movement** *n*. undong 운동, tongjak 동작; idong 이동;
  (*pl*.) haengdong 행동. → **operation** *n*. unjŏn 운전.

  movie *n*. (*motion picture*) yŏnghwa 영화, hwalttongsajin 활동사진.

* **moving** adj. umjiginŭn 움직이는; (touching) kamdongsik'inŭn 감동시키는.

Mr. n. ssi 씨, kun 군, nim 님.

Mrs. n. ...ssi puin ⋯씨 부인, ...yŏsa ⋯여사(女史).

* **much** adj. manŭn 많은. —adv. manhi 많이.

+ **mud** n. chinhŭk 진흙, (mire, swamp) chinch'ang 진창.

murder n. sarin 살인, salhae 살해. —v. salhaehada 살해 하다, chugida 죽이다.

+ **muscle** n. kŭnyuk 근육; (bodily strength) wallyŏk⟨wanryŏk 완력.

museum n. pangmulgwan⟨pakmulgwan 박물관.

mushroom n. (toadstool) pŏsŏt 버섯.

* **music** n. ŭmak 음악; (musical composition) akkok 악곡: Korean ~ kugak 국악, traditional ~ chŏnt'ong ŭmak 전통음악.

+ **musical** adj. ŭmag-ŭi 음악의, (melodious) ŭmaktchŏgin 음악적인. —n. (concert) ŭmakhoe 음악회, (drama) myujikŏl 뮤지컬.

+ **musician** n. ŭmakka 음악가, akssa 악사.

* **must** aux. v. ...haeya handa ⋯해야 한다; ...ham-e t'ŭllimŏptta ⋯함에 틀림없다.

mustache n. k'ossuyŏm 콧수염.

mustard n. kyŏja 겨자(芥子), kat 갓.

mutton n. yanggogi 양고기.

my pron. na-ŭi 나의. —int. M ~! =Oh, m ~! chŏrŏn! 저런! ŏmŏna 어머나! igŏt ch'am 이것 참!

myself pron. na chasin 나 자신.

mystery n. sinbi 신비, isanghan kŏt 이상한 것.

⪦ N ⪧

+ **nail** v. mos-ŭl paktta 못을 박다. —n.(instrument)

mot 못; (*finger*) sont'op 손톱 ; (*toe*) palt'op 발톱 :
~ *clippers* sont'opkkakki 손톱깎이.

naked *adj*. pŏlgŏbŏsŭn 벌거벗은, nach'e-ŭi 나체의;
(*exposed*) noch'uldoen 노출된.

* **name** *n*. irŭm 이름, sŏngmyŏng 성명, (honorific) sŏng-
ham성함. —*v*. irŭmjitta 이름짓다, (*appoint*)
chimyŏnghada 지명하다.

napkin *n*. naepk'in 냅킨.

* **narrow** *adj*. chobŭn 좁은, p'yŏnhyŏphan 편협한.

+ **nation** *n*. (*state*) kukka 국가; (*race*) minjok 민족;
(*people*) kungmin⟨kukmin 국민.

+ **natural** *adj*. chayŏn-ŭi 자연의; (*non-artificial*) chayŏn
kŭdaero-ŭi 자연 그대로의, (*innate*) t'agonan 타고난.

+ **naturally** *adv*. chayŏnhi 자연히, chayŏnsŭrŏpkke 자연
스 럽게;(*by nature*) ch'ŏnsŏngjŏg-ŭro 천성적으로; (*of
course*) tangyŏnhi 당연히.

+ **nature** *n*. chayŏn 자연; (*character*) ch'ŏnsŏng 천성,
sŏngjil 성질; (*sort*) chongnyu⟨chongryu 종류: *things
of this nature* i chongnyu-ŭi samul 이 종류의 사물.

naughty *adj*. (*mischievous*) changnankkŭrŏgi-ŭi 장
난꾸 러기의; pŏrŭtŏmnŭn⟨pŏrŭtŏpnŭn 버릇없는.

navel *n*. paekkop 배꼽.

+ **navy** *n*. haegun 해군. → **soldiers** *n*. kunin 군인.

+ **near** *adj*. kakkaun 가까운. —*adv*. kakkai 가까이. —*prep*.
...ŭi kakkai-e …의 가까이에, ...ŭi kŭnch'ŏe …의 근처에.

+ **nearly** *adv*. (*almost*) kŏŭi 거의; (*narrowly*) kyŏu 겨
우, hamat'ŏmyŏn 하마터면.

+ **neat** *adj*. (*cleanly*) kkyalkkŭmhan 깔끔한, (*shapely*)
santtŭthan 산뜻한: *a ~ design* santtŭthan tijain
산뜻한 디자인.

* **necessary** *adj*. p'iryohan 필요한: *It is ~ to see her
first*. mŏnjŏ kŭyŏja-rŭl mannal p'iryo-ga itta. 먼저
그 여자를 만날 필요가 있다; (*inevitable*) p'ihal ssu
ŏmnŭn⟨ŏpnŭn 피할 수 없는, p'iryŏnjŏgin 필연적인.

+ **neck** *n*. mok 목, mokttŏlmi 목덜미.

necklace *n*. mokgŏri 목걸이.

necktie *n*. nekt'ai 넥타이.

* **need** *n.* (*necessity*) p'iryo 필요 ; (*poverty*) pin'gon 빈곤. —*v.* (*require*) p'iryohada 필요하다; (*must*) ... hal p'iryo-ga itta ...할 필요가 있다; (*be needy*) kon'gung-e ppajyŏitta 곤궁에 빠져 있다.

+ **needle** *n.* panŭl 바늘, chach'im 자침(磁針).

+ **negative** *adj.* pujŏngjŏgin 부정적인; (opp. *positive*) sogŭktchŏgin 소극적인.—*n.* pujŏng 부정(否定) ; (*refusal*) kŏbu 거부. (*film*) wŏnp'an 원판, p'illŭm 필름.

  neighbo(u)r *n.* iut(ssaram) 이웃(사람), → **fellowman** *n.* tongp'o 동포.

+ **neither** *adj.* ŏnŭ tchog-ŭi ...to ...i anin 어느 쪽의 ···도 ···이 아닌.—*pron.* ŏnŭ tchok-tto ``i anida 어느 쪽도 ···이 아니다.

  nephew *n.* chok'a 조카, saengjil 생질.

+ **nervous** *adj.* singyŏng-ŭi 신경의; (*irritable*)ch'ojohae hanŭn 초조해하는, singyŏngjir-ŭi 신경질의.

  nest *n.* saedunguri 새둥우리, saejip 새집. ② pogŭmjari 보금자리. ③ (*retreat*) p'inanch'ŏ 피난처. —*v.* pogŭmjari-rŭl chitta 보금자리를 짓다.

+ **net** *n.* ① kŭmul 그물. ② (*snare*) hamjŏng 함정.-*adj.* (*business*) sunsuig-ŭi 순수익의.

+ **never** *adv.* (used with negative verbs) kyŏlk'o/chŏlttaero/chŏnhyŏ ``ant'a⟨anhta/anida/ŏptta 결코/절대로/전혀 ``않다/아니다/없다.

* **new** *adj.* sae 새, saeroun 새로운, sinsig-ŭi 신식의; (*recently appointed*) sinim-ŭi 신임(新任)의.

+ **news** *n.* nyusŭ 뉴스, sosik 소식, (*article*) kisa 기사. → **rumor** *n.* somun 소문.

+ **newspaper** *n.* sinmun 신문: *daily* ~ ilgansinmun 일간신문, ~ *article* sinmun'gisa 신문기사, ~ *report* sinmunbodo 신문보도.

* **next** *adj.* taŭm-ŭi 다음의.—*adv.* taŭm-e 다음에.—*prep.* ``e kajang kakkaun ``에 가장 가까운.

+ **nice** *adj.* choŭn 좋은, kkaekkŭthan 깨끗한; koun 고운.

  niece *n.* chok'attal 조카딸, chillyŏ⟨chilnyŏ 질녀.

+ **night** *n.* pam 밤, yagan 야간. *all* ~ pamsae(kkŏt) 밤새 (껏), ch'ŏrya 철야. → **evening** *n.* chŏnyŏk 저녁.

nine *n. & adj.* ahop(-ŭi) 아홉(의), ku(-ŭi) 9(의).

nineteen *n. & adj.* yŏl ahop(-ŭi) 열 아홉(의), sipkku (-ŭi) 십구(의).

* **no** *adv.* ani-o 아니오, chogŭmdo ...anida 조금도 …아 니다. —*n.* pujŏng 부정, kŏjŏl 거절. —*adj.* hanado ŏmnŭn 〈ŏpnŭn 하나도 없는, mu-ŭi 무(無)의.

\+ **nobody** *pron.* amudo ...ant'a〈anhta/anida/ŏptta 아무 도 …않다/아니다/없다. —*n.* hach'anŭn saram 하찮은 사람. *He is a mere ~.* kŭ-nŭn hach'anŭn saram-ida. 그는 하찮은 사람이다.

* **noise** *n.* (*clamor*) soŭm 소음.

\+ **noisy** *adj.* sikkŭrŏun 시끄러운, ttŏdŭlssŏkhan 떠들썩 한: *Don't be ~!* ttŏdŭlji ma! 떠들지 마!/sikkŭrŏwŏ! 시끄러워! → **showy** *adj.* yahan 야한.

\+ **none** *pron.* (*no person*) amu-do ... ant'a〈anhta/ anida/ŏptta 아무도 … 않다/아니다/없다. (*nothing*) amukŏt-to ⋯ ant'a〈anhta/anida/ŏptta 아무것도 … 않다/아니다/없다.

nonsense *n.* muŭimi 무의미: hŏt'ŭn sori 허튼 소리, hŏt-ssori 헛소리, nŏnsensŭ 넌센스. —*int.* pabogach'i 바보 같이.

noodles *n.* kuksu 국수.

noon *n.* (*midday*) chŏngo 정오, taenat 대낮.

\+ **nor** *conj.* ...do ttohan ⋯anida ⋯도 또한 ⋯아니다.

\+ **normal** *adj.* chŏngsang-ŭi 정상의, (*usual*) pot'ong-ŭi 보통의, (*regular, standard*) chŏnggyu-ŭi 정규의, (*average*) p'yŏnggyun-ŭi 평균의.

\+ **north** *n. & adj.* puk(-ŭi) 북(의), puktchok(-ŭi) 북쪽(의).

\+ **nose** *n.* k'o 코; (*sense of smell*) hugak 후각.

\# **not** *adv.* ...anida 아니다, ...ant'a ⋯않다, ...ŏptta ⋯없다. *~ only ...but also ...* ...ppunman anira ⋯to⋯뿐만 아 니라 ⋯도.

\+ **note** *n.* (*memo*) memo 메모; (*annotation*) chuhae 주해; (*short letter*) tansin 단신; (banknote) chip'ye 지폐: (Brit. = Amer. *bill*) *a ten-pound ~* sip p'aund (tchari) chip'ye 십 파운드 (짜리) 지폐; (*mark*) puho 부 호. —*v.* (*see*) chumokhada 주목하다; (*write*) kirokhada 기록하다.

+ **nothing** *pron.* (*not anything*) amugŏtto ... ant′a⟨ anhta /anida/ŏptta 아무것도 ⋯ 않다/아니다/없다. --*n.* (*naught*) mu 무(無): *N~ comes out of ~.* mu-esŏ yu-ga saenggil ssu ŏptta. 무에서 유가 생길 수 없다; (*trifle*) pojalkkŏt ŏmnŭn⟨ŏpnŭn kŏt 보잘것없는 것. —*adv.* chogŭmdo ⋯ ant′a 조금도 ⋯ 않다, kyŏlk′o ⋯ ant′a⟨anhta/anida/ŏptta 결코 ⋯ 않다/아니다/ 없다.

+ **notice** *n.* (*information*) t′ongji 통지, t′ongbo 통보, (*warning*) yego 예고; (*observation*) chumok 주목. —*v.* (*perceive*) arach′aeda 알아채다, chumokhada 주 목하다: ~ *hints* hintŭ-rŭl arach′aeda 힌트를 알아채다.

+ **noticeable** *adj.* chumokhal manhan 주목할 만한.

* **noun** *n.* (*gram.*) myŏngsa 명사.

  novel *n.* sosŏl 소설.—*adj.* (*new*) saeroun 새로운, (*strange*) singihan 신기한, kibalhan 기발한.

  November *n.* sibirwŏl 11월.

+ **now** *adv.* ije 이제, chigŭm(-put′ŏ) 지금(부터): *N ~ I would like to tell you about it.* kŭrŏm chigŭm -put′ŏ kŭ iyagi-rŭl hae tŭrigessŭmnida. 그럼 지금 부터 그 이야기를 해 드리겠습니다. —*n.* chigŭm 지금, hyŏnjae 현재. —*conj.* ...han/in isang ⋯한/인 이상, ...nikka ⋯니까: ~ *you mention it* ne-ga kŭ mar-ŭl hanikka 네가 그 말을 하니까.

  nowhere *adv.* amudedo ⋯ŏptta 아무데도 ⋯없다.

+ **nuclear** *adj.* haeg-ŭi 핵의; wŏnjahaeg-ŭi 원자핵의.

  numb *adj.* kamgag-ŭl irŭn 감각을 잃은.

* **number** *n.* (*figure*) sutcha 숫자; (*series*) pŏnho 번호: *phone number* chŏn(h)wabŏn(h)o 전화번호, (*address*) pŏnji 번지, (*suffix*) -pŏn -번: #10 sippŏn 십번.

  nun *n.* sunyŏ(nim) 수녀(님), yŏsŭng 여승.

  nurse *n.* yumo 유모, kan(h)owŏn 간호원. —*v.* (*hospital*) kan(h)ohada 간호하다. ② (*breast feed*) chŏj-ŭl mŏgida 젖을 먹이다.

+ **nut** *n.* (*chestnut, walnut, etc.*) kyŏngwa 견과(堅果), namu yŏlmae 나무 열매; (*vulgar*) mich′in saram 미친 사람.

nylon *n*. naillon 나일론.

＜ O ≥

+ **obey** *v*. poktchonghada 복종하다, (*mal*)-e ttarŭda (말) 에 따르다; (*mal*)-ŭl tŭtta (말)을 듣다.
* **object** *n*. (*aim*) moktchŏk 목적; (*thing*) mulch´e 물체; (*gram.*) moktchŏgŏ 목적어.—*v*. pandaehada 반대하다, hangŭihada 항의하다.
+ **obtain** *v*. ŏtta 얻다, (*procure*) hoekttŭkhada 획득하다.
+ **obvious** *adj*. myŏngbaekhan 명백한, (*evident*) ppanhan 빤한, ppŏnhan 뻔한, (*undisguised*) nugu-na al ssuinnŭn〈itnŭn 누구나 알 수 있는.
+ **occasion** *n*. kihoe 기회; (*case*) kyŏngu 경우.
+ **occasionally** *adv*. ttaettae-ro 때때로, kakkŭm 가끔, chongjong 종종..
　Occident *n*. sŏyang 서양, sŏgu 서구.
　occupation *n*. (*work*) chigŏp 직업; (*military*) chŏmnyŏng〈chŏmryŏng 점령, chŏmgŏ 점거.
　occupy *v*. (*time, place*) ch´ajihada 차지하다; (*territory*) chŏmnyŏnghada〈chŏmryŏnghada 점령하다; → **engage** *v*. (in business) -e chongsahada -에 종사하다.
+ **occur** *v*. irŏnada 일어나다; saenggida 생기다.
　ocean *n*. taeyang 대양: *Atlantic O~* taesŏyang 대서양/*Pacific O~* t´aep´yŏngyang 태평양.
+ **o'clock** *n*. ¨si ¨시(時).
　October *n*. siwŏl 10월.
　octopus *n*. (*giant*) munŏ 문어, (*small*) naktchi 낙지.
　oculist *n*. ankkwa ŭisa 안과(眼科) 의사.
　odd *adj*. (*strange*) isanghan 이상한; (*extra*) yŏbun-ŭi 여분의; (*not even*) kisu-ŭi 기수(奇數)의.
of *prep*. (possessive) ¨ŭi ¨의, (*made of*) ¨ro toen/

mandŭn …로 된/만든.

* **off** *adv.* ttŏrŏjyŏ 떨어져, mŏlli 멀리: *be far* ~ mŏlli ttŏrŏjyŏ itta 멀리 떨어져 있다.

+ **offend** *v.* hwanage hada 화나게 하다: *I am sorry if you are ~ed.* kibun-i sanghaettamyŏn choesonghamnita. 기분이 상했다면 죄송합니다; (*transgress*) pŏmhada 범하다, ŏgida 어기다.

+ **offensive** *adj.* sirŭn 싫은, (*unpleasant*) pulk'waehan 불쾌한, (*impolite*) muryehan 무례한; (*attacking*) konggyŏkchŏk 공격적.

+ **offer** *v.* chech'ulhada 제출하다; cheŭihada 제의하다; (*show*) p'yosihada 표시하다. —*n.* chean 제안, sinch'ŏng 신청.

+ **office** *n.* (*room*) samusil 사무실; (*department*) …pu 부, …ch'ŏng …청, …kuk …국: *the post* ~ uch'eguk 우체국. → **section** *n.* …kwa …과.

+ **officer** *n.* (*public*) kongmuwŏn 공무원, kwalli〈kwanri 관리: *police* ~ kyŏng(ch'al)gwan 경(찰)관; (*army*) changgyo 장교.

* **official** *adj.* (*formal*) kongsig-ŭi 공식의; (*public*) kongmusang-ŭi 공무상의. —*n.* kongmuwŏn 공무원, chigwŏn 직원, kwalli〈kwanri 관리: ~ *in charge* tamdangkwan 담당관.

* **often** *adv.* chaju 자주. → **occasionally** *adv.* kakkŭm 가끔, chongjong 종종.

+ **oil** *n.* & *v.* kirŭm(-ŭl ch'ida) 기름(을 치다): *cooking* ~ sigyongnyu〈sikyongyu 식용유.

ointment *n.* yŏngo 연고, parŭnŭn yak 바르는 약.

* **old** *adj.* (*person*) nŭlgŭn 늙은; (*thing*) nalgŭn 낡은, oraedoen 오래된.

+ **old-fashioned** *adj.* kusig-ŭi 구식의, kop'ung-ŭi 고풍의.

olive *n.* ollibŭ 올리브, kamnam〈kamram 감람(橄欖).

omit *v.* saengnyak'ada〈saengryak'ada 생략하다, ppattŭrida 빠뜨리다. (*neglect*) keŭllihada 게을리하다.

\# **on** *prep.* …wi-e …위에, …e tae/kwanhayŏ …에 대/관하여, …e tae/kwanhan …에 대/관한.

+ **once** *adv.* han pŏn 한 번; (*formerly*) iltchigi 일찍이.

\# **one** adj. (pure Korean number) hana-ŭi 하나의. —n. hana 하나, (Sino-Korean number) il 일.

   oneself pron. chagi chasin-i 자기 자신이, sŭsŭro 스스로, chagi chasin-ŭl[e] 자기 자신을[에].

   onion n. yangp'a 양파, (*green onion*) p'a 파.

* **only** adj. yuilhan 유일한. —adv. taman 다만, -man -만, -ppun -뿐, -pakke (ant'a⟨anhta/ŏptta⟩) -밖에 (않다/ 없다).

\+ **onto** prep. ‥‥ŭi wi-ro ‥‥의 위로.

* **open** v. yŏlda 열다.—adj. yŏllin 열린.

\+ **opening** n. (*beginning*) sijak 시작, (*meeting*) kaehoe 개회: ~ *ceremony* kaemakssik 개막식; (*open space*) tŭm 틈, (*hole*) kumŏng 구멍, (*job*) ch'wijiktchari 취 직자리.

\+ **opera** n. op'era 오페라, kagŭk 가극.

\+ **operate** v. (*conduct*) unjŏnhada 운전하다; (*manage*) unyŏnghada 운영하다; (*surgical*) susulhada 수술하다.

\+ **operation** n. (*machine*) unjŏn 운전; (*management*) unyŏng 운영, kyŏngyŏng 경영; (*surgical*) susul 수술; (*military*) chaktchŏn 작전; (*functional*) chagyong 작용.

* **opinion** n. ŭigyŏn 의견, kyŏnhae 견해, (*pl.*) sosin 소신. *in my* ~ nae saenggag-enŭn 내 생각에는.

   opium n. ap'yŏn 아편.

\+ **opponent** n. chŏkssu 적수, chŏkttaeja 적대자,; kyŏngjaengja 경쟁자. —adj. chŏkttaehanŭn 적대하는, pandaehanŭn 반대하는.

\+ **opportunity** n. kihoe 기회, hogi 호기(好機).

\+ **oppose** v. pandaehada 반대하다, chŏhanghada 저항하다, (*hinder*) panghaehada 방해하다.

\+ **opposite** adj. chŏngbandae-ŭi 정반대의; chŏtchog-ŭi 저쪽의; (*front*) majŭnp'yŏn-ŭi 맞은편의.

\# **or** conj. ttonŭn 또는, hogŭn 혹은.

\+ **orange** n. orenji 오렌지. —adj. orenjisaeg-ŭi 오렌지 색의. → **mandarin(e), Tangerine** n. kyul 귤.

\+ **orchestra** n. kwanhyŏnakdan 관현악단, ok'esŭt'ŭra 오케스트라. *symphony* ~ kyohayangakttan⟨akdan

교향악단.

order n. (command) myŏngnyŏng⟨myŏngryŏng 명령; (sequence) sunsŏ 순서: in (good) ~ sunsŏ-daero 순서대로; (commission to supply) chumun 주문; (decoration) hunjang 훈장. —v. (command) myŏng-nyŏnghada⟨myŏngryŏnghada 명령하다; (goods) chu-munhada/sik'ida 주문하다/시키다: place an ~ chu-munhada 주문하다; chŏngdonhada 정돈하다: put (one's idea) in ~ (mŏri sog)-ŭl chŏngdonhada 머리 속을 정돈하다.

+ **ordinary** adj. (usual) pot'ong-ŭi 보통의, (common) p'yŏngbŏmhan 평범한. —n. pot'ongil 보통일, chŏng-sik 정식.

+ **organ** n. (musical instrument) orŭgan 오르간; (of body) kigwan 기관(器官); (agent) kigwan 기관(機關).

* **organization** n. (system) chojik 조직, (group) tanch'e 단체; (outfit) kigu 기구.

+ **organize** v. chojikhada 조직하다; ch'angnip'ada⟨ch'angriphada 창립하다; chŏngnihada⟨chŏngrihada 정리하다.

orient n. tongyang 동양.—adj. tongyang-ŭi 동양의.

+ **original** adj. ch'oech'o-ŭi 최초의; tokch'angjŏgin 독창적인. —n. wŏnbon 원본, wŏnmun 원문, wŏn-hyŏng 원형.

originality n. tokch'angssŏng 독창성, ch'angŭiryŏk 창의력; ch'amsin 참신, sin'gi 신기(新奇).

+ **ornament** n. changsik 장식.—v. kkumida 꾸미다.

orphan n. koa 고아. —adj. pumoŏmnŭn⟨pumoŏpnŭn 부모없는.

orphanage n. koawŏn 고아원.

other adj. tarŭn 다른, ttan 딴, i/kŭbakk-ŭi 이/그밖의.

otherwise adj. kŭrŏch'i anŭmyŏn 그렇지 않으면, animyŏn 아니면.

+ **ought** aux.v. (obligation) …hayŏya handa …하여야 한다, (naturalness) …hanŭn kŏs-i tangyŏnhada …하는 것이 당연하다, (the best choice) …hanŭn kŏs-i chot'a …하는 것이 좋다; (expectation) …ŭl kkŏsida⟨

　　···ŭl kŏs-ida ···을 것이다: *The bus ~ to be here in a few minutes.* pŏsŭ-ga myŏt ppun nae-royŏgi ol kkŏsida. 버스가 몇 분 내로 여기 올 것이다.

our *pron.* uri-ŭi 우리의, uridŭr-ŭi 우리들의.

* **out** *adv.* pakk-e 밖에, pakk-ŭro 밖으로. —*adj.* pakk-ŭi 밖의.—*prep.* ···eso ···에서.—*n.* pak 밖.

　　outdoors *adv.* yaoe/ogoe-esŏ 야외/옥외에서, chip pakkesŏ 집 밖에서. —*n.* (*wilderness*) yaoe 야외, ogoe 옥외, munbak 문밖.

+ **outer** *adj.* pakk-ŭi 밖의.

+ **outline** *n.* yun'gwak 윤곽, yoyak 요약. —*v.* yungwak-ŭl kŭrida 윤곽을 그리다.

+ **outside** *n.* pakkat 바깥, oebu 외부.—*prep.* ···ŭi pakk-ŭi ···의 밖의. —*adv.* chip pakk-ŭro 집 밖으로, pakkat-e 바깥에: *go ~ the gate* mun pakk-ŭronagada 문 밖으로 나가다. —*adj.* pakk-ŭi 밖의, oebuŭi 외부의.

+ **outward** *adj.* oebu-ŭi 외부의, oemyŏnjŏgin 외면적인,p'yomyŏnjŏgin 표면적인.

+ **oven** *n.* obŭn 오븐, hwadŏk 화덕.

* **over** *prep.* ···ŭi wi-e ···의 위에.—*adv.* (*all over*) toch'ŏ-e 도처에, kkŭnnago〈kkŭtnago (nasŏ) 끝나고〈나서).

+ **overcome** *v.* kŭkppokhada 극복하다, igida 이기다.

　　overshoe *n.* tŏtssin 덧신.

+ **owe** *v.* pij-ŭl chida 빚을 지다, himiptta 힘입다.

　　owing to ···ttaemun-e ···때문에.

　　owl *n.* olppaemi 올빼미, puŏngi 부엉이.

* **own** *adj.* chagi chasin-ŭi 자기 자신의. —*v.* soyuhada 소유하다; (*confess*) chabaekhada 자백하다.

　　oyster *n.* kul 굴; *raw ~* saenggul 생굴.

$$\lessgtr \mathrm{P} \gtrless$$

Pacific Ocean *n.* t'aepyŏngyang 태평양.

pack *n.* chim 짐, (*bundle*) tabal 다발, (*gang*) han p'ae 한 패.—*v.* p'ojanghada 포장하다.

package *n.* (*parcel*) sop'o 소포, chim 짐; p'ojang 포장.

+ **page** *n.* p'eiji 페이지, myŏn 면.

+ **pain** *n.* kot'ong 고통, ap'ŭm 아픔; (*worry*) kŭnsim 근심.

+ **painful** *adj.* ap'ŭn 아픈, koeroun 괴로운; (*toilsome*) him-i tŭnŭn 힘이 드는.

+ **paint** *n.* kŭrimmulkkam 그림물감, p'eint'ŭ 페인트.—*v.* ch'ilhada 칠하다, kŭrida 그리다.

+ **painting** *n.* ① kŭrim 그림. ② p'eint'ŭch'il 페인트 칠: *oil* ~ yuhwa 유화/*water color* such'aehwa 수채화.

+ **pair** *n.* han ssang 한 쌍, (*married couple*) pubu 부부.

+ **pale** *adj.* (*wan*) ch'angbaekhan 창백한.

pan *n.* naembi 냄비: *frying* ~ p'ŭraip'aen 프라이팬.

pantry *n.* singnyop'umsil〈sikryop'umsil 식료품실, sikkisil 식기실.

pants *n.* (*trousers*) paji 바지, (*underwear*) p'aench'ŭ 팬츠.

* **paper** *n.* chongi 종이: *toilet* ~ hwajangji 화장지, *traditional Korean* ~ hanji 한지, *wall* ~ pyŏktchi 벽지; (*newapaper*) sinmunji 신문지; (*essay*) nonmun 논문.

paradise *n.* nagwŏn 낙원; (*Budd.*) kŭngnak〈kŭkrak 극락.

+ **paragraph** *n.* mundan 문단, tallak 단락, chŏl 절(節), hang 항.

paralysis *n.* mabi 마비, chungp'ung 중풍.

+ **parcel** *n.* (*post*) sop'o 소포, (*packet*) sohamul 소하물.

pardon *n.* & *v.* yongsŏ(hada) 용서(하다): *I beg your* ~. choesonghamnida〈choesonghapnida 죄송합니다.

+ **parents** *n.* pumo(nim) 부모(님), ŏbŏi 어버이, yang ch'in 양친.

+ **park** *n.* kongwŏn 공원: *national* ~ kungnip〈kukrip-kongwŏn 국립공원, *amusement* ~ yuwŏnji 유원지; ~*ing lot* (*for automobiles*) chuch'ajang 주차장.

+ **parliament** *n.* kukhoe 국회, ŭihoe 의회.

parrot *n.* aengmusae 앵무새.

* **part** *n.* pubun 부분: *Part one* cheil pu 제일 부/cheil p'yŏn 제일 편; (*district*) chiyŏk 지역; (*role*) yŏkhal 역할. —*v.* (*seperate*) nanuda 나누다, kallajida 갈라 지다.

* **participle** *n.* (*gram.*) punsa 분사(分詞).

+ **particle** *n.* iptcha 입자, mibunja 미분자.

\# **particular** *adj.* (*individual*) kakkag-ŭi 각각의; (*special*) kakppyŏlhan 각별한; (*detailed*) sangse han 상세한. —*n.* (*details*) sahang 사항.

+ **partly** *adv.* pubunjŏg-ŭro 부분적으로.

partner *n.* tongŏptcha 동업자, tchakp'ae 짝패, p'at'ŭnŏ 파트너; chohabwŏn 조합원.

+ **party** *n.* ① (*entertainment*) yŏnhoe 연회, p'at'i 파티. ② (*polit.*) chŏngdang 정당.

+ **pass** *n.* (*passage*) t'onggwa 통과, (*exam*) hapkkyŏk 합격; (*of admission*) iptchangkkwŏn 입장권, p'aesŭ 패스. —*v.* (*way, test, bill*) t'onggwahada 통과하다, (*exam*) hap- kkyŏkhada 합격하다, (*overtake in driving*) ch'uwŏlhada 추월하다; (*elapse*) chinada 지나다; (*pass away,* honorific) toragasida 돌아가시 다. → **die** *n.* chuktta 죽다.

+ **passage** *n.* ① (*passing*) t'onggwa 통과. ② (*voyage*) hang-hae 항해. ③ (*way*) t'ongno⟨t'ongro 통로.

+ **passenger** *n.* sŭnggaek 승객, yŏgaek 여객.

+ **passing** *adj.* chinaganŭn 지나가는, (*transient*) ilssi-jŏgin 일시적인. → **current** *adj.* hyŏnjae-ŭi 현재의.

passport *n.* yŏkkwŏn 여권, p'aesŭp'otŭ 패스포트.

* **past** *adj.* chinagan 지나간. —*prep.* chinasŏ 지나서. —*n.* kwagŏ 과거, yennal⟨yetnal 옛날.

+ **paste** *n.* p'ul 풀.—*v.* p'ulch'ilhada 풀칠하다.

+ **pastry** *n.* panjuk kwaja 반죽 과자, saenggwaja 생과자, p'esŭt'ŭri 페스트리.

patch *n.* hŏnggŏp chogak 헝겊 조각.—*v.* kipda 깁다.

+ **path** *n.* kil 길, (*footpath*) podo 보도: *mountain* ~ sankkil 산길; (*course in life*) insaeng haengno⟨ haengro 인생 행로.

patience *n.* innae(sim) 인내(심), ch'amŭlssŏng 참을성.

+ **patient** *adj.* ch'amŭlssŏng innŭn〈itnŭn 참을성 있는:
~ *person* ch'amkko kyŏndinŭn saram 참고 견디는
사람. —*n.* hwanja 환자, pyŏngja 병자.

+ **pattern** *n.* (*model*) mobŏm 모범, (*sample*) kyŏnbon
견본.

pawnshop *n.* chŏndangp'o 전당포.

* **pay** *n.* chibul 지불: (*salary*) ponggŭp 봉급, posu 보수.
—*v.* chibulhada 지불하다, (ton-ŭl) naeda (돈을) 내다.

+ **payment** *n.* chibul 지불, chibulgŭm 지불금.

peace *n.* p'yŏnghwa 평화, p'yŏngon 평온: (*reconcilia-
tion*) hwahae 화해.

+ **peaceful** *adj.* (*at peace*) p'yŏnghwaroun 평화로운,
(*peaceable*) onhwahan 온화한: (*calm*) choyonghan
조용한.

peach *n.* poksunga 복숭아, poksunganamu 복숭아나무.

pear *n.* pae 배(梨), (*plan*) paenamu 배나무.

pearl *n.* chinju 진주: *articificial* ~ injo chinju 인조진
주/*black* ~ hŭkchinju 흑진주.

pea *n.* wanduk'ong 완두콩.

peel *n.* kkŏptchil 껍질. —*v.* kkŏptchil-ŭl pŏkkida〈
pŏt kida 껍질을 벗기다.

+ **pen** *n.* ① p'en 펜, mannyŏnp'il 만년필: (*writing*)
munp'il 문필. ② (*fold*) uri 우리, ult'ari 울타리.

+ **pencil** *n.* yŏnp'il 연필: ~ *sharpener* yŏnp'ilkkakki 연
필 깎이.

people *n.* saramdŭl 사람들: (*nation*) kungmin〈
kukmin 국민, (*race*)minjok 민족: (*common people*)
minjung 민 중: (*human beings*) in'gan 인간.

pepper *n.* ① (*black*) huch'u 후추. ② (*red*) koch'u 고추.

percent *n.* p'ŏsent'ŭ 퍼센트(%), (colloq.) p'uro 푸로:
paekppun-nyul 백분율.

+ **perfect** *adj.* wanjŏnhan 완전한, wanbyŏkhan 완벽한.
Wanbyŏkhan in'gan-ŭn ŏptta. 완벽한 인간은 없다.
— *v.* wansŏnghada 완성하다.

+ **perform** *v.* (*do*) tahada 다하다, (*accomplish*) suhaeng-
hada 수행하다, (*fulfill*) ihaenghada 이행하다:(*play*)

yŏnju〔kongyŏn〕hada 연주〔공연〕하다.

+ **performance** n. (*duty*) ihaeng 이행, silhaeng 실행: (*drama*) yŏn'gi 연기: (*music, etc.*) kongyŏn 공연: (*entertainment*) yŏhŭng 여흥.

+ **performer** n. (*actor*) paeu 배우, (*musician*) yŏnjuja 연주자, (*doer*) silhaengja 실행자.

  perfume n. (*scent*) hyangsu 향수, (*fragrance*) hyanggi 향기.

+ **perhaps** adv. ama 아마, ŏtchŏmyŏn 어쩌면.

* **period** n. (*time*) kigan 기간, (*historical*) sidae 시대: (*full stop, punctuation*) chongjibu 종지부.

  permanent adj. yŏngsok'anŭn 영속하는, yŏnggujŏgin 영구적인, pyŏnhamŏmnŭn〈pyŏnhamŏpnŭn 변함없는.

+ **permission** n. (*consent*) hŏrak 허락: (*leave*) hŏga 허가, (*licence*) myŏnhŏ 면허: *without* ~ mudanhi 무단히.

person n. saram 사람, (*personality*) inmul 인물: (*character*) inp'um 인품.

+ **personal** adj. kaein-ŭi 개인의, ilssinsang-ŭi 일신상의.

  perspire v. ttamnaeda 땀내다, ttam-i nada 땀이 나다.

+ **persuade** v. sŏlttŭksik'ida 설득시키다, napttŭksik'ida 납득시키다, sŏlboksik'ida 설복시키다.

+ **petrol** n. (*gasoline*) hwiballyu 휘발유.

+ **phone** n. chŏnhwa(gi) 전화(기).—v. chŏnhwa-rŭl kŏlda 전화를 걸다. *public* ~ kongjung chŏnhwa 공중전화. ~ *bill* chŏnhwayogŭm kojisŏ 전화요금 고지서.

  phonograph n. ch'ugŭmgi 축음기.

+ **photograph** n. sajin 사진.—v. sajin-ŭl tchiktta 사진을 찍다, ch'walyŏnghada 촬영하다.

+ **phrasal** adj. ku-ŭi 구(句)의.

+ **phrase** n. ku 구, sukŏ 숙어, kwanyonggu 관용구.

* **physical** adj. (*natural*) chayŏn-ŭi 자연의: (*corporal*) yukch'e-ŭi 육체의, (*bodily*) sinch'e-ŭi 신체의: ~ *beauty* yukch'emi 육체미/ ~ *examination* sinch'e kŏmsa 신체 검사/~ *exercise* undong 운동, ch'ejo 체조. (*science*) mullihag-ŭi 물리학의.

+ **piano** n. p'iano 피아노.

pick *n.* (*pickaxe*) kokkwaengi 곡괭이. —*v.* (*poke*) ssusida 쑤시다; (*dig into*) p'ada 파다; (*fruit*) ttada 따다; (*gather*) moŭda 모으다; (*choose*) korŭda 고르다.

pickpocket *n.* somaech'igi 소매치기.

picnic *n.* sop'ung 소풍, tŭllori〈tŭlnori 들놀이, p'ik'ŭnik 피크닉: go on a ~ sop'unggada 소풍가다.

+ **picture** *n.* kŭrim 그림; (*photo*) sajin 사진. → **movies** *n.* (*movie*) yŏnghwa 영화.

* **piece** *n.* han chogak 한 조각: a ~ of meat han chogak-ŭi kogi 한 조각의 고기, han tchok/kae 한 쪽/개: a ~ of bread han tchok/kae-ŭi ppang 한 쪽의 빵; (*fragment*) p'ap'yŏn 파편.

+ **pig** *n.* (*swine, hog*) twaeji 돼지. → **pork** *n.* twaejigogi 돼지고기.

pigeon *n.* pidulgi 비둘기: ~ hole pidulgijang 비둘기장/carrier ~ chŏnsŏgu 전서구(傳書鳩).

+ **pile** *n.* mudŏgi 무더기, taeryang 대량. —*v.* ssa(h)aollida 쌓아올리다; ssa(h)ida 쌓이다.

pill *n.* hwanyak 환약, allyak 알약.

pillow *n.* pegae 베개; (*wooden*) mokch'im 목침.

pimp *n.* ttujangi 뚜장이; (*pander*) p'oju 포주.

pimple *n.* yŏdŭrŭm 여드름, ppyoruji 뾰루지.

+ **pin** *n.* p'in 핀, app'in 압핀: safety ~ anjŏnp'in 안전핀.

pinch *n.* (*with nails*) kkojipta 꼬집다, choeda 죄다.

pine *n.* sonamu 소나무.—*v.* yŏnmohada 연모하다; (*yearn*) kalmanghada 갈망하다.

+ **pink** *adj.* punhongsaeg-ŭi 분홍색의. —*n.* (*color*) punhongsaek 분홍색.

+ **pipe** *n.* (*for smoking*) tambaettae 담뱃대. (*for liquid, gas*) p'aip'ŭ 파이프, kwan 관(管): water ~ sudogwan 수도관.

+ **pitch** *n.* ① (*tar*) songjin 송진. ② (*throw*) tŏnjigi 던지기.—*v.* tŏnjida 던지다; ch'ida 치다.

piteous *adj.* pulssanghan 불쌍한, kayŏpsŭn 가엾은.

pitiful *n.* pulssanghan 불쌍한, kayŏpsŭn 가엾은, yŏnmin-ŭi chŏng-ŭl chaanaenŭn 연민의 정을 자아내는.

+ **pity** *n.* pulssanghi yŏgim 불쌍히 여김, yŏnmin 연민.
　— *v.* pulssanghi yŏgida 불쌍히 여기다.

\# **place** *n.* changso 장소, kot 곳, te 데.—*v.* tuda 두다.

　plain *adj.* (*clear*) myŏngbaek'an 명백한; (*simple*)
　susuhan 수수한; (*flat*) p'yŏngp'yŏnghan 평평한 →
　moor *n.* p'yŏngya 평야.

* **plan** *n.* (*project*) kyehoek 계획; (*drawing*) tomyŏn 도
　면, (*draft*) sŏlgyedo 설계도. —*v.* kyehoekhada 계획
　하다. *develop a* ~ kyehoek-ŭl seuda 계획을 세우다.

+ **plane** *n.* ① (*flat*) p'yŏngmyŏn 평면; (*airplane*) pi-
　haenggi 비행기. ② (*carpenter*) taep'ae 대패. —*v.*
　taep'aejilhada 대패질하다.

+ **planet** *n.* yusŏng 유성(遊星), hokssŏng 혹성.

* **plant** *n.* (*vegetation*) singmul〈sikmul 식물〉; (*factory*)
　kongjang 공장. —*v.* simtta 심다. (*sow*) ppurida 뿌
　리다.

+ **plaster** *n.* sŏkko 석고; (*medicine*) koyak 고약. —*v.*
　hoech'il-ŭl hada 회칠을 하다.

* **plastic** *adj.* p'ŭllasŭt'ik-ŭi 플라스틱의; (*formative*)
　hyŏngsŏngjŏgin 형성적인; (*pliable*) yuyŏnhan 유연
　한. —*n.* p'ŭllasŭt'ik 플라스틱, hapsŏngsuji
　chep'um 합성 수지 제품.

+ **plate** *n.* (*dish*) chŏpsi 접시; (*of metal*) p'an 판;
　silver ~ ŭnban 은반(銀盤).

+ **platform** *n.* (*stage*) yŏndan 연단; (*station*) p'ŭllaet-
　p'om 플랫폼; (*political*) chŏnggang 정강.

* **play** *n.* (*sports*) undong 운동, kyŏnggi 경기; (*drama*)
　yŏn-gŭk 연극. —*v.* nolda 놀다; (*music*) yŏnjuhada
　연주하다; (*act*) yŏngi-rŭl hada 연기를 하다.

+ **player** *n.* (*of sport*) sŏnsu 선수; (*actor*) paeu 배우;
　(*of instrument*) yŏnjuja 연주자.

* **pleasant** *adj.* kibunjoŭn 기분좋은, yuk'waehan 유쾌한.

+ **please** *v.* chŭlgŏpkke hada 즐겁게 하다; (*in Korean,
　with adverb* pudi) pudi ...ŏ chusipssio 부디 …어 주
　십시오.

+ **pleased** *adj.* kippŏhanŭn 기뻐하는, manjokhan 만족한.

+ **pleasing** *adj.* yuk'waehan 유쾌한, chŭlgŏun 즐거운.

+ **pleasure** n. (*delight*) chŭlgŏum 즐거움, (*enjoyment*) k'waerak 쾌락.

plenty n. manŭm 많음, p'ungbu 풍부, taryang 다량.

* **plural** adj. pokssu-ŭi 복수의.—n. (*gram.*) pokssu 복수.

pocket n. (ho)jumŏni (호)주머니, p'ok'et 포켓.

pocketbook n. chigap 지갑; such'ŏp 수첩.

p.m. n. ohu 오후.

+ **poem** n. si 시(詩).

+ **poetry** n. si 시: *lyric* ~ sŏjŏngsi 서정시, *epic/narrative* ~ sŏsasi 서사시, *a prose* ~ sanmunsi 산문시.

* **point** n. (*dot*) chŏm 점, (*end*) kkŭt 끝, (*view*) kyŏnhae 견해.—v. (*with hand*) karik'ida 가리키다.

+ **poison** n. togyak 독약.—v. tog-ŭl nŏt'a 독을 넣다.

+ **poisonous** adj. yudokhan 유독한, haeroun 해로운.

+ **pole** n. changttae 장대, makttaegi 막대기: kŭk 극, (*plus*) yanggŭk 양극, (*minus*) ŭmgŭk 음극: *South P* ~ namgŭk 남극, *North P*~ pukkŭk 북극.

+ **police** n. kyŏngch'al 경찰: ~ *officer* kyŏngch'al 경찰, *the chief of* ~kyŏngch'alsŏjang 경찰서장, ~ *box* p'ach'ulso 파출소, ~ *station* kyŏngch'alsŏ 경찰서.

policeman n. kyŏngch'algwan 경찰관, sun'gyŏng 순경.

+ **policy** n. chŏngch'aek 정책, pangch'im 방침.

polish n. ① yun 윤, kwangt'aek 광택. ② yŏnmaje 연마제. —v. taktta 닦다, tadŭmtta 다듬다.

+ **polite** adj. (*courteous*) yeŭi parŭn 예의 바른, (*civil*) kongsonhan 공손한; (*elegant*) seryŏndoen 세련된.

* **political** adj. chŏngch'i-ŭi 정치의: ~ *economy* chŏngch'ikyŏngjehak 정치경제학, ~ *party* chŏngdang 정당, ~ *situation* chŏngguk 정국.

+ **politics** n. chŏngch'i 정치, (*political science*) chŏngch'ihak 정치학.

pond n. mot 못(池), yŏnmot 연못, (*swamp*) nŭp 늪.

+ **pool** n. ① murungdŏngi 물웅덩이, (*swimming*) p'ul (jang) 풀(장). ② (*billiards*) tanggu 당구.

+ **poor** adj. (*needy*) kananhan 가난한; (*pitiable*) kayŏpssŭn 가엾은; (*inferior*) yŏlttŭnghan 열등한.

+ **pop** *n.* (*music*) yuhaengga 유행가, taejunggayo 대중가
요, p'apssong 팝송; (*dad*) appa 아빠. —*v.* p'ŏng-
hago t'ŏjida 펑하고 터지다.

+ **popular** *adj.* inkkiinnŭn〈inkkiitnŭn 인기있는. t'ong-
soktchŏk 통속적.

population *n.* in'gu 인구.

porcelain *n.* sagi kŭrŭt 사기 그릇, chagi 자기(瓷器).

porch *n.* hyŏngwan 현관, (*Am.*) peranda 베란다.

pork *n.* twaejigogi 돼지고기.

port *n.* ① hanggu 항구. ② (~ *wine*) p'ot'ŭwain 포트
와인.

porter *n.* (*gatekeeper*) munjigi 문지기, (*carrier*)
chimkkun 짐꾼, unbanin 운반인.

* **position** *n.* (*location*) wich'i 위치, (*social status*)
sinbun 신분, (*job, policy*) chikch'aek 직책.

possess *v.* soyuhada 소유하다.

+ **possession** *n.* soyu 소유, chŏmyu 점유; (*property*)
chaesan 재산.

+ **possibility** *n.* kanŭngssŏng 가능성, kamang 가망.

* **possible** *adj.* kanŭnghan 가능한.

+ **possibly** *adv.* ama 아마, ŏtchŏmyŏn 어쩌면.

+ **post** *n.* (*mail*) up'yŏn 우편: *parcel* ~ sop'o 소포.
(*pole*)kidung 기둥. (*station*)pusŏ 부서(部署). —*v.*
puch'ida 부치다, usonghada 우송하다.

postcard *n.* up'yŏn yŏpsŏ 우편 엽서.

post office *n.* uch'eguk 우체국.

potato *n.* kamja 감자: *sweet* ~ koguma 고구마.

+ **pottery** *n.* togi 도기(陶器), chilgŭrŭt 질그릇.

+ **pound** ① *n.* (*weight*) p'aundŭ 파운드. ② *v.* tudŭlgida
두들기다.

pour *v.* (*flow*) p'ŏbutta 퍼붓다, (*spill liquid*) ssotta
쏟다, ttarŭda 따르다; (*shed*) palsanhada 발산하다.

powder *n.* (*dust*) karu 가루. (*explosive*) hwayak 화
약: *toilet* ~ pun 분(粉).

* **power** *n.* (*strength*) him 힘; (*ability*) nŭngnyŏk〈
nŭngryŏk 능력; (*authority*) kwŏnnŭng 권능: *a world*

~ kangdaeguk 강대국: (force) tongnyŏk⟨tongryŏk 동력: electric ~chŏllyŏk 전력, atomic ~ wŏnjaryŏk 원자력.

+ **powerful** adj. kangnyŏkhan⟨kangryŏkhan 강력한: a ~ engine kangnyŏkhan⟨kangryŏkhan enjin 강력한 엔진.

+ **practical** adj. siryongjŏgin 실용적인: siltchejŏgin 실제적인.

+ **practice** n. (exercise) yŏnsŭp 연습, (habit) sŭpkkwan 습관, (doctor, lawyer) ŏmmu⟨ŏpmu 업무.

+ **praise** n. (commendation) ch'ingch'an 칭찬, (glorification) ch'anyang 찬양. —v. ch'ingch'anhada 칭찬하다, ch'anyanghada 찬양하다. → **worship** n. sungbae 숭배.

pray v. pilda 빌다, kidohada 기도하다.

preacher n. chŏndosa 전도사, sŏlgyoja 설교자. → **minister** n. mokssa(nim) 목사(님).

+ **precious** adj. kwijunghan 귀중한, kach'iinnŭn⟨kach'iitnŭn 가치있는, (colloquial, gross) taedanhan 대단한.

+ **precise** adj. (exact) chŏnghwakhan 정확한: a ~ instrument chŏngmilhan kyegi 정밀한 계기, (meticulous) kkomkkomhan 꼼꼼한.

prefer v. ...(tchog)-ŭl choahada …(쪽)을 좋아하다.

+ **pregnant** adj. (with child) imsinhan 임신한: (inventive) sangsangnyŏg-i p'ungbuhan 상상력이 풍부한: (filled) kadŭkch'an 가득찬.

preparation n. chunbi 준비, maryŏn 마련.

+ **prepare** v. chunbihada 준비하다, maryŏnhada 마련하다.

+ **preposition** n. (grammar) chŏnch'isa 전치사.

prescription n. (medicine) ch'ŏbang 처방: ~ slip ch'ŏbangjŏn 처방전: (order) kyujŏng 규정.

* **present** ① v. (give) chuda 주다, (honorific) tŭrida 드리다, (book, etc.) chŭngjŏnghada 증정하다, (gift) sŏnsahada 선사하다, (document) chech'ulhada 제출하다. —n. sŏnmul 선물. ② adj. ch'ulsŏkhan 출석한:

(*current*) hyŏnjae-ŭi 현재의.

+ **president** *n.* (*of nation*) taet'ongnyŏng⟨taet'ong-ryŏng 대통령; (*of company*) sajang 사장, (*of bank*) ch'ongjae 총재, (*of university*) ch'ongjang 총장, (*of association*) hoejang 회장.

+ **press** *v.* nurŭda 누르다, (*urge*) ch'okkuhada 촉구하다. —*n.* (*newspaper*) sinmun 신문. *the ~* ŏllongye⟨ŏnrongye 언론계.

+ **pressing** *adj.* (*urgent*) kin'gŭphan 긴급한.

+ **pressure** *n.* amnyŏk⟨apryŏk 압력, appak 압박: *atmospheric ~* kiap 기압, *blood ~* hyŏrap 혈압.

+ **pretend** *v.* …ch'ehada …체하다.

  pretty *adj.* koun 고운, ŏyŏppŭn 어여쁜, yeppŭn 예쁜, (*fine*) hullyunghan 훌륭한.—*adv.* (*fairly*) kkwae꽤.

* **prevent** *v.* pangjihada 방지하다.

+ **previous** *adj.* ijŏn-ŭi 이전의, mŏnjŏ-ŭi 먼저의.

+ **price** *n.* kap 값, kagyŏk 가격; (*reward*) posang 보상. *half ~* pankkap 반값, *retail ~* somaekka 소매가, *a bargain ~* harin kagyŏk 할인가격.

  pride *n.* (*self-respect*) chajonsim 자존심, (*satisfaction*) manjok 만족.

  priest *n.* (*monk*) sŭnim 스님, sŭngnyŏ⟨sŭngryŏ 승려,sudoja 수도자; (*holy father*) sinbu(nim) 신부(님), (*minister*) mokssa(nim) 목사(님), saje 사제.

  prime *adj.* ch'ŏttchae-ŭi 첫째의; chuyohan 주요한; pollae-ŭi⟨ponlae-ŭi 본래의: *~ minister* susang 수상.

+ **principle** *n.* wŏnch'ik 원칙; (*doctrine, -ism*) -chuŭi -주의.

+ **print** *n.* ① (*mark*) chaguk 자국. ② (*printing*) inswae 인쇄. —*v.* inswaehada 인쇄하다.

  printer *n.* inswaeŏpcha 인쇄업자; inswaegi 인쇄기.

+ **printing** *n.* inswae 인쇄.

+ **prison** *n.* kamok 감옥, kyodoso 교도소.

+ **prisoner** *n.* choesu 죄수: *~ of war* p'oro 포로.

+ **private** *adj.* satchŏgin 사적인, pimil-ŭi 비밀의.—*n.* (*military*) pyŏngsa 병사(兵士), pyŏngjol 병졸.

+ **prize** ① *n.* (*reward*) sang 상: *Nobel ~* nobelssang 노

벨상. --v. sojunghi hada 소중히 하다. ② n.(booty) chŏl- lip'um 전리품.

+ **probably** adv. ama 아마, siptchungp'algu 십중팔구.

* **problem** n. munje 문제; nanmun 난문.

* **process** n. kwajŏng 과정, (progress) chinhaeng 진행;(method) pangbŏp 방법. —v. kagonghada 가공하다. ~ed food kagong sikp'um 가공식품. ~ an application sin-ch'ŏng-ŭl simsahada 신청을 심사하다.

+ **produce** v. saengsanhada 생산하다, sanch'ulhada 산출하다.

+ **product** n. chep'um 제품, sanmul 산물; (result) sŏngkkwa 성과.

+ **profession** n. chigŏp 직업.

+ **professional** adj. chigŏb-ŭi 직업의; chŏnmun-ŭi 전문의; (businesslike)samujŏgin 사무적인.—n. (athlete) chigŏpssŏnsu 직업선수.

  professor n. kyosu 교수: assistant ~ chogyosu 조교수, associate ~ pugyosu 부교수.

+ **profit** n. iik 이익, idŭkŏng 이득.

+ **program(me)** n. p'ŭrogŭraem 프로그램; (schedule) kyehoek 계획, yejŏng(p'yo) 예정(표).

+ **progress** n. paltchŏn 발전, palttal 발달, chinbo 진보. —v. naagada 나아가다.

+ **project**n. (scheme) kyehoek 계획; (design) sŏlgye 설계; (research topic) yŏn'gugwaje 연구과제. —v. (on screen) yŏngsahada 영사하다; (jut out) tolch'ulhada 돌출하다.

+ **promise** n. & v. yakssok(hada) 약속(하다).

+ **pronoun** n. (gram.) taemyŏngsa 대명사.

* **pronounce** v. parŭmhada 발음하다.

  pronunciation n. parŭm 발음.

+ **proof** n. (evidence) chŭnggŏ 증거, (of book) kyojŏng(swae) 교정(쇄).

  propaganda n. sŏnjŏn 선전(宣傳).

+ **proper** adj. (fit) chŏkttanghan 적당한, chŏktchŏlhan 적절한; (correct) olbarŭn 올바른; (peculiar) tokt'ŭkhan, 독특한.

* **properly** *adv.* chŏkttanghi 적당히, chŏktchŏlhi 적절히.
+ **property** *n.* chaesan 재산, soyumul 소유물: *private/public* ~ 사유/공유 재산.
+ **proportion** *n.* (*ratio*) piyul 비율: (*balance*) kyunhyŏng 균형. → **share** *n.* mok 몫.
+ **proposal** *n.* (*suggestion*) chean 제안, (*proposing*) cheŭi 제의; (*plan*) an 안; (*application*) sinch'ŏng 신청.
  prostrate *adj.* ŏpttŭrin 엎드린, kulbok'an 굴복한.
+ **protect** *v.* pohohada 보호하다, (*defend against*) maktta 막다.
+ **protection** *n.* poho 보호, pangŏ 방어.
+ **protest** *v.* hangŭihada 항의하다, siwihada 시위하다. — *n.* hangŭi 항의. *student* ~ haksaeng siwi 학생시위.
+ **proud** *adj.* charanghanŭn 자랑하는; (*haughty*) kŏmanhan 거만한; (*grand*) tangdanghan 당당한.
+ **prove** *v.* chŭngmyŏnghada 증명하다.
+ **provide** *v.* (*supply*) konggŭphada 공급하다; (*prepare*) chunbihada 준비하다, maryŏnhada 마련하다.
+ **provided** *conj.* manyak ...iramyŏn 만약 …이라면, ...iranŭn chogŏn-ŭro …이라는 조건으로.
  province *n.* to 도(道): (*state*) chu 주; chibang 지방.
+ **pub** *n.* sultchip 술집.
* **public** *adj.* kongjung-ŭi 공중(公衆)의. *a* ~ *library*-kongnip〈kongrip tosŏgwan 공립도서관.
+ **publicity** *n.* sŏnjŏn 선전, hongbo 홍보.
+ **publish** *v.* (*books*) ch'ulp'anhada 출판하다; (*make public*) palp'yohada 발표하다.
  publisher *n.* ch'ulp'anŏpcha 출판업자, palhaengja 발행자: (*company*) ch'ulp'ansa 출판사.
+ **pull** *v.* kkŭlda 끌다, tanggida 당기다.
+ **punish** *v.* pŏljuda 벌주다, ch'ŏbŏlhada 처벌하다.
+ **punishment** *n.* hyŏngbŏl 형벌, ch'ŏbŏl 처벌. *suffer a* ~ pŏr-ŭl patta 벌을 받다.
+ **pupil** *n.* haksaeng 학생; cheja 제자(弟子).
  pure *adj.* sunsuhan 순수한, sun'gyŏlhan 순결한: ~ *gold* sun'gŭm 순금.

+ **purple** *n. & adj.* chajusaeg(-ŭi) 자주색(의).
* **purpose** *n.* (*aim*) moktchŏk 목적, (*motive*) tonggi 동기, (*intention*) ŭido 의도. → **effect** *n.* hyokkwa 효과.
  purse *n.* chigap 지갑.
  pus *n.* korŭm 고름.
+ **push** *n.* milgi 밀기, amnyŏk〈apryŏk 압력.—*v.* milda 밀다; kangyohada 강요하다: ~ *a person to write an answer* nam-ege tab-ŭl ssŭge kangyohada 남에게 답을 쓰게 강요 하다.
* **put** *v.* (*place*) not'a 놓다; (*express*) mal-lo(p'yohyŏn) hada 말로 (표현)하다; (*cause*) ˝sik'ida ˝시키다. → **entrust** *v.* matkkida 맡기다.
  puzzle *n.* susukkekki 수수께끼, k'wijŭ 퀴즈.—*v.* tanghwanghada 당황하다.

+ **qualify** *v.* (*notify*) ...ege chagyŏg-ŭl chuda ...에게 자격을 주다; (*restrict*) chehanhada 제한하다; (*grammar, modify*) susikhada 수식하다. *vi.* chagyŏg- ŭl ttada 자격을 따다. ~ *as typist* t'ajasu chagyŏg- ŭl ttada 타자수 자격을 따다.
* **quality** *n.* (p'um)jil (품)질: *of good* ~ yangjil-ŭi 양질의, (*charateristic, inherent property*) t'ŭkssŏng 특성.
+ **quantity** *n.* (*amount*) yang 양(量), (*numbers*) suryang 수량, (*pl.*) tasu 다수, taryang 다량.
+ **quarrel** *n.* ssaum 싸움, maldat'um 말다툼. --*v.* ssauda 싸우다, maldat'umhada 말다툼하다.
+ **queen** *n.* yŏwang 여왕, wangbi 왕비: *the* ~ *of society* sagyogye-ŭi yŏwang 사교계의 여왕.
  queer *adj.* isanghan 이상한, myohan 묘한.
+ **question** *n.* chilmun 질문; (*doubt*) ŭimun 의문; (*pro-*

blem) munje 문제; nontchŏm 논점. —v. (inquire)
chilmunhada 질문하다; (doubt) ŭisimhada 의심하다.
+ **quick** adj. pparŭn 빠른, sinsokhan 신속한, min'gam-han 민감한.
* **quickly** adv. ppalli 빨리, sinsok'i 신속히.
+ **quiet** adj. (silent) chojonghan 조용한, (still) koyo-han 고요한, (peaceful) p'yŏnghwasŭrŏn 평화스런, (gentle)onhwahan 온화한. —n. koyo 고요, p'yŏngon 평온.
quilt n. ibul 이불, nubi ibul 누비 이불.
quit v. (give up) kŭmanduda 그만두다, p'ogihada 포기 하다, (smoking, etc.) kkŭnt'a 끊다. → **leave** v. ttŏnada 떠나다.
+ **quite** adv. aju 아주, (with negative only) chŏnhyŏ 전혀.

≤ R ≥

rabbit n. chipt'okki 집토끼, t'okki 토끼.
+ **race** n. (contest) kyŏngju 경주, (the human) injong 인종. —v. kyŏngjuhada 경주하다.
radiator n. radieit'ŏ 라디에이터, pangyŏlgi 방열기.
* **radio** n. radio 라디오; (radio message) musŏnjŏnsin 무선전신.
radish n. mu 무; red ~ hongdangmu 홍당무.
raft n. ttenmok⟨ttetmok 뗏목, (abundance) taryang 다량.
rag n. nŏngma 넝마, nudŏgi 누더기.
+ **railroad** n. (American) ch'ŏltto 철도, ch'ŏllo 철로. ~ station ch'ŏlttoyŏk 철도역.
+ **railway** n. (British) ch'ŏltto 철도. ~ station ch'ŏlttoyŏk 철도역.
+ **rain** n. pi 비; drizzling ~ karangbi 가랑비, fine ~ isŭlbi 이슬비.—v. pi-ga oda 비가 오다.

rainy *adj.* pi-ga onŭn 비가 오는: *a ~ day* pionŭn nal 비오는 날. uch'ŏn 우천.

+ **raise** *v.* irŭk'ida 일으키다. ollida 올리다; (*bring up*) kirŭda 기르다.

+ **range** *n.* (*scope*) pŏmwi 범위; (*mountains*) sanmaek 산맥; (*distance*) kŏri 거리.

+ **rank** *n.* (*row*) yŏl 열; (*station*) chiwi 지위.

+ **rapidly** *adv.* (chae)ppalli (재)빨리. sinsokhage 신속하게.

rare *adj.* (*scarce*) tŭmun 드문. chin'gihan 진기한; (*thin*) hŭibak'an 희박한.

rat *n.* chwi 쥐: *like a drowned ~* mur-e ppajin saengjwi-ch'ŏrŏm 물에 빠진 생쥐처럼.

+ **rate** *n.* (*ratio*) piyul 비율; (*charge*) yogŭm 요금; (*grade*) tŭnggŭp 등급: *of the first ~* illyu-ŭi 일류의. *second-rate* igŭp 이급. —*v.* p'yŏngkkahada 평가하다. ŏrimjaptta 어림잡다.

* **rather** *adv.* ohiryŏ 오히려. (*preferably*) ch'arari 차라리; (*somewhat*) taso 다소. → **quite** *adv.* kkwae 꽤.

+ **raw** *adj.* (*uncooked*) nalgŏs-ŭi 날것의: *~ materials* wŏllyo 원료. *~ fish* saengsŏnhoe 생선회. *~ meat* nalgogi 날고기; (*unskilled*) misukhan 미숙한: *a ~ recruit* sinbyŏng 신병.

razor *n.* myŏndok'al 면도칼.

+ **reach** *v.* (*arrive at*) toch'akhada 도착하다. tangdo-hada 당도하다; (*come to*) talhada 달하다. (*extend*) naeppŏtta 내뻗다.

+ **react** *v.* (*act in return*) kŏkkuro chagyonghada 거꾸로 작용하다. (*respond*) paŭnghada 반응하다.

+ **reaction** *n.* pandong 반동. panjakyong 반작용. panbal 반발; (*response*) panŭng 반응.

+ **read** *v.* iktta 읽다. tokssŏhada 독서하다.

+ **reading** *n.* ilkki 읽기. tokssŏ 독서; (*public recital*) nangdok 낭독..

+ **ready** *adj.* chunbi-ga toen 준비가 된.

+ **real** *adj.* (*true*) chinsir-ŭi 진실의; (*actual*) siltche-ŭi 실제의; (*legal*) pudongsan-ŭi 부동산의: *~ estate* (*agent*)pudongsan (ŏptcha) 부동산 (업자).

+ **realize** v. (*accomplish*) silhyŏnhada 실현하다;(*under-stand*) kkaedatta 깨닫다.

* **really** adv. (*actually*) chŏngmal-ŭn 정말은; (*truly*) chŏngmal-lo 정말로, ch'am-ŭro 참으로; (*indeed*) chŏngmal 정말.

+ **reason** n. (*cause*) iyu 이유, kkadak 까닭; (*rational-ity*) isŏng 이성.

+ **reasonable** adj. (*rational*) hamnijŏgin⟨haprijŏgin 합리적인, (*moderate*) chŏkttanghan 적당한; (*inexpen-sive*) almajŭn 알맞은, hapttanghan 합당한: a ~ price almajŭn kagyŏk 알맞은 가격.

  receipt n. yŏngsujŭng 영수증.

+ **receive** v. patta 받다, yŏngsuhada 영수하다.

+ **recent** adj. ch'oegŭn-ŭi 최근의: of ~ date yojŭm-ŭi 요즘의; (*new*) saeroun 새로운.

  recently adv. ch'oegŭn-e 최근에.

+ **recognize** v. (*acknowledge*) injŏnghada 인정하다, (*identify*) araboda 알아보다.

+ **record** n. (*written note*) kirok 기록; (*phonograph*) rek'odŭ 레코드, ŭmban 음반; (*personal history*) kyŏngnyŏk⟨kyŏngryŏk 경력. —v. (*letter*) kirokhada 기록하다; (*voice*) nogŭmhada 녹음하다, (*video*) nokhwahada 녹화하다.

+ **recorder** n. nogŭmgi 녹음기.

+ **recover** v. hoebokhada 회복하다, toech'atta 되찾다.

+ **rectangular** adj. chikssagakhyŏng-ŭi 직사각형의.

+ **red** adj. ppalgan(saeg-ŭi) 빨간(색의): R~ Cross chŏk-ssiptcha 적십자, pulgŏjin 붉어진: be ~ with anger 화나서 얼굴이 붉어지다. —n. chŏkssaek 적색.

+ **reduce** v. (*make less*) churida 줄이다, kamsohada 감소하다; (intransitive v.) chulda 줄다.

  reduction n. ch'ukso 축소; (*discount*) harin 할인.

* **refer** v. chohoehada 조회하다; (*attribute*) ...e tollida …에 돌리다; ch'amjohada 참조하다.

+ **reference** n. ch'amgo 참고: a ~ book ch'amkkosŏ 참고서; (*inquiry*) chohoe 조회; (*testimonial*) chŭngmyŏngsŏ 증명서: *a letter of* ~ ch'uch'ŏnsŏ 추천서 .

+ **refreshment** *n.* wŏn'gihoebok 원기회복; hyuyang 휴
양. (*pl.*) (*light meal*) ŭmsingmul〈ŭmsikmul 음식물.

refrigerator *n.* naengjanggo 냉장고.

+ **refusal** *n.* kŏjŏl 거절, sat'oe 사퇴.

+ **refuse** *v.* (*reject*) kŏjŏlhada 거절하다, (*deny*) kŏbuhada 거부하다.

+ **regard** *v.* yŏgida 여기다; (*respect*) chonkyŏnghada 존
경하다; (*heed*) chuŭihada 주의하다.—*n.* (*considera-*
tion) koryŏ 고려; (*respect*) chongyŏng 존경.

regarding *prep.* ...e kwanhayŏ …에 관하여, ...ŭl tullŏ
ssago …을 둘러 싸고.

+ **region** *n.* chibang 지방, yŏngyŏk 영역.

register *v.* tŭnggihada 등기하다, tŭngnok'ada〈tŭng-
rokhada 등록하다. —*n.* tŭnggi 등기, tŭngnok〈tŭngrok
등록.

+ **regret** *v.* huhoehada 후회하다, yugam-ŭro saenggakhada 유감으로 생각하다. —*n.* (*remorse*) yugam 유감;
huhoe 후회.

+ **regular** *adj.* kyuch'iktchŏgin 규칙적인, chŏnggijŏgin
정기적인.—*n.* (*pl.*) chŏnggyubyŏng 정규병.

+ **reject** *v.* kŏjŏlhada 거절하다, kŏbuhada 거부하다;
(*refuse to grant*) kakhahada 각하하다.

+ **relate** *v.* chinsulhada 진술하다, (*narrate*) iyagihada
이야기하다; (*connect*) kwallyŏnsik'ida 관련시키다.

+ **relation** *n.* (*connection*) kwangye 관계, (*relative*)
ch'inch'ŏk 친척, (*narration*) chinsul 진술.

* **relationship** *n.* (ch'inch'ŏk) kwan'gye (친척) 관계.

+ **relative** *n.*(*kinship*) ch'inch'ŏk 친척; (*grammar*)
kwangyesa 관계사. —*adj.* (*related*) kwangye-ga
innŭn〈itnŭn 관계가 있는, (*comparative*) sangdaejŏgin
상대적인.

+ **relax** *v.* (*loosen*) nŭtch'uda 늦추다; (*rest*) swida 쉬다.

+ **release** *v.* p'urŏnot'a 풀어놓다, (*set free*) sŏkppang-
hada 석방하다; (*remit*) myŏnjehada 면제하다.

+ **relevant** *adj.* kwallyŏntoen〉kwanryŏntoen 관련된,
(*pertinent*) chŏktchŏlhan 적절한.

+ **reliable** *adj.* midŭl ssu innŭn〈itnŭn 믿을 수 있는; hwakssilhan 확실한.
+ **religion** *n.* chonggyo 종교.
+ **religious** *adj.* chonggyojŏkin 종교적인; sinang-ŭi 신앙의.
+ **remain** *v.* mŏmurŭda 머무르다; namtta 남다.
+ **remark** *v.* chumokhada 주목하다; (*speak*) malhada 말하다. —*n.* parŏn 발언; (*comment*) pip'yŏng 비평.
  remedy *n.* (*med.*) ŭiyak 의약; (*cure*) yoppŏp 요법. —*v.* koch'ida 고치다.
+ **remember** *v.* (*recall*) kiŏkhada 기억하다, sanggihada 상기하다.
+ **remove** *v.* (*move*) omgida 옮기다; (*take away*) ch'iuda 치우다; (*get rid of*) ŏpssaeda 없애다.
+ **rent** *n.* (*house*) chipsse 집세, (*room*) pangse 방세; (*land*) chidae 지대(地代); imdaeryo 임대료; (*gap*) kallajin t'ŭm 갈라진 틈. —*v.* (*to somebody*) pillyŏjuda 빌려 주다. (*from somebody*) pillida 빌리다.
+ **repair** *v.* (*mend*) susŏnhada 수선하다, (*correct*) kyojŏnghada 교정하다; (*restore*) hoebokhada 회복하다.
+ **repeat** *v.* toep'urihada 되풀이하다, tasi/kŏtŭphada 다시/거듭하다. —*n.* toep'uri 되풀이.
+ **replace** *v.* chejari-e katta tuda 제자리에 갖다 두다; (*repay*) tollyŏjuda 돌려주다.
+ **reply** *v.* (*answer a question*) taedaphada 대답하다; (*respond to a letter*) taptchanghada 답장하다. —*n.* taedap 대답, taptchang 답장.
+ **report** *v.* podohada 보도하다; pogohada 보고하다, (*announce*) palp'yohada 발표하다; (*present oneself*) ch'uldu hada 출두 하다. —*n.* podo 보도, pogo 보고.
  reporter *n.* pogoja 보고자; (*journalist*) kija 기자.
+ **represent** *v.* nat'anaeda 나타내다 ; (*explain*) sŏlmyŏnghada 설명하다, (*depict*) myosahada 묘사하다; (*stand for*) taep'yohada 대표하다.
+ **reputation** *n.* p'yŏngp'an 평판.
+ **request** *n.* yomang 요망, yogu 요구. —*v.* put'akhada 부탁 하다, (*beg*) kanch'ŏnghada 간청하다, (*ask*) yoguhada 요구하다.

+ **require** v. p'iryo-ro hada 필요로 하다; yoguhada 요구
하다: *required course* p'ilssukkwamok 필수과목.
+ **research** n. (*investigation*) yŏn'gu 연구, chosa 조사.
—v. yŏn'guhada 연구하다,chosahada 조사하다.
  reservation n. (*of hotel room, etc.*) yeyak 예약;
poryu 보류.
  resign v. tannyŏmhada 단념하다; sajik'ada 사직하다.
+ **resource** n. (*natural*) chawŏn 자원, (*financial*) chagŭm 자금; (*means*) sudan 수단. → **expedient** n.
pangp'yŏn 방편.
+ **respect** v. chon'gyŏnghada 존경하다, (*regard*) koryŏhada 고려하다. —n. chonjung 존중. *with ~ to* ...e
kwan-hayŏ …에 관하여.
+ **responsibility** n. ch'aegim 책임: *a sense of ~*
ch'aegimgam 책임감; (*charge*) chikch'aek 직책.
+ **responsible** adj. ch'aegim innŭn⟨itnŭn 책임 있는.
make oneself ~ for ...ŭi ch'aegim-ŭl matta …의 책
임을 맡다.
+ **rest** v. swida 쉬다; (*lean*) kidaeda 기대다. *~ a ladder
against a wall* sadari-rŭl pyŏg-e kidaeda/kŏl-
ch'ida 사다리를 벽에 기대다/걸치다. —n. (*repose*)
hyusik 휴식; (*remainder*) namŏji 나머지.
+ **restaurant** n. sikttang 식당, ŭmsiktchŏm 음식점,
resŭt'orang 레스토랑, yojŏng 요정.
  restless adj. tŭlttŏinnŭn⟨itnŭn 들떠있는, puranhan 불
안한.
+ **restrict** v. chehanhada 제한하다; sokppakhada 속박하다.
* **result** n. kyŏlgwa 결과, sŏngjŏk 성적. —v. (*follow*)
kyŏlgwa-ro irŏnada 결과로 일어나다.
  retail n. & v. somae(hada) 소매(하다).
  retire v. mullŏgada 물러가다, t'oegŏhada 퇴거하다;
(*from office*) t'oejikhada 퇴직하다.
+ **return** v. toraoda 돌아오다; (*borrowed things*) pan-
hwanhada 반환하다. —n. pokkwi 복귀; (*profit*)
suik 수익.*election ~s* sŏn'gŏgyŏlgwa pogo 선거결과
보고.
+ **reveal** v. nat'anaeda 나타내다, poida 보이다; p'ongno-

hada⟨p'okrohada 폭로하다.

reverend *adj.* chon'gyŏnghal manhan 존경할 만한.

reward *n.* ① posu 보수, sang 상(賞). ② hyŏnsanggŭm 현상금.—*v.* posu-rŭl chuda 보수를 주다.

ribbon *n.* ribon 리본, tti 띠.

rice *n.* ssal 쌀, (*cooked*) pap 밥, (*cooked, polite form*) chinji 진지; (*unshelled*) pyŏ 벼.

+ **rich** *adj.* (*wealthy*) tonmanhŭn 돈많은: ~ *people* pujadŭl 부자들.; (*plentiful*) p'ungbuhan 풍부한; (*color*) chit'ŭn 짙은; (*taste*) matchohŭn 맛좋은.

+ **rid** *v.* ŏpssaeda 없애다, (*free*) myŏnhage hada 면하게 하다, (*clear*) chegŏhada 제거하다: *get/be* ~ *of* ...ŭl pŏsŏnada ...을 벗어나다.

+ **ride** *v.* t'ada 타다.—*n.* (*transportation*) sŭngch'a 승차; (*horse*) sŭngma 승마.

+ **ridiculous** *adj.* (*laughable*) usŭkkwangsŭrŏun 우스꽝스러운; (*preposterous*) ŏngttunghan 엉뚱한.

rifle *n.* soch'ong 소총, raip'ŭl ch'ong 라이플 총.

* **right** *adj.* orŭn⟨orhŭn 옳은, chŏngdanghan 정당한; orŭntchog-ŭi 오른쪽의.—*n.* kwŏlli 권리: *human* ~ inkkwŏn 인권.

+ **ring** *n.* (*circle*) kori 고리; (*finger*) panji 반지; (*ear*) kwigori 귀고리.—*v.* ullida 울리다.

ripe *adj.* igŭn 익은, wŏnsuk'an 원숙한.

+ **rise** *v.* (*ascend*) ollagada 올라가다, orŭda 오르다; (*stand up*) irŏnada 일어나다; (*sun*) ttŭda 뜨다. —*n.* sangsŭng 상승, orŭm 오름.

+ **risk** *n.* wihŏm 위험.—*v.* (*venture*) naegŏlda 내걸다 : ~ *one's life* moksum-ŭl kŏlda 목숨을 걸다.

+ **river** *n.* kang 강, nae 내.

* **road** *n.* kil 길, toro 도로: ~ *closed* t'onghaenggŭmji 통행 금지; (*direction*) chillo 진로, (*means*) pangbŏp 방법.

roast *n.* kuun kogi 구운 고기.—*v.* kuptta 굽다.—*adj.* kuun 구운: ~ *beef* pulgogi 불고기.

rob *v.* kangt'alhada 강탈하다, humch'ida 훔치다.

robber *n.* (*bandit*) kangdo 강도, toduk 도둑.

+ **rock** n. pawi 바위.—v. hŭndŭlda 흔들다.
+ **rod** n. changttae 장대, (*stick*) makttaegi 막대기.
+ **role** n. yŏkhal 역할, yŏk 역(役): *play the leading* ~ chuyŏk-ŭl hada 주역을 하다.
+ **roll** n. (*of paper*) turumari 두루마리; (*list of names*) myŏngbu 명부; (*of ship*) yodong 요동. *a* ~ *of sushi* kimppap han chul 김밥 한 줄. —v. kullida 굴리다, urŭrŭ ullida 우르르 울리다.
+ **romantic** adj. nangmanjŏgin 낭만적인.
+ **roof** n. chibung 지붕: ~ *tile* kiwa 기와, *live under the same* ~ tonggŏhada 동거하다; (*summit*) kkok-ttaegi 꼭대기.
* **room** n. (*chamber*) pang 방, (*space*) yŏji 여지. *the main living* ~ anppang 안방. ~ *with heated floor* ondolppang 온돌방.
+ **root** n. ppuri 뿌리, (*base*) kich'o 기초, (*cause, origin*) kŭnwŏn 근원.
+ **rope** n. (pat)chul (밧)줄, saekki 새끼.
  rose n. changmi 장미: ~ *of Sharon* mugunghwa 무궁화.
  rot v. ssŏktta 썩다, pup'aehada 부패하다.
+ **rough** adj. kŏch'in 거친; (*uneven*) ult'ungbult'ung-han 울퉁불퉁한, (*rude*) pŏrŭdŏmnŭn〈pŏrŭtŏpnŭn 버릇없는, (*natural*) chayŏn kŭdae-roŭi 자연 그대로의.
* **round** adj. tunggŭn 둥근.—prep. chuwi-e 주위에.—adv. torasŏ 돌아서.—n. ilhoejŏn 일회전: *the* ~ *of seasons* kyejŏl-ŭi sunhwan 계절의 순환; (*game*) ilhoe 일회: *the first* ~ ilhoe 일회.
+ **route** n. kil 길, (*line*) hangno〈hangro 항로, nosŏn 노선.
+ **row** n. ① (*line*) chul 줄, yŏl 열(列). ② (*disturbance*) pŏpssŏk 법석.③ v. nojŏtta 노젓다.
+ **royal** adj. kugwang-ŭi 국왕의; (*majestic*) wiŏmminnŭn〈itnŭn 위엄있는.
+ **rub** v. pibida 비비다, sŭch'da 스치다: ~ *against a gatepost* munkkidung-ŭl sŭch'ida 문기둥을 스치다. --n. mach'al 마찰.
+ **rubber** n. komu 고무: ~ *shoes* komusin 고무신, ~ *cement* komup'ul 고무풀; chiugae 지우개.

+ **rubbish** *n.* ssŭregi 쓰레기: ~ *bin* ssŭregit'ong 쓰레기통; chapttongsani 잡동사니.
+ **rude** *adj.* (*boorish*) yejŏl ŏmnŭn⟨ŏpnŭn 예절없는, (*impudent*) muryehan 무례한, (*uneducated*) kyoyangŏmnŭn⟨ŏpnŭn 교양없는; (*rough*) nanp'okhan 난폭한.
  ruin *n.* (*destruction*) p'amyŏl 파멸. (*impairment*) hweson 훼손. (*remains*) p'yehŏ 폐허. —*v.* p'agoehada 파괴하다, mangch'ida 망치다.
+ **rule** *n.* kyuch'ik 규칙, (*control*) chibae 지배. —*v.* (*control*) chibaehada 지배하다 ;(*decide*)p'angyŏlhada 판결하다.
+ **ruler** *n.* chibaeja 지배자, t'ongch'ija 통치자; (*measure*) cha 자.
  rumo(u)r *n.* somun 소문, p'ungmun 풍문.
+ **run** *v.* tallida 달리다, ttuida 뛰다; (*flee*)·tomanggada 도망가다; (*manage*) kyŏngyŏnghada 경영하다.
+ **rush** *n.* toltchin 돌진, punmang 분망: ~ *hour* honjaphan sigan 혼잡한 시간, rŏsiawŏ 러시아워.—*v.* toltchinhada 돌진하다; tallyŏdŭlda 달려들다.
  Russia *n.* rŏsia 러시아.
  rust *n.* nok 녹. —*v.* noksŭlda 녹슬다.

⪖ S ⪕

  sack *n.* charu 자루, pudae 부대, pongji 봉지.
+ **sad** *adj.* (*sorrowful*) sŭlp'ŭn 슬픈, (*miserable*) pich'amhan 비참한, (*heartbroken*) kasŭm ap'ŭn 가슴 아픈.
  saddle *n.* anjang 안장, kilma 길마. —*v.* anjang-ŭl not'a 안장을 놓다.
+ **sadness** *n.* sŭlp'ŭm 슬픔, (*sorrow*) piae 비애; (*mournfulness*) pit'an 비탄.
+ **safe** *adj.* anjŏnhan 안전한. —*n.* kŭmgo 금고.

+ **safely** *adv.* anjŏnhage 안전하게, musahi 무사히.

  safety pin *n.* anjŏnp'in 안전핀.

  sail *n.* tot 돛. —*v.* (*navigate*) hanghaehada 항해하다; (*airplane*) chojonghada 조종하다.

  sailor *n.* (*seaman*) sŏnwŏn 선원; subyŏng 수병.

  sake *n.* moktchŏk 목적; iyu 이유; (*interest*) iik 이익: *for the ~ of* …ŭl wihayŏ …을 위하여.

  salad *n.* saellŏdŭ 샐러드, saengch'aeyori 생채요리.

+ **salary** *n.* ponggŭp 봉급, kŭmnyo⟨kŭpryo 급료: *get a high ~* wŏlgŭp-ŭl manhi patta 월급을 많이 받다.

  saliva *n.* ch'im 침, t'aaek 타액.

  salmon *n.* yŏnŏ 연어.

+ **salt** *n.* sogŭm 소금; *the ~ of the earth* sesang-ŭi sogŭm 세상의 소금. —*v.* sogŭm-ŭl ch'ida 소금을 치다.

  salty *a.* sogŭm-ŭi 소금의, tchan 짠.

* **same** *adj.* kat'ŭn 같은, tongilhan 동일한.

  sample *n.* kyŏnbon 견본, p'yobon 표본.

+ **sand** *n.* morae 모래, (*pl.*) moraet'op 모래톱.

  sandwich *n.* saendŭwich'i 샌드위치.

  sanitary *adj.* wisaeng-ŭi 위생의; *a ~ inspector* wisaeng kŏmsagwan 위생 검사관.

  sarcastic *adj.* pikkonŭn 비꼬는, pinjŏngdaenŭn 빈정대는, (*mocking*) nollinŭn 놀리는.

  sardine *n.* chŏngŏri 정어리.

  satin *n.* kongdan 공단.

+ **satisfaction** *n.* manjok 만족, hŭptchok 흡족.

+ **satisfactory** *adj.* manjokhan 만족한, ch'ungbunhan 충분한, (*adequate*) chŏktchŏlhan 적절한.

+ **satisfy** *v.* manjoksik'ida 만족시키다.

  Saturday *n.* t'oyoil 토요일.

  sauce *n.* sŏyang kanjang 서양 간장, sosŭ 소스.

  saucer *n.* patch'im chŏpsi 받침 접시.

+ **save** *v.* (*rescue*) ku(myŏng)hada 구(명)하다, (*hoard*) chŏch'ukhada 저축하다, (*reserve*) namgyŏduda 남겨두다. —*prep.* (*except*) …ŭl cheoehago …을 제외하고.

say *v.* malhada 말하다, (honorific, *elders say*) malssŭm hasida 말씀하시다, (*say to elders*) malssŭm

tŭrida 말씀 드리다: *so to* ~ irŭlt´emyŏn 이를테면. *I* ~ *! ibwa* 이 봐, chamkkanman 잠깐만.

* **saying** *n.* mal 말: *one´s* ~s *and doings* ŏnhaeng 언행;(*proverb*) sokttam 속담.

+ **scale** *n.* ① (*of fish*) pinŭl 비늘. ② (*map*) ch´ukch´ŏk 축척; (*size*) kyumo 규모. ③ (*weighing machine*) chŏul 저울. --*v.* ① pinŭl-ŭl 비늘을 벗기다. ② ch´ukch´ŏk-ŭro chedohada 축척으로 제도하다. ③ chŏul-lo talda 저울로 달다.

scarce *adj.* pujok´an 부족한, (*rare*) tŭmun 드문.

+ **scatter** *v.* hŭtppurida 흩뿌리다, punsanhada 분산하다.

scenery *n.* kyŏngch´i 경치, p´unggyŏng 풍경.

schedule *n.* siganp´yo 시간표, yejŏngp´yo 예정표.

+ **scheme** *n.* (*plan*) kyehoek 계획. (*intrigue*) ŭmmo 음모. (*system*) ch´egye 체계.

scholar *n.* (*learned man*) hakcha 학자; (*student*) hakto 학도.

* **school** *n.* hakkyo 학교, suŏp 수업: *primary* ~ kungminhakkyo〈kukminhakkyo 국민학교, *middle* ~ chunghakkyo 중학교, *high* ~ kodŭnghakkyo 고등학교.*graduate* ~ taehakwŏn 대학원; (*of thought*) hakp´a 학파.

+ **science** *n.* kwahak 과학: *social* ~ sahoekwahak 사회과학, (*skill*) kisul 기술, …hak …학(學): *political* ~ chŏngch´ihak 정치학.

+ **scientific** *adj.* kwahaktchŏgin 과학적인, kwahag-ŭi 과학의.

scissors *n.* kawi 가위.

+ **score** *n.* tŭktchŏm 득점; (*pl.*) tasu 다수. --*v.* tŭktchŏmhada 득점하다, kirok´ada 기록하다.

+ **screen** *n.* k´anmagi 칸막이: *folding* ~ pyŏngp´ung 병풍, (*movie*) yŏngsamak 영사막, sŭk´ŭrin 스크린.

screw *n.* nasa 나사, sŭk´ŭruu 스크루우.

screwdriver *n.* nasa tolligae 나사 돌리개; tŭraibŏ 드라이버.

scroll *n.* turumari 두루마리,(*list*) mongnok〈mokrok 목록.

+ **sculpture** n. chogak 조각, chogakp'um 조각품.

* **sea** n. pada 바다: *the East S~* tonghae 동해, *the Mediterranean S~* jijunghae 지중해.

seal n. ① (*animal*) padap'yobŏm 바다표범. ② (*mark*) tojang 도장, pongin 봉인. —v. narinhada 날인하다; ponginhada 봉인하다.

+ **search** v. ch'attda 찾다, susaekhada 수색하다. —n. susaek 수색, t'amsaek 탐색.

seasickness n. paemŏlmi 배멀미.

season n. kyejŏl 계절, (*right time*) hogi 호기. —v. (*flavor*) kan-ŭl match'uda 간을 맞추다.

+ **seat** n. chari 자리.—v. anch'ida 앉히다.

+ **second** adj. tultchae-ŭi 둘째의, chei-ŭi 제이의. —n. (*time*) ch'o 초(秒).

second-hand adj. mugŭn 묵은, chunggo-ŭi 중고의. —n. chunggop'um 중고품, (*clock*) ch'och'im 초침.

+ **secret** n. pimil 비밀.—adj. pimil-ŭi 비밀의.

secretary n. pisŏ 비서, sŏgi 서기, pisŏgwan 비서관; (*Am. gov.*) changgwan 장관: *the S~ of State* kungmujanggwan〈kukmujanggwan 국무장관.

+ **section** n. kubun 구분; (*area*) chigu 지구; (*office*) -kwa/ bu -과/부: *the second ~* cheikkwa 제이과. *a personnel ~* insakkwa 인사과. —v. kubun/ kuhoek-hada 구분/ 구획하다. → **department** n. -kwa/bu -과/부.

see v. poda 보다; (*meet*) mannada 만나다; (*understand*)ihaehada 이해하다: *I ~.* aratta 알았다; (*see off*) paeunghada 배웅하다; (*attend*) tolboda 돌보다.

+ **seed** n. ssi 씨, chongja 종자. → **fruit** n. yŏlmae 열매.

+ **seeing** n. pogi 보기, (*sight*) sigak 시각(視覺) : *S~ is believing.* paengmun〈paekmun-i puryŏilgyŏn 백문이 불여 일견.

seek v. ch'atta 찾다, (*ask for*) kuhada 구하다.

* **seem** v. (*appear*) …ch'ŏrŏm poida …처럼 보이다, …in tŭthada …인 듯하다.

seize v. (*grasp*) chapta 잡다, (*understand*) p'aak'a-da 파악하다, (*arrest*) ch'ep'ohada 체포하다.

seldom *adj.* tŭmulge 드물게, kanhok 간혹, chomch'ŏrŏm …annŭn 좀처럼 …않는.

select *v.* korŭda 고르다, sŏnt'aek'ada 선택하다. —*adj.* ch'uryŏnaen 추려낸.

+ **sell** *v.* p'alda 팔다, (*be sold*) p'allida 팔리다.

+ **send** *v.* ponaeda 보내다, puch'ida 부치다.

+ **senior** *adj.* sonwi-ŭi 손위의, (*older*) yŏnsang-ŭi 연상의. —*n.* sŏnbae 선배, koch'am 고참, (*superior*) witssaram 윗사람; (*elder*) yŏnjangja 연장자.

+ **sense** *n.* (*perception*) kamgak 감각; (*five senses*) ogwan 오관; (*judgement*) punbyŏl 분별; (*meaning*) ttŭt 뜻.

+ **sensible** *adj.* (*reasonable*) punbyŏlinnŭn⟨itnŭn 분별 있는; (*aware*) ŭisikhan 의식한.

+ **sentence** *n.* munjang 문장; (*for crime*) sŏngo 선고, ŏndo 언도. —*v.* sŏngohada 선고하다.

Seoul *n.* sŏul 서울; taehanmin'guk sudo 대한민국 수도.

+ **separate** *v.* tteŏnot'a 떼어놓다, pullihada⟨punrihada 분리하다.—*adj.* pullidoen⟨punridoen 분리된.

+ **separated** *adj.* pullidoen⟨punridoen 분리된, kallyŏjin 갈려진.

September *n.* kuwŏl 구월.

sergeant *n.* hasagwan 하사관, sangsa 상사, chungsa 중사.

* **series** *n.* (*sequence*) yŏnsok 연속; (*books*) ch'ongsŏ 총서, (*newspaper articles*) yŏnjaegisa 연재기사.

* **serious** *adj.* (*grave*) chinjihan 진지한, (*solemn*) ŏmsukhan 엄숙한; (*critical*) chungdaehan 중대한: a ~ *illness* chungbyŏng 중병.

+ **seriously** *adv.* simgakhage 심각하게, chinjihage 진지하게.

servant *n.* hain 하인, chong 종: a man ~ hain 하인, mŏsŭm 머슴; a maid ~ hanyŏ 하녀.

+ **serve** *v.* sŏmgida 섬기다, sijung-ŭl tŭlda 시중을 들다, (*honorific*) mosida 모시다.

+ **service** *n.* (*employ*) koyong 고용; (*volunteer*) pongsa 봉사; (*official duty*) kŭnmu 근무; (*conscription*)

pyŏng- yŏk 병역; (*treatment in hotels*) chŏpttae
접대; (*devotion to God*) yebae 예배.

sesame *n.* kkae 깨.
* set *v.* (*put*) tuda 두다; (*start*) ch'akssuhada 착수하다;
(*impose*) pugwahada 부과하다; (*adjust*) chojŏnghada 조정하다. —*adj.* (*fixed*) kojŏngdoen 고정된.
—*n.* hancho 한 조(組).

settle *v.* charijapta 자리잡다; (*decide*) kyŏltchŏnghada 결정하다; (*solve*) haegyŏlhada 해결하다.
+ seven *n. & adj.* ilgop(-ŭi) 일곱(의), ch'il 7.
seventeen *n.* yŏrilgop 열일곱, sipch'il 17.
* several *adj.* myŏnmyŏch'〈myŏtmyŏtch'-ŭi 몇몇의,
(*many*) yŏrŏ 여러. —*n.* myŏkkae 몇 개.
+ severe *adj.* (*stern*) ŏmkkyŏkhan 엄격한, (*serious*)
simhan 심한.
+ sew *v.* panŭjilhada 바느질하다, chaebonghada 재봉하다.
sewing *n.* panŭjil 바느질, chaebong 재봉: ~ *machine*
chaebongt'ŭl 재봉틀, *a* ~ *box* panjikkori〈panjitkori
반짇고리.
+ sex *n.* sŏng 성(性), sŏngbyŏl 성별: *the male* ~ nam-
song 남성, *the female* ~ yŏsong 여성.
+ sexual *adj.* sŏngtchŏgin 성적인: ~ *appetite* sŏngyok
성욕, ~ *disease* sŏngppyŏng 성병.
shade *n.* kŭnŭl 그늘; (*blind*) ch'ayang 차양.
shadow *n.* kŭrimja 그림자.
+ shake *v.* hŭndŭlda 흔들다; (*hands*) akssuhada 악수하다.
shall *aux.v.* ...il/hal kŏsida …일/할 것이다.
+ shallow *adj.* yat'ŭn 얕은; (*superficial*) ch'ŏnbakhan
천박한: *a* ~ *idea* ch'ŏnbakhan saenggak 천박한 생각.
shame *n.* pukkŭrŏum 부끄러움, such'i 수치.
* shape *n.* moyang 모양. —*v.* hyŏngsŏnghada 형성하다.
+ share *n.* (*portion*) mok 몫; pundam 분담; (*stock*)
chusik 주식. —*v.* (*apportion*) nanuda 나누다,
paedanghada 배당 하다; (*partake*) kach'ihada 같이
하다.

shark *n.* sangŏ 상어, yoksimjangi 욕심장이.
* sharp *adj.* nalk'aroun 날카로운, (*pointed*) ppyojok-

han 뾰족한; (*temper, appearance*) kkalkkŭmhan 깔끔한. —*adv.* nalk'aropkke 날카롭게; (*alertly*) chosimhayŏ 조심하여.

shave *v.* myŏndohada 면도하다.—*n.* myŏndo 면도.

* **she** *pron.* kŭnyŏ-nŭn/ga 그녀는/가.

shed *v.* (*drop off*) t'ŏlda 털다; (*tears*) hŭllida 흘리다. —*n.* (*hut*) odumak 오두막, hŏtkkan 헛간.

+ **sheep** *n.* yang 양.

+ **sheet** *n.* ibullit⟨ibulit 이불잇, honnibul⟨hotibul 홑이불, sit'ŭ 시트. *a ~ of paper* chongi han chang 종이 한장.

+ **shelf** *n.* sŏnban 선반, sirŏng 시렁.

+ **shell** *n.* kkŏptchil 껍질; (*gun*) p'ot'an 포탄; chogae 조개.

+ **shine** *v.* pinnada⟨pitnada 빛나다, pantchagida 반짝이다. (*polish*) taktta 닦다. —*n.* haeppit⟨haetbit 햇빛, ilgwang 일광. *shoe~* kududakki 구두닦기.

+ **shiny** *adj.* pinnanŭn⟨pitnanŭn 빛나는.

* **ship** *n.* pae 배.—*v.* susonghada 수송하다. *sailing ~* pŏmsŏn 범선, *turtle ~* kŏbuksŏn 거북선 〔an iron-clad warship shaped like a turtle〕, *war ~* kunham 군함, *~ building* chosŏn(ŏp) 조선(업), *~ yard* chosŏnso 조선소.

+ **shirt** *n.* waisyŏssŭ 와이셔쓰. *under ~* sok/rŏning syassŭ 속/러닝샤쓰.

+ **shock** *n.* ch'unggyŏk 충격, syok'ŭ 쇼크.

+ **shoe** *n.* kudu 구두, sin(bal) 신(발): *rubber ~s* komusin 고무신 〔Korean-style〕; *Korean straw ~s/ sandals* chipsin 짚신, *sports ~s* undonghwa 운동화, *mountain- climbing ~s/boots* tungsanhwa 등산화.

shoehorn *n.* kudujugŏk 구두주걱.

shoelace *n.* (*shoestring*) kudukkŭn 구두끈.

shoeshine *n.* kududakki 구두닦기.

+ **shoot** *n.* sagyŏk 사격.—*v.* ssoda 쏘다, sasalhada 사살하다.

+ **shooting** *n.* sagyŏk 사격, (*hunting*) sanyang 사냥.

+ **shop** *n.* kage 가게, sangjŏm 상점: *book ~* chaekppang 책방 /sŏjŏm 서점, *stationery* ~ munbanggu-jŏm 문방구점; (*workshop*) kongjang 공장, chagŏpt-chang 작업장.

shopping *n.* changbogi 장보기, mulgŏnsagi 물건사기, syop'ing 쇼핑. --*v.* mulgŏn-ŭl sada 물건을 사다.

shore *n.* mulkka 물가, kangkka 강가, haean 해안.

* **short** *adj.* tchalbŭn 짧은; (*blunt*) pujokhan 부족한; muttukttukhan 무뚝뚝한. —*n.* (*short pants, shorts*) panbaji 반바지. ~-*sleeve shirt* panp'al syassŭ 반팔 샤쓰.

short cut *n.* chirŭmkkil 지름길.

+ **shot** *n.* t'anhwan 탄환, p'ot'an 포탄, (*shooting*) sa-gyŏk 사격, (*marksman*) sasu 사수.

* **should** *aux. v.* ...hal kkŏsida …할 것이다; (*ought*) ...hayŏya handa …하여야 한다.

+ **shoulder** *n.* ŏkkae 어깨. —*v.* meda 메다.

+ **shout** *n.* koham 고함. —*v.* oech'ida 외치다.

shovel *n.* sap 삽, pusap 부삽, karae 가래.

* **show** *v.* poida 보이다, poyŏjuda 보여주다; (*point out*) karik'ida 가리키다. —*n.* (*ostentation*) kwasi 과시; *for* ~ kwasihagi/poigi wihae 과시하기/보이기 위해; (*events*) kugyŏngkkŏri 구경거리.

shower *n.* sonagi 소나기; (*bath*) syawŏ 샤워.

shrimp *n.* saeu 새우; (*dwarf*) nanjangi 난장이.

shrine *n.* sadang 사당, myo 묘(廟); sŏngdang 성당.

shrink *v.* ogŭradŭlda 오그라들다.

+ **shut** *v.* tatta 닫다, chamgŭda 잠그다.

+ **shy** *adj.* sujup 수줍은, (*bashful*) pukkŭrŏwŏhan 부끄러워하는.

+ **sick** *adj.* pyŏngdŭn 병든; (*nauseating*) mesŭkkŏun 메스꺼운; (*longing*) kŭriwŏhanŭn 그리워하는. *be* ~ *sick* mom-i ap'ŭda 몸이 아프다.

* **side** *n.* tchok 쪽, myŏn 면; (*flank*) yŏkkuri〈yŏpkkuri〉 옆구리.

sidewalk *n.* podo 보도, indo 인도.

+ **sideways** *adv.* yŏp'-ŭro 옆으로, pisŭdŭmhi 비스듬히.

sieve *n.* ch'e 체; (*person*) ib-i kabyŏun saram 입이

가벼운 사람. —v. ch'ejilhada 체질하다.

- sight n. siryŏk 시력: kwanggyŏng 광경, kyŏngch'i 경치. —v. araboda 알아보다.

  sightseeing n. kugyŏng 구경, kwan'gwang 관광.

+ sign n. (symbol) puho 부호, (mark) kiho 기호: (token)chingjo 징조: (signal) sinho 신호: (symbol) puho 부호: (signboard) kanp'an 간판. —v. sŏmyŏnghada 서명하다.

+ signal n. (traffic light) kyot'ongsinho 교통신호. —v. sinhohada 신호하다.

+ significant adj. (important) chungyohan 중요한, (meaningful) ttŭtinnŭn⟨ttŭtitnŭn 뜻있는.

+ silk n. pidan 비단: (Korean) myŏngju 명주.

+ silly adj. ŏrisŏgŭn 어리석은: Don't be ~! ŏrisŏgŭn chin⟨⟨chit)chit mara 어리석은 짓 말아라!

+ silver n. ŭn 은: ~ spoon & chopsticks ŭnsujŏ 은수저.

* similar adj. pisŭthan 비슷한, talmŭn 닮은, yusahan 유사한.

+ simple adj. kandanhan 간단한, (uncomplicated) tansunhan 단순한: (innocent, plain) sobakhan 소박한: ~ manner kkumimŏmnŭn⟨kkumimŏpnŭn t'aedo 꾸밈없는 태도.

+ since conj. (because) ...ttaemun-e …때문에: (time) ...ihu …이후. —prep. ...irae …이래.

+ sincere adj. (honest) chinsilhan 진실한, sŏngsilhan 성실한.

+ sing v. noraehada 노래하다, (chirp) chijŏgwida 지저귀다, ulda 울다: (ring) wingwinggŏrida 윙윙거리다: (praise) yech'anhada 예찬하다.

+ singer n. kasu 가수, sŏngakka 성악가.

+ singing n. noraeburŭgi 노래부르기, ch'angga 창가.

+ single adj. tanil-ŭi 단일의, tan hana-ŭi 단 하나의: (unmarried) tokssin-ŭi 독신의.—n. han gae 한 개.

+ singular adj. koesanghan 괴상한.—n. tanssu 단수.

+ sink n. ssink'ŭ 싱크, sŏlgŏjit'ong 설겆이통: (drain) such'ae 수채, hasugu 하수구.—v. karaanda 가라앉다.

sir n. (*Korean polite title*) nim 님; sŏnsaeng 선생.
+ **sister** n. yŏja hyŏngje 여자 형제. chamae 자매(姉妹); (*boy's older sister*) nuna 누나. (*honorific*) nunim 누님. (*boy's younger sister*) nui/yŏ tongsaeng 누이/여동생; (*girl's older sister*) ŏnni 언니. (*girl's younger sister*) tongsaeng 동생.
+ **sit** v. antta 앉다: ~ *down* antta 앉다: *Please ~ down.* pudi anjŭseyo 부디 앉으세요. ~ *for ch'irŭda* 치르다. ~ *on/upon* ···ŭl chosahada ···을 조사하다.~ *up* irŏna antta 일어나 앉다.
+ **situated** adj. wich'ihan 위치한.
* **situation** n. (*state of affairs*) sangt'ae 상태, hyŏngse 형세, kungmyŏn〈kukmyŏn 국면: the political ~ chŏnguk 정국; (*circumstances*) ch'ŏji 처지; (*place*) changso 장소.
+ **six** n. yŏsŏt 여섯, yuk 육(6). —adj. yŏsŏs-ŭi 여섯의.
  sixteen n. & adj. yŏlyŏsŏt(-ŭi) 열여섯(의), simnyuk(-ŭi)〈sipryuk(ŭi) 십륙(의).
  sixty n. yesun 예순, yuksip 60.
* **size** n. k'ŭgi 크기, ch'isu 치수.
  skating n. ŏrŭm chich'igi 얼음 지치기, sŭk'eit'ing 스케이팅, sŭk'eit'ŭ 스케이트.
  ski n. & v. sŭk'i(-rŭl t'ada) 스키(를 타다).
+ **skillful** adj. nŭngsukhan 능숙한, somssiinnŭn〈somssiitnŭn 솜씨있는.
+ **skill** n. somssi 솜씨, sungnyŏn〈sukryŏn 숙련.
* **skin** n. (*human*) p'ibu 피부; (*fruit, vegitable*) kkŏptchil 껍질; (*animal*) kajuk 가죽.
+ **skirt** n. sŭk'ŏt'ŭ 스커트, ch'ima 치마; (*hem and cuffs, etc.*) charak 자락; (*border*) pyŏnduri 변두리. → **edge** n. kajangjari 가장자리.
+ **sky** n. hanŭl 하늘; (*weather*) nalssi 날씨.
  sled n. ssŏlmae 썰매. —v. ssŏlmae-rŭl t'ada 썰매를 타다.
+ **sleep** n. cham 잠, sumyŏn 수면. —v. chada 자다.
  sleepy adj. chollinŭn 졸리는, chanŭn tŭt'an 자는 듯한.
+ **sleeve** n. somae 소매, (*cuff*) somaetcharak 소맷자락.

slender *adj*. holtchuk'an 홀쭉한, pinyak'an 빈약한: *a ~ income* pinyak'an suip 빈약한 수입.

slice *n*. yalbŭn chogak 얇은 조각. —*v*. yalkke ssŏlda 얇게 썰다.

+ **slide** *v*. mikkŭrŏjida 미끄러지다. —*n*. (*sliding*) hwaltchu 활주, (*projector*) sŭllaidŭ 슬라이드.

+ **slight** *adj*. yakkan-ŭi 약간의, kŭnsohan 근소한. —*v*. kyŏngsihada 경시하다. —*n*. (*disdain*) kyŏngmyŏl 경멸.

* **slightly** *adv*. chogŭm 조금, yakkan 약간; (*flimsily*) kanyalp'ŭge 가냘프게.

slipper *n*. sŭllip'ŏ 슬리퍼.

+ **slope** *n*. pit'al 비탈, kyŏngsa 경사. —*v*. kyŏngsajida 경사지다, pit'aljida 비탈지다.

+ **slow** *adj*. nŭrin 느린, tŏdin 더딘. —*v*. songnyŏk⟨sokryŏk-ŭl nŭtch'uda 속력을 늦추다.

+ **slowly** *adv*. ch'ŏnch'ŏnhi 천천히, nŭrige 느리게, nŭrinnŭrit⟨nŭritnŭrit 느릿느릿.

sly *adj*. kyohwalhan 교활한, ŏngk'ŭmhan 엉큼한; mollae 몰래: *on the ~* ŭnmilhi 은밀히.

small *adj*. (*not large*) chagŭn 작은, (*little*) chŏgŭn 적은; (*trivial, worthless*) pojalkkŏt ŏmnŭn⟨ŏpnn 보잘 것 없는.

+ **smart** *adj*. (*idea*) ttokttokhan 똑똑한, (*wit*) chaech'i innŭn⟨itnŭn 재치있는; (*appearance*) mŏtjin 멋진, maepsiinnŭn ⟨itnŭn 맵시있는.

+ **smell** *n*. naemsae 냄새. —*v*. naemsae matda 냄새 맡다, naemsae-ga nada 냄새가 나다.

+ **smile** *n*. miso 미소. —*v*. misohada 미소하다, saenkutta 생긋 웃다.

+ **smoke** *n*. yŏngi 연기. —*v*. yŏnginaeda 연기내다; (*rette*) tambae(-rŭl) p'iuda 담배(를) 피우다.

smoking *n*. hŭbyŏn 흡연. *No ~.* kŭmyŏn 금연.

+ **smooth** *adj*. maekkŭrŏun 매끄러운, sunt'anhan 평평한: *a ~ road* p'yŏngp'yŏnghan kil 평평한 maekkŭ-rŏpkke hada 매끄럽게 하다.

snack *n*. kandanhan siksa 간단한 식사.

+ **snake** *n.* paem 뱀.

sneeze *n.* chaech'aegi 재채기. —*v.* chaech'aegihada 재채기하다; (*despise*) kkalboda 깔보다.

snore *n.* k'ogonŭn sori 코고는 소리. —*v.* k'o-rŭl kolda 코를 골다.

+ **snow** *n.* nun 눈. —*v.* nun-i oda 눈이 오다.

* **so** *adv.* kŭrŏk'e 그렇게. —*conj.* kŭraesŏ 그래서, kŭrŏmŭro 그러므로. —*pron.* kŭ-wa kat'ŭn kŏt 그와 같은 것.

+ **soap** *n.* pinu 비누: *toilet* ~ hwajang pinu 화장 비누, *laundry* ~ set'akppinu 세탁비누.

* **social** *adj.* sahoe-ŭi 사회의: ~ *problem* sahoe munje 사회문제, ~ *welfare* sahoe poktchi 사회복지; sagyojŏgin 사교적인.

+ **socialism** *n.* sahoejuŭi 사회주의.

* **society** *n.* sahoe 사회; (*academic*) hakhoe 학회.

sock *n.* (tchalbŭ)n yangmal (짧은) 양말.

* **soft** *adj.* pudŭrŏun 부드러운, onhwahan 온화한.

+ **soil***n.* ① hŭk 흙, t'oji 토지; ② (*garbage*) omul 오물. —*v.* (*defile*) tŏrŏphida 더럽히다.

solar *adj.* t'aeyang-ŭi 태양의: ~ *calendar* yangnyŏk 〈yangryŏk 양력(陽曆), ~ *eclipse* ilsik 일식.

+ **soldier** *n.* kunin 군인, (*enlisted man*) sabyŏng 사병.

+ **solid** *adj.* koch'e-ŭi 고체의; tandanhan 단단한; (*firm*) kyŏn'gohan 견고한. —*n.* koch'e 고체.

+ **solution** *n.* haegyŏl 해결: *first step toward a* ~ haegyŏl-ŭi silmari 해결의 실마리; (*dissolution*) yonghae 용해.

+ **solve** *v.* haegyŏlhada 해결하다.

* **some** *adj.* ŏttŏn 어떤, ŏttŏhan 어떠한; yakkan-ŭi 약간의. —*pron.* yakkan 약간, taso 다소, ŏttŏn kŏt 어떤 것.

somebody *n. & pron.* ŏttŏn saram 어떤 사람; (*person of some note*) sangdanghan inmul 상당한 인물.

someone *pron.* ŏttŏn saram 어떤 사람.

something *pron.* ŏttŏn kŏt 어떤 것, (*thing of some value*) sangdanghan kŏt 상당한 것.

sometime *adj.* ŏnjen'ga 언젠가, ŏnjego 언제고.

* **sometimes** *adv.* ttaettae-ro 때때로. → **occasionally** *adv.* ittagŭm 이따금.
* **somewhere** *adv.* ŏdironga 어디론가, ŏdinji 어딘지.
+ **son** *n.* adŭl 아들, (*honorific*) adŭnim 아드님, chason 자손.
+ **song** *n.* norae 노래; (*birds*) unŭn sori 우는 소리.
+ **soon** *adv.* kot 곧, kŭmbang 금방, (*quickly*) ppalli 빨리, (*shortly*) inae 이내.
+ **sore** *adj.* (*painful to the touch*) ap'ŭn 아픈, ssŭrarin 쓰라린; (*sorrowful*) sŭlp'ŭn 슬픈.
+ **sorry** *adj.*(*missing*) sŏpsŏphan 섭섭한, (*feeling regret*) yugamsŭrŏn 유감스런; *I am* ~. (*my fault: apology*) mianhamnida⟨mianhapnida 미안합니다. (*not my fault: sympathy*) andwaessŭmnida 안됐습니다.
+ **sort** *n.* (*kind*) chongnyu⟨chongryu 종류; —*v.* pullyuhada⟨punryuhada 분류하다.
  soul *n.* yŏnghon 영혼, chŏngsin 정신; (*person*) saram 사람.
* **sound** *adj.* (*character*) kŏnjŏnhan 건전한. —*n.* sori 소리; ~ *proofing* pangŭm 방음. —*v.* sori-ga nada 소리가 나다.
  soup *n.* kuk 국, suup'ŭ 수우프.
+ **sour** *adj.* (*acid*) sin 신, sik'ŭmhan 시큼한. ~ *milk* sik'umhaejin uyu 시큼해진 우유.
+ **source** *n.* kŭnwŏn 근원, ch'ulch'ŏ 출처.
+ **south** *n.* namtchok 남쪽.—*adj.* namtchog-ŭi 남쪽의.
  sow *v.* ssi-rŭl ppurida 씨를 뿌리다, p'ŏttŭrida 퍼뜨리다. —*n.* (*a female hog*) amt'waeji 암퇘지.
* **space** *n.* (*room, celestial*) konggan 공간; (*interval*) kan'gyŏk 간격; (*universe*) uju 우주.
+ **spacecraft/spaceship** *n.* ujusŏn 우주선.
  Spanish *n.* sŭp'einŏ 스페인어; (*people*) sŭp'einsaram 스페인사람.—*adj.* sŭp'ein-ŭi 스페인의.
  spare *v.* chŏryakhada 절약하다.
  sparrow *n.* ch'amsae 참새.
* **speak** *v.* malhada 말하다, (*honorific*) malssŭmhasida 말

씀하시다; (converse) iyagihada 이야기하다; (speech) yŏn- sŏlhada 연설하다.

+ **speaker** n. yŏnsa 연사: guest ~ ch'och'ŏng yŏnsa 초청연사, pyŏnsa 변사; (loud speaker) hwakssŏnggi 확성기.

* **special** adj. t'ŭkppyŏlhan 특별한.

+ **specially** adv. t'ŭkppyŏlhi 특별히, t'ŭkhi 특히.

+ **specific** adj. t'ŭktchong-ŭi 특종의; (explicit) myŏnghwakhan 명확한.—n. t'ŭkssaek 특색.

+ **specify** v. (fill in in detail) chasehi kiiphada 자세히 기입하다.

  spectacle n. kwanggyŏng 광경; (pl.) an'gyŏng 안경.

* **speech** n. (address) yŏnsŏl 연설; (language) ŏnŏ 언어, (individual) mal 말; (gram.) hwappŏp 화법.

+ **speed** n. soktto 속도, songnyŏk〈sokryŏk 속력. (swiftness) sinsok 신속.

* **spell** n. ① chumun 주문(呪文). ② (short period) chamsi-gan 잠시간, tchalbŭn kigan 짧은 기간. ③ —v. ch'ŏltchahada 철자하다. ~ing ch'ŏltchappŏp 철자법.

+ **spend** v. (consume) sobihada 소비하다; (money) ssŭda 쓰다, (time) ponaeda 보내다. ~ing ssŭmssŭmi 씀씀이. ~ thrift n. nangbija 낭비자. adj. nangbihanŭn 낭비하는.

+ **spice** n. yangnyŏm 양념, hyangnyo〈hyangryo 향료.

  spill v. ŏptchirŭda 엎지르다, hŭllida 흘리다.

  spinach n. sigŭmch'i 시금치.

  spinning wheel n. mulle 물레.

+ **spirit** n. (soul, mind) chŏngsin 정신; (vigor) ki(un) 기(운); (ghost) mangnyŏng〈mangryŏng 망령; (evil) angma〈akma 악마; (alchohol) alk'ool 알코올, (spirits) tok'an sul 독한 술. —v. (animate) hwalgi-rŭl ttigehada 활기를 띠게 하다.

  spit v. ch'im-ŭl paetta 침을 뱉다. —n. ch'im 침.

+ **spite** n. (intention) agŭi 악의, (resentment) wŏnhan 원한. in ~ of ...edo pulguhago …에도 불구하고. —v. (vex) koerophida 괴롭히다, hakttaehada 학대하다.

  splendid adj. (fire) hullyunghan 훌륭한, (grand)

tang-danghan 당당한, koengjanghan 굉장한.

split v. tchogaeda 쪼개다, tchitta 찢다. —n. kalrajin t'ŭm 갈라진 틈. (*rupture*) pulhwa 불화.

+ **spoil** n. (*goods*) yakt'alp'um 약탈품. —v. (*ruin*) mang-ch'ida 망치다; (*damage*) sonsanghada 손상하다; (rot)ssŏgida 썩이다.

sponge n. haemyŏn 해면, sŭp'ŏnji 스펀지.

+ **spoon** n. sutkkarak 숟가락. sŭp'un 스푼. —v. sutkkarag-ŭro ttŭda 숟가락으로 뜨다.

+ **sport** n. undong 운동, sŭp'och'ŭ 스포츠: ~*man* undong-sŏnsu 운동선수; (*pastime*) nori 놀이; (*jest*) nongdam 농담.

+ **spot** n. (*place*) chijŏm 지점; (*dot*) ŏlluk 얼룩. —v. (*get dirty*) tŏrŏwŏjida 더러워지다.

+ **spread** v. (*map*) p'yŏda 펴다, (*seed*) ppurida 뿌리다, (*rumor*) p'ŏttŭrida 퍼뜨리다, (*information*) pogŭpsik'ida 보급시키다..

+ **spring** n. ① (*fountain*) saem 샘. ② (*season*) pom 봄. ③ (*wire*) sŭp'ŭring 스프링. —v. ttwida 뛰다.

spy n. kanch'ŏp 간첩, sŭp'ai 스파이. —v. chŏngt'amhada 정탐하다, ch'ajanaeda 찾아내다.

+ **square** n. nemokkol 네모꼴, chŏngbanghyŏng 정방형; (*open space*) kwangjang 광장.

squat v. ungk'ŭrigo antta 웅크리고 앉다.

squeeze v. tchada 짜다, kkwak choeda 꽉 죄다.

squirrel n. taramjwi 다람쥐.

+ **stage** n. ① mudae 무대, sŭt'eiji 스테이지, palp'an 발판. ② (*period*) sigi 시기; (*step*) tan'gye 단계.

stair n. sadari 사다리, kyedan 계단.

stamp n. (*postage*) up'yo 우표, inji 인지; (*seal*) tojang 도장.—(*impress*) tchiktta 찍다; (*feet*) par-ŭl kurŭda 발을 구르다, kŏtta 걷다.

+ **stand** n. (*position*) iptchang 입장; (*support*) tae 대 (臺). —v. sŏda 서다; (*endure*) ch'amtta 참다.

+ **standard** n. p'yojun 표준: ~ *time* p'yojunsigan 표준시간. (*level*) sujun 수준: *the* ~ *of living* saenghwalsujun 생활수준; (*flag*) ki 기.

+ **standing** n. (*standing place*) sŏn changso 선 장소;
(*rank*) chiwi 지위, (*reputation*) myŏngmang 명망:
men of high ~ myŏngmang-i nop'ŭn saram 명망이
높은 사람.

+ **star** n. pyŏl 별; (*popular actor, actress*) sŭt'a 스타.

* **start** n. sijak 시작, (*in races*) ch'ulbal 출발; (*shock*)
kkamtchak nollam 깜짝 놀람; (*business*) ch'akssu
착수. —v. sijakhada 시작하다, ch'ulbalhada 출발하
다; ch'akssuhada 착수하다.

* **state** n. (*body politic*) kukka 국가: *head of ~*
kukkawŏn- su 국가원수; (*a province*) chu 주(州): *
universitychuripttaehak* 주립대학, *governor of ~*
chujisa 주지사; (*condition*) sangt'ae 상태. —v.
(*express formally*) chinsulhada 진술하다.

* **statement** n. chinsul 진술; sŏngmyŏng 성명.

+ **station** n. (*of a railway*) yŏk 역: *Seoul ~* sŏullyŏk 서
울역, chŏnggŏjang 정거장; (*bus terminal*) t'ŏminal
터미날: *express bus ~* kosokppŏssŭt'ŏminal 고속 버
스터미날, *local bus ~* sioeppŏssŭt'ŏminal 시외 버스
터미날; (*position*) wich'i 위치; (*rank*) sinbun 신분.
—v. chudunhada 주둔하다, paech'ihada 배치하다.

　stationery n. p'yŏnjiji 편지지, munbanggu 문방구.

+ **statue** n. chosang 조상(彫像): *bronze ~* tongsang
동상.

+ **status** n. (*rank*) sinbun 신분, chiwi 지위: *social ~*
sahoejŏk chiwi 사회적 지위, sinbun 신분; (*condition*) sangt'ae 상태: *current ~* hyŏnhwang 현황.

+ **stay** v. mŏmurŭda 머무르다, (*stop*) mŏmch'uda 멈추
다, (*in a hotel*) muktta 묵다, (*at a friend's place*)
itta 있다:*S ~ here!* yŏgi itkkŏra 여기 있거라. —n.
ch'eryu 체류; chŏngji 정지.

+ **steady** adj. (*fixed*) kojŏngdoen 고정된, (*firm*)
tandanhan 단단한; (*faithful*) ch'akssilhan 착실한,
(*consistent*) hangyŏlgat'ŭn 한결같은; (*smooth*)
sunjoroun 순조로운.

　steak n. sŭt'eik'ŭ 스테이크, pulgogi 불고기.

+ **steal** v. humch'ida 훔치다. —n. (*theft*) chŏltto 절

도; (colloq. *bargain*) hoengjae 횡재.

+ **steam** *n.* chŭnggi 증기, kim 김. —*v.* tchida 찌다. ~*ed*
sweet potato tchin'goguma 찐고구마.

+ **steel** *n.* kangch'ŏl 강철.

+ **steep** *adj.* hŏmhan 험한, kap'arŭn 가파른: *a ~
mountain* kap'arŭn san 가파른 산.

+ **stem** *n.* ① (*of plants*) chulgi 줄기: ~ *of a word*
ŏgan 어간. —*v.* (*stop*) maganaeda 막아내다. ②
(*block*) chŏ-jihada 저지하다: ~ *a torrent against*
kŭmnyu-rŭl maktta 급류를 막다.

+ **step** *v.* (*walk*) kŏtta 걷다; naagada 나아가다; (*tread*)
paptta 밟다. —*n.* kŏrŭm 걸음, (*manner*) kŏrŭmsae
걸음 새, kŏrŭmkŏri 걸음걸이; (pl. *stairs*) kyedan 계
단.

+ **stick** *n.* chip'angi 지팡이.—*v.* (*to*) putta 붙다; (*into*)
tchirŭda 찌르다; (*catch*) kŏllida 걸리다.

+ **sticky** *adj.* kkŭnjŏkkŭnjŏkhan 끈적끈적한.

+ **stiff** *adj.* (*hard*) kudŭn 굳은, ttakttakhan 딱딱한,
ppŏtppŏthan 뻣뻣한. → **dense, thick** *adj.* kŏltchukhan 걸쭉한.

+ **still** *adj.* koyohan 고요한, chŏngjihan 정지한. —*adv.*
ajik(tto) 아직(도): *I still haven't heard from him.*
ajik sosig-i ŏpssŏyo 아직 소식이 없어요; tŏuk 더욱.

  sting *n.* tchillin sangch'ŏ 찔린 상처, (*pain*) simhan
kot'ong 심한 고통.—*v.* (*prick*) tchirŭda 찌르다;
ssoda 쏘다.

  stir *v.* hwijŏtta 휘젓다; umjigida 움직이다.

  stocking *n.* (kin) yangmal (긴) 양말, (*Korean*) pŏsŏn
버선.

+ **stomach** *n.* (*medical term*) wi 위, (*belly*) pae 배.

+ **stone** *n.* tol 돌, tolmengi 돌멩이, sŏktchae 석재.

* **stop** *n.* (*pause*) chungji 중지; (*bus stop*) chŏng-
nyujang〈ryujang 정류장, chŏnggŏjang 정거장. —*v.*
mŏmch'uda 멈추다: ~ *over in* ... ... kyŏngyu-ro ...
경유로, (*quit*) kkŭnt'a 끊다.

+ **store** *n.* kage 가게, sangjŏm 상점, (*suffix*) -chŏm -
점: *convinence* ~ p'yŏnŭijŏm 편의점, *hardware* ~

chŏlmul- jŏm 철물점. —v. chŏjanghada 저장하다.

storm n. p'okp'ungu 폭풍우; sop'ung 소풍: *a ~ warning* p'op'ung chuŭibo 폭풍 주의보.—*v.* (*weather*) sanawŏ-jida 사나워지다.

* **story** n. (*tale*) iyagi 이야기, sŏlhwa 설화: *short ~* tanp'yŏnsosŏl 단편소설. *~ teller* iyagikkun 이야기꾼; (*plot*) chulgŏri 줄거리; (*rumor*) somun 소문.

stove n. nallo〈nanro 난로: *cooking ~* hwadŏk 화덕 /*elec-tric ~* chŏn'gi nallo〈nanro 전기 난로.

+ **straight** adj. (*erect*) ttokpparŭn 똑바른, (*upright*) sujig-ŭi 수직의.—n. (*line*) chikssŏn 직선. —adv. ttokpparo 똑바로, (*honestly*) soltchikhage 솔직하게.

+ **strange** adj. isanghan 이상한, myohan 묘한; natssŏn 낯선.

stranger n. morŭnŭn saram 모르는 사람; munoehan 문외한; (*foreigner*) oegugin 외국인, ibangin 이방인.

+ **strap** n. kajukkkŭn 가죽끈.—v. kajukkkŭn-ŭro maeda 가죽끈으로 매다.

straw n. chip 짚, miljip 밀짚: *~ bag* kamani 가마니.

strawberry n. ttalgi 딸기: *the Alpine ~* yangttalgi 양딸기.

+ **stream** n. (*current*) hŭrŭm 흐름; (*small river*) kaech'ŏn 개천, nae 내. —v. hŭrŭda 흐르다. → **brook** n. kaeul 개울.

+ **street** n. kil 길, kŏri 거리, karo 가로. *main ~* k'ŭngil 큰길, *side ~* kolmokkil 골목(길)

+ **strength** n. him 힘, seryŏk 세력. *physical ~* ch'eryŏk 체력.

+ **stretch** v. (*spread*) nŭllida 늘리다; (*reach out*) naemilda 내밀다; (*goods*) akkyŏssŭda 아껴쓰다. —n. (*width*) nŏbi 너비. → **range** n. pŏmwi 범위.

+ **strict** adj. ŏmkkyŏkhan 엄격한. → **accurate** adj. chŏngmilhan 정밀한.

+ **strike** v. ttaerida 때리다, tudŭrida 두드리다.—n. (*boxing*) t'agyŏk 타격, (*baseball*) sŭtŭraik'ŭ 스트라이크; (*industry*) p'aŏp 파업: *industry-wide ~* tongmaeng- p'aŏp 동맹파업.

+ **string** *n.* kkŭn 끈: *shoe* ~ kudukkŭn 구두끈.

+ **strip** ① *v.* pŏtkkida 벗기다. ② *n.* (*of cloth*) chogak 조
각. *comic* ~ manhwa 만화.

+ **stripe** *n.* chul 줄, chulmunŭi 줄무늬: *the Stars and
S*~ sŏngjogi 성조기.

  stroke ① *n.* (*of Korean characters*) hoek 획:
  (*illness*) choltto 졸도. ② *v.* ssŭdadŭmtta 쓰다듬다.

* **strong** *adj.* (*powerful*) himsen 힘센, kanghan 강한,
kangnyŏkhan⟨ryŏkhan⟩ 강력한, (*sturdy*) t'ŭnt'ŭnhan 튼튼한, (*robust*) kŏn'ganghan 건강한: (*thick,
rich*) chinhan 진한, (*taste*) tok'an 독한.

+ **structure** *n.* kujo 구조: *social* ~ sahoe kujo 사회구조:
(*building*) kŏnmul 건물.

  structural *adj.* kujojŏk 구조적.

+ **struggle** *n.* ssaum 싸움, (*political*) t'ujaeng 투쟁:
noryŏk 노력. —*v.* (*fight*) tat'uda 다투다, t'ujaeng-
hada 투쟁하다: noryŏkhada 노력하다.

+ **student** *n.* hakssaeng 학생: (*researcher*) yŏnguwŏn
연구원. ~ *movement* hakssaeng undong 학생운동, ~
union ch'onghakssaenghoe 총학생회, ~ *id(entifica-
tion)* hakssaengtchŭng 학생증.

+ **study** *n.* kongbu 공부: (*report*) yŏn'gu 연구: (*room*)
sŏjae 서재. —*v.* kongbuhada 공부하다, yŏn'guhada
연구하다.

  stuff *n.* (*material*) chaeryo 재료: multcha 물자:
  (*rubbish*) p'yemul 폐물.—*v.* ch'aeuda 채우다.

+ **stupid** *adj.* ŏrisŏgŭn 어리석은, (u)dunhan (우)둔한.

+ **style** *n.* (*manner*) moyang 모양, (*mode*) hyŏng(sik)
형(식): (*fashion*) yuhaeng 유행: (*of writing*)
munch'e 문체.

* **subject** *n.* (*of a country*) paekssŏng 백성: (*theme*)
chuje 주제: (*of study*) kwamok 과목: (*grammar*)
chuŏ 주어.

* **substance** *n.* (*reality*) silch'e 실체: (*physical matter*) multchil 물질.

  suburb *n.* kyooe 교외(郊外).

  subway *n.* (*underground passage*) chihado 지하도:

(*under-ground railway*) chihach'ŏl 지하철.
+ **succeed** *v.* sŏnggonghada 성공하다; (*follow, come after*) ittara irŏnada 잇달아 일어나다; (*be successor to*) sangsokhada 상속하다, kyesŭnghada 계승하다. → **achieve** *v.* sŏngch'wihada 성취하다.
+ **success** *n.* sŏnggong 성공. → **achievement** *n.* sŏngch'wi 성취.
* **successful** *adj.* sŏnggongjŏg(in) 성공적(인).
# **such** *adj.* kŭrŏhan 그러한, irŏhan 이러한.
+ **suck** *v.* ppalda 빨다; (*breast*) chŏj-ŭl mŏktta 젖을 먹다.
+ **sudden** *adj.* kaptchaksŭrŏun 갑작스러운, (*abrupt*) kŭp(kkyŏk)han 급(격)한, toryŏnhan 돌연한. → **unexpected** *adj.* ttŭtppakk-ŭi 뜻밖의.
* **suddenly** *adv.* kaptchagi 갑자기, pyŏrangan 별안간.
+ **suffer** *v.* (*undergo*) kyŏktta 겪다, (*bear pain*) koerowŏhada 괴로워하다; (*tolerate*) ch'amtta 참다.
+ **suffering** *n.* (*pain*) kot'ong 고통; (*loss*) sonhae 손해.
suffix *n.* (*gram.*) chŏmmiŏ〈chŏpmiŏ 접미어(接尾語).
+ **sugar** *n.* sŏlt'ang 설탕; *cube* ~ kakssŏlt'ang 각설탕.
+ **suggest** *v.* (*imply*) amsihada 암시하다; (*propose*) hada, cheŭihada 제의하다.
+ **suggestion** *n.* amsi 암시; chean 제안, cheŭi 제의.
+ **suit** *n.* (*law*) sosong 소송, koso 고소; (*clothes*) han pŏl ot 한 벌 옷: *a ~ of clothes* han pŏl-ŭi ot 한 벌의 옷 —*v.* (*befit*) ...e chŏkhaphada ...에 적합하다; (*become*) ...e ŏullida ...에 어울리다.
+ **suitable** *adj.* chŏkttanghan 적당한; ŏullinŭn 어울리는.
+ **sum** *n.* (*total amount*) hapkkye 합계; (*outline*) kaeyo; (*pl., calculation*) kyesan 계산.
+ **summary** *n.* yoyak 요약, yoji 요지. —*adj.* yoyakhan 요약한, taegang-ŭi 대강의.
+ **summer** *n.* yŏrŭm 여름, yŏrŭmch'ŏl 여름철. ~ *vacation* yŏ- rŭmppanghak 여름방학.
+ **sun** *n.* hae 해, t'aeyang 태양, haeppit〈haetpit 햇빛. ~ *rise/set* haedoji/haenŏmi 해돋이/해넘이.
sunburn *v.* haeppyŏt'〈haetpyŏt'-e t'ada 햇볕에 타다.

~ *ed* haeppyŏt'-e t'an 햇볕에 탄.

+ **Sunday** *n.* iryoil 일요일, kongil 공일, (*Lord's Day*) chuil 주일.

sunshine *n.* haeppyŏt⟨haetpyŏt 햇볕, ilgwang 일광.

+ **superior** *adj.* hullyunghan 훌륭한, usuhan 우수한. —*n.* (*social relations*) wissaram⟨witsaram 윗사람, sŏnbae 선배, (*in a bureaucracy*) sanggwan 상관.

+ **superlative** *adj.* ch'oego-ŭi 최고의.—*n.* ch'oego 최고.

supper *n.* chŏnyŏksikssa 저녁식사.

+ **supply** *n.* (*supplying*) konggŭp 공급; (*stock*) chaegop'um 재고품; (*provisions*) yangsik 양식.—*v.* konggŭphada 공급하다.

* **support** *n.* chiji 지지.—*v.* (*advocate*) chijihada 지지하다; (*aid*) wŏnjohada 원조하다; (*back up*) huwŏnhada 후원하다.

+ **suppose** *v.* (*assume*) kajŏnghada 가정하다; (*think*) saeng-gakhada 생각하다, ch'uch'ŭkhada 추측하다.

+ **sure** *adj.* hwakssilhan 확실한, (*reliable*) midŭl ssu innŭn⟨itnŭn 믿을 수 있는; (*safe*) anjŏnhan 안전한. --*adv.* (*yes, certainly*) ne 네, mullon 물론.

* **surface** *n.* p'yomyŏn 표면: ~ *of a body of water* sumyŏn 수면; oegwan 외관.

+ **surgery** *n.* (*section*) oekkwa 외과, (*act*) susul(sil) 수술(실).

+ **surprise** *n.* nollam 놀람. —*v.* nollage hada 놀라게 하다.

+ **surprising** *adj.* nollaun 놀라운, nollalmanhan 놀랄만한, ttŭppakk-ŭi⟨ttŭtpakk-ŭi 뜻밖의, nunbusin 눈부신.

+ **surround** *v.* tullŏssada 둘러싸다, ewŏssada 에워싸다; (*battle*) p'o-wihada 포위하다.

+ **surroundings** *n.* chuwi 주위, hwan'gyŏng 환경.

+ **survive** *v.* (*outlive*) poda orae salda 보다 오래 살다, (*disaster*) sara namda 살아 남다.

+ **swallow** *n.* chebi 제비. —*v.* samk'ida 삼키다.

swan *n.* paekcho 백조.

+ **swear** *v.* (*pledge*) maengsehada 맹세하다; (*curse*) yog-ŭl hada 욕을 하다. —*n.* (*oath*) sŏnsŏ 선서; (colloq.*curse*) chŏju 저주.

sweat *n.* ttam 땀. —*v.* ttam hŭllida 땀 흘리다.

sweep *v.* ssŭlda 쓸다, ch'ŏngsohada 청소하다; (*remove*) ilssohada 일소하다. —*n.* ch'ŏngso 청소.

+ **sweet** *adj.* tan 단, talk'omhan 달콤한: ~ *potato* kokuma 고구마; (*pleasing*) yuk'waehan 유쾌한; (*kind*)ch'injŏl-han 친절한; (*charming*) kwiyŏun 귀여운. → **fragrant***adj.* hyanggiroun 향기로운. —*n.* (*candy*) kwaja 과자.

sweetheart *n.* (old-fashioned,*lover*) aein 애인, yŏnin 연인.

sweet-talk *v.* (*to authority figure*) abuhada 아부하다.

swell *v.* pup'ulda 부풀다, k'ŏjida 커지다.

+ **swim** *v.* suyŏnghada 수영하다, heŏmch'ida 헤엄치다; (*float*) ttŭda 뜨다.

+ **swimming** *n.* suyŏng 수영.

swing *n.* (*vibration*) chindong 진동; (*sport*) kŭne 그네. —*v.* hŭndŭlda 흔들다; (*on swing*) kŭne-rŭl ttwida 그네 를 뛰다.

+ **switch** *n.* sŭwich'i 스위치, kaep'yegi 개폐기. —*v.* chŏnhwanhada 전환하다, pakkuda 바꾸다; (*whip*) maejilhada 매질하다.

+ **swollen** *adj.* pup'un 부푼.

sword *n.* k'al 칼: ~ *dance* k'alch'um 칼춤, kŏmmu 검무.

syllable *n.* ŭmjŏl 음절, ch'ŏlja 철자.

+ **symbol** *n.* (*emblem*) sangjing 상징; (*mark*) kiho 기호.

+ **sympathetic** *adj.* tongjŏnghanŭn 동정하는. → **likable** *adj.* (*congenial*) maŭm-e tŭnŭn 마음에 드는.

+ **sympathy** *n.* (*pity*) tongjŏng 동정, (*favor*) tonggam 동감; (*fellow feeling*) konggam 공감.

syrup *n.* sirŏp 시럽.

* **system** *n.* ch'egye 체계, ch'eje 체제: *political* ~ chŏng-ch'i ch'eje 정치체제; chedo 제도: *educational* ~kyoyuk chedo 교육제도; (*method*) pangbŏp 방법, pangsik 방식. → **organization** *n.* chojik 조직.

table   355   taste

$\leq$ T $\geq$

+ **table** n. (*speech*) t'aktcha 탁자, (*food*) sikt'ak 식탁, (*Korean style, eating*) papssang 밥상. → **desk** n.(*study*) ch'aekssang 책상.
  tablecloth n. sikt'akppo 식탁보.
+ **tail** n. kkori 꼬리; kkŭt'ŭmŏri 끄트머리.
  tailor n. chaebongsa 재봉사, (*shop*) yangboktchŏm 양복점.
* **take** v. (*seize*) chwida 쥐다, (*grasp*) chaptta 잡다; (*carry*) kajigo kada 가지고 가다; (*taxi, train*) t'ada 타다; (*eat medicine*) mŏktta 먹다, (*drink*) masida 마시 다; (*time*) kŏllida 걸리다.
* **talk** n. iyagi 이야기, taehwa 대화; (*consultation*) sangdam 상담. —v. malhada 말하다, (*honorific*) malssŭmhasida 말 씀하시다, (*converse*) taehwahada 대화하다, iyagihada 이 야기하다.
+ **tall** adj. k'i-ga k'ŭn 키가 큰, (*building, mountain*) nop'ŭn 높은; ŏmch'ŏngnan 엄청난.
  tangerine n. kyul 귤.
+ **tape** n. t'eip'ŭ 테이프: *cassette* ~ k'asset'ŭ ~ 카세트 ~, *audio* ~ *recorder* nogŭmgi 녹음기; (*tapeline formeasure*) chulja 줄자. --v. (*for video*) nokhwahada 녹화 하다.
+ **target** n. p'yojŏk 표적, (*shooting*) kwanyŏk 과녁; (*goal*) mokp'yo 목표.
+ **task** n. (*job*) il 일, (*duty*) chingmu⟨chikmu 직무, (*lesson*) kwaŏp 과업; (*errand*) simburŭm 심부름: ~ *force*kidongbudae 기동부대.
+ **taste** n. mat 맛, (*food*) immat⟨ipmat 입맛, (*sense*) migak 미각; (*liking*) ch'wihyang 취향, kiho 기호. —v. mappoda⟨matpoda 맛보다, mŏgŏboda 먹어보다.

tasteful *adj.* (*refined*) mŏsinnŭn⟨itnŭn 멋있는.

tattoo *n.* munsin 문신.

+ **tax** *n.* segŭm 세금. ~ *free* myŏnse 면세. —*v.* kwasehada 과 세하다.

taxi *n.* t'aekssi 택시.

+ **tea** *n.* ch'a 차, (*black*) hongch'a 홍차, (*green*) nokch'a 녹 차: *coarse* ~ yŏpch'a 엽차, *ginseng* ~ insamch'a 인삼차.

+ **teach** *v.* karŭch'ida 가르치다, (*explain*) sŏlmyŏnghada 설명 하다.

+ **teacher** *n.* sŏnsaeng (nim) 선생(님), (*honorific*) sŭsŭng 스승, (*primary, secondary school*) kyosa 교사, (*instruc- tor*) kangsa 강사.

+ **team** *n.* t'im 팀, (*group*) p'ae 패.

+ **tear** *n.* ① (*drops of weeping*) nunmul 눈물. ② (*rip*) tchaejin t'ŭm 째진 틈. —*v.* tchitta 찢다.

+ **teeth** *n. pl.* i 이, (*vulgar term*) ippal 이빨, (*honorific*) ch'ia 치아. *brush one's* ~ 이를 닦다. → **tooth** *n.* ~ *pick* issusigae 이쑤시개. ~*paste* ch'iyak 치약. ~ *brush* ch'issol 칫솔.

+ **telephone** *n.* chŏnhwa(gi) 전화(기): ~ *box/booth* kongjung chŏnhwa bakssŭ 공중 전화 박스. ~ *directory* chŏnhwabu 전화부. *mobile* ~ hyudaep'on 휴대폰. ~ *operator* kyohwansu 교환수. *public* ~ kongjung chŏnhwa 공중 전화. —*v.* chŏnhwa-rŭl kŏlda 전화를 걸다.

* **television** *n.* t'ellebijŏn 텔레비전.

* **tell** *v.* malhada 말하다, (*honorific*) malssŭmdŭrida 말씀드리다. iyagihada 이야기하다; allida 알리다: myŏnghada 명하다.

+ **temper** *n.* sŏngjil 성질, (*disposition*) kijil 기질, sŏngmi 성미, (*anger*) nogi 노기.

+ **temperature** *n.* ondo 온도; (*body*) ch'eon 체온, (*air*) kion 기온.

temple *n.* ① (*religion*) sinjŏn 신전(神殿), sawŏn 사원, (*Buddhism*) chŏl 절. ② (*a part of face*) kwanjanori 관자 놀이.

+ **ten** *n. & adj.* yŏl(-ŭi) 열(의), sip(-ŭi) 10(의).

+ **tennis** *n.* chŏnggu 정구, t'enisŭ 테니스.

* **tense** *adj.* kinjanghan 긴장한, (*tight*) p'aengp'aenghan 팽팽한. —*n.* (*gram.*) sije 시제(時制).

   tent *n.* ch'ŏnmak 천막, t'ent'ŭ 텐트.

   terrible *adj.* musŏun 무서운, kagonghal 가공할.

+ **test** *n. & v.* sihŏm(hada) 시험(하다).

* **than** *conj.* ...podado …보다도.

that *adj.* kŭ 그, chŏ 저. —*pron.* kŭgŏt 그것, chŏgŏt 저
   것. —*adv.* kŭrŏk'e 그렇게. —*conj.* ‥hadanŭn/iranŭn
   kŏt ‥하다는/이라는 것.

the *art.* no exact equivalent in Korean and may or
   may not be translated as *kŭ* 그: *the person* (kŭ)
   saram (그) 사람. [When *the* modifies a noun
   mentioned already or contextually definite, it
   may be translated by *kŭ* 그 or *chŏ* 저:‥ ~ *person on
   the bench* pench'i wi-ŭi kŭ/chŏsaram 벤치 위의 그/
   저 사람; but when *the* modifies the unique or
   essentially definite noun, it is usually omitted in
   Korean translation: ~ *sun* t'aeyang 태양,and
   when *the* means a generic group, it is usually
   omitted in Korean translation: ~ *dog is a faithful
   animal.* kae-nŭn ch'ungsilhan tongmurida. 개는 충
   실한 동 물이다. → **A** Cf. *A dog is a faithful animal.*]

+ **theatre** *n.* (*playhouse*) kŭktchang 극장, (*the drama*)
   yŏngŭk 연극.

their *pron.* kŭdŭl-ŭi 그들의.

them *pron.* kŭdŭl-ŭl 그들을, (*to*) kŭdŭl-ege 그들에게.

+ **themselves** *pron.* kŭdŭl chasin 그들 자신.

* **then** *adv.* (*at that time*) kŭttae 그때; (*in that case*)
   kŭrŏ- myŏn 그러면; (*after that*) kŭraesŏ 그래서,
   (*next*) kŭtaŭm-e 그 다음에,kŭrigo-nŭn 그리고는;
   (*moreover*) kŭbakke 그밖에.

+ **theory** *n.* iron 이론; hakssŏl 학설; (*opinion*) ŭigyŏn
   의견.

there *adv.* kŏgi-e 거기에, kŏgi-sŏ 거기서.

+ **therefore** *adv.* kŭrŏmŭro 그러므로, kŭrŏnikka 그러니

까, ttaraso 따라서.

thermometer *n.* ondogye 온도계, hannangye 한난계.

* **these** *pron.* igŏttŭl 이것들. —*adj.* igŏttŭl-ŭi 이것들의: ~ *days* yojŭŭm 요즈음, yosae 요새.

they *pron.* kŭdŭl 그들, kŭdŭl-ŭn 그들은.

* **thick** *adj.* tukkŏun 두꺼운; (*boldfaced*) kulgŭn 굵은, (*rich*) chinhan 진한, (*dense, heavy*) kŏltchukhan 걸쭉한. —*adv.* tukkŏpkke 두껍게, chinhage 진하게.

thief *n.* toduk 도둑, chomdoduk 좀도둑.

thimble *n.* kolmu 골무.

* **thin** *adj.* yalbŭn 얇은; (*fine*) kanŭn 가는, (*slender*) yŏwin 여윈; (*sparse*) tŭmundŭmunhan 드문드문한. —*adv.*

thing *n.* mulgŏn 물건, mulch'e 물체, samul 사물.

* **think** *v.* saenggakhada 생각하다.

+ **third** *n. & adj.* che sam(-ŭi) 제 3(의), setchae(-ŭi) 세째(의).

thirsty *adj.* mongmarŭn〈mokmarŭn 목마른, kaltchŭngnan 갈증난.

thirteen *n. & adj.* yŏlses-ŭi〈yŏlset(-ŭi) 열셋(의), sipsam (-ŭi) 13(의).

thirty *n.* sŏrŭn 서른, samsip 30.

* **this** *adj.* i 이, kŭm 금(今).—*pron.* igŏt 이것.

thorn *n.* kasi 가시.

+ **thoroughly** *adv.* ch'ŏltchŏhi 철저히.

+ **those** *pron.* kŭgŏttŭl 그것들. —*adj.* kŭgŏttŭl-ŭi 그것들의.

+ **though** *adv.* (*however*) kŭrŏna 그러나, (*neverthe-less*) kŭ- rŏch'iman 그렇지만. —*conj.* (*although*) ... ijiman ...이지 만, (*even if*) ...iltchirado ...일지라도. → **despite** *prep.* ˝edo pulguhago ˝에도 불구하고.

thought *n.* sasang 사상, saenggak 생각.

thousand *n. & adj.* ch'ŏn(-ŭi) 천(의): *ten* ~ *man* 만.

+ **thread** *n.* sil 실: *a spool of* ~ silpae 실패.—*v.* sir-ŭl kkweda 실을 꿰다.

+ **threatening** *adj.* wihyŏptchŏk 위협적, (*weather*) hŏmakhan 험악한.

+ **three** *n. & adj.* set(-ŭi) 셋(의), sam(-ŭi) 3(의).

+ **throat** *n.* mok(kumŏng) 목(구멍). *sore* ~ 목이 아프다.

* **through** *prep. & adv.* ¨ŭl t'ongha ¨을 통하여.

+ **throughout** *prep. & adv.* chŏnch'ejŏg-ŭro 전체적으로, to- ch'ŏ-e 도처에, naenae 내내.

+ **throw** *v.* (nae)dŏnjida (내)던지다.

+ **thumb** *n.* ŏmji sonkkarak 엄지 손가락.

thunder *n.* ch'ŏndung 천둥, uroe 우뢰. → **lightning** *n.* pyŏrak 벼락.

Thursday *n.* mogyoil 목요일.

+ **ticket** *n.* p'yo 표; iptchangkkwŏn 입장권: *single/ one-way (bus/train)* ~ p'yŏndo sŭngch'akkwŏn 편도 승차권, *return/roundtrip* ~ wangbokp'yo 왕복표.

tickle *v.* kanjirida 간질이다; (*amuse*) kippŭge hada 기쁘게 하다.

tide *n.* chosu 조수: *ebb* ~ ssŏlmul 썰물. *flood* ~ milmul 밀물; (*tendency*) p'ungjo 풍조.

+ **tidy** *adj.* (*orderly*) chŏngdondoen 정돈된, (*neat*) malssukhan 말쑥한, santtŭthan 산뜻한.

+ **tie** *v.* (*fasten*) maeda 매다, (*bind*) muktta 묶다; (*score*) pigida 비기다. —*n.* nekt'ai 넥타이.

tiger *n.* horangi 호랑이, pŏm 범.

+ **tight** *adj.* (*firm*) tandanhan 단단한, kwak 꽉; (*tense*) p'aengp'aenghan 팽팽한; (*close-fitting*) kkong mannŭn〈kok matnŭn 꼭 맞는.

+ **tightly** *adv.* tandanhi 단단히; kkong〈kkok matkke 꼭 맞게.

\# **time** *n.* sigan 시간, ttae 때.

tin *n.* chusŏk 주석; yangch'ŏl 양철.

+ **tiny** *adj.* chagŭn 작은, chogŭmahan 조그마한.

tip *n.* ① (*top*) kkŭt'ŭmŏri 끄트머리. ② (*money*) t'ip 팁. —*v.* t'ib-ŭl chuda 팁을 주다.

tire *n.* t'aiŏ 타이어. —*v.* (*fatigue*) p'igonhada 피곤하다, (*fore*) siltchŭngnada 싫증나다.

+ **tiring** *adj.* kodoen 고된, chiruhan 지루한.

+ **title** *n.* chemok 제목, ch'ingho 칭호.

\# **to** *prep.* (*up to and including*) ...kkaji ⋯까지; (*place*) ...ŭro ⋯으로, ...e ⋯에; (*purpose*) ...ŭl wihayŏ ⋯을 위하여.

+ **tobacco** *n.* tambae 담배. → **smoking** *n.* hŭbyŏn 흡연.

today *n.* onŭl 오늘; hyŏnjae 현재. onŭllal⟨onŭlnal 오늘날.

+ **toe** *n.* palkkarak 발가락.

* **together** *adv.* hamkke 함께, ta kach'i 다 같이.

+ **toilet** *n.* hwajangsil 화장실. (*lavatory*) pyŏnso 변소.
~ *bowl* pyŏn'gi 변기.

tomorrow *n.* naeil 내일: *the day after* ~ more 모레
/*two days after* ~ kŭlp'i 글피.

tongs *n.* pujŏtkkarak 부젓가락. chipke 집게.

+ **tongue** *n.* hyŏ 혀; (*language*) mal 말: *mother* ~
mogugŏ 모국어.

tonight *n. & adv.* onŭlbam(-e) 오늘밤(에).

* **too** *adv.* (*excessively*) nŏmu 너무. (*also*) ttohan 또한.

+ **tool** *n.* yŏnjang 연장. togu 도구.

tooth *n.* i 이. (*vulgar term*) ippal 이빨.

tooth-brush *n.* ch'isol 치솔.

toothpaste *n.* ch'iyak 치약.

toothpick *n.* issusigae 이쑤시개.

* **top** *n.* ① (*summit*) kkokttaegi 꼭대기. (*head of an
organization*) susŏk 수석. (*first rate*) ŭtŭm 으뜸. ②
(*toy*) p'aengi 팽이.

+ **topic** *n.* hwaje 화제. nonje 논제.

+ **torn** *adj.* tchijŏjin 찢어진.

toss *v.*(*throw*) tŏnjyŏollida 던져올리다. --*n.* (*coin
tossup*) tongjŏndŏnjigi 동전던지기.

+ **total** *n. & adj.* ch'onggye(-ŭi) 총계(의): *the* ~
number ch'ongsu 총수.—*v.* hapkkyehada 합계하다.

+ **totally** *adv.* (*entirely*) wanjŏnhi 완전히. aju 아주.
(*wholly*) chŏntchŏg-ŭro 전적으로.

+ **touch** *v.* (*with hand*) taeda 대다. manjida 만지다.
—*n.* (*contact*) chŏpch'ok 접촉: *be/get in* ~ *with*
...wa yŏllakhada⟨yŏnrakhada …와 연락하다. (*dash*)
p'ilch'i 필치.

+ **touching** *adj.* kamdongsik'inŭn 감동시키는; (*pitiful*)
aech'ŏroun 애처로운.

tough *adj.* (*hard*) tandanhan 단단한. (*strong*) t'ŭnt'ŭnhan 튼튼한; (*sturdy*) wan'ganghan 완강한.

tourist *n.* kwan′gwanggaek 관광객.

* **toward(s)** *prep.*(*direction*) ...tchok-ŭro/e ⋯쪽으로/에; (*about*) tchŭm 쯤, kyŏng 경; (*for*) ...ŭl wihayŏ ⋯을 위하여.

towel *n.* sugŏn 수건, t′awŏl 타월.

+ **town** *n.* ŭp 읍; *big* ~ tohoeji 도회지.

+ **toy** *n.* changnankkam 장난감.

+ **trade** *n.* muyŏk 무역; *international* ~ kuktchemuyŏk 국제 무역, sangŏp 상업. —*v.* changsahada 장사하다; (*barter*) kyohwanhada 교환하다.

+ **traditional** *adj.* chŏnt′ongjŏgin 전통적인.

+ **traffic** *n.* (*transportation*) kyot′ong 교통; ~ *accident* kyot′ongsago 교통사고, ~ *police* kyot′ongkyŏngch′al 교통경찰, ~ *jam* kyot′ongch′ejŭng 교통체증; (*trade*) maemae 매매, kŏrae 거래. —*v.* kŏraehada 거래하다.

+ **train** *n.* kich′a 기차, yŏlch′a 열차, (urban transport) chŏnch′ŏl 전철. —*v.* (*teach*) hullyŏnhada〈hunryŏnhada 훈련하다.

+ **training***n.* hullyŏn〈hunryŏn 훈련, tallyŏn〈tanryŏn 단련, yŏnsŭp 연습, yŏnsu 연수; ~ *school* yŏnsuwŏn 연수원.

translate *v.* pŏnyŏk′ada 번역하다, haesŏk′ada 해석하다.

+ **transport** *v.* (*convey*) susonghada 수송하다.

transportation *n.* kyot′ong 교통. *public* ~ taejung kyot′ong 대중교통.

+ **travel** *n.& v.* yŏhaeng(hada) 여행(하다). ~ *agent* yŏhaengsa 여행사.

tray *n.* chaengban 쟁반; *ash* ~ chaettŏri 재떨이.

treasure *n.* pomul 보물, posŏk 보석, (*wealth*) chaehwa 재화.

+ **treat** *v.* ch′wigŭphada 취급하다; (*hospitality*) taejŏphada 대접하다; (*medical cure*) ch′iryohada 치료하다.

+ **treatment** *n.* taeu 대우, (*medical*) ch′iryo 치료.

+ **tree** *n.* namu 나무; *pine* ~ sonamu 소나무, *ginko* ~ ŭn-haengnamu 은행나무, *willow* ~ pŏdŭnamu 버드나무; sumok 수목.

+ **trial** *n.* (*test*) sido 시도, (*hardship*) siryŏn 시련, (*law*) kongp'an 공판.

+ **trick** n. (*scheme*) kyeryak 계략, (*fraud*) sagi 사기. --v. sogida 속이다.

trip n. yŏhaeng 여행.—v. chalmot tidida 잘못 디디다.

trivial adj. sisihan 시시한, hach'anŭn 하찮은: *a ~ matters* sisihan il 시시한 일.

+ **tropical** adj. yŏlttae-ŭi 열대의. *sub~* ayŏlttae-ŭi 아열대의.

+ **trouble** n. (*worry*) kŏktchŏng 걱정, kŭnsim 근심, (*agony*) konoe 고뇌; (*problem*) munje 문제: *be/get in ~* k'ŭnir-i nada 큰 일이 나다; (*disease*) pyŏng 병: *heart ~*simjangppyŏng 심장병. —v. koerophida 괴롭히다.

+ **trousers** n. (*suit*) (yangbok) paji (양복) 바지.

trout n. songŏ 송어.

truck n. hwamul chadongch'a 화물 자동차, t'ŭrŏk 트럭; sonsure 손수레.

* **true** adj. (*honest*) ch'amdoen 참된, (*genuine*) chinjŏng-ŭi 진정의; (*real*) siltche-ŭi 실제의.

truly adv. chinsillo 진실로; (*loyally*) ch'ungsilhi 충실히; (*correctly*) chŏnghwak'i 정확히.

+ **trunk** n. (*large suitcase*) t'ŭrŏngk'ŭ 트렁크; (*tree*) chulgi 줄기.

+ **trust** n. (*belief*) sinyong 신용; (*responsibility*) sint'ak 신탁.—v. mitta 믿다, sinyonghada 신용하다.

+ **truth** n. chilli〈chinri 진리, chinsilssŏng 진실성, (*fact*) sasil 사실.

* **try** v. sidohada 시도하다, (*attempt, test*) haeboda 해보다, (*endeavor*) noryŏkhada 노력하다; (*law*) chaep'anhada 재판하다.

tub n. t'ong 통: *bath ~* mogyokt'ong 목욕통, yoktcho 욕조.

+ **tube** n. kwan 관, t'yubŭ 튜브.

tuberculosis n. p'yeppyŏng 폐병, kyŏlhaek 결핵.

Tuesday n. hwayoil 화요일.

+ **tune** n. (*melody*) koktcho 곡조, (*tone*) karak 가락. —v. koktcho-rŭl match'uda 곡조를 맞추다.

tunnel *n.* tʼŏnŏl 터널, kul 굴. —*v.* kur-ŭl pʼada 굴을 파다.

turkey *n.* chʼilmyŏnjo 칠면조.

+ **turn** *v.* hoejŏnhada 회전하다, torasŏda 돌아서다; (*curve*)kuburŏjida 구부러지다; (*change*) pyŏnhada 변하다.—*n.* hoejŏn 회전; kulgok 굴곡; pyŏnhwa 변화; (*order*) sunsŏ 순서, chʼarye 차례.

turtle *n.* padagŏbuk 바다거북, kŏbugi 거북이.

+ **twelve** *n.* yŏlttul 열둘, sibi 12.

+ **twenty** *n.* sŭmul 스물, isip 20.

twice *adv.* tu bae-ro 두 배로, tu pŏn 두 번, ihoe 2회.

twin *n.* ssangdungi 쌍둥이, ssangsaenga 쌍생아.

+ **twist** *v.* kkoda 꼬다, (*distort*) waegokhada 왜곡하다,(*wrench*) pitʼŭlda 비틀다,.

* **two** *n.* tul 둘, i 이.—*adj.* tu kae-ŭi 두 개의.

* **type** *n.* (*sort*) hyŏng 형, (*class*) chongnyu〈chongryu 종류, (*model*) yuhyŏng 유형; (*printing*) hwaltcha 활자.—*v.* tʼaipʼŭraitʼŏ-ro chʼida 타이프라이터로 치다.

typewriter *n.* tʼajagi 타자기, tʼaipʼŭraitʼŏ 타이프라이터.

+ **typical** *adj.* chŏnhyŏngjŏgin 전형적인, taepyojŏgin 대표적인.

+ **tyre/tire** *n.* tʼaiŏ 타이어.

≷ U ≷

+ **ugly** *adj.* chʼuakhan 추악한, mot saenggin 못 생긴.

umbrella *n.* (*for rain*) usan 우산, pakchiusan 박쥐우산, (*for sunlight*) yangsan 양산.

+ **unable** *adj.* hal ssu ŏmnŭn〈ŏpnŭn 할 수 없는.

+ **unacceptable** *adj.* padadŭrigi ŏryŏun 받아들이기 어려운.

+ **unattractive** *adj.* maeryŏg-i ŏmnŭn〈ŏpnŭn 매력이 없는, arŭmdaptchi anhŭn 아름답지 않은.

+ **uncertain** *adj.* pulhwakssilhan 불확실한.

uncle *n*. ajŏssi 아저씨, (*sup*.) paekppu 백부, (*inf*.) sukppu 숙부.

+ **unclear** *adj*. maktchi anhŭn 맑지 않은, (*ambiguous*) aemaehan 애매한, (*vague*) punmyŏnghaji anhŭn 분명하지 않은.

+ **uncomfortable** *adj*. pulp'yŏnhan 불편한; pull yuk'waehan 불유쾌한, pulk'waehan 불쾌한.

+ **unconscious** *adj*. muŭisik-ŭi 무의식의.

+ **uncontrolled** *adj*. ŏktche patchi anhŭn 억제 받지 않은.

* **under** *prep. & adv*. arae-e 아래에, mit'-e 밑에.

+ **underground** *adj*. chiha-ŭi 지하의. —*n*. (*Am. subway*) chihach'ŏl 지하철.

+ **underneath** *adv*. arae-ro 아래로.—*prep*. arae-e 아래에.

* **understand** *v*. ihaehada 이해하다, alda 알다.

underwear *n*. sogot 속옷, naeŭi 내의.

+ **undesirable** *adj*. paramjikhaji anhŭn 바람직하지 않은.

undo *v*. wŏnsang-daero hada 원상대로 하다.

undress *v*. os-ŭl pŏtta/pŏtkkida 옷을 벗다/벗기다.

+ **unemployed** *adj*. siltchikhan 실직한. —*n*. sirŏtcha 실업자.

+ **uneven** *adj*. korŭji anhŭn 고르지 않은.

+ **unexpected** *adj*. ttŭppakk-ŭi〈ttŭtpakk-ŭi 뜻밖의, ŭioe-ŭi 의외의, yesangoe-ŭi 예상외의, yegich'i anhŭn 예기치 않은.

+ **unexpectedly** *adv*. ttŭtppakk-e 뜻밖에, yesangoe-ro 예상외로, toryŏnhi 돌연히.

+ **unfair** *adj*. pulgongp'yŏnghan 불공평한, ŏgulhan 억울한

+ **unfavo(u)rable** *adj*. pullihan 불리한: ~ *balance of trade* muyŏk yŏktcho 무역 역조.

+ **unfortunate** *adj*. purunhan 불운한, pulhaenghan 불행한. —*n*. pulhaenghan saram 불행한 사람.

+ **unfriendly** *adj*. (*unlucky*) pulch'injŏlhan 불친절한, uaen〈uaeŏpnŭn 우애없는, paktchŏnghan 박정한.

+ **unhappiness** *n*. pulhaeng 불행.

+ **unhappy** *adj*. (*unlucky*) pulhaenghan 불행한, kipun-i an chohŭn 기분이 안 좋은, (*sad*) sŭlp'ŭn 슬픈.

+ **unhealthy** *adj*. kŏn'ganghaji mothan 건강하지 못한,

mom-iyakhan 몸이 약한.

unification n. t'ongil 통일.

uniform n. chebok 제복. —adj. hanmoyang-ŭi 한모양의, han'gyŏlgat'ŭn 한결같은.

+ **unimportant** adj. chungyohaji anhŭn 중요하지 않은.

+ **uninteresting** adj. hŭngmiŏmnŭn〈hŭngmiŏpnŭn 흥미 없는, chae- miŏmnŭn〈chaemiŏpnŭn 재미없는.

+ **union** n. kyŏlhap 결합; (*labor*) chohap 조합; (*marriage*) kyŏlhon 결혼; (*league*) yŏnhap 연합; (*merge*) t'onghap 통합; (*concord*) ilch'i 일치; (*close union*) hapch'e 합체.

+ **unit** n. tanwi 단위; (*military*) pudae 부대.

+ **united** adj. happyŏnghan 합병한, ilch'ihan 일치한.

+ **university** n. (chonghap) taehakkyo (종합) 대학교.

+ **unjust** adj. olch'i anhŭn 옳지 않은, pujŏnghan 부정한; (*unfair*) pulgongp'yŏnghan 불공평한.

+ **unkind** adj. pulch'injŏlhan 불친절한.

unless conj. …i animyŏn …이 아니면.

+ **unlikely** adj. issŭmjikhaji anhŭn 있음직하지 않은.

+ **unnatural** adj. pujayŏnsŭrŏun 부자연스러운, kigoehan 기괴한.

+ **unnecessary** adj. pulp'iryohan 불필요한, p'iryoŏmnŭn 필요없는.

* **unpleasant** adj. pulyuk'waehan 불유쾌한, yuk'aehajianhŭn 유쾌하지 않은.

+ **unreasonable** adj. pulhamnihan〈pulhaprihan 불합리한; pudang- han 부당한; t'ŏmuniŏmnŭn〈t'ŏmuniŏpnŭn 터무니없는.

+ **unsatisfatory** adj. pulman(jok)sŭrŏun 불만(족)스러운, kidae-e mon〈mot mich'in 기대에 못 미친.

+ **unsteady** adj. puranjŏnghan 불안정한; (*shaking*) hŭndŭllinŭn 흔들리는.

+ **unsuccessful** adj. sŏnggong mothan 성공 못한, silp'aehan 실패한.

+ **untidy** adj. tanjŏngch'i mothan 단정치 못한.

untie v. p'ulda 풀다, kkŭrŭda 끄르다.

* **until** prep. …kkaji …까지.

+ **untrue** *adj.* hŏwi-ŭi 허위의, sasil-kwa tarŭn 사실과 다른.
+ **unusual** *adj.* t'ŭgihan 특이한; (*rare*) tŭmun 드문.
+ **unwanted** *adj.* wŏnhaji annŭn 원하지 않는.
+ **unwilling** *adj.* maŭm naek'iji annŭn 마음 내키지 않는, hago siptchi anhŭn 하고 싶지 않은; sirŏhanŭn 싫어하는.
* **up** *adv. & prep.* ...wi-e …위에 ; ...ŭi wi-ro …의 위로.
  upon *prep.* ...wi-e …위에.
+ **upper** *adj.* witchog-ŭi 위쪽의, sangwi-ŭi 상위의.
+ **upright** *adj.* ttokpparŭn 똑바른; (*honest*) chŏngjik-han 정직한.
* **upset** *v.* twijipŏ ŏptta 뒤집어 엎다.—*n.* chŏnbok 전복.
  upside-down *adj.* twijibŏjin 뒤집어진; chŏndodoen 전도된; ŏngmangin 엉망인.
+ **upwards** *adv.* wi-rŭl hyanghayŏ 위를 향하여, witchog-ŭro 위쪽으로.
  urge *v.* kwŏn'gohada 권고하다, (*push*) chaech'ok'ada 재촉하다, kyŏngnyŏhada〈kyŏkryŏhada 격려하다.
  urinate *v.* sobyŏn boda 소변 보다, ojum nuda 오줌 누다.
  urine *n.* sobyŏn 소변.
  us *pron.* (*accus.*) uri-rŭl 우리를, (*dat.*) uri-ege 우리에게, (*humble*) chŏhi-rŭl/ege 저희를/에게.
use *n.* sayong 사용, yongppŏp 용법. —*v.* ssŭda 쓰다, sayonghada 사용하다, (*take advantage of*) iyong-hada 이용하다. *get ~d to* e iksukhada 에 익숙하다.
+ **useful** *adj.* ssŭlmoinnŭn〈itnŭn 쓸모있는, yuyonghan 유용한.
* **usual** *adj.* pot'ong-ŭi 보통의, p'yŏngso-ŭi 평소의.
* **usually** *adv.* pot'ong 보통, taegae 대개. *as ~* yŏjŏnhi 여전히.

≶ V ≷

vacant *adj.* pin 빈: *a ~ house* pinjip 빈집.

vacation n. hyuga 휴가, (*school*) panghak 방학.

vacuum n. chingong 진공(眞空).

vague adj. magyŏnhan 막연한; (*obscure*) mohohan 모호한.

+ **valid** adj. yuhyohan 유효한; (*authentic*) hwakssilhan 확실한: a ~ *argument* kŭn'gŏ-ga hwakssilhan chujang 근거가 확실 한 주장.

+ **valley** n. koltchagi 골짜기, kyegok 계곡.

+ **valuable** adj. kwijunghan 귀중한; kach'i innŭn〈itnŭn 가치있는. —n. (*pl.*) kwijungp'um 귀중품.

+ **value** n. kach'i 가치: *sense of* ~s 가치관. —v. chonjunghada 존중하다; (*appraise*) p'yŏngkkahada 평가하다.

valve n. p'an 판(瓣): *safety* ~ anjŏnp'an 안전판.

vanish v. sarajida 사라지다, ŏpssŏjida 없어지다.

+ **variety** n. tayang(ssŏng) 다양(성). → **change** n. pyŏnhwa 변화.

+ **various** adj. yŏrŏ kaji-ŭi 여러 가지의, tayanghan 다양한, tach'aeroun 다채로운.

vase n. pyŏng 병, hangari 항아리, tanji 단지; (*for flower*) kkoppyŏng〈kkotpyŏng 꽃병.

+ **vegetable** n. yach'ae 야채, ch'aeso 채소. *mountain* ~ sanch'ae 산채.

* **vehicle** n. ch'aryang 차량, t'al kkŏt 탈 것.

velvet n. udan 우단, pillodŭ 빌로드, pelbet 벨벳.

* **verb** n. (*grammar*) tongsa 동사.

+ **version** n. isŏl 이설(異說), -p'an -판: *modern version* hyŏn- daep'an 현대판. → **translation** n. pŏnyŏk 번역.

+ **vertical** adj. sujig-ŭi 수직의.

very adv. aju 아주, taedanhi 대단히, maeu 매우. --adj. ch'amdaun 참다운, paro kŭ 바로 그.

vest n. (Br. *waistcoat*) chokki 조끼.

+ **video** adj. yŏngsang-ŭi 영상의.—n. video 비디오. → **television** n. telebijŏn 텔레비전.

+ **view** n. (*scene*) kyŏngch'i 경치; (*opinion*) ŭigyŏn 의견. —v. kwanch'alhada 관찰하다.

village *n.* maŭl 마을, ch'ollak⟨chonrak 촌락.

vinegar *n.* ch'o 초, sikch'o 식초.

+ **violence** *n.* p'ongnyŏk⟨p'okryŏk 폭력, (*outrage*) p'ok-haeng 폭행.

+ **violent** *adj.* (*furious*) maengnyŏlhan⟨maengryŏlhan 맹렬한; p'ongnyŏk⟨p'okryŏktchŏk 폭력적, nanp'ok-han 난폭한; (*unnatural*) pujayŏnhan 부자연한: *a ~ death* pyŏnsa 변사.

violet *n.* orangk'aekkot 오랑캐꽃, chebikkot 제비꽃.

+ **violin** *n.* paiŏllin 바이얼린.

virgin *n.* ch'ŏnyŏ 처녀.—*adj.* sun'gyŏlhan 순결한; (*un- trodden*) chŏnin midab-ŭi 전인 미답의.

+ **visit** *n. & v.* pangmun(hada) 방문(하다).

visitor *n.* pangmungaek 방문객, sonnim 손님.

vita *n.* (*personal summary*) iryŏkssŏ 이력서.

vocabulary *n.* ŏhwi 어휘, yongŏ 용어.

* **voice** *n.* mokssori 목소리, ŭmsŏng 음성.

volcano *n.* hwasan 화산.

+ **volume** *n.* (*quantity*) yang 양, (*bulk, size*) pup'i 부 피, k'ŭgi 크기, (*book*) kwŏn 권, (*voice*) sŏngnyang⟨sŏngryang 성량.

vomit *v.* (*spew*) t'ohada 토하다, keuda 게우다, naeppumtta 내뿜다.—*n.* kut'o 구토.

+ **vote** *n. & v.* t'up'yo(hada) 투표(하다).

vulgar *adj.* (*base*) pich'ŏnhan 비천한, chŏsok'an 저속한; (*common people's*) sŏmin-ŭi 서민의.

≦ W ≧

+ **wage** *n.* imgŭm 임금(賃金): *a ~ raise* imgŭm insang 임금 인상.—*v.* (*carry on*) haenghada 행하다.

+ **waist** *n.* hŏri 허리, yobu 요부(腰部).

+ **wait** *v.* kidarida 기다리다, (*serve*) sijungdŭlda 시중들다.

waiter *n.* weit'ŏ 웨이터, kŭpssa 급사.

waiting room *n.* taehapssil 대합실.

waitress *n.* weit'ŭresŭ 웨이트레스, yŏgŭp 여급, .

+ **wake** *v.* kkaeda 깨다, (*awaken*) kkaeuda 깨우다.

+ **walk** *n.* kŏrŭm 걸음, pohaeng 보행; (*stroll*) sanch'aek 산책; (*path*) podo 보도.—*v.* kŏrŏgada 걸어가다, kŏtta 걷다.

+ **wall** *n.* pyŏk 벽, tam 담; (*pl. city walls*) sŏngbyŏk 성벽.

wallet *n.* chigap 지갑, tontchumŏni 돈주머니.

wander *v.* hemaeda 헤매다, kir-ŭl ilt'a 길을 잃다.

* **want** *n.* p'iryo 필요; (*lack*) kyŏlp'ip 결핍. —*v.* wŏnhada 원하다; (*need*) p'iryohada 필요하다.

+ **war** *n.* chŏnjaeng 전쟁, (*fighting*) t'ujaeng 투쟁.

+ **warm** *adj.* ttattŭthan 따뜻한. —*v.* ttattŭthagehada 따뜻하게 하다, teuda 데우다. → **hot** *adj.* tŏun 더운.

+ **warn** *v.* kyŏnggohada 경고하다, t'airŭda 타이르드.

+ **warning** *n.* kyŏnggo 경고, hun'gye 훈계.

+ **wash** *n.* set'ak 세탁. —*v.* (*self*) ssitta 씻다; (*clothes*) set'akhada 세탁하다.

+ **washing** *n.* ppallae 빨래: ~ *machine* set'akki 세탁기.

+ **waste** *adj.* hwangp'yehan 황폐한. —*v.* nangbihada 낭비하다. —*n.* nangbi 낭비; (~ *land*) hwangmuji 황무지.

wastebasket *n.* hyujit'ong 휴지통.

+ **watch** *n.* (sonmok)šigye (손목)시계; (*look out*) kamsi 감시. —*v.* chik'yŏboda 지켜보다, poda 보다: ~ *TV/a game* tellebijŏn/undongkyŏnggi-rŭl poda 텔리비전/운동경기를 보다.

* **water** *n.* mul 물.—*v.* mur-ŭl chuda 물을 주다, kŭpssuhada 급수하다. ~ *melon* subak 수박. *bottled* ~ saengsu 생수. *mineral* ~ yakssu 약수. *tap* ~ sudomul 수도물.

waterfall *n.* p'okp'o 폭포.

watermelon *n.* subak 수박.

waterproof *adj.* pangsu-ŭi 방수의. —*n.* (*clothes*) pangsubok 방수복.

+ **wave** *n.* mulkkyŏl 물결, p'ado 파도. —*v.* mulkkyŏlch'ida 물결치다, pŏllŏgida 펄럭이다.

\# **way** n. kil 길; (*method*) pangbŏp 방법; (*custom*) sŭpkkwan 습관.

+ **we** *pron*. uri-ga/nŭn 우리가/는.

+ **weak** *adj*. yakhan 약한, kanyalp'ŭn 가냘픈.

+ **weakness** n. (*strength*) hŏyak 허약, (*insufficiency*) pagyak 박약, yaktchŏm 약점.

+ **wealth** n. chaesan 재산; (*riches*) pu 부(富); (*abundance*)p'ungjok 풍족.

  wealthy *adj*. chaesan-i manŭn 재산이 많은, puyuhan 부유한: *a ~ person* puja 부자.

+ **weapon** n. mugi 무기, pygi 병기.

+ **wear** v. (*clothes*) iptta 입다. ~ *out* haeŏjida 해어지다.

+ **weather** n. nalssi 날씨, ilgi 일기.

  weather forecast n. ilgi yebo 일기 예보.

  weave v. tchada 짜다, ttŭda 뜨다; yŏktta 엮다.

  Wednesday n. suyoil 수요일.

  weed n. chapch'o 잡초. —v. p'ur-ŭl ppoptta 풀을 뽑다.

+ **week** n. chu 주(週), chugan 주간, iltchuil 일주일.

  weep v. ulda 울다, sŭlp'ŏhada 슬퍼하다.

  weigh v. muge-rŭl talda 무게를 달다; (*consider*) koryŏhada 고려하다; (*importance)* chungyosihada 중요시하다.

+ **weight** n. muge 무게; chungyossŏng 중요성.

  welcome n. & v. hwanyŏng(hada) 환영(하다).

* **well** ① n. umul 우물. —v. sosanaoda 솟아나오다. ② *adv*.chal 잘, hullyunghi 훌륭히.

+ **well-known** *adj*. yumyŏnghan 유명한, allyŏjin 알려진.

+ **west** n. (*direction*) sŏtchok 서쪽, (*region*) sŏbu 서부: *the West* sŏyang/sŏgu 서양/서구. —*adj*. sŏtchog-ŭi 서쪽의. —*adv*. sŏtchog-ŭro 서쪽으로.

+ **western** *adj*. sŏtchog-ŭi 서쪽의, sŏyang-ŭi 서양의.

+ **wet** *adj*. chŏjŭn 젖은.—v. chŏkssida 적시다.

  whale n. korae 고래.

\# **what** *adj*. musŭn 무슨, ŏttŏn 어떤. —*pron*. muŏt 무엇.

+ **whatever** *adj*. (*any ... that*) ŏnŭ ...irado 어느 …이라도. —*pron*. (*no matter what*) ŏnŭ kŏsi ...rado 어느 것이 … 라도; (*all that*) mu modu 무엇이든(지) 모두,

(*any that*) muŏsina 무엇이나.
+ **wheat** *n.* mil 밀, somaek 소맥.
+ **wheel** *n.* pak'wi 바퀴.
# **when** *adv.* ŏnje 언제, ...hal ttae ⋯할 때. —*conj.* ttae-e 때에. —*n.* (*time*) ttae 때; kyŏngu 경우.
  whenever *conj.* (*at whatever time*) ...hal ttae-nŭn ŏnjena ⋯할 때는 언제나; (*no matter when*) ŏnje ...hadŏrado 언제 ⋯하더라도.
* **where** *adv.* ŏdi-sŏ 어디서, ŏdi-e 어디에, ŏdi-ro 어디로.
  wherever *conj.* ŏdidŭn(ji) 어디든(지).
+ **whether** *conj.* ...inji ŏttŏnji ⋯인지 어떤지: *He asked ~ I would help.* kŭ-nŭn towajul kkŏsinji ŏttŏnji-rŭl naege murŏtta. 그는 도와줄 것인지 어떤지를 내게 물었다.
# **which** *adj. & pron.* ŏnŭ (kŏt) 어느 (것).
* **while** *n.* tongan 동안: *for a ~* chamsi tongan 잠시 동안. —*conj.* ⋯hanŭn tongan-e ⋯하는 동안에.
  whip *n.* ch'aetchik 채찍.—*v.* maejilhada 매질하다.
+ **whisky** *n.* wisŭk'i 위스키.
  whisper *n.* soksagim 속삭임, kwienmal⟨kwietmal 귀엣말. —*v.* sokssagida 속삭이다.
  whistle *n.* horŭragi 호르라기, hogak 호각; hwip'aram 휘파 람, hwisŭl 휘슬. —*v.* (*mouth*) hwip'aram-ŭl pulda 휘파람 을 불다; kijŏg-ŭl ullida 기적을 울리다.
* **white** *adj.* hayan 하얀, hŭin 흰, (*pale*) ch'angbaekhan 창백 한. —*n.* hŭinsaek 흰색; hŭinot 흰옷. *W~ House* paegakkwan 백악관.
# **who** *pron.* (*subjective case*) nuga 누가, (*non-subjective case*) nugu 누구, ŏttŏn saram 어떤 사람.
+ **whole** *n. & adj.* chŏnch'e(-ŭi) 전체(의), chŏnpu(-ŭi) 전부 (의).
  wholesale *adj.* tomaehanŭn 도매하는.—*n.* tomae 도매.
+ **whom** *pron.* nugu-rŭl 누구를: *for ~?* nugu-rŭl wihayŏ 누구를 위하여? *from ~?* nugu-egesŏ 누구에게서? *to ~?* nuguege 누구에게?
* **whose** *pron.* nugu-ŭi 누구의, (*honorific*) ŏnŭ pun-ŭi 어느 분의.

+ **why** *adv.* wae 왜, ŏtchaesŏ 어째서. —*int.* ŏmŏ 어머.
+ **wicked** *adj.* nappŭn 나쁜, (*evil*) saakhan 사악한.
+ **wide** *adj.* nŏlbŭn 넓은.—*adv.* nŏlkke 넓게.
+ **wife** *n.* (*own*) anae 아내, manura 마누라, chipssaram 집사람; (*another person's*) puin 부인.
+ **wild** *adj.* yasaeng-ŭi 야생의, (*furious*) nanp'okhan 난폭한. —*n.* (*desert, wilderness*) hwangya 황야, hwangmuji 황무지. → **savage** *adj.* migaehan 미개한;
* **will** *aux. v.* (*be going to*) ...hal kkŏsida …할 것이다, (*be willing to*) ...hagetta …하겠다, ...hal chaktchŏng-ida …할 작정이다, (*promise*) ...halkkeyo …할께요. —*n.* (*desire*) ŭiyok 의욕, (*determination*) ŭiji 의지, (*testament*) yuŏn(tchang) 유언(장). —*v.* (*bequeath*) yu- ŏnhada 유언하다.
+ **willing** *adj.* kikkŏi …hanŭn 기꺼이 …하는.
  willow *n.* pŏdŭl 버들, pŏdŭnamu 버드나무.
+ **win** *v.* (*races*) igida 이기다, sŭngni⟨sŭngrihada 승리하다, (*gain*) tta 얻다.
+ **wind** ① *n.* param 바람. ② *v.* kamtta 감다.
+ **window** *n.* ch'ang 창, ch'angmun 창문.
+ **wine** *n.* (*from grapes*) p'odoju 포도주, (*from rice*) makkŏlli 막걸리. → **alcohol** *n.* sul 술.
+ **wing** *n.* (*of bird*) nalgae 날개; (*of political party*) -ik/p'a -익(翼)/파: *the left* ~ chwaik/p'a 좌익/파.
  wink *n.* nun-ŭl kkambakgŏrim 눈을 깜박거림, wingk'ŭ 윙크. —*v.* kkambakgŏrida 눈을 깜박거리다, nuntchit'ada 눈짓하다.
+ **winner** *n.* sŭngnija⟨sŭngrija 승리자, igin saram 이긴 사람.
+ **winter** *n.* kyŏul 겨울, tonggye 동계(冬季).
  wipe *v.* ssisŏnaeda 씻어내다, taktta 닦다.
+ **wire** *n.* ch'ŏlssa 철사; (*telegram*) chŏnbo 전보. —*v.* chŏnbo- rŭl ch'ida 전보를 치다.
  wise *adj.* hyŏnmyŏnghan 현명한, sŭlgiroun 슬기로운; ŏjin 어진.
+ **wish** *n.* sowŏn 소원, somang 소망. —*v.* (*desire*) hŭi- manghada 희망하다, parada 바라다.

\# **with** *prep.* ...wa hamkke/kach'i〈kat'i ···와 함께/같이, ...rang ···랑, ...ro ···로.

+ **within** *adv.* an-e 안에, sog-e 속에 ; chip an-e 집 안에.

* **without** *prep.* ŏpsi 없이, ...ŭi pakk-esŏ ···의 밖에서.
  —*adv.* pakk-ŭn 밖은. → **outside** *n.* oebu 외부.

  wolf *n.* nŭktae 늑대, iri 이리.

* **woman** *n.* yŏja 여자, puin 부인.

  wonder *n.* nollaum 놀라움, kyŏngi 경이. —*v.* kyŏngt'anhada 경탄하다.

  wonderful *adj.* nollalmanhan 놀랄만한; (*remarkable*) kŭnsahan 근사한, hullyunghan 훌륭한.

* **wood** *n.* namu 나무, (*timber*) moktchae 목재, (*forest*) sup숲.

+ **wooden** *adj.* namu-ŭi 나무의, moktchae-ŭi 목재의.

+ **wool** *n.* yangt'ŏl 양털, (yang)mo (양)모, mojik 모직.

* **word** *n.* tanŏ 단어, (*remark*) mal 말; (*promise*) yakssok 약속.

* **work** n. il 일, (*labor*) nodong 노동; (*employment*) chiktchang 직장, (*occupation*) chigŏp 직업; (*art, literature*) chak- p'um 작품; (*pl. factory*) kongjang 공장: *iron ~s* chech'ŏlgongjang 제철공장. --v. ilhada 일하다, (*labor*) nodonghada 노동하다.

+ **worker** *n.* ilkkun 일꾼, nodongja 노동자.

+ **world** *n.* (*physical*) segye 세계; (*abstract*) sesang 세상; (*mankind*) sesang saramdŭl 세상 사람들; (*sphere*) punya 분야. ~*wide* segyejŏgin 세계적인.

  worm *n.* pŏlle 벌레: *earth* ~ chirŏngi 지렁이.

+ **worry** *v.* (*fret*) kŏktchŏnghada 걱정하다; (*bother*) koerop- hida 괴롭히다. —*n.* kŏktchŏng 걱정.

+ **worrying** *adj.* kwich'anŭn 귀찮은, sŏnggasin 성가신.

  worse *adj.* poda nappŭn 보다 나쁜, ak'wadoen 악화된.
  —*adv.* poda nappŭge 보다 나쁘게.

  worst *adj.* kajang nappŭn 가장 나쁜.

+ **worth** *n. & adj.* kach'i(innŭn〈itnŭn) 가치(있는): *thirty thousand wŏn* ~ sam man wŏn ŏch'i 삼만원 어치.

+ **worthwhile** *adj.* ···hal gach'i-ga innŭn〈itnŭn ···할 가치가 있는.

* **would** *aux. v.* ﹍hal kkŏsida ﹍할 것이다.

\+ **wound** *n. & v.* pusang(hada) 부상(하다).

\+ **woven** *adj.* tchayŏjin 짜여진.

\+ **wrap** *v.* (*pack*) ssada 싸다, (*wear*) turŭda 두르다, (*roll*)malda 말다.

wreck *n.* (*shipwreck*) nanp'asŏn 난파선; (*ruin*) p'agoe 파괴. —*v.* nanp'ahada 난파하다; (*destroy*) p'agoehada 파괴하다.

wrestling *n.* resŭlling 레슬링, ssirŭm 씨름.

wrinkle *n.* churŭm 주름, kugimssal 구김살. —*v.* churŭmjaptta 주름잡다.

\+ **wrist** *n.* sonmok 손목, p'almok 팔목.

* **write** *v.* ssŭda 쓰다, kirokhada 기록하다, chip'ilhada 집필하다.

\+ **writer** *n.* chŏja 저자, chakka 작가, munp'ilga 문필가.

* **wrong** *adj.* nappŭn 나쁜, pujŏkttanghan 부적당한; t'ŭllin 틀린. —*adv.* nappŭge 나쁘게, t'ŭllige 틀리게. —*n.* pudang 부당, chalmot 잘못. —*v.* pujŏng-ŭl chŏjirŭda 부정을 저지르다.

≤ Y ≥

yard *n.* ① madang 마당. ② (*measure*) yadŭ 야드.

yawn *n. & v.* hap'um(hada) 하품(하다).

\+ **year** *n.* hae 해, (*in compounds*) nyŏn 년: *last* ~ changnyŏn- ⟨chaknyŏn 작년/chinan hae 지난해, *next* ~ naenyŏn 내년, *this* ~ kŭmnyŏn 금년/olhae 올해, *every* ~ haemada 해마다, *academic* ~ hangnyŏndo⟨haknyŏndo 학년도; (*pl.*) yŏllyŏng⟨yŏnryŏng 연령.

yell *n.* koham 고함. —*v.* oech'ida 외치다.

\+ **yellow** *adj.* noran 노란. —*n.* noransaek 노란색, hwangsaek 황색.

+ **yes** *adv.* ne 네, ye 예, kŭrŏssŭmnida〈kŭrŏtsŭpnida 그
  렇습니다.
  yesterday *n.* ŏje 어제, ŏjŏkke 어저께: *the day before*
  ~ kŭjŏkke 그저께.
+ **yet** *adv.* ajik 아직. —*conj.* kŭrŏm-edo pulguhago 그럼
  에도 불구하고. → **usual** *ad.* yŏjŏnhi 여전히
you *pron.* tangsin(dŭl) 당신(들), (*to inferiors*)
  chane(dŭl) 자네(들), nŏhŭi(dŭl) 너희(들).
+ **young** *adj.* chŏlmŭn 젊은, ŏrin 어린.
# **your** *pron.* tangsin(dŭl)-ŭi 당신(들)의, (*to inferiors*)
  chane(dŭl)-ŭi 자네(들)의, nŏ(hŭidŭl)-ŭi 너(희들)의,
  (contraction of 너의) ne 네.
* **yourself** *pron.* tangsin chasin 당신 자신, ne chasin 네
  자신.
  youth *n.* ch'ŏngch'un 청춘, chŏlmŭm 젊음.

≤ Z ≥

zero *n.* yŏng 영(零), kong 공.
zipper *n.* chip'ŏ 지퍼, (*slide fastener*) chak'ŭ 자크.
zither *n.* (*Korean*) kayagŭm 가야금, kŏmun'go 거문고.
zone *n.* chiyŏk 지역, chidae 지대, (*in compounds*) tae
  대(帶): *safety* ~ anjŏn chidae 안전 지대.
zoo *n.* tongmulwŏn 동물원.

Difficulties with Korean Grammar

I. Verbs

Irregular Verbs

Although most verbs [in a broad sense, including descriptive verbs, i.e. adjectives] in Korean follow a regular pattern of conjugation, several categories of irregular verbs are difficult for many learners of Korean. These verbs can be classified into the following six categories: "ㄷ" verbs, "ㄹ" dropping verbs, "ㅂ" verbs, "ㅅ" dropping verbs, "르" verbs, and "ㅎ" dropping verbs. These changes affect the stem of the "아/어 form" of the verb only, except in the category of "ㄹ" dropping verbs. In this category, "ㄹ" is dropped from the stem in the "-ㅂ 니다" form and is maintained in the "아/어 form." In the following examples, the honorific form of the verb (stem + 시다) is formed instead of the "(으)면 form" for the "ㄹ" dropping category.

"ㄷ" Verbs

When verb stems ending in "ㄷ" are followed by a vowel, the "ㄷ" changes to "ㄹ" as in the following examples:

걷다	걸어요	걸으면	걷습니다
깨닫다	깨달아요	깨달으면	깨닫습니다
듣다	들어요	들으면	듣습니다
묻다	물어요	물으면	묻습니다
싣다	실어요	실으면	싣습니다

Note that the following verbs do not fit this rule: 닫 다, 믿다, 받다, 얻다, etc. These verbs follow regular rules (e.g., 닫다 → 닫아요).

"ㄹ" Dropping Verbs

When verb stems ending in "ㄹ" are followed by a "ㄴ", "ㅂ" or "ㅅ", "ㄹ" is dropped from the stem as in the following examples:

놀다	놉니다	노시다	놀아요
들다	듭니다	드시다	들어요
만들다	만듭니다	만드시다	만들어요
살다	삽니다	사시다	살아요
알다	압니다	아시다	알아요
열다	엽니다	여시다	열어요
울다	웁니다	우시다	울어요
팔다	팝니다	파시다	팔아요

There are no exceptions to this rule.

"ㅂ" Verbs

When verb stems ending in "ㅂ" are followed by a vowel, "ㅂ" is dropped from the stem. The compound vowel "와" is added to stems ending in "오", whereas the compound vowel "워" is added to stems ending in all other vowcls.

반갑다	반가워요	반가우면
고맙다	고마워요	고마우면
아름답다	아름다워요	아름다우면
돕다	도와요	도우면
곱다	고와요	고우면
맵다	매워요	매우면

Note that the following verbs do not fit this rule: 씹다, 업다, 입다, 잡다, etc. These verbs follow regular rules (e.g., 입다 → 입어요, 입으면).

"ㅅ" Dropping Verbs

When verb stems ending in "ㅅ" are followed by a vowel, the "ㅅ" is dropped from the stem and is replaced by "아" if the vowel in the stem ends in "아" or "오", and "어" if the vowel in the stem ends in any other vowel.

굿다	그어요	그으면
낫다	나아요	나으면
붓다	부어요	부으면
잇다	이어요	이으면
짓다	지어요	지으면

Note that the following verbs do not follow this rule: 벗다, 빼앗다, 씻다, 웃다, etc. These verbs follow regular rules (e.g., 웃다 → 웃어요, 웃으면).

"르" Verbs

When verbs stems ending in "르" are followed by "아" or "어", "으" is dropped from the stem and the "ㄹ" is attached to the end of the stem that precedes the part of the stem containing the "—"; the "아" and "어" are change to "라" and "러" respectively as in the following examples:

고르다	골라요	고르면
기르다	길러요	기르면
나르다	날라요	나르면
다르다	달라요	다르면
부르다	불러요	부르면
빠르다	빨라요	빠르면
서두르다	둘러요	서두르면
서투르다	서툴러요	서투르면
오르다	올라요	오르면
흐르다	흘러요	흐르면

Note that the following verbs do not follow this rule: 따르다, 치르다, etc. These verbs follow regular rules (e.g., 따르다 → 따라요, 따르면).

"ㅎ" Dropping Verbs

When verb stems ending in "ㅎ" are followed by "ㄴ", "ㄹ", "ㅁ", "ㅅ" or "ㅇ", "ㅎ" is dropped from the stem. Verbs in this category are mainly adjectival verbs.

어떻다	어떤	어떨까요?	어떠면	어떠세요	어때
이렇다	이런				이래
그렇다	그런	그럴까요?	그러면	그러세요	그래
저렇다	저런				저래
까맣다	까만				까매
노랗다	노란				노래
빨갛다	빨간				빨개
파랗다	파란				파래
하얗다	하얀				하얘

Note that conjugations for the other words in this chart follow the same pattern as in the examples ("어떻다" and "그렇다"), but these are not given because they are used rather infrequently. The following verbs do not follow this rule: 낳다, 넣다, 놓다, 닿다, etc. These verbs follow regular rules (놓다 → 놓아요).

Irregular verbs appear in the "dictionary form" (stem + 다) in this dictionary.

Auxiliary and Compound Verbs

Korean has a large number of auxiliary verbs that are used by adding the auxiliary verb to the "아/어 form" of the first verb. Auxiliary verbs intensify or modify the meaning of the main verb by giving the meaning greater specificity. Compound verbs, on the other hand, take on a new meaning that combines elements from both parts of the compound. The following chart is a list of auxiliary verbs (with an example) that are commonly juxtaposed to the main verb in "아/어 form" stem and written with a space in between the two verbs:

Nuance/Meaning of Auxiliary Verbs

Attempt   보다

"김치를 들어/드셔 보셨어요?"
(Have you tried (to eat) kimch'i?)

Completion   버리다, 내다

"미안해. 그 책을 잊어 버렸어."
(I'm sorry, but I forgot the book.)
"일을 다 해 냈으니까 내일 좀 쉬려고 그래요."
(I've finished everything,
so I'm going to take it easy tomorrow.)

Giving/Receiving   주(시)다, 드리다

"언제든지 도와 드리겠습니다."
(I'll help you whenever you want.)
"선생님께서 나한테 추천서를 써 주셨어."
(Prof. (name) wrote a recommendation for me.)

Maintaining/Keeping   두다, 가지다

"제가 정리 다 할 테니까 그대로 놓아 두세요."
(Please leave it as it is. I'll take care of it.)
"한국어를 배워 가지고 다시 오세요."
(Learn Korean and come again.)

Movement   가다, 오다

"공사가 잘 되어 갑니다."
(The construction is going well.)
"준비를 많이 해 오셨네요."
(Wow, you've done a lot of preparation.)

Placing/Preparing   놓다

"지금은 휴가 철이니까 미리 예약을 해 놓고 가는 것이 좋을 것 같아요."
(I think it would be a good idea if you made a
reservation in advance because it's peak season now.)

Repetition   쌓다, 대다

"며칠동안 원고를 써 대니까 정신이 없어요"
(I'm worn out because I've been doing
so much writing recently.)

Common Compound Verbs

The following is a list of commonly used compound verbs that take on a new meaning by com-
bining elements of the first and second verb, which
are written without a space in between:

가져가다	take
가져오다	bring
갈아입다	change clothes
갈아타다	change (method of transportation)
나오다	come out, appear, attend, originate from
넘어가다	go over, pass
돌아가다	go back, leave, pass away
돌아보다	look back, reflect on
돌아서다	turn around
돌아오다	come back, return
들어가다	go in, enter
들어오다	come in, enter
바라보다	look up at
알려주다(드리다)	inform
알아듣다	understand
올라가다	rise, go up
일어나다	get up
해내다	accomplish

381

받아들이다	accept
나가다	go out, leave, move out, sell
알아보다	inquire, check, look into

Some commonly used compound verbs are listed as separate entries ins this dictionary.

Stative Verbs

The auxiliary verb "있다" is placed after the "아/어 form" of many verbs to describe a particular state or condition. These verbs are used to emphasize that the effects of the action of the first verb are continuing at the time of speaking. Examples:

"우리 동생이 거기 서 있어요."
(My [younger] brother is standing over there.)
"김선생님께서 벌써 와 계세요."
(Prof. Kim has already come.)

The use of "있다" in the stative form should not be confused with the "있다" in the present progressive tense (verb stem + 고 있다). This form can be used with various tenses and forms of the verb.

Stative verbs are not listed as separate entries in this dictionary.

Passive Verbs

The passive in Korean differs from English in that it is generally used for situations that lack a clear performer (agent) of the action of the verb. The passive is thus limited to situations which describe a general state that did not result from active intervention on the part of the agent. The following chart is describes how the passive is formed:

Suffix	Examples
-기-	안기다, 끊기다, 감기다, 빼앗기다
-리-	들리다, 물리다, 풀리다, 빨리다, 밀리다, 열리다, 걸리다, 눌리다
-이-	꺾이다, 놓이다, 섞이다, 쌓이다, 보이다, 쓰이다, 파이다
-히-	먹히다, 닫히다, 업히다, 잡히다, 뽑히다, 얹히다, 묻히다, 밟히다

Uses of the passive are illustrated in the following examples:

"오늘은 맑아서 관악산이 잘 보입니다." (Mt. Kwanak is clearly visible [can be seen well] because it's clear today.)

"눈이 길거리에 많이 쌓였어요." (The street is full of snow [Snow is piled up in the street].)

Verbs that are formed by the stem of the "아/어 form" and "지다" are often considered as passive verbs. The meaning of verbs formed in this way includes a stronger emphasis on the process of evolution to the state describe in the verb than do strictly passive verbs. For this reason, they are excluded from the discussion here on passive verbs.

With certain passive verbs, it is possible grammatically to include the agent in the sentence as in "범인이 경찰에게 잡혔어요." (The criminal was caught by the police.). This type of sentence, however, often sounds awkward; in such cases, the active verb is preferred.

Causative Verbs

Korean contains a class of verbs called causative verbs that are used to indicate that the action of the verb is being caused by the direct intervention of the subject of the clause or sentence. Certain verbs in this group are the transitive equivalents of intransitive verbs (verbs that do not take an object). The following chart illustrates the formation of passive verbs:

Suffix	Examples
-이-	죽이다, 먹이다, 속이다, 높이다, 보이다, 줄이다, 붙이다
-히-	익히다, 앉히다, 좁히다, 넓히다, 밝히다, 읽히다
-리-	날리다, 돌리다, 울리다, 살리다, 얼리다, 놀리다, 알리다
-기-	웃기다, 남기다, 숨기다, 감기다, 벗기다, 맡기다
-우-	지우다, 깨우다, 채우다, 비우다, 세우다, 새우다
-구-	떨구다, 돋구다, 일구다
-추-	낮추다, 늦추다, 맞추다

The use of the causative form is best illustrated by the difference between "죽다" (to die) and "죽이다" (to kill [to cause to die]) as used in the following sentences: "고양이가 죽었어요" (The cat died) and "고양이를 죽였어요" (Someone killed the cat). The verb in the second sentence is in the causative form, thus indicating that someone caused the action of the cat's death.

The causative can also be formed in two other ways: one way is the form "-게 하다" and the other is the use of "시키다" after a noun. "-게 하다" means "make + verb"; for example, "슬프게 하다" (to make sad, to sadden) or "따뜻하게 하다" (to heat up [to make warm]). This form is commonly used with adjectives. "시키다" means "strong causation" or "forced causation" as in the following examples: "어학 연습을 많이 시켜야 되요." (We need to have [make] our students learn languages more) or "우리 고향에 오시면, 구경을 시켜 드릴게요. (I'll show you around if you come to my hometown).

Certain verbs with a causative form can also be used with the "-게 하다" form. In such cases, the nuance varies somewhat. The causative form contains a clearer reference to the subject of the sentence as the cause of the action, whereas the "-게 하다" form allows for a broader interpretation of the subjects role in causing the action. Notice the following examples:

Causative Verbs: "학생에게 이 책을 읽혔어요." (I made my students read this book)
"-게 하다" Form: "학생에게 이 책을 읽게 했어요" (I had my students read this book)

The second sentence could mean that the teacher required that his or her students read the book or that the teacher suggested that his or her students read the book.

Most of the commonly used causative forms are listed in this dictionary, either as separate entries or under the entry from the equivalent non-causative or non-transitive verb.

Ⅱ. Adverbs

Adverb Formation

Korean contains a number of adverbs (words that modify a verb or an entire sentence) that are derived from nouns, verbs, or adjectives by changing the ending of the word. There are generally five major ways to change a noun, verb or adjective into an adverb or adverbial form:

Type	Example
1. Verb stem + "이"	없이(없다), 같이(같다), 깊이(깊다)

많이(많다), 가까이(가깝다)

　　　Verbs stems in this group come from "non-하다" verbs, verbs that end in "ㅂ", verbs that end in "ㅅ", and repeating verb stems.

2. "하다" adjective　　　상당히(상당하다), 안녕히(안녕하다),
   stem + "히"　　　　충분히 (충분하다)

　　　Native Korean and Sino-Korean adjectives that end in "하다" belong to this group.

3. "르/ㄹ" verbs + "리"　　빨리(빨리), 다르다(달리), 멀리(멀다)

4. Noun + "로"　　　정말로(정말), 실로(실), 때때로(때때)

5. Word repetition　　　줄줄, 반짝반짝, 구석구석

　　　Adverbs are formed by repeating a word that represents a particular feeling or concept by the sound of the language. This type of adverb intensifies the meaning of the verb and is thus used mainly for emphasis.

　　　Some of the most commonly used adverbs that are formed from nouns, verbs, or adjectives are listed as separate entries in this dictionary. These are in addition to adverbs that are not formed from other parts of speech.

Regular Adverbial Conjugation

　　　There are also "adverbial forms" that are derived from a regular verb conjugation. The ending -게 can be added to all verb and adjective stems to create an adverbial form of the verb that is equivalent to an adverb.

Verb/Adjective stem + -게　　크게(크다), 바쁘게(바쁘다),
　　　　　　　　　　　　다르게(다르다), 맛있게(맛있다)

These adverbial forms generally focus on the way the action of the main verb of the sentence takes place.

Ⅲ. Speech Levels and Honorifics

Speech Levels in Korean

Koreans alter the formality of their speech depending on the context of the conversation. Regular patterns in these changes make up several broadly defined levels of language usage in Korean.

These speech levels can be divided into the following four broad categories: the intimate (아/어), the informal (아/어요), the informal polite (-[으]세요), and the formal (-[으]ㅂ니다). The sentence "어디 가십니까?" will be used to illustrate this difference. The intimate level is used between siblings, husband and wife, close friends and associates of the same age or younger (어디 가?). The informal level is used between people who know each other, but may not be intimate friends or when there is a slight difference in age (어디 가요?). The informal polite level is used between people who know each other, but who need to show respect because of age or social status to each other by making use of honorific forms (어디 가세요?). This form is also common between strangers, particularly younger people and women. The formal level is used in formal settings and in situations that demand a high level of respect for the addressee (어디 가십니까?). Men often use this level when speaking with strangers. The plain form of the verb (-다) is used in written Korean (journalism, academic writing, novels, etc.), but rarely in speech.

Many speakers mix features from one language level twith those from another idiosyncratic in different contexts, but moves toward informal and intimate ways of speaking require the consent of the speaker and the addressee to avoid being rude.

Formality vs. politeness

For proper usage, it is necessary to distinguish between formality and politeness. Formality is a characteristic of a situation, often with 'andience'. In formal situations, one uses formal sentence final endings such as *-pnita*. Politeness is a deferential attitude held by the speaker towards the hearer or the referent. To be polite to the hearer use polite sentence-final endings such as *-seyo* or *-pnita* and humble words (see below). To be polite to the referent, use honorific *-si-* and honorific words (see below).

Age and the Korean Language

A person's age has a profound influence over language use in Korea. Age influences not only the type of language level that is used in a conversation, but who can say what, when. The greater the age gap between the speakers, the greater respect the younger person needs to show to the older person. Thus, in addition to using proper honorific words and verb endings, the younger person should show a deferential attitude toward the older person by not asserting his or her ideas in the conversation and by not taking control of the flow of the conversation. These tendencies are greater when there is greater social distance or greater differences in social status.

Older people, on the one hand, may use the informal speech level to younger people. This varies greatly from person to person, but older people generally use the informal speech level when the age gap is large and when there is relatively little social distance. University professors, for example, often use the informal speech level to their students for this reason, and parents use the most intimate informal speech level to their children. This is not considered rude in Korean because the informal speech level reflects avuncular intimacy which is comforting to younger people. Among strangers in an urban setting, however, the use of the informal speech level, regardless of age, is generally rude.

The importance of age in Korean personal relationships is reflected in the question, "How old are you?" The answer to this question helps to clarify the relationship between the speakers, which determines which level of language should be used.

Honorific Words

Some words in Korean have a special honorific equivalent that is used, along with appropriate honorific verb endings, to convey proper respect for the addressee. Age, social status, and social distance determine how much respect needs to be expressed to the addressee in a given situation.

Situations that require the use of honorific words vary greatly from one to another, but generally the speaker should address the addressee in honorifics if there is a difference in either age, social status, or emotional distance. For example, children are expected to use honorifics to their parents out of deference for parental authority. Two strangers who are similar in age and social status would also use honorifics so as not to offend each other. Honorific forms are also used in talking about someone in the third person (the referent) who should be respected, such as one of the addressee's parents or superior at work.

The following is a list of such expressions:

	Common Word	Honorific
Nouns		
	말	말씀
	나이	연세, 춘추
	밥	진지
	병	병환
	집	댁
	이름	성함
	이	치아
Pronouns		
	그 사람	그 분
	자기	당신(께서)
Verbs		
	자다	주무시다
	먹다	잡수시다/드시다
	있다	계시다
	죽다	돌아가시다
Particles		
	-이/가	-께서
	-는/은	-께서는
	-에게	-께
	-에게서	-께서

Humble Words

Korean has a few humble words which are used to lower the speaker and elevate the addressee in formal polite situations. Two humble pronouns are commonly used: "저" for "나" and "저희" for "우리." Most formal and informal polite conversations require the use of "저" instead of "나", especially if there is a difference in age between or among the speakers. "저희" is used to lower the level of a particular group that the speaker represents, such as the family or place of employment, but is less common than "저" in everyday speech. The word "말씀" is also used as a humble word to refer to what the speaker is saying to the addressee. In this case, 말씀 is often combined with the verb "드리다" to become "말씀 드리다" (literally: "I give [honorific] you my humble words"). The following is a list of humble words:

Common Word	Humble Form
나	저
우리	저희
주다	드리다
묻다	여쭙다
보다	뵙다

"있다/없다" for Possession and Existence

The words "있다" and "없다" are used for the English word "to have" in many situations in Korean. "있다" and "없다" refer to possession of a material object. These words are also used to describe relationships between people. Examples of this use of "있다" and "없다" are as follows: "차 있어요?" (Do you have a car?), or "형제가 몇이 있어요?" (How many brothers and sisters do you have?).

The last example can also be described as "있다" and "없다" referring to the existence of human beings and things: "차고에 차가 있다" (The car is in the garage) or "한국은 중국과 일본 사이에 있다" (Korea is between China and Japan).

In honorifics, "possession" and "existence" are differentiated by two different forms respectively: "있으시다" vs. "계시다"; "없으시다" vs. "안계시다." "있으시다" and "없으시다" are used in situations in which respect should be shown to the owner of a particular object; for example, "컴퓨터 있으세요?" (Do you have [honorific] a computer?).

The other honorific form of "있다," "계시다" is used to refer to the existence of the addressee or to people associated with the addressee; for example, "교수님 어디 계세요?" (Where's the professor?).

Ⅳ. Numbers and Dates

Native Korean Numbers and Sino-Korean Numbers

Korean has two sets of numbers: numbers of an indigenous Korean origin ("native Korean numbers") and numbers that originated from Chinese characters ("Sino-Korean numbers"). The native Korean numbers are as follows (native Korean numbers beyond 99 are now obsolete):

1	하나	10	열
2	둘	20	스물
3	셋	30	서른
4	넷	40	마흔
5	다섯	50	쉰
6	여섯	60	예순
7	일곱	70	일흔
8	여덟	80	여든
9	아홉	90	아흔

Numbers such as 25 or 76 are formed in the following way: "스물 다섯" for 25 and "일흔 여섯" for 76. Native Korean numbers are used mainly in counting things and in counting someone's age.

Sino-Korean numbers are as follows:

1	일	20	이십
2	이	30	삼십
3	삼	100	백
4	사	1,000	천
5	오	10,000	만
6	육	100,000	십만
7	칠	1,000,000	백만
8	팔	10,000,000	천만
9	구	100,000,000	억
10	십	1,000,000,000	십억

Numbers such as 37 and 84 are formed in the following way: "삼십칠" for 37 and "팔십사" for 84. Sino-Korean numbers are used in dates, in mathematics, with weights and measurements, and in counting money.

Counting Words with Native Korean Numbers

Korean has special counting words that are combined with Korean numbers in counting. The following counting words are used exclusively in with native Korean numbers in counting:

개	general for various shapes
명	for people
분	honorific for people
잔	for cups or glasses of liquid
병	for bottles of liquid
권	for books (different titles)
부	for copies of the same thing
통	for letters
장	for flat things such as paper and photographs
쪽	for pieces of a larger thing
갑	for package of something such as cigarettes
마리	for animals
벌	for clothes, sets of things
켤레	for pairs of things, such as socks and shoes
자루	for long narrow things
그릇	for bowls of food such as rice
대	for vehicles
채	for detached houses
평	traditional Korean counting word for area

These words follow native Korean numbers as in "물 한 잔" (one glass of water) (Note: "하나" changes to "한", "둘" to "두", "셋" to "세", "넷" to "네" when followed by a counting word). The above list contains the most commonly used counting words only.

Counting Words with Sino-Korean Numbers

Although most counting words are used with native Korean numbers, several are used with Sino-Korean numbers. A common combination is a the counting word "개" used in front of another word to create a new counting word that is used with Sino-Korean numbers. For example, "개" in front of the word "국" (country) "개국" becomes the counting word for countries; "개" in front of "국어" (languages) "개국어" becomes counting word for languages. Sino-Korean numbers are also used with words of the metric system and counters of Chinese origin such as "인분" (portion) "2인분" (a portion for two) and "세", the Sino-Korean counter for age (Native Korean numbers with the counter "살", however, are more common for counting age, particularly younger ages).

Dates and Counting Periods of Time

Dates in Korean use the Sino-Korean numbers with words for year, month, and day, in that order. The following example is typical: 1994년 12월 31일. At times, this is also written as 1994.12.31.

Numbers of years are referred to in Sino-Korean numbers as in "삼 년" "three years." Both native Korean numbers and Sino-Korean numbers are used respective counters, "달" (native Korean) and "개월" (Sino-Korean) to count numbers of months as in "세 달" (three months) and "삼 개월" (native Korean numbers tend to be used for smaller numbers of months).

[Weeks are counted in Sino-Korean numbers with the counter "주일" as in "이주일" (two weeks). Days are counted in the following native Korean numbers:

1	하루	4	나흘
2	이틀	5	닷새

3	사흘	6	엿새
7	이레	9	아흐레
8	여드레	10	열흘

Native Korean numbers are generally used for smaller numbers of days; Sino-Korean numbers tend to be used for larger numbers of days and almost exclusively for numbers of days beyond ten. When Sino-Korean numbers are used, the word "일" (day) becomes the counter for days as in "십 일" (ten days). In counting any of the above periods of time, the suffixes "간" and "동안" may be placed behind the words "년", "달/개월", "주일", or "하루(etc.)/일" to focus more sharply on the period of time.

V. Sino-Korean Words

Often a pair of synonyms are distinguished by etymology: one is of native Korean and one of Sino-Korean origin. The Sino-Korean word ismore formal, academic and (morphologically) productive, while the native Korean word is more casual, familiar and less productive. Also Sino-Korean words tend to be used more in written Korean, native words in spoken Korean. It would be helpful for students to know, that Sino-Korean words tend to be pedantic, precise and (semantically) sterile, whereas native words tend to be vulgar, emotional and laden with overtones of extra semantic function.

VI. Contracted Forms

Contracted forms are common in speaking and in written Korean, particularly in novels. Most contracted forms are a combination of a noun or pronoun and a particle. The following is a list of the most common contracted forms:

난	나는
내	나의
넌	너는
네	너의
-대(요)	-다고 그래(요)
뭘	무엇을
에선	-에서는
이건	이것은
이게	이것이
-재(요)	-자고 그래(요)
전	저는
제	저의
-케	-게 하다

In speech, contracted forms are generally used in more informal language; they should be used with care in formal situations. The print media occasionally uses contracted forms in headlines to draw attention to the article.

VII. Word Order

Unlike English, Korean can be said to be a head-final language. This means that the head of any phrase (e. g. the main verb in a verb phrase or noun in a noun phrase) comes at the end of the phrase. In particular, Korean modifying words and phrases come 'before' the word they modify, instead of after them, as in English. English has prepositions; Korean has suffixes which function as 'post-positions.'

Eng.	the BOOK	that is [on the desk]	
Kor.	책상 위에	있는	책
	[desk-on]	[is-MOD]	BOOK

Eng.	RUNS	quickly
Kor.	빨리	뛴다
	quickly	RUNS

The basic word order for English is S-V-O: the subject is followed by the verb, which is followed by the direct object: "I eat the apple." The basic order of a Korean sentence is S-O-V: "I the apple eat."

The main predicate of a complex Korean sentence always comes at the end, whereas in English it almost always comes near the beginning, immediately after the subject.

  I STUDY Korean because it's interesting.
  재미있기 때문에 한국말을 공부한다
  [interesting-is] because [Korean-OBJ] STUDY

In general, the structure of an English sentence begins with the broadest concepts and fills in the details later, while a Korean sentence give the reader a lot of details at the beginning and then places them in context.

A rabbit is a small animal with big ears.
  토끼는 몸이 작고 귀가 큰
  [rabbit-TOP] [body-SUBJ] [small-AND] [ear-SUBJ] [big-MOD]
  동물이다
  [animal-is]

Usage Notes

1. Terms of Address (-님)

Terms of address are very important in conveying a sense respect for other people in Korean society. Terms of address are generally taken from the title of a person's position in a company or organization. For example, if some one is a director of a research institute "연구소", the suffix "장" is attached to the last syllable of "연구소", -소 to form the word "소장", "director." To show appropriate respect in addressing the director "소장" directly, the suffix "-님" is added to the word "소장" to form "소장님."

2. Figurative Use of Kinship Terms (형, 누나, 오빠, 언니)

Koreans often use kinship terms to refer to older friends and senior associates in an organization that are close to each other. Words such as "형" and "누나" and "오빠" and "언니" follow the person's given name. For example, a man would call a friend of his named "철수", who is one year older, "철수형"; a woman would call the same person "철수 오빠" (Women at university often use the word "형" instead of "오빠"). Older friends and associates, however, do not use word "동생" after a person's name. Women often use the word "언니" as a general term of address for women who look like they are similar in age to the speaker.

3. Words for "You"

Korean does not have a word that is equivalent to the English word for "you", which is used to the addressee regardless of the context. The word "당신" (you [polite]) is often used between husband and wife. "당신" is often considered a personal attack in other situations. The informal "너" (you [informal]) is used only among close friends of the same age and an older person to a younger person (inside and outside the family); it should be used with care. In general, overt second person reference is avoided wherever possible.

In more formal social settings, Koreans use a variety of titles and kinship terms to refer to the addressee. The honorific suffix "-님" is often used to show respect to the addressee as in the following example "과장님, 어떻게 생각하십니까? (What do you think [Section chief, what do you think?]). In this case, the word "section chief" is being used as "you" to refer to the addressee. The context of the sentence usually clarifies whether the reference is to the second person addressee or a third person.

The suffix "씨" is also used after the addressee's full name to refer to the addressee. This form is polite, but the use of title + "-님" is preferred when the speaker knows the addressee's title or position in society. In summary, names and/or titles, with or without honorific suffixes, are often used for "you".

4. The use of "우리"

Koreans often use the word "우리" (our) or "저희" (our [humble]) for "my". This reflects the importance of the group in Korean society. The use of "내" (my) or "제" (my [humble]) sounds unnatural to Koreans, particularly in reference to people or group-based organizations (schools, companies, etc). Examples: "우리 누나가 고등학교에서 가르치고 있어요" (My sister teaches at a high school) or "우리 집사람이 다음주에 한국에 돌아올 것 같아요" (My wife is coming back to Korea next week). While the Korean expression is literally "our wife", English speakers often use the singular my in the same case. "내" and "제" can be used to refer to material things that are not or cannot be possessed by or shared with a group. "내 열쇠가 없어졌어요." (My key disappeared).

5. Difference between "-아/어+서", "-(으)니까", "-기 때문에", and "(으)므로"

There are four major ways of expressing "because" in Korean, but each way differs somewhat in meaning and usage.

The "아/어 form"+서 is used to indicate a subjective and loose connection between two clauses. The event or state in the first clause causes the event or state in the second clause; for example, "날씨가 좋아서 어디 나가고 싶어요" (I want to go out somewhere because the weather's nice).

"-(으)니까" is used to indicate the speaker's subjective judgment about cause and effect. This form is stronger than "아/어 form"+서 because it emphasizes the cause or reason, stated in the first clause, of the event or state in the second clause. An example is: "지금 바쁘니까 오후에 전화해 줄래?" (Can you call me this afternoon because I'm busy right now?).

"-기 때문에" also expresses a clear cause and effect relationship, but from a more objective stance. Rather than emphasizing the cause from a subjective point of view, this form places emphasis on the logical relationship of the cause, stated in the first clause, and the effect or state in the second clause; for example, "서울은 사람이 너무 많기 때문에 집 값이 비싸요" (Housing is expensive in Seoul because it is overcrowded).

"(으)므로" is similar in meaning to the "-기 때문에", but is mainly used in writing or formal situations, such as academic presentations.

6. Difference between "-에게(서)" and "-한테(서)"

The particles "-에게" and "-한테" both mean "to" in reference to a person other living creature. The difference between these two words is stylistic: "-에게" is the more formal form and should be used when speaking in a formal situation, whereas "-한테" is more colloquial and should be used only in informal situations. "-에게" is preferred in writing, except for informal letters. The same distinction applies to "-에게서" and "-한테서".

7. Use of the Plural Suffix "-들"

Plurality of nouns in Korean is indicated by the plural suffix "-들". Unlike English, the plural suffix is optional in situations in which the plurality of the subject is understood. For example, in "our students [the students in our department]" would be expressed more commonly as "우리 학생", rather than as "우리 학생들". When a definite pronoun, such as "이", "그", and "저", is placed before the noun, "-들" is required to indicate plurality because "그 학생" (that student) refers to only one student, whereas "그 학생들" (those students) refers to a group of several students.

8. Difference between Nominalizing Forms "-(으)ㅁ", "-기", and "-는 것"

There are three major ways to turn a verb into a noun in Korean. "-(으)ㅁ" is used to indicate abstract ideas and states of being. It is also used at the end of a clause or sentence in public announcements to make the sentence sound more formal and objective, such as "전화카드 있음" (Telephone Cards for Sale). This form is used more commonly in writing than in speech because of its formality. Certain commonly used nouns, however, are derived from this form: "걸음" (walk, pace), "웃음" (laugh, smile), "아픔" (pain), "잠" (sleep), "기쁨" (feelings of gladness), "슬픔" (sadness).

"-기" is used in situations where a certain degree of the action of the verb is preserved. The use of this form resembles the use of the gerund form in English to some degree; for example, "날씨가 도우니까 공부하기가 어려워요" (It's hard to study today because it's hot [Studying is hard today because it's hot]). This form is also used in a variety of patterns that make use of a verb that has been changed into a noun.

"-는 것" is similar to "-기" in meaning, but is used in situations in which the speaker wants to focus on the action of the verb, but which require a nominalized form grammatically. For example, "이번 토요일 에 등산 가는 것이 어때요?" (How about going mountain climbing this Saturday?).

9. Difference between "일" and "것"

The words "일" and "것" are often confused, particularly in relation to various grammatical structures. "일" means "an event", "a thing", "an errand", "something to do", and "an experience", and is often combined with the verbs "있다/없다". The context of the sentence determines which of these meanings is appropriate; for example, "내일 할 일이 많이 없을 것 같아 요" (I don't think that I'll be very busy tomorrow [I don't think that I'll have much business to attend to tomorrow]).

"것", on the other hand, means "thing", "thing to do", and "fact", and it is used more frequently than "일" in various grammatical patterns. "것" is more abstract than "일"; for example, "말씀 드릴 것이 있습니다" (There's something I'd like to tell you).

10. Cultural Differences

Korean Age : In the traditional Korean way of counting age, a baby is one year old at birth, and becomes one year older every New Year. Thus everyone born in the same year is considered the same age.

For more precise distinctions in legal and other contexts Koreans have adopted the Western way of counting age as well, with a baby turning one year old on its first birthday and gaining one year of age on every subsequent birthday

When Western age is referred to, the expression denoting the age is generally prefixed by *man: man vǒsǒs sal, man sip p'alse*.

In addition to "How are old", Korean speakers often ask "What year were you born?" or "What's your sign?"(see "Cycle of years")

Lunar calender (birthdays, holidays) : Birthdays and many holidays are traditionally celebrated accoring to the lunar calendar (umnyǒk) rather than the solar calendar *(yangnyǒk)*.

Lunar holidays include Lunar New Year's (kujǒng, sǒllal: 1/1), Buddha's birthday (puch'ǒnim osin nal:4/8), and the Harvest Moon Festival (ch'usǒk: 8/15)

Cycle of years(tti) : In Korea, as in China and Japan, each year is associated with one of a cycle of twelve animals (see chart). These are called *tti*, and a person born in the year of a particular animal is believed to have certain characteristics or to be a good or bad match for someone born in another year.

The twelve animals correspond to the twelve "earthly" signs (*chiji*), and each year is further associated with one of a cycle of the "heavenly" signs (*chǒnkan*). Each cycle repeats in order, so every 60 years the same combination of two symbols reoccurs.

Commonly Used Prefixes and Suffixes

Knowledge of commonly used native Korean and Sino-Korean prefixes and suffixes helps greatly in learning new words. The following is a list of commonly used prefixes and suffixes:

Native Korean Prefixes

맨–	bare, naked, just as is	맨발	barefoot
한–	big, main	한겨울	the middle of winter
헛–	false, wrong, empty	헛소문	groundless rumor

Sino-Korean Prefixes

과–	excessive	과소비	excessive consumption
구–	old, ancient	구식	old-fashioned
대–	big, great	대금	a large sum of money
대–	against, opposite	대립	confrontation
무–	no-, non-, -less, ir-	무관심	no interest
미–	not yet, un-, in-	미정	undecided
반–	anti-	반전	anti-war
부–	non-, in-, un-, ir-	부도덕	immorality
불–	non-, in-, un-, ir-	불편하다	uncomfortable
비–	un-, non-, a-	비민주적	undemocratic
신–	new	신도시	new town
재–	re-	재활용	recycle
전–	all, entire, whole	전세계	the whole world
전–	former, ex-	전대통령	former president
특–	special, particular	특집	special edition

Native Korean Suffixes

-껏	degree, extent(utmost)	정성껏	with utmost sincerity
-꾼	doer/performer(of something)	장사꾼	merchant ("wheeler-dealer")
-살이	way of living	고생살이	a life of hardship
-씨	mode	말씨	accent
-장이	type of behavior	멋장이	stylish person
-질	activity	낚시질	fishing
-짓	act, gesture, behavior	나쁜 짓	bad behavior

Sino-Korean Suffixes

-가	professional	소설가	writer
-계	area of activity	미술계	art world ("scene")
-과	department	국문과	Department of Korean Literature
-관	building	도서관	library
-구	entrance, exit	비상구	emergency exit
-기	records, annals	일기	diary
-당	large room, auditorium	강당	auditorium
-대	generation	30대	one's thirties
-사	company	여행사	travel agency
-성	nature, possibility	필요성	necessity
-소	place	파출소	police station
-식	style, method	한국식	Korean-style
-실	room	휴게실	lounge
-원	academy, institute	연수원	training institute
-적	-ic, -ical, like	사회적	social
-제	system, institution	실명제	real-name system (banking)
-화	-ization	기계화	mechanization

APPENDIX

I. 기초 숙어 Basic Idioms

고개(를) 들다
[(Unconscious thoughts) come to mind, gradually grow stronger and reach consciousness]

구멍(이) 나다/뚫리다 [A setback occurs]

구멍(을) 메우다   [Make up for a weakness]

군침(을) 삼키다   [Covet someone else's possessions]

국수(를)/떡(을) 먹다 [(Someone else) gets married]

금(이) 가다
[A relationship (between people) becomes strained]

금을 긋다/넘지 않다 [Limit (something)]

기름을 짜다   [Forcibly take away possessions, etc.]

김(이) 새다   [Be disappointed, dispirited]

깡통/쪽발(을) 차다 [Beg, come to ruin]

나팔(을) 불다   [Advertise (some fact) widely and noisily]

날(이) 새다   [(Something) goes wrong]

눈(을) 감다   [(Someone) dies: lit. close one's eyes]

눈(을) 감아주다   [Feign ignorance, look the other way]

눈(을) 뜨다
[Come to understand the logic (of something)]

눈(을) 붙이다　　　[(Briefly) fall asleep]

눈(이) 어둡다/멀다　[Lose one's judgment (because of greed)]

다리(를) 걸다/걸치다 [Have a connection or relationship]

다리(를) 놓다　　　[Function as an intermediary]

다리(를) (쭉) 뻗다 [Be relieved, get along comfortably]

담(을) 쌓다　　　　[Be uninterested, make a boundary, be out of touch cut off relations]

덜미(가) 잡히다　　[Have someone take advantage of one's weak point]

덜미를 누르다/짚다 [Urge strongly, take to task]

등(을) 돌리다　　　[Cut off relations with (someone)]

등(을) 치다　　　　[Take away (someone's) possessions through force]

머리(를) 깎다　　　[Become a Buddhist monk]

머리(를) 들다　　　[Gain confidence]

목(을) 매(달)다　　[Be extremely tenacious (about work, etc.); lit. hang (a person/oneself) by the neck]

목(을) 자르다　　　[Fire (someone); lit. cut one's throat/head]

목(이) 잘리다　　　[Be fired, given the sack]

몸(을) 던지다　　　[be absorbed (in one's work)]

무릎(을) 꿇다   [Give in, surrender; lit. kneel down]

무릎(을) 꿇리다   [Make (someone) surrender; lit. make one kneel down]

문(을) 닫다   [Close up (a shop), quit (a business)]

물 샐 틈(이) 없다   [Have no weakness]

물(을) 들이다   [Influence (someone else's) thoughts, actions, habits, etc.]

물(이) 들다   [Thoughts, actions, habits, etc. come to be alike]

미역국(을) 먹다   [Fail an examination]

바가지(를) 긁다   [Nitpick, find fault with (someone)]

바람(을) 맞다   [Have a promise broken (by someone)]

발목(을) 잡다   [Get into an awkward situation]

발목(이) 잡히다   [Be unable to get out of an awkward situation]

발에 채이다   [Be scattered widely here and there]

발(을) 들여놓다   [Get involved (in something)]

발(을) 묶다   [Have (someone) completely in one's power]

발(을) 빼다   [Sever connections with, quit]

발(이) 묶이다   [Be totally unable to move]

발(이) 저리다   [Be unjust, unfair]

배(가) 아프다 [Be green with envy; lit. have a stomach-ache]

배(를) 아파하다 [Make (someone) jealous]

벼락(을) 맞다 [Get punished; lit. be struck by lightning]

벼락이 떨어지다 [(Someone) gets punished; lit. thunderbolts strike]

변죽(을) 울리다 [Hint (at), allude (to)]

보따리(를) 싸다 [Completely quit something (one) had been involved in]

불을 끄다 [Resolve an urgent matter]

비행기(를) 태우다 [Pump (someone) up, encourage]

사족(을) 못 쓰다 [Be completely charmed and in (someone's) power]

산통(을) 깨다 [Ruin something that had been planned]

손(을) 내밀다/벌리다 [Get help]

손(을) 놓다 [Quit (something)]

손(을) 대다 [Become involved (in a matter)]

손(을) 들다 [Give up]

손(을) 떼다 [Quit (something)]

손(을) 뻗치다 [Try to become involved in (something)]

손(을) 쓰다 [Take action]

409

손(을) 잡다 　　　　[Act in concert, cooperate (with)]

손이 크다 　　　　[Be generous with expenses]

시집(을) 가다 　　　[(A woman) gets married]

시집(을) 보내다 　　[Marry off (a woman)]

신물(이) 나다 　　　[Get tired of (something)]

싹수가 노랗다/누렇다 [Have no future, be hopeless]

아픈 데를/곳을 찌르다/건드리다 [Bring up (someone's) weak point, etc.]

오리발(을) 내밀다 　[Talk about unrelated matters]

오지랖이 넓다 　　　[Meddle in many things]

이(가) 갈리다 　　　[Become enraged]

이(를) 갈다 　　　　[Harbor a grudge]

이를 악물다 　　　　[Endure hardship]

입맛(이) 당기다/동하다 [Desire, covet (something)]

입맛(이) 떨어지다 　[Lose interest, have no interest (in something)]

입맛(이) 쓰다 　　　[Be distressed, have things not work out the way one wants]

입(을) 다물다 　　　[Keep a secret]

입(을) 떼다 / 열다 [Give away a secret]

입을 (틀어)막다/봉하다 [Make (someone) keep a secret]

입(을) 씻다   [Seize a benefit for onself and feign ignorance about it]

자리(가) 잡히다   [Order, discipline, system, etc. takes shape]

자리(를) 잡다   [An emotion, thought, or the like becomes fixed in one's mind]

잠(을) 자다   [Remain unused, unutilized]

재(를) 뿌리다   [Spread abuse, slander]

주름(을) 잡다   [Take control of]

죽(을) 쑤다   [Ruin, spoil something]

큰소리(를) 치다   [Be pompous, boastful]

틈(이) 나다/생기다/벌어지다
     [A relationship (between people) sours]

파리(를) 날리다   [Business, work, etc. goes badly]

피(를) 빨다   [Exploit, use (someone)]

학(질)(을) 떼다   [Grow tired of, get out of a distressing task]

호박씨(를) 까다   [Furtively do something bad]

Ⅱ. 속담과 성어 (Proverbs and Set Phrases)

1. 가까운 이웃이 먼 일가보다 낫다.
   A near neighbour is better than a far-dwelling kinsman.

2. 가난이 죄다.
   Poverty is the mother of crime.

3. 가는 세월 오는 백발.
   Time and tide wait for no man.

4. 가랑이가 찢어지게 가난하다.
   1) As poor as a church mouse.
   2) As poor as Job.

5. 같은 값이면 다홍치마.
   Better a castle of bones than of stones.

6. 개같이 벌어서 정승같이 쓴다.
   Narrow gathered, widely spent.

7. 개구리 올챙이 적 생각 못한다.
   The parish priest forgets that ever he has been holy water (parish) clerk.

8. 걷기도 전에 뛰려 한다.
   Children learn to creep ere they can go.

9. 고생 끝에 낙이 온다.
   No pleasure without pain (repentance).

10. 고슴도치도 제 새끼는 함함하다고 한다.
    1) The owl thinks her own young fairest.
    2) The crow thinks her own birds fairest.

11. 곡식 이삭은 잘 될수록 고개를 숙인다.

The more noble, the more humble.

12. 공자 앞에 문자 쓴다.
   Don't teach your grandmother to suck eggs.

13. 공중누각.
   To build castle in the air.

14. 구르는 돌은 이끼가 끼지 않는다.
   A rolling stone gathers no moss.

15. 구슬이 서말이라도 꿰어야 보배.
   No pains, no gains.

16. 궁하면 통한다.
   1) Where one door shuts, another opens.
   2) Necessity is the mother of invention.

17. 꿩 먹고 알 먹는다.
   1) To catch two pigeons with one bean.
   2) To kill two birds with one stone/bolt.

18. 귀한 자식 매로 키워라.
   Spare the rod and spoil the child.

19. 그림의 떡.
   Pie in the sky.

20. 금강산도 식후경.
   1) A loaf of bread is better than the song of
      many birds.
   2) Better are meals many than one too merry.

21. 나쁜 소문은 빨리 퍼진다.
   Bad news travels fast.

22. 남의 떡이 더 커 보인다.

1) The grass is always greener on the other side of the fence.
2) The apples on the other side of the wall are the sweetest.
3) Our neighbour's ground yields better corn than ours.

23. 남의 짐이 가벼워 보인다.
Every horse/one thinks his pack/sack heaviest.

24. 남의 집 금송아지가 우리집 송아지만 못하다.
A feather in hand is better than a bird in the air.

25. 남의 흉이 한 가지면 제 흉은 열 가지라.
The eye that sees all things else sees not itself.

26. 낫 놓고 기역자도 모른다.
He cannot say B to a battledore.

27. 낮말은 새가 듣고 밤말은 쥐가 듣는다.
1) Fields have eyes, and woods have ears.
2) Walls have ears.

28. 내 것도 내 것, 네 것도 내 것.
What's mine is mine and what is yours is mine.

29. 누울 자리 보고 발 뻗는다.
1) Stretch your arm no further than your sleeve will reach.
2) Everyone stretchs his legs according to the length of his coverlet.

30. 누워서 떡 먹기.
As easy as lying.

31. 눈 뜬 장님.

1) There is no blindness like ignorance.
2) As blind as a bat.
3) Blind as a mole.
4) Blind as an owl.

32. 다다익선.
The more the merrier.

33. 달도 차면 기운다.
Every flow has its ebb.

34. 닭 벼슬이 될 망정 쇠꼬리는 되지 마라.
1) Better be the head of a dog (ass, mouse, fox, lizard) than the tail of a lion.
2) Better be first in a village than second at Rome.
3) Better be the head of the yeomanry than the tail of the gentry.

35. 대장간에 식칼이 논다.
1) None more bare than to shoemaker's wife and the smith's mare.
2) The shoemaker's son always goes barefoot.

36. 떡 줄 놈은 생각도 않는데 김칫국 찾는다.
1) Don't spread the cloth till the pot begins to boil.
2) Make not your sauce, before you have caught the fish.

37. 도둑이 제 발 저리다.
1) He that has a great nose thinks everybody is speaking of it.
2) He that commits a fault thinks everyone speaks of it.

38. 돈에 침 뱉는 놈 없다.

Money is welcome, though it comes in a dirty clout.

39. 돈이 돈을 번다.
    1) Money draws money.
    2) Money makes/breeds money.

40. 돈이 장사라.
    1) Money is power.
    2) Money will do anything.
    3) What will not money do?

41. 돌다리도 두들겨 보고 건너라.
    Look before you leap.

42. 되로 주고 말로 받는다.
    To sow the wind and reap the whirlwind.

43. 돼지 목에 진주.
    To cast pearl before swine.

44. 두 손뼉이 맞아야 소리가 난다.
    It takes two to make a quarrel.

45. 뜻이 있는 곳에 길이 있다.
    Where there's a will, there's a way.

46. 등잔 밑이 어둡다.
    1) You must go into the country to hear what news at London.
    2) Go abroad and you'll hear news of home.
    3) If you will learn news, you must go to the oven or the mill.

47. 등 치고 간 내 먹는다.
    To give one roast meat, and beat him with the spit.

48. 마른 하늘에 날벼락 친다.
   The unexpected always happens.

49. 마이동풍.
   1) Talk to the wind.
   2) To sing psalms to a dead horse.
   3) To whistle psalms to the taffrail.
   4) Knock at a deaf man's door.

50. 모로 가도 서울만 가면 된다.
   The end justifies the means.

51. 모르면 약이요, 아는 게 병이다.
   1) Where ignorance is bliss, 'tis folly to be wise.
   2) Ignorance is the peace of life.

52. 목구멍이 포도청.
   1) The devil dances in an empty pocket.
   2) Need makes the old wife trot.
   3) Poverty is an enemy to good manners.

53. 무소식이 희소식.
   No news is good news.

54. 물에 빠지면 지푸라기라도 잡는다.
   A drowning man will catch at a straw.

55. 물에 빠진 놈 건져 놓으니까 내 봇짐 내라 한다.
   1) Save a stranger from the sea, and he'll turn
      your enemy.
   2) Save a thief from the gallows and he'll cut
      your throat.

56. 믿는 도끼에 발등 찍힌다.
   1) In trust is treason.
   2) Trust makes way for treachery.
   3) Trust is the mother of deceit.

57. 바늘 구멍으로 황소 바람이 들어온다.
   1) A small leak will sink a great ship.
   2) A little fire burns up a great deal of corn.
   3) Of a small spark, a great fire.

58. 바늘 도둑이 소 도둑이 된다.
   1) He that will steal a pin, will steal a better thing.
   2) He that will steal an egg will steal an ox.

59. 발 없는 말이 천리 간다.
   Give a lie twenty-four hours' start, and you can never overtake it.

60. 백문이 불여일견.
   1) Seeing is believing.
   2) One picture is worth a thousand words.

61. 백짓장도 맞들면 낮다.
   1) Many hands make light work.
   2) Many a little makes a mickle.

62. 번개가 잦으면 천둥을 친다.
   There is lightning lightly before thunder.

63. 법은 멀고 주먹은 가깝다.
   Where drums beat, laws are silent.

64. 보기 좋은 떡이 먹기도 좋다.
   Names and natures do often agree.

65. 부뚜막의 소금도 집어 넣어야 짜다.
   No pains, no gains.

66. 부전자전.
   Like father, like son.

67. 빈대 잡으려 초가삼간 태운다.
   1) To burn one's house to get rid of the mice.
   2) Don't cut off your nose to spite your fault.

68. 빈 수레가 요란하다.
   1) Empty vessels make the greatest sound.
   2) Shallow streams/waters make most din.

69. 빛 좋은 개 살구.
   1) Never judge from appearance.
   2) Appearance are deceptive.
   3) It is not the beard that makes the philosophers.

70. 사공이 많으면 배가 산으로 간다.
   Too many cooks spoil the broth.

71. 사람은 죽으면 이름을 남기고 호랑이는 죽어서 가죽을 남긴
   다.
   He who leaves the fame of good works after him
   does not die.

72. 사촌이 땅을 샀나, 배는 왜 앓아?
   An envious man waxes with the fatness of his
   neighbour.

73. 사후 약방문.
   1) Prescription after death.
   2) While men go after a leech, the body is buried.

74. 산 입에 거미줄 치랴.
   Everyday brings its bread with it.

75. 상부상조.
   1) Claw me, and I'll claw thee.
   2) Scratch me and I'll scratch you.
   3) Roll my log and I'll toll yours.

76. 설상가상.
   Out of the frying pan into the fire.

77. 세 살 먹은 버릇이 여든 간다.
   1) Habit is a second nature.
   2) Old habit die hard.
   3) What is learned in cradle is the carried to the
      tomb.

78. 세월이 약이다.
   1) Time cures all things.
   2) Time is a healer.

79. 소 귀에 경 읽기.
   1) To sing psalms to a dead horse.
   2) To whistle psalms to the taffrail.
   3) Knock at a deaf man's door.

80. 소 잃고 외양간 고친다.
   It is too late to shut the stable door when the
   steed is stolen.

81. 쇠뿔은 단 김에 빼라.
   1) Strike while the iron is hot.
   2) Hoist your sail when the wind is fair.

82. 숯이 검정 나무란다.
   The kettle calls the pot black(-brows).

83. 시작이 반이다.
   Well begun is half done.

84. 시장이 반찬.
   Hunger is the best sauce.

85. 식자우환.
   A little learning is a dangerous thing.

86. 십인십색.
   1) So many men, so many opinion.
   2) So many herds, so many wits.
   3) Many lords, many laws.

87. 아는 것이 힘, 배워야 한다.
   Knowledge is power.

88. 아는 길도 물어 가라.
   Better ask the way than go astray.

89. 아니 땐 굴뚝에 연기 날까?
   No smoke without some fire.

90. 아이 자라 어른 된다.
   The child is the father of the man.

91. 안 되는 놈은 자빠져도 코가 깨진다.
   The bread never falls but on its buttered side.

92. 암탉이 울면 집안이 망한다.
   1) It is a sad house where the hen crows louder than the cock.
   2) It is a sorry flock where the ewe bears the bell.

93. 어부지리.
   1) Two dogs strive for a bone, and a third runs away with it.
   2) One beats the bush and another catches the bird.

94. 엎친 데 덮친다.
   Ill comes often on the back of worse.

95. 연목구어.
   It is very hard to shave an egg.

96. 열번 찍어 안 넘어가는 나무 없다.
    Little strokes fell great oaks.

97. 오는 말이 고와야 가는 말이 곱다.
    Soft answer turneth away wrath.

98. 오는 정이 있어야 가는 정이 있다.
    To give one as one gets.

99. 옥에도 티가 있다.
    1) No silver/gold without its dross.
    2) There are spots even in the sun.
    3) The best cloth may have a moth in it.

100. 옷이 날개라.
    1) Fine/fair feathers make fine birds/fair fowls.
    2) Apparel makes the men.
    3) The tailor makes the man.
    4) Good cloths open all doors.

101. 용두사미.
    1) To start off with a bang and to end with a whimper.
    2) He who begins many things, finishes but few.
    3) Great cry and little wool.

102. 우는 아이 젖 준다.
    The squeaking wheel gets the grease.

103. 우물에 가 숭늉 찾는다.
    To seek hot water under cold ice.

104. 웃는 낯에 침 뱉으랴.
    1) A soft answer turned away wrath.
    2) Good words are good cheap.
    3) Good words cost nought.

105. 웃물이 맑아야 아랫물이 맑다.
    1) Parents are patterns.
    2) One sheep follows another.

106. 원숭이도 나무에서 떨어진다.
    Accidents will happen in the best regulated
    families.

107. 유유상종.
    Birds of a feather flock together.

108. 음지가 양지되고 양지가 음지 된다.
    1) Sadness and gladness succeed each other.
    2) Joy and sorrow are next door neighbours.
    3) Bad luck often brings good luck.
    4) The worse luck now, the better another time.

109. 이열치열.
    1) One poison drives out another.
    2) The smell of garlic takes away the smell of
       onions.
    3) Fight fire with fire.

110. 일거양득.
    1) To catch two pigeons with one bean.
    2) To kill two birds with one stone/bolt/sling.

111. 일장춘몽.
    The mirth of the world dureth but a while.

112. 입에 쓴 약이 병에는 좋다.
    1) No pains, no gains.
    2) Bitter pills may have blessed effects.

113. 자라 보고 놀란 가슴 솥뚜껑 보고 놀란다.
    1) Birds once snared fear all bushes.
    2) He that has been bitten by a serpent, is afraid

423

of a rope.
3) Whom a serpent has bitten. lizard alarms.

114. 자업자득.
1) To sow the wind and reap the whirlwind.
2) As you make your bed. so you must lie on it.

115. 잘 자랄 나무는 떡잎부터 알아 본다
First impressions are the most lasting.

116. 장님이 장님을 인도한다.
When the blind lead the blind. both shall fall into the ditch.

117. 재주는 곰이 넘고 돈은 되놈이 번다.
1) One beats the bush and another catches the birds.
2) Two dogs strive for a bone. and a third runs away with it.

118. 적반하장.
1) Save a stranger from the sea. and he'll turn your enemy.
2) Save a thief from the gallows and he'll cut your throat.

119. 제 눈에 안경.
Beauty is in the eye of the beholder.

120. 제 버릇 개 줄까?
It is hard to break a hog of an ill custom.

121. 제 발등 불을 먼저 끄랬다.
Meddle not with another man's matter.

122. 죽고 보면 여섯 자.
Six feet of earth make all men equal.

123. 죽은 자는 말이 없다.
Death men tell no tales.

124. 쥐구멍에도 볕들 날 있다.
Fortune knocks once at least at every man's gate.

125. 지렁이도 밟으면 꿈틀한다.
Tread on a worm and it will turn.

126. 천리길도 한 걸음부터.
Step after step the ladder is ascended.

127. 천생연분.
Match made in heaven.

128. 철나자 망령난다.
Life is half spent before we know what it is.

129. 칠전팔기.
If at first you don't succeed, try, try, try again.

130. 콩을 팥이라 해도 곧이 듣는다.
To say the crow is white.

131. 타산지석.
1) Let another's shipwreck be your sea-mark.
2) It is good to learn at other men's cost.

132. 털어서 먼지 안 나는 사람 없다.
1) Every man has his faults.
2) No man is infallible.

133. 토끼 둘을 잡으려다 하나도 못 잡는다.
If you run after two hares, you will catch neither.

134. 티끌 모아 태산.

1) Little and often fills the purse.
2) Penny and penny laid up will be many.
3) Many a little makes mickle.
4) Many small/drops make a great/shower.

135. 팔이 안으로 굽는다.
Men are blind in their own causes.

136. 피는 물보다 진하다.
Blood is thicker than water.

137. 하룻강아지 범 무서운 줄 모른다.
Fools rush in where angels fear to tread.

138. 하늘 보고 침 뱉기.
Who spits against the heaven, it falls in his face.

139. 하늘이 무너져도 솟아날 구멍이 있다.
If it were not for hope the heart would break.

140. 한 번 엎지른 물은 주워 담지 못한다.
1) It is no use crying over spilt milk.
2) Grieve when the chance is past, it is too late.
3) What's done cannot be undone.

141. 한 부모는 열 자식을 거느려도 열 자식은 한 부모를 못 거느린다.
1) One father can support the children; ten children cannot support one father.
2) One father is enough to govern one hundred sons, but not a hundred sons one father.

142. 호랑이 굴에 가야 호랑이 새끼를 잡는다.
Nothing venture, nothing win.

143. 호랑이 제 말하면 온다.
1) Talk of the devil, and he is bound to appear.

2) Talk of the devil, and he'll either come or send.

144. 혹 떼러 갔다가 혹 붙여 온다.
Many go out for wool and come home shorn.

Index in alphabetical order

the gentry. 34.
Birds of a feather flock together. 107.
Birds once snared fear all bushes. 113.
Bitter pills may have blessed effects. 112.
Blind as a mole. 31.
Blind as an owl. 31.
Blood is thicker than water. 136.
Children learn to creep ere they can go. 8.
Claw me, and I'll claw thee. 75.
Death men tell no tales. 123.
Don't cut off your nose to spite your face. 67.
Don't spread the cloth till the pot begins to boil. 36.
Don't teach your grandmother to suck eggs. 12.
Empty vessels make the greatest sound. 68.
Every flow has its ebb. 33.
Every horse/one thinks his pack/sack heaviest. 23.
Every man has his faults. 132.
Everyone stretchs his legs according to the length of
    his coverlet. 29.
Fair feathers make fair fowls. 100.
Fields have eyes, and woods have ears. 27.
Fight fire with fire. 109.
Fine feathers make fine birds. 100.
First impressions are the most lasting. 115.
Fools rush in where angels fear to tread. 137.
Fortune knocks once at least at every man's gate.
    124.
Give a lie twenty-four hours' start, and you can
never overtake it. 59.
Go abroad and you'll hear news of home. 46.
Good clothes open all doors. 100.
Good words are good cheap. 104.
Good words cost nought. 104.
Great cry and little wool. 101.
Grieve when the chance is past, it is too late. 140.
Habit is a second nature. 77.
He cannot say B to a battledore. 26.

He that commits a fault thinks evryone speaks of it. 37.

He that has a great nose thinks everybody is speaking of it. 37.

He that has been bitten by a serpent, is afraid of a rope. 113.

He that will steal a pin, will steal a better thing. 58.

He that will steal an egg will steal an ox. 58.

He who begins many things, finishes but few. 101.

He who leaves the fame of good works after him does not die. 71.

Hoist your sail when the wind is fair. 81.

Hunger is the best sauce. 84.

If at first you don't succeed, try, try, try again. 129.

If it were not for hope the heart would break. 139.

If you run after two hares, you will catch neither. 133.

If you will learn news, you must go to the oven or the mill. 46. ˙

Ignorance is the peace of life. 51.

Ill comes often on the back of worse. 94.

In trust is treason. 56.

It is a sad house where the hen crows louder than the cock. 92.

It is a sorry flock where the ewe bears the bell. 92.

It is good to learn at other men's cost. 131.

It is hard to break a hog of an ill custom. 120.

It is no use crying over spilt milk. 140.

It is not the beard that makes the philosophers. 69.

It is too late to shut the stable door when the steed is stolen. 80.

It is very hard to shave an egg. 95.

It takes two to make a quarrel. 44.

Joy and sorrow are next door neighbours. 108.

Knowledge is power. 87.

Knock at a deaf man's door. 49. 79.

Let another's shipwreck be your sea-mark. 131.

Life is half spent before we know what it is. 128

Like father, like son. 66.

Little and often fills the purse. 134.

Little strokes fell oaks. 96.

Look before you leap. 41.

Make not your sauce, before you have caught the fish. 36.

Many a little makes mickle. 61. 134.

Many go out for wool and come home shorn. 144.

Many hands make light work. 61.

Many lords, many laws. 86.

Many small/drops make a great/shower. 134.

Match made in heaven. 127.

Meddle not with another man's matter. 121.

Men are blind in their own causes. 135.

Money draws money. 39.

Money is power. 40.

Money is welcome, though it comes in a dirty clout. 38.

Money makes/breeds money. 39.

Money will do anything. 40.

Names and natures do often agree. 64.

Narrow gathered, widely spent. 6.

Necessity is the mother of invention. 16.

Need makes the old wife trot. 52.

Never judge from appearance. 69.

No màn is infallible. 132.

No news is good news. 53.

No pains, no gains. 15. 65. 112.

No pleasure without pain (repentance). 9.

No silver/gold without its dross. 99.

No smoke without some fire. 89.

None more bare than to shoemaker's wife and the smith's mare. 35.

Nothing venture, nothing win. 142.

Of a small spark, a great fire. 57.

One beats the bush and another catches the birds. 93. 117.

One father can support the children; ten children cannot support one father. 141.

One father is enough to govern one hundred sons, but not a hundred sons one father. 141.

One picture is worth a thousand words. 60.

One poison drives out another. 109.

One sheep follows another. 66. 105.

Old habit die hard. 77.

One beats the bush and another catches the birds. 93. 117.

Our neighbour's ground yields better corn than ours. 22.

Out of the frying pan into the fire. 76.

Parents are patterns. 105.

Penny and penny laid up will be many. 134.

Pie in the sky. 19.

Poverty is an enemy to good manners. 52.

Poverty is the mother of crime. 2.

Prescription after death. 73.

Roll my log and I'll toll yours. 75.

Sadness and gladness succeed each other. 108.

Save a stranger from the sea, and he'll turn your enemy. 55. 118.

Save a thief from the gallows and he'll cut your throat. 55. 118.

Scratch me and I'll scratch you. 75.

Seeing is believing. 60.

Shallow streams/waters make most din. 68.

Six feet of earth make all men equal. 122.

So many men, so many opinion. 86.

So many herds, so many wits. 86.

Soft answer turneth away wrath. 97.

Spare the rod and spoil the child. 18.

Step after step the ladder is ascended. 126.

Stretch your arm no further than your sleeve will reach. 29.

Strike while the iron is hot. 81.

Talk of the devil, and he is bound to appear. 143.

Talk of the devil, and he'll either come or send. 143.

Talk to the wind. 49.

The apples on the other side of the wall are the sweetest. 22.

The best cloth may have a moth in it. 99.

The bread never falls but on its buttered side. 91.

The child is the father of the man. 90.

The crow thinks her own birds fairest. 10.

The devil dances in an empty pocket. 52.

The end justifies the means. 50.

The eye that sees all things else sees not itself. 25.

The grass is always greener on the other side of the fence. 22.

The kettle calls the pot black(-brow). 82.

The mirth of the world dureth but a while. 111.

The more the merrier. 32.

The more noble, the more humble. 11.

The owl thinks her own young fairest. 10.

The parish priest forgets that ever he has been holy water (parish) clerk. 7.

The shoemaker's son always goes barefoot. 35.

The smell of garlic takes away the smell of onions. 109.

The squeaking wheel gets the grease. 102.

The tailor makes the man. 100.

The unexpected always happens. 48.

The worse luck now, the better another time. 108.

There are spots even in the sun. 99.

There is lightning lightly before thunder. 62.

There is no blindness like ignorance. 31.

Time and tide wait for no man. 3.

Time cures all things. 78.

Time is a healer. 78.

To burn one's house to get rid of the mice. 67.

To build castle in the air. 13.

To cast pearl before swine. 43.

To catch two pigeons with one bean. 17. 110.

To give one as one gets. 98.

To give one roast meat, and beat him with the spit. 47.

To kill two birds with one stone/bolt/sling. 17. 110.

To say the crow is white. 130.

To seek hot water under cold ice. 103.

To sing psalms to a dead horse. 49. 79.

To sow the wind and reap the whirlwind. 42. 114.

To start off with a bang and to end with a whimper. 101.

To whistle psalms to the taffrail. 49. 79.

Too many cooks spoil the broth. 70.

Tread on a worm and it will turn. 125.

Trust is the mother of deceit. 56.

Trust makes way for treachery. 56.

Two dogs strive for a bone, and a third runs away with it. 93. 117.

Walls have ears. 27.

Well begun is half done. 83.

What is learned in cradle is the carried to the tomb. 77.

What's done cannot be undone. 140.

What's mine is mine and what is yours is mine. 28.

What will not money do? 40.

Well begun is half done. 83.

When the blind lead the blind, both shall fall into the ditch. 116.

Where drums beat, laws are silent. 63.

Where ignorance is bliss, 'tis folly to be wise.51.

Where one door shuts, another opens. 16.

Where there's a will, there's a way. 45.

While men go after a leech, the body is buried. 73.

Who spits against the heaven, it falls in his face. 138.

Whom a serpent has bitten, lizard alarms. 113.

You must go into the country to hear what news at

London. 46.

Index (in the order of subjects)

(Numbers refer to the counterparts in Korean proverbs.)